W9-BUG-521

The Official
Learn-to-Sail Manual
of the American
Sailing Association
and the United States
Coast Guard Auxiliary
Revised and Updated

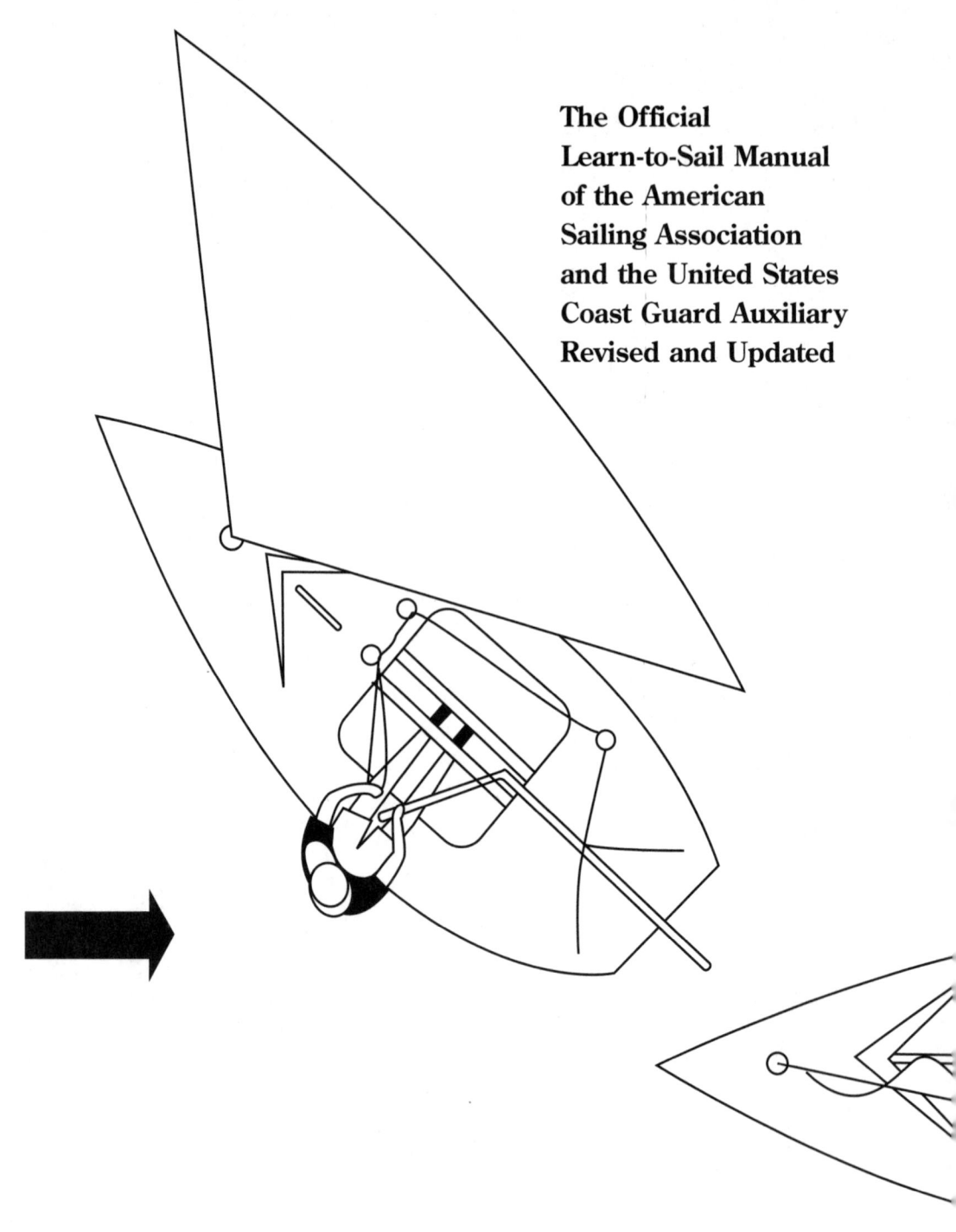

ILLUSTRATIONS BY MARTI BETZ

SAILING

FUNDAMENTALS

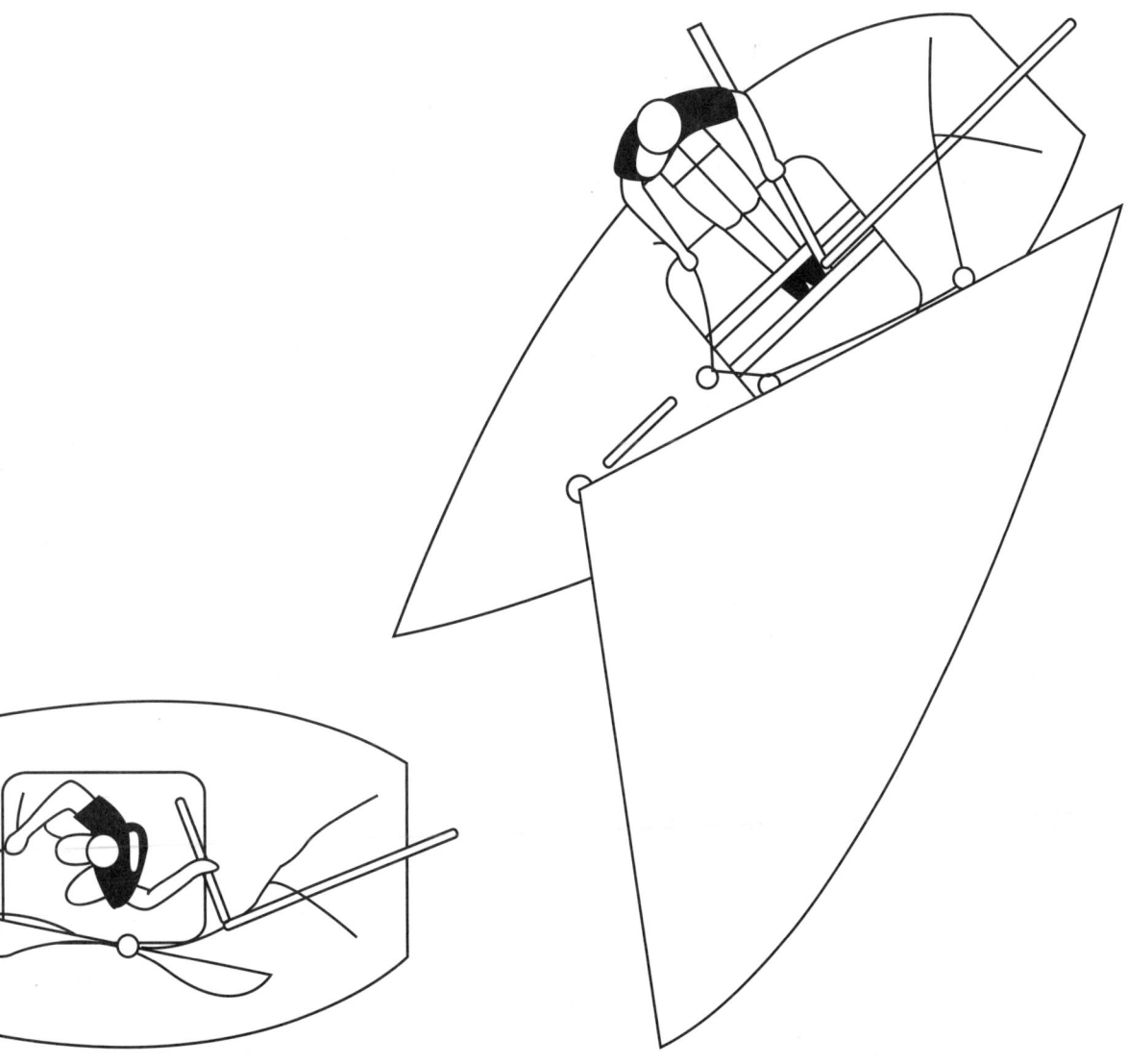

BY GARY JOBSON

A FIRESIDE BOOK
PUBLISHED BY SIMON & SCHUSTER

FIRESIDE
Rockefeller Center
1230 Avenue of the Americas
New York, NY 10020

Copyright © 1984 by American Sailing Association
Copyright © 1987, 1998 by American Sailing
Association and Gary Jobson

All rights reserved, including the right of reproduction in whole or in part in any form.

FIRESIDE and colophon are registered trademarks of Simon & Schuster Inc.

Designed by Barbara Marks

Manufactured in the United States of America

10

Library of Congress Cataloging-in-Publication Data
Jobson, Gary
Sailing fundamentals.
Includes index.
1. Sailing. 2. American Sailing Association.
1. American Sailing Association. II. Title.
GV811J62   1986   797.1'24   86-20338
ISBN-13: 978-0-7432-7308-4
ISBN-10:   0-7432-7308-7

DUE TO ONGOING CHANGES IN GOVERN-
MENTAL SAFETY AND NAVIGATION REGU-
LATIONS, THE PRUDENT SAILOR SHOULD
KEEP ABREAST OF ANY SUCH CHANGES
SINCE THE DATE OF THIS PUBLICATION
BY CONTACTING THE NEAREST U.S.
COAST GUARD REPRESENTATIVE.

CONTENTS

THE AMERICAN SAILING ASSOCIATION

by Harry Munns, Executive Vice President, ASA

The American Sailing Association is a nationwide network of sailors, sailing instructors, sailing schools, and charter fleets. Since 1982, the ASA has created and maintained professional standards within the sailing community. We promote boating safety through education. Our mission is to ensure that every sailor learns to sail properly and that he or she is rewarded with valuable credentials.

A comprehensive set of sailing standards lies at the heart of the ASA system. Detailed outlines of the standards are printed in the ASA Sailing Log Book. These performance objectives provide sailors with a credible evaluation of their sailing knowledge and seamanship skills.

ASA certification provides individual sailors with the most accepted means of proving their abilities to rental and charter fleets throughout the world. With the ASA Log Book–which also includes space for certification seals and a record of sailing experience–the ASA sailor has a passport to present to charter and rental agents in any of the thousands of sailing areas to which he or she may travel. Charter/rental agents use the ASA *Sailing Log Book* as an efficient way to gauge a prospective client's qualifications. Without it, they may have to decipher pages of resumes that often contain vague accounts of training and experience. With the ASA system, agents simply examine the internationally recognized logbook, which documents both knowledge and experience in a clear, concise format.

Sailing Fundamentals contains the knowledge and skills necessary to achieve Basic Keelboat Sailing and Basic Coastal

---

Progression of Training
- **BASIC KEELBOAT SAILING**
- **BASIC COASTAL CRUISING**
- **BAREBOAT CHARTERING**
- **COASTAL NAVIGATION**
  (within sight of land)
- **ADVANCED COASTAL CRUISING**
  (by day and night)
- **CELESTIAL NAVIGATION**
- **OFFSHORE PASSAGE MAKING**

CONTINUING EDUCATION

Cruising certification. The material is divided into parts one through seven. Satisfactory completion of the first four parts qualifies students for certification to ASA Basic Keelboat Sailing. By completing parts five and six, sailors qualify for the Basic Coastal Cruising rating. Anyone planning to take the ASA or United States Coast Guard Auxiliary written exam for Basic Keelboat Sailing should read the entire book. Students who pass Basic Keelboat Sailing also achieve certification for having passed a National Association of State Boating Law Administrators (NASBLA) – recognized safe boating class. (An ASA membership application form is included in the back of this book.)

To qualify for ASA Basic Keelboat Sailing, you must be able to sail a boat about 20 feet long in light to moderate winds and sea conditions in familiar waters without supervision. This is a preparatory standard with no auxiliary (engine) or navigation skills required. For the Basic Coastal Cruising standard, you must be able to cruise safely in familiar waters as both skipper and crew of an auxiliary powered sailing vessel 20 to 30 feet long, in moderate winds and sea conditions.

UNITED STATES COAST GUARD AUXILIARY

Sailing Fundamentals is also the official sailing textbook of the United States Coast Guard Auxiliary (USCGAUX). The USCGAUX is the volunteer civilian component of the United States Coast Guard (USCG). It consists of approximately 35,000 members who wish to further their boating education and who provide administrative, operational, and other support to the USCG.

Safe boating education is one of the major missions of the USCGAUX. USCGAUX courses include both classroom and distance-learning (home-study) classes. The USCGAUX does not offer on-the-water courses to the general public, although such training is made available to members who wish to engage in search and rescue (SAR), aids to navigation (ATON), and other operational activities that require boat-crew qualification.

The USCGAUX public education program includes special courses for children and the Boating Safely Course (BSC), an eight-hour course for powerboaters, operators of personal watercraft (PWC), hunters and fishermen, and others interested in boating safety. The Skipper's Safe Boating course is a distance-learning course for those whose schedules do not permit classroom attendance. The core program includes the Boating Skills and Seamanship (BS&S) course for powerboaters and the Sailing Fundamentals course for sailors. Boaters with an interest in coastal navigation may take the USCGAUX Basic Coastal Navigation (BCN) and Advanced Coastal Navigation (ACN) courses. Members of the USCGAUX are eligible to take advanced training in a variety of topics, including communications, seamanship, SAR, and navigation, and courses on related topics offered through the USCG Institute.

The Skipper's Safe Boating Course, BSC, BS&S, and Sailing Fundamentals courses are approved by the National Association of State Boating Law Administrators (NASBLA) and graduates may satisfy state requirements for certification in those states that have mandatory education requirements. (Check with your state Boating Law Administrator [BLA] to see if this course is approved in your state.) Additionally, students who graduate from the S&S course also pass the classroom portion of the ASA Basic Keelboat Sailing Standard.

HOW TO USE THIS BOOK

Each of the first six parts of this book is divided into two sections, Sailing Knowledge and Sailing Skills.

Sailing Knowledge covers terminology, sailing theory, safety, and government regulations–all the things you need to know before going out on the water. To reinforce what you have learned, you will find review questions at the end of each Sailing Knowledge section. Answers are provided in Appendix A.

The Sailing Knowledge sections are covered in detail in the USCGAUX Sailing Fundamentals course. Questions in the written final Sailing Fundamentals examination cover material from the Sailing Knowledge section of each chapter. USCGAUX students are not tested on topics covered only in the Sailing Skills sections (see below), but are encouraged to read this material as a course supplement and in preparation for later on-the-water training offered by ASA schools.

Although this is principally a text about sailing, some of the topics covered in the Sailing Knowledge sections of this book apply to powerboats. This material is included to give the reader additional background and to satisfy the boating–safety education standards set by NASBLA and the USCG. If your vessel has an engine (as many sailboats do) and the engine is in operation–regardless of whether or not the sails are raised–you are considered to be operating a powerboat under the navigation rules and must comply with all regulations applicable to these craft. Moreover, engine equipped vessels must satisfy other federal and state regulations, such as carriage of additional required safety equipment.

The Sailing Skills sections describe exercises and maneuvers designed to teach boat handling. Although the basic principles of sailing are the same for all craft from sailboards to 12-meter yachts, the exercises in this book are designed for a boat of about 14 to 30 feet with at least two people aboard. In practicing each maneuver, switch roles with your fellow crew members so that everyone learns every skill.

Each exercise teaches a particular task. Many of the skills will build upon lessons learned in previous exercises. Each Sailing Skills section is designed to take two to three hours to complete on the water. The ideal way to learn is with the hands-on knowledge imparted by a qualified instructor or experienced sailor. The sequence of exercises in this book allows for a knowledgeable sailor on board with you, although the book itself can be your instructor.

Certain fundamental maneuvers–such as leaving the dock under sail–have purposely been left to later parts. By that point, your skills will have been developed sufficiently for you to attempt these more complicated maneuvers. We deal only with sailboats in Parts One through Four; we will cover handling a vessel under power in Part Five.

Important terms are explained in the text as well as defined in the Glossary beginning on p. 205. Illustrations or photographs give a more detailed explanation of terms when necessary. Each subject area is explored in increasing depth in subsequent parts as you gain knowledge and develop basic skills.

Good luck and smooth sailing.

PART ONE

Introduction to Sailing

OVERVIEW: THE SAILBOAT AND THE WIND

To illustrate the way the wind interacts with the sails, let me tell you a story.

In my early days of sailing I was once sailing a little ten-foot boat on Toms River, a body of water off Barnegat Bay along the coast of New Jersey. It was a particularly difficult day to be out on the water. Not only was the wind strong, but it was frequently shifting direction. Every time I got settled down on a desirable course, with the sails set at a correct angle to the wind and the boat moving fast, the wind would shift. I often had to make an unscheduled, drastic change in course to keep the sails filled with wind. Sometimes I did not move fast enough, and my boat was left lying stopped in the river with her sails flapping helplessly.

An older friend, named Tom Chapman, was watching from the nearby shore. At the time, Tom was one of the top sailors on Barnegat Bay, but he understood my frustration. Instead of watching in amusement as some people might do, he coached me back to shore, hopped into the boat with me, and gave me some good advice.

"First, he said, "you must understand where the wind is coming from. Your problem is that you aren't aware of any changes in direction. Here's what I do," he continued. "Before I head out, I stand on the shore and simply look at wind indicators. I look at flags on shore and on boats. I study the direction that water ripples blow in, and I watch other boats that are out sailing. This helps me understand how the wind is shifting in direction and strength so I'm not surprised once I push out.

"The next thing I do is plan in advance where I want to sail. Say I want to sail from here to that island." He pointed into the wind. "Obviously, I can't sail straight to it because that would mean sailing directly into the wind, and this boat can't sail closer to the wind than about 45 degrees. So I'll sail a series of short legs on a course of 45 degrees to the wind, first with the wind on one side and then with the wind on the other, and so on back and forth until I get to my destination. To get started, I push off, pick the first course, get sailing at 45 degrees to the wind, and adjust the sail so it catches the wind just right, without flapping. When a boat is sailing that close to the wind, the sail should be pulled in quite far, until it is right over the boat.

"Now, suppose that I'd decided to sail to that marina down there." He pointed directly downwind. "Then I'd be sailing with the wind behind me. That means that the sail should be adjusted so it is way out over the water at about a right angle to the boat. As you can see, the way I adjust the sail depends entirely on the course I choose."

Tom and I pushed off and sailed out into the river. I decided to sail toward the island upwind, so I headed about 45 degrees to the wind and pulled the sail in close. Tom resumed coaching. "I watch what the wind is doing to my sail," he said, "and adjust the course so I stay at that 45-degree angle. If the sail begins to flap, I'm probably sailing too close to the wind. I should change my course to get back to that 45-degree angle. On the other hand, if I let the sail out a little and it does not flap, that means I'm sailing too wide and should alter my course until I'm sailing closer to the wind."

"But don't look only at the sail. I spend about half my time watching the water beyond the bow of my boat so I can try to understand what the wind will do. I try to remember what I observed while I was on shore, but I also learn through experience. For example, if the wind shifts 20 degrees to the left side, it will ripple the water at a new angle. Whenever I see that kind of ripple on the water," he said, pointing and adjusting our course, "I anticipate another wind shift to the left".

"When you're sailing in a shifty wind, at first you'll be making big swoops between sailing either too close to the wind or too wide off it," Tom warned. "But with experience and practice you will be able to steer a straighter course, and you won't find your boat sailing quite as high or quite as low."

On the way back to shore, Tom had one last bit of advice. "In shifty winds, it's important to be able to make rapid adjustments to the sail. So keep the sheet (the rope leading to the sail) in your hand so you can adjust it whenever the wind changes direction."

That afternoon, in less than an hour, Tom's lessons set me on the right course. I was learning how to sail.

In this first lesson, the parts of the boat and the two most frequently used knots are introduced. Knots are an essential part of a sailor's knowledge and should be attempted before the first lesson. Upon completion of this part you will be able to raise the sails, come about, jibe, and leave the boat in shipshape fashion after a sail.

SAILING KNOWLEDGE

ALL ABOUT BOATS

PROPULSION TYPES

Recreational boats are designed to use one or more of three propulsion types. Self-propelled vessels, including kayaks, rowboats, rafts, and canoes, are designed to be propelled by people using paddles, oars, or poles. Power-driven vessels (powerboats) typically use gasoline or diesel motors for propulsion. Sailing vessels (sailboats) are wind powered, using sails to capture the wind's power (see below).

POWERBOAT–a recreational boat typically powered by a gasoline or diesel engine. Powerboats may be subdivided into several types, including utility boats (prams, skiffs, dinghies, inflatables, and utility outboards), runabouts (bowriders, open fishermen, center consoles), cruisers (trawlers, houseboats, larger sportfishing vessels), pontoon boats, and personal watercraft (PWC). Each type has certain uses, characteristics, and limitations. Utility boats, for example, are used as tenders for larger craft and as platforms for fishing and hunting in protected waters. Because utility boats are generally small with limited stability, boaters should enter them carefully to avoid overloading. Caution should also be exercised when moving within these boats to avoid tipping them over. Runabouts are generally fast, maneuverable craft, used for fishing, hunting, cruising, and waterskiing. Cruisers are generally larger, more seaworthy (except for houseboats) craft, equipped with berths (sleeping areas), a head (marine toilet), galley (marine kitchen), and other facilities necessary for living aboard. Powerboats are subject to particular navigation rules and have specific responsibilities under those rules.

PERSONAL WATERCRAFT–also called "water scooters" as well as a variety of trade names. They are highly maneuverable, fast, fun-to-operate, low-cost, power-driven (jet drive) craft capable of operation in very shallow water. Many PWC are designed for one person, but larger models are available for use by two or three people. PWC are not toys and are governed by navigation rules applicable to power-driven vessels. In addition, most states and many localities have established specific laws that regulate PWC activities, such as prohibition of night operations, speed limitations, prohibitions of specific activities (e.g., wake jumping), limitations on operator age, and education requirements. These popular craft have unique operating capabilities (e.g., high speed, shallow draft), but are also subject to limitations. For example, PWC are steered by altering (via handlebars) the direction of the jet drive, and if power is not applied, steering is lost (the so-called off-throttle steering problem). Operators who are unfamiliar with this design feature may have difficulty controlling the vessel. PWC are designed for operation in relatively calm waters, have limited fuel capacity, and are not stable or very maneuverable at slow speeds.

PWC operators often focus their attention on nearby waves or wakes, which can impair their ability to maintain a proper lookout. Operators of other vessels should exercise caution when operating in the vicinity of PWC to minimize the likelihood of collision.

Persons using PWC can expect to be thrown into the water and should wear personal flotation devices (PFDs) suitable for PWC use. The ability to swim and knowing how to reboard a PWC from the water are also essential. Many PWC are equipped with engine kill switches rigged to shut the engine off if the riders are thrown from the craft. Fuel management is very important for PWC. Not all PWC are equipped with fuel gauges. Instead, they have reserve tanks and riders need to know how to switch to the reserve tanks and must know the PWC's endurance when using the reserve tanks. Weight and balance are important for PWC operators. Thorough familiarity with owners' manuals and strict adherence to the published limitations are essential. Finally, it is important that operators of PWC (as well as other craft) display environmental sensitivity. Operations in shallow water areas may disturb a fragile ecosystem and its inhabitants.

PWC operators must observe restrictions on loud noise in populated areas. This can be both a matter of courtesy and regulation.

SAILING VESSEL–as noted above, this is a wind-powered vessel that uses only sails for power. Many sailboats are also equipped with gas or diesel motors for use (either as primary or supplemental power) when winds are light or from the wrong direction, for docking or other precise maneuvering, and for operation in waters (e.g., certain canals) where use of sails is prohibited. A sailboat is a power-driven vessel, as defined in the navigation rules, when the motor is in operation, and must observe regulations applicable to this type of vessel. When powered solely by sail, a sailboat is termed a sailing vessel and is subject to other specific regulations and (because of its limited maneuverability) enjoys certain privileges under the navigation rules. Various types of sailboat are discussed later in this text.

Most large powerboats like this one do not have the ability to plane.

SAILBOARD–a modified surfboard with a mast attached that holds a sail and is capable of swiveling. They are one-person craft, so the "skipper" operates the sail, steers, and acts as lookout. Visibility on these high-speed craft may be limited when the operator is positioned behind the sail. Skippers of other craft should understand this limitation and exercise caution when operating in the vicinity of sailboards.

HULL

The hull is the basic boat minus the rigging. The hull comprises the bottom, topsides, buoyancy tanks, and deck. One way to classify boats is based on hull design. Displacement-hull boats move through the water and push it aside or displace it. Planing-hull vessels move faster and, after gaining speed, ride more nearly on top of the water. All boats at rest or moving slowly are displacement boats. Each displaces a volume of water equal in weight to its own weight when operating in displacement mode.

A displacement-hull vessel always displaces a volume of water equal to its own weight, regardless of its speed. At slow speeds, it is easy for a displacement-hull boat to push the water aside, forming a bow wave. As speed increases, the bow wave becomes higher and the boat tries to climb it. But the boat is not designed to do this so there is a practical limit to its speed. Displacement vessels with longer waterlines have the capability of attaining higher speeds as long as they have adequate power. Most sailboats (except sailboards and certain other light-weight boats such as racing dinghies), tugs, freighters, and true trawlers are displacement-hull vessels. The theoretical upper limit (the hull speed) of a displacement hull can be calculated with relative precision. Hull speed in knots (nautical miles per hour) is approximately 1.34 times the square root of the waterline length in feet. Thus, a displacement-hull vessel with a waterline length of 36 feet has a maximum speed of approximately 8 knots (9.2 statute miles per hour). Despite their slow speed, displacement–hull vessels have many advantages and special uses. They are steady and comfortable and can handle rougher water than their planing hull cousins (see below). Engine-powered displacement-hull vessels are typically fuel efficient.

Above hull-speed a planing-hull vessel rides on its bow wave or "on-plane." When planing, it uses most of its power to move forward instead of pushing the water aside and displaces a volume of water less than its own weight. Generally, flatter hull bottoms allow boats to plane more easily. Runabouts, speedboats, sportfishing boats, and PWC are examples of planing-hull vessels. Power-driven planing-hull vessels are generally less fuel efficient than displacement-hull vessels of comparable size and weight.

As the name implies, a semidisplacement hull has both displacement and planing characteristics. Up to a certain power and speed, a semidisplacement hull behaves as a displacement hull. Beyond that point, the hull can rise to a partial plane. Increasing the power of a semidisplacement hull vessel increases its speed. It never gets fully "on top," however, and is not as fast as a vessel with a true planing hull. Most trawlers and many cruisers fit into this category.

Multihull vessels include sailing catamarans (two hulls) and trimarans (three hulls). Although technically a displacement-hull vessel, a multihull is able to escape the restriction of hull speed because the narrow hulls create very little wave resistance and because this type of vessel typically carries a great deal of sail. These boats may be difficult to maneuver at docking speeds because they lack the momentum that heavier, ballasted boats use to maintain forward motion.

There is no single, all-purpose, perfect hull design. Boat builders strive to find a happy compromise among conflicting design objectives.

THE BASIC BOAT

Learning to sail is rather like going to a foreign country. Everyone seems to speak a different language. But don't let this trouble you, for the language will soon become familiar. Once you cast off from shore, your boat becomes a self-contained world. To function within that world you need to learn the parts of your boat and their uses. Go over them often so there is no question in your mind.

KEEL–a weighted fin that, when attached to the bottom of a sailboat, keeps the boat from capsizing or slipping sideways in the water, which allows it to sail upwind.

CENTERBOARD–A sailboat without a keel may have a centerboard. A centerboard is a wooden or metal fin housed in a centerboard trunk. It can be lowered to overcome the boat's lateral motion.

BEAM–the maximum width of the hull.

DECK–the horizontal upper surface of the boat.

STERN–the back of the boat.

BOW–the front of the boat.

AFT, AFTER–toward the stern.

FORWARD–toward the bow.

WINDWARD–toward the wind.

LEEWARD–away from the wind.

ALOFT–overhead.

RUDDER–the fin at the stern of the boat used for steering.

TILLER–the wooden or metal steering arm attached to the rudder. It is used as a lever to turn the rudder.

TILLER EXTENSION–a wooden or metal pivoting extension attached to the tiller. It is usually found in dinghies and enables the skipper to steer accurately while hiking out.

WHEEL–on larger boats the wheel replaces the tiller and is used to turn the rudder.

MAST–the vertical pole or spar that supports the sails and boom. The top of the mast is called the masthead.

BOOM–the horizontal spar which is attached to the mast to support the bottom part of the mainsail.

HIKING OUT–leaning the weight of the crew over the windward side to help keep the boat on an "even keel."

PORT–the left side of the boat as you face forward.

STARBOARD–the right side of the boat as you face forward.

MAINSHEET–the line used to make major adjustments to the trim of the mainsail.

BOOM VANG–an adjustable tackle or rod that prevents the boom from lifting. A rod type boom vang also keeps the boom from dropping on deck.

LIFELINES–plastic-coated wires enclosing the deck to keep the crew from failing overboard. Lifelines are suspended from metal supports, called pulpits and stanchions.

TRAVELER–a slide, running across the boat, to which the mainsheet is led. The crew can change the trim of the mainsail by adjusting the slide position.

TOPSIDES–the sides of the hull above the waterline.

The **STANDING RIGGING** is a collection of

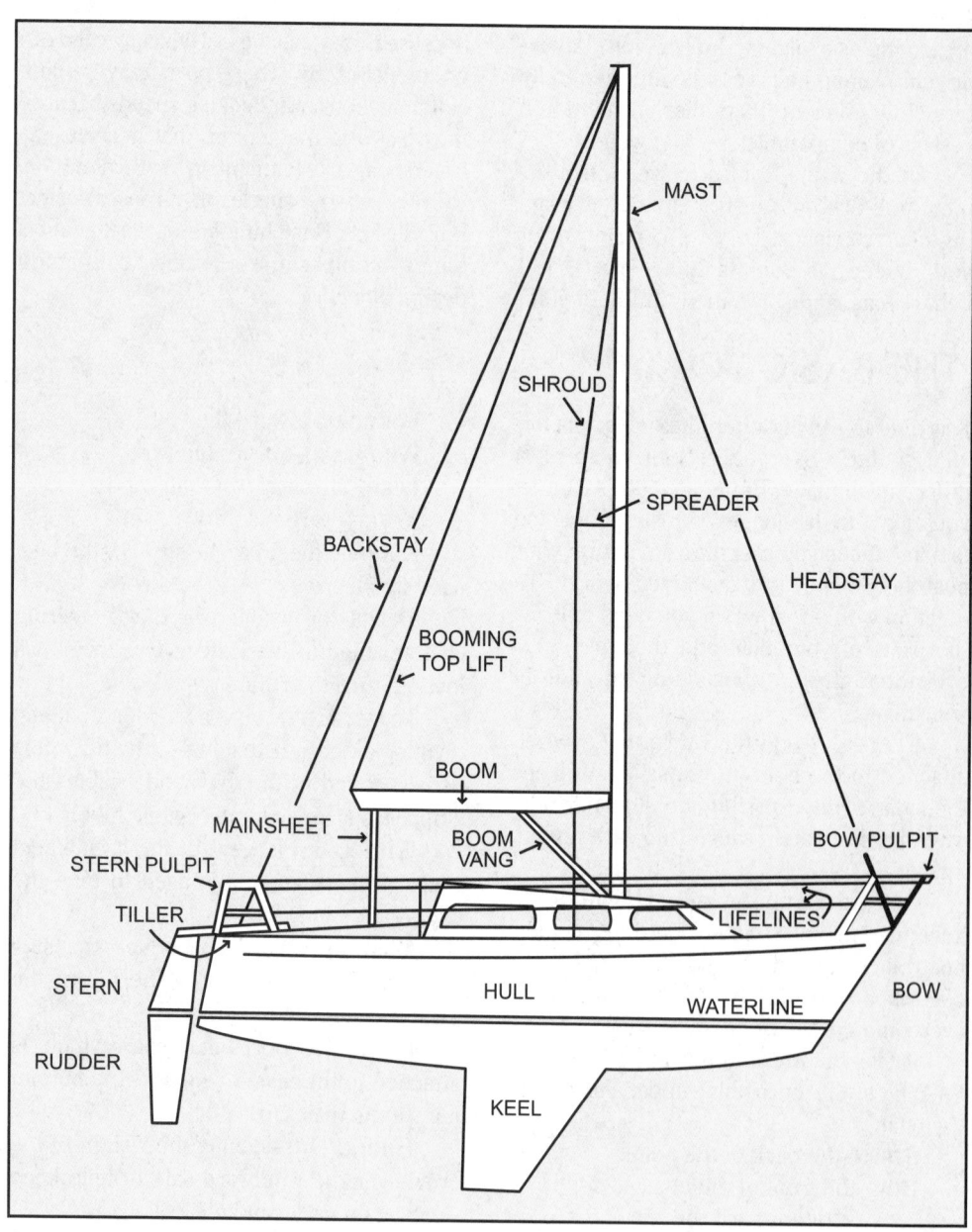

Boat parts

wires that supports the mast. On more sophisticated boats, the standing rigging is more complex and can be adjusted to optimize a sail's performance. The basic standing rigging consists of:

HEADSTAY–a wire that runs from the top of the mast (or near the masthead) to the bow and onto which the jib is attached. It supports the mast, preventing it from falling backwards.

BACKSTAY–a wire that runs from the top of the mast to the stern and supports the mast.

SHROUDS (SIDESTAYS)–wires that run from the masthead (or near the masthead) to the sides of the boat to support the mast and prevent it from swaying.

SAILS–are the power supply of the sailboat. They are most frequently made of Dacron, a synthetic fiber, used because of

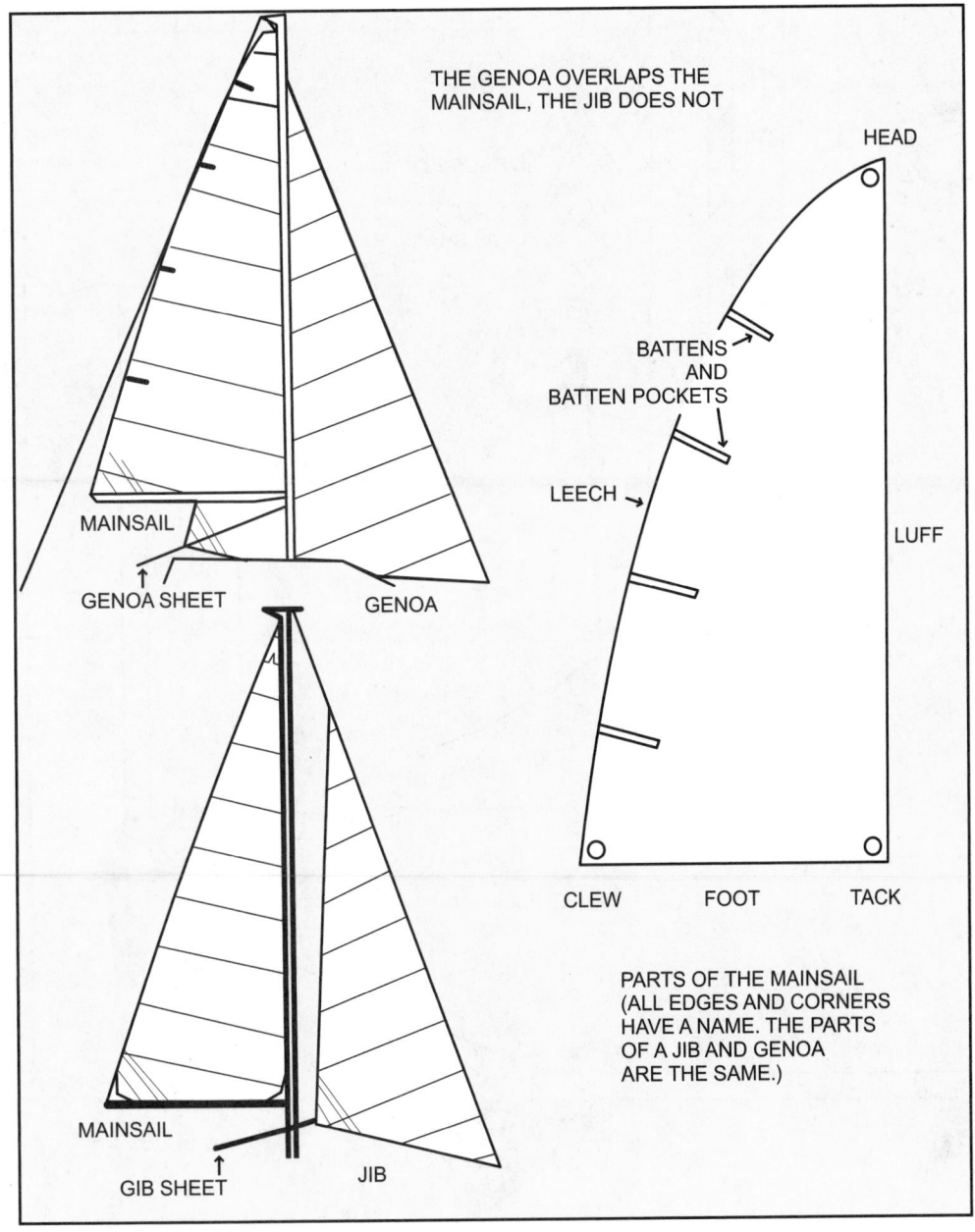

THE GENOA OVERLAPS THE MAINSAIL, THE JIB DOES NOT

HEAD

BATTENS AND BATTEN POCKETS

LEECH →

LUFF

MAINSAIL

↑ GENOA SHEET

GENOA

CLEW   FOOT   TACK

PARTS OF THE MAINSAIL (ALL EDGES AND CORNERS HAVE A NAME. THE PARTS OF A JIB AND GENOA ARE THE SAME.)

MAINSAIL

↑ GIB SHEET

JIB

Sail parts

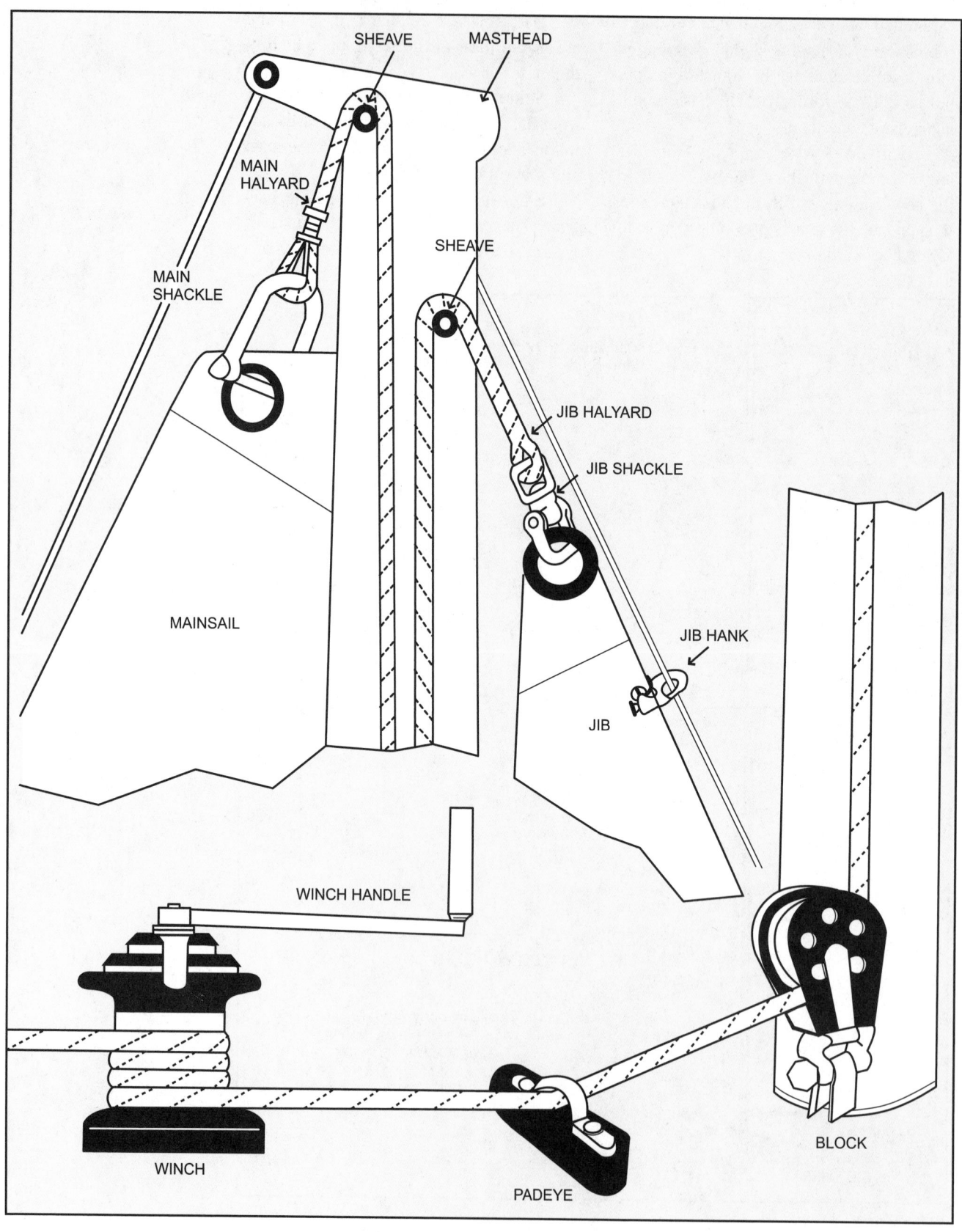

its resistance to stretching. Other materials such as nylon, Mylar, and Kevlar are also used in sailmaking. Types of sails are:

MAINSAIL–the primary and most easily controlled source of sail power, attached to the aft edge of the mast and the top edge of the boom.

SPINNAKER (CHUTE)–a balloonlike sail, often colored, used when running (sailing downwind).

JIB (HEADSAIL)–the sail set forward of the mainsail and attached to the forestay using jib hanks or a headfoil track for a bolt rope.

GENOA (HEADSAIL)–a large jib with an overlap aft of the mast.

Each part of a sail has a name:

HEAD–the top corner of the sail.

TACK–the forward lower corner of a sail.

CLEW–the back lower corner of a sail.

LUFF–the leading edge (front) of a sail. The luff of the mainsail attaches to the mast, and the luff of the jib attaches to the forestay.

FOOT–the bottom edge of a sail. The foot of the mainsail attaches to the boom. The foot of the jib is unattached and consequently more difficult to control.

LEECH–the trailing (back) edge of a sail.

BATTENS–support sticks held in pockets to keep the leech from flapping and to add support to the sail.

DRAFT–the fullness or roundness of a sail.

The **RUNNING RIGGING** consists of ropes (called lines) that pull the sails up and adjust the sails' shape. Unlike the standing rigging, the running rigging is not stationary. When sailors speak of "trimming" sails to find the most efficient shape, they mean that the sheets are being let out (eased) or pulled in (trimmed).

The running rigging includes:

HALYARDS–lines used to raise (hoist) sails and hold them up.

MAINSHEET–a line used to trim the mainsail; it is led through a series of blocks to form a block and tackle.

JIB SHEETS TWO lines, one on each side of the boat, to trim the jib.

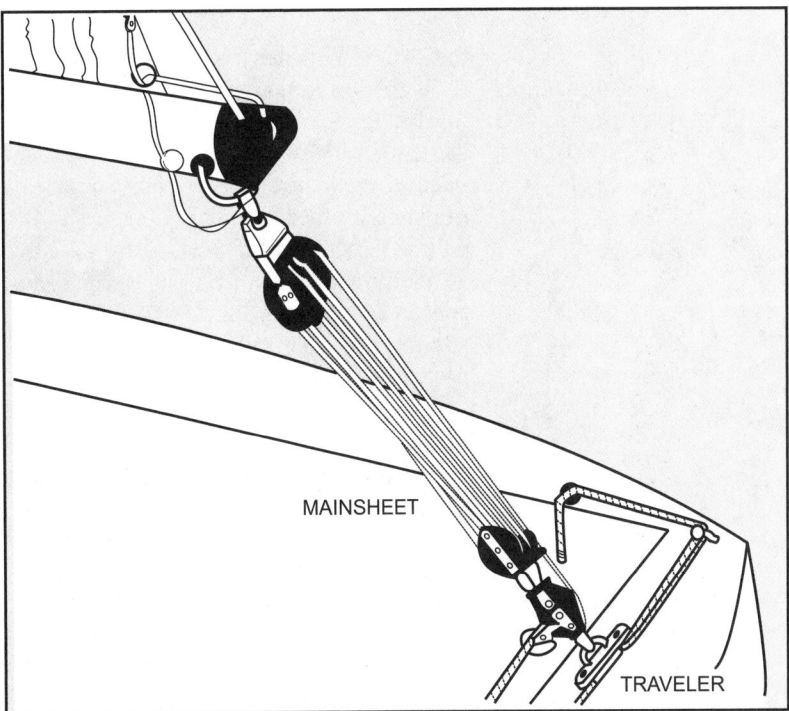

MAINSHEET

TRAVELER

The **TOPPING LIFT**, which prevents the boom from dropping on deck, is part of the running rigging. The **DOWNHAUL, OUTHAUL,** and **CUNNINGHAM** are also running rigging. We will discuss them later.

HALYARDS attach to the top or head of a sail. Halyards run through the top of the mast by means of a **SHEAVE** or **BLOCK** (pulley) and then down to the bottom of the mast. A halyard can be **INTERNAL**, inside the mast, or **EXTERNAL**, outside the mast. The **MAIN HALYARD** raises the mainsail and the **JIB HALYARD** raises the jib.

Halyards sometimes terminate at the base of the mast, requiring the crew to be at the mast when hoisting and lowering the sails. A better system is to have the halyard lead back to the cockpit through **TURNING BLOCKS** and **PADEYES** (blocks and eyes through which a line is threaded to give it a clear, safe run). The sail can then be hoisted by the crew without leaving the safety of the cockpit.

Most boats have **WINCHES** on the mast or on the deck to aid in the hoisting of sails. Winches pull on lines mechanically and safely. They consist of a drum that rotates only in a clockwise direction around which

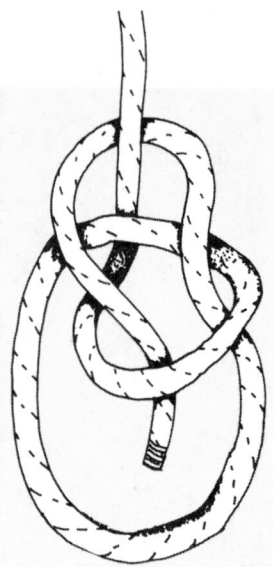

Bowline knot

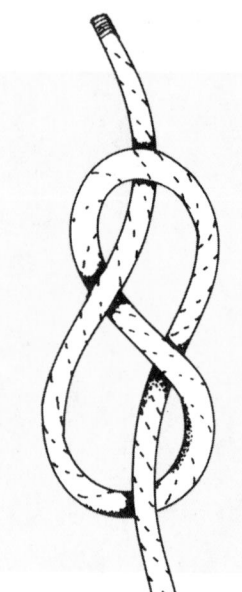

Figure eight knot or "stopper knot"

The windward or "lazy" jib sheet becomes the new working sheet when the boat tacks.

the line is wrapped. A crank handle rotates the drum. Winches are discussed in the Sailing Skills section of this part.

SHEETS control the shape of the sail and **SAIL TRIM** or position of the sail. The mainsheet and jib sheets are quite different from one another. The mainsheet is a multiple-part block and tackle used to increase an individual's pulling power. By giving a sheet a 2:1, 4:1, or 8:1 advantage, the device lets you trim your sails more easily. This is particularly helpful in strong winds.

The jib sheet consists of two lines connected to the clew of the jib that lead along each side of the boat to the cockpit. Although the actual leading of the jib sheets varies from boat to boat, the system illustrated in this book is among the most common.

The jib sheets are attached to the clew of the jib with a knot called a **BOWLINE** This knot provides a temporary loop that allows the jib sheet to be securely attached to the sail. The key feature of the bowline, like any property tied knot, is that it unties remarkably easily, even after being under prolonged, heavy strain.

The other end of the jib sheet leads through a **BLOCK** (a pulley), or series of blocks, around a winch, to a cam cleat or deck **CLEAT** (a wooden, plastic, or metal fitting used to secure lines). The crew controls the sail trim by pulling in or letting out

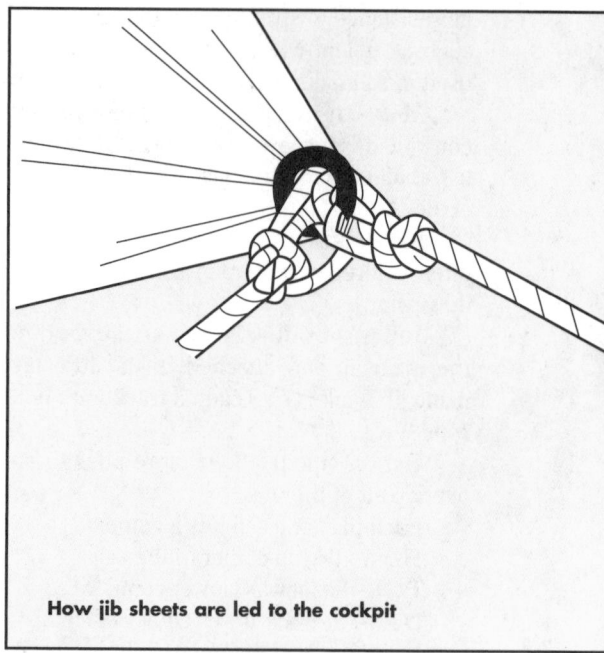

How jib sheets are led to the cockpit

the sheet.

Since the jib sheets are led along both the **WINDWARD** (toward the wind) and the **LEEWARD** (away from the wind) sides of the boat, they are referred to as the **LEEWARD** and **WINDWARD SHEETS**. The leeward sheet is led along the leeward side of the boat. It is the working sheet and will be taut when the jib is in use; the windward sheet is the nonworking or "lazy" sheet and will be slack. Of course, as the side of the boat

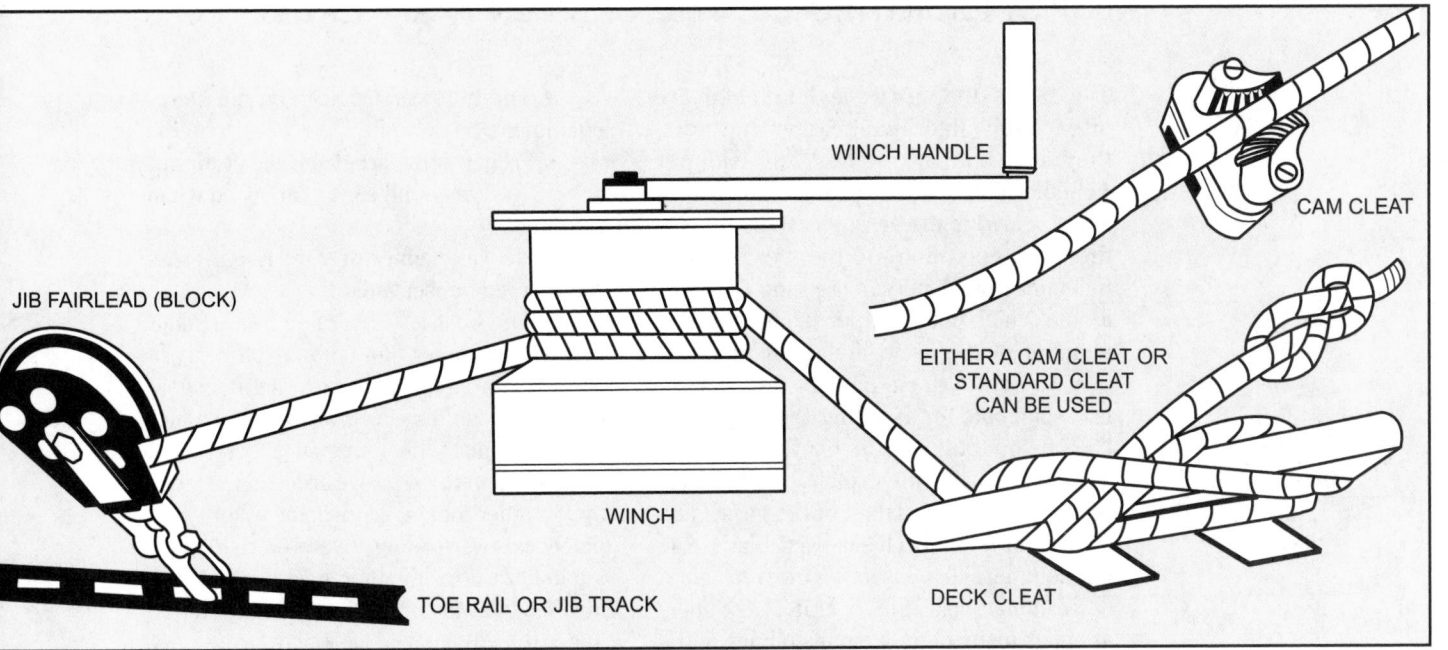

JIB FAIRLEAD (BLOCK)

WINCH HANDLE

CAM CLEAT

EITHER A CAM CLEAT OR
STANDARD CLEAT
CAN BE USED

WINCH

TOE RAIL OR JIB TRACK

DECK CLEAT

the wind is blowing from changes, reference to the windward or leeward jib sheets also changes.

At the tail end of the jib sheet will be a **FIGURE EIGHT** or **STOPPER** knot. The knot will keep the line from pulling through the turning block or fairlead.

The topping lift, or boom lift, holds the boom off the deck when the sail is not being used. If the mainsail is lowered without the topping lift attached, the boom will fall to the deck.

A topping lift should be adjustable, either from the cabin top or from the boom itself One of the simplest types of topping lift attaches to the backstay and consists of a few feet of wire with a clip or shackle on the end. Although this type of topping lift serves the basic purpose of support for the boom, it is difficult to use and almost impossible to adjust or disconnect once the sail has been raised.

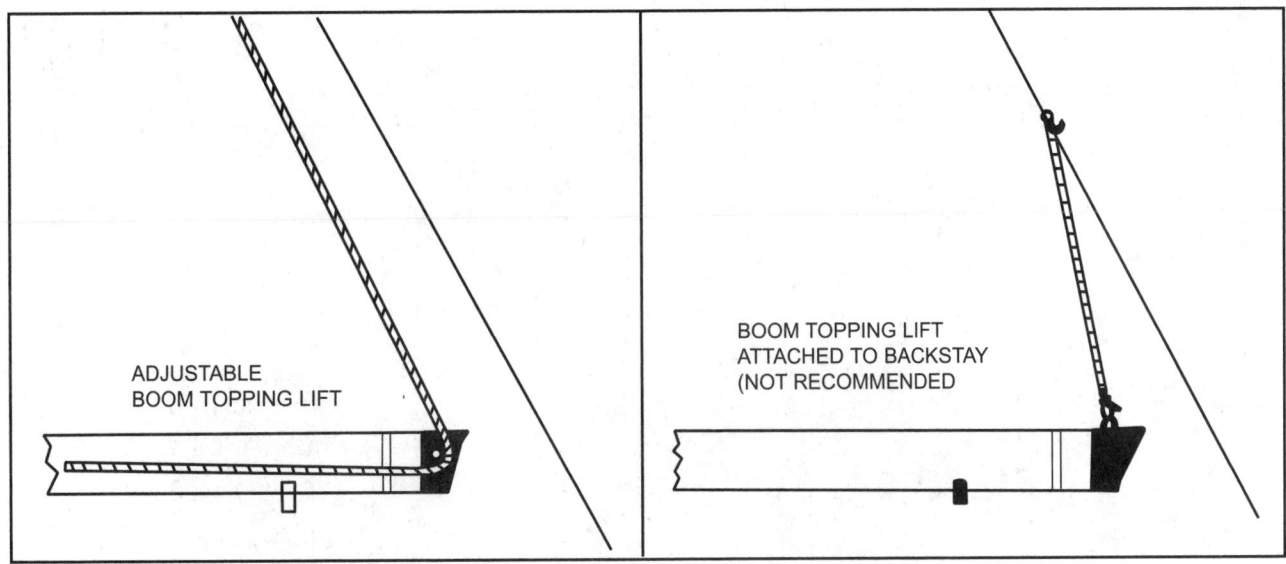

ADJUSTABLE
BOOM TOPPING LIFT

BOOM TOPPING LIFT
ATTACHED TO BACKSTAY
(NOT RECOMMENDED

RESPONSIBILITIES OF THE SKIPPER AND CREW

The terms **HELMSMAN** and **SKIPPER** are often used interchangeably; however, they are not the same. The skipper (whether on deck, at the wheel, or taking a nap below) is the person responsible for the safe operation of the vessel. The helmsman is the person steering the boat, a role which may be performed by any member of the crew, including the skipper. The crew (including the helmsman) is responsible for assisting the skipper in the safe operation of the boat.

Traditionally, the captain of a vessel is responsible for the safety of the vessel and all persons aboard. This is particularly true on commercial vessels. However, on a recreational boat the operator (skipper) assumes many of the responsibilities of the captain. If the boat is boarded by federal, state, or local law-enforcement personnel, the skipper must answer for the condition and conduct of the boat. For example, the skipper is responsible for ensuring that:

Organize the crew by giving each person a specific task

• The boat carries all required safety equipment.

• Proper lights are displayed at night.

• Correct sound signals are used when required.

• No-wake zones and restricted areas are correctly observed.

• The boat isn't operated in a manner that will endanger life, limb, or property of any person. Negligent or grossly negligent operations could include: operating in a hazardous manner, operating in a designated swimming area, excessive speed in the vicinity of other boats, hazardous waterskiing practices, overloading, overpowering, boating in hazardous weather, bowriding (or riding on a gunwale or transom), and operating under the influence of alcohol or drugs.

• The boat complies with the rules for preventing collisions.

• Proper registration numbers are displayed and the certificate of number is carried on board.

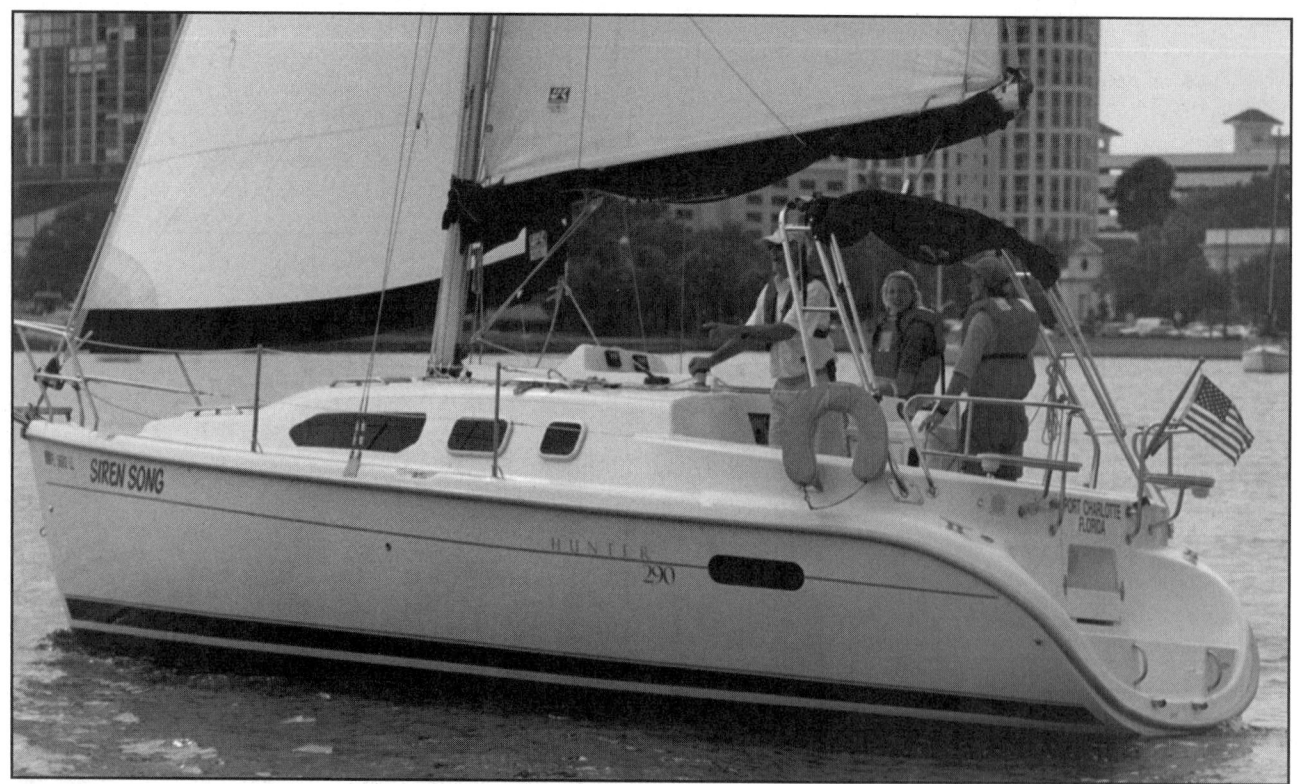

• An accident report is prepared if the boat or persons aboard are involved in an accident that involves a fatality or disappearance (Report within 48 hours), injuries requiring more than first aid, more than $2000 damage to vessels or property, or the complete loss of a vessel (within 10 days).

• Assistance is rendered to persons overboard and to other boats needing help. (The operator or any person in charge of a vessel is obligated by law to provide assistance that can be safely provided to any individual in danger at sea. The Good Samaritan rule in the Federal Boat Safety Act of 1971 will protect you from liability if you act reasonably and prudently. The operator is subject to a fine and/or imprisonment for failure to do so.)

• Trash, oil, and other pollutants are properly disposed of, and that permanently installed marine toilets comply with United States Coast Guard (USCG) regulations.

• The owner is responsible along with the operator if an injury occurs or if the boat causes damage.

The above list is illustrative, not exhaustive. It identifies some of the specific required actions and responsibilities of the skipper. Being a good skipper, however, entails more than satisfying the specific requirements listed above. It is also a matter of attitude. To a degree unmatched by many other forms of transportation, passengers and other boaters are dependent upon the skipper's skills and responsible approach to boating. In boating, responsibility and fun go hand in hand.

To ensure the safety of the crew, the skipper must organize the operation of the boat so that tasks will be performed efficiently. This means delegating jobs according to the abilities of different crew members.

As a skipper, be tactful when giving an order; as a crew member, be willing and able to obey all reasonable commands. The great General "Stonewall" Jackson once said, "Obedience to orders, instant and unhesitating, is not only the life blood of armies and navies, but the security of states." This statement applies perfectly on sailboats.

Give orders in a friendly but firm tone of voice. Never shout: it only makes the crew nervous and leads to mistakes. Explain commands to inexperienced crew members in advance so they feel more relaxed. Give commands in exact terms. For example, ask for sails to be trimmed in four inches instead of "a little." By putting commands in precise terms, you leave no doubt as to what you want. The best skippers are those who ask the advice of the rest of the crew. However, in times of quick action, the crew must obey commands immediately and ask questions later.

One of the greatest yachtsmen of all time, Ted Turner, establishes the role of each crew member when that person steps on board the yacht. He clearly defines the job of every person on the boat. In case there is an emergency or an important maneuver, each person is assigned a specific task. Turner has earned great loyalty from his crews over the years because they have faith in his ability to make clear decisions in the heat of battle. His secret? Taking good advice when asked for, assigning specific duties, and motivating the crew by giving everyone on board a reason to excel.

This book will introduce and develop the skills you must have to be a good skipper and crew member. Whether you are tending docking lines, trimming the mainsail, or maneuvering through a crowded marina, each task undertaken and learned in this course will make you a better and safer sailor. More on the duties and responsibilities of a skipper will be discussed in part six, Basic Coastal Cruising.

ALCOHOL AND DRUG ABUSE

The National Transportation Safety Board (NTSB) estimates that between 37 and 76 percent of all boating fatalities can be traced to operators with measurable levels of alcohol in their blood. Moreover, studies show that, compared with sober operators, legally drunk boaters are ten times more likely to be fatally injured.

Alcohol consumption while boating is problematic for several reasons:

• Boating exposes the operator to natural stressors (e.g., noise, shock, extreme temperatures, vibration, sun, glare, and wind) that increase fatigue, decrease dexterity, and interfere with judgment. Alcohol exacerbates these effects.

• Complex reaction time (that associated with more difficult tasks or divided attention) is increased with moderate alcohol use. In tasks requiring vigilance (i.e., prolonged periods of task concentration or attention to task) accuracy decreases and the time required for correct response increases with blood alcohol content.

• Alcohol impairs the psychomotor performance of tasks that are vital to safe boat operation, such as steering and signal anticipation. Visual acuity is reduced in low contrast situations such as twilight and night conditions.

• Fatigue increases with alcohol consumption.

• Intellectual functions are sensitive to the effects of alcohol. Verbal performance, problem solving, and short-term memory are adversely affected by alcohol.

• Balance is adversely affected by alcohol, increasing the likelihood of falling from the boat.

• Judgment is adversely affected by alcohol. Persons under the influence appear to be willing to take greater risks and to underestimate their degree of impairment.

These are all excellent reasons to refrain from consumption of alcohol while boating. Nonetheless, the American Red Cross National Boating Survey reveals that 29 percent of all boaters reported using alcohol during typical outings, and the percentages for operators of cabin cruisers and cabin sailboats were higher, 44.6 percent and 41.6 percent respectively.

Here are some ideas to reduce alcohol related risks:

• Refrain from alcohol consumption until safely tied up at the end of the day. This is the best strategy.

• Limit consumption to one drink or less per hour.

• Eat before and while drinking.

• Alternate between drinking alcoholic and nonalcoholic beverages. Use nonalcoholic beverages to quench thirst before drinking alcoholic beverages.

• Don't invite people who characteristically drink to excess.

• Don't bring large amounts of alcohol.

• Don't stop at waterside drinking establishments.

Operating a vessel while intoxicated became a specific federal offense effective January 13, 1988. The final rule set standards for determining when an individual is intoxicated. If the blood alcohol content (BAC) is 0.10 percent or greater for operators of recreational vessels being used solely for pleasure, violators are subject to a civil penalty not to exceed $1,000 or a criminal penalty not to exceed $5,000, one-year imprisonment, or both. State laws may have other penalties, such as forfeiture of vessel (or motor vehicle) operating privileges. Most states have an implied consent law and refusal to take a blood alcohol test can be used against the boater.

A 160-pound person who consumes five drinks (twelve ounces of beer equals five ounces of wine equals one ounce of eighty-proof liquor equals one drink) in a two-hour period will raise his or her BAC to 0.1 percent.

Intoxicating drugs may not show up in a sobriety test designed for alcohol. However, many jurisdictions give law-enforcement officers great latitude in determining the probability of drug use by operators. If behavior and/or other outward signs indicate that drugs may be present, the officer may charge the operator with boating under the influence (BUI).

FEDERAL REQUIREMENTS FOR RECREATIONAL BOATS

As noted above, the prudent skipper ensures that the recreational vessel carries all required safety equipment (e.g., personal flotation devices, fire extinguishers, appropriate lights, sound-producing devices) and operates the vessel in full conformity with the navigation rules (both topics are covered in parts two and five). Additionally, the operator must comply with other federal and state requirements, such as registration or documentation, numbering, display of capacity information, ventilation systems, use of approved backfire-flame arresters, appropriate pollution placards, and marine sanitation devices (MSDs).

REGISTRATION AND DOCUMENTATION

A vessel of five or more net tons may be documented through the USCG. Documentation is a form of national registration available to citizens or corporations of the United States. In the documentation process, USCG issues papers similar to those issued for large ships. Bills of sale, mortgages, and other papers of title may be recorded with federal authorities, giving legal notice that such documents exist. Documentation may provide additional security and aids in financing and transfer of title. Many states also require that you register documented vessels (see below). If a documented vessel is registered, a decal issued by the state is displayed in lieu of the usual registration number. The decal must be in a clearly visible location. The name and hailing port of a documented vessel must be displayed on an exterior surface that is clearly visible (typically a transom). The original documentation papers (not copies) must be carried aboard.

If your vessel is not documented, registration in the state of its principal use is probably required. Check with state authorities to determine if your vessel must be registered. If you use it mainly on an ocean, gulf, or other similar water, register it in the state where you moor it. Registration fees vary with state, vessel length, and type of propulsion. The period of registration also varies with the state and may be one year or more.

All states, except Alaska, register boats. (The USCG issues the registration numbers in Alaska.) You must have the original registration certificate (certificate of number) aboard (not a copy) when the boat is in use. Some states will issue duplicate originals for a small additional fee for operators concerned over the certificate's security or susceptibility to water damage.

***In most cases, a boat which is legally registered in one state can travel to another state without a specific application to do so. The operator bears responsibility for determining whether any additional legal obligations prevail when operating in another state. ***

An alpha-numeric sequence (the registration number) is provided on the certificate of registration. It usually consists of three groups: two letters (indicating the state), up to four numerals, followed by one or two additional letters. Registered vessels must have their registration number painted or permanently attached on both sides of the forward half of the hull. This registration number must be clearly visible in block characters (of contrasting color to the background) at least three inches high, which can be read from left to right. The three character groups must be separated by a space or hyphen. Most states issue a decal, along with the registration, which identifies the expiration date of the registration. This decal must be affixed in close proximity to the registration number.

Unlike state registration numbers that appear near the boat's bow, the Hull Identification Number is quite small and is attached to the transom.

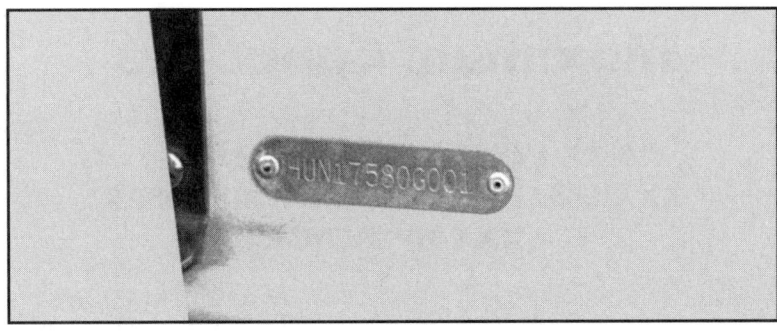

HULL IDENTIFICATION NUMBER

A boat manufactured for use in the United States after 1972 must have a hull identification number (HIN) permanently attached to the transom on the starboard side, above the waterline. The number must also be located in an unexposed location. The vessel's HIN should be recorded by the owner. It may be helpful in identifying a lost or stolen boat. Moreover, the HIN is required on many state registration forms.

CAPACITY INFORMATION

Manufacturers must put capacity plates on most monohull recreational motorboats less than 20 feet long. Sailboats, canoes, kayaks, and inflatable boats are exempt. Outboard boats must display the maximum permitted horsepower of their engines. The plates must also show the allowable maximum weight of the people on board. And they must show the allowable maximum combined weights of people, motors, and gear. Inboards and stern drive boats need not show the weight of their engines on their capacity plate.

The capacity plate must appear where it is clearly visible to the operator when getting underway. This information reminds the operator of the vessel's maximum capacity under normal circumstances. On windy days or in rough water, don't load your boat as heavily as on calm days in smooth water. Overloaded boats can swamp, capsize, and sink. Law-enforcement officers may consider operation of an overloaded boat to be an act of reckless endangerment or negligent operation. For home-built or other boats not required to have a capacity plate the following formula can be used to estimate the maximum number of persons who can safely ride in the boat on a calm day. Multiply the length (in feet) by the width (in feet) and divide this by 15. Round the result down to the nearest whole number. For example, a boat with a length of 20 feet and a beam of 6 feet could safely carry $(20 \times 6) / 15 = 8$ persons on a calm day. This formula assumes that the average weight of a person is 150 pounds-adjustments should be made if this assumption is incorrect. Note that the length of the boat is measured along a straight line from its bow to its stern. The length does not include bowsprits nor does it include rudders, brackets, outboard motors, diving platforms, or other attachments.

Remember that the number of seats in a boat is not a reliable indicator of how many people the boat can safely carry!

VENTILATION

The largest cause of fire and explosions aboard recreational boats is gasoline vapor collecting in the lower compartments of the boat. Gasoline vapor is heavier than air and sinks to the lower compartments. If a flow of air is not present to ventilate gas vapors, a spark from a source such as a cigarette ash, an electric switch, or static electricity could cause trapped gasoline vapors to explode.

Technology has not as yet provided us with a completely foolproof ventilation system. However, natural or powered ventilation systems are required by law because they significantly reduce the chance of explosion. Both powered and natural ventilation are required for boats with permanently installed gasoline engines that have cranking motors. An engine compartment is exempt if its engine is open to the atmosphere. Diesel-powered boats are also exempt.

Fresh air is directed into engine and fueltank compartments using wind scoops (cowls), often assisted by electric blowers. A tube leads to the exhaust cowl

---

U.S. Coast Guard

Maximum Capacities

XX PERSONS OR XXX LBS.
XXX LBS. PERSONS, MOTORS, GEAR
XXX HP MOTOR

where the collected vapor is vented overboard. The tubes connecting the lower areas with the intake and exhaust cowls should be at least two inches in diameter. A powered blower should have a marine-type, spark-proof switch.

Ventilation systems are particularly important for inboard, engine-powered sailboats. The engine location in the lower portion of a deep hull can make routing the ventilation ducts very difficult. It is important that ventilation in this type of boat not be neglected. Because sailboats spend a great deal of time operating with the engine shut down, engine "breathing" doesn't help ventilate the engine compartment. When the wind dies and it's time to start the engine, the engine compartment must be free of vapors.

A ventilation system will not remove spilled fuel or oil from the bilge or bottom of a boat! Wipe up any spilled fuel or oil (and dispose of it properly)! Remember the following points:

• Always ventilate the engine compartment before turning on any switches or starting the engine.

• Operate the bilge blower for at least five minutes before starting an inboard engine. If the blower fails to operate, fix or replace it before attempting to start the engine.

• Even if your boat is equipped with fuel vapor detectors, sniff your bilges. Your nose is the best fuel and vapor detector.

A BRIEF DIGRESSION:
SAFE FUELING PROCEDURES

While on the subject of ventilation, it is useful to provide a few pointers on safe fueling procedures. Most boat fires occur just after fueling and most are preventable. Fuel can leak from punctured hoses, lines, and tanks. Fittings, loosened through normal operation, can also fail. Periodically inspect the entire fuel system and tighten fittings when necessary. Gasoline that requires an oil mixture (for two-stroke motors) should have the oil added on shore in a separate container. (This procedure minimizes the impact of an oil spill

and reduces the hazard.) The gas-oil mixture should then be poured into the boat's tank. Leave air space for expansion at the top. If it is necessary to keep additional gasoline onboard, keep it in a safety-approved tank with adequate air supply. All combustibles should be kept away from the boat's engine(s) and batteries.

Here are key safety tips to follow when fueling. You may wish to summarize these in a checklist for onboard review:

• Ensure that you are familiar with the locations of all fire extinguishers.

• Label your deck-mounted fuel fill to prevent mistaking it for the water or sewage tank.

• Portable tanks must not be fueled on the boat.

• Refuel during daylight hours to minimize the likelihood of spills.

• Turn off motor or any other source of sparks or heat. Electrical equipment and compressed cooking-gas tanks should all be off.

• Close all hatches and ports and seal off all cabin areas. Ventilating cabins during fueling can allow fumes to be trapped below.

• Ask your crew to stand on the dock away from the fueling operation.

• No smoking!

• Verify that the correct fuel pump (gas or diesel) is being used. Hold the spout or nozzle firmly against the tank or filler pipe. This keeps the two grounded and prevents sparks from static electricity. Remember that the automatic shut-off on the fuel nozzle may not work on your boat. Never leave a fuel hose unattended while refueling!

• Do not overfill the tank (see below). To minimize the likelihood of a spill, estimate the amount of fuel that you will need and have one of your crew call out the amount delivered if you cannot see the dial on the fuel pump.

• Wipe up all spills. Your clean-up rags should be allowed to dry in the open air, not in the boat. If rags must be stored, store them in an air-tight container. Better yet, use disposable rags.

• When fueling is completed, open all hatches and ports. Enclosed areas should be allowed to air-out for at least five minutes. Use the blower for at least five minutes before starting the engine.

• Check all fuel lines and connections again for leaks. Check enclosed areas for fumes. Start the engine and invite your crew back aboard.

BACKFIRE-FLAME ARRESTERS

Gasoline engines, other than outboards, must have acceptable means of backfire control. Backfires occur when flames from an engine exit through the carburetor instead of the exhaust system. A backfire control keeps the flames from entering the engine compartment. The usual method of controlling backfires is by a backfire-flame arrester mounted atop the engine's carburetor. A flame arrester works by rapidly dissipating the heat of the flame. Thus, the flame is kept out of the engine compartment. An acceptable backfire-flame arrester bears a Coast Guard approval number, or it shows that it complies with Underwriters Laboratories Standard UL 1111. The label may also state that it complies with the Society of Automotive Engineers Standard SAE J-1928.

To be effective, flame arresters must

be free of oil, grease, and dirt. Grease dissolving detergents are available for this purpose. Other than periodic cleaning, backfire-flame arresters do not need servicing or replacement.

MARINE SANITATION DEVICES

There is no requirement to equip your boat with a marine toilet. However, installed toilets must have Type I, II, or III marine sanitation devices (MSDs), certified by the Coast Guard. Most pleasure boats have Type III MSDs, which use holding tanks to contain waste until it can be properly disposed of onshore. Vessels over 65 feet long must use Type I or Type 11 MSDs. Pumpout stations-shoreside facilities designed to empty the holding tank-can be found at many marinas.

Additives are often used to sanitize and deodorize waste while it is stored onboard. These additives may contain chlorine, quaternary ammonia, or formaldehyde. Marine life and septic systems can both suffer when these substances are introduced. Boaters should make an effort to use products that do not contain environmentally damaging substances.

Some systems use Y valves to direct

Typical dumping placard.

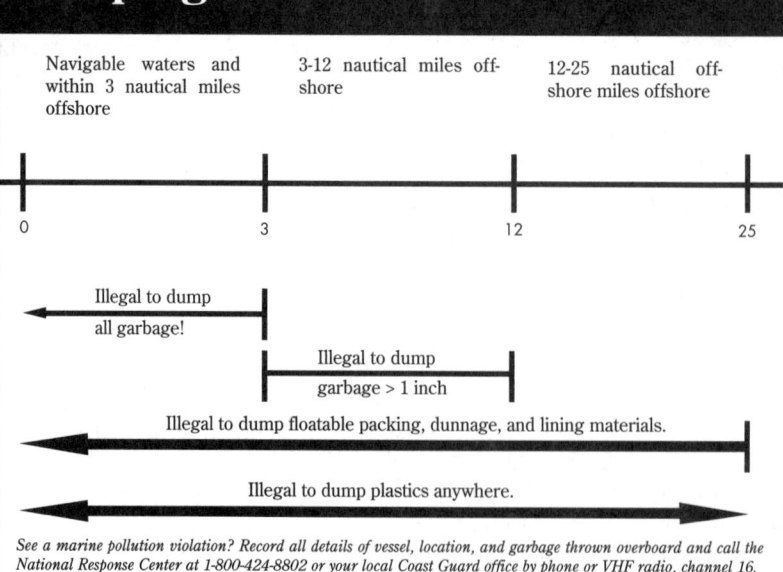

Garbage Dumping Restrictions

Under Federal law, it is illegal to discharge plastic or garbage mixed with plastic into any waters. Regional, state, or local regulations may also apply. All discharge of garbage is prohibited in the Great Lakes and their connecting or tributary waters.

Violators are subject to substantial civil penalties and/or criminal sanctions, including fines and imprisonment.

Navigable waters and within 3 nautical miles offshore

3-12 nautical miles offshore

12-25 nautical off-shore miles offshore

0   3   12   25

← Illegal to dump all garbage!

Illegal to dump garbage > 1 inch

← Illegal to dump floatable packing, dunnage, and lining materials. →

← Illegal to dump plastics anywhere. →

See a marine pollution violation? Record all details of vessel, location, and garbage thrown overboard and call the National Response Center at 1-800-424-8802 or your local Coast Guard office by phone or VHF radio, channel 16.

waste into the holding tank or directly overboard. Boats with a Y valve that can direct waste overboard must use special caution on inland waters, in a "No-discharge Area," or within the three-mile coastal limit. Consult state and local rules regarding the operation of this system.

POLLUTION

For too many years, it was thought that the sheer volume of rivers, bays, and oceans was so great that there was little man could do to cause significant environmental damage. Today, we recognize the fallacy of that assumption and understand that we all share a responsibility to help keep our waters clean and to avoid damage to fragile wetlands and other sensitive areas. There is much that all boaters (both power and sail) can do to reduce environmental impacts. Here are a few suggestions:

• Observe dumping restrictions (see below). These are easily complied with and can significantly reduce environmental impact. Stow all loose items, plastic bags, drink cups, and other articles properly so that they do not fall into the water. Use onshore toilet facilities instead of MSDs whenever possible.

• Develop a waste-management plan that specifies the measures you will take to comply with applicable laws and the procedures you will use to collect, process, and move waste for proper disposal. Identify the person responsible (usually the skipper) for implementing this plan. Vessels more than 40 feet in length with a galley and berths are required to have such a plan. A simple written statement to the effect that the skipper is in charge of trash and trash disposal in accordance with the Act to Prevent Pollution from Ships (MARPOL Annex V) is all that is required.

• Check the bilge frequently for signs of oily wastes and use approved absorbent pads to collect this waste. (This is a good safely measure as well as an environmentally sound practice.) If you spill fuel or oil into the water, do not disperse it with detergent or soap. This only sends the problem down to the seafloor where it becomes more toxic and more difficult to clean up.

• Keep engines properly tuned to reduce hydrocarbon emissions. This will improve your fuel efficiency and lower fuel bills as well. Clean your boat's bottom regularly to reduce drag and improve performance.

• Exercise care when fueling. To minimize the likelihood of a spill through the vent tube, do not fill fuel tanks to the top.

• Use only environmentally friendly antifouling bottom paints.

• Use environmentally friendly cleaning products (look for the words phosphate-free and biodegradable on the label) when washing your boat. Rinsing your boat with clean water after each use will reduce your need for cleaners and heavy-duty products.

• Do not anchor in rubble, coral reefs, or sea grass. This practice is unsafe and will damage the underwater environment.

• Stay in marked channels whenever possible to lower the likelihood of running aground and damaging bottom vegetation.

• Take steps to prevent the introduction of zebra mussels into uninfested waters. These steps include: use of antifouling paints, cleaning your vessel with hot water, removal of all bait and emptying bait wells and bait buckets and flushing them with water containing chlorine bleach.

• Operate at slow speeds in manatee areas to lower the likelihood of harming this vulnerable mammal. In general, do not disturb wildlife.

DISCHARGE OF OIL

All vessels under 100 gross tons must have a fixed or portable means of discharging oily bilge stops into a container-a bucket or bailer is acceptable. Any discharge that causes a sheen on the water is a violation of the Federal Water Pollution Control Act. If your vessel is 26 feet or more in length you must post a placard stating the federal requirements. The placard must be at least 5 by 8 inches and made of a durable material. Post it in the machinery space or at the bilge and ballast pump control station. The placard must state:

DISCHARGE OF OIL PROHIBITED

The Federal Water Pollution Control Act prohibits the discharge of oil or oily waste into or upon the navigable waters of the United States or the waters of the contiguous zone if such discharge causes a film or sheen upon, or discoloration of the surface of the water or causes a sludge or emulsion beneath the surface of the water. Violators are subject to a penalty of $5,000.

These placards are commonly available at marine supply stores. You are encouraged (required, if you are the source) to report any pollution discharge to the nearest USCG office. Report its location, source, size, color, substance (if known), and the time you saw it. If you are uncertain what substance has been discharged, keep flames away from it and avoid physical contact and inhalation of vapors. The USCG oil spill and pollution telephone number is 1-800-424-8802.

PLASTICS

It is illegal to dump plastics anywhere on the water. Plastics are lightweight, strong,

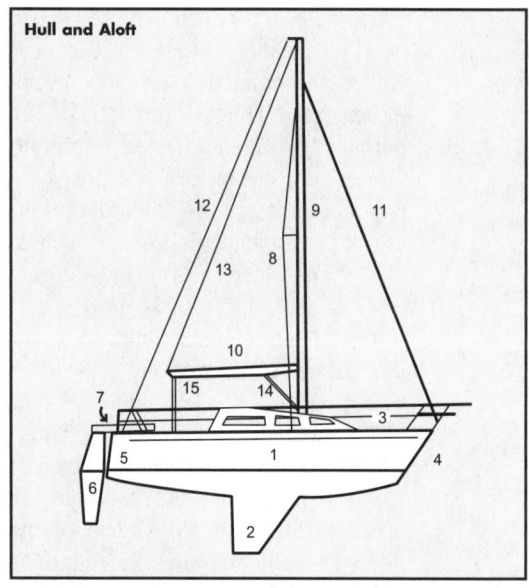

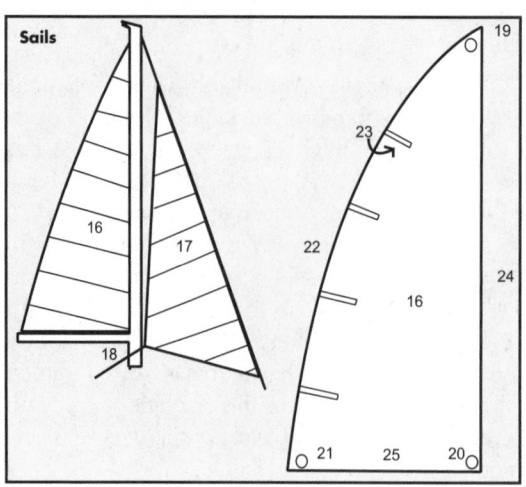

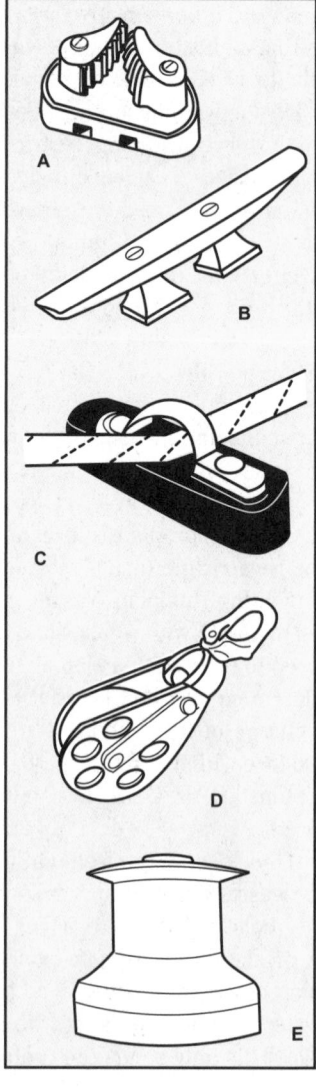

and durable. On land, these may be very desirable qualities; but on the water these same characteristics are responsible for environmental damage. Because plastics are lightweight, they tend to float or remain in the water column. Birds, marine mammals, and fish can either ingest or become entangled in plastics. Both are major problems. Because plastics are strong, it may be difficult or impossible for marine animals to break free once they have become entangled. And, because plastics are durable, the threat to marine animals is persistent.

GARBAGE

It is illegal to dump garbage in any U.S. lakes, rivers, bays, harbors, and so on. Limited dumping offshore of trash and garbage is permitted beyond the 3-mile limit. If you have a vessel 26 feet or more in length, you are required to have a placard summarizing dumping restrictions. This placard (shown in the illustration on page 30) notifies guests and crew of applicable discharge restrictions. It is available in most marine stores.

Regional, state, or local regulations may impose additional restrictions.

REVIEW QUESTIONS

1. Match the following parts of the boat with the numbers on the illustrations.

A. Aloft
headstay ——————————
backstay ——————————
shroud ——————————
mast ——————————
boom ——————————
boom vang ——————————
topping lift ——————————
mainsheet ——————————

B. On Deck and Below
tiller ——————————
lifelines ——————————
rudder ——————————
stern ——————————
hull ——————————
bow ——————————
keel ——————————

C. Sails
jib ——————————
jib sheet ——————————
mainsail ——————————
head ——————————
clew ——————————
tack ——————————
luff ——————————
foot ——————————
leech ——————————
batten ——————————

2. In what direction can a boat not sail?
a) with the wind blowing across the boat (abeam)
b) into the wind
c) with (in the same direction as) the wind

3. From the illustrations, identify:
deck cleat ——————————
winch ——————————
block ——————————
padeye ——————————
cam cleat ——————————

4. Two major types of boat hulls are _____ hulls and _____ hulls.

5. A sailboat with an operating engine is considered a _____ under the navigation rules even if the sail is raised.

6. True or false: A backfire-flame arrester is required on a diesel engine.

7. True or false: Any discharge that causes a sheen on the water is a violation of the Federal Water Pollution Control Act.

8. A boat with a length of 16 feet and a width of 5 feet can carry a maximum of _____ 150 pound passengers on a calm day.

Answers in Appendix A, p. 201.

SAILING SKILLS

BOARDING

Boarding a sailboat for the first time is an exciting experience for everyone, but it can be traumatic. This is normal. Be careful when boarding a boat; even experienced sailors have fallen in the water. Always wear nonskid deck shoes for better footing, and also to protect the deck. Wearing socks with your shoes will increase traction.

Board the boat quickly. To steady yourself, hold onto a shroud or rail while stepping on board, or hold the steadying hand of a person already on the boat. Don't step from dock to deck with an armful of gear. Pass your gear across to the boat first. Step into the boat as close to the middle (between bow and stern) as you can. On smaller boats it is imperative to step into the middle of the boat while keeping your weight low. It often helps to put the centerboard down to give the boat added stability while you're loading. Keep the deck clear by stowing your gear as it is passed on board. Most importantly, relax when boarding, but don't take unnecessary chances. Falling into the water between the boat and dock can be dangerous because a wave might push the boat back against the dock, causing you injury.

Each crew member should have a specific place to sit when the boat is leaving the dock and when it's underway. Make sure the helmsman has room to move the tiller, and always keep your head low to avoid being hit by the boom. Normally, most of the crew weight is kept at the beamiest (widest) part of the boat.

The helmsman has to sit near the tiller. He or she should try to sit so that the tiller extension or "hiking stick" is at a 90 degree angle to the tiller. On a boat with a wheel, standing may give the helmsman a better view of the sails and the boat's heading.

Run through all the motions of boarding on land first, then practice from a dock to get the feeling of the boat in the water.

Sit with the hiking stick at about a 90-degree angle to the tiller.

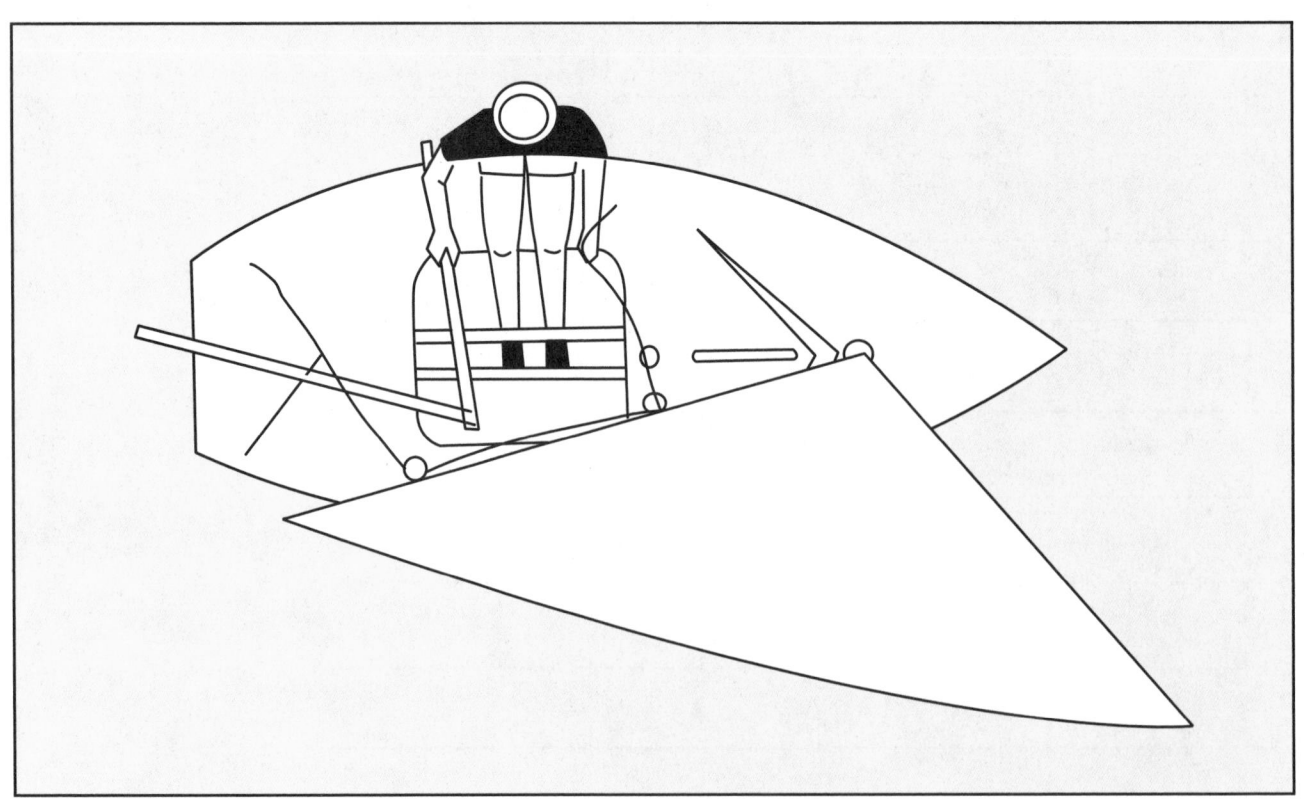

SAILING CHECKLIST

It is now time for your first sail. Use the following checklist to ensure that all required equipment is on board and that the boat is properly prepared to sail.

1. Check the weather report (see Part Six, Weather, p. 166).

2. Open hatches and ventilate the boat. Check below. If gasoline, stove fuel, or a holding tank for the **head** (toilet) are on board, the crew must check to make sure there are no fumes present before any flames are lit or the engine is started.

3. Check bilges and pump. The floor boards in the bottom of the boat should be lifted. They cover the **bilge** (the lowest part of the interior of the boat), and water will collect there from the natural "sweating" of a closed boat or from rain. Water will also seep in around loose keel bolts (the bolts that attach the keel to the boat). Use the bilge pump or a bucket and sponge to empty the bilge so the water won't slosh around while you're sailing.

4. Make sure there is one **PFD** (personal flotation device or life jacket) for each person aboard, plus one Type IV. (See Essential Safety Equipment, p. 144 for more details.)

5. Stow all gear in a safe, accessible place. Equipment must be close at hand in case of an emergency. Loose gear may roll around and injure someone during the sail. Be sure gear is stowed securely so it doesn't fall into the cabin when the boat heels over.

6. Make sure that the horn or whistle is operational.

7. Plan the day's sail and course.

8. Check the rigging and sails. Are the halyards clear and the sails ready to go up? Are the battens in their pockets? It is important that all lines be uncoiled and ready so they do not foul up in a block while you are attempting to leave the dock.

9. Assign specific jobs to each member of the crew and spell out the goal for the day.

ATTACHING THE SAILS

THE MAINSAIL

The mainsail may be furled (folded or rolled) on the boom, secured with sail ties, and protected with a sail cover, or it may be stored off the boom, folded and kept in a sail bag below. Newer Mylar and Kevlar sails are best rolled when lowered. This keeps the material from cracking. In either case, there are several steps necessary to prepare the mainsail for hoisting.

If the sail is off the boom, it will be taken out of the bag and laid along the deck. The crew will feed the clew into the groove in the boom. The sail will then be slid onto the boom until the tack is at the **gooseneck** (the fitting that attaches the boom to the mast). The **tack pin** (the pin that holds the tack of the sail to the boom) will be attached, as well as the **outhaul** (the line that attaches to the clew and is used to tension the foot of the sail).

If the mainsail is stored on the boom, the crew simply has to remove the sail cover, feed the luff or the attached plastic slugs into the groove of the mast, and attach the **main halyard shackle** to the head of the sail. Ensure that the battens are in the batten pockets, flexible end first. The crew should take up any slack from the halyard.

THE JIB

Hank-on jibs are always stored in a sail bag when not in use. To set the jib, remove it from the sail bag and spread it on the foredeck. Locate the head, tack, and clew of the sail, the head being the narrowest angle of the three corners. Many sailmakers will mark the corners of the sail with *head, tack,* and *clew.* If this has not been done, it is easy to do with an indelible marker providing an easy reference.

The luff of the jib will usually be **hanked**

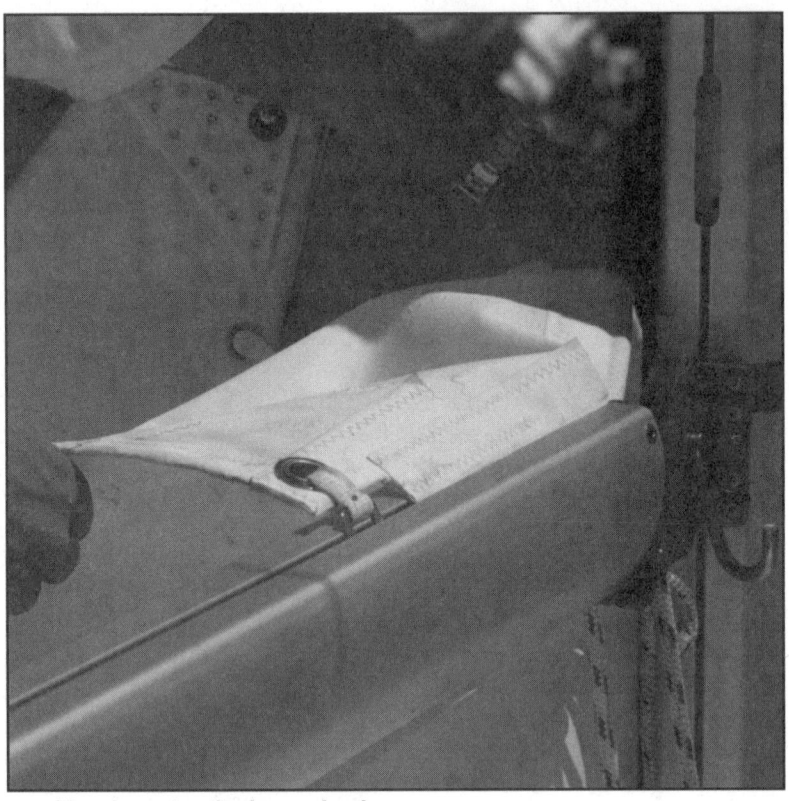

Attaching the mainsail's clew and tack

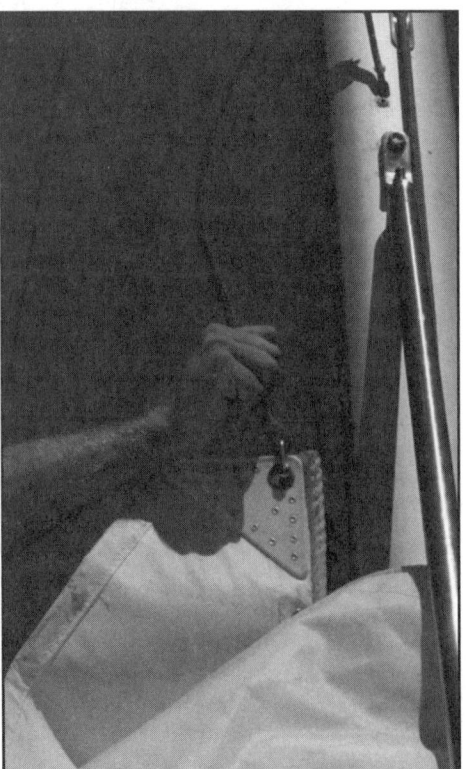
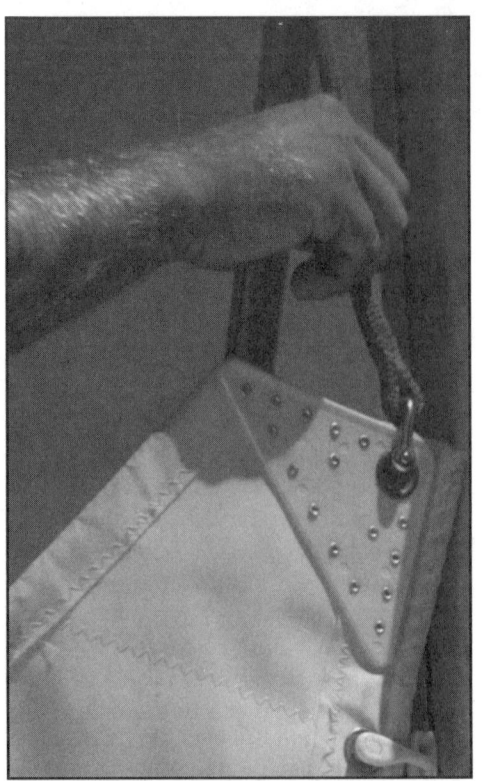

Attaching the mainsail's head and halyard

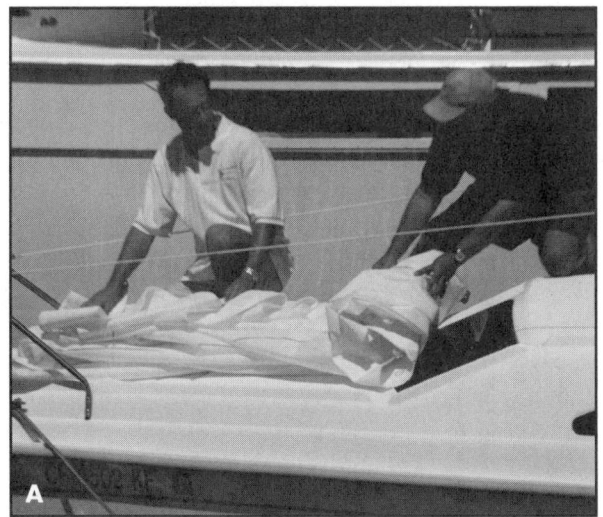

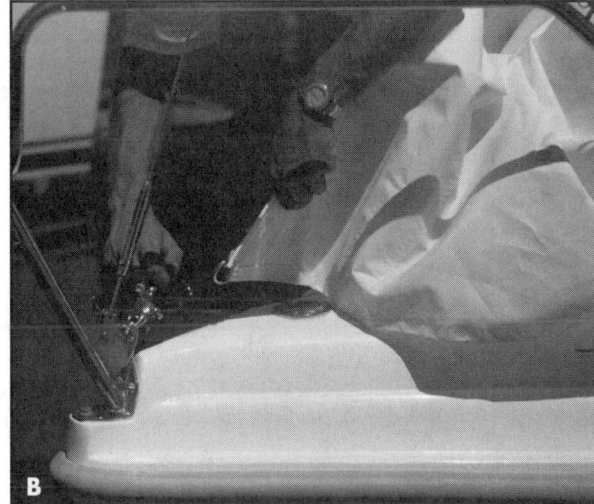

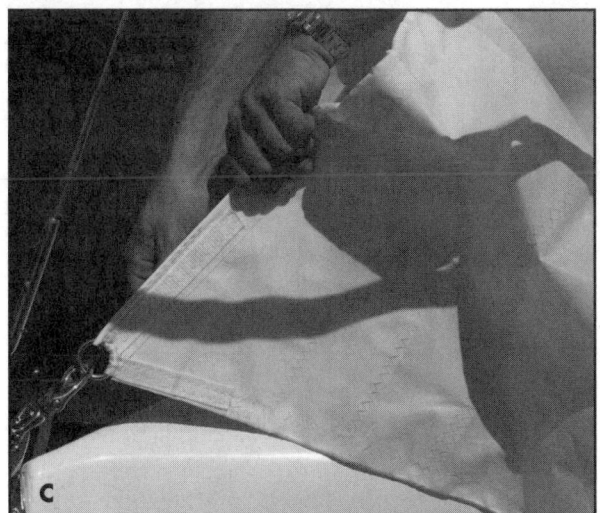

Attaching the jib

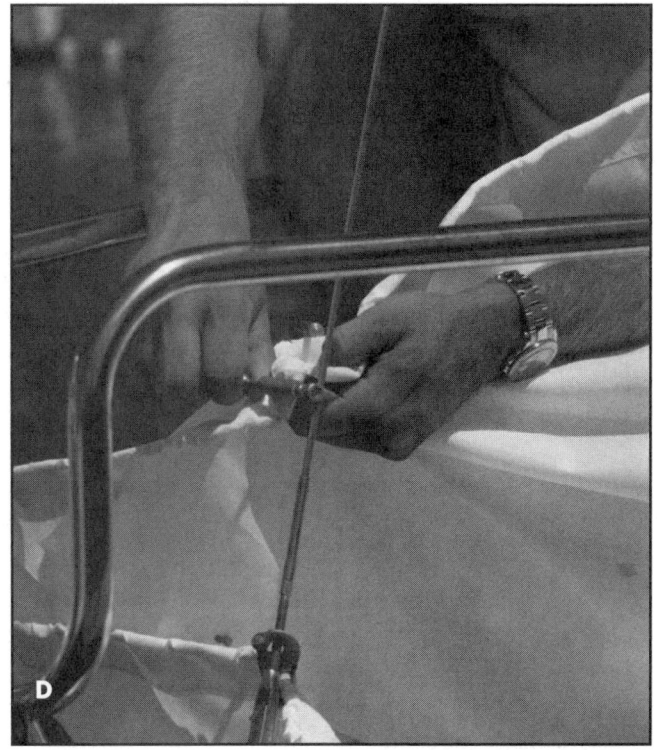

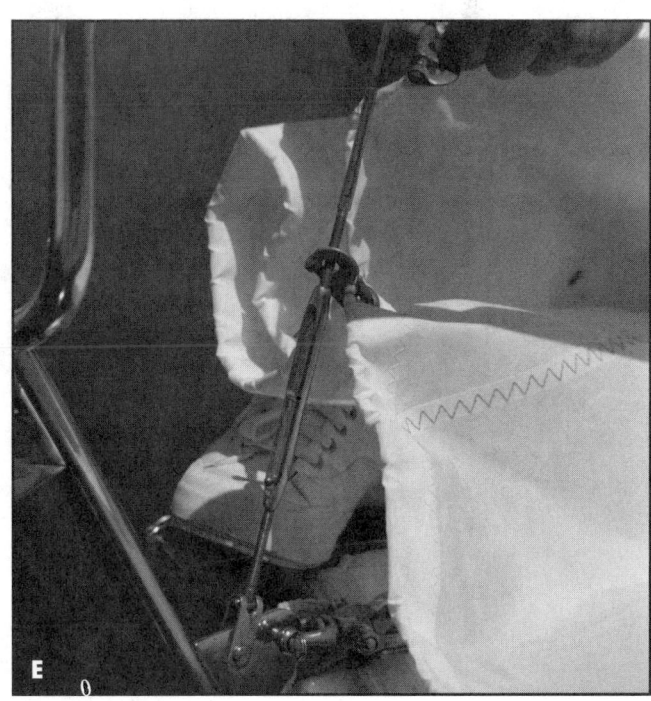

(with small brass or plastic snip fittings on the jib) onto the headstay and the jib sheets will be attached to the clew of the jib with bowline knots. If the headstay has a groove, then the jib will have a **bolt rope** (rope sewn into the luff of the sail) instead of hanks. In that case, insert the bolt rope into the **prefeeder** (a device which makes raising sails easier) and then into the groove.

The next step is to lash the jib to the side of the boat farthest from the dock. This will keep the sail out of the way while you leave the dock. To keep the jib from creeping up the forestay before it is time to hoist the sail, either tie a line around the sail and halyard or undo the top hank of the sail and attach it to the lifeline.

RIGGING CHECKLIST

The mainsail:
1. Remove sailcover.
2. Attach outhaul to the clew.
3. Attach tack pin to tack.
4. Attach main halyard to head of sail.
5. Uncoil and uncleat mainsheet.
6. Loosen boom vang.

The jib:
1. Attach jib to headstay.

2. Attach jib halyard to head.
3. Attach jib sheets to clew of jib with bowlines.
4. Lead jib sheets according to your particular boat's design, either inboard or outboard of shrouds.
5. Lead jib sheets to winches.
6. Tie the jib to lifelines to keep deck clear and secure head of jib to lifelines or bow pulpit.

Winches make many jobs on a sailboat easier and safer.

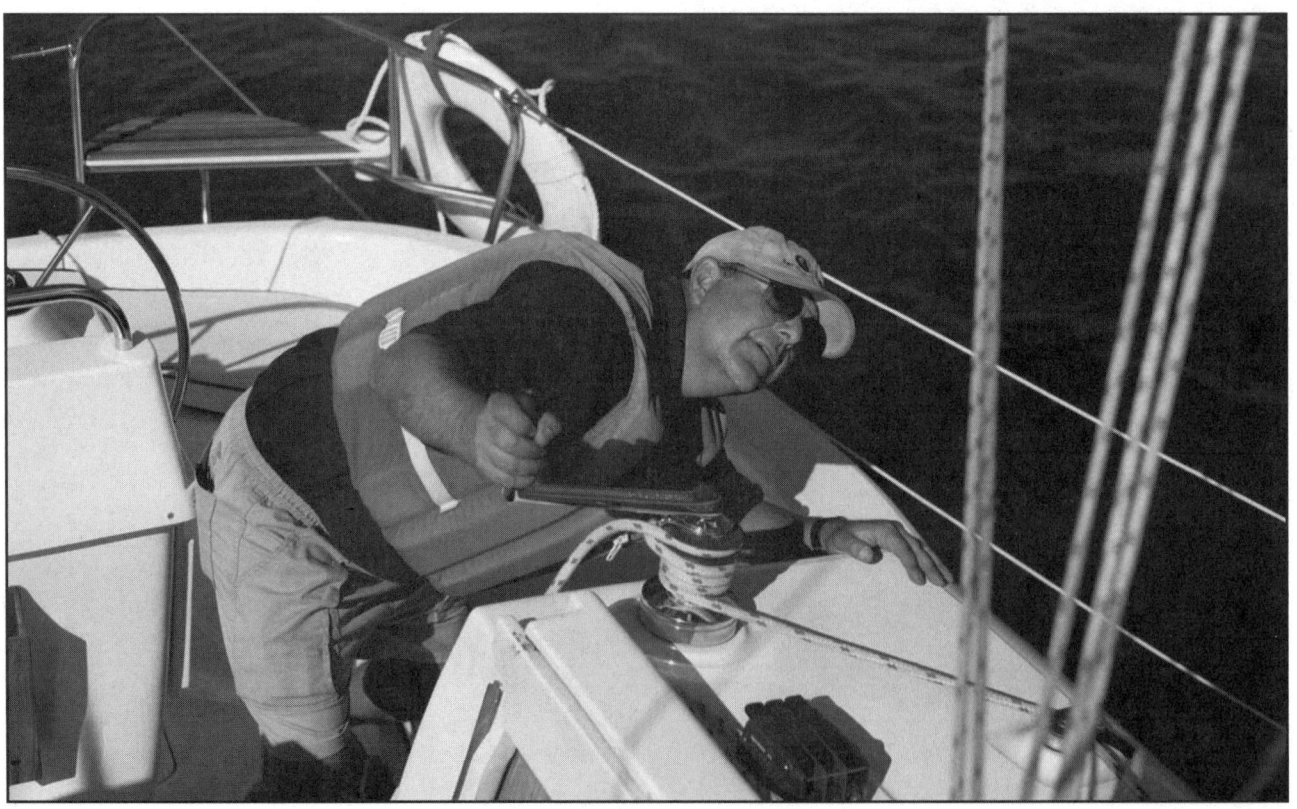

USING WINCHES

An important piece of gear on boats larger than about 20 feet is the winch, a drum turned by a handle that gives a mechanical advantage when hoisting sails and trimming sheets. All winches work the same way:

1. Before there is a strain on the line, make one or two clockwise loops around the drum.

2. Pull on the line hand-over-hand until the strain is heavy.

3. Make one or two more clockwise loops depending on load.

4. Insert the winch handle. With one hand, rotate the handle. With the other hand, pull on the line. (In some boats, the winch handle is permanently installed. When sailing on larger boats with very heavy strains, it may be necessary to have one crew member turn the handle with two hands while another crew member "tails," or pulls on the line.) Keep winching the line in until the halyard is hoisted or the sheet is trimmed properly. Be careful not to let fingers, hair, clothing, watch straps, etc., catch in the turns.

5. Once the line is cleated, remove the winch handle from the winch. If it's left in, it may trip somebody or fall out and be lost overboard.

RAISING THE MAINSAIL

The mainsail is always hoisted first because it is the primary source of power and because a sailboat handles better under mainsail alone than under jib alone. Since the mainsail is attached to the mast and boom, it is also easier to control than the jib.

Whether you raise the mainsail at the dock or while motoring out of the harbor, the bow of the boat should point into the wind. Check all shackles to be sure they are secure. Many are of the twist-locking type with a little groove for the pin. Make sure the pin is in the proper place. Keep enough slack in the mainsheet so that the sail can be fully hoisted. It is best to keep passengers and extra crew out of the way of the boom, which will swing radically during the hoisting procedure. Keep the mainsheet clear of winches, cleats, and the stern of the boat. Be sure to stay low so you don't get hit in the head as the boom swings while the main is raised.

PREPARATION

1. Position one person at the mast at the point where the sail enters the luff groove.

2. A second crew member should be at the end of the halyard, prepared to raise the sail.

3. A third crew member (if there is one) should keep the end of the boom from jumping around by controlling the mainsheet as the sail is being raised.

4. Crew members in the cockpit should slacken the topping lift, the mainsheet, and the boom vang. Some boats use the main halyard for the boom lift, so someone will have to hold the boom while the sail is being raised.

5. Don't begin hoisting until the bow is aimed directly into the wind.

PROCEDURE

When the skipper orders, "Hoist the mainsail":

1. Wrap the main halyard once around the winch.

2. Release sail ties.

3. Pull the halyard to start raising the sail.

4. Feed the luff of the sail into the slot to keep it from jamming. If it jams, lower the sail a few inches and hoist again.

5. The crew member on the halyard will

keep pulling by hand until the sail reaches the top of the mast. Use the winch to raise the halyard if the sail gets too heavy to hoist.

FINISHING OFF

1. When the sail reaches the top of the mast, take an additional wrap or two around the winch.

2. Place the winch handle in the winch and turn slowly until one vertical wrinkle appears in the luff of the sail, indicating proper tension. This wrinkle will smooth out when the boat begins sailing.

3. Coil and stow the halyard.

The jib may be hoisted now, or hoisting may be delayed until the boat is in open water if you leave the dock under power.

Raising the mainsail

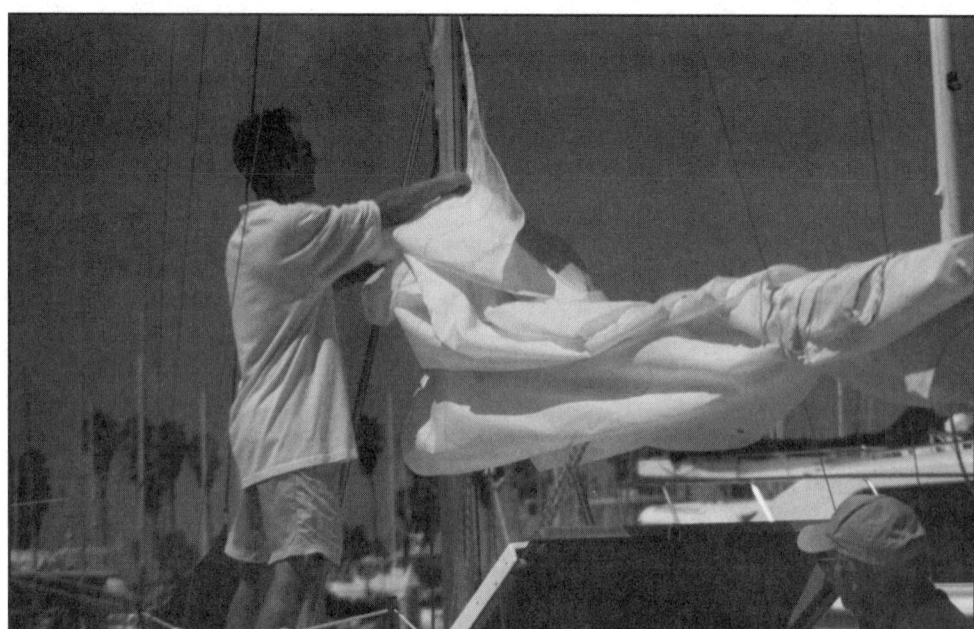

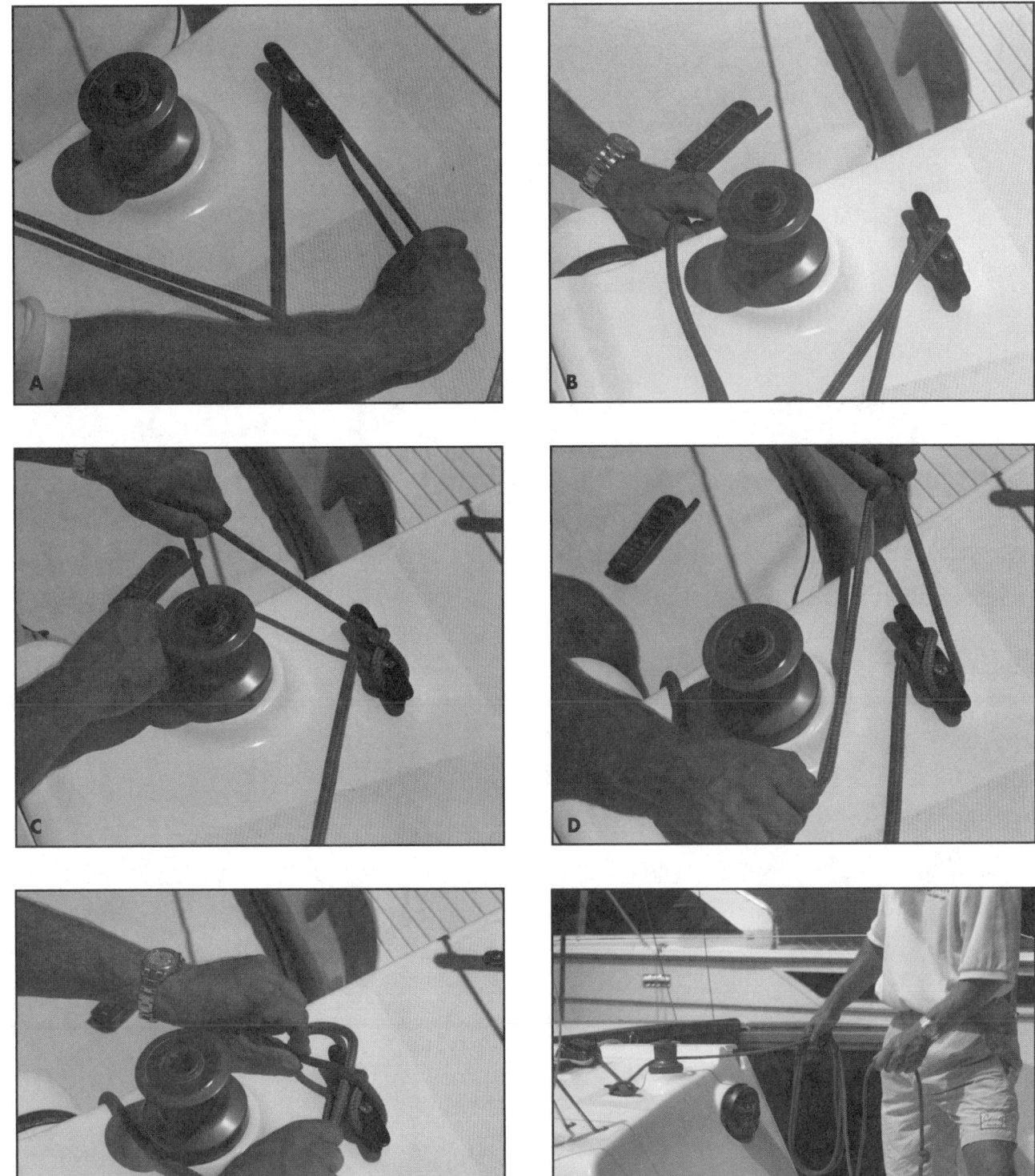

Cleating and coiling a line

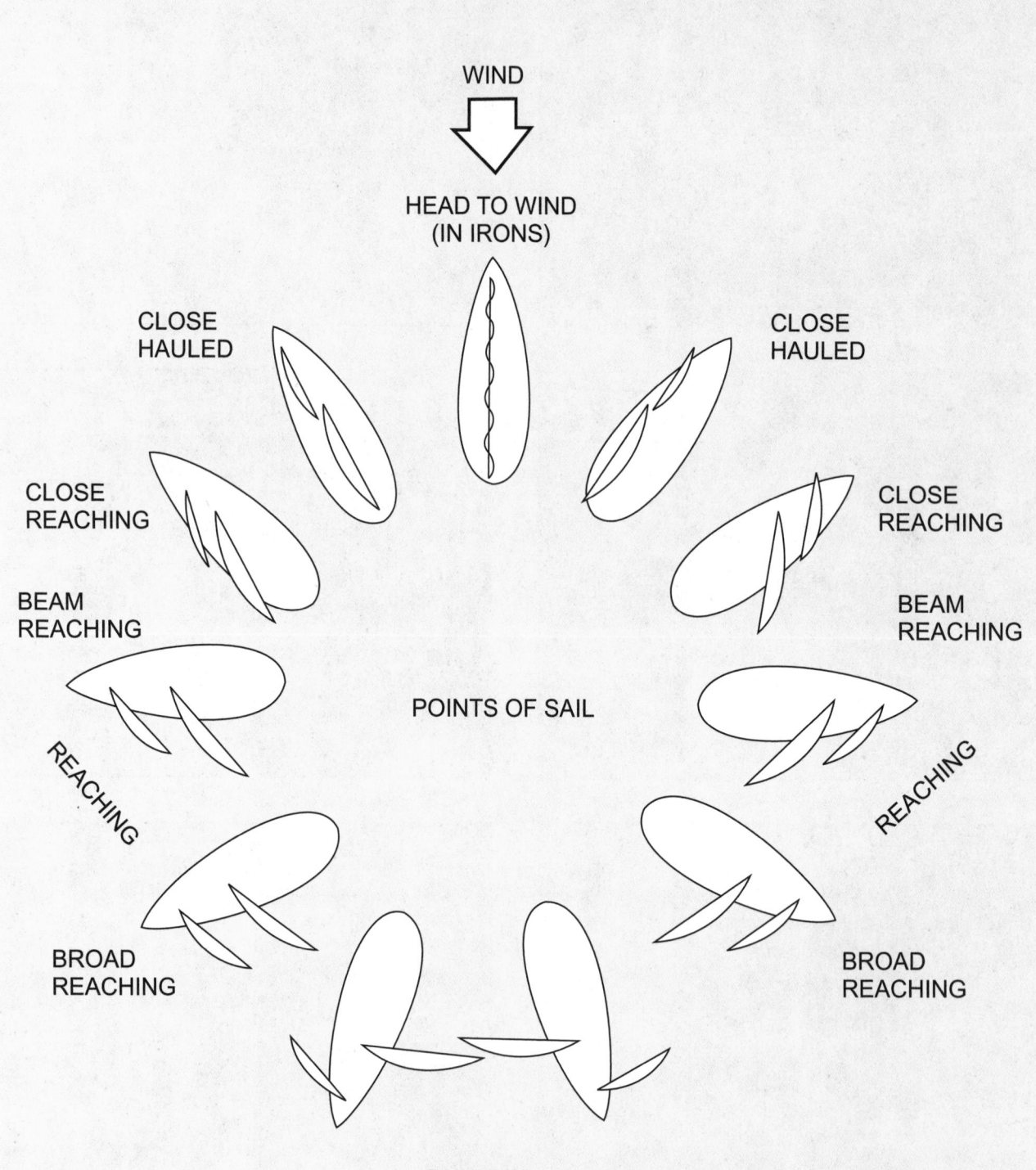

GETTING THE BOAT MOVING

The best wind for learning lies between 4 and 12 knots. Lighter winds make it difficult to maneuver, while heavier winds require greater skill. Light to moderate breezes and small waves allow the boat to sail easily. In addition, the crew feels more secure. Here, we'll look at basic skills while sailing under mainsail alone.

When steering, sit on the windward side where you can see the sail working while watching the approaching wind and waves. The windward side gives you the clearest view of where you are heading and what is happening on your boat.

When picking a course to sail, keep in mind that sailboats cannot sail directly into the wind. A sailboat's directional heading with respect to the wind is called her point of sail. There are three basic courses: beating (wind is from ahead), reaching (wind is from the side), and running (wind is from astern). The three different types of reaching and more will be explained in Part II, Basic Sailing.

Sailing around with just the mainsail is an excellent way to learn the principles and mechanics of changing direction, but it is not as much fun as sailing with both the jib and mainsail. Sailing with the jib requires more coordination between the helmsman and crew, while providing better boat performance and more pleasurable sailing.

Understanding how the wind acts on sails will enable you to sail to any destination you choose. The set of the sail in relation to the boat and the wind is called sail trim. To trim a sail is to adjust its position by pulling in or letting out its sheet.

Without going too deeply into the physics of what makes a sailboat sail, let's look at the airflow over a well-trimmed sail. A sail acts much like the wing of an airplane. As air flows over the two surfaces of the sail, lift develops, just like the lift on an airplane's wing. This lift pulls the sail forward and with it the boat.

As long as the sail's angle relative to the wind is correct (properly trimmed), smooth airflow over the sail will be main-

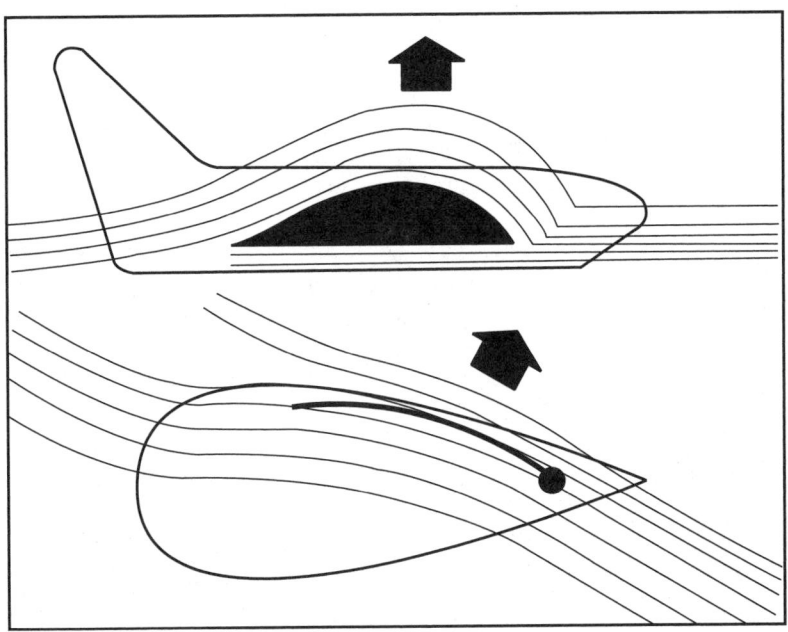

tained and a strong lift will result. If for some reason the sail is pointing too close to the wind or too far away from it, the flow of air on the sail will be turbulent, destroying the lift effect. Imagine an airplane with its wings installed improperly. How well do you think it will fly? The same thing happens to the sailboat if the sails are not properly trimmed. The sailboat will not perform any better than an airplane would with vertically mounted wings.

Good airflow is most critical when you're beating and reaching. Although airflow does affect the other points of sail, it does so to a lesser degree.

Trimming sails is a fascinating game all sailors can play. The techniques are logical and simple if you follow a few basic principles. Our first sailing exercise requires trimming just the mainsail. The main objective will be to gain a feel for how the boat sails, to learn to steer, and to learn to control the trim of the mainsail while sailing in a straight line.

Most sailors enjoy steering. You become attuned to the boat and feel close to the wind and waves.

The wind powers a sailboat just as it helps an airplane lift off.

EXERCISE: **GETTING THE BOAT MOVING**

1. The helmsman should position the boat so it is about 90 degrees to the wind. This is a reaching course and the easiest point of sail.

2. The crew should ease (let out) the mainsheet until the sail starts to luff (flap), then pull in slowly until the sail just stops luffing. This will indicate the best trim. In other words: Let the sail out as far as it can go without luffing.

3. To double-check whether this is exactly the right trim, the crew will again ease the sheet out slowly until the sail starts to luff and then pull it back, just until the luffing stops. This is a fine tuning in which the crew will move the mainsheet only a few inches.

Note: As the boat starts to move, the sail will begin to luff again. Don't question it now, just sheet in (pull in the sheet) until the luffing stops.

4. The helmsman will steer a straight course to the mark. The crew will continue to test the trim of the sail by easing it out until it luffs and then pulling it back in until it stops. Your goal is to steer a straight line. Make a game out of sailing. As the boat begins to sail, pick an object on shore or on the water to head for. Having a target to point the boat toward makes it easy to watch where you go. If the target is an object in the water, such as a buoy, channel marker, or an anchored boat, watch the motion of your reference in relation to the shoreline in the background. It's easy to see if you are altering course inadvertently. Another technique is to watch the wake, or the trail of waves, coming from the stern of your boat. If you have a straight trail, you have been sailing a straight line. Don't write your name in the water. When you reach the object you have been heading for, pick another and start again.

WIND

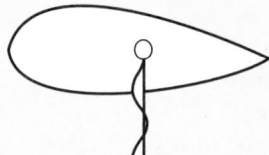

MAINSAIL LUFFING

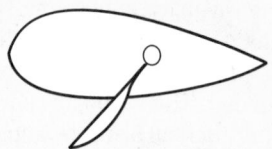

CREW SHEETS IN MAINSAIL

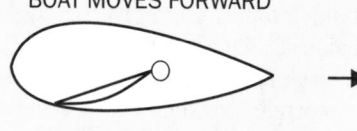

MAINSAIL FULL . . .
BOAT MOVES FORWARD

GETTING OUT OF IRONS

Many beginning sailors find themselves **in irons.** The term means that the boat is stopped, pointing directly into the wind, having lost all headway. It will not sail off on either tack. Not to worry, being caught in irons is an everyday occurrence. It happens to everyone at one time or another. Just be patient. Relax.

The term *irons* comes from the great days of sail, when a battleship stuck in irons could not maneuver away from its foe and therefore was unable to escape attack. The term refers to handcuffs or leg irons, since the boat cannot move. A boat in irons was certain to be sunk as the enemy circled it. Captains were very careful to keep their boat from getting stuck in irons, but of course this was difficult, since one error in sail trim could be fatal to the vessel. These great ships were slow to maneuver, taking as long as thirty minutes to tack (change direction). A boat in irons might be stuck for several hours.

Even 12-meters can find themselves in

A boat is in irons when stopped and aimed directly into the wind. To get out of irons, back the jib to one side and the bow will move away from the wind in the opposite direction. Then release the jib and trim it on the leeward side to begin sailing.

irons. And, when sailing under a mainsail alone, I've found that it is almost impossible to get a 12-meter out of irons. I remember we were taking a lunch break while sailing on Defender during a testing session off Newport, Rhode Island, when we inadvertently got the 12-meter in irons. Our stablemate, Courageous, recognized our predicament and made continual passes by the boat lobbing spare bits of food in our direction and causing a great mess on deck. Since Defender was in irons, she was pow-

erless to do anything about it, but the incident made for a great water fight back on shore after the day's sail testing. Defender's escape was finally made by hoisting the jib and getting the 12-meter underway.

To get out of irons, push the boom out until the sail fills with wind and the boat begins to sail backwards. This is called backing the mainsail. Now you've got to steer in reverse until the wind is coming over the side and the boat once again moves forward. To steer backwards, push

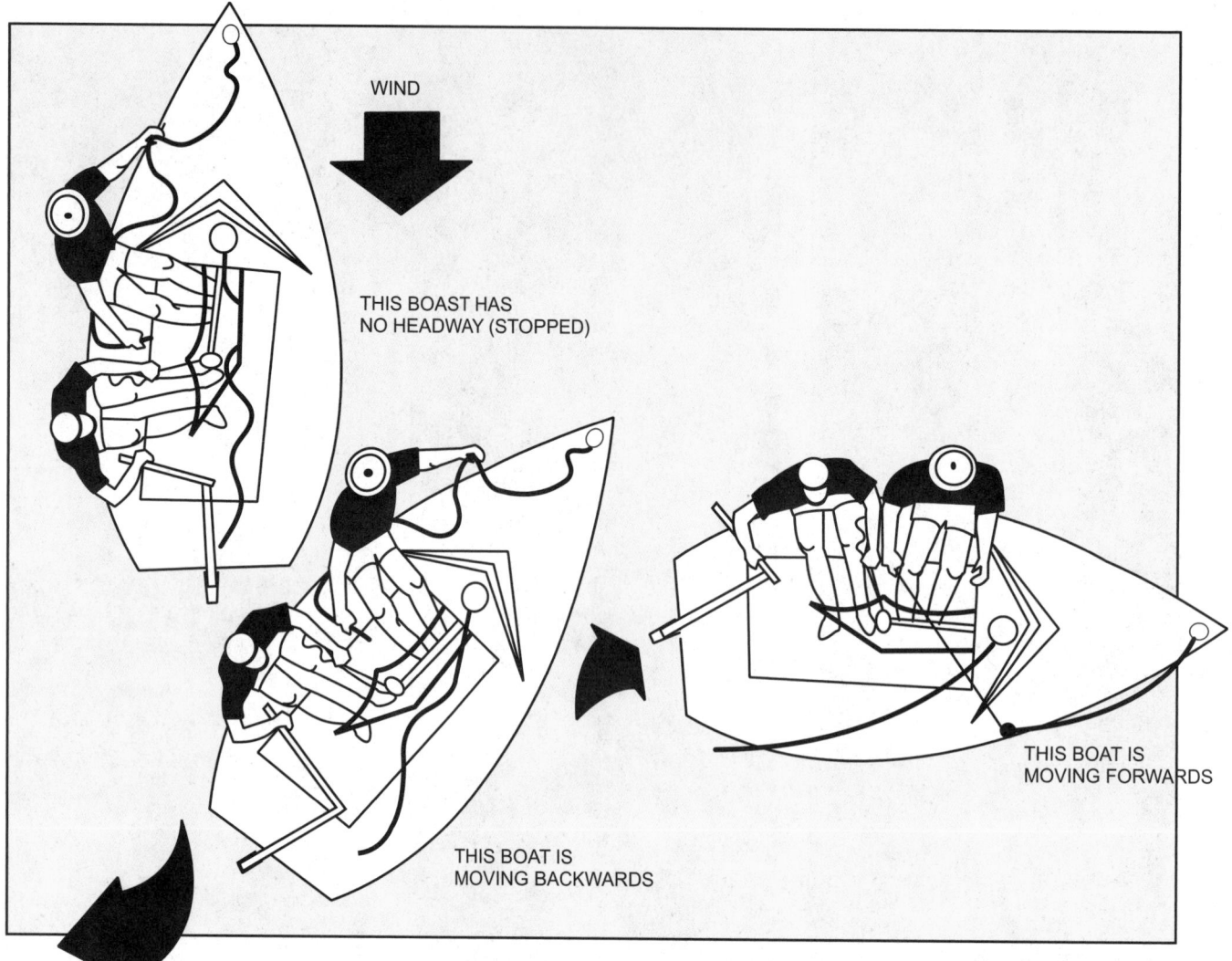

WIND

THIS BOAST HAS
NO HEADWAY (STOPPED)

THIS BOAT IS
MOVING BACKWARDS

THIS BOAT IS
MOVING FORWARDS

**Getting out of irons
(backing a jib)**

the tiller in the opposite direction that you want the stern to go, but turn the top of the steering wheel in the same direction that you want the stern to go. When the wind is coming over the side, let go of the boom, trim the mainsheet a bit, and get moving slowly. If you pull the mainsheet in too much, the boat will simply head right back into the wind again.

It's a lot easier to get out of irons when the jib is up. Although we haven't said much about sailing with the jib, let's assume that one is flying. If you're caught in irons, simply back the jib by holding the clew out to one side. You'll sail backwards slowly and the jib will push the bow off to the opposite side. For example, if you back the jib to starboard (the right-hand side), the bow will swing to port. When the wind is coming

over the starboard side, let go of the jib and trim its sheet normally, on the port side. Then trim in the mainsheet a little. The boat will quickly get sailing on a reach.

A well-balanced boat will more or less sail itself. A helmsman controls the boat and guides it along its course once the sails are set. Many sailors, particularly novices, over-correct for changes in the wind and deviate from the course steered.

Light boats are easy to maneuver because the rudder is large compared to the weight of the boat. Therefore you can rely on the rudder for all course changes. As a new sailor, you will find yourself using the rudder as a crutch. The key is to use the rudder in combination with your weight and the sails to help control and steer your boat.

COMING ABOUT OR TACKING (Mainsail Only)

Coming about or **tacking** means changing course by turning the boat into and through the wind until the sails move from one side of the boat to the other.

Coming about changes the **tack** of a sailboat. In this context the noun *tack* is not to be confused with the forward lower center of a sail, also called a tack. The tack you are sailing on is determined by the side of the boat over which the wind blows.

You can sail on either a starboard or port tack. On a **starboard tack** the wind comes over the starboard or the right-hand side of the boat. The boom is always on the port side of the boat when you sail on the starboard tack. A boat is on a **port tack** when the wind is coming over the port or left-hand side of the boat and the boom is to starboard.

I love tacking a sailboat. When I first learned to do a crisp roll tack while attending the Maritime College, I could spend hour after hour tacking back and forth. It feels so good because your body and the boat become one as you balance from tack to tack. In a **roll tack** you use your weight and sail trim and very little rudder to change the course of the boat. This is only possible in smaller boats. You can actually accelerate because you create the wind in your sails as you rock from one tack to the other.

Although roll tacking is an art form in itself that takes years of practice, it is one of the things that make sailing so special to me. The one-on-one competition found in match racing is the best. Tacking well is the essence of match-racing championships. The real goal is to turn the boat as quickly

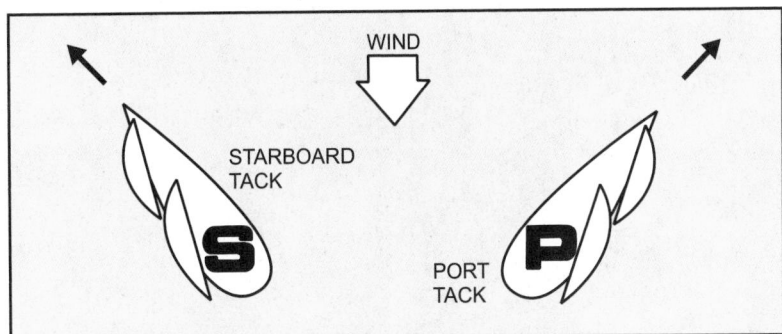

as possible without losing speed. The boat that does this best will often win a race. Even if you're not racing, you should learn to tack efficiently.

The closest angle most boats can sail from the wind is about 45 degrees, although some boats, like 12-meters, can sail 35 degrees off the wind. If you wish to reach a point directly upwind, sail as close as you can to the wind until you reach a point at which if you were to come about, you would be able to sail directly to your destination. The destination can also be reached by sailing close hauled and coming about in a series of short tacks.

SAFETY

When coming about, the helmsman and crew should always watch for other boats.

To avoid getting hit in the head, everyone must keep his head down as the boom crosses the boat during the tack. It is best to face forward when coming about so you see where your boat is heading.

The helmsman must establish a course (steer in a straight line) as soon as the mainsail fills. This will prevent the boat from going in circles and out of control.

JIBING (Mainsail Only)

There is another way to change tacks–jibing, or turning the boat away from the wind until the wind crosses the stern of the boat and the sail moves to the opposite side of the boat. To jibe, the helmsman turns the

boat in the direction away from the wind. This is called bearing away or bearing off. (In coming about, remember, the boat turns into the wind or heads up).

Jibing is one of sailing's greatest chal-

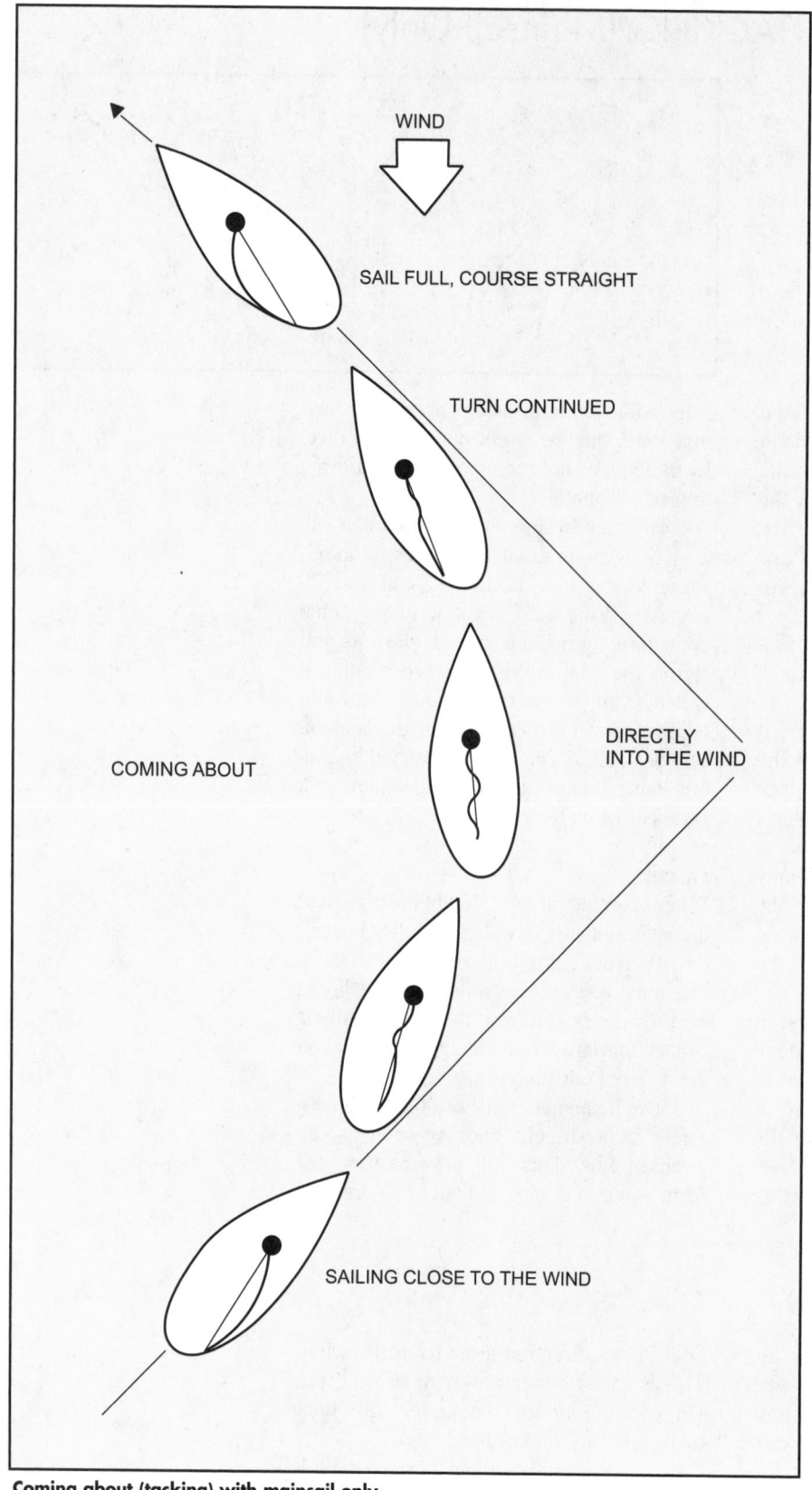

WIND

SAIL FULL, COURSE STRAIGHT

TURN CONTINUED

COMING ABOUT

DIRECTLY
INTO THE WIND

SAILING CLOSE TO THE WIND

WIND

SAIL FULL

BATTENS START
THE JIBE

SAIL JIBES
(QUICKLY EASE
THE MAIN SHEET)

JIBE COMPLETE

Coming about (tacking) with mainsail only

Jibing with mainsail only

lenges. In a dinghy, the possibility of capsizing is greater while jibing than at any other time. Since the sail shifts sides so rapidly, it is important to duck at the right moment to avoid being hit in the head by the boom. It takes many beginning sailors a couple of good bumps before they learn this important lesson.

The boat will feel unstable while running; therefore you want to jibe quickly. In jibing, the mainsail stays full of wind at all times, unlike in tacking, where the sail loses its power and luffs through the maneuver. For this reason, we must control the movement of the boom and sail during a jibe. The boom should not be allowed to fly across the cockpit in a potentially dangerous uncontrolled or accidental jibe.

In light breezes you may change course quickly and pull the boom across the boat onto the new tack. However, with a stiff breeze the boom will fly across violently. An accidental jibe can wipe out your rig.

In one regatta in San Francisco we were sailing cat-rigged (single sail) boats. All twelve competitors capsized at a jibe mark. The real race became how fast you could right your boat. I remember that the twelfth person to capsize came screaming in on a reach in a 35-knot gust going into a jibe, with the rest of us all trying to right our boats and watching the fellow. He started to jibe but lost control at the last second as his bow buried into a wave. The boat capsized, throwing the skipper head over heels into the water to the applause of all the rest of us who had reached a similar fate moments before.

There is a story about a Hudson River sloop captain who discovered an interesting jibing technique for boats with large mains. This captain was sailing his loaded vessel down the Hudson River when for navigational reasons it came time to jibe. The helmsman pushed the tiller over too far and the boat went on a flying jibe. Considering that the boom on this boat was over sixty feet long, it looked as if the sail was going to continue out on the new side and take the mast with it. But the gods, being with this sailor, allowed for the sail simply to

EXERCISE: **COMING ABOUT**

1. The helmsman should sit on the windward side of the boat, where he can measure the effect of the wind on the sail and have clear sight lines forward.

2. Before coming about, sight 90 degrees across the boat on the windward side to see the new course. Line up your new course with an object on shore or an object on the water as a reference point. Be sure before you come about that your new course is clear of other boats. A boat that is coming about should always stay clear of a boat that is on a tack.

3. The helmsman will turn the boat toward the direction of the wind by pushing the tiller to leeward slowly until the boat begins to head into the wind. This is called heading up.

4. As the boat reaches head-to-wind, the sail will luff. At that point, push the tiller over fast.

5. As the boom crosses over the center of the boat, the skipper and crew will smoothly change from one side of the boat to the other, taking as few steps as possible.

6. As the mainsail fills, the helmsman will steer the new course.

7. Repeat this maneuver, sailing an upwind, zigzag course until the helmsman can turn the boat smoothly.

The faster you turn the wheel or push the tiller over, the faster the boat will turn, but the more it will slow down. Your object when tacking is to maintain speed when turning. This takes practice.

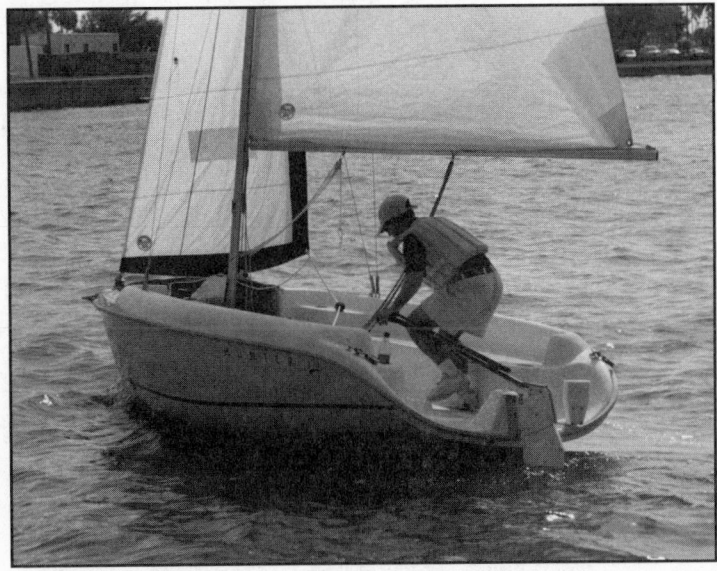

The skipper changes from one side to the other as the boom crosses the centerline.

EXERCISE: **JIBING**

1. Bear off (or bear away) so the boat is sailing straight downwind.

2. Keep your sail overtrimmed slightly. Otherwise the force on a run may cause you to "heel" or lean to weather (windward). (Heeling to windward, the boat can capsize to windward on top of you. Heeling to leeward and overtrimmed, the boat will round itself up into the wind.) The sail will indicate when it is ready to be jibed. The leech starts to jibe first.

3. Hold onto the tiller while jibing to keep the boat from spinning out of control.

4. The crew should assist the mainsail by quickly pulling in on the mainsheet until the sail starts to cross the boat. Keep the traveler centered and securely cleated. A fast-moving traveler can cause injuries and damage.

5. The crew then releases the mainsheet as the boom passes the centerline of the boat. This allows the boom to swing fully to the new side.

6. After the jibe, resume your normal course as soon as possible. Staying dead downwind keeps the boat off balance. If the boat seems to be out of balance, sail more on a reach, heeling (leaning) the boat slightly to leeward until you are under control.

7. Repeat this exercise, sailing a downwind, zigzag course, until the boom passes from one side of the boat to the other without banging into the rigging on the other side. The helmsman and crew must be able to change sides of the boat smoothly, just as the boom crosses.

Changing hands behind during jibe

back itself as it fluttered into place. The speed of the sail as it changed sides created so much force that a wind was generated on the back side of the sail. Did the captain discover this jibing technique by accident or plan? I think he found it by accident. It might be a good technique for you to use any time you are sailing in a boat with over five thousand square feet of mainsail.

Try to keep the boat flat when jibing. Put the centerboard down halfway. Too little board will allow the bottom to spin out from under the mast; too much board will cause the board to steer the boat and tip it. In stronger winds, keep your weight aft during the jibe so the bow does not dip into the water.

Important: When steering, change hands early in a jibe so you do not get twisted up in the boat. If you are forward of the tiller, move it by passing it from one hand to the other behind you.

Getting your boat moving quickly after a jibe is difficult. The heavier the boat, the longer it will take to accelerate. A square-rigger will take minutes before it is moving at full speed. Even a 12-meter sloop will sometimes take a full minute to get up to top speed. A smaller boat, like a Sunfish, can easily reach top speed in ten seconds. To accelerate a boat, keep it on course as close to a reach as possible. Trimming your sails to the most efficient point and keeping the boat flat are essential. These combined forces will help the boat to sail at full speed.

S-JIBE AND ROLL JIBE

There are two special methods of jibing. One is the **S-jibe,** used when the wind is blowing hard and there is a chance of capsizing. In strong-wind jibing, the main boom comes over with such force that it goes too far out on the new side and the boat begins to round into the wind. At its worst, this loss of control can capsize dinghies or **broach** (spin out of control into the wind) larger keel boats. To stay upright, you must keep the boat under the mast and the boat in balance. Steering an S course when jibing can accomplish this.

As you go into an S-jibe, bear off and

keep the boat sailing slightly by the lee. This is the point of sail where the wind is coming over the corner of the stern that the boom is still on. It is a temporary point of sail only. Keep the main overtrimmed at this time. Then, as the mainsail is coming across the boat, steer back in the direction in which the main is going. This change of course reduces the power in the sail and doesn't allow the boat to round into the wind. As the main fills on the new side, keep it overtrimmed and resume course, having completed your jibe.

When there is little sea and the air is calm, use the **roll jibe** in sailing small dinghies. The advantage of this technique is that you can jibe the boat without changing course and accelerate rapidly. Basically, you sail dead downwind or slightly by the lee. With your weight, roll your boat to leeward about 10 degrees, then roll it hard to windward, giving a rapid trim on the mainsheet. Have the crew throw the boom over. When the sail is just reaching the other side, roll the boat back to the new windward side. You are, in effect, rocking the sail from one side to the other. This method will take considerable practice to master.

COMING ABOUT VERSUS JIBING

We can change tacks either by turning into the wind (coming about) or by turning away from the wind (jibing). The choice between the two depends upon which direction the boat is sailing. If you're sailing upwind, you come about; if you're sailing downwind, the obvious choice is to jibe.

There are times, however, particularly in heavy winds, when jibing can be dangerous. Since the sail does not lose any power during a jibe, it will swing with tremendous force as the boom slams across the boat and the sail crashes to a stop at the shrouds. Consequently, in strong winds coming about is the preferred maneuver even though it takes slightly longer when you're sailing downwind. Instead of jibing through, for example, a 90-degree arc, you head up and come about through 270 degrees.

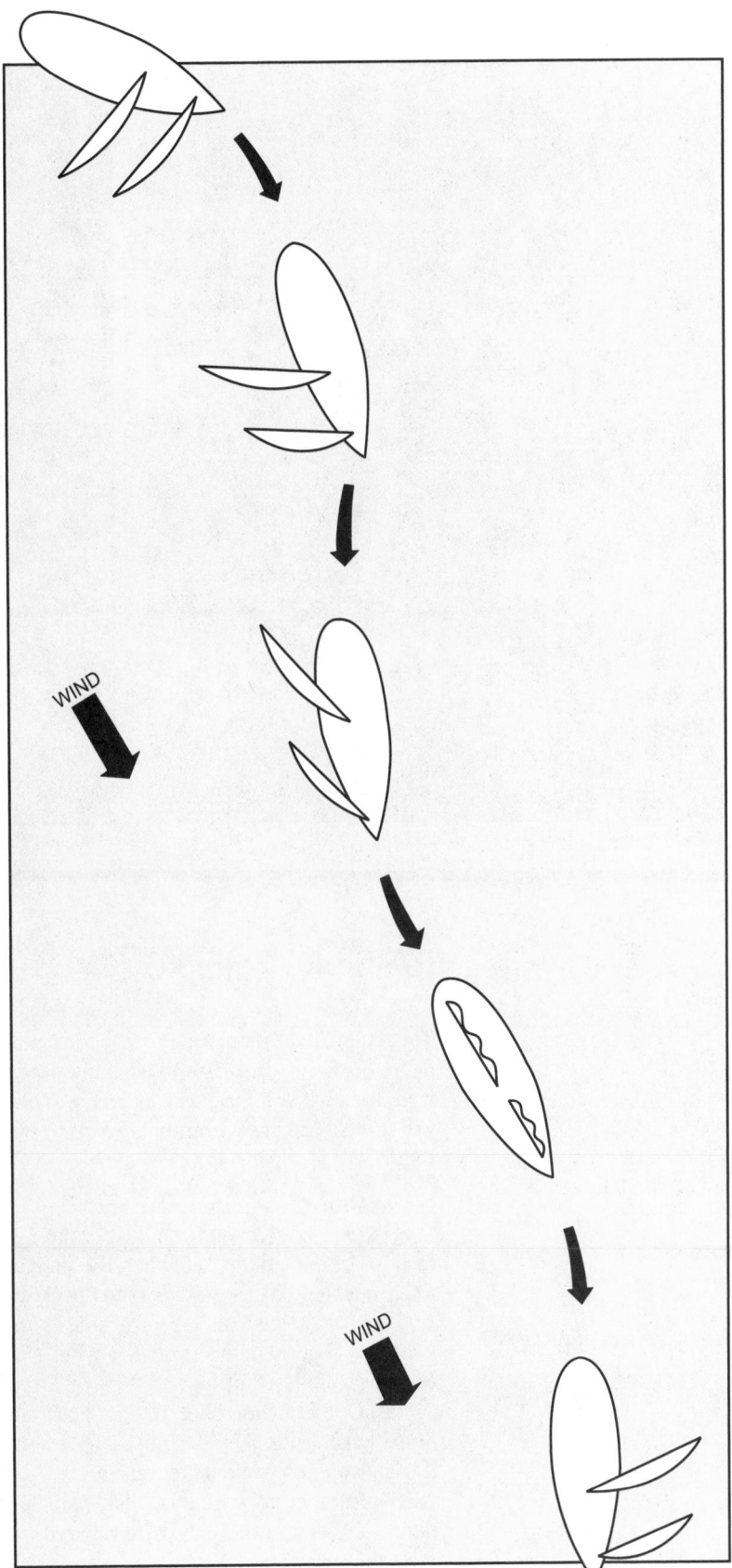

S-jibe

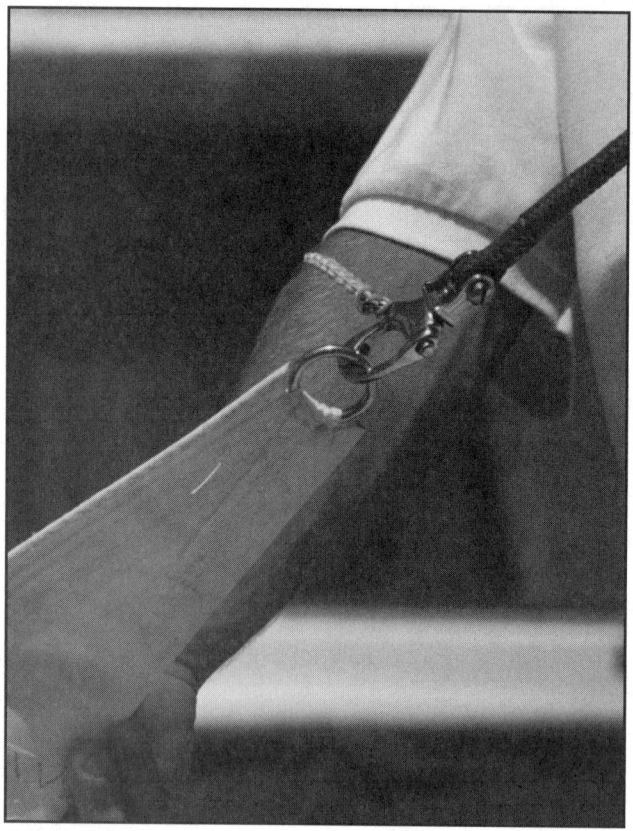

Attaching the jib halyard

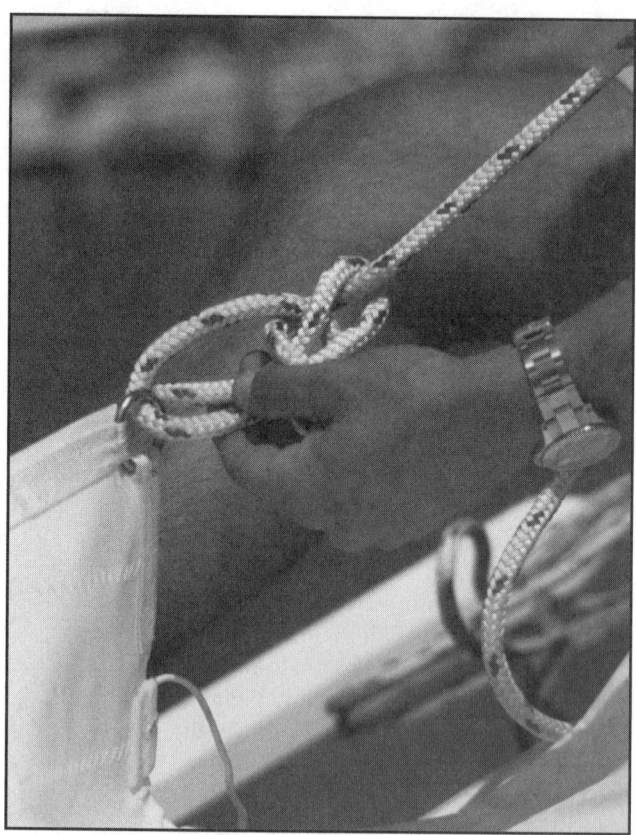

Attaching the jib sheets to the clew

RAISING THE JIB

The helmsman should point the bow 30 degrees off the wind. The jib will blow away from the boat and mast as it is raised. This will protect the crew from being beaten by the flailing jib sheets and clew of the sail.

PREPARATION

1. One crew member attaches the jib tack to the tack fitting, attaches the luff to the headstay, and ties the sheets to the clew.

2. The helmsman steers a course to keep the boat 30 degrees off the wind (so the mainsail is just luffing).

3. One crew member takes a position at the headstay to feed the sail and prevent it from jamming while being raised.

4. Another crew member takes a position at the end of the halyard, prepared to raise the sail.

5. The crew unties the jib and ensures the jib sheets are clear (free of knots and tangles).

6. The helmsman makes sure the crew members are ready.

PROCEDURE

1. Foredeck crew watches to make sure the sail goes up properly (no snags).

2. The crew pulls the sail all the way up by hand with one wrap around the winch.

3. Use the winch for the final tightening of the luff.

4. The crew coils and stows the halyard.

Note: When the skipper gives commands, the crew should respond with an acknowledgment.

REACHING WITH MAINSAIL AND JIB

This exercise is a repeat of the first exercise, performed when sailing under the mainsail alone. The helmsman positions the boat so the wind is blowing over the beam (90 degrees off the bow). The crew eases both sails so they are luffing (shaking).

SAFETY

Make sure there are at least two or three wraps of the jib sheet around the winch at all times. The friction of the line around the winch will relieve some of the pressure of the sail and make it easier for the crew to hold the sheet.

Never allow fingers or clothing inside the area where the sheet comes onto the winch.

For now, the crew should not cleat the

EXERCISE: REACHING

1. The crew trims the mainsail until the sail just stops luffing.

2. The helmsman keeps the boat in a straight line by using a buoy or an object on shore as a guide.

3. When the mainsail is full, the crew begins trimming the jib sheet on the leeward side of the boat (this is the side on which the sails are set).

4. As the jib starts to fill, the boat will heel and gain speed.

5. The sails will start to luff (flutter) slightly as the boat accelerates. The crew then retrims the sails until the luffing stops.

---

jib sheet. If the boat has to be slowed, the jib sheet need only be released from someone's hand rather than taken off a cleat. Sheets should never be cleated in puffy winds or during a maneuver.

COMING ABOUT WITH MAINSAIL AND JIB

Remember how easy it was to come about under mainsail alone? It will be that easy with both sails, if the proper system is used. Remember, the helmsman should keep his weight on the windward side (the side opposite the mainsail) to balance the boat, and he should face forward. The exercise on page 49 or 56 shows how the boat is tacked.

SAILING A FIGURE EIGHT

Using two marks set in a line at right angles to the wind, sail a figure eight course, tacking only. As we'll see later, this maneuver is vital in rescuing a man overboard, so practice until you can complete every part of it smoothly. To ensure that the roles of helmsman, mainsheet trimmer, and jib sheet trimmer are learned by everyone on board, each person should rotate through each of these duties. The best-sailed boats are ones on which every crew member can perform every function.

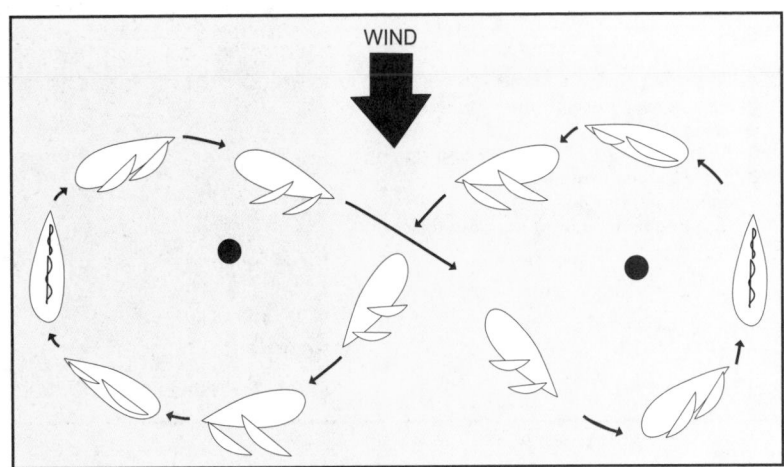

Sailing a figure eight course, tacking only, with mainsail and jib.

EXERCISE: **COMING ABOUT**

1. One crew member prepares to cast off the leeward jib sheet (the one under pressure holding the jib in).

2. Another crew member prepares to pull in on the windward sheet (the slack or "lazy" one).

3. The helmsman checks to see that no other boats are in his path and that the crew is prepared to come about.

4. The helmsman informs the crew that the boat is ready to come about by hailing, "Ready about." When prepared, the crew should respond, "Ready."

5. The helmsman pushes the tiller to the leeward side of the boat and says, "Hard alee. "

6. As the jib begins to luff, one crew member releases the leeward jib sheet.

7. As the jib is blown to the opposite side of the boat, another crew member pulls in on the jib sheet.

8. When the mainsail has filled on the new tack, the helmsman steers to the next buoy.

This exercise should be repeated until releasing **(casting off)** and trimming the jib is a smooth and coordinated effort on the part of the crew at helmsman. At this stage, the objective is to be able to keep the boat moving in a zigzag course without stopping.

A. Preparing to come about
B. Bow passes through the wind back-winding the jib
C. Jib blows clear of the mast and rigging
D. Crew begins trimming jib
E. Cruw trimming jib
F. boat begins to sail on the new tack

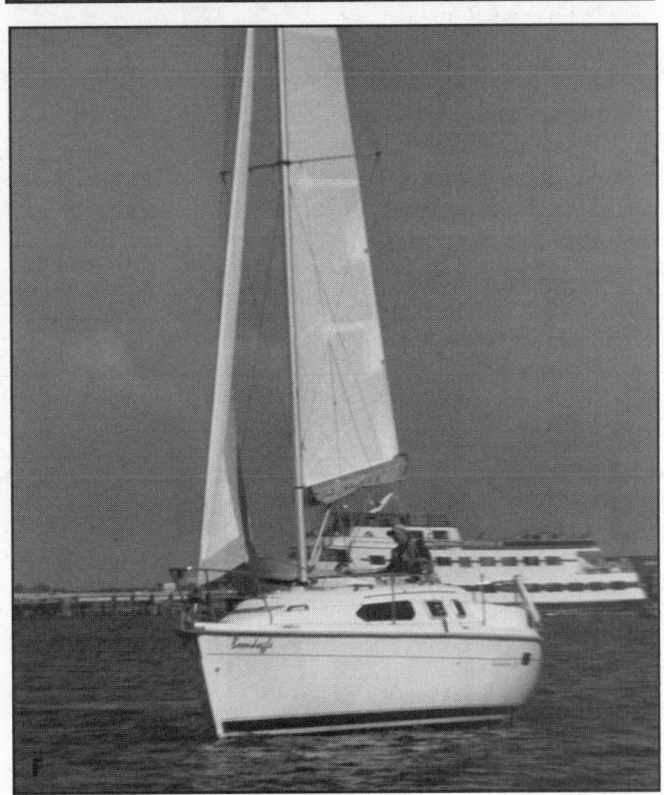

JIBING WITH MAINSAIL AND JIB

Here is how the boat is jibed under mainsail and jib:

EXERCISE: **JIBING**

1. A crew member prepares to cast off the leeward jib sheet with one hand and pull in the other sheet with the other hand.

2. Another crew member or helmsman takes hold of the mainsheet, checking that it is not tangled. This person should have plenty of elbow room, because he or she will have to trim the sheet quickly in the middle of the jibe.

3. The helmsman (who should be sitting to windward) makes sure that no other boats are in his path both during and after the maneuver.

4. The helmsman says, "Prepare to jibe." If they are ready, the crew say, "Ready." If not, they say, "Wait."

5. When the crew is ready, the helmsman says, "Jibe ho, " and pulls the tiller to windward with a steady motion.

6. As the boat heads off, the crew members ease their sheets.

7. When the jib is blanketed by the mainsail and hangs limply, the crew knows that the boat is running almost directly before the wind. At this point, one crew member trims the mainsheet rapidly and the other crew member lets go of the old leeward jib sheet and takes a strain on the other sheet.

8. The helmsman continues to make the turn until the boom has swung across the boat (the crew must duck their heads). The crew members trim the sails properly for the new point of sail.

As the boat either comes about or jibes, the crew and helmsman should shift from one side of the boat to the other to keep the boat balanced and to give the helmsman an unobstructed view in front and to one side of the boat.

A. Sailing on a broad reach
B. Boat turns downwind backwinding the jib
C. Jib and main jibe putting the boat on a new tack
D. Crew begins trimming jib
E. Boat sails away on the new tack

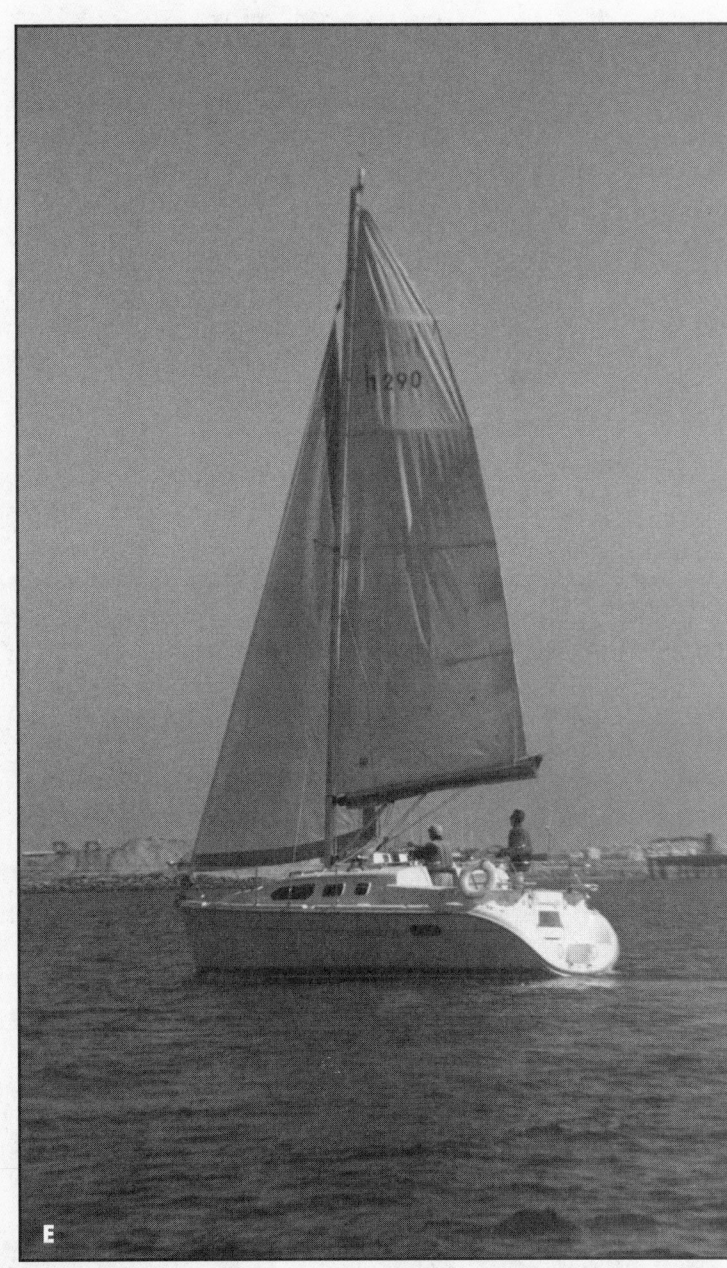

ENDING THE SAIL

When heading back to dock, first lower the jib, then the mainsail. How and when the sails are lowered will depend on your particular docking situation. The skipper will have to make this decision. We will assume the dock is easily accessible.

The biggest danger is approaching a dock with too much speed or on a downwind course. The key to docking is maintaining control.

LOWERING THE JIB

The jib can be lowered by one of three methods. In the first, the helmsman positions the boat into the wind, a crew member releases the halyard, and the foredeck crew pull the sail onto the foredeck.

In the second method, as the helmsman brings the boat about, with the jib sheet cleated, a crew member releases the jib halyard. As the sail drops to the deck, one of the crew pulls the luff of the sail down the forestay. The helmsman continues to turn the boat until it is sailing on the new tack.

The third way of dropping the jib is for the helmsman to head the boat directly downwind. This makes the procedure easy because the boat is upright and in a stable position. It is also easier on the foredeck crew because they will not be getting wet, since the boat is sailing with the wind.

LOWERING THE MAINSAIL

The helmsman steers the boat back to the mooring or marina under mainsail alone. The mainsail must be lowered with the boat heading into the wind so that the sail drops neatly onto the deck, but this shouldn't be done too early since the boat needs the mainsail for propulsion. If the boat is to be tied up to a mooring, the sail may be dropped after the mooring buoy is picked up. However, if she will be tied up to a float or pier, it may be best to head up into the wind, lower the mainsail several yards upwind of the float, and then drift down to it with the little bit of momentum that is left over. Sometimes, the wind and the pier may be aligned, so the mainsail can be dropped as the boat approaches the pier. Obviously, the boat should not be going so fast that she can't be easily stopped by somebody standing on the pier.

Here's how to drop the mainsail:

1. Tighten the adjustable topping lift to lift the boom parallel with the deck.

2. Close the main hatch to ensure that no one falls into the cabin.

3. Lower the halyard while a crew member pulls down the mainsail luff and gathers in the sail.

Flaking the mainsail

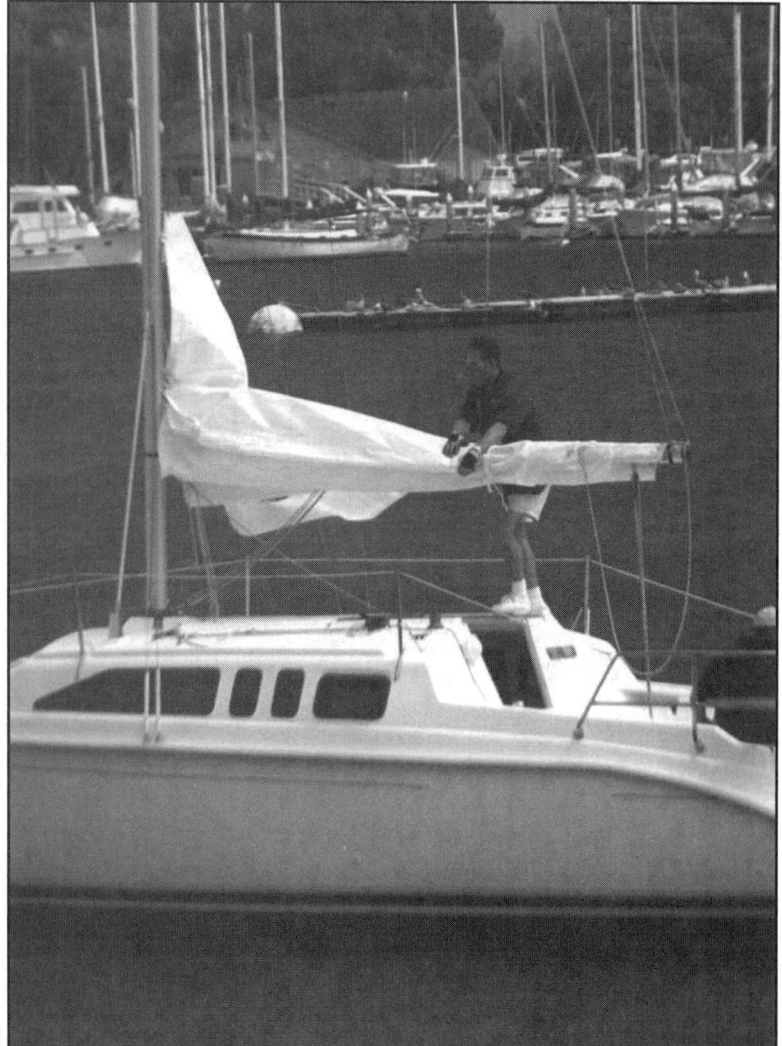

STOWING SAILS

Sails are stowed (put away) primarily to protect them. Two of the most damaging things to a sail are direct sunlight and chafing. The ultraviolet rays in direct sunlight break down the synthetic fibers in the sail while chafing wears the sail cloth thin.

FLAKING THE MAINSAIL

Flaking is the preferred method of stowing the mainsail. To flake the sail, a crew member should be positioned at each side of the sail (the luff and the leech).

The crew then pulls on the sail to take the wrinkles out and simultaneously layers the sail over the boom accordion-style. Keep the battens parallel when folding. Wrap the last few feet of the sail (the head) around the mainsail and boom to form a cumberbund, and then secure it with at least three sail ties.

Rubber shock cords should not be used to tie the sail down, since the end of the tie may fly around if released unexpectedly and could cause a serious eye injury.

ROLLING THE MAINSAIL

Rolling the mainsail is one of the best ways to protect it from wrinkles. Starting at the

Flaking a sail on the dock

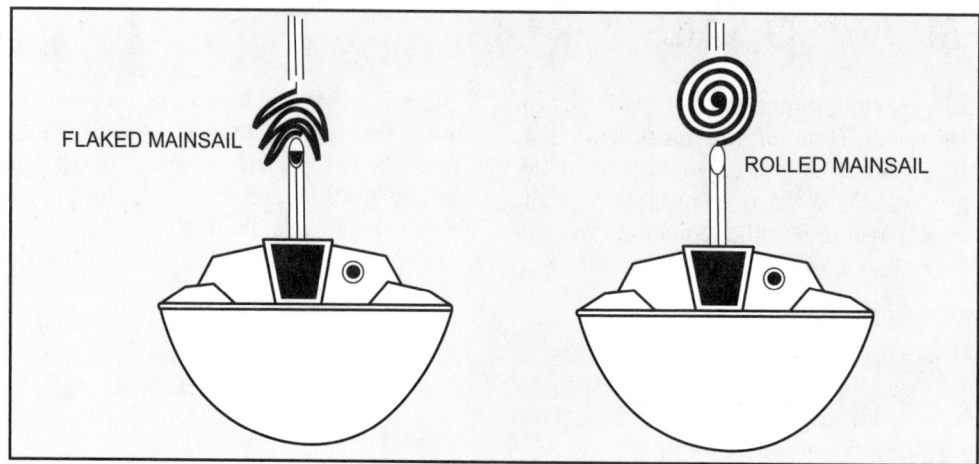

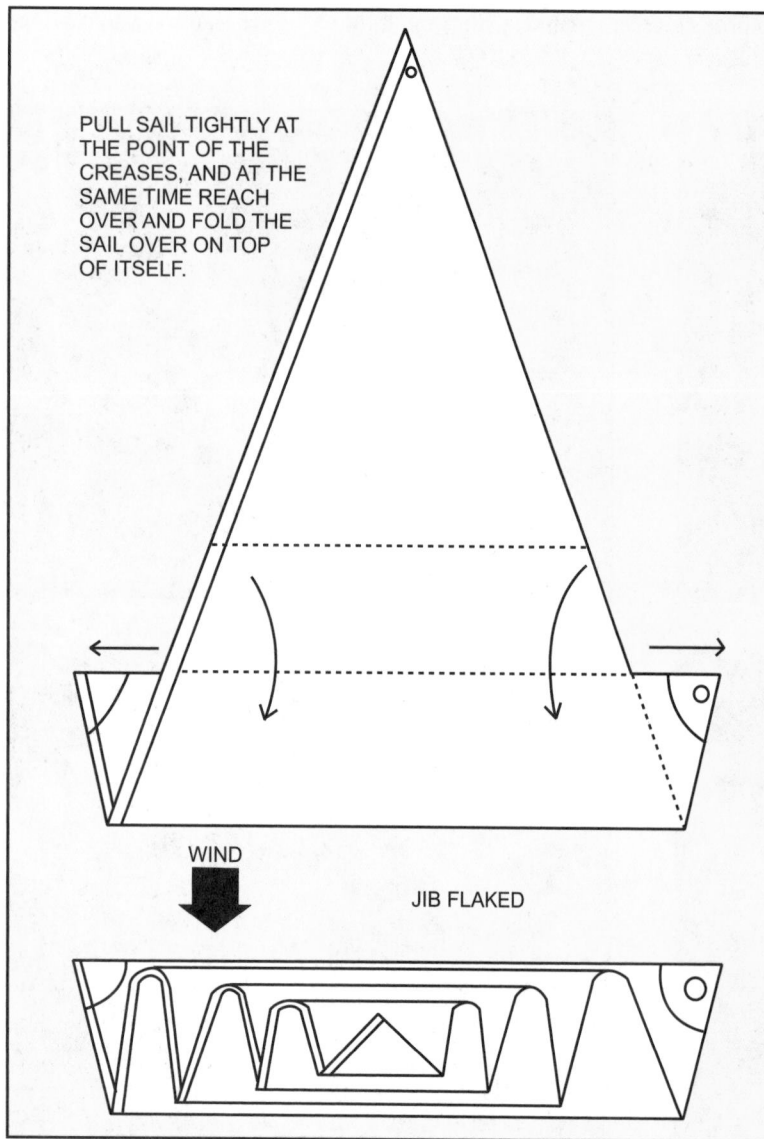

PULL SAIL TIGHTLY AT THE POINT OF THE CREASES, AND AT THE SAME TIME REACH OVER AND FOLD THE SAIL OVER ON TOP OF ITSELF.

WIND

JIB FLAKED

Flaking a jib or genoa

head of the sail, the crew rolls the sail until it sits on the boom as a neat bundle. Then it is tied to the boom with sail ties.

Taking the sail off altogether is another option if there is no sail cover; in that case the mainsail would be flaked in the same manner as the jib or genoa.

FOLDING THE JIB OR GENOA

To fold the jib or genoa, the crew spreads the sail out on a clean dry area such as a lawn or a clean dock. Wash the salt from your sails, using fresh water so they will dry properly. Salt water dries very slowly, sometimes taking days. Unless the sail is going to be used within a day or two, it should be dried completely before being folded.

The proper sail folding procedure is as follows:

1. Spread the sail flat with the foot into the wind.

2. Fold the sail accordion-style from the foot to the head, making the width of each fold slightly shorter than the length of the sail bag. Continue folding until the entire sail is folded. If the sail has a plastic window, first fold the foot of the sail over it so as not to crease the window. You'll find that the sail will fold more easily if you tension (pull) at the fold line while making the fold.

3. Fold over the ends.

4. Without pressing hard, roll or fold the sail into a rectangular shape to fit the sail bag. Slide the folded sail into the bag. Avoid stuffing; it causes creases.

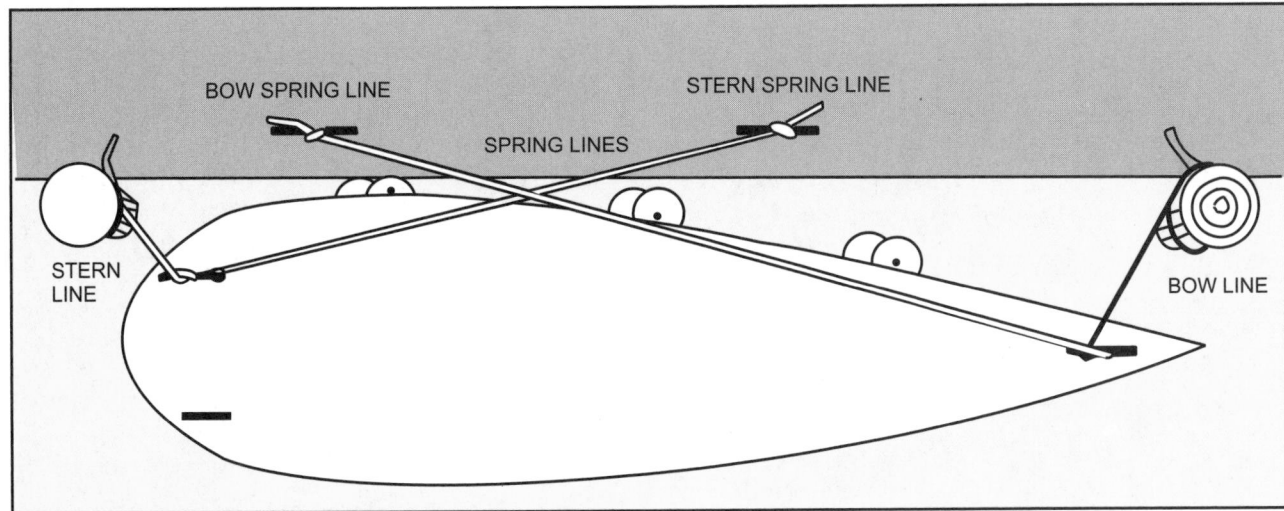

The boat is tied side-on at the dock and protected by fenders.

DOCKING

To prevent damage to the boat while it is not in use, the vessel must be secured properly. There are many types of docking and mooring systems. The most common is the side-on to the dock, as illustrated.

The crew must make sure the fenders (inflated protectors hung between the boat and a float or pier) are in place. Position at least half of the fender under the edge of the dock. If they are placed too high, the boat may scrape against the dock.

The crew secures the bow and stern lines to position the boat on the dock and then secures bow and stern spring lines to keep the boat from rotating or moving forward and backward at the dock

SUMMARY

We have covered a lot of material in this part, which should be reviewed often. The next five parts of the book will help you refine these skills and sail better and safer.

By this point, you as helmsman should be able to make the boat go in any direction by turning the tiller. Maneuvers, such as coming about and jibing, will need practice. As a crew member you should be able to trim the sails properly by easing them until they luff and pulling them back until the luffing stops. You should be able to secure the boat properly and fold the sails.

Basic Sailing

SAILING KNOWLEDGE

In Part One you were introduced to many aspects of sailing, including the parts of the boat, U.S. Coast Guard requirements for pleasure boats, the parts of the sails, how to raise and lower sails, the basic maneuvers of coming about and jibing, and putting the boat away.

Now in Part Two we will learn more about turning the tiller and sheeting the sails to achieve smooth sailing. This knowledge will be incorporated into more sophisticated maneuvers, such as stopping the boat in a predetermined location.

It is easy to understand the relationship a boat has with water: the hull "slices" through the waves as the boat moves. At the same time, the sail is "carving" its way through the wind, but this relationship is not so easy to see. The action of the wind on the sail must be seen by its results—the boat's forward motion and **heeling** (leaning).

You will learn more about how to sail a boat to an upwind destination and how to sail across the wind at the boat's greatest speed. The coordination of helmsman and crew will also be studied. By the end of this section, you will be able to describe:

• The duties of the helmsman and crew on each point of sail

• The Rules of the Road

• How to stop a boat to pick up an object or tie up to a mooring buoy or can.

SAIL TRIM

Let's begin by learning more about the importance of sail trim. While trimming your sails, watch the luff, the forward edge of the sail. Trim is correct when the wind flows evenly on both sides of the leading edge of the sail, with very little or no luffing.

If the sail is luffing, trim it in until it barely stops. When the sail is luffing you are moving slower than you should be. You'll gain speed by keeping your sails trimmed correctly at all times. As a rule of thumb, a boat will sail faster as the sails are eased just short of letting them luff. This may mean easing the sail out slowly until you see the first sign of a luff near the mast. Practice watching the luff of the sail to keep track of what the wind is doing.

TELLTALES

One of the best ways of knowing whether the flow of air over a sail is as smooth as it should be is to use telltales, or pieces of yarn attached to the sails and rigging. Telltales are very sensitive to changes in the flow of air over the sail's surface and therefore are good wind indicators. Any turbulence caused by even small alterations of wind direction or change of the sail's angle can be detected by the telltales long before the sail luffs or before the boat slows down and stalls.

The best locations for telltales are at the top of the mast, on the shrouds, and on the sails themselves. They should be about six inches long and as thin as possible to flow easily. A dark color is best since it will contrast with the sails. Polyester and mohair are better than wool because they are water resistant.

When adding telltales, place them along the luff six inches from the forward edge on both sides of the jib. Space your telltales equally, with one at the top, one in the middle, and one at the bottom. Telltales are also helpful on the outer edges of the mainsail, particularly along the leech.

Reading the telltales is relatively easy. When the wind is flowing smoothly on both sides of the sail, the windward and leeward telltales flow straight aft and the sails are trimmed correctly. If the boat is pointing too close to the wind, the sail is under-trimmed and the windward telltale will flutter up and down. Change your course away from the wind or trim your sails in until both telltales flow aft evenly.

If your boat is pointing too low or the sail

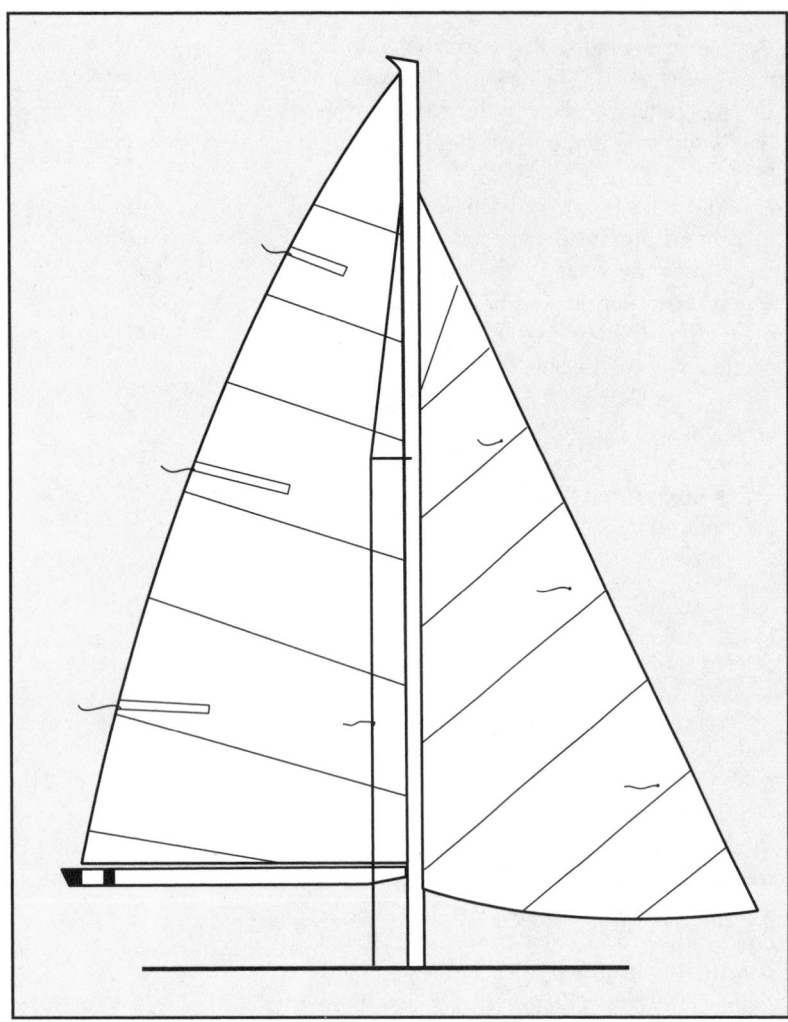

Placement of telltales

is overtrimmed (trimmed too tightly), the leeward telltale will flutter up and down. Head closer to the wind or ease your sails out until both telltales luff evenly.

READING THE WIND

Since you cannot see the wind, you must learn to read its signs. Observe how the wind affects flags on shore, trees, wind pennants, smoke from stacks, clouds, and other boats. The angle and intensity of the ripples on the water are very important wind indicators. You'll be able to predict what's about to happen if you study the effect of wind on these. Your face, neck, and ears are also very sensitive to changes in wind direction and strength.

The wind is always changing patterns during the day. Use a wind pennant at the top of your mast so you can tell what the wind is doing. This pennant is called a masthead fly. With practice, you will be able to forecast the wind. Try to predict from distant signs what the wind will do as it approaches your boat. Estimate its velocity and direction. You will get a feeling for the patterns. As studying the wind becomes a habit, you will be able to forecast wind changes accurately.

Although people smile at them, old wives' tales can be useful in forecasting the

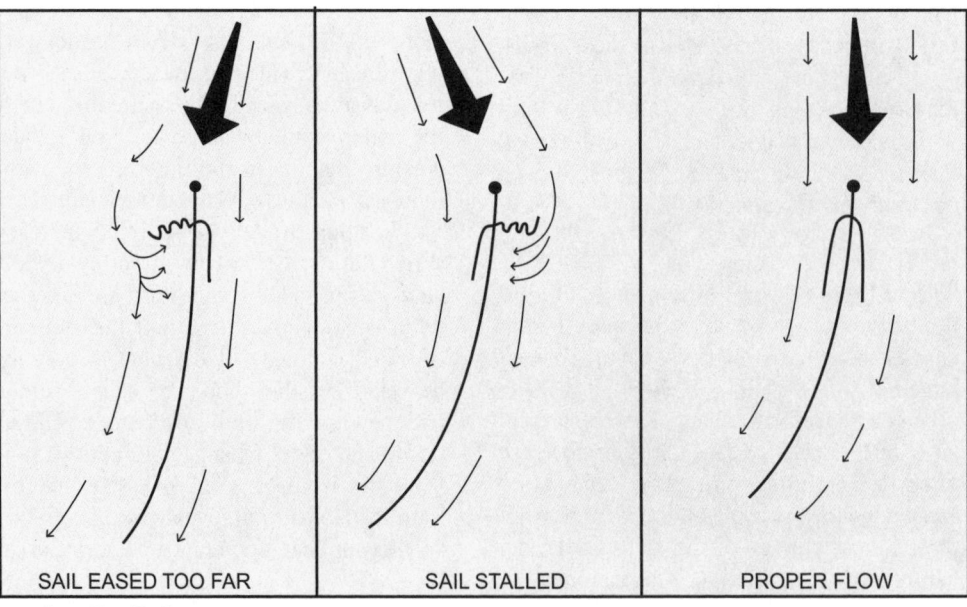

SAIL EASED TOO FAR   SAIL STALLED   PROPER FLOW

Reading jib telltales

wind. Cornelius Shields of Long Island Sound wrote a paper several years ago entitled "Corny Shields' Lore of Long Island Sound." Some of his old wives' tales are helpful. Dew in the morning means an early strong southerly wind. Cobwebs in the rigging mean a northwester in the near future. Wind from the northeast generally brings rain, at least on the eastern seaboard. Wherever you sail, you can learn from the local folk wisdom. There are other sayings that tell a story concisely: "Red sky at night, sailors delight. " "Wind before rain, set sail again. " "Rain before wind, take her in. "

Pay attention to the water. By comparing different colors in the water with the constant color of the sail, with your boat, or with an object on land, you will be able to note differences in the wind. This will help you read the direction of puffs and predict when the wind will shift and where the lulls in the wind are.

When watching the wind on the water, use both eyes and let them relax. Blink often and try not to stare. Concentrate on one section of the horizon at a time rather than making sweeping glances.

Since the wind is constantly shifting (changing direction), the sails often go out of trim without any action on the part of the helmsman or crew. Therefore, the helmsman must continuously adjust for the subtle wind changes when sailing into or away from the wind, and the crew must adjust the sails when crossing the wind.

APPARENT WIND AND TRUE WIND

There is a difference between the **apparent wind** and **true wind.** True wind is the actual direction and speed the wind is blowing over the water. Apparent wind is the wind you feel while sailing. Because a sailboat is moving, it creates its own wind. The wind you feel when sailing will be the apparent wind, a product of the true wind and your relative wind due to your motion. The apparent wind direction will be forward of the true wind.

For example, if you were on a bicycle and were stopped with the wind blowing from the side, you would feel the

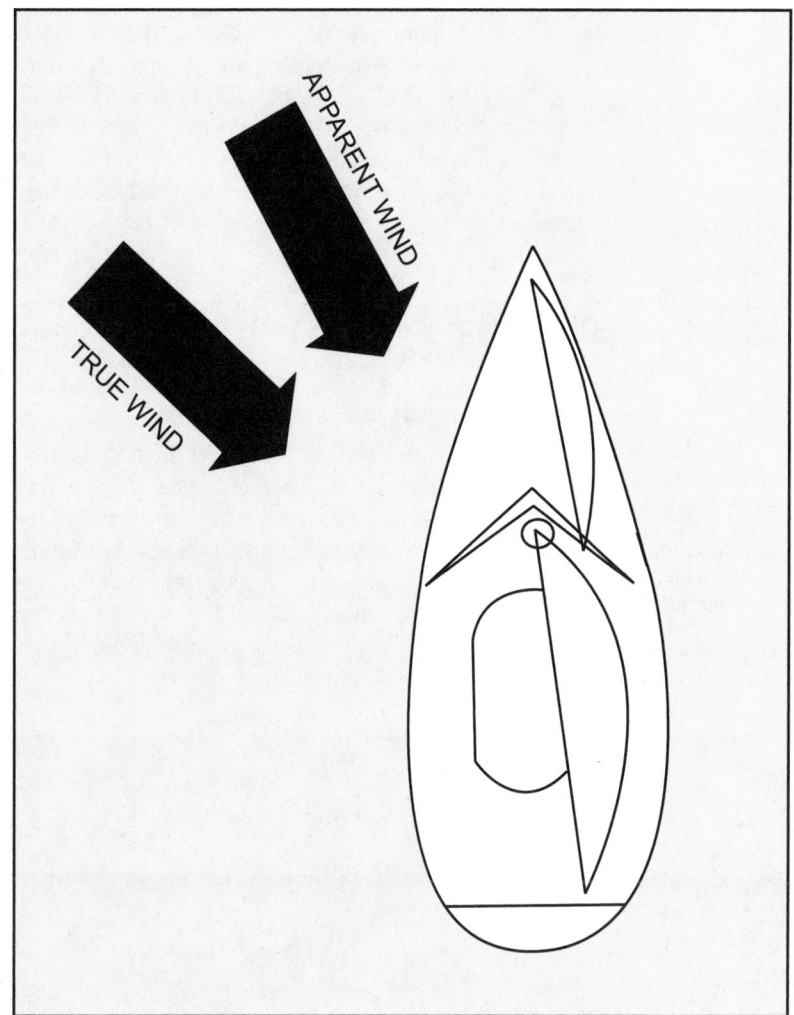

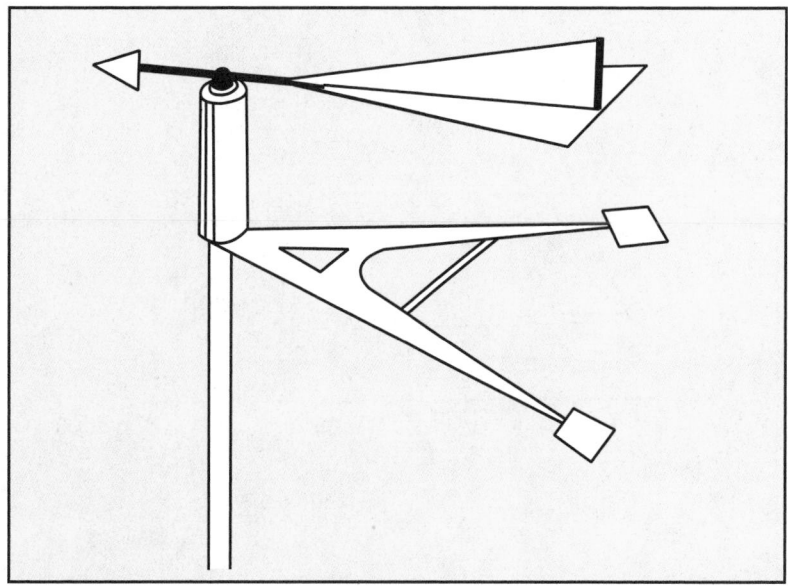

Masthead fly

wind on your side. But once you start pedaling, the faster you go, the more forward the wind will feel until it is directly ahead. Again, the combined effect of the true wind and the wind you are creating is the apparent wind. The apparent wind will be at a 30 to 35 degree angle when sailing upwind. The faster your boat is going, the farther forward the apparent wind will be. The direction of the apparent wind is indicated by any telltale or masthead fly.

WHAT MAKES A BOAT SAIL

When the sail's center of effort is directly over the hull's center of lateral resistance, the boat is balanced, with neither lee nor weather helm. Heeling the boat will change this relationship and cause windward (weather) helm.

LATERAL RESISTANCE AND HEEL

The centerboard or keel is critical to a boat's windward performance. If there were no centerboard or keel, the force of the wind would push the boat sideways. But the counteracting force of the water on the keel or centerboard allows the boat to go forward. This resistance to sideslipping is known as **lateral resistance.**

The **center of lateral resistance** is the point on the centerboard, keel, or hull under the water that acts like a pivot for the whole area of lateral resistance: one-half of the lateral resistance is to one side of the center and the other half is to the other side. In a way, the center functions like a pivot on a seesaw. There is another important center, called the **center of effort,** which acts as a pivot for the sails. When the two centers are in the same vertical plane, the boat will **balance,** which means that she will be easy to steer. (In a moment, we will have more to say about balance.)

Designers try to come up with hull shapes that work efficiently on all points of sail in all wind conditions. One major concern, besides balance, is that the boat be **stable,** which means that it not heel (tip) very far. Larger boats have keels made of lead or iron that provide stability against heeling. These boats should sail efficiently upwind at an angle of heel of 20 degrees or less. However, centerboard boats, which do not have keels, are kept upright by the weight of their crews. For best performance, they should not be allowed to heel more than 5 to 10 degrees.

Heeling has one advantage in that it lengthens the boat's waterline. Generally, a longer waterline will help the boat go faster by creating a longer wave length,. But if the boat heels too far over, it will begin to slide sideways, or make leeway. The weight of the helmsman and crew or that of the keel can keep the boat sailing "on its lines," at the optimum angle of heel; otherwise the water flow will be inefficient.

If the boat heels too much because of a

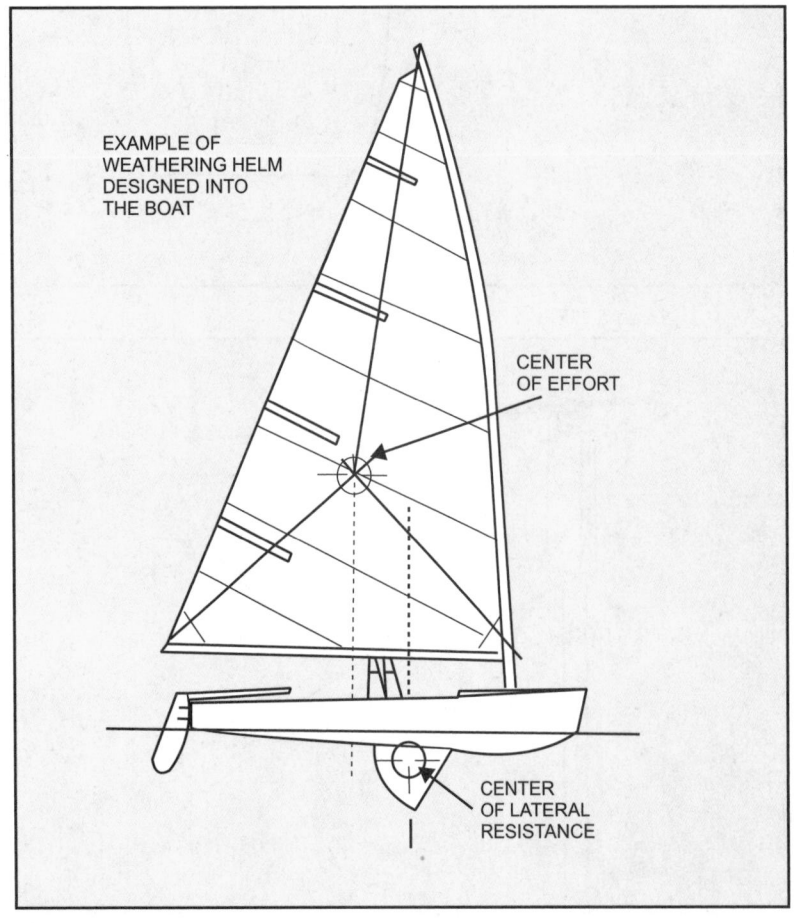

EXAMPLE OF
WEATHERING HELM
DESIGNED INTO
THE BOAT

CENTER
OF EFFORT

CENTER
OF LATERAL
RESISTANCE

sudden gust or too much wind, you must reduce the angle of heel by flattening your sails to reduce their power, heading into the wind, hiking out farther, or easing your sails. In puffy winds, ease your sails in a hard puff when the boat begins to heel too much. You'll discover that easing the sails and using your weight in combination with your steering will get you through the heaviest puffs while maintaining the same angle of heel. The gustier the wind, the more suddenly the boat will heel over and the more attention must be paid to sail trim.

WEATHER (WINDWARD) AND LEE (LEEWARD) HELM

Another factor to be aware of, especially while sailing close into the wind, is weather and lee helm. Weather helm is created by heeling and the wind on the sails. It is the tendency of a boat to round up into the wind when you let go of the tiller. The more the boat heels or the greater the force on the sails, the more the boat will want to round up into the wind. To reduce the windward helm force, you have several options, including hiking out until the boat is flat, heading the boat slightly into the wind to reduce heel, easing your sails, or flattening your sails.

Lee helm is the opposite of weather helm. When you let go of the tiller and the boat steers away from the wind, you have lee(ward) helm. If your sailboat has lee helm, allow it to heel to leeward somewhat until you get some weather helm. Most sailors prefer a slight amount of weather helm when sailing upwind.

Extra waterline length when heeling

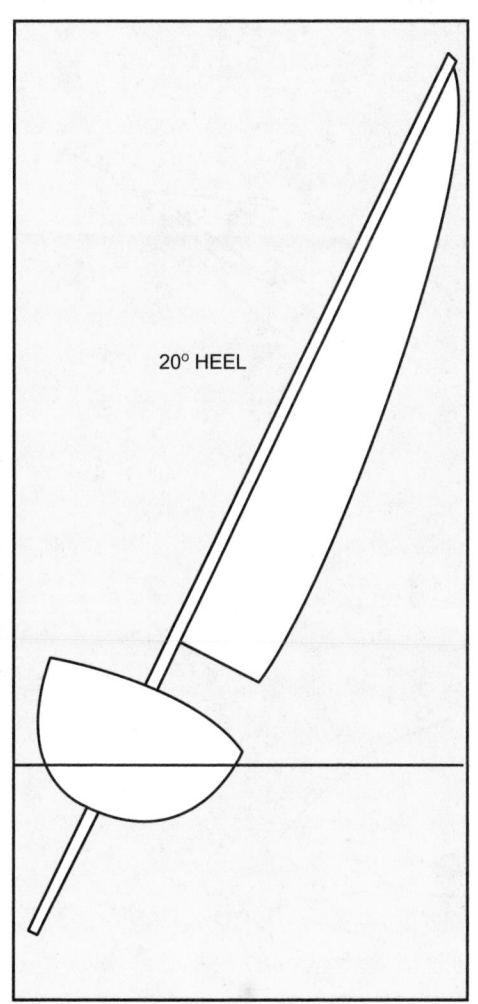

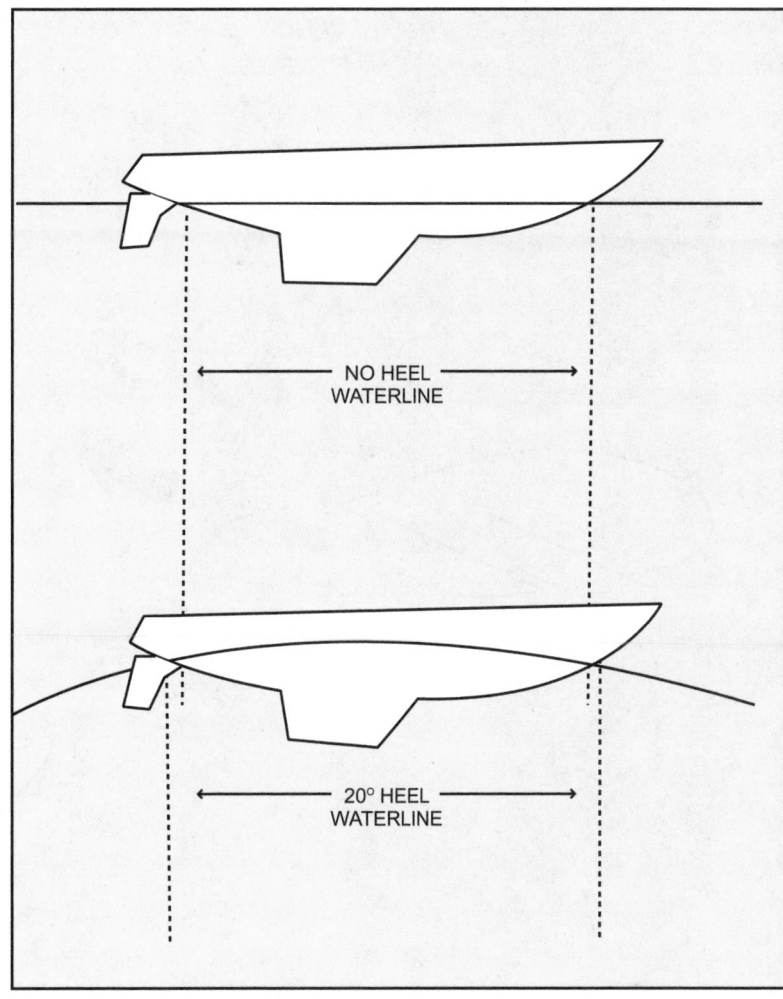

POINTS OF SAIL

Altering course from one point of sail to another can be compared to changing lanes on a highway. In going from one point of sail to another (changing lanes) you steer the boat either closer to or farther away from the direction of the wind. Steering toward the wind is called **heading up,** and steering away is referred to as **bearing away**. (To carry this analogy one step further, changing tacks by coming about or jibing can be compared to moving from one highway to another.)

As we have already learned, a boat cannot sail directly into the wind. Instead, a boat sails at various angles to the wind, the closest of which is about 45 degrees, although America's Cup 12-meter yachts can sail as close as 35 degrees. The point of sail closest to the wind is **close-hauled.** The sails are sheeted in close to the boat, and the vessel is steered as close to the wind's direction as possible without the sails luffing.

If a boat is sailing in the same direction as the wind, it is **running** with the wind coming from directly behind. A boat sailing across the wind, at an angle between close-hauled and running is on a **reach.** On each of these points of sail, sail trim varies and the duties of crew and helmsman vary as well.

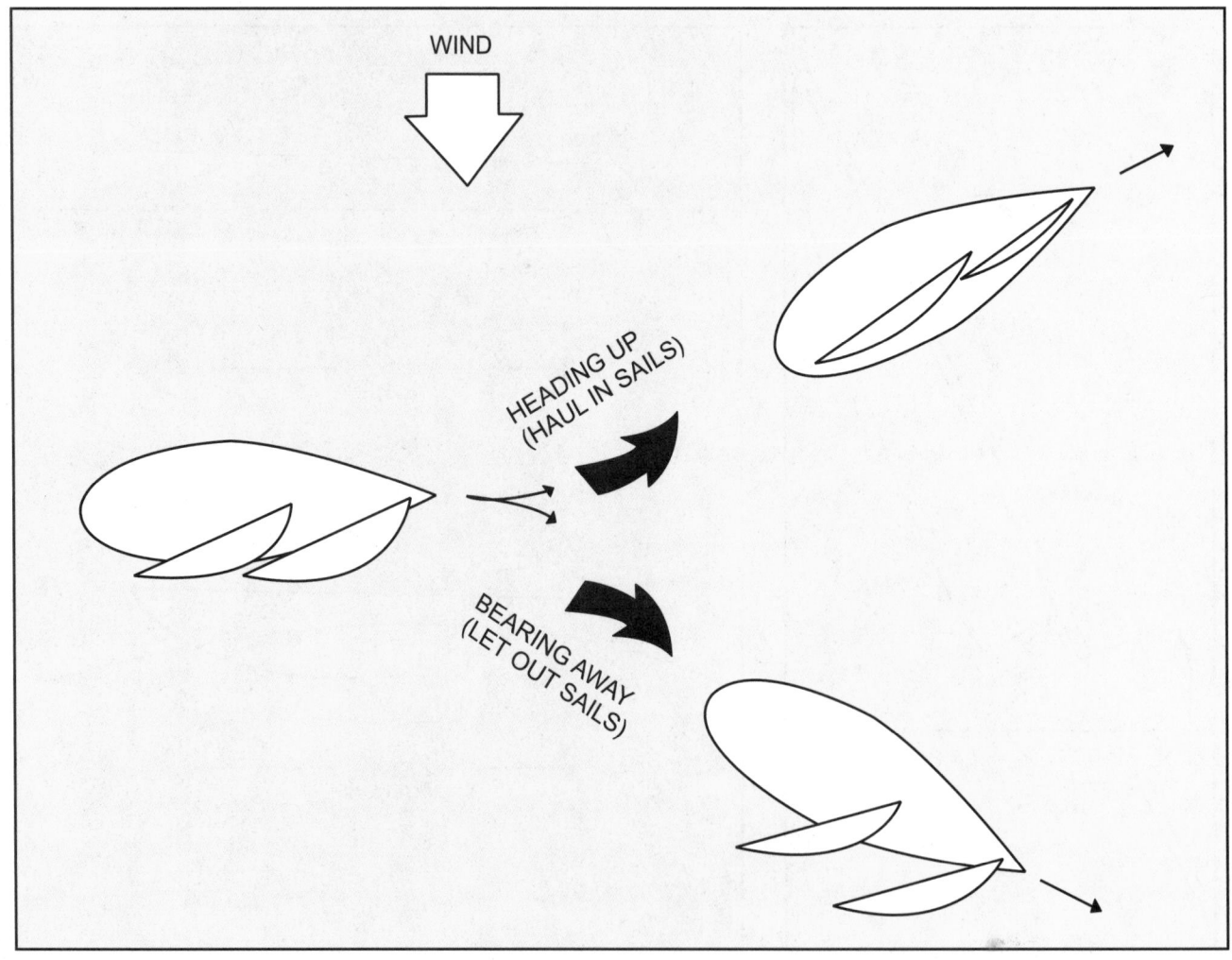

WIND

HEADING UP
(HAUL IN SAILS)

BEARING AWAY
(LET OUT SAILS)

SAILING CLOSE-HAULED

Sailing close-hauled is also known as **beating to windward.**

At point A, the sail appears to be well trimmed and the boat is moving through the water. To ensure efficient wind flow, the helmsman heads up (steers the boat toward the wind) until the sail just starts to luff (point B). When the helmsman bears away again (point C, the sails fill, and the boat is once more sailing close-hauled (as close to the wind as possible).

If the helmsman bears away (point D) and the crew does not ease the sheets, the boat will continue to sail, but less effectively. The boat will slow down.

Sailing close-hauled is exciting. The wind is in your face and the boat works through the waves. Sailing to windward on a balanced boat is a thrill because you and your boat become one being as you feel every wave and puff of wind.

A boat is **balanced** when it will sail in a straight line with little action on the tiller. In fact, it is possible to balance the boat so there is no need to use the tiller at all. However, most boats perform best when there is some weather helm. This means the wind on the sails pushes the boat to turn toward the wind. It should take approximately 2 to 3 degrees of rudder to counter this force and keep your boat in balance.

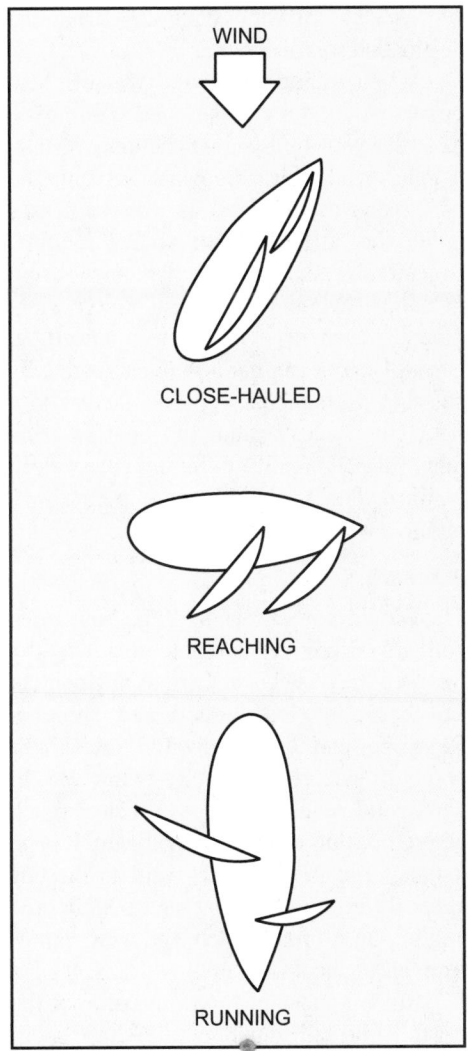

Correct sail trim

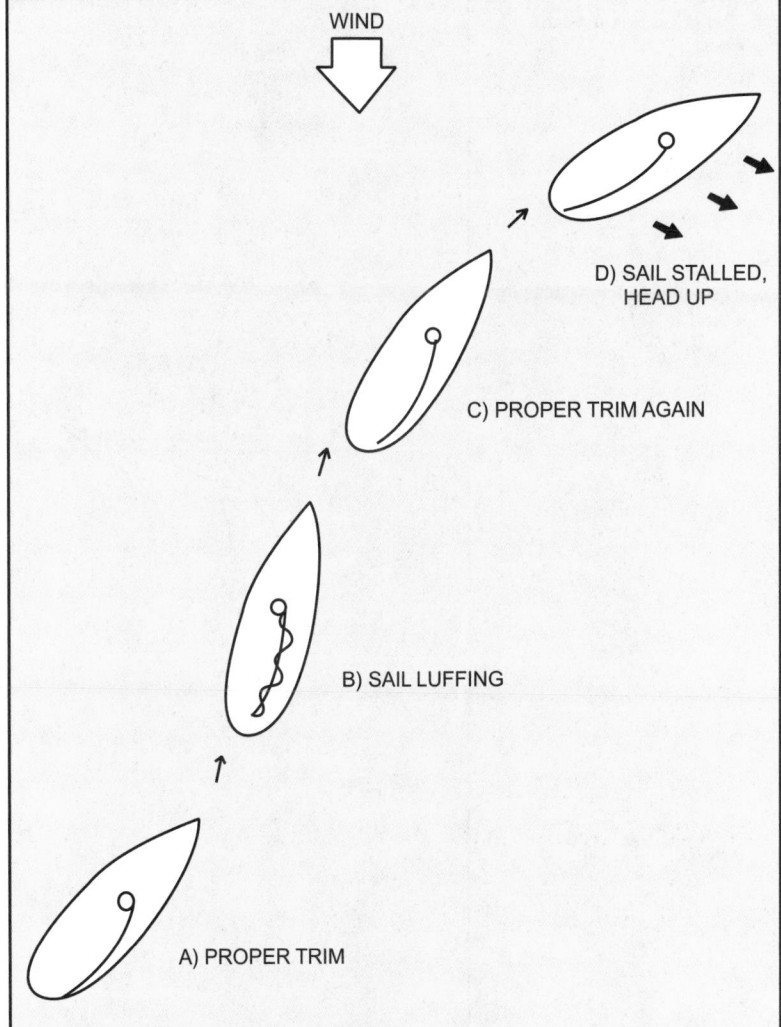

Adjusting course to correct sail trim

To get to an upwind destination as quickly as possible, sail as close to the wind as you can without allowing your sails to luff. You want to keep the boat moving at optimum speed at the closest possible course to the wind. Therefore, it is important to have a better understanding of sail trim and helm tendencies. Learning to gauge the wind by your telltales and a masthead fly will help you sail to windward efficiently.

RUNNING

A sailboat is running when the wind is blowing from behind the boat. On a run, the lifting effect of the sail is replaced by a pushing effect of the wind.

When you're sailing on a run, the wind has a pushing effect.

WIND

When running, the boat stands upright and moves freely along as the wind pushes the boat from astern. Running with the wind is particularly gratifying after a long beat to windward with the boat pounding into the waves, hiking for long periods of time, and tacking (coming about) back and forth. Now you can sail with the wind, running free. Like a cross-country skier coming to a slope, you simply stop pushing and let gravity take you along.

Sailing downwind is the goal of many sailors. Early skippers always made a point of sailing in the trade winds or in other reliable prevailing winds. They could be assured of sailing with the wind for long periods of time. This was particularly important in older sailing vessels, since they could not sail very close to the wind; going to a windward destination was arduous.

When sailing downwind you will also be pushed by the waves. As each one passes under your hull you will actually be able to gain speed. This is known as surfing. The boat gains extra speed as a wave passes under the hull. Although surfing requires considerable skill and practice, it will begin to happen whenever you encounter wind-driven waves or even after a powerboat passes by. You can get a sailboat surfing by steering it on a course perpendicular to a wave, then accelerating the boat by trimming the sail rapidly or shifting your weight forward. The first time you get a boat surfing on a wave is quite a thrill.

REACHING

The wind is from the side of the boat when you are sailing on a reach. Reaching-the fastest point of sail-is defined as any point of sail between close-hauled and running. Reaching can be subdivided into three points of sail: **close reach, beam reach, and broad reach.** A boat is on a close reach when the wind is forward of abeam. It is on a beam reach when the wind is directly abeam (hitting the boat at a 90 degree angle). On a broad reach, the wind comes from aft of abeam.

More important than the name of the reach is the sail adjustment. We have seen

that a sail has to be trimmed all the way in on a close-hauled course and eased all the way out on a run. On a reach, the sail is somewhere between these two extremes. Sails should be eased until they begin to luff, then trimmed in just a little bit to keep them from luffing.

Sometimes it's difficult to steer a straight course when reaching, because the waves as well as the wind approach from the side. In small (smooth) seas no problem exists. However, in large (choppy) seas difficulties can arise. You may need to adjust your course, sailing either higher (on a closer reach) or lower (on a broader reach), to keep from rolling too much.

Reaching, the boat will heel. Correct for this by sitting to windward. If the boat continues to heel too much, ease the sail until it luffs a little. For temporary relief, head the boat into the wind to luff the sails, or steer a new course farther away from the wind (on a broader reach) and ease your sails. This will reduce your heel angle, making the boat easier to sail.

HEAD TO WIND AND BY THE LEE

There are two final points of sail to be discussed: **head to wind** and **by the lee**.

A sailboat can surf with the waves in windy conditions, giving the crew an exhilarating ride.

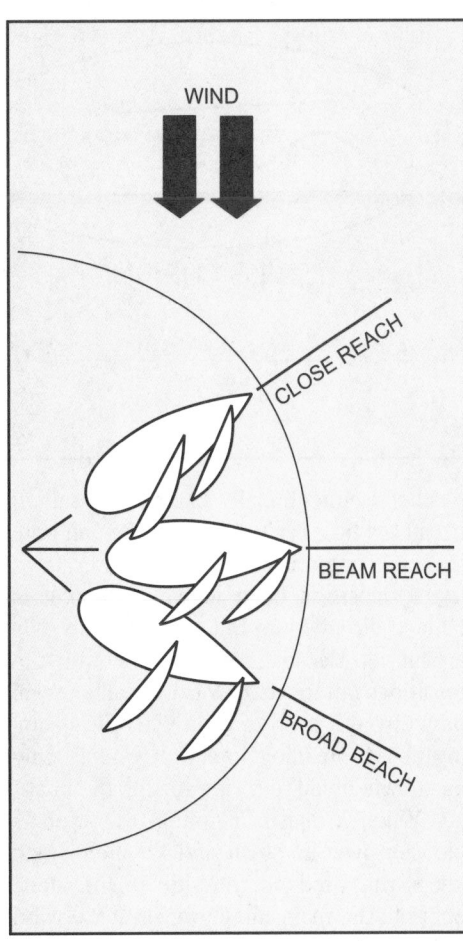

Three kinds of reaches

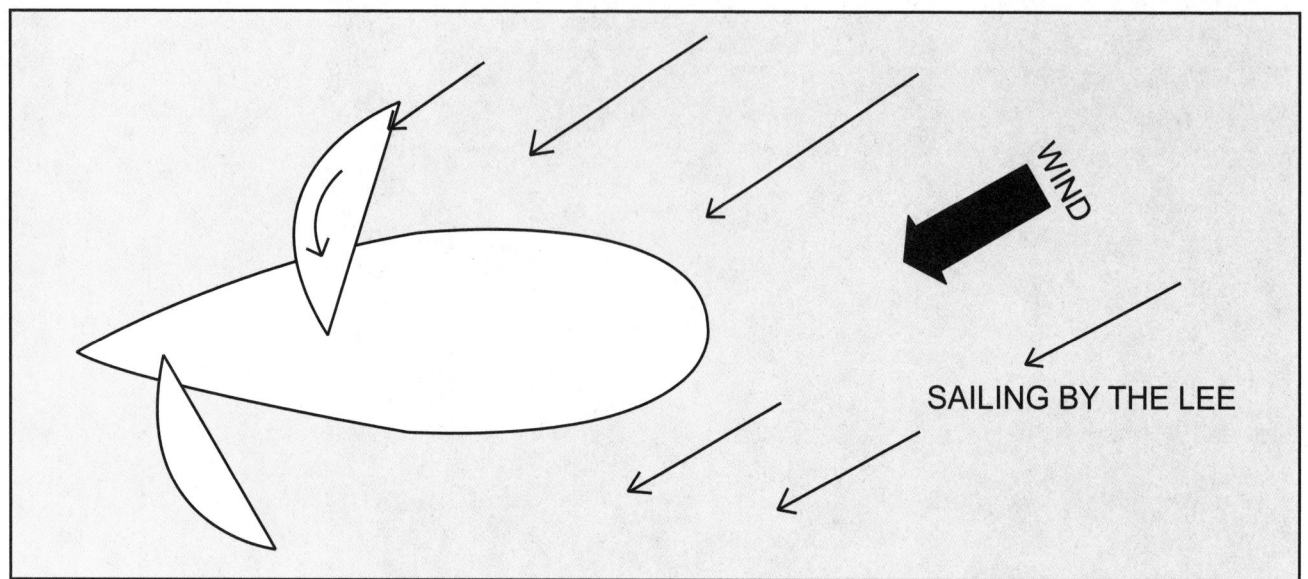

SAILING BY THE LEE

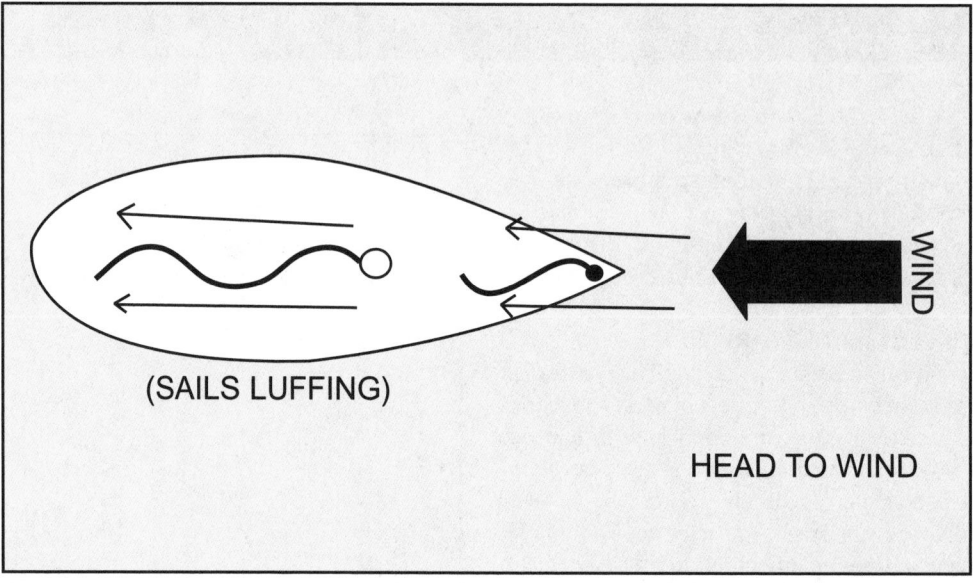

(SAILS LUFFING)

HEAD TO WIND

Neither is intentionally used while sailing because a boat can't sail on the first and the second is potentially dangerous.

A vessel is head to wind when it is pointed directly into the wind and the sails are luffing. Because the sails do not fill, the boat does not move forward. A sailboat will pass through head to wind when it is coming about. Heading into the wind is only useful when you're trying to stop the boat.

When a boat is running, the wind is blowing over its stern and the helmsman keeps the wind on the side of the stern opposite the mainsail. However, if the wind

shifts or the helmsman is unable to steer a true course, the wind could begin to blow over the same side of the boat as the side on which the mainsail is set. This situation is called sailing by the lee.

Sailing by the lee carries the inherent danger of an accidental jibe. An accidental jibe is an inadvertent changing of the mainsail from one side of the boat to the other and can result in damage to the boom, rigging, and sails. Even worse, an unprepared crew member could get in the way of the flying boom and be knocked overboard and seriously injured.

RULES OF THE ROAD UNDER SAIL

There is often a chance of collision between two or more boats approaching one another. There are rules to cover these situations. These are known as the rules of the road or more properly as Navigation Rules (NAVRULES) or Collision Regulations (COLREGS). Every sailor must follow these rules for his own safety and that of others. You may think that it is impossible for two boats to collide when they have wide open spaces of water around them in which to maneuver, but it is all that open space that causes people to relax and be less vigilant.

When the helmsman and crew are sitting to windward, they are unable to see boats approaching from leeward behind the sails. One crew member should be assigned to check to leeward occasionally to be sure the course is clear. If someone other than the skipper notices a boat in their path, he should immediately report its position to the skipper. A decision is then made as to which boat (or boats) must stay out of the way and which is (or are) allowed to stay on course. The terms used to describe the boats are give-way vessel and stand-on vessel. The first is obligated to give way (or stay clear), and the second is allowed to hold its course.

There are several different sets of water traffic rules. Which set applies to you depends on where you sail. Most American sailors come under the jurisdiction of the Inland Rules of the Road, which apply to boats in bays and estuaries connected with the Atlantic or Pacific oceans or the Gulf of Mexico. Such major boating areas as Long Island Sound, Chesapeake and Biscayne bays, San Francisco Bay and the Great Lakes are covered by the Inland Rules. In the ocean or the Gulf of Mexico, you are subject to the International Rules of the Road. The boundary between these two jurisdictions is an imaginary line drawn across the mouths of rivers, harbors, and inlets along the coasts; the two sets of rules are very similar. You can purchase a copy of the U.S. Coast Guard's "Navigation Rules, International-Inland" from most marine or ship stores, or contact your local Coast Guard office for information.

This section provides some general information and some specific rules that apply to sailing vessels (without operating engines). Additional material on the navigation rules relevant to powerboats is presented in part five.

Both Inland and International Navigation Rules require that every vessel shall maintain a proper lookout at all times-including use of all appropriate means to assess the risk of collision. Failure to maintain a proper lookout is one of the major causes of accidents. It may be advantageous to assign sec-

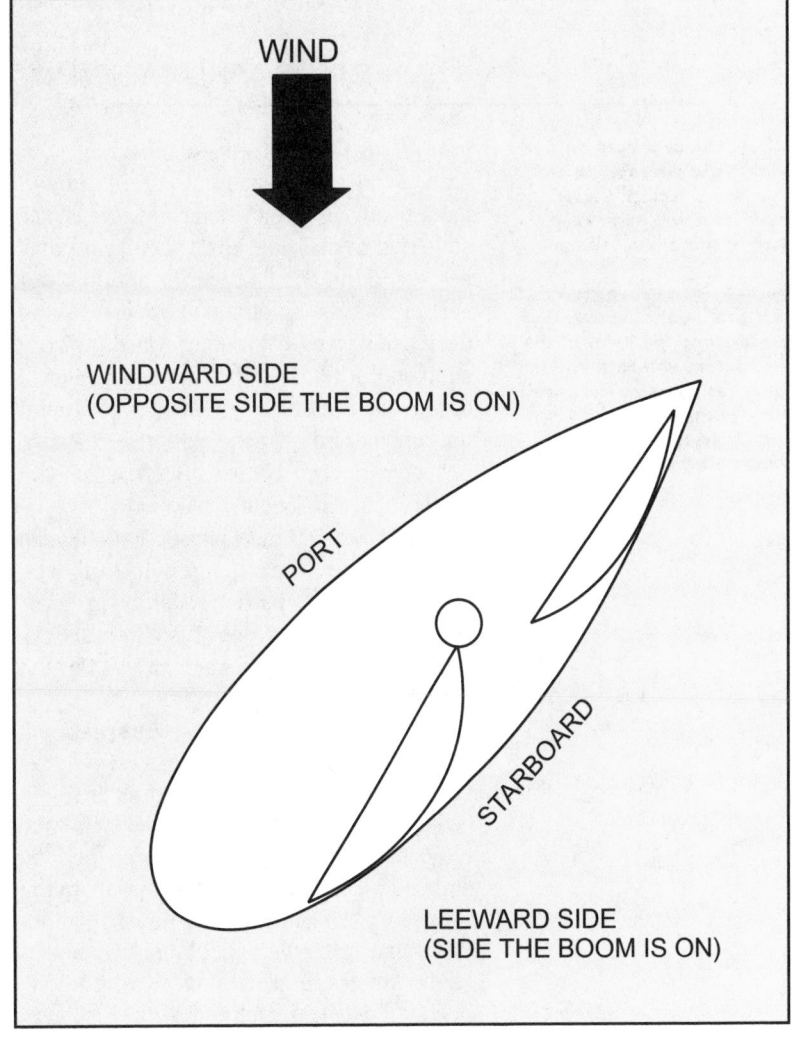

WIND

WINDWARD SIDE
(OPPOSITE SIDE THE BOOM IS ON)

PORT

STARBOARD

LEEWARD SIDE
(SIDE THE BOOM IS ON)

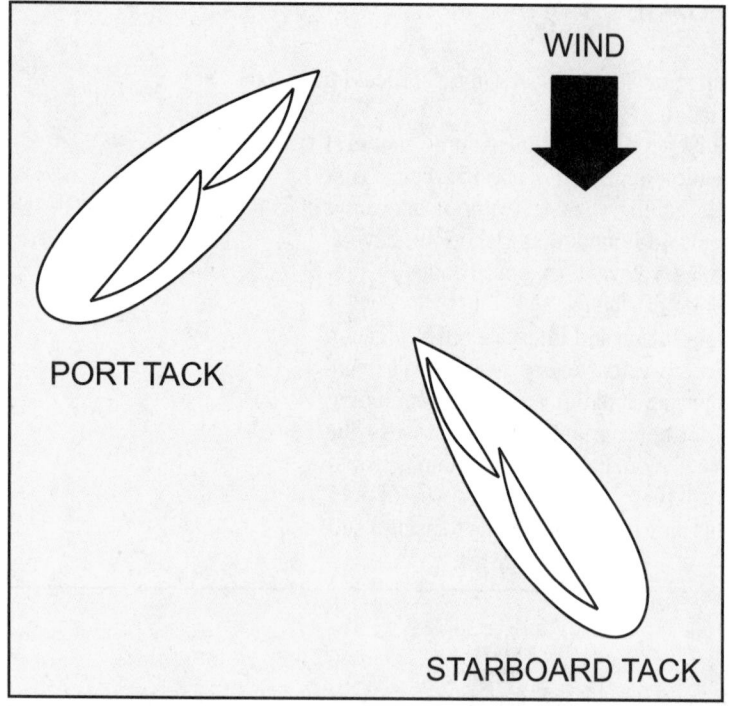

PORT TACK

WIND

STARBOARD TACK

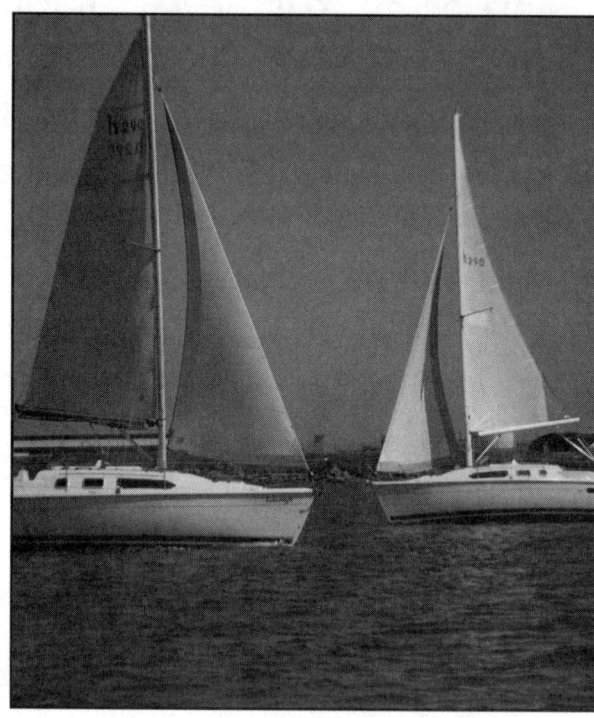

Above: Since a boat on port tack gives way to one on starboard tack, the port tack boat will be at fault here if there is a collision.

Above right: When crews are proficient at sailing and understand the Rules of the Road, they can race in close quarters as here. The port-tack yacht on the right is staying clear of the star-board-tack boat on the left.

tors of responsibility to members of your crew, or in any event to stress the importance of advising you whenever there is possible risk of collision. Risk of collision may be deemed to exist whenever another vessel maintains a constant bearing and decreasing range. In other words, if you sight another boat at the same spot relative to your boat just off the bow for example) for any period of time and the distance between the two boats is decreasing, you are probably on a collision course.

Maintenance of a proper lookout can be a particular challenge on sailboats, where the sails restrict visibility in some sectors. Difficult or not, it is the responsibility of the skipper to keep an alert watch for other traffic.

Both Inland and International Navigation Rules require that every vessel shall proceed at a safe speed at all times, in order to insure that the vessel can take effective action to avoid collision and be stopped within a distance appropriate to the prevailing circumstances. Many sailors think that this rule applies only to powerboats, but there are instances where sailboats have been charged with negligent

operation as a result of excessive speed.

Both Inland and International Navigation Rules require that every vessel shall use all available means to determine if risk of collision exists and, if in doubt, to assume that such risk exists. "All available means" includes the proper use of radar equipment, if fitted and operational.

Both Inland and International Navigation Rules require that actions to avoid collision shall be positive and made in ample time. Alterations in course or speed shall (where possible) be large enough to be readily apparent to another vessel. If necessary to avoid collision or to allow more time to assess the situation, you should reduce your speed or take all way off (stop).

WHEN APPROACHING ANOTHER SAILBOAT

Use the following to agree with current NAVRULES:

• When each has the wind on a different side, the vessel, which has the wind on the port side shall keep out of the way of the other.

• When both have the wind on the same side, the vessel which is to windward shall keep out of the way of the vessel, which is to leeward.

• A boat that is astern or overtaking shall keep out of the way to a boat ahead.

• A boat coming about or jibing shall give way to a boat on a tack.

The give-way vessel always alters course to pass astern of the stand-on vessel. The stand-on vessel is obligated to maintain a steady course during any crossing situation. However, if a collision is imminent, the stand-on vessel should alter course to stay clear as well.

• If one boat is running and the other is close-hauled and they are on the same tack, the close-hauled boat must hold its course and speed while the running boat stays clear. This is because the running boat is to windward of the close-hauled boat.

• If a vessel with the wind on the port side sees a vessel to windward and cannot determine with certainty whether the other vessel has the wind on the port or on the starboard side, she shall keep out of the way of the other.

• If both vessels are running, but one of them is on port tack and the other is on starboard, then the boat on starboard tack is the stand-on vessel.

• For the purposes of this rule, the windward side shall be deemed to be the side opposite to that on which, the mainsail is carried or, in the case of a square-rigged vessel, the side opposite to that on which the largest fore-and-aft sail is carried.

WHEN APPROACHING A POWERED VESSEL

Use the following to agree with current NAVRULES:

In general, sailboats are stand-on vessels when approaching power-driven vessels, but there are four exceptions:

• When overtaking a power-driven vessel, a sailboat is the give-way vessel.

• A sailboat must stay clear of a vessel not under command, i.e., unable to maneuver.

• A sailboat must stay clear of a vessel engaged in fishing with nets, lines, trawls or any other fishing apparatus which restricts maneuverability, but does not include a vessel fishing with trolling lines or other fish-

The windward boat to the left must stay clear of the leeward boat (right).

In restricted channels, stay clear of passing freighters with limited visibility and steerage. This cruising boat is much too close.

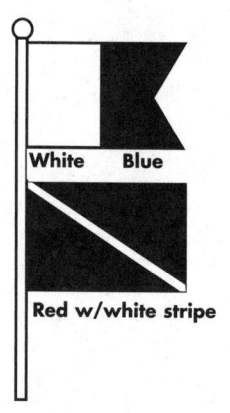

White   Blue

Red w/white stripe

Diver's flags

ing apparatus which does not restrict maneuverability.

• In a narrow channel or confined area, a sailboat must not hamper the safe passage of power-driven vessels that can navigate only inside such a channel or area. Large ships are not very maneuverable and often have poor visibility from the bridge. Therefore it is important for sailing vessels to stay away as far as possible from large steamers.

WHEN APPROACHING DIVERS

All vessels are required to keep clear of divers displaying the international code flag alpha ("A"). Although the red and white diver's flag is more readily recognized, the legal requirement is the blue and white international code flag. For safety and legal reasons, divers often fly both flags, and boaters should avoid any vessel displaying either one.

These Rules of the Road have been presented in detail because they are important. The skipper of any vessel is morally and legally responsible for avoiding collisions. Know the rules and abide by them.

A final note on sailing etiquette: When daysailing, you will undoubtedly encounter sailboat races. Although racing sailboats have no special privileges, for your own safety and enjoyment, and out of courtesy to them, try to steer clear. If that is impossible, make your way through the fleet carefully, passing to leeward of racing boats to avoid disturbing their wind.

REVIEW QUESTIONS

1. When the telltales stream straight back, they indicate
a) turbulent air flow
b) smooth air flow
c) no air flow

2. The sails are trimmed in tight when the boat is
a) close reaching
b) close-hauled
c) in a close call
d) in irons

3. On a run, the sails are
a) trimmed all the way in
b) trimmed halfway in
c) eased out all the way

4. One of the major safety concerns when sailing on a run is
a) coming about
b) reaching
c) an accidental jibe

5. On which point of sail will a boat not sail?
a) by the lee
b) head to wind
c) broad reach

6. In drawings A, B, C, and D at right, circle the boat which is stand-on vessel whenever approaching. Add arrows to indicate what course the give-way vessel should take.

7. When one sailboat is overtaking another, the _____ is the stand-on vessel.
a) boat ahead and being overtaken
b) boat behind and overtaking

8. Sailboats are stand-on vessels whenever approaching power-driven vessels except
a) when overtaking
b) when sailing on port tack
c) when the power vessel is limited in its maneuverability by a narrow channel
d) when the sailboat is also under power

9. A _____ tack boat shall give-way to a boat on _____ tack

10. When two sailboats are approaching on the same tack, the _____ boat shall stay out of the way of the _____ boat.

Answers in Appendix A, p. 201.

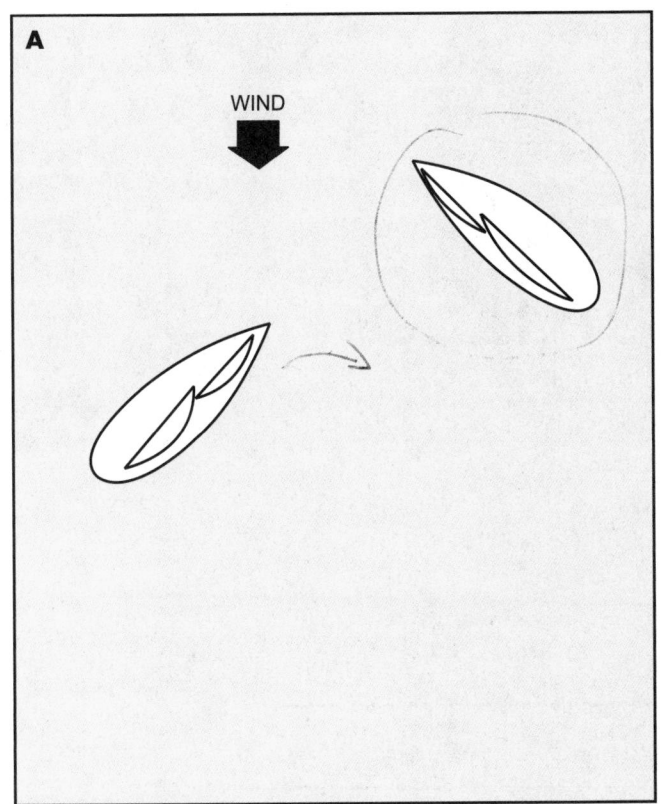

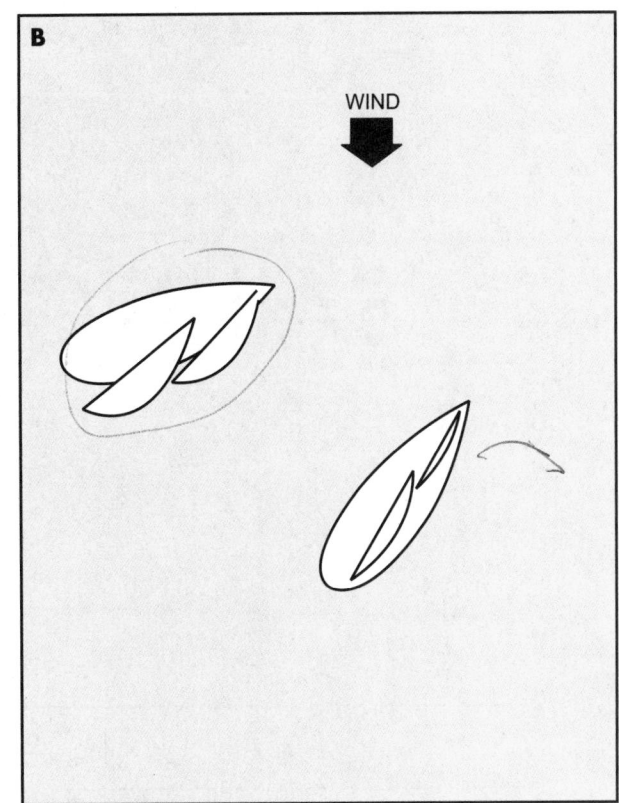

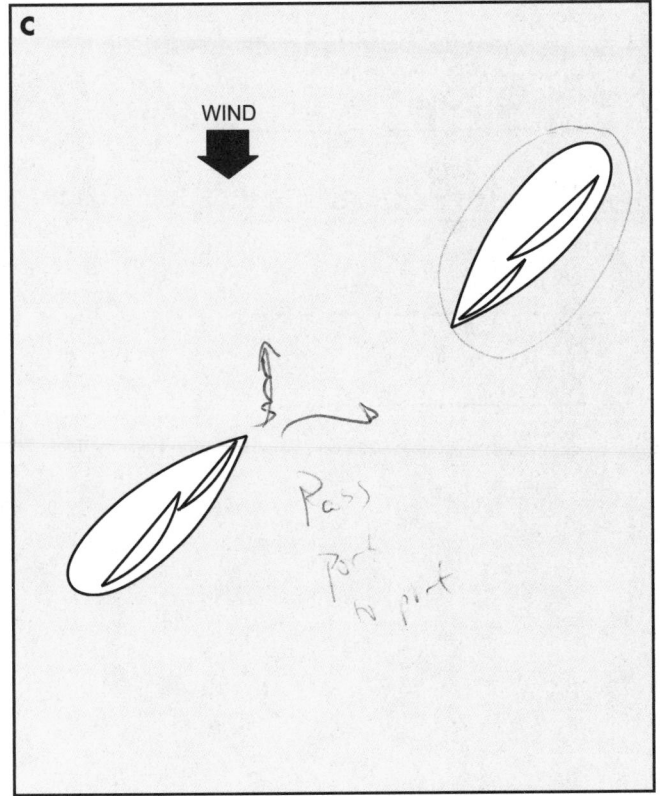

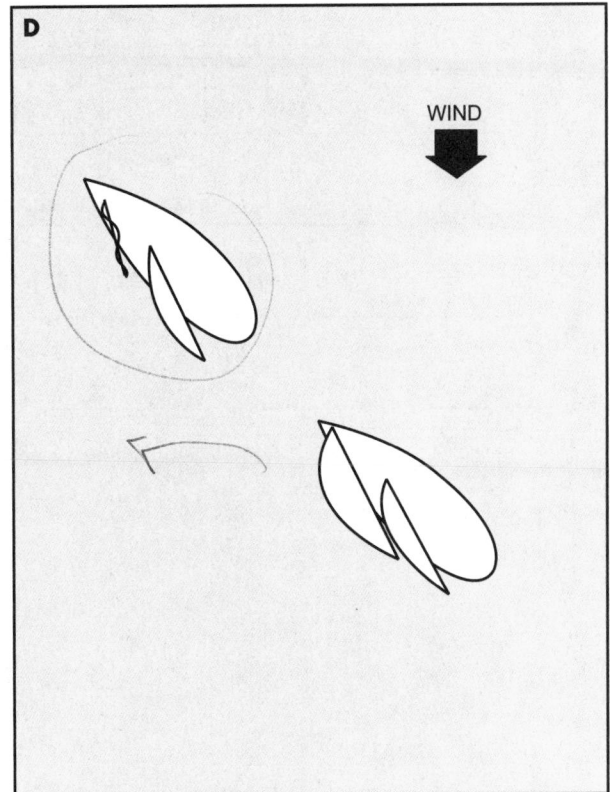

SAILING SKILLS

The following exercises have been devised to increase the competence and confidence of both helmsman and crew. They will help you evolve from the mechanical approach we took in Part One to a more intuitive or reflexive approach. Review the sail raising procedures in Part One, then let's go sailing.

Sailing close-hauled, reaching, and running each involves different techniques and skills for the person at the helm and for the crew. A good sailor will be able to perform all functions on the boat, so read the instructions once from the point of view of the helmsman, and again from the crew's point of view. Then practice each on the water. In Part One we developed the technique of sailing across the wind (reaching). By learning how to sail close-hauled, we will be able to sail closer to the wind; and, by coming about from time to time, sail to an upwind destination.

COMMUNICATIONS

When the boat is leaving the dock or maneuvering, only one voice should be heard. The helmsman should be the skipper, and he or she gives the orders. The boat will be better organized and there will be less confusion than if authority is shared. Murphy's rule of sailing confusion is, "For every additional person you add to a boat you square your problems."

To ensure that the crew understands the helmsman's intentions (and vice versa), simple, standard verbal commands have been developed. These commands should be learned and used at all times. Each time the vessel alters course and the trim of the sail is changed, the proper commands must be used to alert the others on the boat that such changes are about to take place. Although the actual wording of the commands may vary from boat to boat and from skipper to skipper, the meaning and the reason for them is the same-communication and safety. For sailing upwind and coming about these are the most frequently used commands:

HELMSMAN: "Ready about." (This means the crew will get ready to come about by putting the windward jib sheet around the winch.)

CREW: "Ready." (The crew has made sure that the jib sheets are clear and the boat is ready to come about.)

HELMSMAN: "Hard alee. " (The tiller is being pushed to the leeward side of the boat, and the boat is starting to turn.)

Another series of commands is used when heading up (steering closer to the wind):

HELMSMAN: "Prepare to head up." (The crew prepares to pull in on the sheets.)

CREW: "Ready." (The crew has made sure that all is ready.)

HELMSMAN: "Trim sheets." (The tiller is moved slightly to leeward, and the sheets are pulled in as the boat is turning.)

You probably noticed that there was a preparatory command" and then a "command of execution." It's important to have both.

SAILING CLOSE-HAULED

Sailing close-hauled is perhaps the most difficult point of sail for a helmsman because it is the least forgiving. If the helmsman steers too close to the direction of the wind or too far from it, or if the crew pulls the sails in too tight or not tight enough, the boat will not perform efficiently. The happy medium of best angle to the wind is often referred to as the "groove."

As a rule, the closer you sail to the wind, the slower the boat will go. For upwind sailing with the sails trimmed, you as helmsman should head up, easing the tiller to leeward and turning the boat until the sail

EXERCISE: SAILING CLOSE-HAULED

1. The helmsman starts the boat from a beam reach position.

2. The crew trims the sails for a beam reach, with the wind flowing evenly on both sides of the sail as indicated by the telltales. Watch the luff or leading edge of your mainsail along the mast and the luff of your jib. The boat should be steered so that the sails remain full, but keep testing your course by slowly heading the boat toward the wind. If the sail begins to luff, either trim it in until it stops or, if the sail is already trimmed in all the way, bear away from the wind by pulling the tiller to windward (constantly looking at the "luff " in the sails) until the sail fills.

3. When the boat has picked up speed, the helmsman gives the command "Prepare to head up." The crew responds with "Ready" when they are prepared to sheet in the sails.

4. With the command "Trim sheets," the helmsman turns the boat closer to the direction of the wind and the crew sheets the sails to prevent luffing.

5. Counteract any heeling action by moving crew weight to the windward rail as the sails are trimmed in. If you feel uncomfortable or if the boat heels excessively, ease out your mainsail while trying to maintain your close-hauled course. A normal reaction is to bear away from the wind without letting the sails out. This will cause too much heel and weather helm. Keep the boat balanced by adjusting your mainsail trim to maintain a constant angle of heel. In strong breezes upwind, you can control the angle of heel by your mainsail trim.

6. When the sails have been sheeted in, the helmsman tests to see if the boat can be steered any higher toward the wind by heading up until the jib luffs, and then bearing away from the wind until the luffing just stops.

7. The helmsman needs to be in a position to see the telltales at all times. By indicating when the boat is a few degrees out of the groove, the telltales allow the helmsman to steer a close-hauled course. Slight tiller adjustments are required to keep both telltales streaming properly. If the windward telltales rise up in the air, your sail is probably beginning to luff and you should sail a lower course by bearing away. If your leeward telltales begin to flutter, you are sailing too low a course and you should head toward the wind or ease your sails out.

8. The helmsman sails on a close-hauled course for a minute or two and then signals coming about with the command "Ready about." When the crew replies "Ready," the helmsman turns the tiller, saying, "Hard alee."

9. The helmsman comes to a close-hauled course after each tack, and the helmsman and crew shift to the opposite side of the boat. Avoid oversteering. Since a sailboat sails about 45 degrees off the wind, coming about should be a turn of 90 degrees-45 degrees to the wind and another 45 to the opposite tack. If this 90-degree turn is anticipated and practiced, the helmsman will be able to come about from closehauled to close-hauled every time.

10. After a few minutes of testing the trim of the sails, come about again. Repeat this exercise until a predetermined upwind objective (a mark or buoy) is reached. This should require coming about at least four or five times. The helmsman will then prepare to head the boat downwind with the command: "Prepare to bear away." When the crew replies "Ready," the helmsman orders "Ease sheets" and pulls the tiller to windward.

just begins to luff. When the sails luff, bear away slightly (pull the tiller to windward to turn away from the wind) just until the sails cease luffing. Now you have found the upwind groove. Constant retesting is required to keep you in this groove.

Remember to go through maneuvers slowly and gradually both to give the crew time to react and to maintain the speed of the boat. Most maneuvering problems occur because the helm is turned too quickly.

For crew members, close-hauled is a relatively easy point of sail. Once the sails have been sheeted in, the crew's main duty is to watch for other boats. The helmsman, on the other hand, has to continually steer the boat, making small course adjustments for the inevitable wind shifts. The most common problem for the new sailor is oversteering. Try to sail a straight course by using a compass or heading for a fixed object.

A good way to learn to sail to windward is to sail alongside another boat. You will feel more comfortable with another boat nearby, and it will give you a reference point or a benchmark. When doing this exercise, sail about two or three boat lengths apart.

In this exercise, being able to sail from the leeward to the windward mark repeatedly and efficiently is your goal. It's a major

accomplishment; don't be concerned if you do not perform well at first. Many new sailors have difficulty getting the boat on a close-hauled course the first time, but with practice you will learn to sail a close-hauled course at optimum speed.

SAILING ON A RUN

Although sailing downwind (running) may seem less demanding than upwind sailing. It takes concentration to maintain sail control and crew coordination. When running, the boat is being pushed by the wind. Running with the wind efficiently is a matter of exposing as much sail as possible. The more proficient the crew and helmsman become at sailing downwind, the more sail area they can set to catch the wind.

When sailing close-hauled, the helmsman continually tests the set of the sails by steering a few degrees into the wind until the sails luff and then back until the luff stops. Similarly, on a run, the helmsman continually tests the sails by steering away from the wind a few degrees. The idea is to sail as low a course as possible and yet maintain speed.

Sailboats can be difficult to steer dead (directly) downwind, particularly lightweight dinghies in which the weight of the crew exceeds the weight of the boat. If you reach up slightly toward the wind, the boat will gain stability and be easier to sail.

It is a good practice to position your crew so that you do not feel any pressure on the helm-that is, your boat will maintain a steady course if you let go of the tiller. Your boat will heel slightly to windward (or to leeward) to balance the helm. Don't worry, this is normal. With a balanced helm, the center of effort of the sails is directly over the center of lateral resistance of the hull under the water.

Ease your sails out as far as you can without letting them luff. Keep easing the sail out until it just begins to luff, then trim in slightly until the luffing stops.

In cat-rigged (mainsail only) boats, sailing downwind is simply a matter of bearing away from the wind and easing the mainsail out. However, in a sloop (a boat with two sails) it will help to wing your jib to wind-

EXERCISE: **SAILING ON A RUN**

1. Pick the course that you would like to sail by locating an object downwind in the water or on shore to steer toward or simply by noticing the wind direction.

2. As the boat gets onto a run, the jib is blanketed by the mainsail and loses wind. This is the first indication that the boat is on a run.

3. The crew pulls the jib to the opposite side of the boat by releasing the leeward jib sheet (the one on the same side as the mainsail). They then tighten the windward sheet. Try to keep the wind flowing slightly to one side of astern so both sails will fill. When sailing downwind in a strong breeze, the boat will have a tendency to plow into the waves ahead of you. Moving the weight of your crew aft helps to lift the bow up out of the waves. You can also head up slightly so that you are sailing at an angle to the waves.

4. The helmsman must watch the wind indicators. A masthead fly or telltale can be particularly helpful when you're sailing downwind. Watching the direction from which the wind is coming helps you to steer. Masthead flies always tell the truth. Keep the wind over your quarter. If you feel the boat become unstable or start to rock back and forth, head the boat toward the wind by pushing the tiller to leeward. Ease the sail until the boom is at a right angle to the wind. The masthead fly should create a right angle with the boom and the foot of the jib.

5. After maintaining this course and point of sail for a few minutes, the helmsman gives the command to prepare to jibe the mainsail, "Prepare to jibe. " The crew replies "Ready, " and the helmsman gives the order "Jibe ho. "

6. The jib is always jibed after the mainsail has crossed the boat, since it is less important on a run than the main.

7. In small boats, the helmsman and crew should sit on opposite sides of the boat to keep it level and to allow each crew member to watch for other boats and obstructions.

ward (set it on the opposite side from the mainsail). This helps both sails to capture the air more efficiently. If the jib is kept to leeward of the mainsail,` the main will block the wind from the jib. One crew member may hold the jib sheet on the windward side of the boat to capture the wind.

The jibe, as you learned in Part One, is the most direct approach to changing tacks downwind. This running exercise will involve a series of jibes, and with practice the helmsman should be able to jibe the mainsail without steering the boat more than a few degrees from a dead downwind course.

The commands for jibing are:
HELMSMAN: "Prepare to jibe." (The crew gets ready on the sheets.)
CREW: "Ready."
HELMSMAN: "Jibe ho." (The tiller is pulled to windward, and the boat starts to turn away from the wind.)

Sailing upwind and sailing downwind are actually two parts of the same exercise. While working through the upwind exercise for sailing close-hauled, you'll have to sail on a run to get back downwind to the leeward mark or buoy. Let us look at how to improve downwind sailing skills by doing the "Sailing on a run" exercise.

SAILING ON A REACH

Reaching differs from sailing close-hauled and running because the crew cannot just set the sails and then leave the trimming to the helmsman's course. When sailing close-hauled or on a run, the helmsman must maintain the trim of the sails by steering the boat to adjust for changes in the wind direction. On a reach, the helmsman maintains a straight course to a destination and the crew trims the sails by easing them out until they luff and pulling the sheets in until the luffing stops.

Three buoys with anchors are needed for the next exercise. Anchor them in a triangular pattern so that in order to sail the entire circuit, the helmsman must steer on a beam reach, a close reach, and a broad reach.

EXERCISE: **SAILING ON A REACH**

1. On each leg of this exercise, the helmsman steers directly for the next mark while the crew trims the sails by easing them out until they luff and then trimming them until they stop luffing.

2. Telltales are less effective on a beam reach than on an upwind course and virtually useless on a broad reach and run. On a broad reach, ease the sail until it luffs and then trim until the luffing stops. The crew continually tests to make sure the sails are properly trimmed.

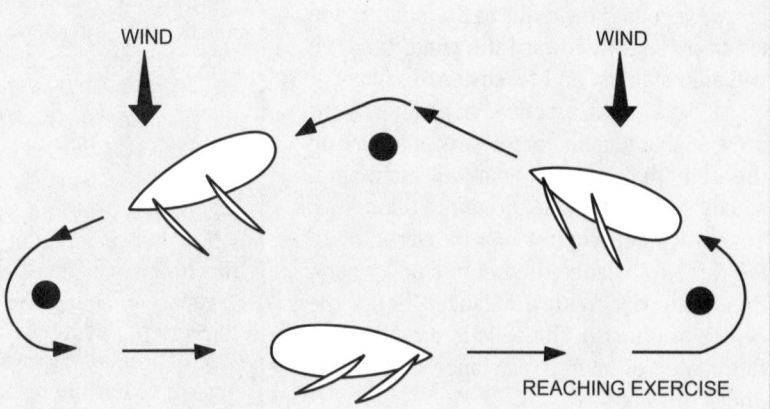

WIND

WIND

REACHING EXERCISE

STOPPING THE BOAT

So far, we have been concerned with keeping the boat moving through proper trim and steering. This exercise will help the helmsman and crew to stop the boat wherever they want. Control in stopping a boat is as important as control when moving. At the end of this exercise, the helmsman should be able to stop the boat within six feet to windward of an object in the water.

In Part One, we were concerned with getting the boat moving. We started with the sails luffing and the boat at right angles to the wind (on a beam reach). To stop the boat, we have to be able to position the boat so that the wind cannot possibly fill the sails. This is done by easing the sails out as far as possible when the boat is on a close reach.

It might seem that the best way to stop the boat is to point it into the wind-head to wind-so the sails just luff. Although the boat will definitely stop when head to wind, the helmsman has the least control of the boat on this point of sail. Control is a primary goal of all helmsmen.

For example, suppose someone's hat blew into the water while the boat was sailing, and the helmsman and crew managed to get the boat turned around and headed back to the point where the hat was lost. If the helmsman headed the boat up until it was head to wind, the boat would stop. However, if the boat stopped a few feet short of the object, the crew would have to get the boat turned away from the wind, start sailing again, and repeat the exercise until the timing of the stop was exactly right.

I will never forget sailing in one major championship in E-Scows on the New Jersey shore. The skipper of the boat I was sailing on had a favorite hat which had followed him for years. As soon as we had rounded the leeward mark to the finish in a race that we were doing well in, his hat, for the first time, blew off his head. He reached to grab it-almost going overboard-but missed. The hat was now in the water. Was

losing the race worth the hat? It seemed foolish at the time to hesitate even for an instant to go back for a hat. But the helmsman reeled around, barely missing another competitor, came up on the breeze; leaning overboard, two of us dived for the hat, picked it up, and on we went. Reflecting on the race later that night, the skipper said, "We might have lost a couple of places in that race, but it would have been tragic for the rest of the summer without my hat."

The following weekend he showed up again with the same hat, this time with a strap underneath his chin.

While you may never have to pick up a treasured hat in the middle of a race, learning how to make a controlled approach toward an object while under sail will reward you in many situations, for example, when approaching a pier. The key is always to make the approach on a close reach. On this point of sail, the boat can both sail fast and be stopped quickly. A good way to practice is to throw a cushion overboard, and then make a wide circle and head back to it.

EXERCISE:
STOPPING THE BOAT

1. Sail toward the object on a close reach.

2. As you near it, let the sails luff to slow the boat gradually until you are stopped with the object just to one side, either windward or leeward.

3. If you stop short of the object, simply trim the sails a little to pick up speed.

Do this exercise until you can stop the boat beside the object every time. This maneuver becomes the heart of a very important exercise that we will describe in the next chapter—making a man overboard rescue.

SUMMARY

In this part, we have introduced the points of sail. These are the angles, relative to the direction of the wind, that a boat can sail. Remember that the point of sail chosen depends on your destination.

If you want to sail upwind, your boat must be close-hauled and you must come about a number of times until the destination is reached. Downwind destinations are attained by running with (in the same direction as) the wind.

If a destination is across the wind, reaching is the necessary point of sail. The boat is easy to control on a reach. The wind comes over the side and the crew eases the sails until they luff and trims them until the luffing just stops.

When there is any doubt as to whether a sail is properly trimmed, ease it to find out. The rule is "when in doubt, let it out. " The coordination of helmsman and crew is essential on all points of sail.

The drills on the water in this part further developed the mechanics of sailing the various points of sail and refined tacking and jibing. The final exercise-stopping the boat-will become an integral part of more complex maneuvers in Parts Three and Four.

Safety and Seamanship

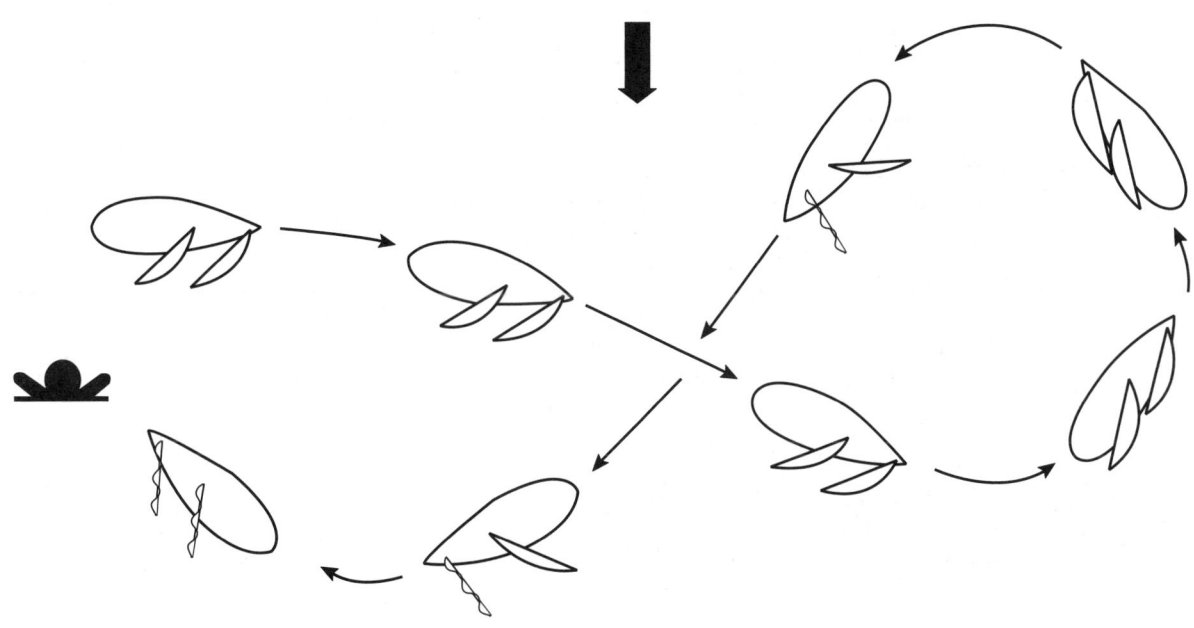

SAILING KNOWLEDGE

Sailors enjoy one of the best safety records of any recreational activity. The U.S. Department of Transportation (Safety Branch) has rated sailing as the safest of all sports. By and large, sailors have themselves to thank for this impressive record. Sailors take the time to prepare for potentially hazardous situations by knowing both their own limitations and those of their boat and equipment. However, even the most knowledgeable sailor can be surprised by a gust of wind or by a wave. For this reason, a good sailor anticipates difficult situations and prepares for them.

High wind and large waves (heavy weather) lead to the majority of unsafe situations aboard a boat. Anticipation and preparation are required of the skipper and crew. We will look at the causes, prevention, and then rescue of a man overboard. The rescue is an important drill; with luck you'll never need it, but be prepared. Further guidelines for heavy-weather sailing are covered in Part Six.

THE SAFETY HARNESS

A safety harness is an important protection against falling overboard. It is a simple web harness that fits around the upper body. There are two steel D rings secured to the front. Attached to these rings is a tether with a quick release shackle at one or preferably both ends. The shackle allows the wearer to attach and detach quickly, using only one hand.

The purpose of the safety harness is to keep a person on board by attaching the individual to a strong part of the boat: the base of a stanchion, the pulpit or stern rail, or a safety line ("jackwire" or "jackline") attached to strong deck cleats. Experts recommend that a person not shackle a safety harness to lifelines, the mast, or rigging because the rigging can fail in extreme conditions.

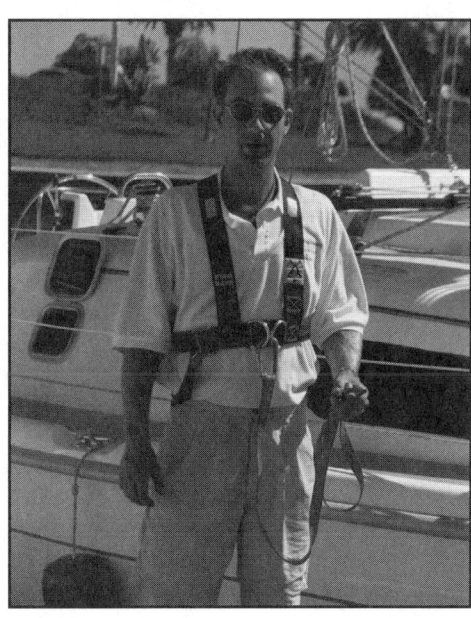

This crew member is prepared for heavy weather in a safety harness with a tether approximately six feet in length. The tether should not be hooked to lifelines.

DECK SAFETY

Certain areas of the boat are less safe than others. As a crew member moves forward out of the protection of the cockpit, there is an increasing need to hook on with a safety harness. Keeping a low stance with knees bent also reduces the chances of being thrown from the deck. There are times when crawling along the deck while holding on to a secure hand hold is the only safe way to move around the boat. Even with a safety harness, an important rule for all sailors is "One hand for the boat and one hand for yourself. " This simply means hold on to something solid. Move about a boat in rough weather as if you're eighty years old (apologies to you spry octogenarians).

The afterdeck, sidedeck, and foredeck are areas of reduced safety.

Some afterdecks have lazarettes for storing equipment. If a hatch to one of these is left open, a crew member may slip and fall. into the opening. A more common

Areas of reduced safety on deck. Lifelines, stanchions, grabrails, and shrouds are excellent handholds.

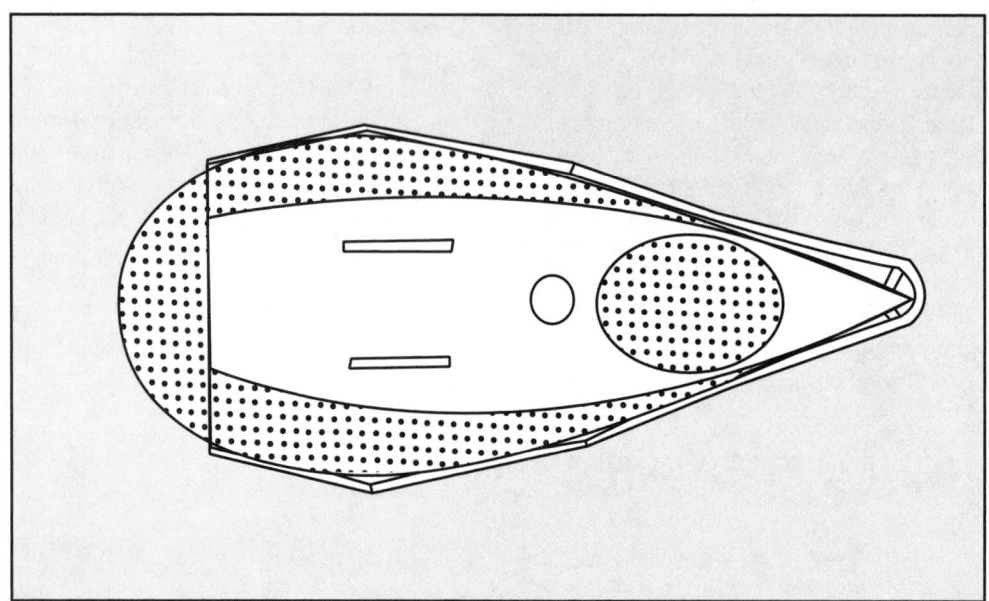

The safety line is led from the cockpit to a cleat on the bow. The safety line is sometimes called a jackline.

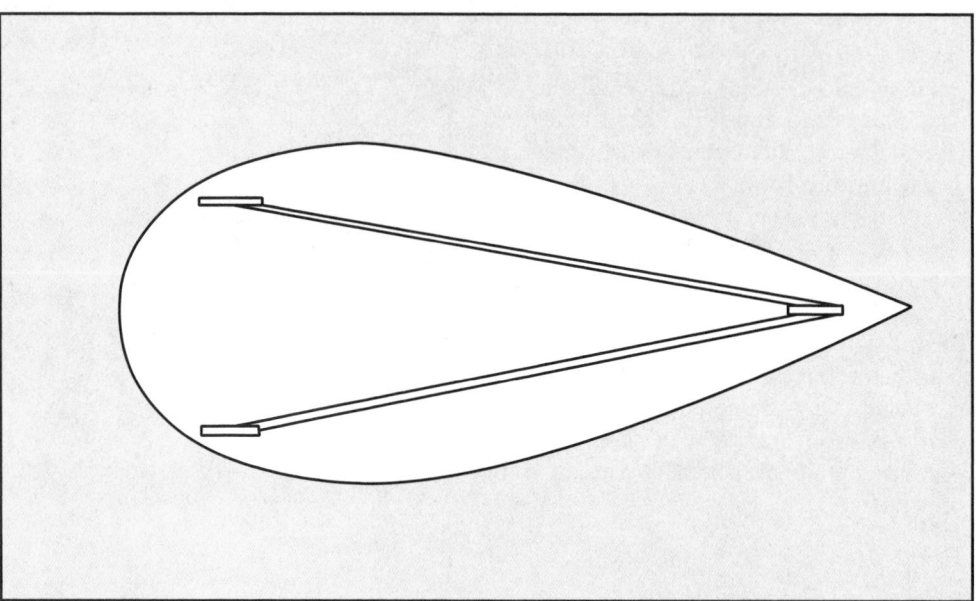

problem is failing down the forward hatch on the foredeck. Further, a sailor moving around on the afterdeck can fall overboard if the boat suddenly pitches.

A crew member moving along the sidedeck to the foredeck should do so along the windward side. It is easier to move on the windward side because the sails are set to the leeward side. Moving past the leeward shrouds requires bending and ducking, while on the high side there is ample room to pass.

The foredeck can be hazardous because there is only a small surface to work on.

Anytime a crew member has to move forward or work on the deck in heavy weather, a safety line, or "jack line," should be led from a deck cleat near the cockpit to a cleat on the bow. This gives the sailor a secure place to attach the safety harness tether and allows him to move forward without having to detach it at any time. Safety lines should be led down both sides of the boat.

HYPOTHERMIA AND CLOTHING

Although the possibility of drowning by falling into the water from a sailboat is a great concern, another real threat is hypothermia, a condition that exists when the body's core temperature drops below 95 degrees F. The loss of body heat results in loss of dexterity, loss of consciousness, and eventually loss of life.

Hypothermia is not only a danger in very cold water. In fact, the only time it is not a threat is when the water temperature is over 91 degrees. It is rare to experience water this warm in the United States. For example, the water off the coast of California in the summer rarely exceeds 70 degrees. Even the shallow, sun-drenched waters of the Bahamas reach only 85 degrees in the summer. Waters in the United States are cold enough to be a threat year-round.

In 65-degree water, the norm in summer throughout most of the United States, the average person without protective clothing could lose consciousness in just two hours. Survival time is greatly reduced if the individual is swimming, for example, from an overturned boat to shore.

Hypothermia can easily occur on deck when the air temperature is between 30 and 50 degrees. It is important to take precautions. I once spent a day on the water when the temperature never went above 35 degrees and I was so excited about being out on the boat that I didn't realize how cold I was until the day was over. Two hours later I started shivering and was sick for two days.

Hypothermia is a progressive problem. The body passes through several stages before an individual lapses into unconsciousness. Each of these stages provides signs to a rescuer of what immediate treatment is appropriate. The treatment of the victim depends on the level of hypothermia.

The extent of an individual's hypothermia can be ascertained from the following symptoms:

mild hypothermia
    feeling cold
    violent shivering
    slurred speech
medium hypothermia
    loss of muscular control
    drowsiness, incoherence, stupor
    and exhaustion
severe hypothermia
    collapse and unconsciousness
    respiratory distress and/or cardiac
    arrest probably leading to death

The first stage occurs when the body temperature drops to 95 degrees-just 3 degrees below the body's normal temperature. The body, in an attempt to reduce heat loss and at the same time replace the heat that has dissipated into the surrounding water, restricts circulation by reducing the flow of blood to the arms and legs. With less blood flowing, there is less heat drawn away from the body core and lost into the surrounding water. At the same time, the muscles involuntarily start to shiver as a means of generating more heat. These visual symptoms can be seen in a small child at the beach-blue lips (from reduced blood flow) and shivering.

Mild hypothermia is dealt with the same way you would treat a shivering child at the beach. The person is removed from the elements (wind and water), wrapped in a warm towel, and given warm fluids. Just as with a child, *no alcohol.*

In a state of medium hypothermia, an additional drop in the body's core temperature results in more violent shivering and a loss of coordination and manual dexterity. Simple tasks, such as grasping a thrown line, become difficult. The victim is less aware of his or her mental condition. If the limbs are cold and stiff, damage may result from trying to remove clothing. At this level, simply wrapping the individual in a blanket or towel is virtually useless because the body cannot generate enough heat to rewarm itself. The person has to be reheated by application of external direct warmth. The most practical and accessible source of heat aboard a boat is another human being. Simply sharing a sleeping bag

MINIMUM INSULATION FOR IMMERSION IN COLD WATER	
Water Temp. (F)	**Insulation (Foam Neoprene)**
60° or higher	3/16" vest or V8" jacket
50-60°	3/16" jacket, pants, boots, and gloves
40-50°	3/16" jacket, pants, hood, boots, and mittens
below 40°	1/4" jacket, pants, hood, boots, and mittens

or a blanket will provide the proper amount of heat at the right temperature.

Do not administer fluids to someone who is not totally coherent. Having to deal with a choking victim will take away from the essential treatment of warming the individual.

Do not massage the victim's arms and legs. Massage will cause the circulatory system to take cold blood from the surface into the body's core, resulting in further temperature drop. And, due to numbness, the victim cannot discern if the massage is too rough. Damage to skin tissue and nerve endings can result.

Do not administer alcohol, which causes loss of body heat, or coffee or tea. Stimulants may have the same effect as massage.

Even if the victim is breathing and does not require mouth-to-mouth resuscitation, emulating the rescue breathing technique by timing the rescuer's breathing rate with that of the victim will allow warm air to enter the victim's lungs and supply direct heat to the body core.

Severe hypothermia requires the same treatment as the medium stage. An added risk, however, comes from the chance of respiratory distress or cardiac arrest. A person in a severe stage of hypothermia may appear dead, without apparent pulse or breath. This should not stop the rescuer from using mouth-to-mouth or cardiopulmonary resuscitation (CPR) to revive the victim. These techniques are beyond the scope of this learn-to-sail text, but courses in first aid and CPR should be a high priority for all sailors, especially those in cold water.

As the core temperature continues to drop, the shivering stops and the muscles become rigid. Loss of consciousness soon follows and, if the victim does not receive prompt medical attention, the result can be fatal.

Hypothermia in severe stages is a medical emergency. Medical assistance is a must.

CONSERVING HEAT IN THE WATER

Conservation of heat is the foremost objective for a person in the water. To accomplish this, limit body movement. Any action generates heat, which is absorbed by the water and taken away from the body. Movement, such as treading water, will also cause the water warmed by the body to be moved away, and new, colder water will take its place. This exchange of water accelerates the cooling of the body.

A person without a personal flotation device (PFD) has to tread water to keep afloat. This uses up precious body heat and further exposes the high heat loss areas to the cold water. Heat loss, therefore, is greatly accelerated. A prudent sailor dons a PFD as soon as sailing conditions deteriorate. If someone who has fallen overboard does not have one, then a PFD must be thrown to the victim immediately. (See Sailing Skills in this part for Rescuing a Man Overboard.)

The PFD allows the person in the water to assume the heat escape lessening position-H.E.L.P. This position, commonly referred to as the fetal position, permits the victim to float with little effort and to concentrate on reducing heat loss. The areas of greatest heat loss-those requiring the greatest protection-are around the head, armpits, sides of the chest, groin, and backs of the knees.

Some survival suits and float coats are approved PFDs that provide life-saving insulation. In 60-degree water, a full survival suit considerably extends survival time.

A person without a flotation device should restrict movements to just those required to keep the head out of the water, since over 50 percent of the body heat loss in water is through the head. If possible,

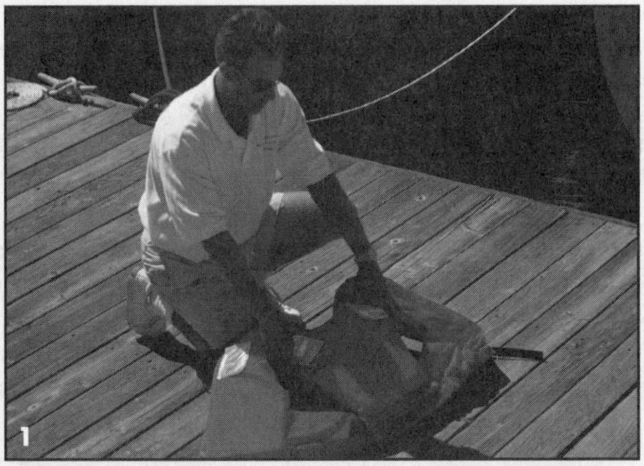

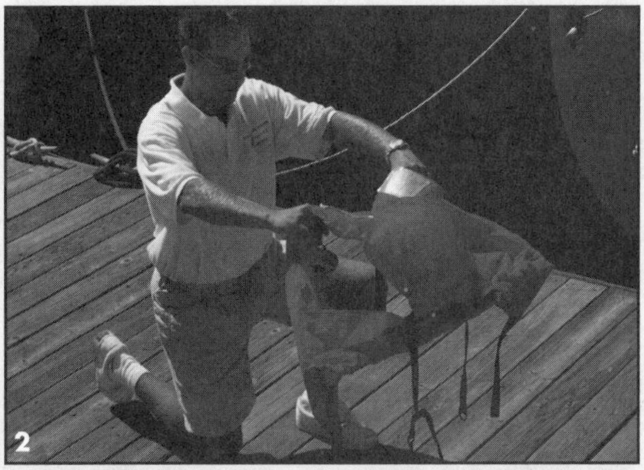

To don a PFD while in the water:

1. Place the PFD in front of you, inside out with the collar toward you.

2. Place arms in armholes.

3. Raise arms, bringing PFD over the head.

4. Lower arms, allowing PFD to be pulled down into place. Fasten zipper.

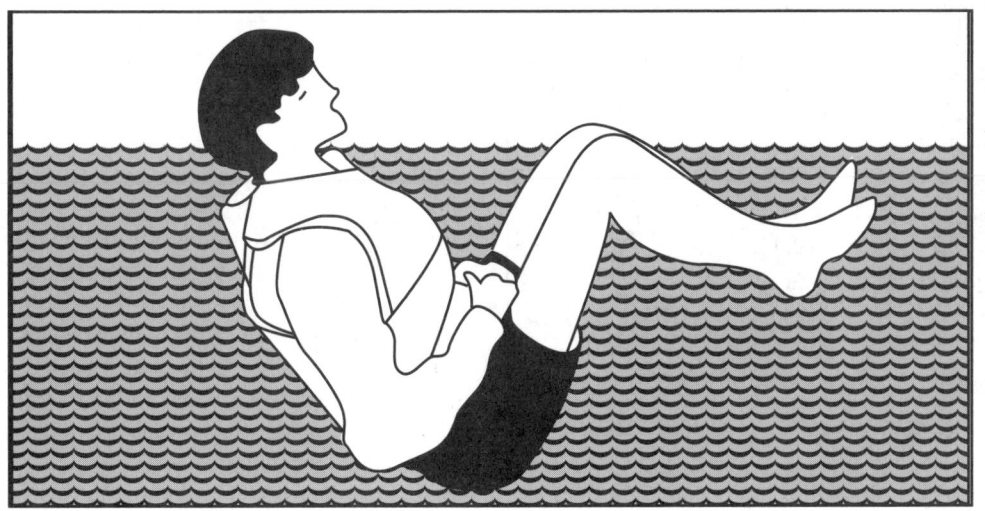

Heat Escape Lessening Position (H.E.L.P.)

get out of the water (possibly into an overturned boat). Water conducts heat away from the body twenty-five times faster than air. Never attempt to swim to shore from an overturned boat. The combination of increased circulation from swimming and exposure of high heat-loss areas (head, neck, and groin) to the water will greatly increase the risk of hypothermia. Always *stay with the boat.*

A huddle should be formed to trap water warmed by heat loss.

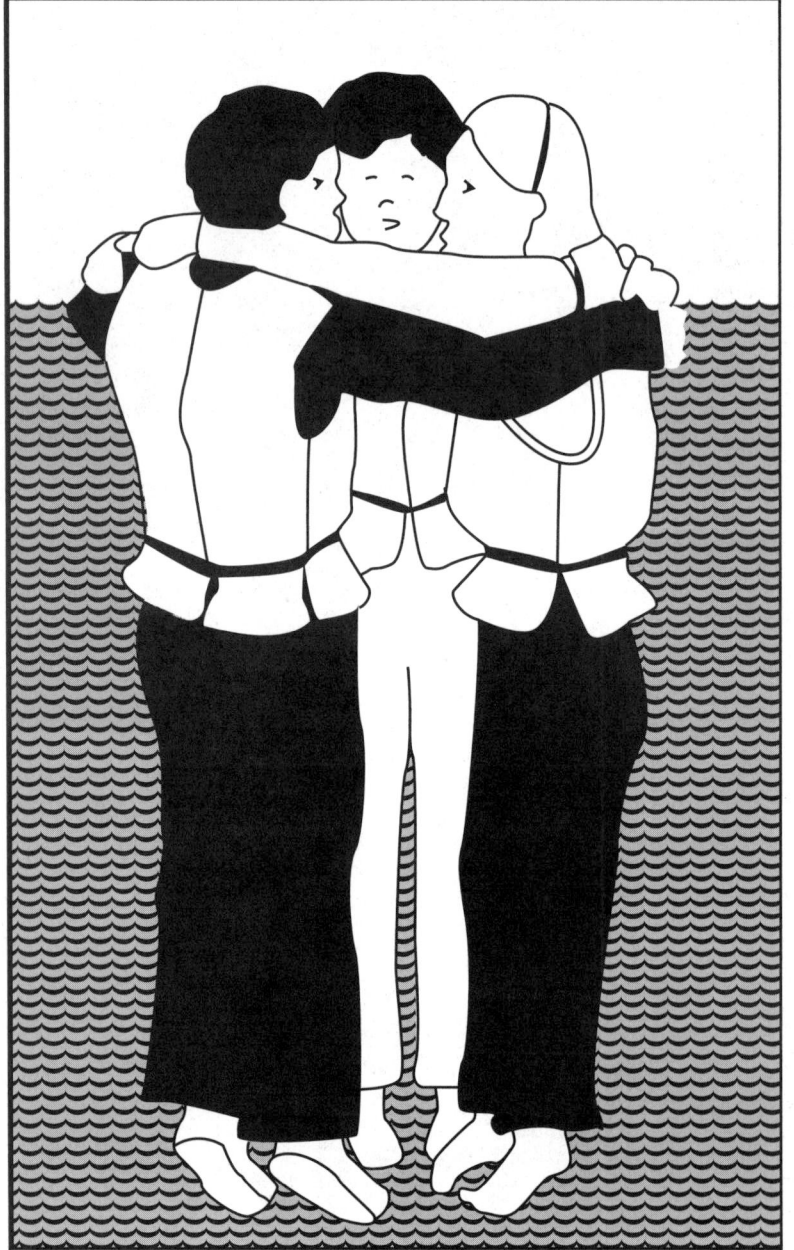

Another word of caution: "Drownproofing, " a rescue swimming and breathing method taught in the sixties and seventies, will accelerate the progression of hypothermia. Do not use drownproofing techniques.

A group of people in the water together should form a huddle. In this position, the water warmed by the heat loss of the group is trapped in the huddle. Once the water has been warmed, it draws less heat from the individuals into the water. This is the same principle behind the protection provided by a diver's wet suit. Small children should be kept in the center of the huddle. They are greatly protected by the relatively warmer water there.

THE RIGHT CLOTHES

The best way a sailor can prevent hypothermia out of the water is to wear the right clothes and stay warm and dry. The chill factor gets worse rapidly as the wind increases.

In no other sport is there a greater variety of clothing, ranging from nothing at all (as I found sailing in St. Tropez) to wearing every stitch of clothes you own. On one race from Chicago to Mackinac Island I was shivering in my bunk waiting for the next watch at 3:30 A.M. One of the crew came below to wake our watch and told us, "Put on everything you have. " I was already wearing everything I had, and it was a cold morning.

One of the secrets to sailing well is to be comfortable while on the water. Although foul-weather gear is an expensive investment, it's worth it.

Wear sneakers or nonskid shoes with soft soles at all times. Although I generally don't wear socks on shore, I always wear them while sailing to give me better traction. It is a bad habit to sail barefoot, since you may lose your balance.

There are many styles of boots. On offshore yachts, calf-high boots are best. For dinghy sailing, wear boots that fit tightly around the ankle. These are particularly comfortable for hiking.

The warmest sailing clothes are thermal

polypropylene underwear and socks under wool or pile pants and shirt, goose-down vests or jackets, topped off with foul-weather pants and a waterproof parka.

Wind takes heat right away from the body. Even a light breeze can reduce the air temperature between the layers of clothing. Ideally, the outer layer of clothing should act as a windbreaker, keeping the wind and water away from the body.

The goal is to contain as much body heat as possible. Many sailors wear towels around their necks to keep water from trickling in. Gloves can be useful, particularly on long passages. Plan your sail in advance so you can take the right clothes with you. In boats that are particularly wet, a wet suit will keep you warm and comfortable and give you some flotation. A wet suit or dry suit should be used on wet boats when the water temperature dips below 72 degrees. In a wet suit, a thin layer of moisture that develops under the rubber suit gets warmed by your body and acts as insulation. Wear foul-weather gear over your wet suit in particularly cold weather.

Headgear (a hat or visor) is helpful in sunny weather because it shades you from the sun and helps keep you cool. In cold weather, a hat is important since a great deal of body heat escapes from your head. I find the best for cold weather are wool ski hats because they stay on your head and are designed for warmth.

An oiled woolen sweater is particularly good in cold weather since it resists water. I generally wear a T-shirt underneath my sweater to absorb perspiration. Wear sneakers, deck shoes, or boots with soft soles at all times. But be careful. If you end up in the water, all of this clothing will soak up water and restrict your movements. To counteract all of this weight it is best to wear a life jacket (PFD) so that you will stay afloat in the water.

A float coat is a jacket with flotation material sewn into the panels. Float coats are popular because they keep you warm and provide flotation if you do go into the water. Some sailors use a float coat with a strobe light sewn into a pocket in case they

fall overboard at night. Some sailors sew a safety harness into their coats as well. Short jackets can be annoying, as they ride up and leave part of your back exposed. Longer float coats are best since they stay down to keep you covered.

There are many excellent brands of foul-weather gear on the market. Find an outfit that fits you comfortably, slightly loose so that it is easy to move around in, yet able

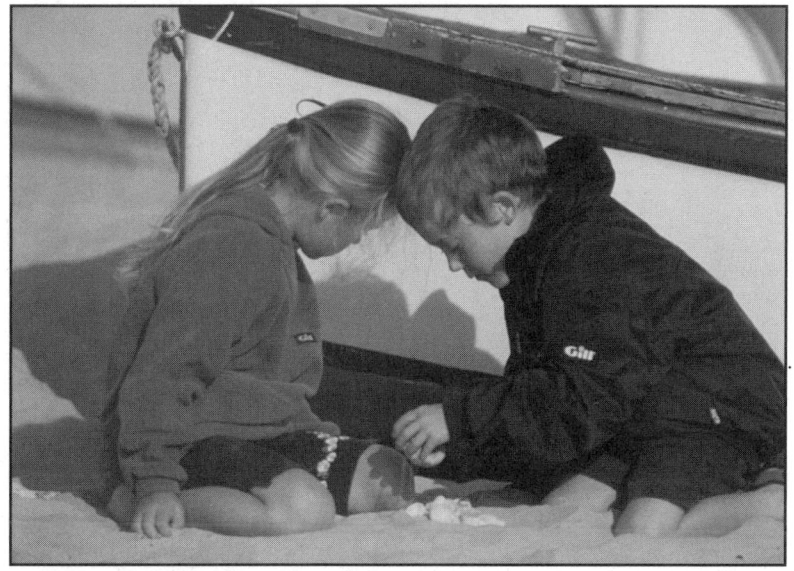

Insulated sailing gear comes in all sizes and colors.

 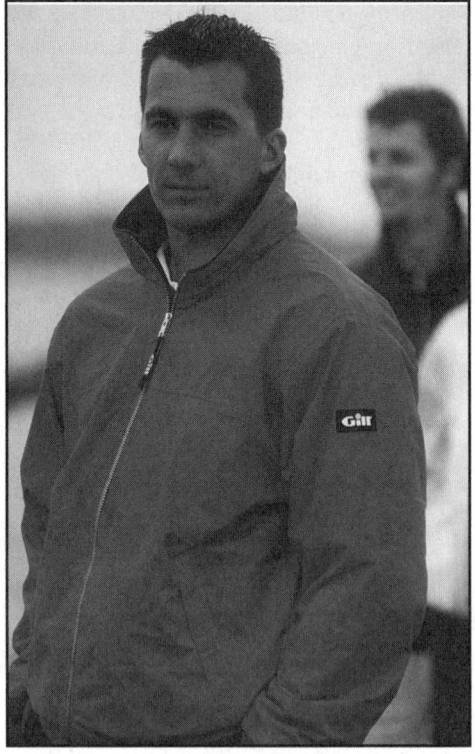

Raising the hoods on this foul weather gear (left) gives head to toe protection. A windbreaker with a high neck (right) offers comfort in less severe conditions.

to keep you dry in all kinds of weather. There really is no substitute for a good set of foul-weather gear. Pick a foul-weather jacket with a good hood and front designed to prevent rain from trickling in. Traditionally, foul-weather gear is bright yellow, orange, or red so that a person can be easily spotted if he falls in the water. I favor sweaters or chamois shirts instead of heavy jackets underneath my foul-weather gear, since they permit better movement.

Remember, the pleasure of sailing is directly proportional to your comfort. Proper clothing for different weather conditions makes it that much more enjoyable.

SEASICKNESS

Seasickness is generally less dangerous than hypothermia (although a severe case of motion sickness can be incapacitating), and its symptoms are easier to spot. Motion sickness afflicts many sailors, particularly at night. Some people are more prone to it than others, but no one ever escapes it entirely. A primary contributor to motion sickness is becoming overheated or chilled. It is important to wear the right clothing to maintain normal body temperature. Early symptoms of motion sickness are nausea, overheating, or feeling uncomfortable just moving around. Swallowing helps, although chewing gum doesn't since it creates too much saliva.

The first thing to do when you start feeling ill is to get some fresh air. Try to be active but relaxed. Don't be uptight about it. Fighting it off can make it worse. Often when you are feeling seasick you may not have eaten for a while; it may help to eat saltine crackers and drink a noncarbonated beverage. There are pills you can take, although they may make you drowsy. The motion sickness medicine used on the NASA space shuttle is the disc Transderm Scop (scopolamine), a prescription drug. Transderm Scop helps provide protection against motion sickness by delivering the drug scopolamine through the skin at a consistent, controlled rate. The adhesive disc is worn behind the ear and delivers the drug for up to three days. Tests show, however, that one out of six users of Transderm Scop experience drowsiness and two out of three users experience dryness of mouth. Other common side effects include vision problems in persons with glaucoma and urinary problems in older men as a result of the drug's effect on the prostate. Avoid overuse! Persons complaining of problems on cruises in the Caribbean have been found to have as many as four patches adhered to their body. Even replacing the patch daily can result in an overdose, as patches are meant to release a predetermined dosage over a few days. Read the product literature carefully and consult your doctor if you have questions.

If you do get seasick, head for the leeward rail.

YOU ARE WHAT YOU EAT

How well you eat determines how well you sail. The night before you sail, try to avoid exotic foods. Stay away from alcohol. Acidic (gas-producing) and greasy foods help induce motion sickness. Try to eat foods that store energy. Carbohydrates, such as pasta, potatoes, and bread, are best. It is best to have a good, solid breakfast about two to three hours before you go out so that you will have plenty of stored energy for the day's sail. Eat lightly if you are tense. On the water it is best to drink water and iced tea in hot weather; hot soup is best when the weather is cold. Stay away from carbonated beverages, as they produce gas. Sugary foods are good for short bursts of energy, but in the long run they are fatiguing.

This adhesive disc on the author's neck delivers scopolamine through the skin.

REVIEW QUESTIONS

1. The purpose of the safety harness is to _____ .

2. If alone in the water, wearing a PFD, an individual can extend his or her survival time by assuming the h _____ e _____ l _____ position.

3. List three *dos* when treating a hypothermia victim.

_____

_____

_____

4. List three *do nots* when treating a hypothermia victim.

_____

_____

_____

Answers in Appendix A, p. 201.

SAILING SKILLS

SAILING A TRIANGULAR COURSE

Each set of on-the-water exercises in this book builds upon the previous exercises. The following exercise will give you an opportunity to consolidate some of the skills you have acquired thus far. Once you can successfully sail a triangular course, you will be able to sail anywhere. This is because all points of sail, as well as coming about and jibing, are required to sail around the triangle.

The course for this exercise consists of three marks set far enough apart to allow five to seven tacks on the upwind leg. The key to success with this exercise is repetition.

By now, the helmsman and crew should be working as a coordinated team. Communications should be excellent and proper commands should be used during every maneuver. On the upwind leg, the helmsman should be able to sail a close-hauled course without having to adjust the boat's course except for changes in wind direction.

When coming about, the helmsman should try to complete the 90-degree turn without oversteering. The turn should be executed fast enough so that the boat does not slow down or stall, but slow enough for the crew to handle the sails properly and safely.

The crew's goal is to respond to the helmsman's commands quickly. When coming up to a close-hauled course from a reach, the crew sheets the sails in as the boat is heading up-not before or after the turn. When coming about, the crew releases the jib just as it starts to backwind and blow through the **foretriangle**—the space between the mast and forestay.

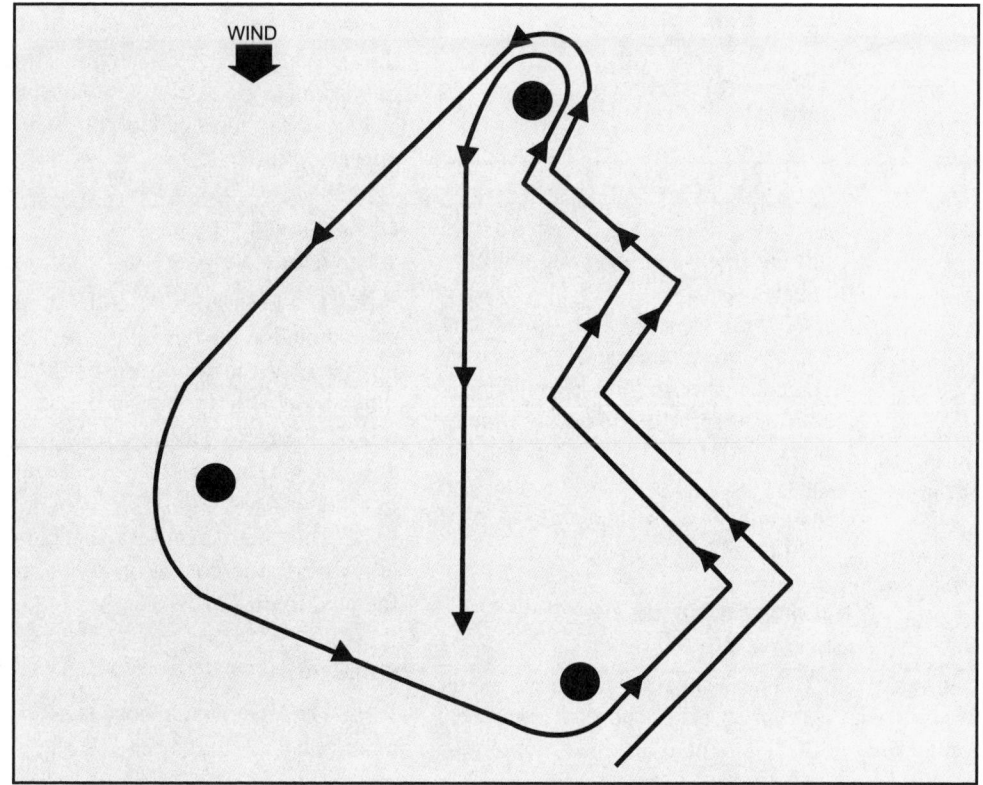

A triangular course. The windward leg is between marks 1 and 2; the reach legs are 2 to 3 and 3 to 1; the downwind leg is from mark 2 back to 1.

EXERCISE: **SAILING A TRIANGULAR COURSE**

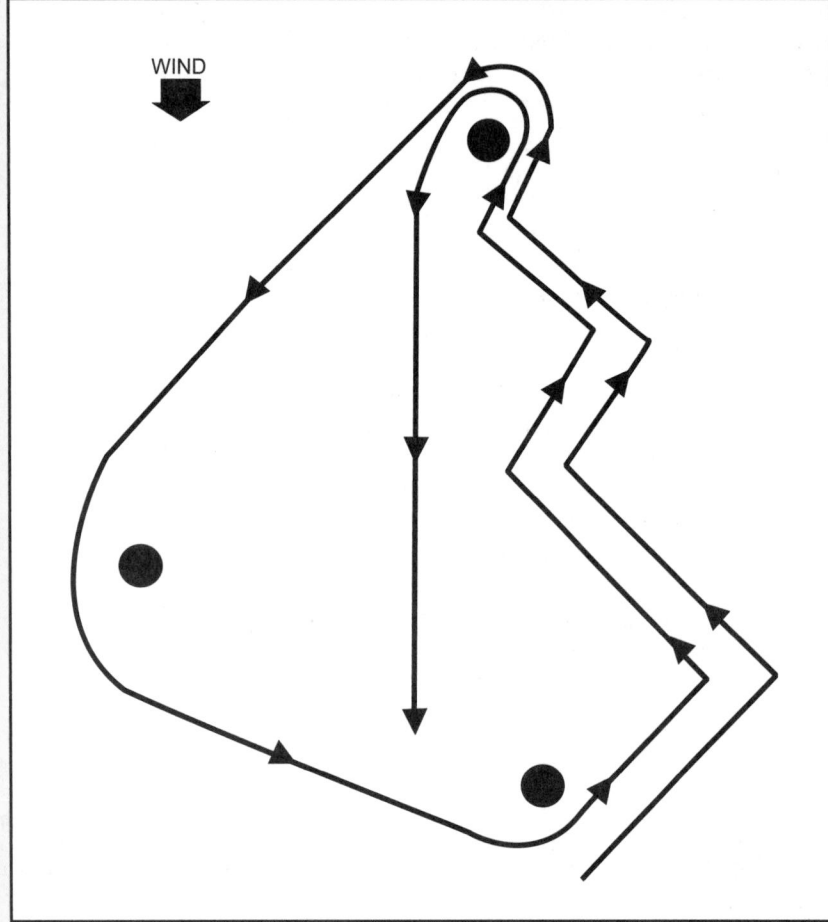

WIND

man makes sure the boat is actually sailing close-hauled by heading up until the telltales luff and then bearing away until the luffing stops.

3. To ensure that the turn is as close to 90 degrees as possible, the helmsman looks to windward to select a landmark for reference. This reference point will be off the windward beam of the boat (90 degrees off the bow).

4. With the command "Hard alee," the helmsman initiates a smooth turn to windward.

5. The crew member tending the leeward jib sheet releases the sheet just as the sail starts to move across the boat. Of course the sailor must be careful not to release the sheet too soon, or the boat will not come about as efficiently as possible. If he is too late in releasing the jib sheet, the sail will backwind and the helmsman will have difficulties in preventing the boat from oversteering.

6. As the boat completes its 90-degree turn, the crew member trims the jib on the new tack and the helmsman again tests that the boat is sailing on a close-hauled course by observing the telltales.

ON THE FIRST LEG, YOU WILL BE SAILING CLOSE-HAULED:

1. Starting from a reach at the leeward mark (**1**, the mark farthest away from the wind), the helmsman will be on the windward side of the boat, the best position for watching the telltales and water ahead. He gives the command to head up to a close-hauled course.

2. The helmsman or a crew member trims the mainsail as the boat comes up to close-hauled. One crew member trims the jib.

3. The helmsman tests to make sure the boat is sailing close-hauled by gradually heading up until the

windward (inside) telltales start to luff and then bearing away until the telltales stream aft.

4. If the wind gusts, the boat may become overpowered. The crew should then ease the mainsail slightly to allow some of the excess wind to be "spilled" from the sail * When the gust passes, the crew retrims the mainsail. The jib remains sheeted tight for upwind sailing.

COMING ABOUT ON THE UPWIND LEG:

1. The helmsman and crew use all appropriate commands and responses.

2. Before coming about, the helms-

BEARING AWAY AT THE WINDWARD MARK:

1. The helmsman gives the proper commands to bear away as the boat rounds the windward mark (**2**, the mark closest to the wind).

2. The crew eases the mainsheet and jib sheet as the helmsman bears away.

3. The helmsman lets the crew know when the boat is on course to the next mark (**3**).

REACHING:

1. The helmsman now steers a straight course to the third mark.

2. The crew ensures the correct trim of jib and mainsail by continually adjusting the sails as the wind direction varies. The crew sets the jib by easing the sheet until the inside telltale luffs and then sheeting in until the telltales are streaming aft. One of the most common. problems experienced by new crew is sheeting the jib too tight. The rule of thumb for preventing this remains "When in doubt, let it out."

3. Trim the mainsail concurrently with the jib, easing it until the sail backwinds from the wind coming off the jib. Retrim until the sail is just full again.

JIBING AT THE THIRD MARK:

1. While approaching the third mark, the helmsman prepares the crew with the appropriate commands for jibing.

2. As the boat starts to turn, one crew member begins sheeting in the mainsail. Optimal timing would have the boom coming to the centerline of the boat just as the wind passes over the stern. The mainsheet is then eased to allow the sail to swing out to the opposite side of the boat.

If this action is smooth and coordinated, the mains" movement will be continuous, without pause in the center of the jibe and without the boom banging into the rigging or the mainsheet taking a great shock as the boom swings out.

The reach back to the leeward mark **(1)** will require the same coordination as the first reach.

HEADING UP TO BEGIN AGAIN:

1. At the leeward mark the helmsman gives the commands to head the boat up to a close-hauled course.

2. Giving the command "trim sheets," the helmsman heads the boat up and the crew trims the mainsheet and jib sheet.

3. The crew trims the mainsail and jib to the close-hauled setting.

4. The crew tells the helmsman when the sails are trimmed for sailing on a close-hauled course.

5. The helmsman tests that the boat is actually sailing close-hauled by sailing toward the wind until the sails luff.

The second windward leg is just like the first.

SAILING DOWNWIND:

1. When the boat rounds the windward mark (2) for the second time, the helmsman bears away to a run, setting a course for the leeward mark (1).

2. As the boat bears away, the helmsman gives the command "ease sheets, " and the crew eases the sheets.

3. The helmsman watches the masthead fly to determine when the boat is on a run. The jib will become blanketed by the mainsail and will no longer fly to leeward.

4. One of the crew releases the old jib sheet, while the other crew member pulls in on the new jib sheet to guide the jib to the opposite side of the boat.

5. The jib sheet is eased until the jib is full and parallel to the mainsail. This is called sailing **wing-and-wing.**

6. Practice jibing while sailing downwind toward Mark 1. Avoid sailing by-the-lee (where the wind is coming from the same side the boom is on) and accidental jibes.

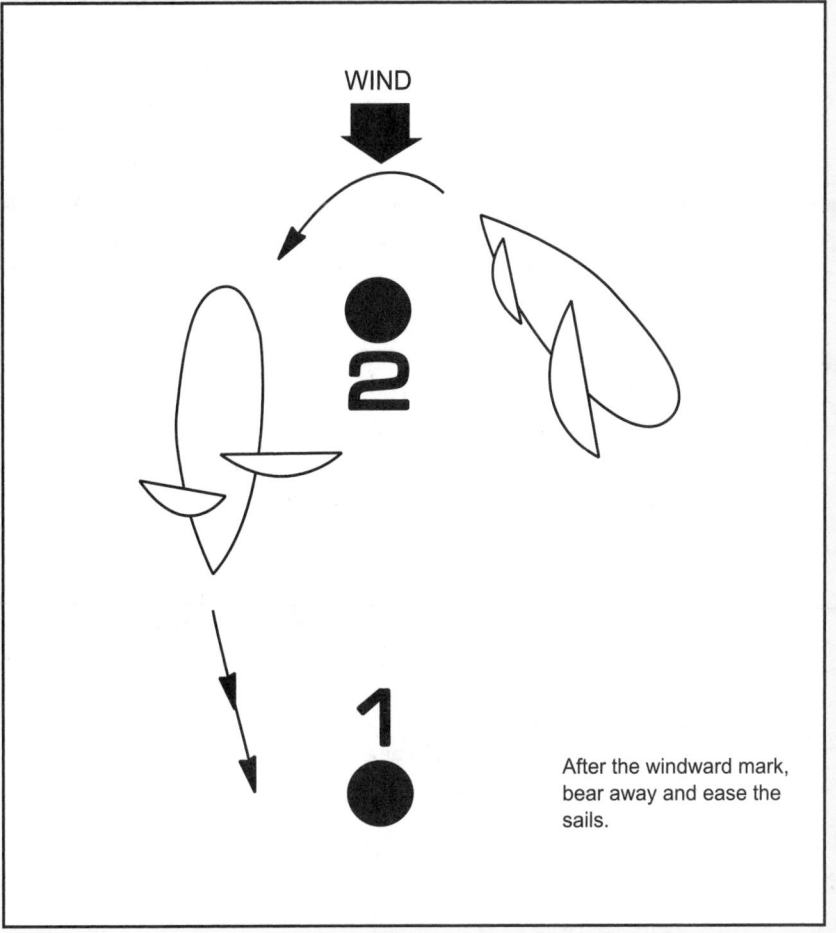

WIND

After the windward mark, bear away and ease the sails.

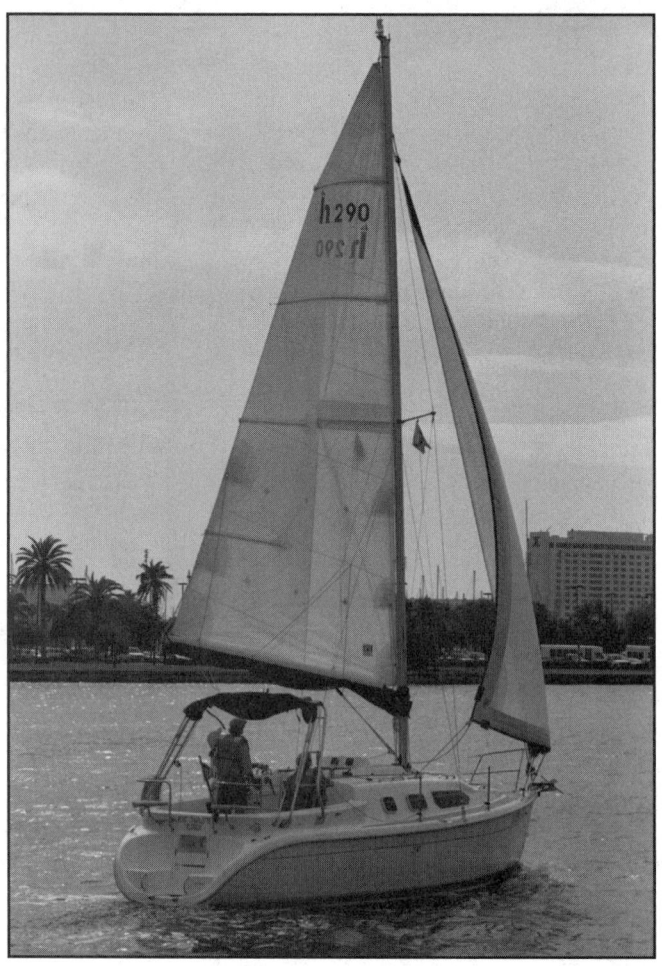

Winging the jib to windward on a run

RESCUING A MAN OVERBOARD

Man overboard is a serious situation on all boats. Consequently, the best method for returning to someone who has fallen in the water is one of the most hotly debated subjects s in sailing. Of the three popular basic methods, we feel that the following is the most efficient method of rescue and includes some safeguards which make it preferable for new sailors. Others may choose alternate methods, but the objective for everyone is the same-safe, efficient, and reliable recovery of someone who has fallen overboard.

The following method involves sailing a figure eight course with one tack and no jibe. It places the rescuing vessel on a close reach approaching the victim. You will remember from Part Two that a sailboat is easiest to stop with control on a close reach; that's why the following method is recommended for beginners. Crews should practice it many times in all types of weather.

THE FIGURE EIGHT METHOD

1. As soon as the person falls overboard;

a) Someone must shout "Man overboard!"

b) The nearest person must throw a PFD, life jacket, life ring or any other large, buoyant object to the person in the water.

c) Another person must be assigned to

watch the person in the water. This spotter points to the victim and gives verbal directions to the helmsman as to where the man overboard is. The spotter must never take his eyes off the person in the water.

2. The helmsman immediately steers to a beam reach from whatever point of sail the boat has been sailing.

3. The crew prepares a heaving line, boarding ladder, blankets, and jackets.

4. After sailing long enough for the crew to get prepared (about 100 yards), the helmsman commands the crew to prepare to come about.

5. As the boat comes about, the crew trims the mainsail but not the jib. This slows the boat's speed. Not having to tend the jib also frees up one member of the crew to assist the spotter or prepare to rescue the man overboard. The loop formed by the jib sheet in the water also gives the man overboard something to grasp as the boat comes near.

6. The spotter continues to give verbal and visual directions to the helmsman.

7. The helmsman, before getting too close to the victim, will have to test to see if the boat is actually on a close reach by having the crew luff the mainsail. If the mainsail luffs fully, the boat is on a close reach and the helmsman and crew carry on as if this were a stopping exercise. The helmsman stops the boat a few feet to windward of the victim. (The helmsman can also look to see that the masthead fly is pointing 40 to 50 degrees off the bow. This too indicates a close reach, but requires the helmsman to take his eyes off the spotter or the person in the water.)

8. As soon as the boat is stopped to windward of the victim, a line should be thrown and the individual secured to the vessel.

9. Once the person is alongside, the crew must bring him aboard. If he is unconscious or exhausted, he will not be able to help himself, so all crew members will have to haul him up by the armpits. Alternatively, a line may be led under his armpits and pulled up with a halyard. However, if the swimmer is self-sufficient, the crew should lower the boat's swimming ladder (if there is one). Obviously, the boat must be at a dead stop,

10. After the victim is aboard, treat him or her for hypothermia.

Picking up a man overboard

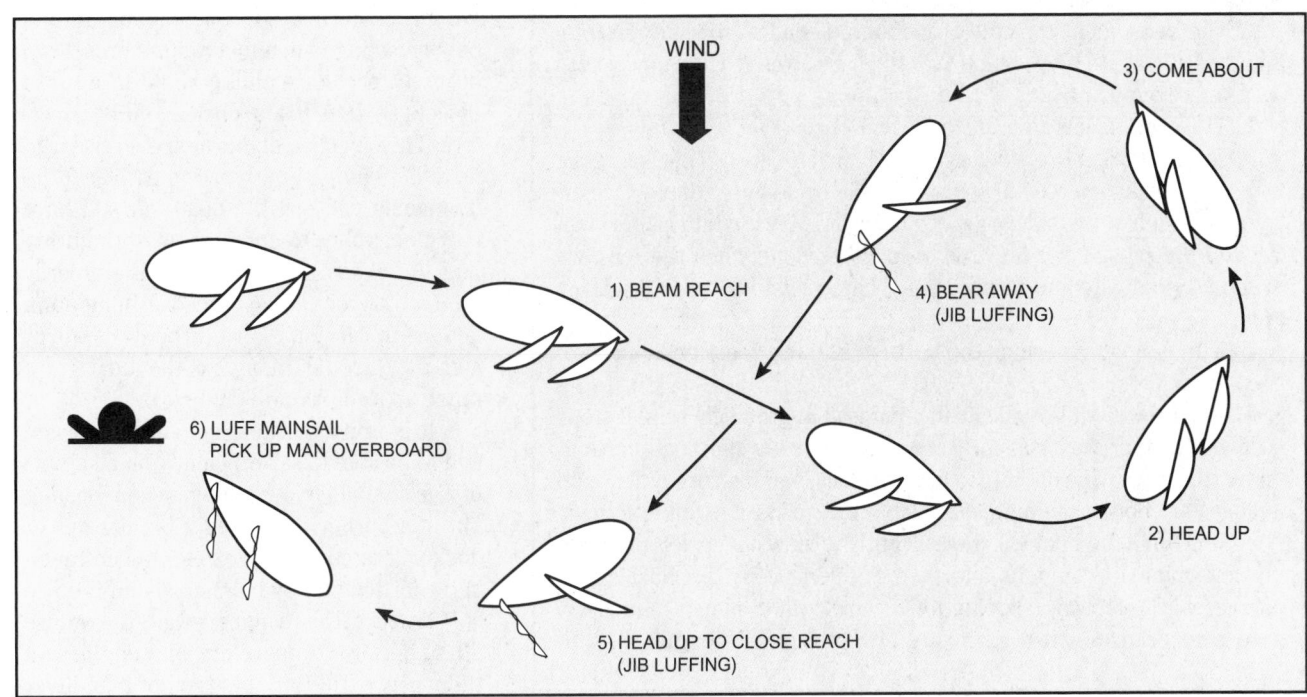

WIND

6) LUFF MAINSAIL
PICK UP MAN OVERBOARD

1) BEAM REACH

4) BEAR AWAY
(JIB LUFFING)

3) COME ABOUT

2) HEAD UP

5) HEAD UP TO CLOSE REACH
(JIB LUFFING)

SAILING IN CONFINED WATERS

A sailboat does not require auxiliary power, although there are times when entering and leaving a crowded anchorage or mooring area can be greatly assisted by an engine. In these exercises, we will develop the skills required to handle a sailboat in confined or crowded conditions.

BOAT SPEED

The single most important factor in handling a vessel in an area with restricted maneuverability is control of boat speed. If a boat is stopped, it cannot be steered any more than it is possible to turn a parked car by turning the steering wheel. The crew will have to keep the sails trimmed properly at all times. The slightest luffing or stalling will result in loss of speed.

The faster you turn a boat, the faster it will stop. I recall one time sailing into a small harbor where a cocktail party was being held on the seawall near its opening. Any maneuvers would have to be sharp and precise. At the time I was seventeen and in a mood to do a little "hot dogging. " I was sailing a 28-foot E-Scow, a boat known to sail at speeds in excess of 20 knots. In entering the marine basin, we were sailing fast on a beam reach. Just before crashing into the seawall where the party was being held, I pushed the helm over as hard and as fast as I possibly could, forcing the boat to round up into the wind. The maneuver was made so sharply that the boat came to a complete stop. One of the crew marched forward to the bow, took the painter (bow line) and wrapped it around the cleat on the dock. We all stood up and took a bow to the cheering crowd. It must have looked spectacular to everyone except the owner, who was hesitant to loan us his boat again.

Once out of the slip, it is important to accelerate as quickly as possible, since speed equals control. Practice the following exercise in open water before trying it in a crowded area.

COMING ABOUT IN A CONFINED AREA

We have learned to come about around buoys. Sailing in confined waters presents a different problem-coming about in front of objects such as boats, docks, and breakwaters. The objective of this next exercise is to be able to judge how close to an object the helmsman can sail the boat and still have sufficient room to come about without hitting the object. Success depends primarily on two factors: boat speed (momentum needed to carry the boat through the turn) and the turning radius of the boat (how much space it requires to turn).

It is important to maintain boat speed and to be able to sail efficiently on all points of sail. Sailing close-hauled when beating out of a harbor or around a breakwater or dock will require the greatest concentration and coordination by helmsman and crew.

Practice this confined waters exercise often, because even sailors with engines on their boats will find this type of maneuver

---

EXERCISE: **SAIL TRIMMING**

This exercise is designed to illustrate the effects of proper sail trim techniques by comparing them with improper methods. The first part of the exercise is what not to do:

1. The helmsman stops the boat about fifteen feet to windward of a buoy on a beam to close reach with the sails luffing. The buoy serves as a reference point.

2. The crew sheets the sails quickly and abruptly.

The boat will move sideways rather than forward. This is a result of the sail being sheeted in so fast that the boat is not able to accelerate and simply drifts sideways with the wind blowing into rather than around the sail. To see how the boat will respond when the sails are trimmed gradually and to the proper angle relative to the wind, try this:

3. The helmsman brings the boat back to the same position as in step 1.

4. One crew member sheets the mainsail in gradually until it stops luffing. Another will trim the jib concurrently. As the boat starts to move, the crew will continue to trim the sails, making sure that the jib telltales are both streaming aft and that the mainsail is not luffing.

This time, the boat will move slightly to leeward (watch the buoy to determine how much) and then accelerate. As the boat speed increases, the leeway (slipping to leeward) will diminish. This exercise gives dramatic proof of the need for proper sail trimming.

ing necessary should the engine fail when they're coming into a mooring area or anchorage. The difference between making a boat sail and making it sail well is the difference between someone who owns a boat and a sailor.

OBSTRUCTIONS

If an obstruction or another boat is in your path, you must maneuver to stay clear. Always keep a sharp lookout when you approach another boat: don't lose sight of it. As a rule it is best to pass astern, although on starboard tack you have the right-of-way and will be the stand-on boat. A yacht on port tack is obligated to stay clear. Remember that many sailors do not know the rules and are uncertain about what to do. Any time it looks close, stay clear to avoid a collision.

If you encounter a boat that has the right of way (or one that does not but whose crew thinks it does), but are obstructed by other boats or shallow water from passing on either side, there's not much you can do except stop, luff your sails, and wait for the boat to get out of your way. Sometimes you may be able to turn around and backtrack. Either way, try to stay to windward of the other boat. If it's downwind of you, there's no way that it can drift down onto you.

EXERCISE: **COMING ABOUT IN A CONFINED AREA**

Practice in open water before attempting this exercise in confined sailing conditions.

1. The helmsman approaches a buoy on a close-hauled course. (The buoy should be plastic, or use a plastic drop mark, since we will attempt to turn as close to the buoy as possible and there may be some contact.)

2. When approximately one-half boat length from the buoy, the helmsman comes about with the proper commands.

3. The helmsman watches the bow closely throughout the turn. If the boat comes too near the mark after the boat is past head to wind (over halfway through the turn), the helmsman straightens out the vessel's course slightly to avoid contact with the buoy.

The helmsman must judge how close the boat is able to turn to the buoy. Repeat the exercise until the bow passes within a few feet. This is as close as the boat should come to the buoy.

SUMMARY

The emphasis of the Sailing Knowledge part of Part Three has been on safety and seamanship. From preparation to execution, the skipper of a sailing vessel must keep the safety of crew and vessel as his or her primary concern.

We have discussed hypothermia. In the cold waters of the United States and elsewhere, this is a subject that should never be taken lightly. Adequate clothing, sensible diet, and attention to deck safety are your insurance against medical emergencies on the water. The use of safety harnesses and PFDs goes a long way toward ensuring the safety of the crew.

The Sailing Skills part of this section continued this safety theme. Recovering someone who has fallen overboard is a drill we all hope we'll never have to use. However, the helmsman and crew must still be properly prepared.

Finally, the sailing exercises (around a triangular course and in confined waters) test skills acquired so far. We are now only one lesson away from completing the ASA Basic Sailing standard.

PART FOUR

Basic Seamanship Skills

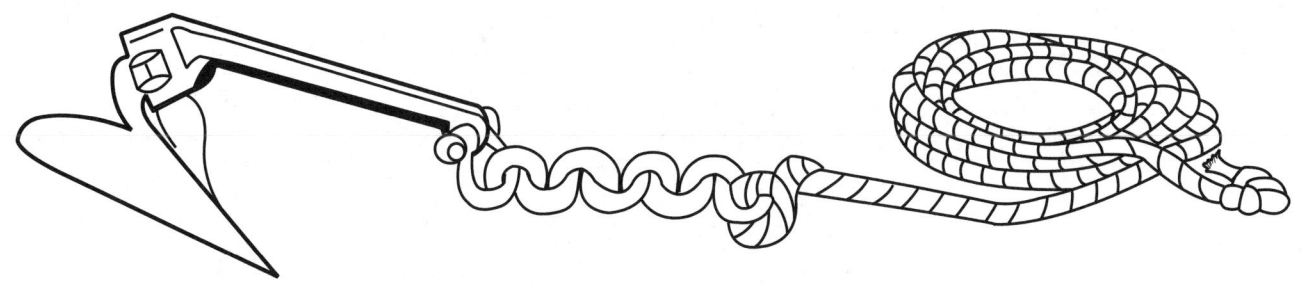

SAILING KNOWLEDGE

In this section, our concern is with special seamanship skills: chart reading, anchoring, heaving to (a way of stopping the boat while underway), and docking under sail. All of the skills taught so far will be practiced and polished in the sailing exercises, but in addition the new skills will make the handling and sailing of the boat more controlled and much safer.

DAYSAIL PLANNING

Before you go sailing, the following factors (other than the boat) have to be considered:
• weather
• season and time of day
• clothing
• the crew and their abilities

WATCH THE WEATHER

Before I go sailing I call the National Weather Service to get their report. I find that they are generally accurate in most parts of the country. Special continuous weather broadcasts are available on VHF radio channels. A marine weather radio will receive these broadcasts. Radio stations, particularly in cities along the coasts, have regular boating forecasts. Forecasters usually mention the barometric pressure, which indicates variation in air pressure. The direction and rate of change of the barometric pressure is important when forecasting weather. Weather changes are caused by the movement of pressure systems. A steadily failing barometer normally indicates unsettled or wet weather. A rapidly falling barometer usually forecasts the development of strong winds or a storm. A slowly rising barometer is normally associated with lighter winds.

Clouds are also helpful weather indicators. In general, thickening and lowering cloud layers are a sign of approaching wet weather. When layers of clouds show holes and openings or are frayed and indistinct at the edges, you can expect improving weather or a delay in the development of foul weather. An old adage says "Red sky at night, sailors delight; red sky at morning, sailors take warning. "

There are many helpful indicators, including the following:

• bright blue sky: good sailing
• dark, gloomy sky: wind
• bright yellow sky at sunset: wind
• sunrise from a gray horizon: fair day
• weak and washed-out sun: rain in the future
• sunset with diffused and glaring white clouds: storm
• ring around the moon: rain
• soft clouds: fine weather with light to moderate wind
• hard-edged, oily clouds: wind
• small, inky clouds: rain

Be familiar with the coastal warning displays issued by the U.S. Weather Service. These indicate foul weather. The following displays are normally shown at marinas, yacht clubs, and some Coast Guard stations (the Coast Guard is moving away from using storm signals):

Small craft advisory. One red pennant displayed by day and one red light above a white light at night. Indicates wind and sea conditions dangerous to small craft.

Gale warning. Two red pennants displayed by day and a white light above a red light at night. Indicates conditions dangerous to all boats.

Storm warning. A single square red flag with black center displayed by day and two red lights at night. Indicates very dangerous conditions.

Hurricane warning. Two square red flags with black centers displayed by day and a white light between two red lights at night. Indicates the most dangerous conditions.

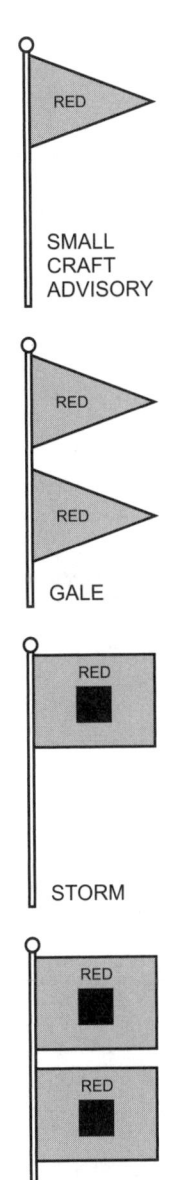

Daytime signals

SEASON AND TIME OF DAY

If your daysail is to last three to four hours, it naturally would be started during daylight. In the summer, a pleasant evening sail can be started at 6 P.M. and be over by sundown. In the fall or winter (if you live in an area where winter sailing is possible), you should start just after noon so you can have the boat back and tied to the dock before sunset. Evening sails are fun, but sailing in the dark shouldn't be attempted by a new sailor until boat-handling skills and knowledge are more developed.

CLOTHING

In warm weather wear light clothing, but keep in mind that the sun, particularly on hazy days, can give you severe sunburn. The sun's rays are intensified as they reflect off your deck and sails. Therefore stay covered for a good portion of the day. It doesn't take long to get sunburned. I have seen the rays burn through T-shirts. Use a sun screen lotion with a high SPF (sun protection factor). It is better to use too much sun screen than too little. Constant exposure to the sun and wind also ages your skin and increases your chances for skin cancer. Sun screens will help counteract this.

THE CREW AND THEIR ABILITIES

New sailors cannot wait to take their friends sailing. However, this usually results in a crew consisting of one not very experienced sailor and a group of novices. The workload and responsibilities of the skipper in this situation increase dramatically with each nonsailor who comes aboard.

A new skipper should take along at least one other experienced sailor on a daysail. There is always someone at the local sailing school, sailing club, or marina who has some experience and who would enjoy the opportunity to sail.

While they are putting on the sails and preparing the boat, the skipper and the experienced guest should take some time to discuss their duties and responsibilities once they are underway. In this situation, it's all too easy for each person to defer to the other, the end result being that nobody knows who's in charge. It's very important that one person, able to give decisive commands, is given clear authority. This may prevent disaster in such situations as near collisions or approaching thunderstorms. It's also a good idea for everybody on board to agree on a common terminology. Sailors of different generations, backgrounds, and levels of experience often find themselves speaking remarkably different languages when they're sailing, and this, too, can lead to trouble.

CHART SYMBOLS

It is not our intent to teach navigation. However, even on a daysail, you need to be able to read the symbols on a nautical chart to determine the depth of the water, the hazards in the area (such as wrecks or rocks), and the composition of the bottom under the water in case you wish to anchor.

Chart symbols are bits of concise information on a nautical chart. The placement of the symbols is accurate and important. They give the skipper a clear map of the bottom over which the boat is sailing. The full list of chart symbols is found in the publication Chart No 1, "Symbols Abbreviations and Terms," that is the key to all chart symbols and an essential part of any vessel's sailing equipment.

SOUNDINGS

Soundings, or water depths, are listed in fathoms (one fathom equals six feet), feet, and meters. Nautical charts are being converted to the metric system and an increasing number of charts are now labeled in meters. The vertical reference plane–or datum–for soundings is mean lower low water, which means that charted depths are generally conservative. However, the actual water depth can be less than that charted and the prudent mariner allows a safety margin.

A common and embarrassing error is to read four feet as four fathoms and to find the boat in four feet of water and not twenty-four feet (4 fathoms). A skipper who reads a chart in fathoms, when it is actually in feet, will find that a boat does not sail well when it is sitting on the bottom, aground.

Running aground is easy to do. If you are sailing in new waters that you have not been in before, it is helpful to have a chart on deck and keep track of the course you are steering and your position on the chart. On the bright side, if you run aground you become a warning mark for other vessels that are passing. Never laugh at a boat that has run aground; you may be the next to hit the bricks.

Even the famous America's Cup helmsman, Dennis Connor, once ran aground off Newport, Rhode Island, cutting between a series of rocks and the mainland. Although the chart showed that passage was risky at low tide, Connor and his crew took a chance. The crew was forced to stay on the rocks for at least twenty-five minutes while the tide rose. In the meantime, thirty-eight other competitors all sailed by. Connor's boat was named *Lobo*, and today local watering holes in Newport have a special drink called "Lobo on the rocks" in honor of the occurrence.

DISTANCE

Distance on a nautical chart is measured in **nautical miles.** A nautical mile equals 1.15 statute miles (the miles used on land and on inland charts). Unlike the statute mile, which has evolved from the whims of kings

Sounding - Symbols for Water Depths

No.	Symbol	Description	No.	Symbol	Description
1	SD	Doubtful sounding	10		Hairline depth figures
2	65	No bottom found	10a	8₇ 19	Figures for ordinary soundings
3	(23)	Out of position	11		Soundings taken from foreign charts
4		Least depth in narrow channels	12		Soundings taken from older surveys (or smaller scale chts)
5	30 FEET APR 1972	Dredged channel (with controlling depth indicated)	13	8₇ 19	Echo soundings
6	24 FEET MAY 1972	Dredged area	14	8₂ 19	Sloping figures
7		Swept channel (See Q 9)	15	8₂ 19	Upright figures (See Q 10a)
8	2₁	Drying (or uncovering) heights above chart sounding datum	16	(25) (2)	Bracketed figures (See O 1, 2)
9	17 119	Swept area, not adequately sounded (shown by purple or green tint)	17	6	Underlined sounding figures (See Q 8)
9a	29 23 3 30 8 21 7	Swept area adequately sounded (swept by wire drag to depth indicated)	18	3₂ 6₁	Soundings expressed in fathoms and feet
			22		Unsounded area
			(Qa)	6 5 21t	Stream

and politicians, the nautical mile is not an arbitrary measure. The circumference of the earth is measured in degrees. If measured through the poles (north and south), the degrees of the circumference are referred to as *latitude* (degrees north and south from the equator). *Longitude* (east and west) is the measure of the earth's circumference around the equator.

One degree of latitude is equal to sixty nautical miles. Annapolis, Maryland is about 39 degrees north latitude. Therefore, Annapolis, the home of the U.S. Naval Academy, is approximately 2,340 miles north of the equator (39 degrees of latitude times 60 nautical miles per degree of latitude).

One sixtieth of one degree of latitude (called a minute) is one nautical mile. The scale for this measurement (the latitude scale) is found on the side of a nautical chart. One nautical mile can be divided into tenths or sixtieths (one second of arc is one sixtieth of one minute). Most charts, however, will be in tenths of nautical miles, because a sixtieth is too small a distance with which to be concerned on a boat.

AIDS TO NAVIGATION

Aids to navigation (ATONs) are devices found on waterways, such as buoys and beacons, that identify the locations of channels where safe passage is assured, warn boaters of dangers and obstructions, and help boaters determine their positions. This section provides an introduction to ATONs. Other courses offered by ASA and USCGAUX provide more information on navigation and ATONs.

The United States has an excellent system of ATONs. Indeed, the density of buoys and beacons in U.S. waters is quite high compared to those of most other countries.

BUOYS

Buoys are floating ATONs. Depending upon their use, buoys are identified by color (green, red, green/red bands, red and white striped, or yellow), shape (can or conical), and usually by either a number or letter(s). Buoys may be lighted (green, white, or red) or unlighted. Numbering (or lettering) and light rhythms on buoys help the boater to identify a particular buoy on a nautical chart.

Unlighted green buoys that resemble vertical cylinders are called CANs and have odd numbers. Unlighted red buoys that look like cylinders with conical tops are called NUNs and have even numbers.

Storms, wave action, and damage caused by collisions can move a buoy, so prudent boaters should not rely on buoys alone to determine their positions. Report any buoys or other ATONs that may be out of position, damaged, or defective to the USCG.

Do not moor your vessel to a buoy or other ATON. This practice is prohibited, among other reasons, because it may prevent other boaters from observing the ATON and cause an unsafe situation!

Do not pass too close to buoys. They may be very close to the danger they mark.

Channel with buoys and daymarks

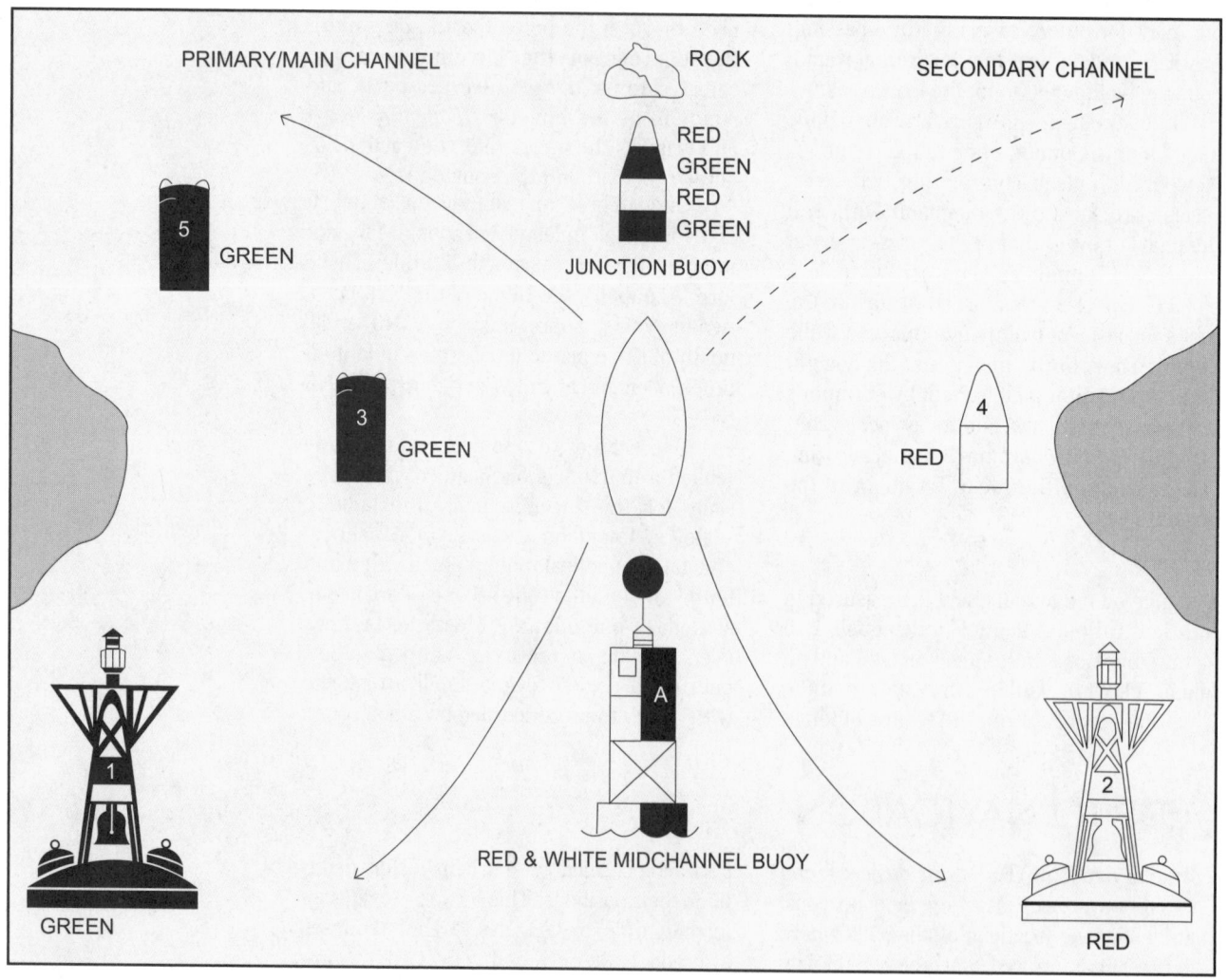

Daymark #4 is attached to a structure marking the entrance to this harbor.

Moreover, buoys are anchored to the bottom with chains and may shift location (within a so-called watch circle) as a result of wind and current action.

BEACONS

Beacons are fixed ATONS. Daybeacons, used in shallow water, have one or more signboards (daymarks) on them. Depending upon their use, daymarks are identified by color (green, red, green/red bands, red and white stripes, or yellow), shape (square, octagonal, or triangular), and usually by either a number or letter(s). Green daymarks are square and have odd numbers. Red daymarks are triangular and have even numbers. Octagonal daymarks have eight sides and are marked with letters. Daymarks may be mounted on posts or on groups of pilings tied together (dolphin). Daybeacons may have lights that correspond to the daymarks.

ATON SYSTEMS

There are two general ATON systems used in the United States: the U.S. Aids to Navigation System and the Uniform State Waterway Marking System (USWMS). The waters of the United States and its territories are marked by the U.S. Aids to Navigation System. The U.S. Aids to Navigation System has two variations, the

		11 Wreck showing any portion of hull or superstructure (above sounding datum)
(25) ⬭(25)		
†1 Rock which does not cover (height above MHW)		⫶⊞⫶ Masts 12 Wreck with only masts visible (above sounding datum)
* Uncov 2 ft ❋ Uncov 2 ft * (2) ❋ (2)		13 Old symbols for wrecks
		13a PA Wreck always partially submerged
2 Rock which covers and uncovers with height above chart sounding datum (see Introduction)		14 ⊞ Sunken wreck dangerous to surface navigation (less than 11 fathoms over wreck) (See O 6a)
⊹ 3 Rock awash at (near) level of chart sounding datum ⊕ Dotted line emphasizes danger to navigation		15 5⅟ Wk Wreck over which depth is known

Chart danger symbols

Intracoastal Waterway Aids to Navigation System and the U.S. Aids to Navigation System on the Western River System. There are slight differences between these systems. ASA publishes an insert card, ASA-152, on ATONs, which displays the various types and colors of ATONs.

Intracoastal Waterway System

This system is used on the Intracoastal Waterway (ICW), an inland waterway running parallel to the Atlantic and Gulf coasts from

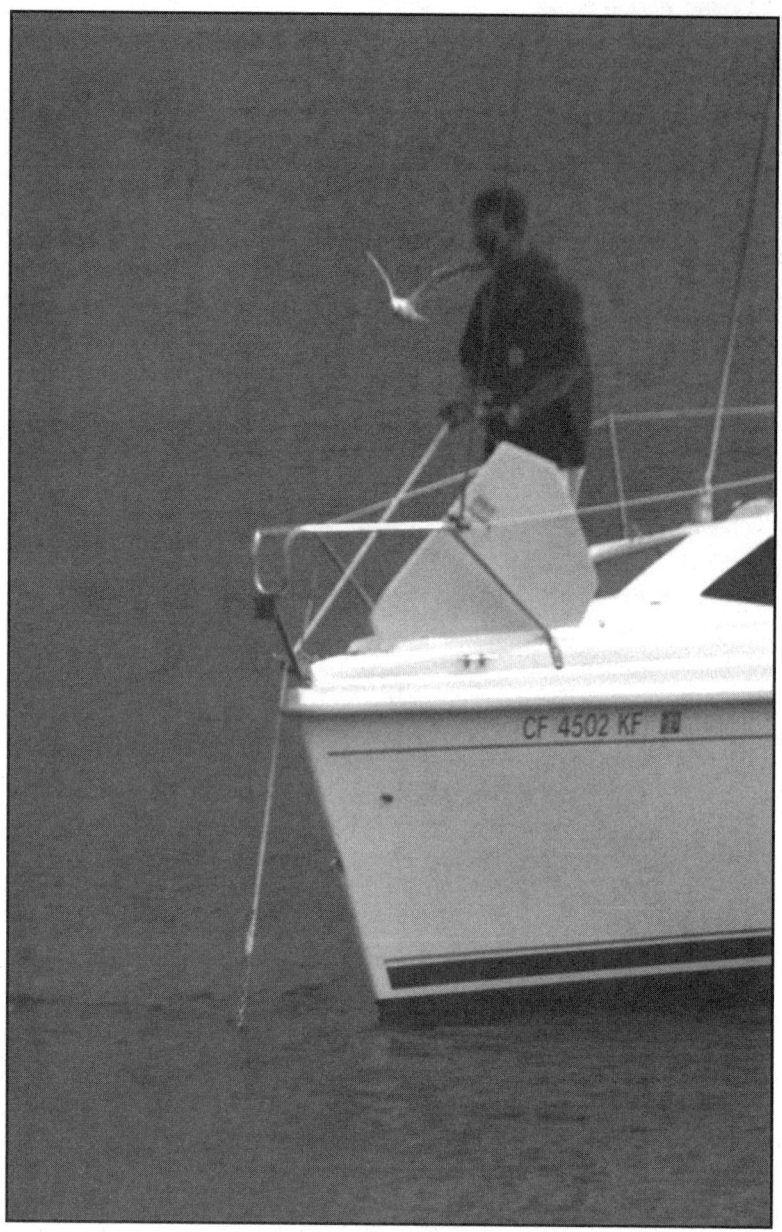

Gloves and a firm grip will reduce the possibility of injury during anchoring.

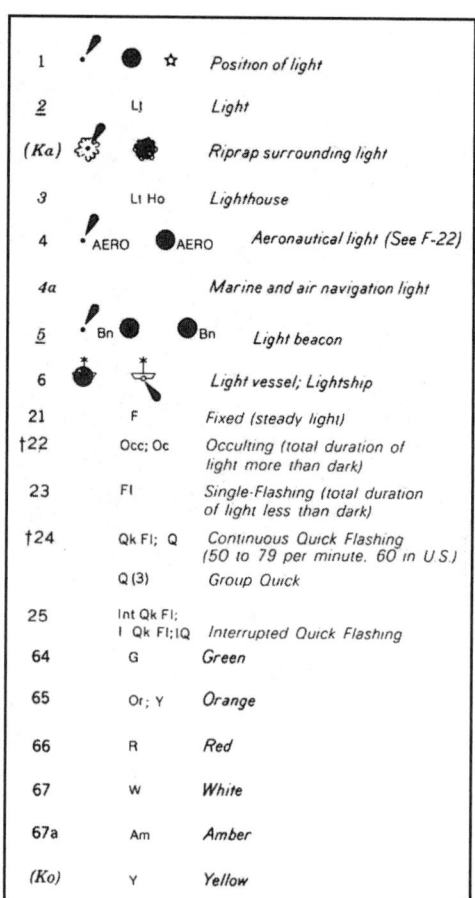

Lights

1				Position of light
2		Lt		Light
(Ka)				Riprap surrounding light
3		Lt Ho		Lighthouse
4	AERO	AERO		Aeronautical light (See F-22)
4a				Marine and air navigation light
5	Bn	Bn		Light beacon
6				Light vessel; Lightship
21		F		Fixed (steady light)
†22		Occ; Oc		Occulting (total duration of light more than dark)
23		Fl		Single-Flashing (total duration of light less than dark)
†24		Qk Fl; Q		Continuous Quick Flashing (50 to 79 per minute. 60 in U.S.)
		Q (3)		Group Quick
25		Int Qk Fl; I Qk Fl; IQ		Interrupted Quick Flashing
64		G		Green
65		Or; Y		Orange
66		R		Red
67		W		White
67a		Am		Amber
(Ko)		Y		Yellow

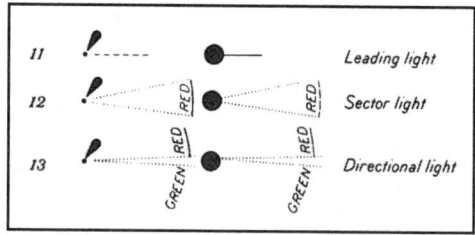

Limit symbols

11		Leading light
12		Sector light
13		Directional light

Manasquan Inlet, New Jersey, to Brownsville, Texas. ATONs marking these waters follow the same coloring and numbering system as the U.S. Aids to Navigation System, except that some portion of each ATON is marked with a yellow square, a yellow triangle, or a yellow band. When following the ICW in a southerly direction from New Jersey to Florida and/or westerly to Texas:

Yellow Square: Keep the ATON on your left.

Yellow Triangle: Keep the ATON on your right.

Horizontal yellow bands are found on safe-water daymarks and buoys. These identify aids as marking the ICW.

Note that the shape of the yellow marker (not the shape of the buoy or daymark) determines the side to pass on when in the ICW.

The Western River System

This system is used on the Mississippi River and its tributaries above Baton Rouge,

Louisiana, as well as on certain other rivers that flow toward the Gulf of Mexico. Buoys and daymarks are shown in the figure.

The USWMS

The USWMS supplements and is generally compatible with the U.S. Aids to Navigation System. This system was developed in 1966 to provide an easily understood navigation system for operators of small boats. Although the USWMS is intended for use on lakes and other inland waterways that are not depicted on nautical charts, it is authorized for use on other waters as well. This system has specific variations from the U.S. Aids to Navigation System evident in the figure. (Note: black buoys in the USWMS are being phased out in favor of green buoys to achieve greater harmonization with the U.S. Aids to Navigation System.)

TYPES OF ATONS

The U.S. Aids to Navigation System uses two basic types of ATONs: lateral marks, including preferred-channel marks, and nonlateral marks.

Lateral Marks

Lateral marks are buoys or beacons that indicate the port and starboard sides of a route to be followed. Both are used in conjunction with a conventional direction of buoyage. "Red, right, returning," is a helpful phrase in figuring out how to use lateral marks. When returning from seaward (proceeding in the conventional direction of buoyage) keep red buoys or daymarks on your starboard (right) side as you pass them and green buoys on your port (left) side. When proceeding toward the sea, reverse the rule, leaving green buoys or daymarks on your starboard side as you pass them and red buoys on your port side.

In U.S. waters, returning from seaward and proceeding toward the head of navigation is generally considered to be moving southerly along the Atlantic coast, westerly along the Gulf coast, and northerly along the Pacific coast. In the Great Lakes, the conventional direction of buoyage is gener-

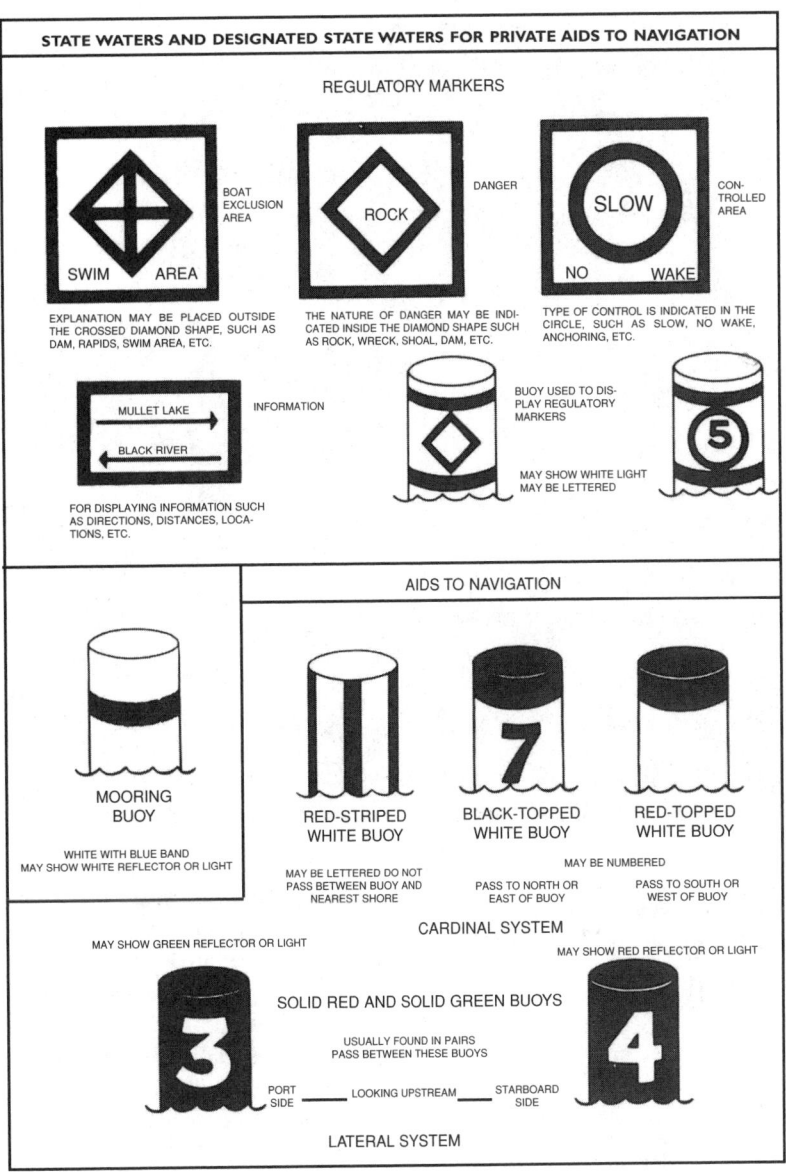

Private aids to navigation

ally considered westerly and northerly, except on Lake Michigan, where southerly movement is considered as returning from the sea. These general principles are not always sufficient to enable boaters to know the direction of buoyage in a particular area. The nautical chart should always be consulted.

Preferred-channel marks, which are colored with green and red bands, mark channel junctions or splits. Preferred-channel marks may also indicate wrecks or obstructions. Normally, preferred-channel marks

Communication between bow crew and helmsperson is essential during anchoring.

may be passed on either side, but your intended route should dictate how you pass the mark. If you wish to follow the preferred channel, be guided by the color of the topmost band on the mark. That is, if the topmost band is red, leave it on the right, if green, leave it on the left when proceeding in the conventional direction of buoyage. Always check your chart to determine if there is sufficient water depth in the preferred or alternate channels. Channel depths vary greatly. This is important with all craft, but particularly to sailboats, which because of their generally deeper drafts require more water for safe passage.

Nonlateral Marks

As the name implies, these marks have no lateral significance, but are used to supplement lateral ATONs. Nonlateral marks include information and regulatory marks used to provide warnings or regulatory information, isolated-danger marks to warn of specific dangers, lighthouses, range lights to mark the centerlines of certain channels, safe-water (fairway) marks, and special marks to alert the boater to special features or areas, such as spoil areas, pipelines, water intakes, anchorage areas, and so on.

Information and regulatory marks provide warnings and regulatory information. These marks use orange diamonds, circles, squares, or rectangles on a white background. For example, an open-faced diamond means danger, a circle denotes restrictions of various types (e.g., no-wake area), and a diamond containing a cross means that boats are excluded.

CHARTING OF ATONS

The locations and descriptions of most ATONs are shown on nautical charts. This is designed to help boaters determine their positions. In some cases, such as inlets subject to frequent shoaling and consequent repositioning of buoys, buoys are not charted and a note is appended to this effect on the chart.

ANCHORS AND THEIR USES

The combination of anchor, chain, and rode (rope) is commonly called ground tackle. This entire system keeps the boat securely fastened to the bottom. The chain and rode are as important for keeping the vessel from dragging as the anchor itself.

Anchors hold by one of two means: weight or digging into the bottom. A pleasure boat does not have the crew or the machinery to pull up a very heavy anchor like the ones found on naval vessels and commercial ships, so small craft anchors have to be designed to hold by digging into the bottom.

The proper anchor varies with the type of bottom one is anchoring in. Wise sailors carry more than one type of anchor so that they're prepared for any anchoring situation. The two most popular cruising anchors are the Danforth and the plough.

The **Danforth** is an all-purpose anchor, and it will hold in any bottom soft enough to allow the flukes to dig in. If the bottom is too soft (soft mud), however, the flukes will simply drag through the mud and the anchor will not hold.

The flukes of the Danforth have sharp edges to dig into harder mud or soft clay, and a wide flat surface to resist dragging once the anchor is buried in the bottom. Suited for hard mud, sand, and soft clay, the Danforth, or an anchor of similar design, is the choice for the weekend sailor and cruiser alike.

The **plough** anchor is so called because the shape of the fluke is like that of a plough share. This heavy-duty cruising anchor digs into harder surfaces than the Danforth anchor can penetrate; it also grabs into rocks. The plough is able to dig through some weeds and into the bottom. A plough must be heavier than a Danforth to provide the same holding power for the same size boat.

The **rode** is the rope line. When anchoring you should normally let out approximately four to seven times as much anchor rode as you have depth in water. In other words, in ten feet of water you should let out forty to seventy feet of anchor rode.

Danforth anchor

Plough anchor

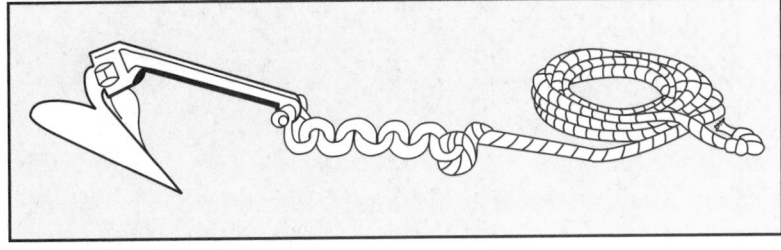

Ground tackle

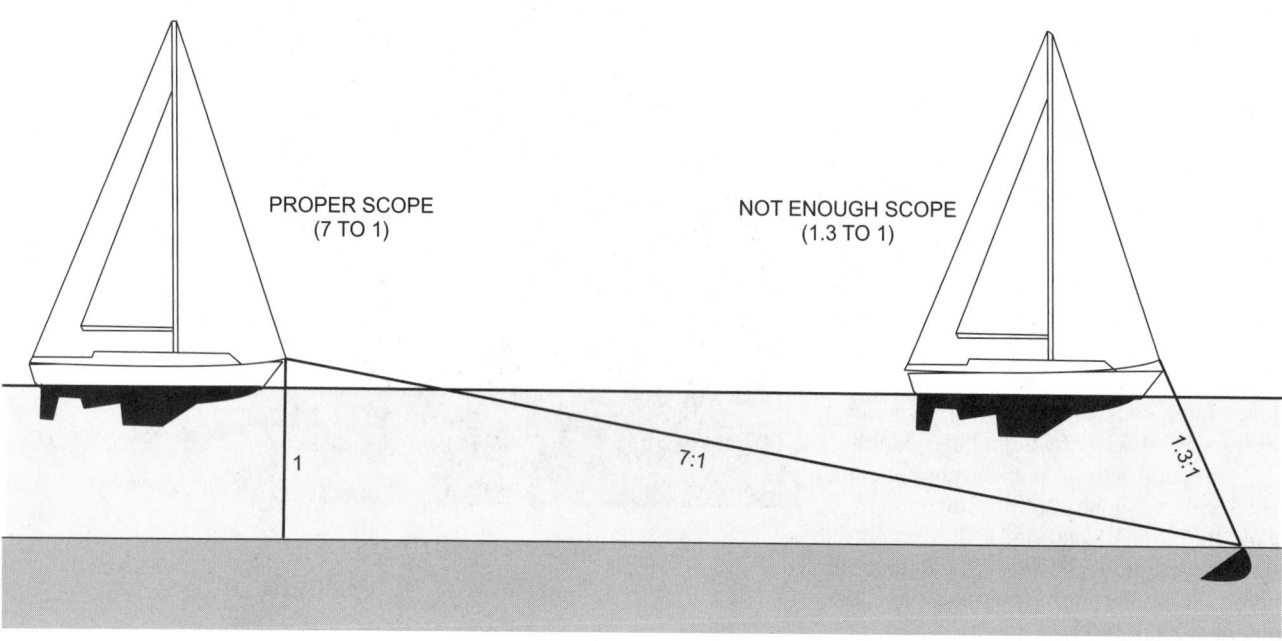

PROPER SCOPE
(7 TO 1)

NOT ENOUGH SCOPE
(1.3 TO 1)

1

7:1

1.3:1

Anchor scope

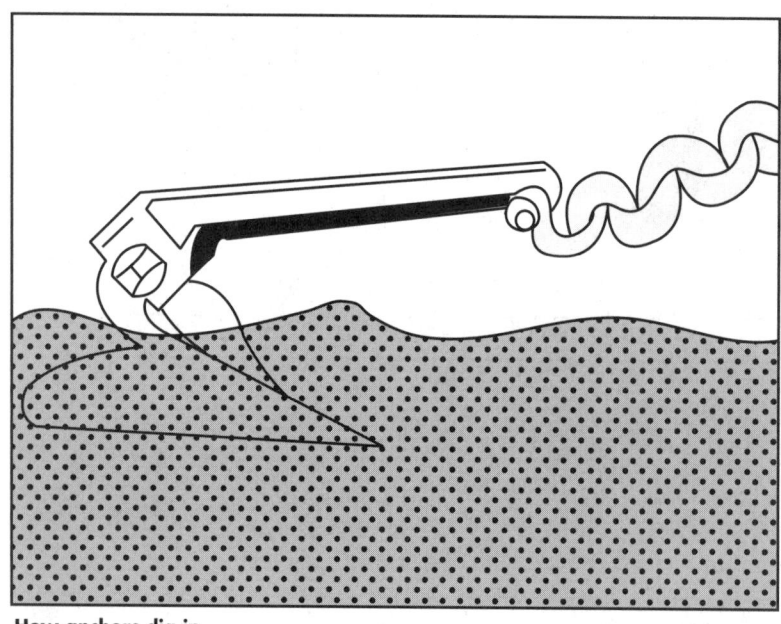

How anchors dig in

The rode should be marked at regular intervals. If the winds are heavy or the seas high, more anchor rode may be required.

The **chain** connects the anchor to the rode. A chain will absorb shock from a pitching boat in heavy seas, allowing the anchor to stay dug into the bottom. Also, a chain keeps the rode from chafing on the bottom, particularly important when the anchor is passing over jagged coral or rocks.

The anchor, rode, and chain combine to hold a boat in place. The most common anchoring errors are not letting out enough rode and using an anchor that is too light or not suited to the type of bottom. To make sure the ground tackle holds together, tighten with a wrench the pins in the shackles joining the anchor to the chain and rode, and wire them closed.

THE ANCHORAGE

A safe anchorage must have:
- shelter
- room to swing on the anchor
- sufficient depth of water
- good holding ground (bottom)

SHELTER

The ideal anchorage is out of wind, waves, and traffic; however, it is difficult to have all of these advantages at once. Therefore, compromise may be necessary. The best place to anchor is in the lee of an island or shore. You are in the lee of an island when the island is between you and the wind. To be in the lee of something (or to leeward of it) is to be protected from the wind. A lee shore, however, is to leeward of the boat (on the side of the boat away from the wind).

ROOM TO SWING ON THE ANCHOR

If we pay out seventy feet of rode to maintain sufficient (7: 1) scope, a wind shift will cause the boat to swing through a very large circle. The result could be embarrass-ing or even dangerous if the boat is anchored too close to a pier, the shoreline, or another boat that is not swinging in the same size circle.

The boat's swinging circle can be reduced by setting more than one anchor. For now, we are concerned with basic anchoring skills. Advanced anchoring (setting two anchors) is covered in the ASA Bareboat Chartering and Advanced Coastal Cruising standards. For now, simply allow enough room for the boat to swing through 360 degrees. Seventy feet of rode will result in a swinging circle of approximately 140 feet in diameter.

SUFFICIENT DEPTH OF WATER

We have learned that the amount of rode let out to maintain scope depends on the depth of water. If the water is too deep, it is possible there will not be enough rode aboard to maintain a scope of 7: 1. If the water is too shallow at any place in the swinging circle of the boat, or if a tide change reduces the water depth, the boat

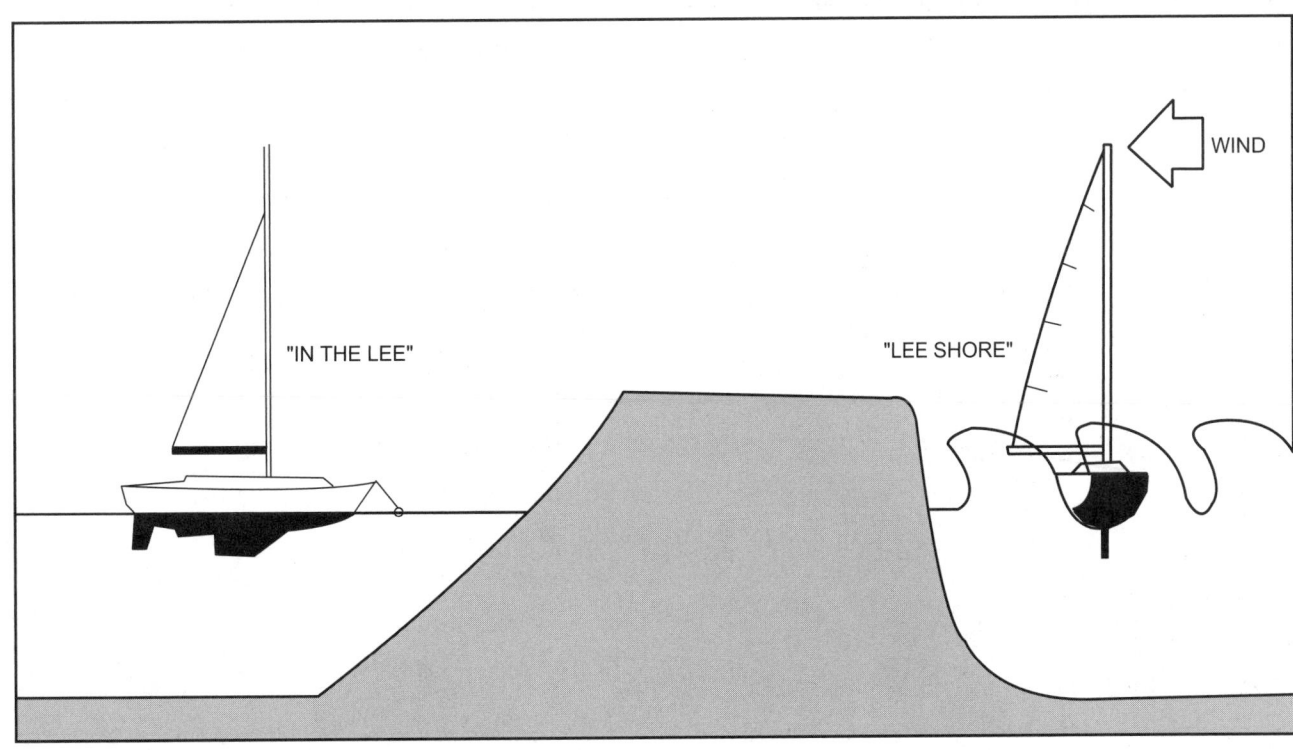

"IN THE LEE"

"LEE SHORE"

WIND

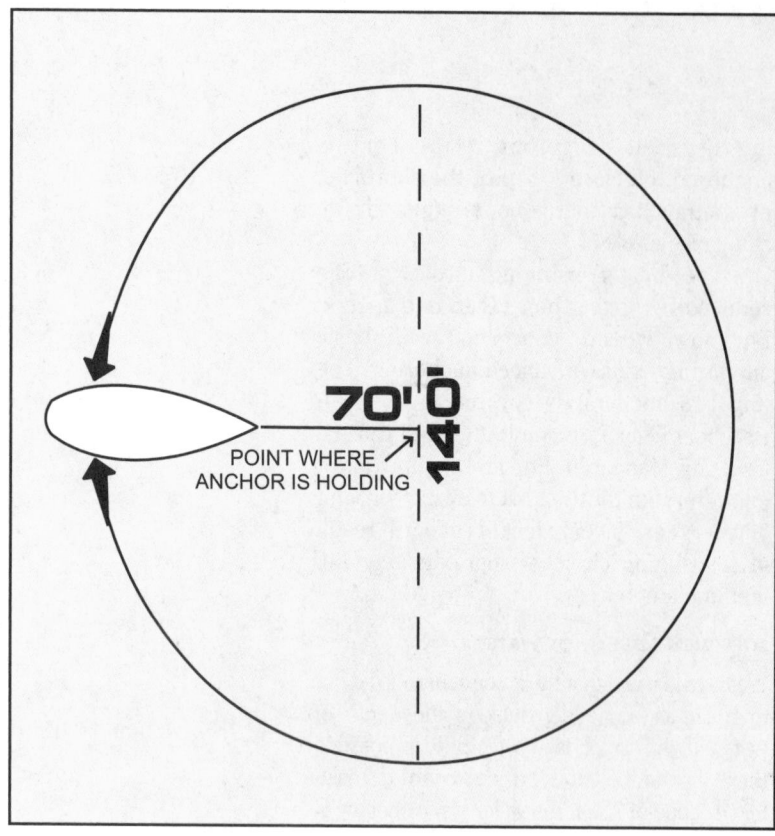

Swinging circle at anchor

may ground (come in contact with the bottom).

Note: Grounding occurs when a boat is left aground and dry by an outgoing tide. Running aground is the act of hitting bottom when in shallow waters; it will be covered in Part Six. If a vessel runs aground on a falling tide, it is in double trouble.

In tidal waters, the scope of the boat's anchor rode may be sufficient at low tide. At high tide, the water will be deeper and more rode will have to be paid out in order to maintain proper scope. It may therefore become necessary to post an anchor watch to correct the scope during tide changes and to warn the crew if, for any other reason, the anchorage becomes unsafe. This rarely becomes a concern on a daysail, as the boat is normally anchored only for a short times such as a lunch break, when there is usually someone on deck to assess the situation.

GOOD HOLDING GROUND

The type of bottom will affect the anchor's ability to dig in. If the bottom is too soft,

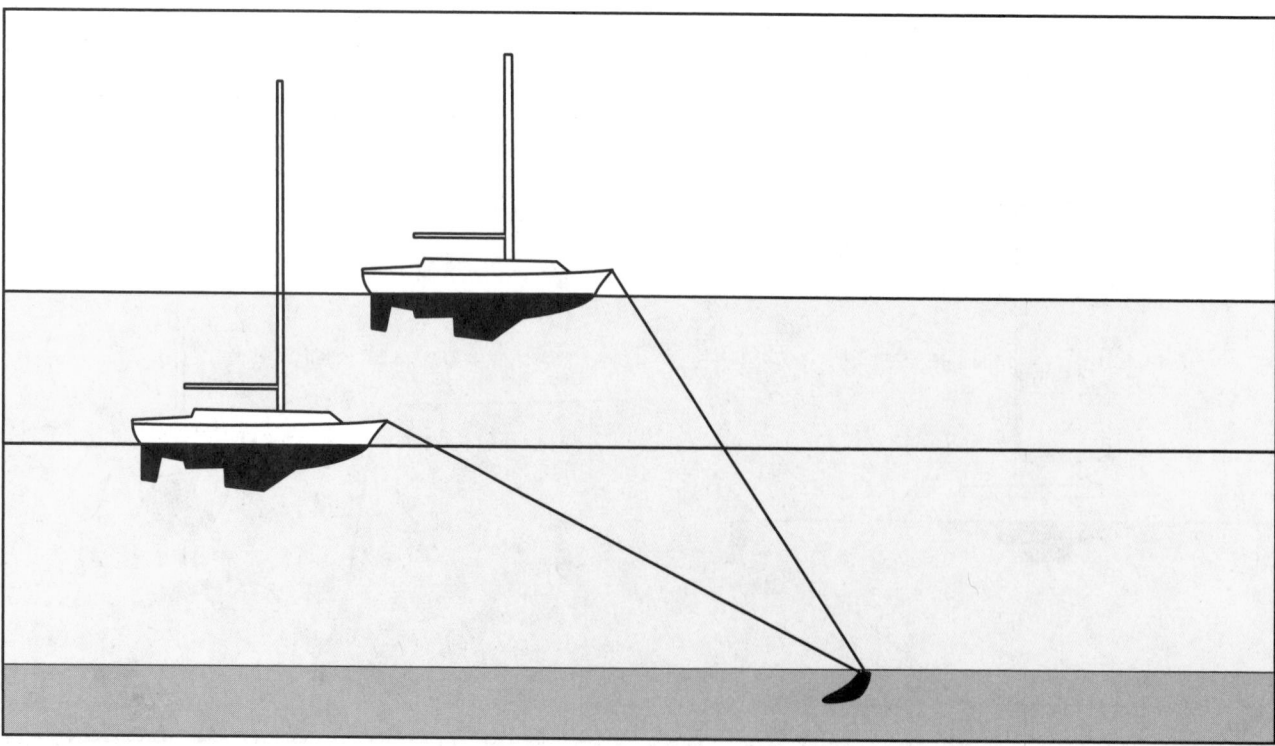

Rising tide reduces scope.

the anchor will just slide through. If it is too hard, the flukes will not be able to grab.

In areas like the Florida Keys, quite often it's a matter of simply looking down through the crystal clear water to see if there is sand, weed, or coral under the boat. Most water, however, is not that clear. Therefore, our best reference is the nautical chart. The chart symbols for a suitable bottom type are

S–sand   **M**–mud   **Cl**–clay

Chart symbols for usable but less than desirable anchorages are

Oz–ooze (very soft mud or sludge)
Rk–rocks or rocky bottom

Selecting a suitable anchorage is a matter of practice, patience, and wisdom to know when to leave an anchorage before it deteriorates and becomes unsafe. Proper selection, based on the four factors we have discussed, will lessen the chances of anchoring in a dangerous location.

KNOTS

In the Sailing Skills section of this part, we will be practicing docking under sail. Some docks will not have mooring cleats. Therefore it may be necessary to tie to a piling or rail when docking. The **clove hitch** and the **round turn** and **two half hitches** are used to secure a vessel to a piling.

The clove hitch is used for temporary docking or for securing fenders to a lifeline before docking. A clove hitch will undo if left for any length of time. For anything more than a few minutes, secure the clove hitch by making one or two half hitches on the line. But before leaving the boat unattended, always replace a clove hitch with a round turn and two half hitches, which is a more secure knot.

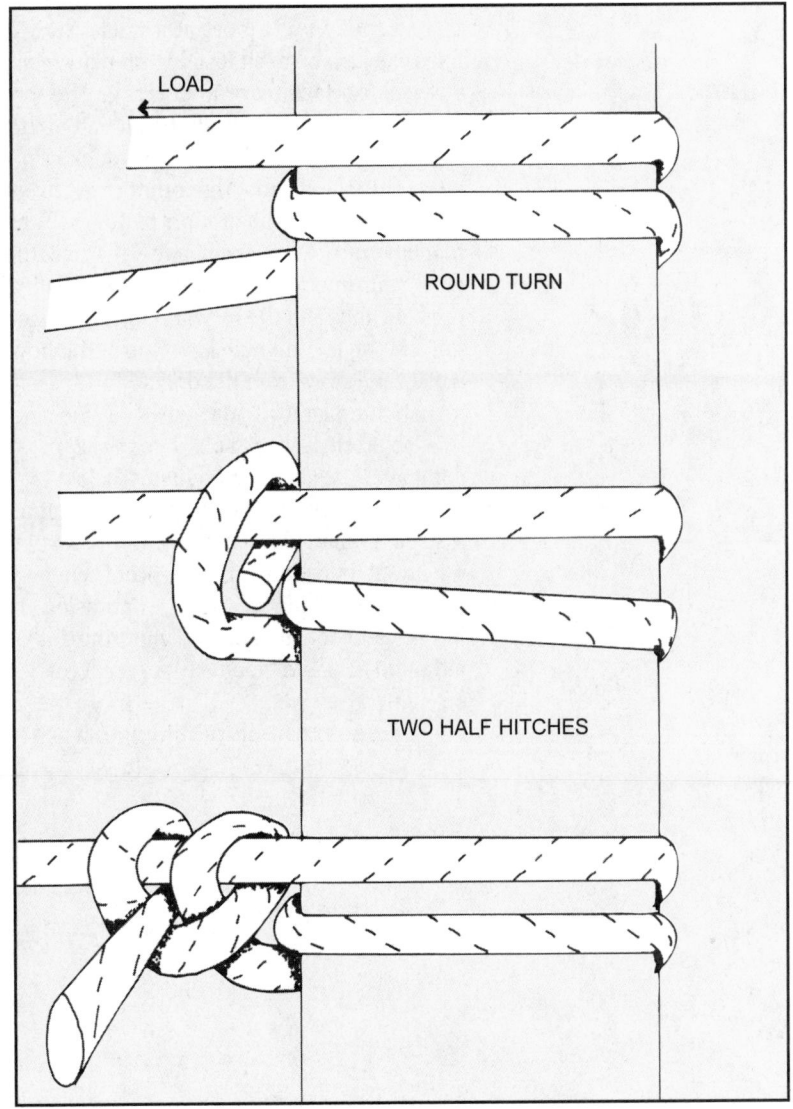

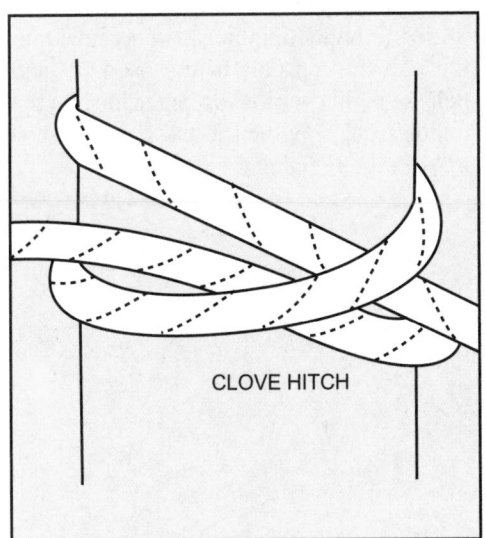

DOCK LINES AND THEIR USES

The proper use of dock lines can simplify the docking and undocking of a boat and protect the boat during rough weather. Below are the lines necessary for docking.

Bow lines secure the bow to the dock. The inshore bow line runs from an onboard cleat and through a chock to a cleat on the dock. The offshore bow line runs through the offshore chock to a separate cleat on the dock.

Stern lines secure the stern. The inshore stern line runs from a cleat through an inshore chock to a cleat on the dock.

Spring lines are used to control fore and aft motion of a boat at a dock. Spring lines can also be used to aid in maneuvering a vessel for docking or undocking. The forward spring line runs from the aft end of the boat forward to a cleat on the dock. The aft spring line runs the other way, from the bow aft (see illustration p. 157). When maneuvering away from a berth, use the aft spring line to turn the boat. With all of the bow lines and the forward spring line let go, and the engine put slow astern, the bow will swing away from the dock.

Be familiar with the types of line and the job each is best suited for. The most common types of lines are listed below.

Nylon has superior strength as well as a stretch characteristic with high recovery quality. It is rot and mildew-proof, easy to handle, and highly resistant to abrasion. It is excellent for anchor and mooring lines, although it loses about 10 percent of its strength when wet.

Dacron retains its full strength when it is wet and has only slight stretch under loads. It is as strong as nylon with similar characteristics. It is used for sheets, halyards, and other running rigging.

Polyethylene is made in a variety of colors and has little stretch. Its floatability makes it popular for ski tow ropes and dinghy painters. Polyethylene is adversely affected by heat and friction.

Polypropylene has a higher melting point than polyethylene, is more abrasive-resistant, and not as slippery. It is used for ski tow ropes and where low stretch is important.

Cotton is soft, pliable, and easy to handle except when wet. Cotton lines are used mostly in small sizes for flag halyards and lanyards.

Lines should never be left in a heap, whether on deck or down below. A line is always coiled so it will be ready in a hurry without kinks or tangles. To coil a line, hold one end (or the part near where the line is cleated) in one hand, and with the other hand make two-foot-long loops, which you then drop into the first hand. Don't twist the line as you coil it, or it will kink. When all but the last 4-6 feet of the line has been coiled, finish the coil off by wrapping half the remaining line around the middle of the loops three times, forming a figure-8. Then push the bight (middle) of the remainder through the top hole in the open "8" and pull the bight over the top, and slide it to the middle again. Tighten it and hang the coil up with the remaining bit of line.

REVIEW QUESTIONS

1. Soundings are measured in units of _____, _____, and _____. Soundings are being converted to the metric system and will be given in _____ in the future.

2. When entering a harbor, green buoys are kept to which side?
a) port
b) starboard

3. A junction buoy indicates where a river or channel
a) crosses the road.
b) stops.
c) splits into two routes.

4. Identify what each of the following buoys means:

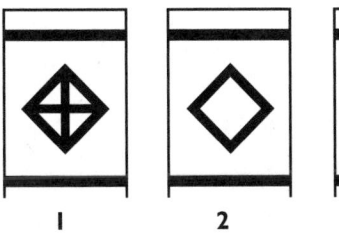

1. _____

2. _____

3. _____

5. Label the three parts of the ground tackle.

6. list two functions of the chain in the ground tackle system.

a) _____

b) _____

7. What are four prerequisites of a good anchorage?

a) _____

b) _____

c) _____

d) _____

8. What is the best kind of rope to use for

a) dock lines _____

b) sheets _____

c) anchor rodes _____

d) halyards _____

e) ski tow lines_____

9. Spring lines are used to control the _____ and _____ motion of a boat at a dock. Spring lines can also be used to aid in _____

Answers in Appendix A, p. 201.

SAILING SKILLS

SAILING SKILLS • 127

ANCHORING

Anchoring is an art. The helmsman and crew have to orchestrate their efforts with the wind, current, and vessel. Earlier in this part, we looked at the anchor and the anchorage. By the end of this exercise, you should be able to select a suitable anchorage, set the anchor with a scope of 7:1, retrieve the anchor, and properly stow the ground tackle.

To check whether the anchor is dragging, take simple sightings on objects ashore or observe the relative position of other boats in the anchorage. Use a compass to take bearings. If the bearings begin changing, your anchor is dragging. For more on how to handle a boat that is dragging anchor, see Part Six, Running Aground and Other Nuisances.

Another way to determine if an anchor is dragging is to place your hand on the rode. If it is bounding, the anchor is dragging over the bottom. The vibrating of the rode indicates that the anchor is skipping over the bottom.

EXERCISE: **VESSEL AND CREW PREPARATION**

1. The crew takes down the jib and clears it from the foredeck. This will give the crew room to work on the foredeck and will prevent the sail from being damaged when the anchor is raised and lowered. It also keeps the crew from slipping on the sail.

2. The crew then lays the anchor on the foredeck.

3. The end of the rode not attached to the anchor-the bitter end-is then tied around the mast. This is to prevent the ground tackle from being lost overboard should the crew lose control of it.

4. The rode is then coiled into a basket or onto the foredeck to make sure that there are no snags or tangles when the rode pays out.

A coiled line will invariably knot and tangle unless it is properly flaked, or laid out on deck in long loops. This reduces the tendency of the anchor rode to snarl.

5. One crew member positions himself to signal the helmsman when the anchor is on the bottom.

6. When the deck is clear, the anchor rode is flaked, and everyone is prepared, the helmsman makes a first approach to the selected anchorage. The helmsman and crew survey the site: the number of boats already in the anchorage, location of docks and channels, and overall suitability.

The helmsman should not attempt to anchor on this first pass. Once the skipper is sure the anchorage has shelter, swinging room, sufficient water depth, and good holding ground, the final approach can be planned. After the first approach is complete, the helmsman heads the boat back into open water and turns to make the final approach.

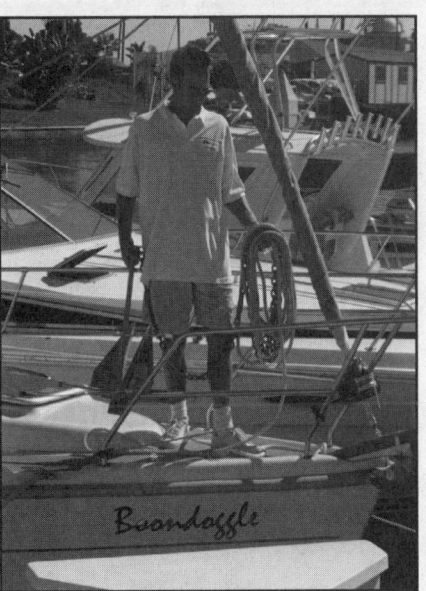

The rode should be carefully coiled so it does not kink when running out.

EXERCISE: **THE FINAL APPROACH**

The anchoring technique is the same whether the boat is under sail or power. If under power, simply reverse the engine (see Part Five, p. 159) instead of backing the mainsail.

If there is any confusion, or if the anchoring is not going well, the helmsman can abort the final approach and return for another try. It is better to start again than to try to salvage a poor situation.

1. The helmsman steers on a close reach course to a point two or three boat lengths downwind of the spot selected.

2. At this point, the helmsman heads the boat directly into the wind to stop its forward motion. This is different from the stopping drills previously practiced.

3. As the boat stops (and not before), the crew should lower-not throw-the anchor. As the anchor is being lowered, the crew backs the boat down by backing the mainsail.

4. As the boat drifts backwards,

one crew member continues to ease the anchor rode. The others will indicate to the helmsman in which direction the anchor is lying in order to keep the helmsman backing the boat directly away from the anchor.

5. The boat should drift backwards after the anchor is on the bottom.

6. When a scope of 4:1 is reached, the crew snubs the rode around the deck cleat to set (dig in) the anchor.

7. Once the anchor has been set, the crew continues to pay out the rode until a scope of 7:1 is reached.

8. Once the scope is let out, tug on the anchor line to make sure that the anchor is secured to the bottom. Then secure to the deck cleat.

9. Once the crew is certain the anchor has been properly set, the mainsail will be lowered to prevent the boat from sailing.

A

C

To anchor, this bow crew, A. points the bow into the wind and drops the jib, B. secures the halyard, C. folds and removes the jib from the deck, D. carefully lowers the anchor into the water and E. pays out rode while the helmsman backs the boat.

D

B

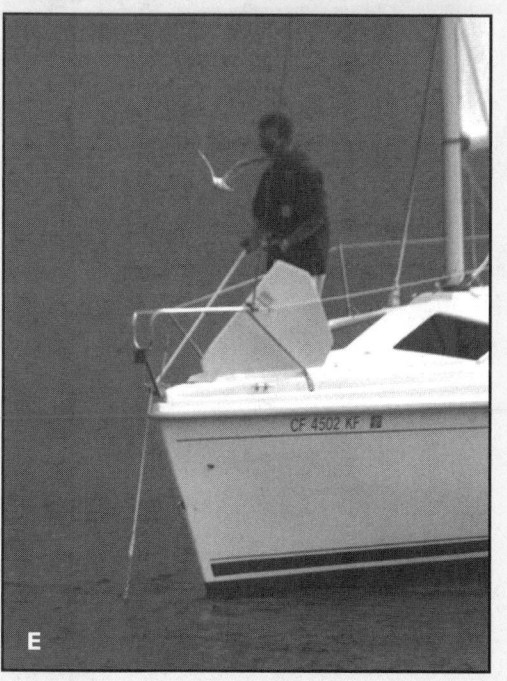

E

EXERCISE: **RECOVERING THE ANCHOR**

1. Before raising the anchor, raise the mainsail, for once the anchor breaks free of the bottom, the boat has to be able to maneuver. Even if the boat will be maneuvered under power, it is wise to have the mainsail hoisted in case the engine fails.

2. The crew then leads the anchor rode to a winch and wraps it around three or four times. With the foredeck crew guiding the helmsman toward the location of the anchor with hand signals, the crew winches the rode and anchor aboard.

3. As the anchor breaks free, the helmsman bears away and sails to open water, while the crew coils or flakes and stows the ground tackle. The crew should dunk the anchor repeatedly to clean any mud or clay from its flukes. Mud is difficult to clean from the deck and sails, and it may be tracked into the cabin if the crew is not careful.

HEAVING TO

It is sometimes necessary to stop a boat in order to make repairs, fix meals, or reef the sails (see Part Six, Reefing Systems). **Heaving** to is a technique for laying a boat across the wind so that it makes slow progress to leeward. The major safety concern when hove to is to check that there are no obstructions to leeward in your path of drift.

Once the boat is hove to, the jib will be backed (trimmed on the windward side of the boat), the mainsail will be either luffing or partially luffing and the tiller will be lashed to the leeward side of the vessel.

With the tiller to leeward, the boat tends to steer into the wind. As the boat heads up, the wind catches the backed jib and pushes the bow away from the wind. These two actions cancel each other, and the net result is a slow zigzag course with very little progress.

EXERCISE: **HEAVING TO**

The maneuver and commands for heaving to are similar to those for coming about.

1. With the command "Ready to heave to," the helmsman instructs the crew to prepare. When ready, the crew responds "Ready."

2. The helmsman brings the boat about with the command "Hard alee," as the tiller is pushed to the leeward side of the boat.

3. As the bow of the boat passes through the wind, the crew eases the mainsail but leaves the jib sheeted to weather.

4. As the boat slows, the helmsman pushes the tiller to the new leeward side of the boat. This causes the bow to head toward the wind. With the jib backed, the motion will be stopped and the boat successfully hove to. A little trimming of the mainsail might be regained to balance the boat and provide a little headway.

TO GET UNDER WAY AFTER HEAVING TO:

5. The crew releases the windward jib sheet.

6. The helmsman centers the tiller or wheel.

7. The crew trims the mainsheet.

Repeat the maneuver until everyone on board understands the procedure.

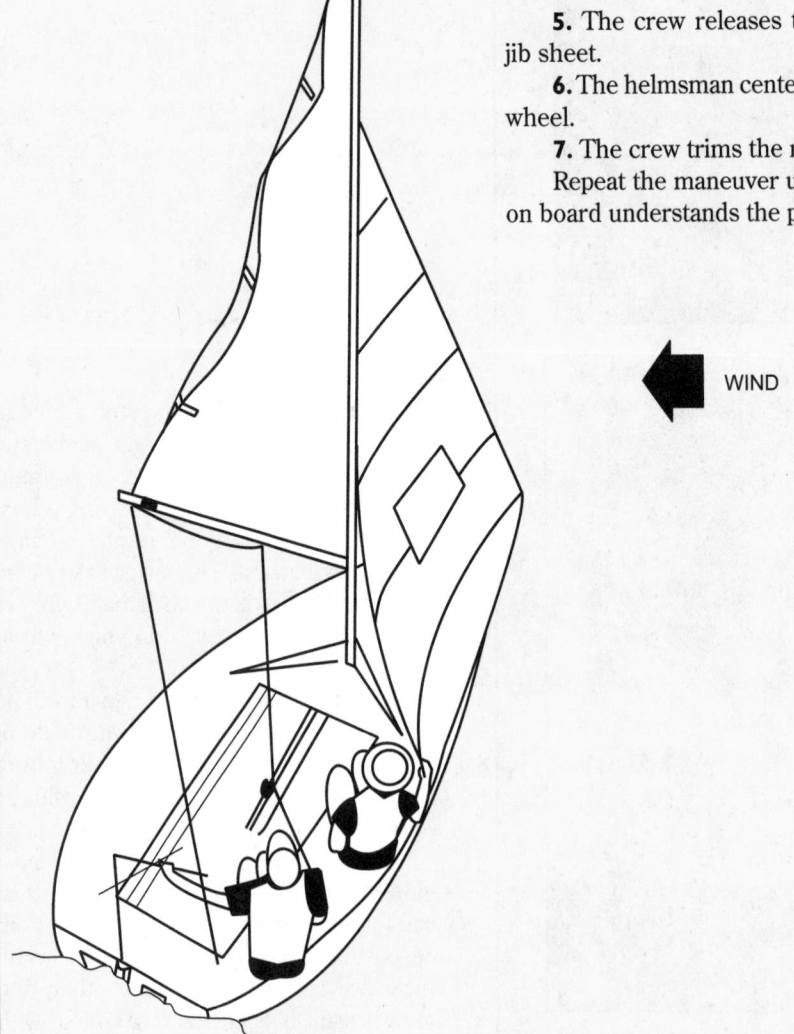

WIND

Hove to

DOCKING UNDER SAIL

Docking under sail requires the same reaching approach as picking up a marker (Part Four) or the man overboard drill (Part Three). It also requires the same control of boat speed. Remember that a boat under sail has no brakes. The momentum of the boat will continue to carry it forward even after the sails have been eased and are luffing.

Wind and current are determining factors in whether to approach the dock on a close reach or broad reach. If the slip is upwind, the approach will be easier than if the slip is crosswind or downwind. Let us first concentrate on the easier approaches. Techniques learned in the early exercises will make the more complicated situations easier to handle.

As a precaution, the end of the slip should be padded with a fender or rubber bumper. Even veteran sailors misjudge distances, and accidents do happen. It is easier to repair a damaged ego than the bow of a sailboat.

CREW PREPARATION

Before you approach the dock, dock lines must be secured to the cleats on the boat and led through the appropriate chocks. Using a beam spring line (as opposed to a bow or stern line) will allow a boat to stop at a dock or in a slip without the bow being pulled into the dock.

The crew, positioned on the sidedecks outside the lifelines and holding onto the shrouds, should be prepared to step ashore. This is normally the safest position for stepping onto or off the boat because it

Docking in a slip under sail

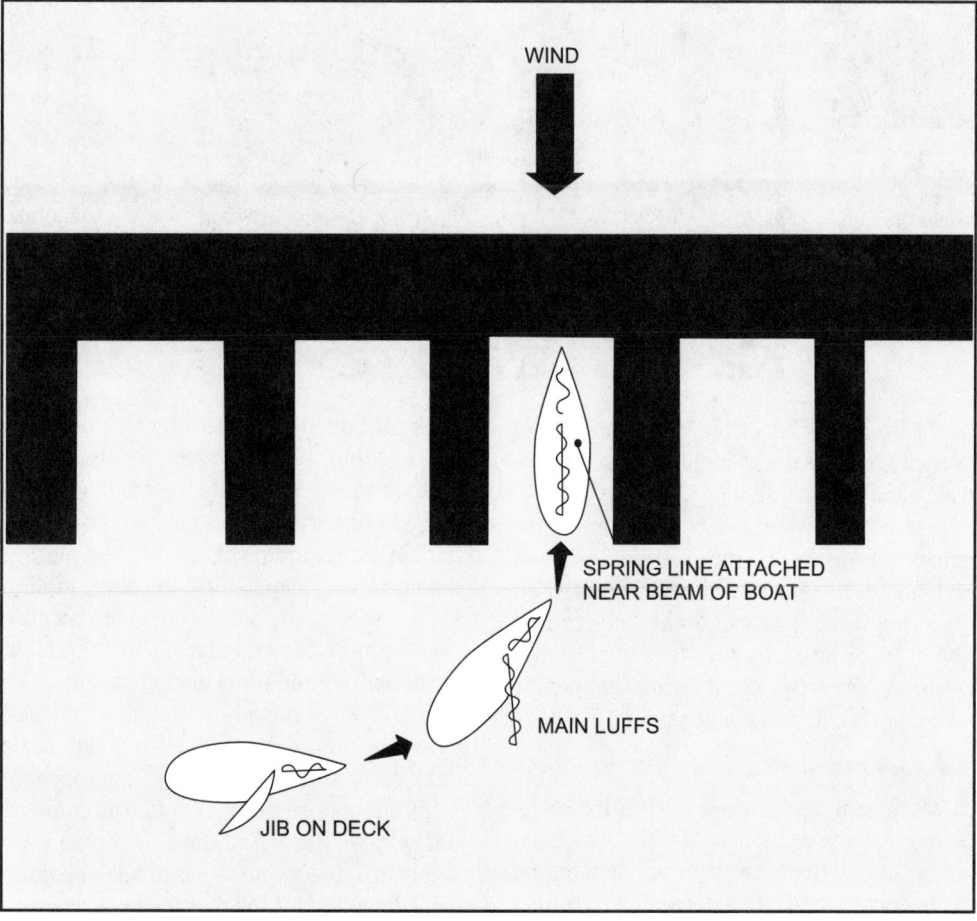

WIND

SPRING LINE ATTACHED
NEAR BEAM OF BOAT

MAIN LUFFS

JIB ON DECK

On first approaching a dock, A. the jib comes down, B. the boat sails toward the dock on a close reach and C. the mainsheet is eased allowing the mainsail to luff and slow the boat. Bow crew prepares to step onto the dock from the boat's beam.

is the widest point of the boat (and therefore nearest the dock) and the shrouds provide excellent handholds.

It is important when docking to use chocks or blocks and cleats as well as good nylon line. Big waves or heavy winds when you are off the boat can break lines or pull the boat away from the dock if it is not secured correctly. Avoid using lifelines or running rigging to tie a boat up.

DOCKING IN A SLIP

A slip is just an enclosed dock. The enclosure creates a complication. If he makes an error in judgment while approaching an open dock, the helmsman can turn the boat back into open water and try again. When approaching a slip, however, the helmsman is faced with a dead-end street and nowhere to go. Forward motion can be slowed by backing the mainsail or by zigzagging through the water. Any turning motion slows the boat, and repeated turning (zigzagging) before entering the slip is an excellent method for reducing speed.

The only time a boat should be docked when heading downwind is in a slip. On a dock, it is a simple matter of approaching from the opposite direction to overcome an unfavorable wind. And the only way to dock safely in a downwind slip is to take all of the sails down before turning the boat down-

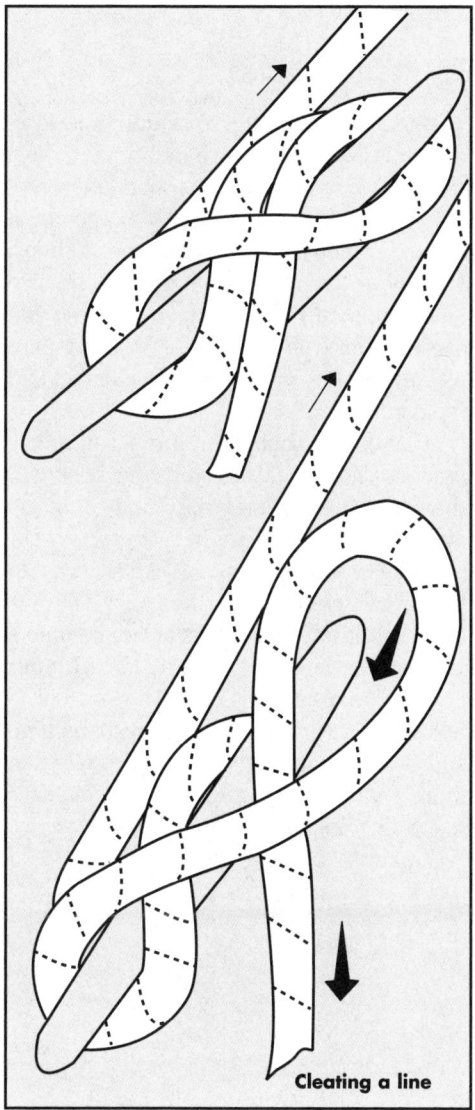

Cleating a line

EXERCISE: **DOCKING UPWIND (no current)**

Practice this first exercise approaching a pier, as opposed to a slip, to allow yourself greater escape possibilities. Winds in and around docks can be affected by buildings and land masses and will challenge the helmsman more than winds in open water. So, make a pass at the dock to determine how the wind is blowing off the dock and whether there are any drastic changes in wind direction. Then make a second approach to complete docking.

1. As with all other boat-stopping exercises, the helmsman, for control, approaches the dock on a close reach under mainsail alone.

2. The crew luffs the mainsail two or three boat lengths from the dock. If the boat is moving too slowly, the crew retrims the mainsail to accelerate.

3. As the bow nears the dock, the helmsman heads up into the wind, parallel to and at least six feet from the dock. The dock provides a reference point for judging the speed of the boat and the stopping distance required.

4. Just before the boat comes to a stop, the helmsman bears away and returns to open water. The crew sheets in the mainsail.

With the stopping distance of the boat determined, the second approach is made.

5. This time, the helmsman steers parallel to and about three feet out from the dock.

6. Just before the boat stops its forward progress, the crew steps ashore and secures the dock lines to the cleats on the dock.

This procedure will work on all docks where the wind direction is off the dock. If the wind is blowing onto the dock, the procedure is similar however, the helmsman will stop the boat on a beam reach four to six feet from the dock and the wind will carry the vessel onto the dock.

wind. Crew work and control of boat speed become very important during this maneuver.

As soon as the boat turns downwind, it will start to accelerate. A crew member with a dock line attached to the beam of the boat must step ashore at the first possible moment and take one wrap of the dock line around a dock cleat to stop the boat before it reaches the end of the slip. Do not tie off the dock line at this point; let it slip controllably until the boat is fully stopped.

SECURING THE VESSEL

Once the boat has stopped alongside the dock or is in the slip, the crew ties off the bow and stern lines with **cleat hitchs**. The crew then rigs spring lines forward and aft to keep the boat from pivoting in the slip. Longer lines to more remote dock cleats may be necessary to allow lines to stretch in areas of extreme tides. Take a look at how your neighbors have set their lines in unfamiliar areas.

MOORING

A mooring is a buoy connected to an extremely heavy anchor or weight (such as an engine block). Many yacht clubs, marinas, and harbors have moorings where you can tie your boat temporarily or permanently for a fee. Picking up a mooring has three advantages over anchoring. First, you don't have to go to the bother of using your anchor. Second, the mooring's anchor probably is never going to drag. And third, because the mooring's anchor is so heavy and deeply imbedded in the bottom, less

scope is needed on the rode and, therefore, the boat will swing around in a tighter radius than it would on its own anchor.

A mooring consists of an anchor, a chain, a mooring pendant, and a buoy. Usually, each mooring has a distinctive mark (generally a number or color) so you can tell one from the other. Moorings are usually located out of the main channel and rapid currents.

Landing a sailboat at a mooring takes practice. Your goal is to stop your boat with the bow directly into the wind right up against the mooring, so that a crew member can take hold of the pendant and secure it to the bow cleat. Moorings are always attached through the bow chock and onto a cleat so the boat swings around it. If your boat sails past the mooring, do not try to hold onto it from the stern. Instead, let it go and sail around until you make a better, more controlled landing. The maneuver is much like anchoring. Once again, practice is the key.

EXERCISE: **MOORING**

1. The skipper checks to be sure the boat may be kept at the mooring.
2. If so, the crew lowers and removes the jib.
3. The helmsman approaches the mooring from downwind.
4. The crew picks up and secures the mooring line.
5. The crew lowers and flakes the mainsail.
6. The crew double-checks all the mooring lines and secures the halyards.

SUMMARY

In this part we have learned about planning a daysail. We have studied the aids to navigation and learned how a skipper uses a local chart and Chart No. 1 to find the safest sailing waters.

In Sailing Skills we learned how to anchor and how to heave-to. There is nothing quite like setting an anchor and having lunch off a secluded beach. Heaving-to is a way of stopping the boat so that repairs can be made or so that you can have lunch if

you do not wish to anchor or if there is no suitable anchorage nearby.

Finally, we looked at the skills required to dock a boat under sail and secure a boat to a mooring. These are valuable skills for all sailors. Whether or not you have an engine aboard, you will eventually need or want to dock your boat under sail.

In the next part we will begin to learn about cruising.

Basic Coastal Cruising I

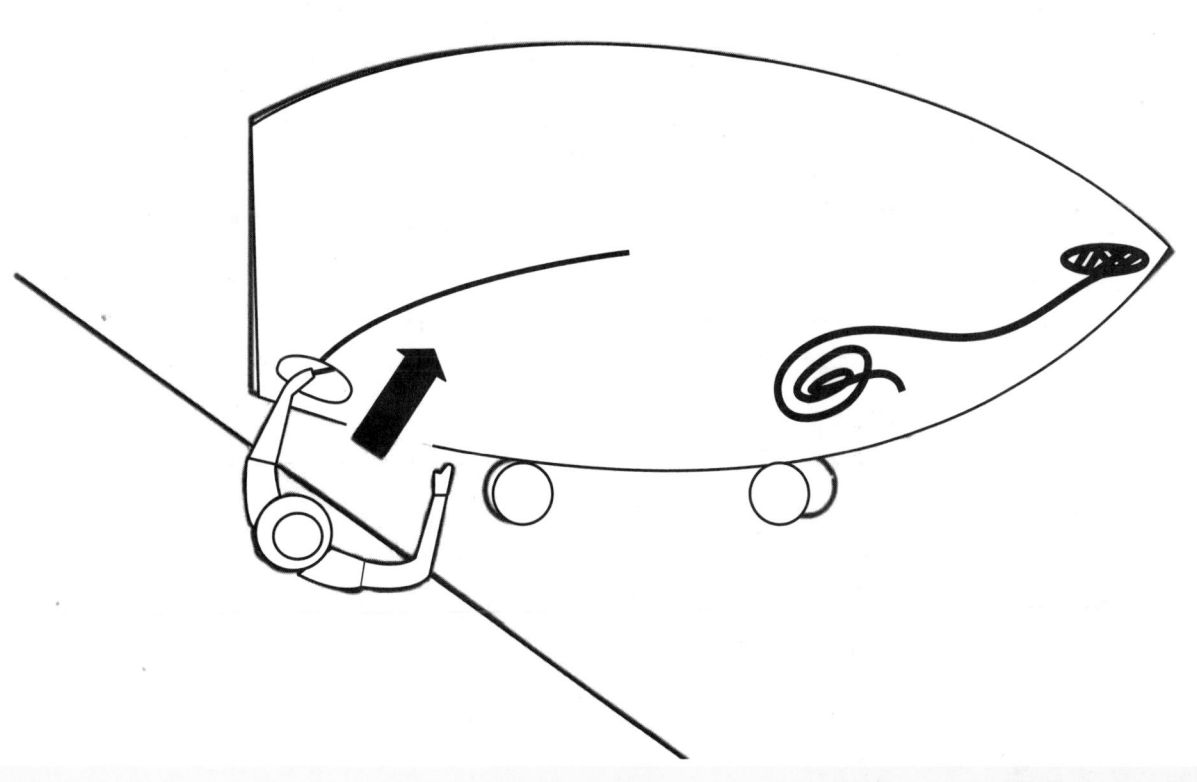

SAILING KNOWLEDGE

The first four parts of this book were designed to teach a person to sail a 16 to 26-foot sailboat. This part and the next build on that knowledge and introduce the new sailor to some of the skills and knowledge required to cruise a small sailboat.

The word cruise conjures up a different notion in every individual. For our purposes, a cruise is a journey by boat from a home harbor to another harbor or anchorage. A cruise may take as little as an afternoon or it may take weeks or years.

In this part we will add some new sailing terms. As you prepare to venture farther from home, it is essential to know the language of the sea. When there is a lot of activity on the boat, you don't want to run the risk of misinterpreting an instruction or command. Precise and accurate terms must be learned and used at all times.

TERMS AND DEFINITIONS

A **self-bailing cockpit** is one that allows the water to run out as it enters, automatically. It is no different from the drain in a kitchen sink. The floor of the cockpit is above the waterline of the boat and the **through-hull fitting** is below the waterline. The drains in the cockpit **sole** (floor) allow any water to drain out the through-hull fitting.

Earlier in the book we discussed the purpose and action of the rudder. What we haven't considered is how the rudder attaches to the boat. There are two methods, depending on whether the rudder is suspended from the **transom** (flat surface across the stern) or placed under the boat.

If the rudder is mounted on the transom (as is usual on smaller boats), it must be connected with hinges, like a door. The parts of the hinges are called the **pintle** (the pin) and **gudgeon** (the opening into which the pin fits). Most rudders use a stop just above the pintle and gudgeon to prevent the rudder from popping out. All rudders should have a fixed system. If the rudder is suspended through the hull, it is done so on a post called the **rudderpost.** The rudderpost is an integral part of the rudder and must pass through the hull and into the cockpit. Some boats have swing rudders which tilt up in shallow water. They should be secured in the lowered position.

The tiller attaches to the top of the rudderpost or to the top of the rudder if it is mounted on the transom. A steering wheel

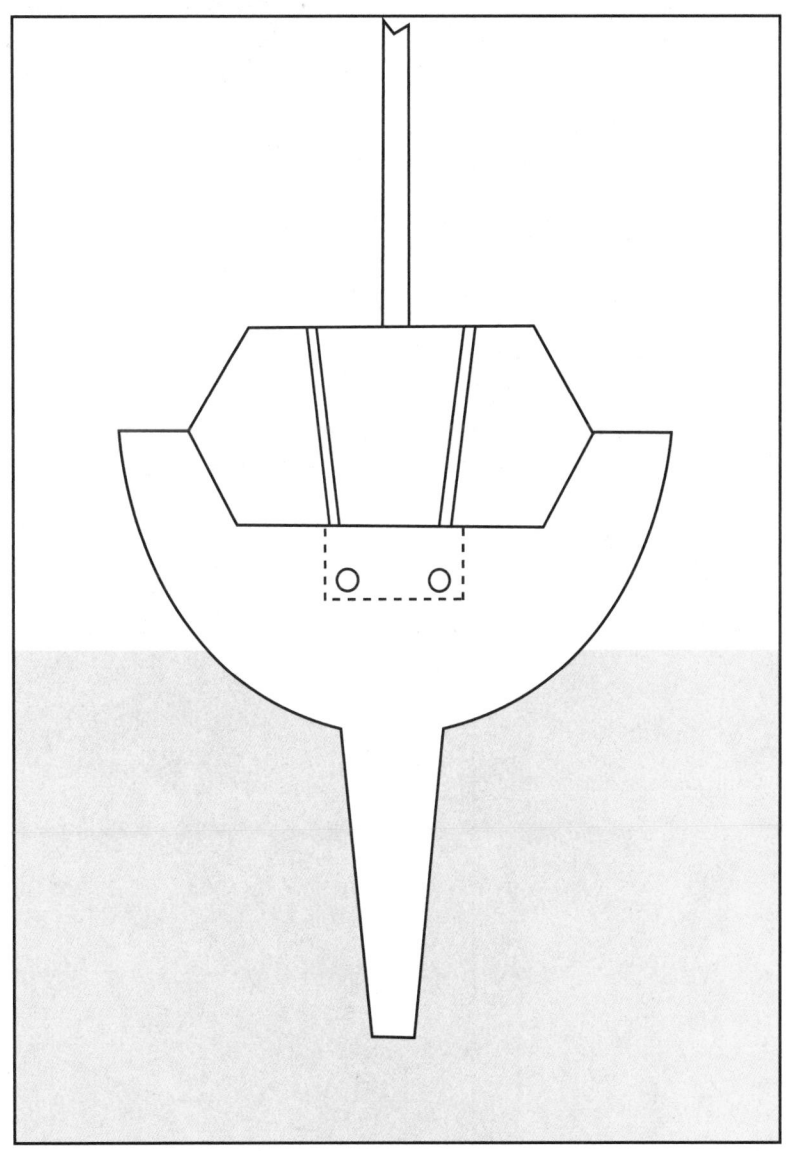

Self-bailing cockpit

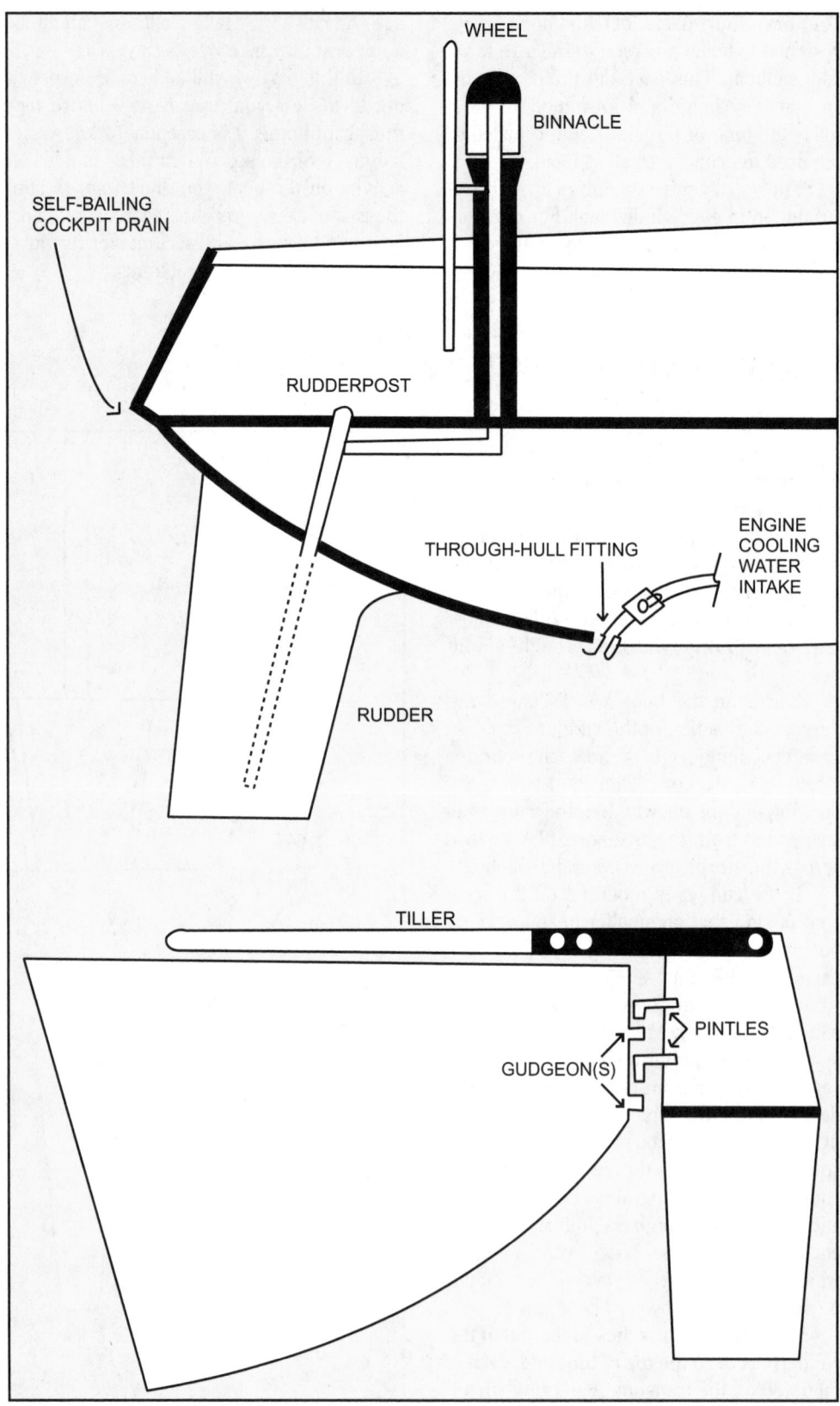

Rudder and tiller assembly

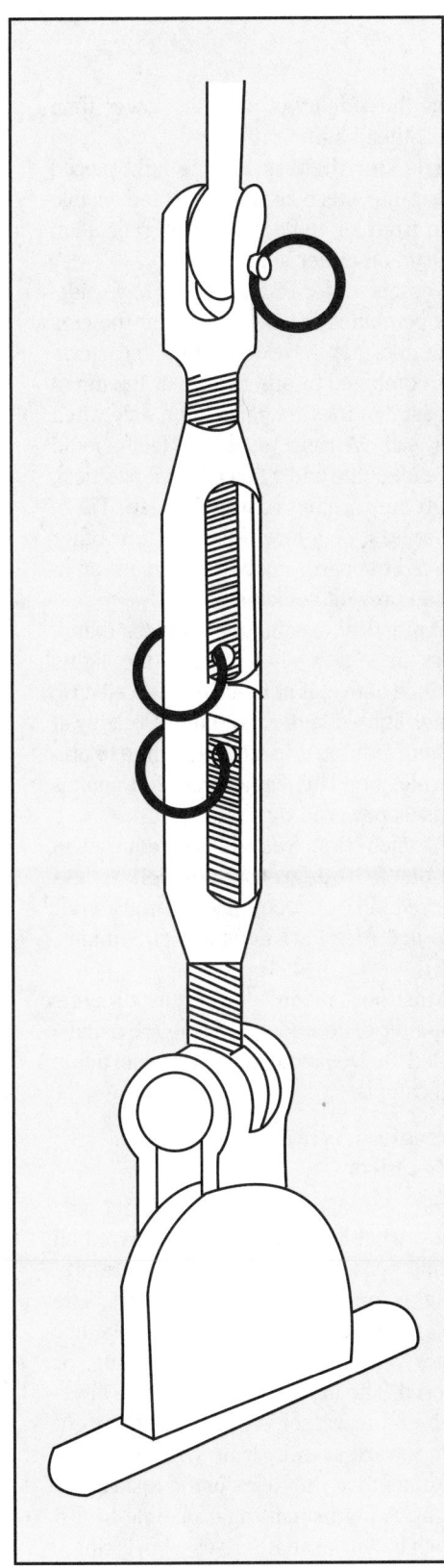

attaches to the rudderpost under the cockpit by one of many mechanical means; however, the top of the post is still exposed in the cockpit as an attachment point for the emergency tiller, if the steering wheel should fail.

The shrouds, forestay, and backstay support the mast. The strong metal fittings that attach these wires to the mast are called tangs. The other end of each shroud and backstay is attached to an adjustable device called a turnbuckle. The turnbuckle allows the shrouds and stays to be adjusted to the proper tension. Proper tensioning, or tuning of the mast, is a subject for an intermediate cruising course.

The shroud and backstay turnbuckles attach to the boat's hull by means of chainplates. These stainless steel straps are fastened securely to the boat's hull and form a secure base to keep the mast standing. The forestay is attached to the stem fitting, an integral part of the bow construction.

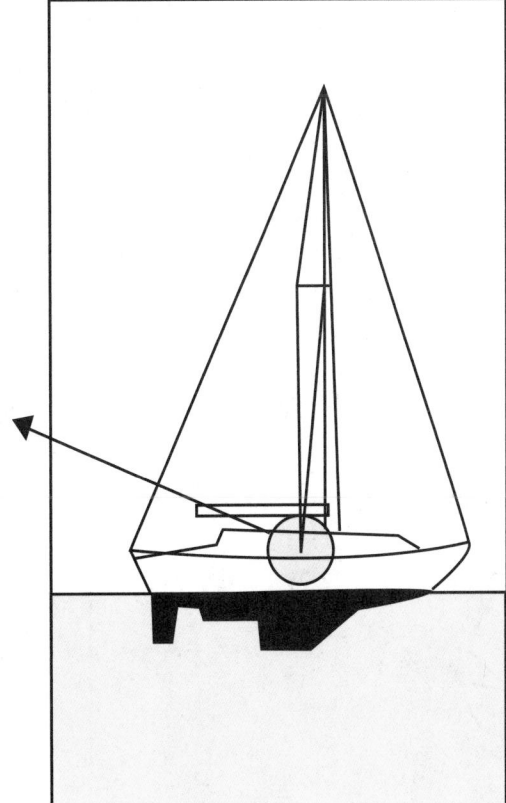

RUNNING LIGHTS

All boats must show the correct lights at night and at other times when visibility is restricted, whether at anchor or under way. It is against the law to sail at night without them.

The **masthead light** is a fixed white light over the fore-and-aft centerline of the vessel. Attached to the mast, it is visible from ahead around to an angle of 22.5 degrees abaft the beam on both sides. A masthead light is also called a **bow** or **steaming light.** It indicates a boat moving under engine power. Note: the masthead light should be extinguished on a sailboat when the engine is not operating.

Sidelights are red and green lights visible on the port and starboard sides respectively from directly ahead to an angle of 22.5 degrees abaft the beam. On a boat under power, the sidelights must be lower than the masthead light.

The **sternlight** is a white light placed as near the stern as possible and visible astern from an angle of 22.5 degrees abaft the beam on either side.

Vessels under 65.5 feet may have sidelights combined in one lantern on the centerline and may have sidelights and sternlights combined in one lantern at the top of the mast, but they may use them only when under sail. Vessels under 23 feet should carry sidelights and a sternlight if practical, though they are not required by law. There must at least be a bright flashlight or other white light aboard, ready to be displayed in order to prevent collisions.

If practical, a sailing vessel less than 7 meters in length shall exhibit the lights described above, If not, however, an electric torch or lighted lantern should be readily at hand and exhibited in sufficient time to prevent collision. This same provision applies to vessels powered by oars.

At anchor, all vessels are required to show one **360-degree white light** unless anchored in a recognized small craft anchorage (see Part Four, Chart Symbols, p. 112).

Most boat manufacturers install lights as a matter of course, and these are usually installed to Department of Transportation specifications.

INTERPRETING ANOTHER BOAT'S LIGHTS

For the new sailor, it is important not only to know what lights should be displayed on a sailing vessel but to be able to interpret the lights on another boat at night. The color and position of lights indicate whether another vessel is under power, sailing, or anchored. The lights also indicate the direction the other vessel is moving-to the right or left, toward or away from you.

Remember, the Rules of the Road apply at night. A helmsman must be able to discern what course another vessel is taking,

Lights that may be used under sail only. Only boats smaller than 65.5 feet may use the combination masthead light.

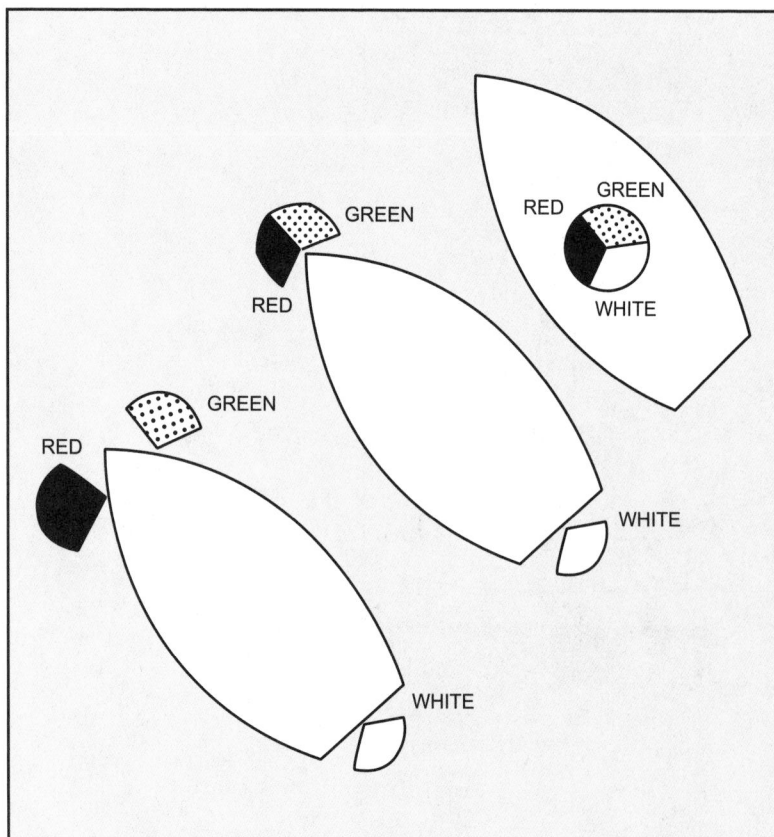

what rule applies, and what action, if any, is to be taken.

Let us look at the lights shown by recreational vessels under 65.5 feet in length. For pleasure boats, there are only three colors of lights with which to be concerned: white, red, and green.

The red light is shown from forward to just past the beam on the port side. To help recall which side is red, try this aid: Port wine is red. The starboard sidelight is green. The sternlight, which completes the circle of light, is white. If a vessel is propelled by sails alone, it will show just these three colors on the appropriate sides of the boat.

A powerboat (or sailboat under power) will show the following lights: sidelights, masthead light (higher than the sidelights), and sternlight.

The above description of required lights illustrates the key lighting requirements for sail- and powerboats. However, there are many other light configurations that apply to vessels of particular types, such as tugs, barges, vessels constrained by draft, and pilot vessels. It is possible to learn a great deal about the nature and activities of an unknown vessel when only its lights can be seen through the darkness. These are fully described in the International/Inland Navigation Rules and should be studied by boaters.

Running lights

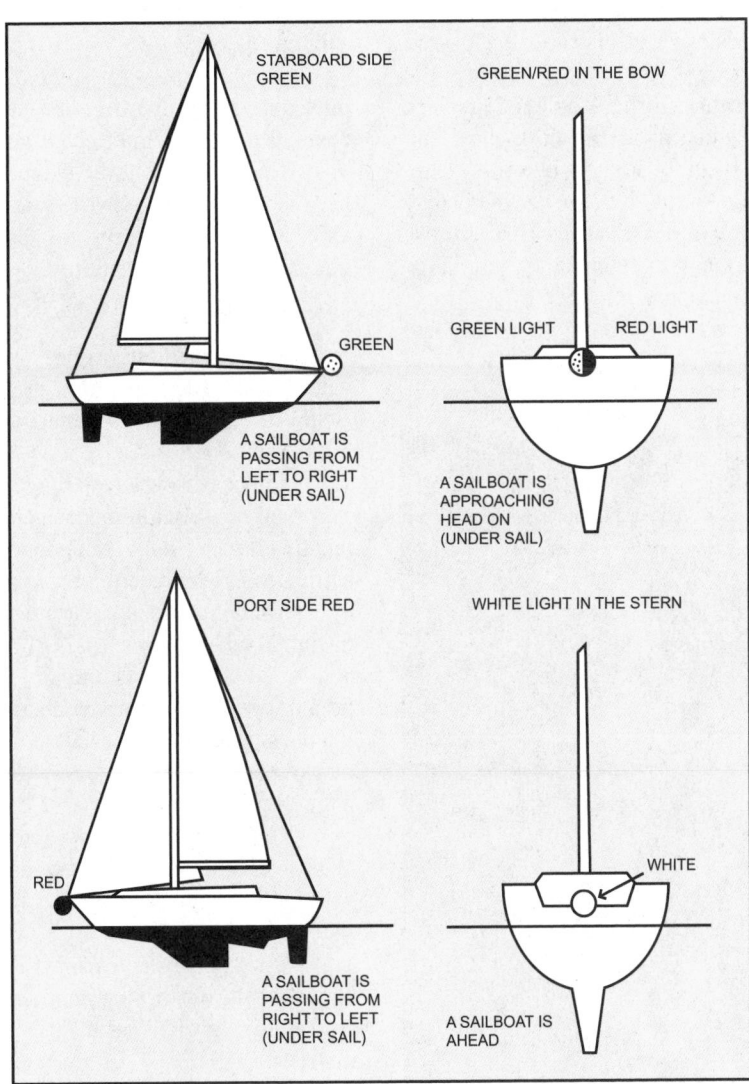

STARBOARD SIDE GREEN

GREEN

A SAILBOAT IS PASSING FROM LEFT TO RIGHT (UNDER SAIL)

GREEN/RED IN THE BOW

GREEN LIGHT   RED LIGHT

A SAILBOAT IS APPROACHING HEAD ON (UNDER SAIL)

PORT SIDE RED

RED

A SAILBOAT IS PASSING FROM RIGHT TO LEFT (UNDER SAIL)

WHITE LIGHT IN THE STERN

WHITE

A SAILBOAT IS AHEAD

DUTIES OF SKIPPER AND CREW FOR CRUISING

In Part Two we discussed the duties of the skipper-the safe operation of the vessel and the safety of the crew. The crew's duty is to assist the skipper in the safe operation of the vessel.

The skipper is responsible for the safety of the crew and must be able to delegate tasks and responsibilities to those who have the capacity to carry them out. Some of the tasks, such as steering the boat, are not necessarily part of the skipper's role, although in tough situations the skipper may want to assume the duties of helmsman.

If a crew member does not know how to do something on the boat, it is the skipper's responsibility to instruct that person in the required techniques. Among the skipper's most difficult decisions are whether to set sail in the first place and whether to head for home when the weather turns bad. Although these decisions may be made after a discussion with the crew, the decision and responsibility ultimately rest with the skipper.

The crew's duty to assist in the safe operation of the boat includes cleaning up dock lines and other boat equipment without being asked and taking a hand in the operation of the vessel. Tending sheets, steering, assisting with the anchor, and cooking, as well as assisting with the navigation, are all part of the crew's responsibilities.

A good crew member will always be invited back for the next sail. One way to ensure a second invitation is to bring along refreshments for an afternoon's sail. A crew member who packs some extra sandwiches, soft drinks, or other staples shows respect for the skipper and owner, who picks up the tab for the expensive parts of sailing.

If the crew pays for some of the fuel or puts money toward the slip fees or other costs, the crew is, in effect, **chartering** the boat. This means that the skipper has to be licensed by the U.S. Coast Guard. Skippers and boat owners should be careful not to get caught in this situation.

BOAT ETIQUETTE

Sailing is more enjoyable for everyone when basic good manners are observed. Below are some fundamental rules of boating etiquette.

- Do not throw any garbage overboard.
- Arrange your mooring before landing; this is easily done by a phone call before setting sail or by hailing people on shore.
- Do not tie up to government buoys or navigational aids (this is a law).
- Anchor in areas that are clear of traffic and away from narrow channels. Many harbors have specific anchorage areas marked by special buoys. Stay clear of other anchored boats.
- Follow the right-of-way rules and stay clear to avoid confusion. Stay clear of boats with fishing lines or boats that are sailing in races.
- Ask permission from the owner or skipper before boarding another boat.
- Always offer assistance to a boat in distress.

The most important thing in sailing is to enjoy yourself.

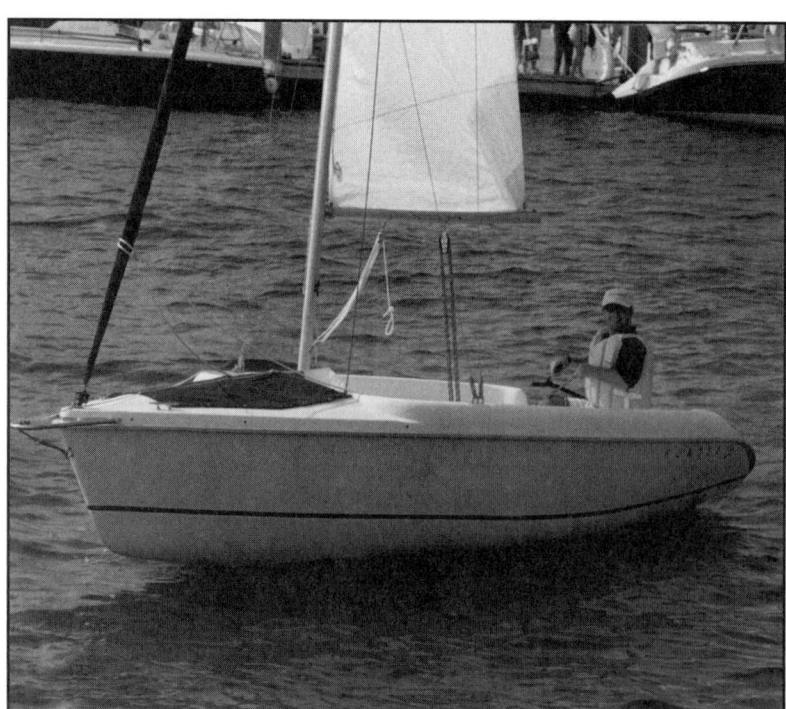

RULES OF THE ROAD UNDER POWER

A sailboat is only defined as a sailboat under the Rules of the Road when propelled by the wind alone. If the engine is running and in gear, the vessel is considered a powerboat and must follow the powerboat rules. The three basic right-of-way situations for powerboats are:

1. Two powerboats approaching each other should pass port side to port side (give way to the right), just like two cars on the highway.

2. When two powerboats are crossing, the vessel that has the other vessel to its starboard side is to keep clear. When getting out of the way, the helmsman of the vessel giving way must not attempt to cross ahead of the other vessel by speeding up. The best action is to alter course and pass astern or to slow down and wait for the other vessel to pass.

3. When one boat is overtaking another, the overtaking vessel shall keep out of the way of the vessel being overtaken. Thus, for example, a sailboat (operating under sail alone) is required to keep out of the way of any vessel it is overtaking.

Whistle (horn) signals are also required in meeting, crossing, and overtaking situations between powerboats in sight of one another. Although the precise meaning of these horn signals differs depending upon whether Inland or International Navigation Rules apply, the rules are generally similar. Briefly, for Inland Rules:

One short (1 second) blast indicates that you intend to leave the other boat to port.

Two short blasts indicate that you intend to leave the other boat to starboard.

Three short blasts should be sounded to indicate that you are operating in reverse.

Under the Inland Rules, these whistle signals indicate intention, and a response to these whistle signals is required by the other vessel. Under International Rules, these are signals of action (e.g., one short blast means that you are altering course to the right), and no response is required. Under Inland Rules, the response consists of the same signal (e.g., one or two blasts) if the proposed maneuver is agreeable to the other vessel or five or more short blasts-the danger or doubt signal-to indicate that a dangerous situation exists. Under no circumstances should "crossed" signals be sounded (e.g., answering one short blast with two short blasts or the converse).

International Rules require unique signals when overtaking in a narrow channel or fairway. If you are in the overtaking vessel in this circumstance, you must sound two prolonged blasts and one short blast to indicate that you intend to pass the other vessel on your port side, or two prolonged blasts followed by two short blasts to indicate that you intend to pass the other vessel on your starboard side. If the vessel being overtaken is in agreement, it should sound one prolonged, one short, one prolonged, one short, blast in response or, if not in agreement, sound the danger signal of five or more short blasts.

Under both Inland and International Navigation Rules, a boat nearing a bend or an area of a channel or fairway where other boats may be obscured by obstructions is required to sound one prolonged (4-6 seconds) blast. Additionally, under Inland Navigation Rules, a powerboat leaving a dock is required to sound one prolonged blast.

The above sound signals are widely misunderstood and many boaters either fail to use these signals or use them incorrectly. Nonetheless, they are required by the navigation rules and you may be cited for failure to sound them correctly. Moreover, if you do not properly sound these signals and then get into an accident, the failure to observe the rules may have consequences in terms of the liability for damages.

The navigation rules also require sound signals when operating in circumstances of reduced visibility. For example, a sailboat (without engine running) is required to sound one prolonged blast followed by two short blasts at intervals of not more than 2 minutes when operating in or near an area of restricted visibility. More information on sound signals in restricted visibility is provided in part six of this text.

ESSENTIAL SAFETY EQUIPMENT

Sailing is a great way to escape the hassles of the everyday world. People become involved in sailing to gain the freedom and independence of needing only the wind to power a boat. To protect this independence, a sailor has to prepare for almost any eventuality. As we have already seen, the Department of Transportation has prescribed the minimum safety equipment to be carried on sailboats without auxiliary power (see Part One, Federal Requirements for Recreational Boats, p. 27). A prudent sailor would take much more gear to sea.

There are legal requirements as well for safety equipment on boats with auxiliary power. The United States Coast Guard maintains one of the finest search and rescue forces in the world, but there are times when the Coast Guard may not be available to assist a vessel unless there is a life-threatening situation. The required safety equipment enables the skipper and crew to cope with many annoying or potentially dangerous situations.

Here is a list of some of the required safety equipment that should be aboard your vessel:

• **Personal Flotation Devices (PFDs):** the official name for life preservers or life jackets. They are available in a variety of sizes and types. To be acceptable, they must be Coast Guard approved, in good condition, and readily accessible. Here is a brief summary of the various types of PFDs:

Type I (Off-shore life jacket): Type I PFDs will turn most unconscious people from face-down positions to vertical or nearly face-up positions. Type I PFDs come in two sizes to fit most children and adults. The adult size provides a minimum of 22 pounds of buoyancy. Type I PFDs provide more protection than other types, but are bulky and less comfortable. Type I PFDs will keep swimmers afloat for extended periods in rough water and are recommended for offshore cruising where a delayed rescue is probable.

Type II (Near-shore buoyant vest): Type II PFDs will turn some unconscious people from face-down to vertical or nearly face-up positions. Type II PFDs come in several sizes, including infant, child, and adult. The adult size provides a minimum of 15.5 pounds of buoyancy. The Type II is more comfortable than a Type I but does not have as much buoyancy. Type IIs are recommended for inshore and inland cruising on calm water. Use these when prompt rescue is likely.

Type III (Flotation Aids): Type III PFDs are similar to Type II PFDs in terms of minimum buoyancy (although they may not turn unconscious swimmers face up), but are designed for greater comfort. Type IIIs are usually worn where freedom of movement is necessary, such as when waterskiing, sailing in small boats, and hunting and fishing. Type IIIs come in several sizes from small child through large adult.

Type IV (Throwable Device): Type IV Ring Life Buoys, Buoyant Cushions, and Horseshoe Buoys are Coast Guard approved devices designed to be thrown to persons in the water. Type IV throwables are not designed as PFDs for unconscious persons, nonswimmers, or children. Use these only in an emergency. Ring buoys come in 18-, 20-, 24-, and 30-inch diameter sizes and have grab lines. You should attach about 60 feet of polypropylene line to the grab line to aid in retrieving someone in the water. If you throw a ring, be careful not to hit the person.

Type V (Special-Use Devices, Hybrids): There are two kinds of Type V PFDs: special-use devices and hybrids. Special-use devices include boardsailing vests, deck suits, work vests, and others. They are approved only for the special uses or conditions indicated on their labels. Each is designed for the particular application shown on its label. They do not meet legal requirements for general use aboard recreational boats. Hybrid life jackets are inflatable devices with some built-in buoyancy provided by plastic foam or kapok. They can be inflated orally or with cylinders of compressed gas. Inflating a Type V increases its buoyancy In some hybrids the gas is released manually. Others inflate automatically when the PFDs are immersed in water. Hybrids manufactured before February 8,1995, must be worn whenever a boat is underway and persons wearing them are not below decks or in an enclosed space. Otherwise, they are not considered part of the required number of PFDs (see below). Those manufactured after this date need not be worn in order to count toward carriage requirements.

By law, a Coast Guard–approved wearable PFD-that is, a Type I, II, III, or V–must be carried for each person on board. Additionally, if your boat is 16 feet or greater in length and not a canoe or kayak, you must also have one Type IV on board. Life jackets should be readily accessible-not enclosed in the original wrapping materials or in a remote location. Store PFDs in a dry place. PFDs should be fitted to each person aboard. PFDs are important safety equipment and not fenders or seat cushions.

In addition to ratings for type (I, II, III. IV and V), PFDs are rated for buoyancy and a person's size and weight. All rating information is listed on a tag attached to the device. Lay-out all PFDs before getting underway and match them to the people on board.

PFDs come in several colors: red, blue, green, camouflage, and so on. However, from a safety standpoint, international orange is easiest to see in the water, especially in rough seas.

If possible, you and your crew should have some experience in swimming while wearing a PFD.

The safety margin around a boat pulling a skier or other towed device increases as a result of the length of tow line and the rapid speed with which most towing boats travel. Maintain a distance of at least 100 feet on either sided of a towing boat to avoid interfering with the skier.

If your interest in boating expands to include hunting and fishing from a boat, remember that all safety rules still apply. In the excitement of getting off the perfect cast or shot, hunters and fisherman might feel the urge to move into unbalanced positions. Always remain seated.

Studies estimate that as many as 80 percent of boating fatalities could have been prevented if the victims had been wearing PFDs. Make it a policy to wear a PFD whenever there is any risk of falling overboard. Nonswimmers, children, physically challenged, and elderly persons should always wear life jackets whenever they are aboard and not below. In potentially hazardous waters or at night, ensure that everyone is wearing a PFD.

FIRE AND FIRE EXTINGUISHERS

Fire at sea is a frightening prospect. Fire prevention is the first line of defense-for example, using proper fueling practices, avoiding stowage of oily rags in bilges, inspection of fuel tubing for proper fit, inspection of all electrical systems for poor connections and bare wires that could cause a short circuit. But fire extinguishers are essential if prevention measures fail. Fires are subdivided into three major classes: Class A-ordinary combustible material, such as paper or wood; Class B-gasoline, oil, grease, and other flammable liquids; and Class C-electrical fires. Fire extinguishers are also classified in terms of their suitability of use for the various classes of fires. For example, carbon dioxide is suitable for use on all three classes of fires. Water is only suitable for use against Class A fires.

MINIMUM NUMBER OF FIRE EXTINGUISHERS REQUIRED		
Vessel Length	No Fixed System	Approved Fixed System
Less than 26 feet	1 B-1	None
26 feet to under 40 feet	2 B-I or 1 B-II	1 B-1
40 feet to 65 feet	3 B-I, or 1 B-II and 1 B-I	2 B-I or 1 B-II

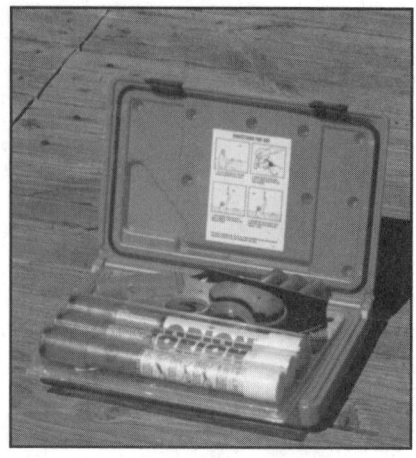

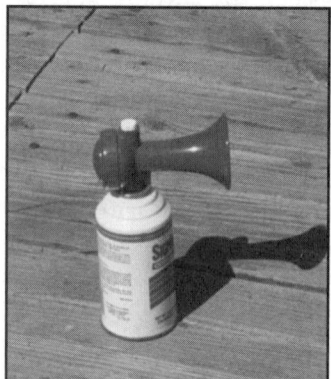

Safety equipment: flares, throwable lifering, PFD, running lights, fire extinguisher, compressed air horn, bell

Fire extinguishers must be Coast Guard approved, in serviceable condition, and mounted in fixed brackets.

Fire extinguishers come in two basic types of canister: portable and approved fixed systems (for machinery spaces). Portable systems are further classified among type and size. A B-I extinguisher, for example, contains 4 pounds of carbon dioxide or 2 pounds of dry chemical or 2.5 pounds of Halon. A B-II extinguisher contains 15 pounds of carbon dioxide or 10 pounds of dry chemical or 10 pounds of Halon. Required fire extinguishers for powerboats (including sailboats equipped with auxiliary engines) depend upon the vessel length and whether or not an approved fixed system is installed. The table on p. 145 provides a brief summary of the minimum requirements.

Fire extinguishers should be checked frequently to ensure that they are properly stored, are undamaged, have adequate pressure, and (in the case of Halon or carbon dioxide extinguishers) have appropriate weight. Do not "try out" an extinguisher to see if it will work. If an extinguisher has been discharged, replace or refill it promptly.

Fire Preparedness

All crew and guests aboard should know the location of and how to use all fire extinguishers and should inform the skipper whenever a fire or related symptoms occur (e.g., heat, the smell of burning wire insulation, smoke). You should conduct periodic fire drills to ensure that your crew are ready to help if necessary

In the event of fire, get everyone into PFDs (in case evacuation is required). Stop the boat immediately if possible; wind from the boat's motion could fan the flames. Position the boat so that the fire is downwind if possible (e.g., head the bow into the wind if the stern is on fire). If time permits, instruct a crew member to get on the radio to advise rescue authorities of the boat's problem and position. React quickly and decisively to attempt to put out the fire. Fire extinguishers usually have a device (locking pin) to keep them from being discharged accidentally. Remove the locking pin, point the nozzle at the base of the fire, and squeeze the handle to discharge the contents while sweeping the nozzle from side to side. Be careful. Smoldering materials may ignite. Dunk cushions and other smoldering materials on the downwind side of the boat to prevent reignition. If the fire is controlled and rescue authorities have been contacted by radio, make sure that you call to let them know that help is no longer required.

If fire starts in the engine compartment, shut off fuel to the engine(s) and discharge the fixed engine-fire-suppression system (if not automatic). Do not open engine hatches immediately, as a fresh supply of oxygen may restart the fire. After an engine fire is extinguished, do not attempt to restart the engine(s) without a careful assessment of the possible cause of and damages resulting from the fire.

If it appears that the fire cannot be controlled, prepare to abandon ship. Account for all persons aboard, ensure they are all wearing PFDs. Break out a life raft or tender if available, and depart the vessel.

• A **horn, whistle, or bell,** audible for one mile, must be carried on all vessels over 39.4 ft. but less than 65.5 ft.

• Vessels less than 12 meters (39.4 ft.) need not carry a whistle, horn, or bell. However, the navigation rules require sound signals to be made under certain circumstances, and you should carry some means for making an efficient signal.

• A vessel operating at night must show the required **running lights.**

• **Visual distress signals** (flares) suitable for day and night must be carried on all boats in coastal waters.

The two most common types of flares are, aerial and hand-held. Both types burn at high temperatures to produce brilliant light and smoke. Avoid injury and damage to the boat by holding or launching flares downwind and away from the boat.

SAFETY EQUIPMENT RECOMMENDED BY ASA AND USCGAUX

The ASA and USCGAUX recommend that boats heading out on long cruises or into rough weather carry the following equipment. Of course, some of this gear-flashlights, for example-should be on any boat that is used for cruising.

Anchors: A well-equipped cruising boat should carry two anchors with no less than 200 feet of cable, rope, or chain on each. When the usual means of propulsion on a sailboat-the wind or motor-fails, it may be necessary to stop the movement of the boat. A vessel can be easily carried onto a lee shore by waves and current, even after the wind has stopped blowing. A well-set anchor will prevent a boat from going aground. The second anchor may be slightly smaller than the first. A lighter anchor is often used if the boat is only stopping briefly, perhaps for lunch.

One anchor is not enough to hold a boat in very strong winds, so a second anchor should always be carried to be set as a reserve. On a cruising boat the anchor should be stowed neatly on deck. If an anchor is stowed below deck or in a cockpit locker, it must be easily accessible in an emergency and, therefore, should not be stowed under sails or other gear. Anchor rodes must be kept neatly coiled or flaked into a basket.

Bailer or manual bilge pump: Boats tend to collect water in the bilge (lowest part of the hull) from rain, condensation, or from stray waves that find their way into the cabin. Although a plastic bucket will serve as a bailer, a hand-operated bilge pump is required to remove large quantities of water in a short time. Two buckets should always be carried as a backup.

Flashlight and extra batteries: A flashlight is invaluable for looking into dark corners or for illuminating the sails at night. The flashlight should have a focused beam for distances and be rubberized to protect it from corrosion. Spare batteries and light bulbs should be kept in a safe, dry place. Plastic Ziploc bags are great for storing small items that have to be kept dry.

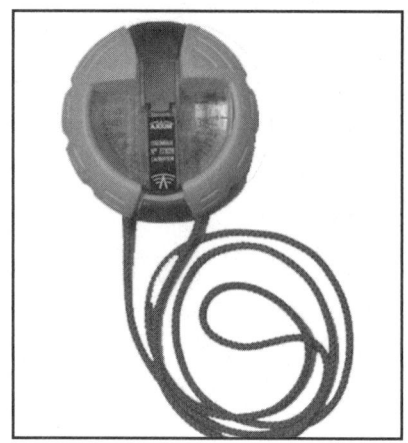

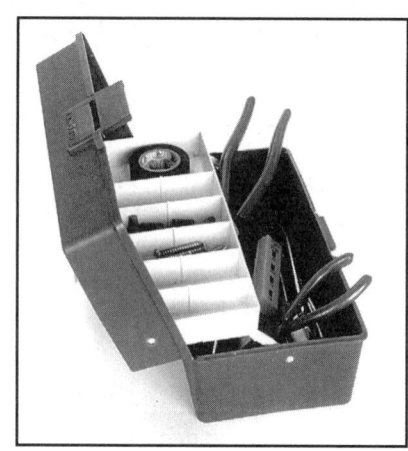

VHF marine radio, bulk-head-mounted compass, hand bearing compass, radar reflector, tool kit

First aid kit. A good first aid kit is needed for dealing with common problems, among them sunburn, scrapes, bruises, minor burns from the galley stove, seasickness, and bug bites. Here is a minimum inventory.

first aid manual
adhesive bandages in various sizes
3-inch sterile pads
triangular bandages
1-inch and 3-inch rolled bandages
tweezers and blunt scissors
cotton balls or cotton wool
antiseptic
sun screen (min. SPF15)
calamine lotion
motion sickness pills (or scopolamine patches)
aspirin or substitutes
eyewash cup

Tool kit and spare parts: Every boat should have a tool kit and spare parts. The kit should contain:

large and small screwdrivers
Phillips screwdriver
wrench for every type of fastening, nut, or bolt on the boat
sailmaker's needle and thread to sew sails and lines
sail ties
coil of nylon line
assorted shackles, nuts, bolts, and screws
vice grips
hammer
sharp knife and sharpening tool (a seaman's best friend)
high-quality duct (silver) tape
lubrication spray
hacksaw and several sharp blades

Tools should be kept well lubricated with spray to prevent rust.

Navigation charts and equipment: Even for a short daysail in familiar waters, it will be necessary to refer to a large-scale (the most detailed) chart of the area to determine the location of any hazards (see Part Four, Chart Symbols, p. 112). The latest editions should be kept on board and these should be corrected with information from the *Local Notices to Mariners,* published by the Coast Guard. Buoys and other ATONs are sometimes relocated, navigational hazards are discovered, and other pertinent information may have changed since the chart was issued. In addition to charts, a copy of the local *Coast Pilot,* Chart No. 1 (the chart symbols), and the *Light List* should be on board at all times. These publications are available from stores that sell charts and other navibation books. Also carry a compass!

Other safety items:

Soft wood plugs, tapered and of various sizes to plug any leaky valve or through-hull fitting.

A **VHF radio** to receive weather reports, to transmit emergency information, and for general ship-to-ship and ship-to-shore communications. At the very least, a boat should have an inexpensive weather radio.

An Emergency Position Indicating Radio Beacon (EPIRB) is a small, battery-powered radio transmitting buoylike device. When activated by immersion in water or a manual switch, an EPIRB transmits a distress signal that can be detected by SAR units, which can increase the speed of location and rescue. The recently introduced 406 MHz EPIRBs are more expensive but preferable, due to their ability to transmit a code identifying a database of information specific to your vessel (if the unit is properly registered).

Every boat less than 16 feet long should carry an alternate means of propulsion, such as a paddle, oar, or small outboard engine. Even if this second means of propulsion is impractical for getting all the way home, it can be used to move the vessel to a safer location. Safety often requires moving a distressed boat out of a shipping channel or to shallow water where secure anchoring is possible.

Personal safety equipment:

Safety harnesses, one for each person. One or more for each person on motor cruisers as may be needed when on deck. Wear a safety harness on deck in bad weather or at night. Make sure it is properly adjusted.

Rescue equipment for man overboard:

Life buoys, at least two. One life buoy should be kept within easy reach of the helmsman. For sailing at night, it should be fitted with a self-igniting light.

Buoyant heaving line, at least 100 feet, with breaking strain of 250 pounds. This should be kept within easy reach of the helmsman.

Inflatable life raft, large enough to carry everyone on board. It should be stowed on deck or in a locker opening directly to the deck and should be serviced annually; or

Rigid dinghy with permanent, not inflatable, buoyancy and with oars and oarlocks secured. It should be carried on deck. It may be a collapsible type; or

Inflatable dinghy, built with two compartments, one at least always kept fully inflated, or built with one compartment, always kept fully inflated, and having oars and oarlocks secured. It should be carried on deck.

In sheltered waters the equipment listed below is usually adequate.

Distress flares, six with two of the rocket/parachute type.

Daylight distress (smoke) signals.

Tow rope, of adequate size to tow the boat.

Water-resistant light.

Fog horn.

Name and sail number of the boat should be marked on all pieces of large equipment and on the vessel itself. If you're sailing offshore, display the number and name so they may be easily read from an aircraft flying overhead.

REVIEW QUESTIONS

1. Identify the following parts of the boat on the diagram.

self-bailing cockpit _____

through-hull fittings_____

pintle _____

gudgeon _____

rudderpost _____

tiller _____

turnbuckle _____

chainplate _____

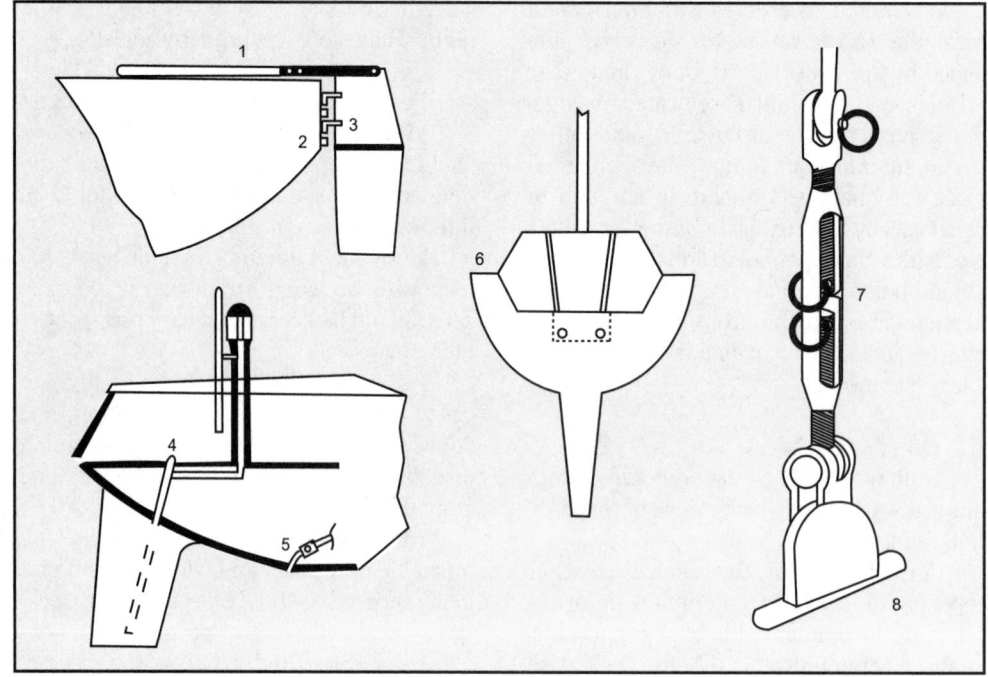

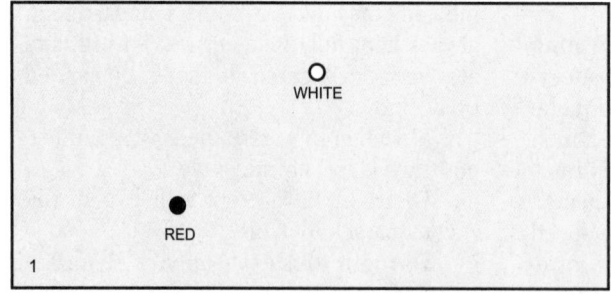

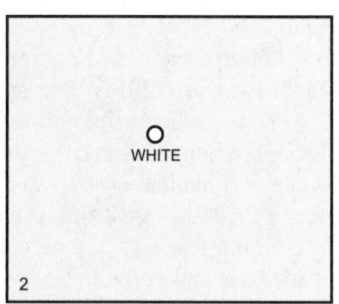

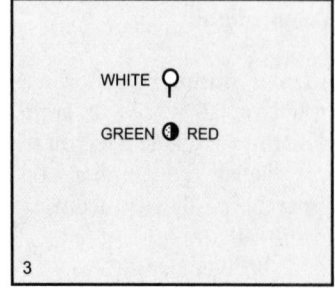

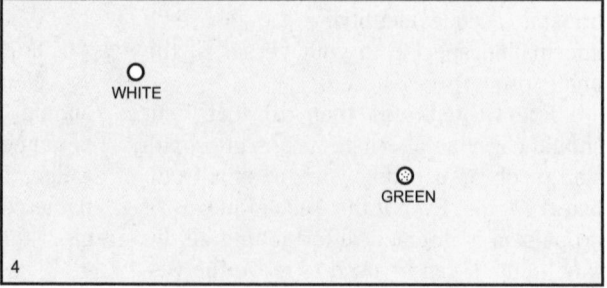

2. In what directions do the lights on the bottom of page 160 indicate a powerboat is heading?
a) left to right _____
b) right to left _____
c) toward us _____
d) away from us _____

3. Circle the vessel that may stand on (hold its course) in each of the following situations and indicate which direction the other boat should turn to avoid a collision.

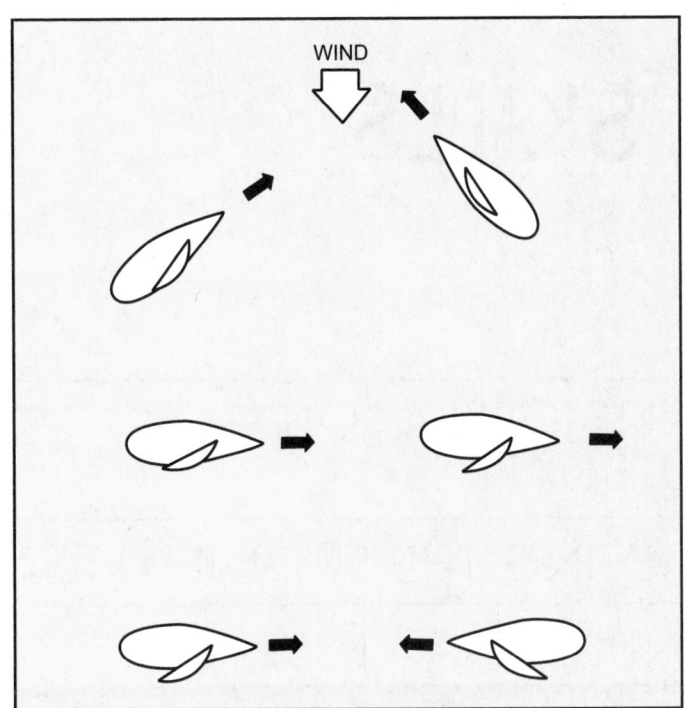

4. Under the Inland Navigation Rules, a power-driven vessel that proposes a port-to-port passage in a head-on situation should sound _____ blast(s). If in agreement, the other vessel should sound _____, if not, it should sound _____.

5. A power-driven vessel nearing a bend or an area of a channel or fairway where other vessels may be obscured by an intervening obstruction should sound _____.

6. A _____ PFD can turn most unconscious wears face-up in the water and is recommended for open, rough, or remote waters.

7. An auxiliary-engine equipped sailboat between 26 and 40 feet in length without an approved fixed fire extinguisher installed is required to carry _____ fire extinguishers on board.

8. Burning oil or gasoline is a Class _____ fire.

9. On discovering a fire in the engine compartment, you should,
a) Ensure that all crew members put on PFDs
b) Stop the boat
c) Shut off fuel to the engine, if possible
d) All of the above

10. Water is only suitable to extinguish a _____ fire.

Answers in Appendix A, p.201.

SAILING SKILLS

As you move up from small daysailers to auxiliary-powered sailboats, you will find that at least a minimum knowledge of outboard motor operation is essential to your pleasure and security on the water.

ENGINE OPERATION-OUTBOARDS

Outboard motors are mounted on the transom of sailboats, either by a bracket or in a stern lazarette. To raise and lower bracket-mounted motors follow the manufacturer's instructions.

REFUELING

To prevent a fire or explosion, take the following precautions when refueling.

1. Moor the boat securely.

2. Shut off the motor and make sure all passengers are ashore.

3. Don't smoke. Extinguish all open flames and close all windows and hatches.

4. Don't use electrical switches.

5. Don't overfill the tank. Ground (touch) the nozzle against the filler pipe.

6. Wipe up any spills and turn the blower on for five minutes.

7. Check for vapor odor; when clear, start the motor and reload your passengers.

Improper maintenance of an outboard engine will lead to frustration and loss of sailing time. The proper gas and oil mixture and clean spark plugs go a long way in ensuring the efficient operation of the motor.

STARTING THE ENGINE PRIOR TO LEAVING THE DOCK/MOORING

Before starting:

1. Check the gas tank by shaking or lifting the can to determine how much fuel is in the tank (don't rely on gauges-they have a tendency to stick).

2. Check the fuel line to make sure the 0 ring is in place and intact. Connect the fuel line to the motor.

3. Pump fuel into the carburetor by squeezing the priming bulb until the bulb feels firm.

4. Place the gear shift in neutral.

5. If the motor is attached to a two po-

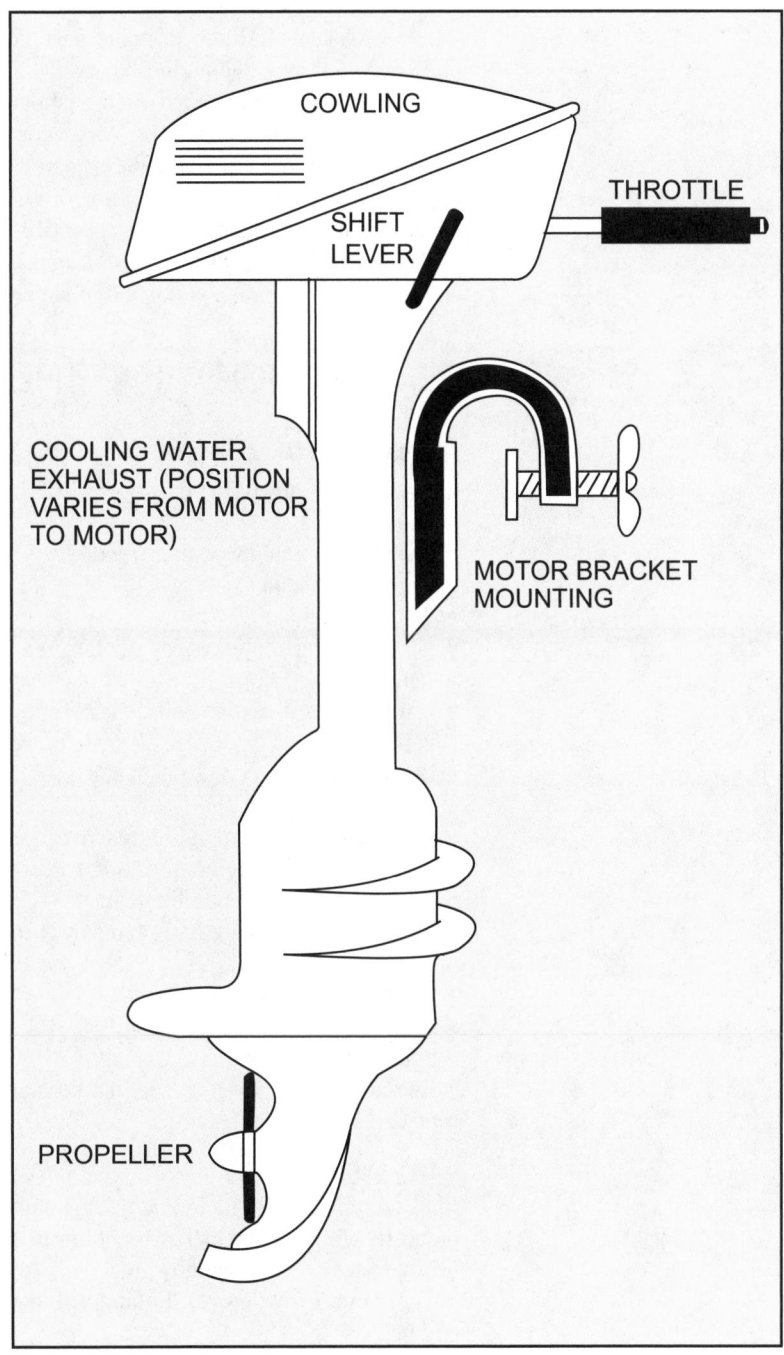

Outboard motor

sition motor mount, make sure the motor is in the down position to allow for proper water intake for the cooling system.

6. Set the throttle to the start position.

7. Pull out the choke.

Starting procedure:

1. Pull the starter cord slowly until you feel resistance.

2. Check behind you to make sure no one will be hit by a flying elbow.

3. Pull the starter cord with a short, quick motion. Do not pull the cord more than about 18 to 24 inches. If the starter cord is pulled too far and too hard, it will eventually be pulled from the starting coil.

4. Once the engine has started and is running well, the choke is pushed in slowly (first) and the throttle turned to the idle position.

5. The engine operator will check to see if there is cooling water flowing from the back of the motor. If not, the motor must be turned off immediately.

6. While the boat is tied securely to the dock, check the transmission by first putting the motor into forward and then into reverse. It is better to discover the transmission will not shift while in the slip or mooring rather than when you're already halfway down the channel.

If the starter cord breaks off, the motor can still be started. Put a figure eight knot in the end of the starter cord and wind it around the flywheel.

TROUBLESHOOTING THE ENGINE

BATTERY AND STARTER MOTOR

- Battery run down. Recharge or start engine by hand.
- Battery terminal loose or corroded. Tighten or clean.
- Battery lead faulty.
- Starter switch, solenoid, or starter motor faulty.
- Starter motor brushes dirty. Clean or replace.
- Bendix gear jammed. Loosen starter motor to free.
- Starter motor not engaging. Starter motor turns but engine does not. Caused by a faulty or dirty Bendix gear.
  Starter motor turns engine too slowly to start it:
- Battery run down.
- Battery lead or terminal faulty.
- Starter motor faulty.
- Engine oil of wrong grade. Drain and replace.

DIESEL ENGINES

Fuel faults: Detach fuel pipe at injection pump to see whether fuel is reaching it. If not, suspect one of the following:

- Fuel tank low or empty. Refill and bleed engine.
- Fuel tap turned off.
- Fuel pipe or filter blocked. Clear and bleed engine.
- Fuel tank vent blocked.
- Fuel pipe fractured or leaking. Repair and bleed engine.
- Fuel lift pump faulty.

If fuel is reaching the injection pump, suspect one of the following:

- Stop control not released.
- Injection pump faulty. Control rod may be sticking.
- Injector faulty. Normally requires expert adjustment.

Warning: The spray from an injector is powerful enough to penetrate the skin.

Mechanical faults:

- Injection timing wrong.
- Compression poor. Normally the result of wear.
- Valve faulty.
- Air cleaner blocked.

Engine stops: This may be caused by a fuel system fault. In rough seas dirt or water may be stirred up from the bottom of the tank, or air may be drawn into the fuel pipe if fuel is low. It may also be caused by a mechanical system fault:

- Valve sticking.
- Governor idling setting incorrect.
- Injection timing too far advanced. Retard.

Engine loses power: This may be caused by a fuel system fault, a mechanical system fault, or overheating. In addition, it may be caused by the following:

- Propeller fouled.
- Stern gear bearings seizing. Regrease.

Engine misfires: This may be caused by a fuel system fault or overheating. Also suspect one of the following:

- Injector pipe fractured.
- Piston ring sticking.
- Valve sticking.

In diesel engines overheating may also be caused by a faulty injector.

Bleeding the fuel system: Air may enter the fuel system of a diesel engine as a result of running out of fuel, leaks in pipes or connections, disconnection of pipes, or changing filters. The following procedure is generally applicable to most diesel engines. However, the exact procedure varies from model to model.

1. Trace fuel pipe from lift pump to fuel filter. Open bleed screw on inlet side.

2. Operate priming lever until fuel, free of air bubbles, emerges around screw.

3. Open bleed screw on outlet side of filter and repeat procedure above.

4. Trace fuel pipe to injection pump. Open bleed screw and repeat procedure above.

If the engine runs for a few minutes and then stops, there is probably still air in the system, so the whole procedure must be carried out again. If there is air in the system, the engine may in fact run satisfactorily until stopped, then fail to start.

GASOLINE ENGINES

Fuel faults: Detach fuel pipe at the carburetor to see whether fuel is reaching it. If not, suspect one of the following:

- Fuel tank low or empty. Refill.
- Fuel valve turned off.
- Fuel pipe or filter blocked. Clear.
- Fuel tank vent blocked.
- Fuel pump faulty.

If fuel is reaching the carburetor, suspect one of the following:

- Engine flooded. Remove spark plugs and turn engine several times.
- Fuel contaminated with water. Drain fuel tank and clean fuel pipes and carburetor.
- Choke defective. Check valve and cable.
- Jets blocked. Clear.
- Carburetor faulty.

Mechanical faults:

- Intake manifold air leak. Check by squirting oil around intake connections. Tighten manifold.
- Cylinder head gasket leaking. Replace.
- Spark plug loose. Tighten.
- Compression poor. Normally the result of wear.
- Valves faulty.

Ignition faults: Check for spark at plugs. If none, suspect the following:

- Plugs fouled. Clean tip with sandpaper.
- Plug gaps incorrect. Reset or replace.
- Porcelain cracked. Replace plug.

Check for spark at plug leads. If none, suspect the following:

- Plug lead loose or faulty. Tighten or replace.
- Distributor cap wet or dirty. Clean and dry.
- Distributor cap cracked. Replace.
- Condenser faulty. Replace.
- Rotor arm not making contact with carbon brush in distributor cap. Adjust.

Check for spark at HT lead. If none, suspect the following:

- HT lead loose or faulty. Tighten or replace.
- Ignition coil faulty. Replace.
- Contact breaker points out of adjustment. Reset.

Engine stops: This may be caused by a fuel system fault or an ignition system fault.

- LT lead loose. Tighten.
- Contact points dirty. Clean.
- Ignition switch faulty.

Engine loses power: This may be caused by a fuel system fault. It may also be caused by one of the following:

- Fuel mixture too lean.
- Carburetor flooding.
- Valve faulty.

• Ignition timing incorrect. Advance or retard.

• HT lead shorting.

• Propeller fouled.

• Plug leads crossed.

Engine Overheats:

• Header tank low or empty. Refill with fresh water.

• Drive belt slipping or broken.

• Seawater intake closed or blocked. Check that water is coming out of the system.

• Water pump faulty.

• Thermostat sticking.

• Engine oil low. Refill.

• Air in cooling system.

In gasoline engines overheating may also be caused by the following:

• Fuel mixture too weak.

• Ignition timing incorrect.

OUTBOARD MOTORS

If the engine will not start, suspect one of the following:

• Fuel tank empty or supply turned off.

• Fuel line blocked or kinked.

• Fuel system not primed. Squeeze priming bulb until hard.

• Fuel tank vent closed.

• Engine flooded. Release choke, shut off fuel, turn engine over several times, and wait one or two minutes.

• Engine not choked.

• Spark plug fouled or faulty. Clean or replace.

• Throttle low.

If the engine lacks power, suspect one of the following:

• Fuel line blocked or kinked.

• Carburetor out of adjustment.

• Spark plug faulty.

• Engine overheating.

If the engine will not idle, suspect one of the following:

• Spark plugs dirty or faulty.

• Carburetor out of adjustment. Adjust idling speed.

• Fuel mixture incorrect.

If the engine overheats, suspect one of the following:

• Water intake blocked.

• Water pump faulty.

• Prolonged low speed running.

Outboards dropped in the water must be serviced quickly because corrosion sets in within about three hours. If you think sand may have been drawn into the engine or if there is any sign of binding when the flywheel is turned, do not turn the engine over.

1. Rinse motor with fresh water.

2. Remove plugs and dry them.

3. Clean carburetor, preferably with kerosene.

4. Turn engine over several times with plug hole facing downward.

5. Squirt oil into cylinders.

6. Refit plugs and carburetor.

7. Try to start engine.

If engine fails to start, remove plugs and repeat procedure. If all attempts fail, take the engine to a dealer.

HANDLING A VESSEL UNDER POWER

Getting a vessel safely away from a dock or out of a slip involves more than just proper technique. It requires awareness and coordination of the entire crew. A predetermined sequence of events as well as clear, concise instructions from the helmsman will ensure a seamanlike exit from any dock.

Determine the wind's direction and strength. Remember that the wind will push the bow away faster than the rest of the boat. Plan the best route for leaving the dock. Be alert to hazards, especially moving boats.

Before taking a boat away from the dock, review how the boat is tied up. It will be left this way at the end of the on-the-water session.

DEPARTING FROM A DOCK-WIND OFF THE DOCK

When the wind is blowing off the dock, it will push the bow away from the dock. The helmsman takes advantage of this to simplify leaving the dock.

1. The helmsman tells the crew to "Prepare to cast off."

2. The crew removes the spring lines and takes the hitches out of the bow and stern lines. The crew leaves the bow and stern lines wrapped once around the dock cleats to prevent the boat from moving until the helmsman gives the command. When this is done, the crew replies, "Ready."

3. With the command "cast off the bow line," the crew casts off the bow line from the dock and steps aboard at the shrouds, the widest and closest part of the boat to the dock.

4. With the command "cast off the stern line," the crew will cast off the stern line from the dock while the helmsman puts the gear shift lever into forward (slow speed) and steers the boat away from the dock.

5. Both the helmsman and the crew member on the dock should make sure the stern does not hit the dock, and as soon as possible, the crew member should step aboard at the stern of the boat.

6. Once clear of the dock, the crew removes and stows fenders and dock lines in their proper places.

DEPARTING FROM THE DOCK-WIND TOWARD THE DOCK

When the wind is blowing toward the dock, the bow of the boat will be pushed into the dock faster than the stern. Therefore, backing away from the dock will be easiest.

A crew member should always have a fender ready to place between the boat and the dock. It is important to have instantly available one fender that is not tied in place.

1. The helmsman tells the crew to "Prepare to cast off. " Once the spring lines have been cast off, the bow of the boat will start to drift into the dock.

2. When the crew has undone the half hitches in the bow and stern lines and there is one wrap of each remaining on the cleat, the crew responds, "Ready."

3. The helmsman instructs the crew

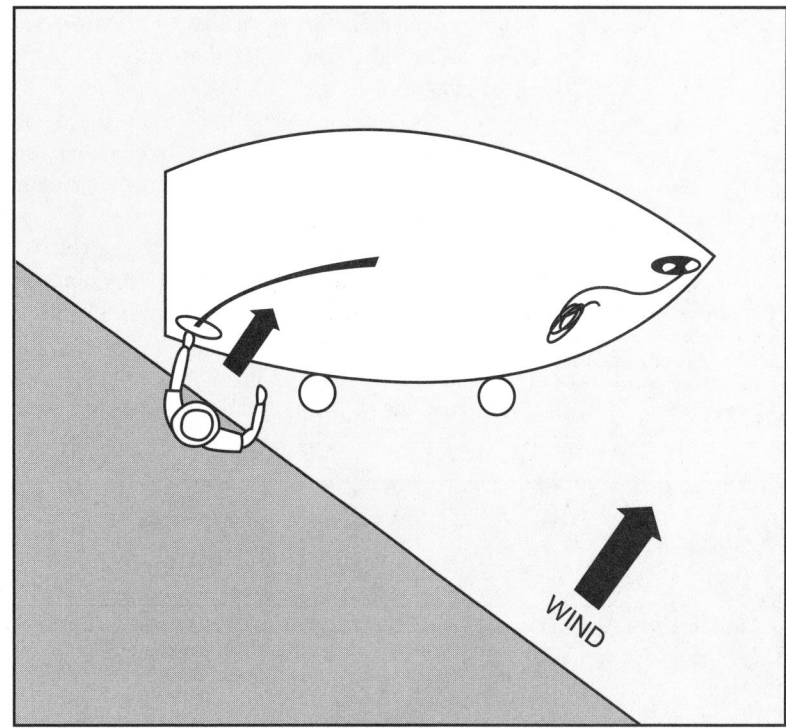

A crew member on the dock casts off the stern line and watches that the stern does not hit the dock.

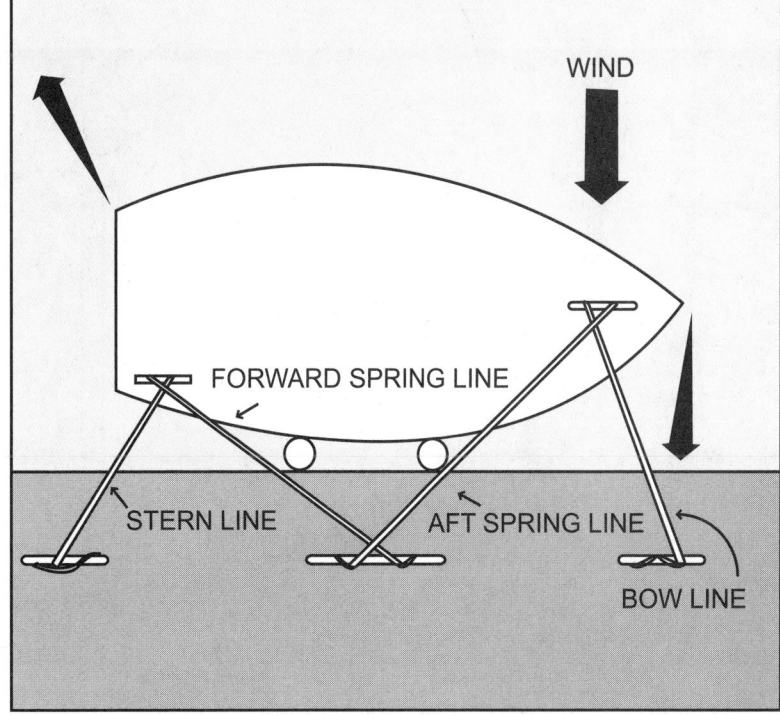

The boat is properly secured to the dock with bow and stern lines, and forward and aft spring lines.

member on the stern line to 'Cast off the stern line." The sailor does this and steps aboard.

4. As the bow is blown into the dock, one of the crew has to move a fender forward to protect the bow from being damaged.

5. As the stern starts to swing clear of the dock, the helmsman puts the engine in reverse and commands the bow crew member to "Cast off the bow line." This time, the sailor on the bow line does not push the bow away from the dock, casts off, and

Departing from a slip: A crew member steps aboard at the shrouds (the most stable part of the boat) as he casts off.

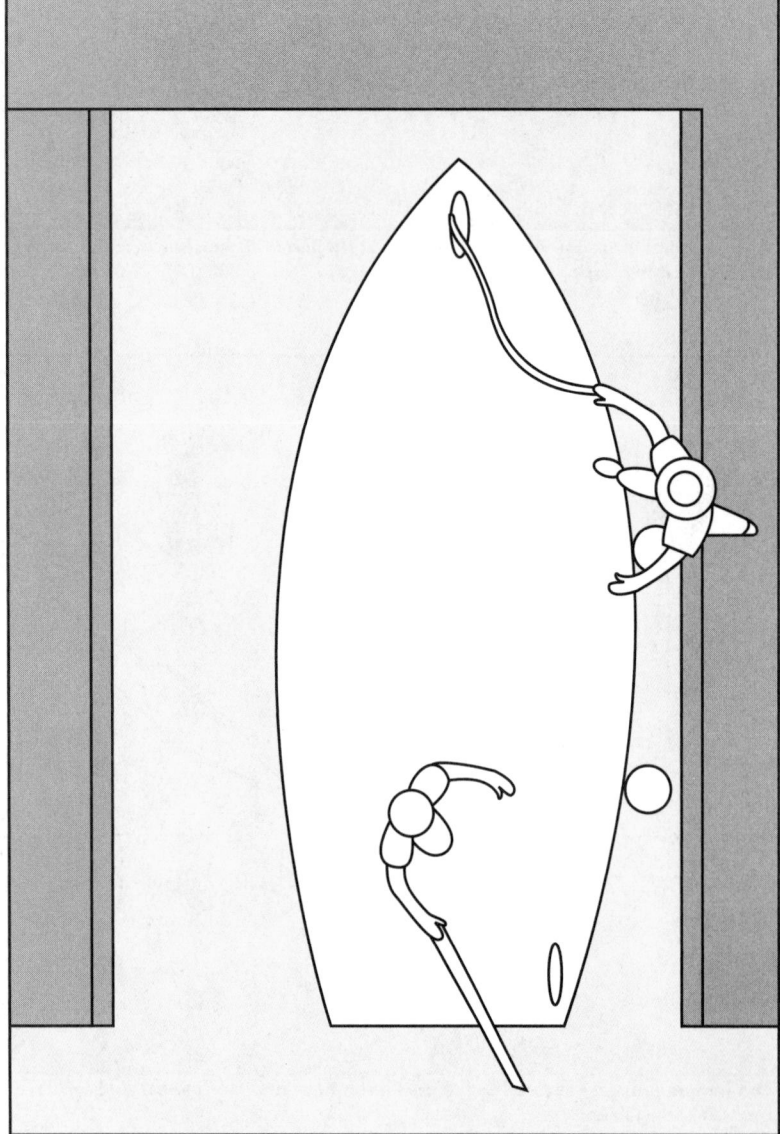

boards the boat.

6. The boat continues to back away from the dock until it is in open water. At that time, the helmsman shifts into forward and proceeds away from the dock.

DEPARTING FROM A SLIP

1. The helmsman instructs the crew to "Prepare to cast off."

2. The crew releases the spring lines and unties the hitches in the bow and stern lines. Then the crew replies, "Ready."

3. On the command "Prepare to reverse," the crew releases the bow and stern lines and starts to walk the sailboat out of the slip. (Remember to use fenders and lines to protect the boat rather than relying on your strength.)

4. Just before the beam (widest part) of the boat passes the end of the slip, the crew steps aboard on the beam.

5. The helmsman continues to back the boat out until it is clear of the slip.

6. After clearing the slip, the helmsman shifts the engine into forward and throttles up until the boat starts moving forward. Don't turn the helm until the boat is moving forward.

Every sailboat handles differently under power. The best way to discover how a particular vessel will respond in a tight situation (especially in a crowded marina) is to practice in the open water. Boats with inboard engines turn faster in one direction

EXERCISE: **POWER**

The purpose of this exercise is to gain a feel for the boat's movement through the water. It will also show how the boat responds to easy and abrupt turns.

1. In open water, clear of other boats, bring the boat up to half speed.

2. First turn the boat to starboard, straighten it out, and then slowly turn to port.

3. Repeat the exercise, this time at full throttle.

EXERCISE: **FIGURE EIGHT AT HALF THROTTLE AND FULL THROTTLE**

The purpose of this exercise is to illustrate the area required to turn a vessel to port and to starboard. You will find the turning radius increased and stability reduced (resulting in increased heeling) as your speed increases.

1. Using two buoys or markers as in the original sailing exercises, turn to starboard in a complete circle at half throttle.

2. When the boat crosses its wake (the trail from the stern), turn the boat to port, completing a figure eight in the water. You should note if your boat turns better in one direction than the other (due to propeller rotation). This will be useful to know in tight maneuvering situations.

3. Repeat the exercise at full throttle and note the larger turning radius required.

The direction of rotation of the propeller will also have an effect on how well the sailboat stops. If the propeller turns to port in reverse, the stern of the boat will be pulled to port as forward motion is lost.

FIGURE EIGHT REVERSE

Repeat the figure eight exercises in reverse and notice the difference in handling. Be careful to hold the tiller or wheel tightly, since reverse gear puts a lot of pressure on the rudder.

EXERCISE: **FAST STOP**

The objective of this exercise is to determine how long it takes to stop the boat.

1. As the boat passes a marker or buoy at full throttle, throttle down, shift to neutral, then to reverse, and slowly throttle up. Be sure to shift into neutral at very low engine speed, for otherwise the transmission will break down.

2. When the boat comes to a stop, throttle down and shift to neutral.

The helmsman and crew should take notice of how long it takes the boat to stop.

3. Repeat this exercise going upwind, downwind, and across wind. Notice how the wind helps stop the boat upwind and virtually keeps the boat from stopping downwind. Across the wind, as the boat slows, the bow begins to blow away from the wind. The helmsman must keep this in mind when docking in a crosswind slip.

than the other due to the rotation of the propeller. It's important to determine which direction your boat favors.

Although these exercises are designed for beginners, any sailor who steps aboard an unfamiliar boat should use them to test its maneuverability and handling characteristics.

When getting underway, we start from a stationary position and therefore have more control than when docking. In docking we must be prepared before we approach the dock.

The key to all maneuvers under power is controlled speed. The approach must not be so fast that the boat cannot be stopped before it hits the dock, nor so slow that the helmsman loses steerage. As when leaving the dock, consider wind and current when planning the approach.

The stopping exercises were designed to test the distances required to stop a sailboat upwind, downwind, and across the wind. Your are now ready to practice docking at an open upwind dock.

Some docking facilities are designed in

EXERCISE: **LANDING AT AN UPWIND DOCK**

Preparing to dock:

1. Once the sails are lowered, the crew ties dock lines to the bow and stern docking cleats and also readies spring lines. As in docking under sail, a dock line rigged to the widest part of the boat will be used to stop it at the dock without pulling the bow into dock.

2. If the dock is unfamiliar the helmsman makes an initial approach to survey the placement of dock cleats and determine how high the fenders need to be set. This done, the helmsman returns the boat downwind.

3. The crew sets the fenders, keeping one fender free to be quickly placed between the boat and the dock should anything unexpected happen.

The boat then makes the final approach:

4. The helmsman approaches parallel to and about three feet away from the dock, while two crew members position themselves holding on to the shrouds, each with a dock line in his hand.

5. The helmsman puts the boat into neutral three to six boat lengths from the point where the boat will be docking. When the boat is about one boat length away, the helmsman steers slightly closer, to within one foot of the dock.

6. To stop the boat, the helmsman shifts into reverse at low revs (otherwise you might lose the coupling or transmission).

7. The crew steps (do not jump) from the boat as soon as it is safe to do so. The crew stops the boat with the after spring, uses the stern line to keep the stern in.

8. As soon as the boat has come to a stop, the helmsman shifts the engine to neutral.

9. The crew centers the boat in the docking space, then completes the cleat hitch on each dock line.

10. Once the boat is secured, the crew secures the spring lines on the dock cleats.

line with the prevailing winds so that the winds blow either along or off the dock. This makes docking easier. Some docks may not be so well designed, and the helmsman may have to dock across the wind or, in the worst case, downwind.

Preparing to land at a dock under power is similar to preparing to land under sail, except that you must lower the sails before entering the docking area. The mainsail should be tied to the boom, but the sail cover should never be put on the mainsail until the boat is securely tied at the dock. If the motor fails, the crew must be able to raise the sail and maneuver out of trouble.

SUMMARY

Part Five has brought us closer to being a skipper-the decision maker. We have learned the care and handling of a sailboat under power. A motor prevents the sailor from being left at the total mercy of the elements. If the wind dies, all we have to do is "hoist the iron genoa" (start the motor).

Learn to take good care of your motor. Always use the proper fuel mixture, warm the motor before putting the transmission in gear, and check the lubrication levels regularly. Do these things and, when you need to use the motor, it will be there to assist you.

Abide by the rules governing the operation of power-driven vessels. Remember, a sailboat under power is a power vessel, whether the sails are raised or not.

PART SIX

Basic Coastal Cruising II

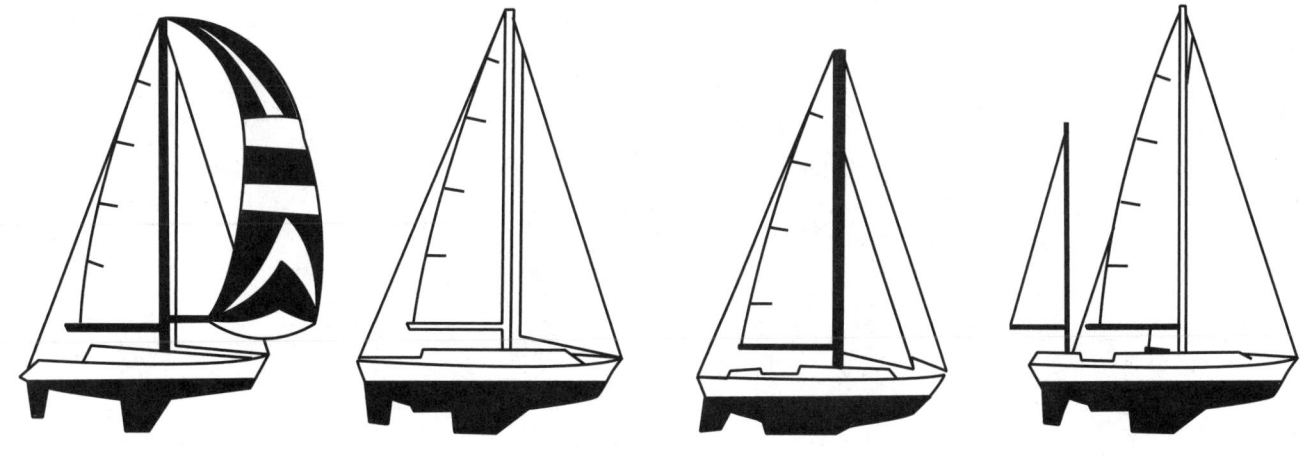

SAILING KNOWLEDGE

As you advance from daysailing to cruising, the boat you sail may change as well. You may move on to a larger **sloop**-rigged sailboat. Others will choose a more traditional rig such as a **ketch, yawl,** or **schooner.** The boat may be of a different construction–steel, fiberglass, or aluminum. The keel may change from the fin shape that we have seen so far to a full-length keel on an offshore cruising yacht.

In this part, we will discuss the selection of sails on a cruising boat. Sails, like tires for a car, come in different designs, sizes, and materials. Cruising sails have qualities different from those of some racing sails, while other characteristics are the same.

The ASA Basic Coastal Cruising standard states that you should be able to perform as a helmsman and crew member on a 20- to 30-foot boat in moderate weather and in local waters. You should be able to anchor the boat, reef the mainsail, change the foresail, and safely negotiate the boat in and out of its slip under sail or power. In short, you should be able to sail.

SAIL SELECTION

Contrary to popular belief, new sailboats are seldom sold with sails included. It may seem strange for a sailboat to be sold without sails, but the selection of a sailmaker is a personal choice.

Cruising sails are usually cut from slightly heavier sailcloth than racing sails, and the seams are reinforced. Racing sails may also be constructed from more exotic and expensive materials such as Mylar and Kevlar.

Sails can be divided into four main categories: mains (and **mizzens**), **foresails** (what we have been calling jibs), **staysails,** and **spinnakers.** We have already discussed the mainsail at great length. The mizzen, the furthest aft sail on a yawl or ketch, is simply another type of mainsail and is handled in the same manner.

The foresails (jibs and genoas) are set from the headstay. The difference between a jib and a genoa is size. A genoa, when it

Different sailing rigs

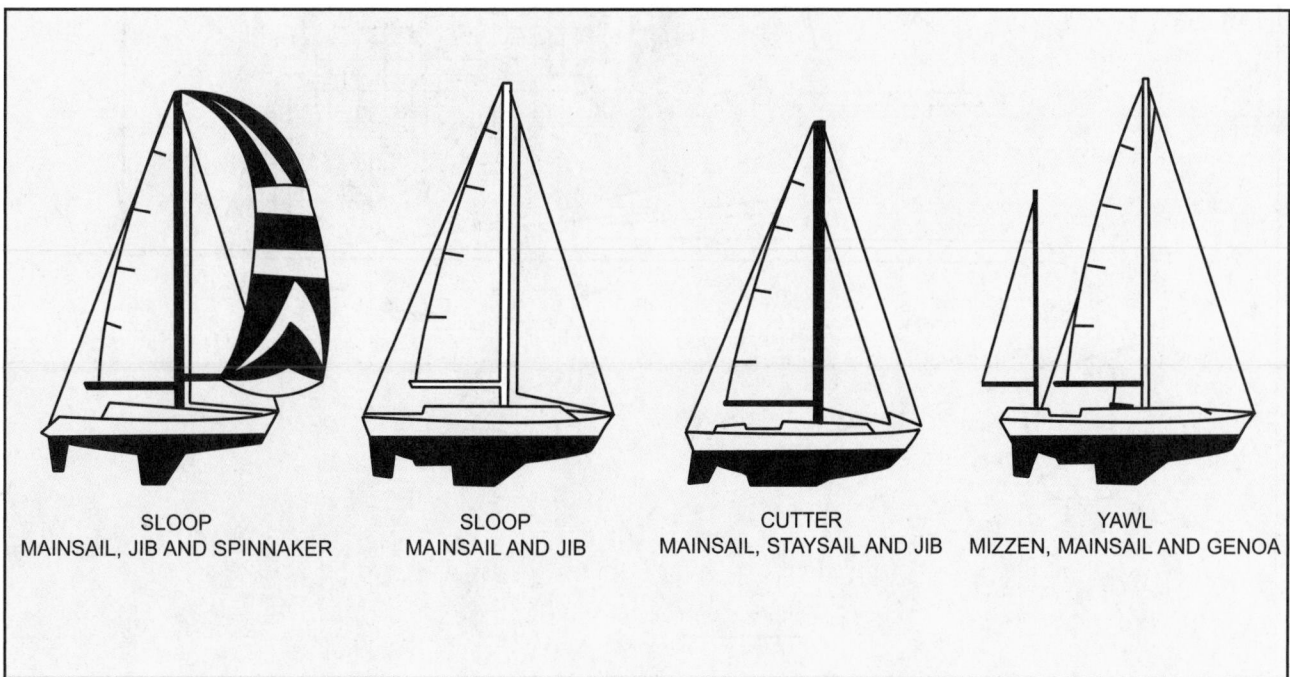

SLOOP	SLOOP	CUTTER	YAWL
MAINSAIL, JIB AND SPINNAKER	MAINSAIL AND JIB	MAINSAIL, STAYSAIL AND JIB	MIZZEN, MAINSAIL AND GENOA

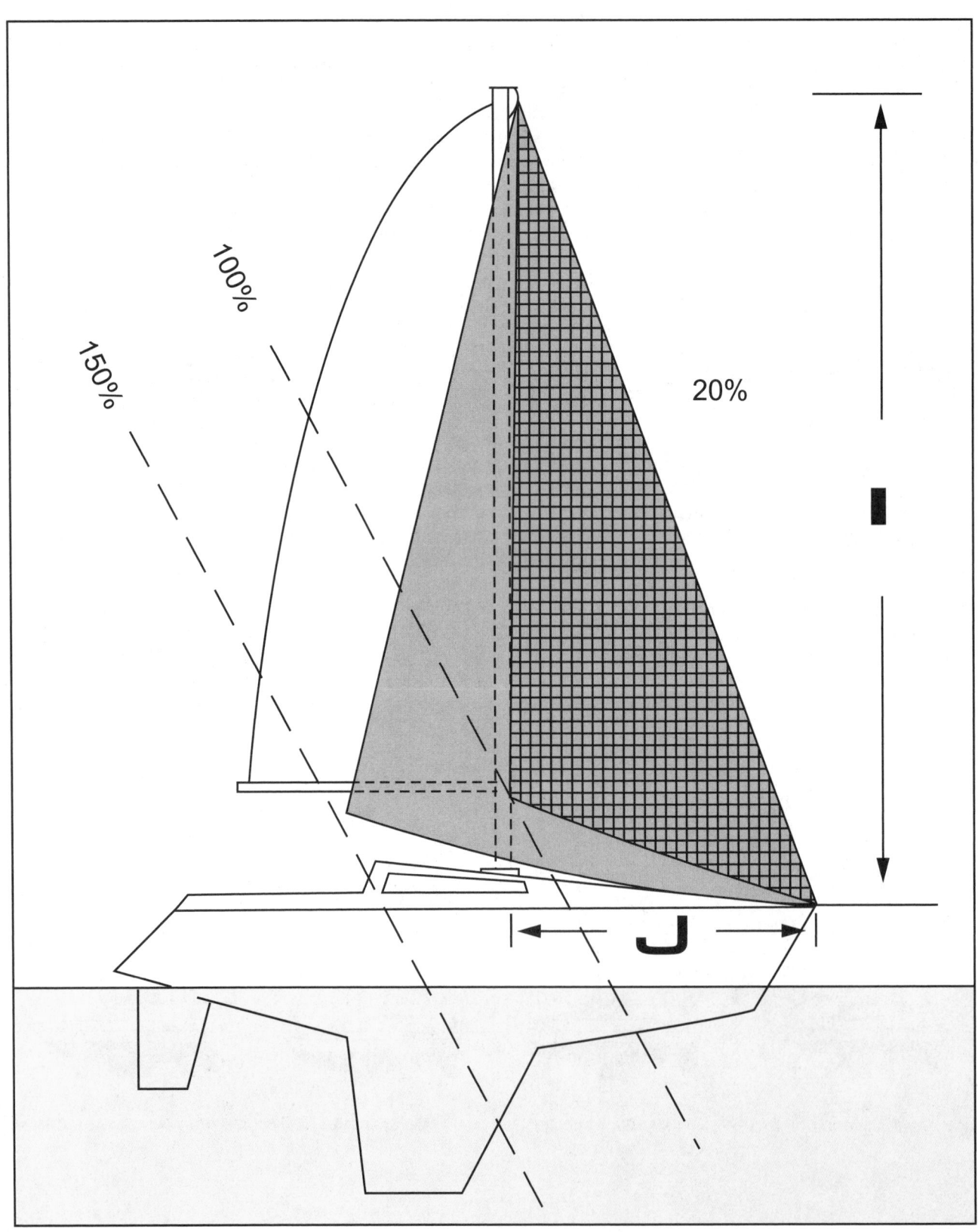

Foretriangle, 100% jib, 150% genoa

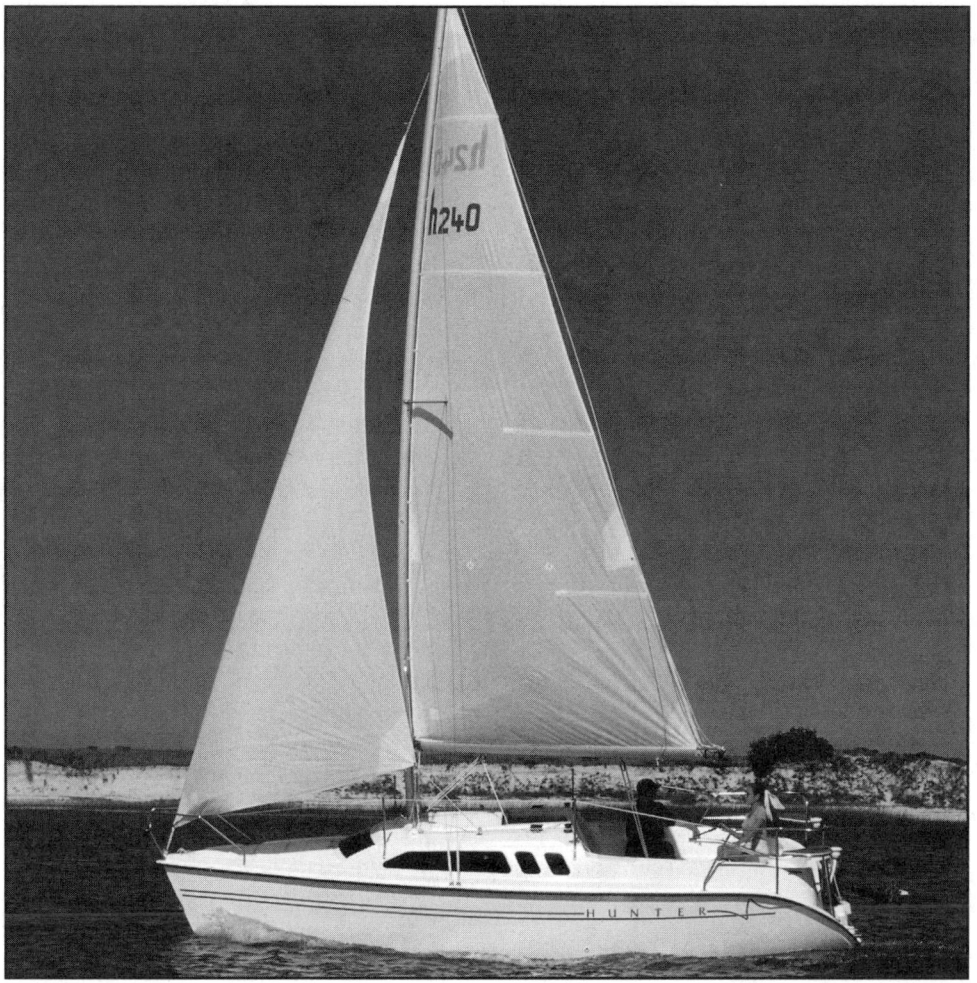

100% jib

is set for close-hauled sailing, will overlap the mast, while a jib is smaller and will not. Genoas and jibs are named according to size, and two systems are used. They may simply be numbered 1, 2, 3, etc. (1 being the largest). If the foresails are labeled according to their foot length relative to the distance between the mast and forestay, then percentages are used-100 percent, 120 percent, 150 percent, etc. The number 1 genoa, with the largest overlap, is 150 percent.

Sails are sometimes rated according to how much wind they will withstand without stretching. This is a measure of the strength of the sailcloth used and the construction of the sail. The wind the sail is designed to withstand is usually stronger than the strongest wind in which a new skipper can control the boat. Therefore, a new skipper doesn't have to be concerned with a sail's rating. In strong winds, the skipper should choose a smaller and heavier sail based on the handling characteristics of the boat and the ability of the skipper and crew.

A sloop-rigged cruising sailboat should have a minimum sail inventory of a mainsail with two sets of reef points (see Reefing Systems, p. 173), a regular number 1 genoa (150 to 170 percent), and a working jib (80 to 100 percent). This minimum selection of sails will allow the boat to sail in light winds (using the genoa), while still being able to cope with stronger winds (using the jib and a reefed mainsail).

WEATHER

Armed with some simple facts, the knowledgeable sailor can predict most weather. Thus, the skipper can take appropriate action-in crew preparation, destination plans, and sail reduction-to ensure the safety of the crew and vessel.

WEATHER REPORTS

First, a prudent sailor must know where to get accurate weather information before going sailing. There are many reliable sources for the large-scale weather picture, but local weather forecasting is a matter of being able to read the weather signs. What is experienced at the local weather station or at the airport may not be the same as what you experience on the water.

The primary source of marine weather information is the marine weather bands on VHF radio. Channels W1 and W2 broadcast continuous weather reports, updated regularly every three to six hours. Listen to the VHF before setting out, then monitor it on a regular basis throughout your sail. The broadcast contents vary, but in general they contain:

• a description of weather patterns affecting the broadcast area, including coastal waters

• regional and state forecasts with the outlook for three days ahead

• marine forecasts and warnings for coastal waters

• observations from selected National Weather Service and Coast Guard stations

• radar summaries and reports

• local weather observations and forecasts

• special bulletins and summaries concerning severe weather

• tide reports

Another source of weather information is commercial radio stations. Most stations in coastal areas (including lakes) broadcast a marine weather forecast periodically. The frequencies of these commercial stations and the broadcast times of weather reports are available from a local boating almanac (source of local marine information). Keep the published broadcast schedule on the boat beside the AM/FM radio.

Although no longer required, some Coast Guard installations and marinas at harbor mouths still display storm-warning flags to warn sailors of what to expect past the calm of the sheltered harbor. They have boats on the water reporting local weather that may not be covered in the more general forecasts. Reports transmitted through the local Coast Guard station are often available. Depending upon the size of the station, you may get a recorded message; or you might get lucky and be able to talk directly to someone. Look in the federal government listings in the phone book under Department of Transportation for USCG Weather Information.

If the small craft warning flags are flying, only experienced sailors should go out. The higher wind warnings mean no small craft should sail that day.

All airports have a weather reporting service. Large airports will use a telephone recording, while in smaller communities you may be able to talk to the meteorologist on duty. If this is the case, you may be able to learn some things not included in the official forecast such as an approaching storm front which has just appeared on the local radar. Airport weather information is also listed under the Department of Transportation heading in the phone book.

WIND FORCES

The Beaufort scale is one way to measure and describe the wind velocity. Most U.S. weather reports refer to wind velocity in **knots** - nautical miles per hour.

Beaufort Scale (expressed as "force X" such as "force 5".

0 calm: sea like a mirror

1 light air: Ripples with the appearance of scales but without foam crests; wind 1-3 knots

2 light breeze: small wavelets, short but pronounced; crests have a glassy appearance and do not break; wind 4-6 knots; wave height 1 foot

3 gentle breeze: large wavelets with crests beginning to break, foam of glassy appearance, occasional whitecaps; wind 7-10 knots; wave height 2 feet

4 moderate breeze: small waves, becoming longer; fairly frequent whitecaps; wind 11-16 knots; wave height 3 feet

5 fresh breeze: moderate waves, taking a more pronounced long form; many whitecaps formed (chance of some spray); wind 17-21 knots; wave height 6 feet

6 strong breeze: large waves beginning to form; the white foam crests more extensive (probably some spray); wind 22-27 knots; wave height 10 feet

7 near gale: sea heaps up; white foam from breaking waves beginning to be blown in streaks; wind 28-33 knots; wave height 13 feet

8 gale: moderately high waves of greater length; edges of crests beginning to break into spindrift; foam blown in well-marked streaks; wind 34-40 knots; wave height 18 feet

9 strong gale: high waves; dense streaks of foam; crests of waves beginning to topple, tumble, and roll over; spray may affect visibility; wind 41-47 knots; wave height 22 feet

10 storm: very high waves with long overhanging crests; great patches of foam blown in dense white streaks; the whole surface of the sea taking on a white appearance; the tumbling of the sea heavy and shocklike; visibility affected; wind 48-55 knots; wave height 29 feet

11 violent storm: exceptionally high waves (small and medium ships may be lost to view behind the waves); sea completely covered with long white patches of foam; everywhere the edges of the wave crests blown into froth; visibility affected; wind 56-63 knots; wave height 36 feet

12 hurricane: air filled with foam and spray, and the sea completely white; visibility greatly reduced; wind speed 64-71 knots; wave height 45 feet.

WHAT CAUSES WEATHER

Before we discuss the visual signs that precede thunderstorms, line squalls, or other types of severe weather, we will look at what causes such disturbances. Weather features such as wind, rain, and storms result from the collisions between air masses of different temperatures.

When a warm air mass meets a cold air mass, the result is a low pressure system. Associated with the low is a series of cold and warm fronts. There are distinctive weather and cloud formations related to each of these fronts. For safety's sake, you must learn which ones can result in severe weather.

Weather associated with a warm front: As a warm front catches up with cooler air, the warmer air rises over the cooler mass. The typical shape is a wedge. As the warm air rises, it cools. Moisture in the air condenses and forms clouds along the wedge.

The first clouds identifying an approaching warm front are hazy thin layers (**cirrus**). These indicate that rain will be

Typical warm front

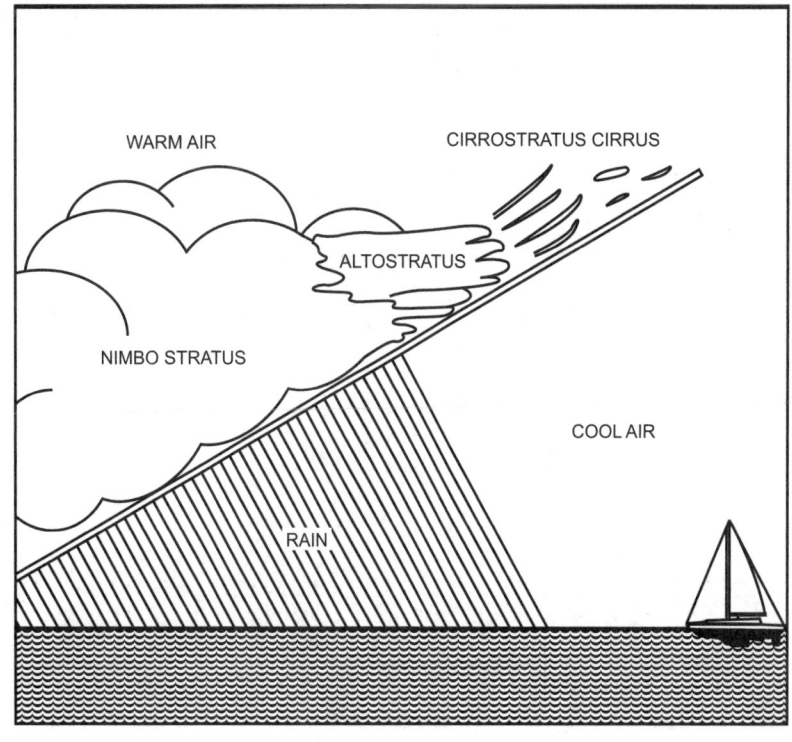

following in less than twenty-four hours. As the cloud layer becomes more defined (**cirrostratus**), the rain is getting closer. With the thicker **altostratus** and **nimbostratus** clouds comes the rain, which is then followed by clear and warmer weather.

Weather associated with a cold front: A cold front tends to produce more severe weather than a warm front. The cooler front forces its way under the warmer air mass. As the warm air is forced up, it condenses rapidly and forms **altocumulus** clouds. These are full and fluffy. As the clouds grow thicker and darker (**nimbostratus** and **cumulonimbus**), the rain comes, and along with it come stronger wind and changes in the wind direction. This weather system can develop into either a thunderstorm or a line squall.

Thunderstorms usually occur along a cold front but can also occur along a warm front. One sign is the formation of large anvil-shaped clouds. There is a discharge of static electricity between the clouds and the earth, causing lightning and thunder. If the wind of the cold front is very strong, it may blow the top off the cumulonimbus cloud before the cloud has the opportunity to build. This results in a quickly passing storm called a **line squall.** The winds of a line squall are short-lived but can be extremely severe. A sign of an approaching line squall is a low rolling cloud. If you see one coming, look for shelter or quickly reduce sail area (double-reef the mainsail) to ride out the storm.

Fog is formed when warm moist air comes into contact with cooler water or land. The warm air may be the leading edge of a warm front. In colder climates (from San Francisco to Vancouver and from Maine to north of Nova Scotia), fog (and rain) on the water are quite common. The colder northern Great Lakes-Superior and Huron-are also very susceptible to fog.

Fog may appear as a whitish haze on the horizon or may form in pockets in harbors and inlets. Fog may fully encompass some sailing areas, while other areas within a few hundred yards remain quite clear.

NAVIGATING IN FOG

In fog the greatest danger to any vessel is collision with either the shore or another vessel. The following procedures are all designed to minimize one or both of these risks. It is also especially important in fog to handle the boat cautiously.

Slow down. As well as giving you more time to take avoiding action, slowing down in a motor boat will also make it easier to hear the sounds of other vessels.

Keep a good lookout. This includes "listening out" too. Every available person should be posted on deck, away from engine and other noise, to look and listen. In particular, someone should be posted at the bow. Sounds can be deceptive in fog; the source of a sound may not lie in the direction from which it appears to be coming.

Make sound signals. For the appropriate signals for a power-driven vessel,

Typical cold front

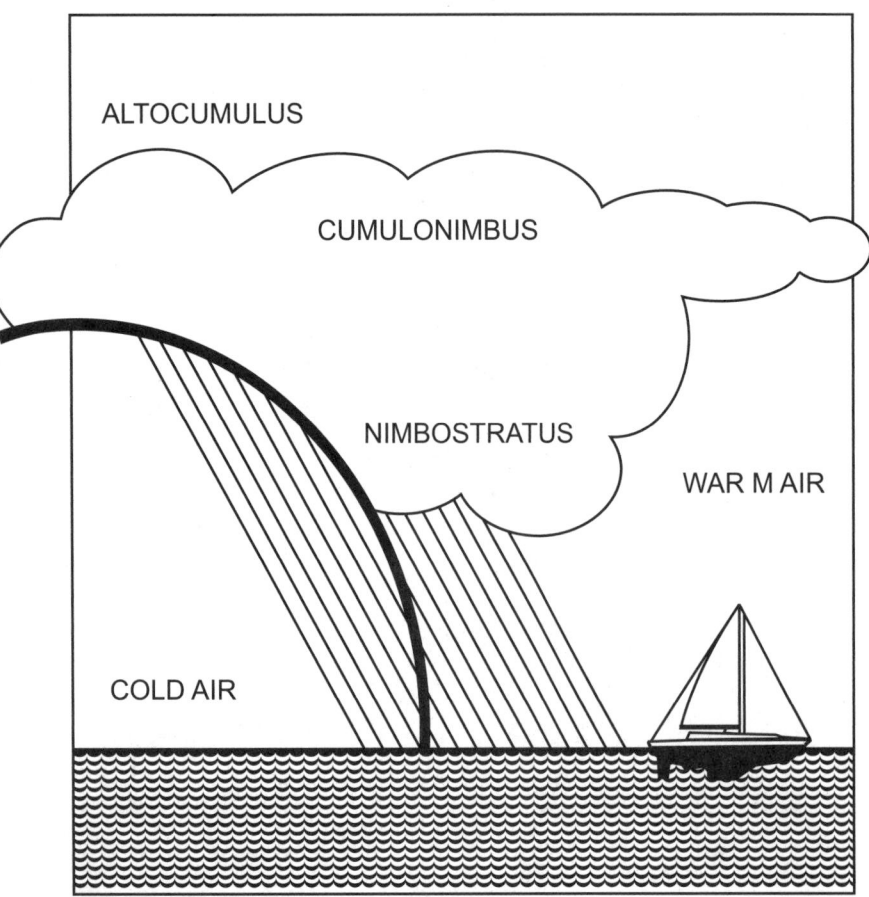

ALTOCUMULUS

CUMULONIMBUS

NIMBOSTRATUS

WAR M AIR

COLD AIR

sailing vessel, and vessel at anchor in restricted visibility, see the chart below.

Hoist a radar reflector. The larger it is and the higher it is, the better. In any event it should be at least eighteen inches from comer to comer and not less than twelve feet above sea level. It should be hoisted with one straight edge, not a corner, uppermost.

Keep clear of shipping lanes. If you must cross one, do so at right angles to the flow of traffic. The safest place for a small boat is in water too shallow for big ships. If you find yourself becalmed or moving very slowly across a shipping lane, you should start the engine to get clear of it. Stop the engine at intervals to listen, as you would in any other power-driven vessel.

SOUND SIGNALS IN RESTRICTED VISIBILITY

— power vessel making way

— — power vessel under way but not making way through the water

—•• vessel not under command, vessel restricted in her ability to maneuver, vessel constrained by her draft, sailing vessel, vessel engaged in fishing, vessel towing or pushing

—••• vessel being towed

vessel at anchor. In the case of a vessel more than 328 feet long, the bell is rung in the fore part of the vessel and followed by a five-second sounding of a gong aft.

•—• warning signal to an approaching vessel made in addition to the signal above

vessel aground

It is particularly important in fog to keep an accurate record of your course and distance run and to plot your position regularly on the chart. This means steering as straight a course as possible (use a compass), which is easy to forget when you are concentrating on keeping a lookout.

It is dangerous to get too close to the shore in thick fog, even if you know it well and it is free from outlying dangers. It is often better to anchor and wait for the fog to lift, provided you are clear of shipping lanes

and other hazards. If you must approach the shore, do so at right angles to the coast and go in slowly, using the depth sounder. On a shore with cliffs, echoes of your fog signals may also give you some warning of when land is just ahead.

General precautions: All members of the crew should wear life jackets, and the life raft should be ready for immediate launching. Keep some flares ready for instant use to draw attention to yourself if there is a danger of collision with a larger vessel.

VISUAL SIGNS

In the absence of an official forecast or to supplement an official forecast, you can tell a good deal about the likely development of the weather in your own area from the barometer and your own observations. Of course, these layman forecasting methods are by no means infallible.

Barometric pressure. Rapid changes of pressure usually indicate strong winds. A rise or fall of eight millibars (mb) or more within three hours is often followed by a gale, perhaps in four to eight hours' time. A less rapid change of, say, five mb may indicate strong winds of less than gale force.

A falling barometer is a sign of an approaching depression, but the worst of the wind may not come until the barometer has begun to rise again.

First rise after low
Foretells a stronger blow.

Gales with a rising barometer are usually more squally than gales with a falling barometer.

Normal barometric pressures vary from area to area, but if the barometer is lower than normal, and steady or falling, unsettled weather is indicated. If the barometer is high, and steady or rising, settled weather may be expected.

Clouds are useful weather indicators. For a description of seven different cloud types and their implications, (see p. 167-168). Cirrus and cumulus combinations are particularly noteworthy:

Mackerel skies and mares' tails
Make tall ships carry low sails.

In general, lower clouds indicate bad weather. If a lower cloud formation (or the wind) is moving at an angle to high clouds, a change of weather can be expected. When you stand with your back to the wind or oncoming lower clouds and if the upper clouds are moving from left to right, the change will be for the worse; if the upper clouds are moving from right to left, the change will be for the better. These directions are reversed for the southern hemisphere.

Wind direction. As a very rough rule, in the northern hemisphere the wind backs (changes direction counterclockwise) with the approach of bad weather and veers (changes direction clockwise) with the coming of an improvement, although it may not come immediately. The reverse is true in the southern hemisphere.

You can also tell the direction of the center of a low pressure system from the wind. If you stand with your back to the wind, low pressure is on your left in the northern hemisphere (right in the southern).

Sunsets. A bright yellow sunset often means wind, a pale yellow sunset rain, and a pink sunset fair weather. A "high" sunset, when the sun sets behind a bank of clouds, often gives warning of bad weather, assuming the cloud is approaching from the west. Conversely, when the sun's rays light the upper clouds after it has gone below the horizon, the sky to the west must be clear.

Deteriorating weather is often preceded twenty-four to forty-eight hours ahead of time by some or all of these signs, indicating the approach of a depression:

• barometer falling
• feathery cirrus at high altitude (mares' tails), followed by cirrostratus, then altostratus becoming a thick gray sheet of cloud
• wind veering (backing in the southern hemisphere). If the wind moderates rapidly, then begins to back one more time (veer in the southern hemisphere), and the barometer starts falling again, be prepared for a secondary depression following the first one.

Good weather can be expected to continue when the barometer is high and continues to be steady or rises slowly or when small fleecy cumulus (fair weather cumulus or cirrus) dissolve at high altitude.

Sea fog is formed when relatively warm, moist air comes into contact with a relatively cool sea. In winter and spring the water is normally coldest inshore, so that is where fog forms; in summer and fall the pattern is reversed. Fog also forms over cold ocean currents and where tidal streams stir up cold water from below the surface. Sea fog may persist even in winds of 22 to 27 knots and may not disperse until the arrival of a cold front.

Radiation fog, which forms in damp places inland, sometimes drifts out over the coast, but it tends to lift as it comes into contact with the sea and so it is less of a hazard.

Local winds. Sea breezes occur when the heating of the air over land, often marked by small cumulus clouds, draws in air from the relatively cool sea. Such winds reach their peak in the afternoon and die toward evening. Sea breezes may attain 11 to 16 knots but do not generally occur if the pressure system wind is 17 knots or more. They are a summer phenomenon in temperate latitudes. At night the sea breeze may be replaced by a land breeze, not usually so strong.

Winds tend to be influenced quite substantially by the direction and height of the coastline, being channeled up estuaries or around headlands and often becoming more concentrated in strength. When blowing roughly parallel to the coast, or at a slight angle onto it, the wind often increases in strength within about ten miles of land. This is especially marked on the edges of a high pressure system.

INTERPRETING CLOUDS

Other factors must be taken into consideration when interpreting a cloud formation, apart from the mere appearance of the cloud itself. Do not rely solely on the cloud pattern at any particular moment. Cirrus followed by cirrostratus (see below) often precedes a depression, but cirrus or cirrocumulus may also be visible when a depression has passed and better weather is on the way. Wind direction at sea level, unless it is a sea breeze, is important when interpreting cirrus.

High cloud developments are often not visible because of the presence of clouds at a lower level.

Learn to interpret the following cloud formations:

cirrus (mares' tails): high wispy clouds, often an early warning of bad weather if followed by a buildup of cloud, but wind direction is important. Cirrus dissolving means an improvement.

cirrostratus with a solar halo: a sign of bad weather, especially if it follows cirrus. The larger the halo, the sooner the onset of bad weather.

altocumulus: white and gray, formed in round masses, often partly fibrous. Sometimes a sign of rain, especially when masses break off higher than the rest; these can indicate thunderstorms.

altostratus: a gray cloud sheet formed when cirrostratus thickens. Usually followed by rain, it resembles stratus without its blackness.

nimbostratus with long, ragged clouds (fractostratus) below: may follow cirrostratus. It often accompanies rain and strong winds.

cumulonimbus with characteristic anvil-shaped top: thunderclouds bringing heavy rain and perhaps violent squalls. Such clouds may mark isolated storms or may indicate an approaching front.

cumulus: Small fluffy clouds are a fair weather sign. A buildup of small cumulus over land in the morning may bring sea breezes later. If they grow large, thundery showers can follow.

HEAVY-WEATHER SAILING

Throughout this text we have discussed preparing for each situation and then have built exercises to either simulate or create situations requiring particular sailing skills. Severe weather conditions, however, cannot be simulated in exercises.

In the Sailing Skills section that follows we will preview some routines that should be learned in nice weather so that they will be familiar and can be more easily executed in heavy weather. The keys to being prepared for heavy-weather sailing are practice and routine.

CREW PREPARATION

As bad weather approaches, assuming that it has not been possible to reach a sheltered harbor or marina, the skipper of the vessel will start preparing the crew by assigning the following tasks:

• Put on life jackets and foul weather gear.

• Put on safety harnesses.

• Rig safety lines.

• Reef the mainsail (later in this section).

• Change to a smaller foresail (later in this section) or drop it altogether.

• Stow or tie down all loose gear above and below decks.

• Plot your position on the chart. (This is a subject for the advanced reader and goes beyond the scope of this book.)

REDUCING SAIL AREA AND ITS EFFECT ON BOAT HANDLING

To discover the effect of excess wind on a sailboat, let us return to the simple cat-rigged boat from Part One. As the wind blows into the mainsail, lift is produced. This lift pulls the boat to the side and forward.

As the wind speed increases, there is more power developed than is required to propel the boat through the water. This extra force from the increased wind overpowers the boat. The boat heels excessively and the helmsman now has to pull the

Lift pulls the boat forward.

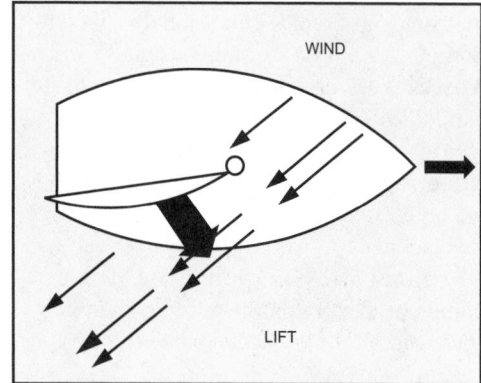

Too much lift creates windward helm and overpowers the boat, causing excess heeling.

The helmsmen is overpowered and uses too much helm to hold a steady course. Note the extreme angle of the tiller.

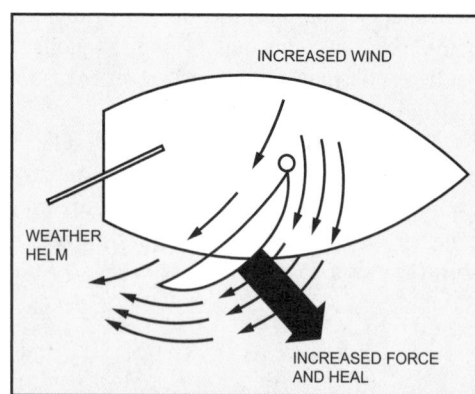

tiller far to windward to keep it sailing in a straight line.

All of this extra force on the sail causes:

- excessive heeling
- weather helm, as the boat wants continually to turn itself into the wind
- added strain on the helmsman, who has to work harder at steering
- added strain on the boat, including more strain on the standing rigging and more strain on the rudder and tiller caused by oversteering to compensate for the weather helm.
- an uncomfortable ride for the passengers and crew. Sailing at an extreme heel is not everyone's idea of a good time.

The quick, short-term solution is to ease the mainsail and spill some of the wind. This works if the wind comes in gusts. If the increase in wind speed is sustained, the remedy is to reduce the amount of sail exposed to the wind so that the boat is propelled efficiently through the water without the added strains and hazards listed above. We reduce mainsail area by reefing.

REEFING SYSTEMS

Looking at the illustration of the mainsail, we see above the tack and clew two reinforced points, the **reefing tack** and **clew.** When the sail is reefed, the reefing tack is secured to the boom by a hook or by a line in the same place the original tack was fastened. What we call the **reefing clew** is an eye, called a **reefing grommet,** set into the leech of the sail. A line called the **reefing line** is led through the grommet, down to the boom, and forward to a cleat (on larger boats, there's a winch to help tighten the line). After the reefing tack is secured, finish taking in the reef by pulling down on the reef line while the sail is luffing. Most cruising boats have two or three pairs of reefing tacks and clews. Each reef shortens the mainsail area by about 25 percent.

After the reef is taken in by securing the tack and pulling down on the leech reefing line, the reefed part of the sail will flap about. To keep this from happening, lead a light quarter-inch line through small holes in the sail, called **reef points,** and around the boom. This line takes the place of old-fashioned short lines dangling from the middle of the sail that you see in pictures of traditional sailing vessels.

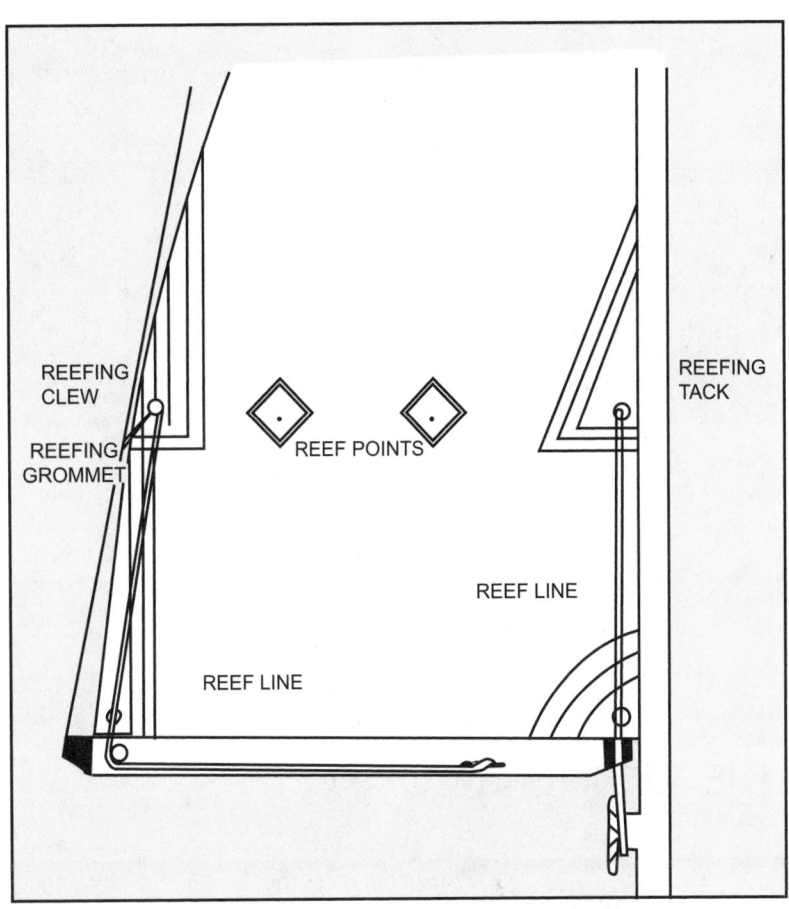

Jiffy reefing

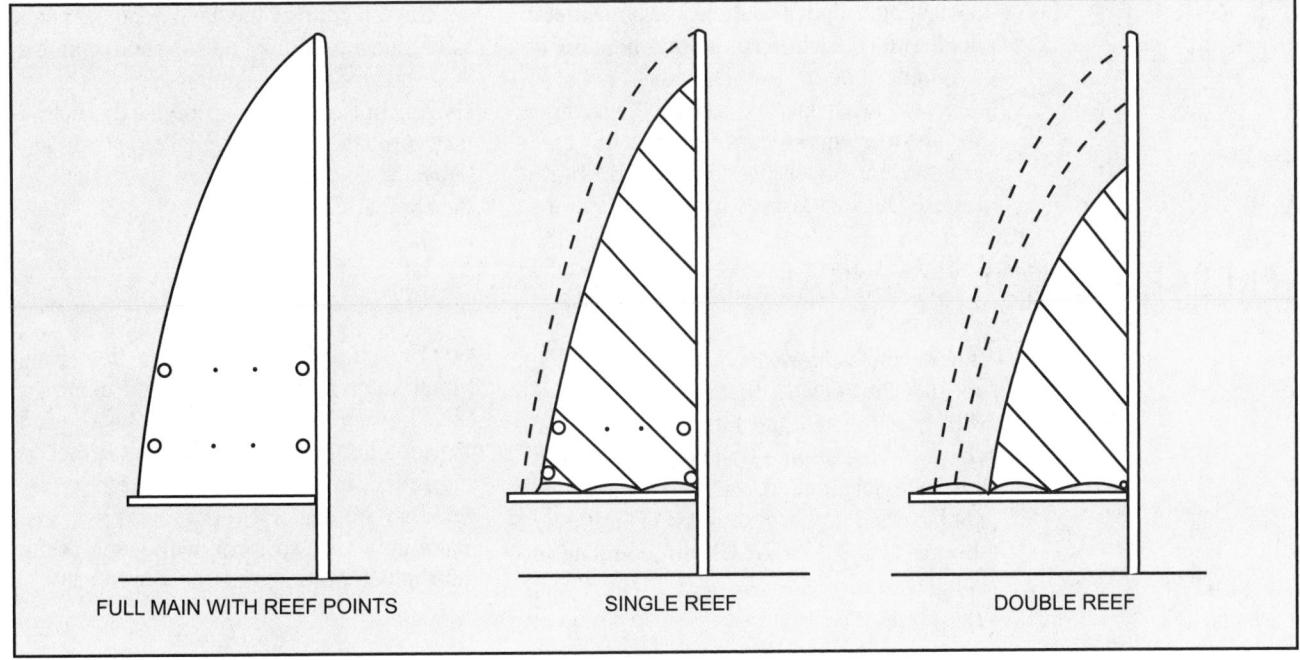

FULL MAIN WITH REEF POINTS   SINGLE REEF   DOUBLE REEF

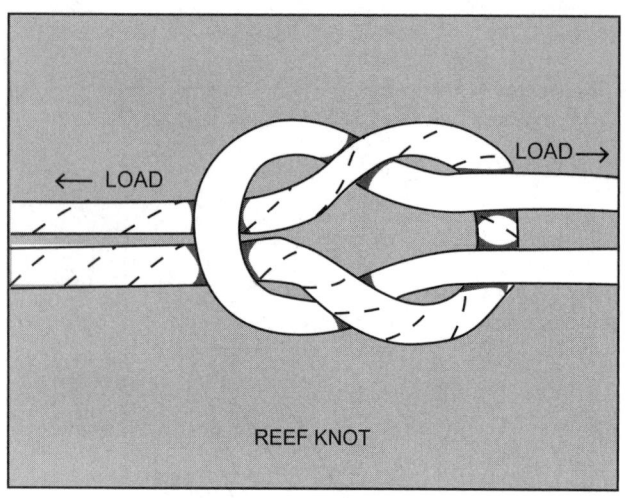

REEF KNOT

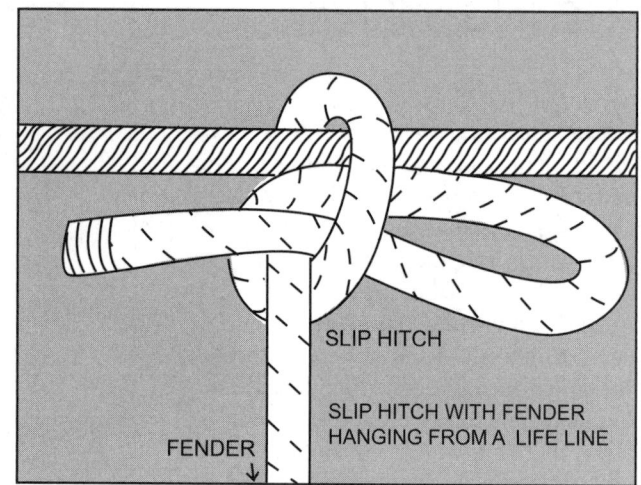

SLIP HITCH

SLIP HITCH WITH FENDER
HANGING FROM A LIFE LINE

FENDER

REEF KNOT AND SLIP HITCH

The reef knot (also called the square knot) is used to tie lines of equal diameter together. A piece of rope through the reef points to secure a sail after being reefed is tied with a reef knot.

The slip hitch is a variation of the reef knot and is not much different from the knot used when tying your shoes. A slip hitch is used when sail ties are nylon webbing, as opposed to rope. A slip hitch is also used on a fender that may have to be moved quickly. When entering an unfamiliar harbor, a fender may have to be adjusted at the last minute. The slip hitch makes this an easy task.

THE MAGNETIC COMPASS

The compass is one of the most important instruments on the boat-if not the most important instrument-because it provides a constant reference point for steering and navigating. Aligned to the earth's magnetic field, with its north arrow always pointing at magnetic north, the compass has 360 degrees clearly marked around the perimeter of the compass card. Around the card are several small posts called **lubber's lines.** The forward, or front, lubber's line lies right over the direction in which the boat is heading.

The compass must be located where the helmsman can see it clearly. In clear weather and during the daytime, most boats sailing near land may be steered by aiming at a buoy or a landmark (an object on shore). But in fog and at night, the helmsman probably won't be able to see any buoys or landmarks, and so must steer by the compass.

PREPARING FOR COASTAL CRUISING

Before you venture from familiar waters, you need to ensure that you are familiar with how to read and interpret a nautical chart and have some basic familiarity with coastal navigation. Coastal navigation is not included in this text, but it is taught by the ASA and USCGAUX in companion courses.

You should also prepare a float plan, which summarizes your planned itinerary, lists the names of persons on board, and provides information about your vessel. A suggested format for this float plan is provided in Appendix B. (You may wish to make up your own form, with some of the information preprinted.) Be sure to leave the float plan with a responsible party (friend, relative, your marina) and with instructions to call the Coast Guard if you do not return at the planned time. (Most maritime law-enforcement agencies-including the Coast Guard-will not act as a repository for your float plan.) Be sure to call this person when you return or if you make changes to the itinerary to let them know that you have arrived safely or changed your plans. Otherwise the Coast Guard or other search and rescue agencies may waste valuable time looking for you.

RUNNING AGROUND AND OTHER NUISANCES

There are three types of sailors in the world: those who have run aground, those who are about to run aground, and those who lie. In 90 percent of the situations, running aground is merely a nuisance and an embarrassment.

Running aground occurs when the navigator misreads the chart, the skipper tries to cut a corner on a harbor entrance, there is **silting** (moving of soft sand and mud) at a harbor mouth, or the tide table is misinterpreted. Running aground can be prevented by avoiding all of the causes listed above, but that is easier said than done.

Listening to the local notice to mariners on the VHF radio (channel 22) will alert a skipper to local hazards such as silting of a channel or **seiches**–changes of water depth caused by strong pressure and/or winds blowing water out of a harbor. Silting is prevalent along the east coast of the United States, and seiches occur regularly on the top end of Chesapeake Bay.

Many pretty anchorages are missed when the skipper of a boat stays in only the deepest water. By all means, avoid running aground on rock and coral-a shipwreck can ruin your whole day. On the other hand, being able to free a vessel after running aground on sand or mud is a skill that all cruising sailors need to acquire and will use.

A vessel runs aground when the depth of water is not sufficient for the draft of the boat. As soon as the boat touches bottom, the helmsman should attempt to reverse direction by coming about or jibing, depending on which point of sail the vessel was on when it started to run aground. This quick maneuver may well save the skipper and crew from having to use the techniques explained below to free the vessel.

Since it is difficult in the short term to make the water deeper (except in tidal water), once you are aground it will be necessary to take other steps, such as:
• heeling the boat
• kedging off, using an anchor
• shifting weight (Put the crew on the boom.)
• taking a tow from another boat
• Waiting for high tide (tidal area only), or
• any combination of the above

HEELING THE BOAT

If sailing off the shoal is not effective, heeling is often a successful solution. When a boat heels to leeward it does not need as much water depth. The skipper of the boat must be quick to assign each member of the crew a job. The largest crew members will all be placed on one side of the boat to make it heel. This effectively reduces the draft and may permit the vessel to be sailed off.

At the same time the engine should be started. A check for lines in the water should be made before the engine is put into gear. This is not the time to add a fouled prop to the predicament.

It may be possible to turn the boat with the aid of the engine until the bow is pointing into deeper water. With the boat heeled and the engine in forward, the helmsman will attempt to drive the boat off the bottom. The helmsman and crew will watch the engine guages to make sure it doesn't overheat. Sand and mud churned up by all the activity may clog the cooling water intake valve. With the sails down and the boat heeled over, it may be possible to motor off in reverse, providing the wind is not too strong.

The boat can be heeled even further by placing some of the crew out on the boom. You can also tie a line into a halyard and secure it to something on shore, to an anchor, or to another boat.

Towing with a bridle (note: deck cleats have been used because the bridle line is too short to reach the mast).

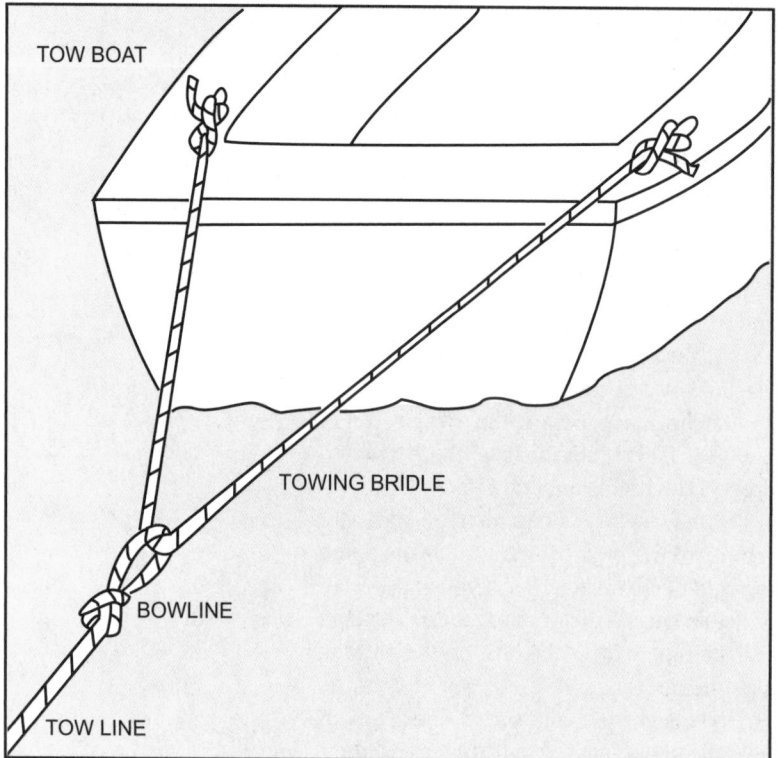

KEDGING OFF

Since an anchor may be used to keep a vessel from going aground in a storm, it seems reasonable that an anchor can be employed to pull a vessel off when it has run aground. This maneuver is called kedging off. To deploy the anchor, row it out in a dinghy. If a small boat is not available, it is possible (but only as a last resort) to have someone swim the anchor offshore by floating it on a PFD or float cushion.

The anchor rode will be led through the bow chock and back to a winch. By winching in the rode, you may be able to pull the bow into open water and refloat the stranded vessel.

TAKING A TOW

When all else fails, the only solution may be to take a tow from a passing boat or from a commercial towing service. Caution must be used to protect the crew of both boats when towing. Don't let anyone stand by the towing line. If it breaks, the recoil can cause severe injury.

The cleats used to tie the boat at night probably aren't constructed or intended to be used for towing. Use them only if you have no other alternative.

Instead, the towed boat should tie one of the dock lines in a loop through one of the bow chocks (or at least under the pulpit), around the mast, in through the other bow chock and then tie the two ends of the rope together using a reef knot or a pair of bowlines. This towing bridle will distribute the towing pull over the greatest area of the boat. The major part of the load will be taken by the strongest part of the boat-the mast.

The towing boat, if it is a sailboat, should rig a line the same way through the stern chocks. A powerboat should attach a bridle around the cabin or at least two deck cleats if that is all there is available. Taking up speed very slowly, the towing boat will then attempt to free the boat that is aground.

The tow line should be attached to the towing bridle with a bowline. Towing puts a great strain on a line, and the bowline knot is easy to untie. Also, the loop formed by the bowline around the towing line helps ensure the tow boat can maneuver properly.

DEALING WITH TIDES WHEN AGROUND

It is easier to get off if the tide is rising. If it is high or falling at a fast rate, speed in getting off is essential. If the boat is stranded by the retreating tide, you should try to make sure, by weight distribution or a line from the top of the mast, that she settles against the uphill slope (if any) of a bank or shoal. The most critical time is as the boat settles on her bilge, when damage may be caused by pounding.

If the tide is flooding (coming in) when the boat goes aground, an anchor should be set offshore to keep the boat from going further aground. The crew can just sit until the boat is refloated by the tide.

If aground on an ebb tide (tide going out), and all attempts to free the boat have failed, follow these steps:

1. An anchor is set further offshore to keep the boat from going further aground.

2. The crew pads the side of the hull to protect against damage if the bottom uncovers (dries) at low tide.

3. The navigator or skipper reads the tide tables to determine when the tide will come back in.

4. The crew then tries to figure out how to prevent the same situation from happening again.

DAMAGE CONTROL

When you're sailing in waters with muddy or sandy bottoms, running aground will not cause much damage. However, you should check for leaks immediately if the impact was a hard one. Minor damage can often be stopped temporarily by covering it on the inside with a bunk cushion or something similar, then wedging it in place with an oar, boat hook, or anything nearby.

SPRINGING A LEAK

One of the most disconcerting things that can happen on a boat is to find water in the bilge after it has supposedly been pumped dry (see bilge pumps, p. 147). This usually means the boat has a leak someplace.

One of the most obvious places is around the through-hull fittings-the valves that let water into the boat for cooling the engine or that let water out from the sink and head. Inspect each fitting to find the problem. It may be as simple as a loose clamp or a broken hose that can be stopped by closing the valve or plugging it with a tapered wood plug (see Essential Safety Equipment, p. 144). Also check the keel bolts for leaks.

If the leak is more serious, plug it with rags, use a sail bag, or even wrap a sail around the outside of the hull. If the leak is at the waterline, heel the boat to the opposite side. If there is any doubt as to the seriousness of the leak, radio the Coast Guard for advice and assistance.

RIGGING FAILURE

If a piece of equipment breaks or is on the verge of breaking, the first step is to remove any pressure from it. There are four major parts of the rig that may fail: the mast, forestay, backstay, and shrouds.

If the mast breaks, the most important concern is to keep the broken section of the mast from damaging the hull. This could mean cutting away the wire supports and the mast. If the sails and mast can be salvaged without any risk to the safety of the crew or boat, they should be.

If a shroud breaks, the helmsman should tack immediately to put the strain on the opposite side of the rigging.

If the forestay fails, the helmsman should immediately bear away to a broad reach or a run. This will cause the pressure on the sails and mast to be forward, taking any additional strain off the luff of the jib. The jib should be left hoisted to support the mast temporarily from the front until a spare halyard can be rigged to the bow and tightened to act as a headstay.

If the backstay breaks, sheet in the mainsheet as hard as possible. The support of the mast normally borne by the backstay will be taken over by the leech of the main sail. Heading upwind will reduce the pressure on the leech. Rig a halyard aft to the stern and tighten. This will act as a temporary backstay allowing you to ease the main,

STEERING FAILURE

If the tiller breaks, the wheel ceases to turn the rudder, or the rudder falls off, the boat can be steered with the sails. In our first exercise in Part One, we found that under mainsail alone the boat tended to head toward the wind. This caused weather helm. Under jib alone, the opposite happens: a lee helm develops and the boat tends to turn away from the wind.

By using these two forces and balancing them when we want to travel in a straight line, we can steer the boat and even come about or jibe. We will practice steering with the sails in the Sailing Skills section that follows.

DRAGGING ANCHOR

If the boat is dragging anchor, the first action is to increase scope (let out more rode) and possibly rig another anchor. If this does not work, the anchor should be hauled up and the vessel re-anchored. If the decision is to re-anchor, the skipper should reconsider the suitability of the anchorage. If the conditions that caused the anchor to drag make the anchorage dangerous to the boat, then the skipper will have to decide whether to select a new site or simply to sail until conditions change. Don't get pinned in an unsafe anchorage.

FOULED PROP

Occasionally a line will get tangled in the propeller. The helmsman should stop the engine immediately (if the engine has not already stalled). Pulling on the line that has committed the impropriety may remedy the situation, but don't count on it. The second option is to send someone over the side to unravel, or as a last resort, cut away the line. The crew on deck should be watching for other vessels or obstacles. It may be necessary to sail to a dock or mooring and secure the boat before cutting the line.

BROKEN HALYARD

If a halyard or shackle breaks while sailing, the next step is to pull the sail down and hoist it again on another halyard, if available.

SERIOUS EMERGENCIES

Most situations are nuisances and nothing more. Prepare for them. Have the proper equipment to handle any of these annoyances quickly and in a seamanlike manner. Don't panic. Sometimes, however, you may find yourself in a serious emergency. Somebody may be badly injured or ill, or the boat may be sinking or her mast may break. If that happens, stay calm, do the best you can to cope with the situation using aids and equipment that you have on board, and call for help. To summon help, use the boat's radio, if there is one, or any of several approved visual signals. These signals are taken from the U. S. Coast Guard's "Navigation Rules."

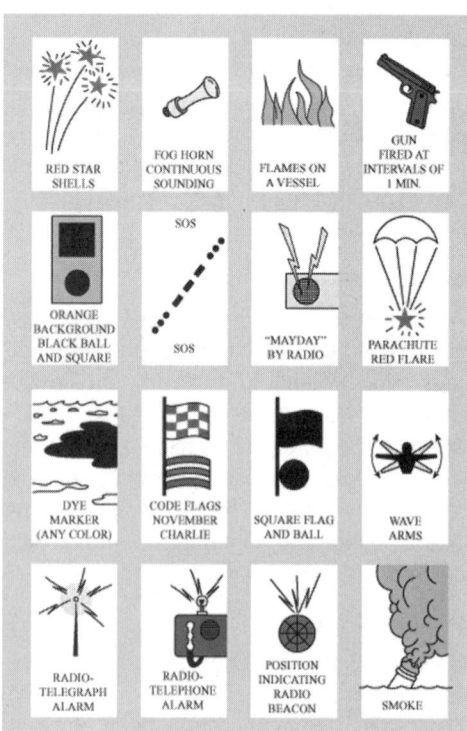

Official distress signals

REVIEW QUESTIONS

1. Knots have been taught throughout the book. Identify the knots from the following pictures and give one use for each.

KNOT   USE

a) _____ _____
b) _____ _____
c) _____ _____
d) _____ _____
e) _____ _____

2. Which sail would you be most likely to choose for very light wind?
a) 90 percent jib
b) 150 percent genoa
c) storm jib

3. Bad weather comes from
a) high pressure systems
b) low pressure systems

4. More violent weather is usually associated with
a) warm fronts
b) cold fronts

5. What kinds of weather do the following clouds precede?
a) cumulonimbus clouds
b) low rolling clouds

6. Describe the first action to be taken in each of the following situations:

a) You run aground (no tide)._____
_____

b) The boat springs a leak. _____
_____

c) Part of the standing rigging fails. _____
_____

d) The steering fails. _____
_____

e) The prop fouls. _____
_____

Answers in Appendix A, p. 201.

SAILING SKILLS

In this Sailing Skills section, three new skills will be presented: reefing, sailing a compass course, and steering with sails only. The balance of the on-the-water session will be devoted to evaluating your ability to act as skipper and crew. To preview the evaluation, we introduce the ASA Basic Coastal Cruising checklist (see p. 184-185).

You should be able to perform the role of both skipper and of crew for each of the performance objectives on the list. The completed checklist will help you identify weaknesses in your sailing skills. You are not expected to achieve a perfect score. The aim is to perform each maneuver safely and with control. If any item cannot be completed, you will know exactly what has to be practiced. Review the section in the book, and go out and work on those skills in your next on-the-water session. Some items just need practice. But now, on to new skills.

REEFING

Reefing-reducing sail area-can be accomplished in a number of different ways. It is important to reef before there is so much wind that the process becomes too difficult or dangerous. On a windy day, the reef should be taken in before leaving the dock so that the sail is raised in a reduced form. The reef can also be taken in at anchor or when hove to. It is always easier to take out a reef that is not required than it is to put one in when it is too windy. Better safe than sorry.

The crew has rigged first and second reef lines. A reef line should be led any time heavy weather is anticipated.

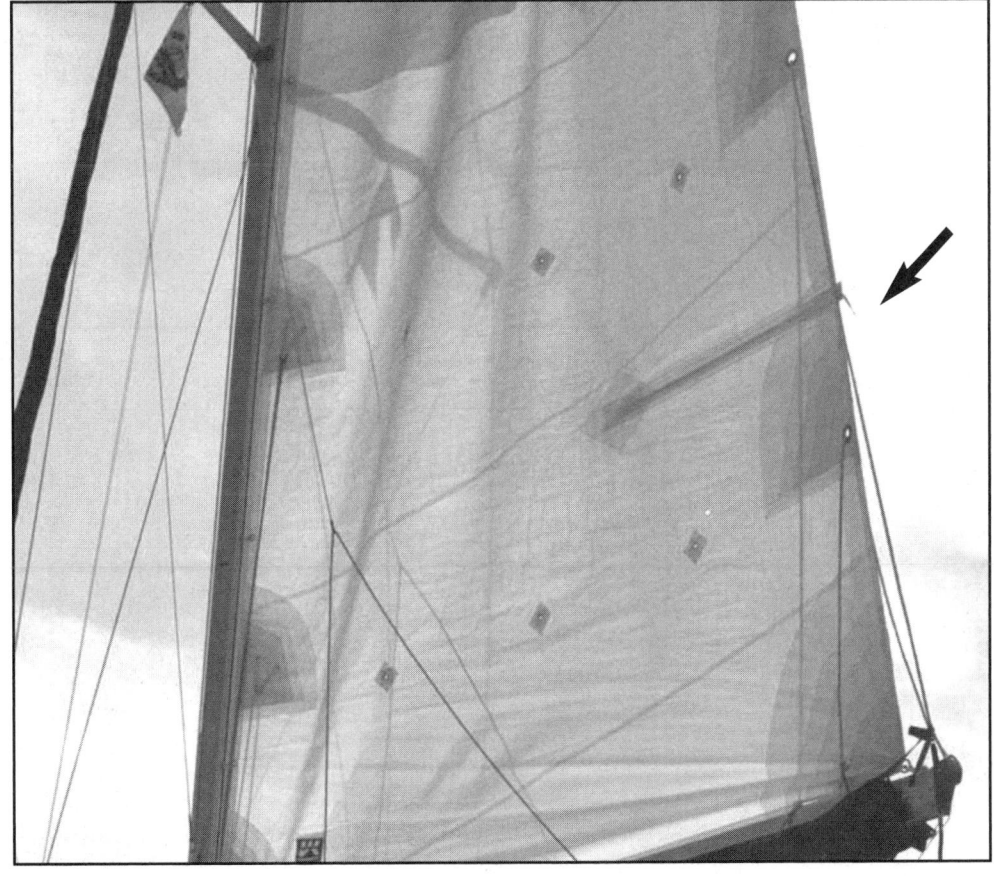

EXERCISE: **REEFING IN**

Practice this procedure while the boat is docked, moored, anchored, or hove to.

1. The helmsman positions the boat so that the wind is at least 30 degrees off the bow, as when raising sails.

2. The crew checks that the topping lift is secured so that the boom will not fall to the deck as the main halyard is released. The mainsheet and boom vang are then released.

3. Luff the mainsail by easing the sheet.

4. One of the crew at the main halyard lowers the sail until the reefing tack is at the boom.

5. Secure the reefing tack of the sail by the hook or reefing line and rehoist the halyard to the proper tension. Better too tight than too loose.

6. Pull in the reefing line through the leech grommet and cleat it to secure the clew close to the boom. (Use a winch if necessary.)

7. Tie the excess sail area to the boom with fight lines or sail ties led through the grommets in the sail.

8. Sheet in the mainsail.

To undo or shake out the reef, reverse the procedure. It is possible to reef underway by sailing on the jib and letting the main luff.

Reefing greatly reduces sail, making the boat easier to handle in heavier winds.

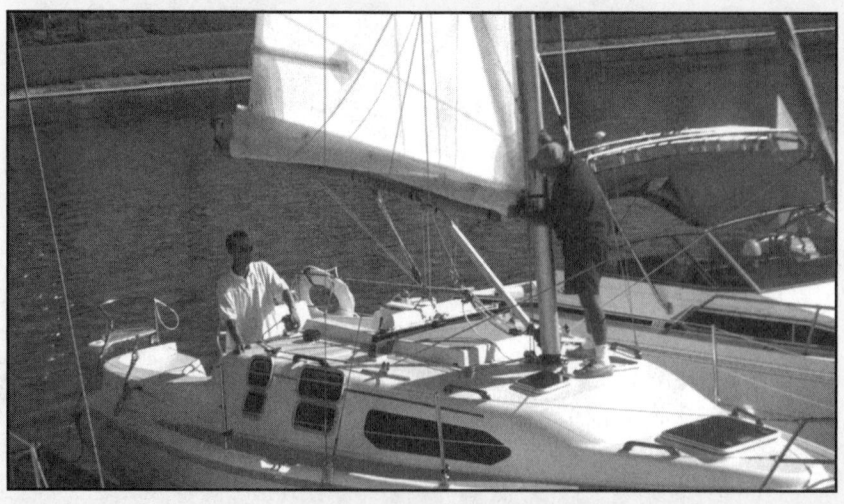

SAILING A COMPASS COURSE

The helmsman should learn how to use the various indicators that are available to help steer a course.

In very calm water, the helmsman should be able to steer a very accurate course. But if there are waves, steering the precise compass course will be impossible. The boat will wander to either side of the course, perhaps as much as 5 degrees. This is acceptable. Using an object ahead as a guide, the helmsman should try to balance out the wanders to either side so that the boat averages the original compass course as it makes way toward the object. This will take some practice. It is important that the helmsman not simply stare at the compass. Doing so distracts him from the destination and from the sails, weather, waves, objects in the water, and boat traffic around him.

EXERCISE: **SAILING A COMPASS COURSE**

1. While sailing on a reach, the helmsman selects a buoy or a landmark (for example, a water tower or a large building) that lies ahead at a distance of half a mile or more.

2. The helmsman aims the boat directly at the object, and the crew trims the sails properly and keeps a lookout for other boats.

3. The helmsman then looks at the compass to see what compass course the boat is sailing. This is the number just under the forward lubber's line (the front post inside the glass dome).

4. Moving his eyes back and forth between the compass and the object ahead, the helmsman tries to steer a steady compass course.

STEERING WITH THE SAILS

In case your steering equipment ever fails, you should know how to steer a boat by sails alone. Practice this technique in open water, away from land and other boats.

EXERCISE: **STEERING WITH THE SAILS**

1. The helmsman ties the tiller or wheel in a central position.

2. The crew releases the jib and trims the mainsheet. This will cause the boat to head up.

3. The crew releases the mainsheet and trims the jib. The boat will bear away.

4. The crew then trims the mainsheet and eases the jib sheet until the boat is sailing in a straight line.

5. When this has been accomplished, the crew trims the mainsheet, releases the jib sheet, and holds this trim until the boat is head to wind.

6. The crew then trims the jib sheet on the windward side to back the jib. This will force the bow of the boat away from the wind on the new tack. By balancing the sails, steer the boat in a straight line on the new tack.

BASIC COASTAL CRUISING CHECKLIST

This checklist for the Basic Coastal Cruising standard can be used as a guide for what you have learned or are about to learn. It itemizes the minimum skills an individual should possess when taking an auxiliary-powered sailboat on the water.

PRELIMINARIES

Put on life jacket.
Give verbal checklist (Appendix C).
Produce equipment on checklist and note deficiencies.
Put on sails.
Furl sails neatly.

GETTING UNDER WAY

Check for gas leaks (sniff or smell).
If outboard, check motor secure on bracket with safety line.
Bilge blower turned on.
Start motor in neutral. Check cooling water.
One man only on the bow.
All lines on board and shipshape.
Cast off all lines.
Engage motor.

Demonstrate Proper Winch Techniques

When to use winches
Proper wrapping technique on winch (hand safety)
Removal of winch handle after use

MANEUVERING UNDER POWER

Stop the boat (with bow half a boat length from mark, using reverse).
Steer straight course on approach.
Use a speed slow enough.

Parallel Docking

Correct approach
Slow speed
Correct distance from dock
Boat stopped without using lines
Bow stopped before mark

Anchoring

Choose good location for anchoring.
Use safe foredeck procedures.
Lower anchor properly.
Pay out good scope for depth and tide.
Check the drag.
Raise the anchor.
Override the anchor.
Use slow speed when hauling in anchor.

BOAT HANDLING UNDER SAIL

Hoisting Sails

Check topping lift.
Hoist and set mainsail.
Tension mainsail luff.
Coil and hang halyard.
Check figure eight used as stopper knot on halyard and sheets.
Bear off slightly and hoist jib.
Tension jib luff.
Coil and hang halyard.

Lowering Sails

Start motor in neutral.
Bring boat near head to wind.
Check jib sheets inboard.
Check main hatch closed.
Lower jib and secure halyard.
Secure jib.
Attend to topping lift.
Lower mainsail.
Furl mainsail neatly.
Secure halyard and sheets.

SAILING

Beating

Helmsman sails close to wind.
Crew sets sails appropriately.

Reaching

Helmsman sails a compass course.
Crew trims sails appropriately.

Running

Helmsman keeps wind slightly off the stern.
Crew sets sails as full as possible.

Tacking

Helmsman uses proper commands.
Helmsman selects new heading.
Helmsman executes maneuver smartly.
Crew gives proper responses.
Crew releases sheets at proper time.
Crew retrims sheets correctly.

Jibing

Helmsman uses correct commands.
Helmsman selects new heading.

Helmsman controls mainsheet.
Helmsman executes maneuver smartly.
Crew releases sheets with proper timing.
Crew controls mainsheet.
Crew retrims sheets correctly.

Heading Up

Helmsman sails closer to wind.
Crew trims sails correctly.

Bearing Away

Helmsman sails farther downwind.
Crew trims sails correctly.

Luffing Up

Helmsman brings boat higher up to
wind, without sail adjustment.
Crew eases sheets to cause luff.

REEFING

Boat has sufficient sea room.
Helmsman maintains control.
Crew is safe during procedure.
Complete reefing procedure carried out.

Man Overboard Drill

Hail "Man overboard."
Post lookout.
Toss life ring.
Turn vessel to a beam reach or
downwind.

Use proper approach to victim.
Secure victim.
Bring victim aboard.
Explain one method of bringing victim
aboard when shorthanded.

Securing the Vessel for the Night

Shut off fuel.
Leave motor in neutral.
Run bilge blower if inboard.
Remove key from switch.
Leave proper lines in place and secure.

Making Fast

Bow and stern lines in place
Spring lines in place
Fenders placed correctly
Dock lines coiled where applicable
Halyard secured and away from mast
Lines coiled and hung
Valuables below (winch handles, etc.)
Boat locked
Belongings and garbage ashore

Knots

Tie the following knots:
Reef
Round turn and two half hitches
Bowline
Figure eight
Clove hitch
Sheet bend

SUMMARY

In these six parts we have presented all the basic information you need to sail a small boat. We have not discussed big boat cruising, navigation, or offshore (ocean) sailing, all of which require more experience and training. Sailing is a continual learning process. That is why ASA standards promote continued education.

Now that you have completed the basic instructional part of this book, you are ready to enjoy sailing with your friends and family. For those of you seeking special tips on dinghies, sailboards, and catamarans, continue on to Part Seven. But whatever you sail, you will find every trip a new experience. Learn from each one. There's a new world of fun and adventure ahead of you. Learning to sail is the key to that world.

Special Sailing Information

SPECIAL SAILING INFORMATION

DINGHY SAILING

There are some principles of sailing that apply equally to a Sunfish or a 12-meter yacht. Mastering one helps you master the others.

Small boats such as dinghies have grown in popularity over the past decades due to their affordability. Recently there has been a huge growth in sailboards, catamarans, and even small cruising boats. The trend is toward easier-to-handle, self-righting boats. Generally, small dinghies are relatively unstable and capsize following the simplest mistake. It is valuable to hone your skills with dinghy sailing before moving up in size. The best large boat sailors are the ones who learned on small boats first.

SAILING TO WINDWARD

Sit on the windward side so you can watch the sails working together and see where you are heading. Keep your back to the wind, face the sail, and sit up on the side of the deck to keep the boat flat.

In very light winds (under 6 knots), sit toward the middle of the boat, allowing it to heel to leeward slightly (see illustration on p. 190). Heeling to leeward helps the sails take shape and the boat sail on its lines.

The centerboard or keel is critical to a boat's performance to windward. If there were no centerboard or keel, the force of the wind would push the boat sideways. Raising the centerboard a few inches will help reduce your helm and your angle of heel in very strong winds. With a force of wind hitting your sail, the larger the centerboard the greater the heeling force. Reducing the area of your centerboard reduces the amount of heel.

TACKING

When tacking, changing sides of the boat can be hard if you are handling both mainsheet and tiller. Take as few steps as possible crossing from one side of the boat to the other. In dinghies only one step is necessary. As you cross you must change hands as well. Hold on to the mainsheet while preparing to tack. Keep your sheet uncleated so it does not get caught on the old leeward side. As you change sides, bring the hand holding the mainsheet back to the tiller behind you, keeping the mainsheet in that hand. For a split second one hand will hold both the mainsheet and the tiller. At this point change hands behind your back. The mainsheet and the tiller will be under control at all times.

Face forward during your tack. You will see where you are going and be able to shift your weight at the right moment to keep your boat on an even keel. Common errors in tacking are holding the tiller over to one

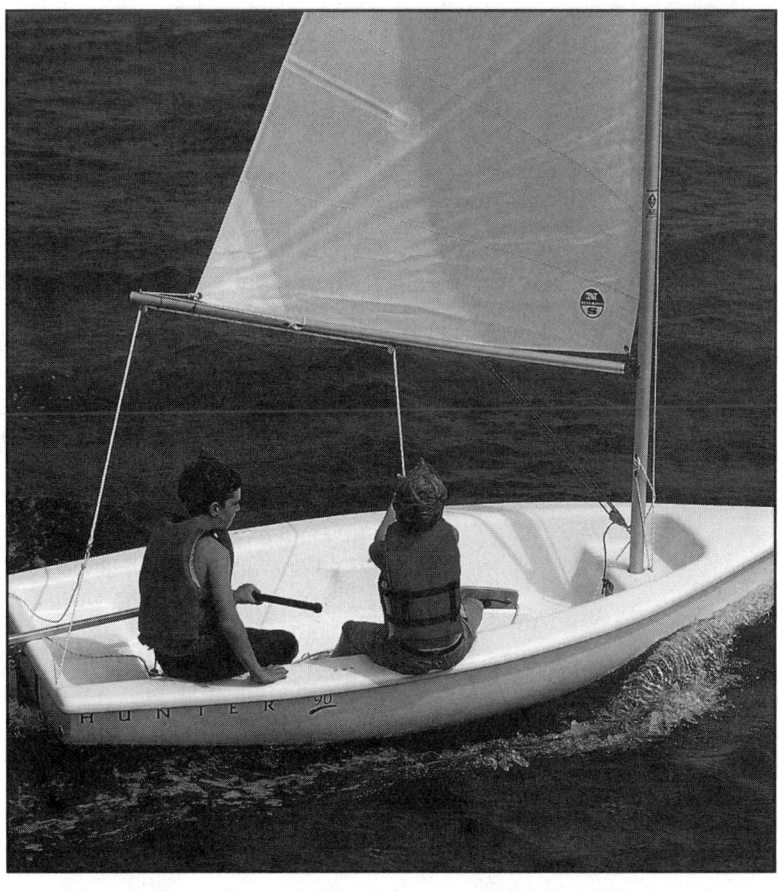

Build your foundation with dinghy sailing before moving up in size. Cat-rigged boats come in many forms, such as the Hunter 90.

Crew and skipper sit in positions where they can watch both sails and see traffic and obstructions.

side too long and not changing hands soon enough.

As you complete your tack, the action of the wind on your sails (whether you are luffing or not) tells you if you are on your new course. You must concentrate on where you are heading and what is happening to your sails.

JIBING

Try to keep the boat flat when jibing. Put the centerboard down halfway. Too little board down will allow the bottom to spin out from under the mast; too much board will cause the board to steer the boat and tip it. Keep your weight aft during the jibe in heavier air so your bow does not dip into the water. Change hands early in a jibe so you do not get twisted.

After the jibe, resume your normal course as soon as possible; staying dead downwind keeps the boat off balance. If the boat is out of balance, head up, heeling the boat slightly to leeward until you are under control. Hold on to the tiller while jibing to keep the boat from spinning out.

ACCELERATING

Part of the fun of sailing small boats is quick acceleration. The heavier the boat, the

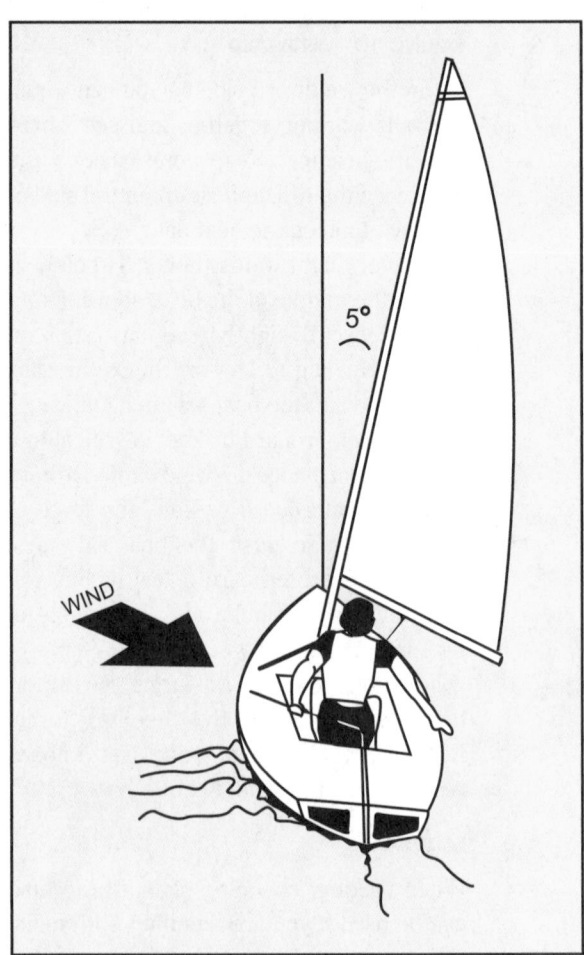

Heeling to leeward in light air.

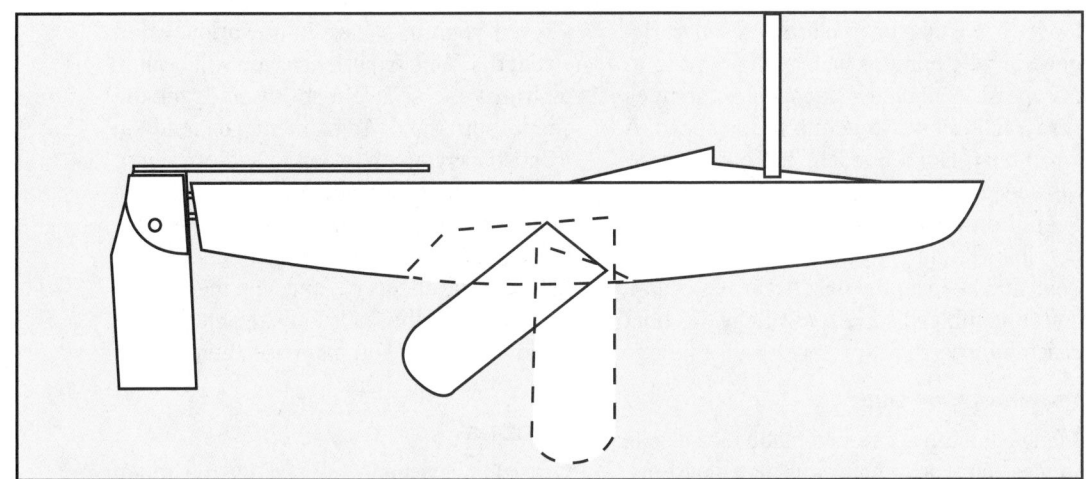

Reduce centerboard area to reduce heel in strong winds.

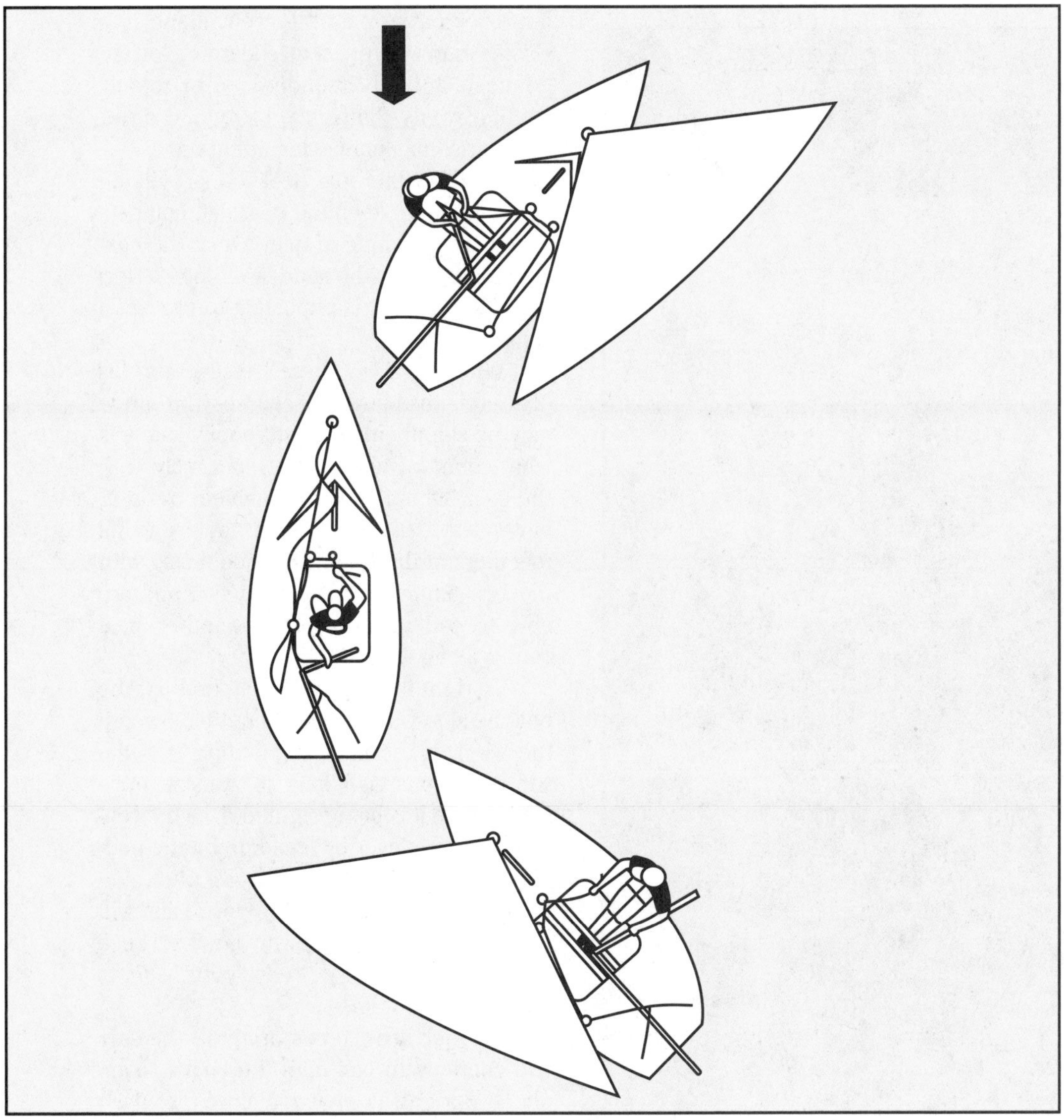

Changing hands during a tack

longer it will take to accelerate. A squarerigger will take minutes before it is moving at full speed. A 12-meter sloop will sometimes take a full minute to get up to top speed. A small boat, like a Sunfish, can easily reach top speed in seconds. To accelerate a boat, keep it on a course as close to a reach as possible. Trimming your sail to the desired point and keeping the boat flat are essential. These combined forces will help the boat reach full speed.

TRIMMING YOUR SAILS

Many adjustments can be made to the sails to give them any shape you may desire for a given point of sailing in all various wind strengths. With experience, you will be able to trim your sails effectively and get the shape you want. Adjustments depend on what shape you are trying to achieve. First, it is important that whenever you are trimming sails to never cleat the sheet, especially in smaller boats. If a sudden gust of wind hits with the sheets cleated, you may not be able to ease the sails quickly enough to avoid capsizing. You can ease them at any time if you hold them.

CAPSIZING

Capsizing is usually caused by too much wind for the amount of sail being carried; improper balance by the crew, jibing in a strong wind with the centerboard up too far, not keeping the boat under control, rapidly shifting winds (both in velocity and direction), or simply not paying attention.

Don't let the boat heel too far. Hiking out will help to keep the boat flat, compensating for the angle of heel. Once the boat gets too far over, the rudder will be ineffective. Therefore, it is important to prevent a capsize early.

When capsized, there are several rules of thumb to follow. Of course your pride may be slightly injured, but bodily safety is what counts. Once in the water, stay with the boat. Even if you are unable to right it, never leave the boat. This applies to all members of the crew. You should stay with the boat until you have righted it and are able to sail again, or until another boat comes along to help.

To right the capsized boat, first put the boat head to wind by swinging the bow into the wind. If the mast is pointing into the wind, the boat is likely to capsize once again while it is being righted. Use the centerboard as a lever by standing on the middle of it. Be sure your sheets are uncleated so that as the boat pops up your sails will not fill, causing the boat to go over once again. In a dinghy keep your sheets uncleated at all times.

As your boat comes up, grab the side and continue to pull until the boat is completely upright. Try not to make a mad dash

This sailor could flatten his boat easily by shifting his weight to the windward side of the boat.

to get on the boat, as you will probably want to; the sharks won't get you yet. Instead, hold on to the side of the boat and rest for a moment to regain your energy. The toughest thing will be climbing back into the boat. When you have rested and feel strong enough, pull yourself into the middle of the boat or over the transom.

If the mast begins to sink and the boat begins to turn turtle (completely upside down), try to place a fife jacket under the tip of the mast to help keep it floating. If the boat does turtle, pulling on the centerboard will slowly bring the boat back. If the mast is wedged tightly in the mud, you may need the assistance of another boat. Have this boat anchor directly upwind and throw a line to you. Eventually, the force of the wind and waves will pivot your boat into the wind, pulling the mast out of the mud and making it easy to right. Training boats are often equipped with Styrofoam, sewn into the head of the sail to stop the boat from turtling.

If the boat is swamped, sit down and begin to bail it out once it is righted. Keep one person in the water to steady the boat. If the rail is awash with one person in, best keep everyone in the water. When the boat is towed by a powerboat, the water proba-

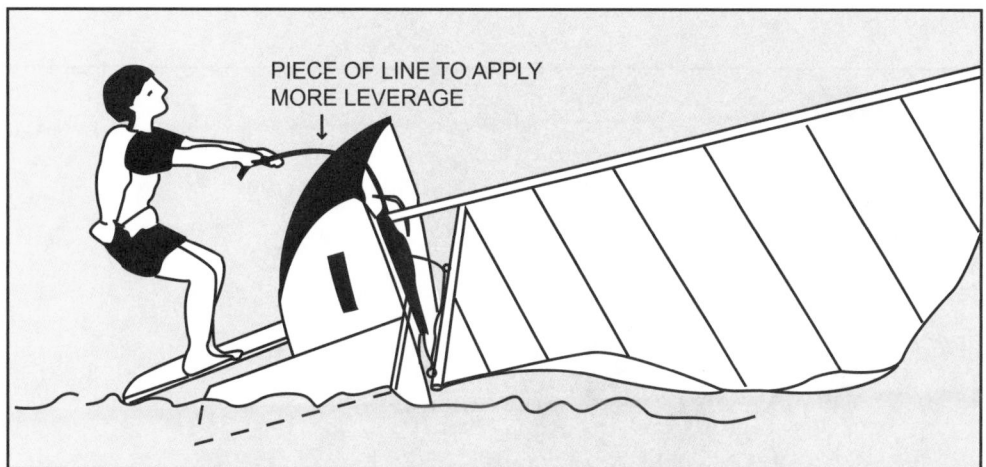

PIECE OF LINE TO APPLY MORE LEVERAGE

Using a centerboard as a lever for righting and a piece of line as shown will help a small (light) person right a boat.

The skipper is preparing to use her weight on the centerboard to right her capsized dinghy, as shown in the diagram above.

bly will flow out. First let your sails down and secure all equipment to prevent it from floating away. Have the rescuing boat throw you a line. Attach it around the base of the mast. The water will begin to empty out. Have your boat towed straight into the wind at a slow speed. Keep the centerboard up. You may capsize again if the centerboard is down. Water-filled boats are very unstable. Handle with care. Head into the wind a little more if your boat feels unstable. When a swamped boat is being towed, have at least one person in the stern to keep the bow from nose-diving and to balance the boat. As the boat is towed, the bow will rise and the water will pour over the stern. Keep

Using a jib sheet to right a turtled dinghy.

your fife jacket on. If you weren't wearing one when you capsized, put one on now. You may find swimming more difficult, but at least you will be safe.

Be prepared. Sometimes all the preventative efforts in the world can't keep the boat from capsizing. If you suddenly find yourself in the water, locate your crew and passengers. Double check to see everyone's PFD is on and keeping them afloat. Stay with the boat unless it's drifting toward some hazard like breaking surf or a power plant intake. Anything that floats such as an ice chest or fender might help elevate you and make you more visible for potential rescuers.

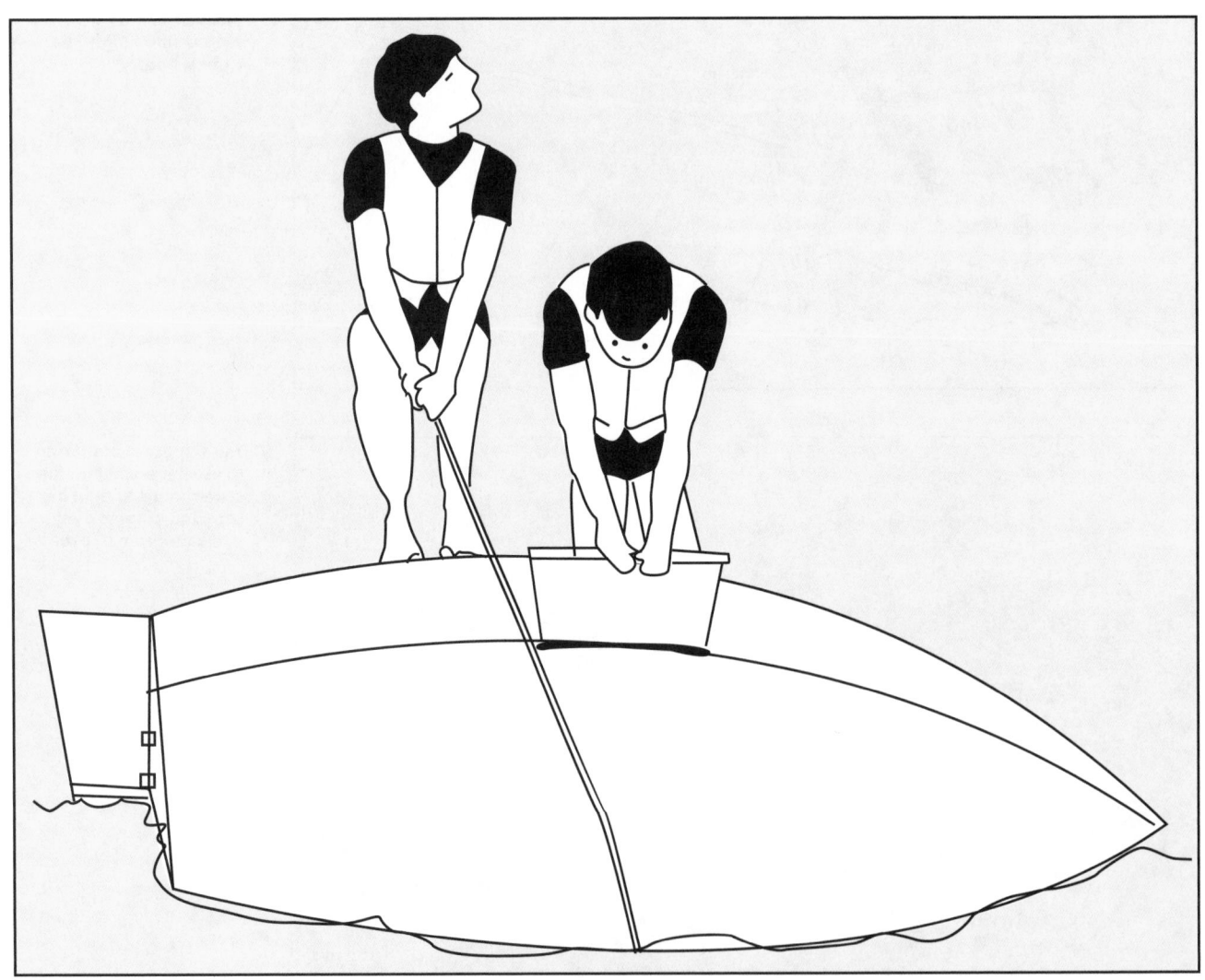

SAILBOARDS

Learning to sail a sailboard can be very enjoyable or extremely frustrating. A successful first attempt requires ideal conditions; it's beneficial to have the use of some type of training equipment and helpful if you have some good instruction.

Under ideal conditions, the wind is less than 8 knots, seas are calm, and the water is warm. The area in which you sail should be relatively free of boat traffic and obstructions. The smaller the area the better, so long as the breeze is not excessively obstructed by buildings.

EQUIPMENT

The basic and most common training sailboard for a beginner has a small sail, usually around 43 square feet. (Stock sails are 56 square feet.) A smaller sail takes a lot of the power out of the rig and reduces the tendency for the beginner to become overpowered. There are several specially designed trainer boards that are wider and more stable and the rig (boom and mast) is made of aluminum and fiberglass, easy to pull out of the water and to hold on to.

INSTRUCTION

Qualified sailboarding instruction is available around the world. Many instructional programs consist of two three-hour lessons. Certified instructors teach the classes using special equipment. Classes start with sailing theory. The instructor demonstrates each step of sailboarding on a land simulator, and each student then practices the steps. The instructor corrects the students' mistakes on land, before they go onto the water, thus saving a lot of time. Later, on the water, students use training boards with small sails.

SAILBOARDING STEP-BY-STEP

There is no substitute for good instruction in sailboarding. However, the steps fisted below give you an idea of what it's all about.

Getting ready: Determine the wind direction and aim the board perpendicular to the wind. Point the mast straight downwind horizontal to the water, so that the mast and the board form a right angle.

Stance: Face the sail with your back to the wind. Place your feet on the centerline of the board. The forward foot should be in front of the mast and the back foot over the centerboard. Bend your knees for more

Sailing takes many forms. Here, an energetic person sails a sailboard.

stability. Keep your feet centered unless tacking or jibing. Straighten your back and keep your hips forward.

Getting started: Be sure the board is crosswise to the wind. Now pull the mast straight up out of the water. To do this, hold the uphaul (a line on the mast) with both hands, reach across with your forward hand (the one closest to the bow), and grab the boom about six inches from the end. Next, move the mast forward using your forward hand, until it is close to your forward leg. Reach back with your back hand and grab the boom. To fill the sail with wind, pull in with your back hand. At the same time, tip the mast and sail toward the nose of the board to keep it from rounding up into the wind.

Control: Hold the rig out of the water by the uphaul. To turn the board away from the wind, tip the mast forward. To turn the board into the wind, tip the mast back. Keep the mast in the center plane. Remember, your body weight and the sail control the board.

Turning: The sail is used to effect all turns including the tack and jibe. To tack, lean the luffing sail back and step around to the bow of the board as it turns into the wind. Stand on the bow with a foot on either side of the center as the sail luffs over the stern. Lean the sail to the left or right to complete the turn, then step back to the centerline of the board.

To jibe, lean the sail forward. As the board turns downwind, step around aft of the sail. Stand on the stern of the board as the sail luffs over the bow. Next, lean the sail to the left or right to complete the turn. As the board moves crosswise to the wind, step back to the centerline.

Tips: If you become overpowered, release the boom with your back hand and pull in with your front hand. This will let the wind out of the sail, just as easing a mainsheet would. If you release the boom with your forward hand, the board will react as if you had cut a shroud (that is, the mast will fall over).

It is important to keep your feet on the centerline. To improve balance, bend at the knees and lean against the sail. If overpowered, let out the sail; if falling backwards, pull in with your back hand to catch more wind.

Advanced technique: Sailing in strong winds requires some special expertise. In high winds you must hang from the boom out over the water and use your body weight to its utmost. This means you will grip the boom farther back and keep your feet much farther back on the board. In extreme winds it is necessary on some boards to change the daggerboard (or centerboard). Use a high-wind centerboard or kick up the adjustable centerboard to reduce the planing surface and move the center of lateral resistance aft when the winds are over 15 knots. Since the partially hoisted centerboard or high-wind daggerboard is small and swept back, it reduces the board's tendency to round up into the wind and makes it possible to bear off and surf on the waves in a strong wind.

Recently sailboarding has grown tremendously in popularity. A new breed of sailboards–short, surfboardlike boards–are being used by sailors to jump and surf waves or just blast around at amazingly high speeds. Design innovations on these high-speed boards keep the entire sailboarding world advancing by leaps and bounds.

CATAMARANS

Catamarans have two hulls of equal length, with the mast supported in the center of a bridge deck between them. Some designs have flexible connections between the hulls and accommodations within the hulls, and some designs have large bridge deck structures with no accommodations at all within the hulls.

Smaller day-racing catamarans fall into several additional groups. One group, whose only function is high speed and maximum performance, includes the Tornado, which has semirounded hulls, pivoting centerboards, and a fully articulating mast with full battened mainsail. This group also includes C class catamarans, among the most sophisticated sailboats in existence and the most close-winded boats afloat. C class catamarans are easily identified by their wing masts and airplane like structure.

Finally, there is a group of day-racing catamarans which might be called "off the beach" boats. Some of these boats, such as the Hobie 14, the Hobie 16, and the various sizes of Prindles, have no daggerboards. Some get their lift to windward from asymmetrical hulls, which work the same way the sails do. Others have kick-up centerboards and rudders. These cats, capable of spirited performance and high speed, are designed for beachability and rugged recreational use.

TRIMARANS

Trimarans have three hulls; beyond that, there is little that is standard. The length of the outer hulls, spacing from the main hulls, percentage of buoyancy, and shape all vary a great deal. There are very few day-sailing trimarans.

WHY A CATAMARAN?

The first advantage in catamaran sailing is high speed; no vessel except for the tiny, speed-oriented sailboards can compare with the potential speed of a catamaran. The second advantage of a catamaran is its great stability. It is easy to board and disembark. It's an easy boat to rig, and you can walk around on it without tipping it over. It is also easy to beach, easy to trailer, and much lighter than many of its single-hulled counterparts.

HANDLING

There are some handling differences between catamarans and most single-hulled boats. The chief difference with the majority of designs is in tacking. Most catamarans, because of their extremely light weight, have no momentum to carry them through a tack and must be backwinded. In many cases it is necessary to backwind the jib to bring the boat completely around onto the other tack. (The secret is to not release the jib sheet until the main has filled on the new tack.) However you do it, it's slow. In a racing situation this means that the short tacking that might work for a very nimble monohull will probably be disastrous for a catamaran. In catamaran racing, try to make as few tacks as possible.

Catamarans are designed to sail with both hulls in the water or with the windward hull just kissing the water. Hotdogging, or "flying a hull," is a lot of fun and very exciting, but detrimental to the performance of the boat.

Keeping the boat flat is an acquired skill done mostly with the tiller. The secret of keeping the boat flat on a reach is to turn downwind when the hull begins to rise. If you turn upwind, the forces that are lifting the hull in the first place will accelerate. A basic difference in handling a catamaran as opposed to a single-hulled boat is that you turn downwind when the boat becomes overpressed, rather than turning upwind and letting the sail luff. This is because in a single-hulled boat the additional momentum gained by turning upwind heels the boat a little farther, allowing the rig to spill the wind. In a catamaran, the same forces apply. However, if the boat heels farther, the threat of capsize becomes greater; since you are trying to bring the hull back down to the water, you must turn downwind rather than up. In winds too heavy for using the tiller alone, turn by easing the traveler and if necessary the mainsheet.

A catamaran sailor seldom sails directly downwind because a run is the slowest point of sail. When sailing dead downwind, a boat can achieve only a percentage of the true wind speed. On a reaching course you develop your own wind, and you can increase your speed enormously downwind by "tacking downwind." To do so, reach across the wind and turn downwind until you are getting less drive out of the sails. At this point, head back up slightly and maintain that course. Find the best possible downwind course, so that your sails are full but you're not heading dead downwind. This is often about 15 degrees to either side of the true wind. A simple jibe then brings you onto the other tack. Tack downwind toward a mark in the same manner that you would tack upwind. If you have boards, raise them fully to take advantage of your leeway.

Occasionally you may be overpowered going downwind. In smaller boats this usually becomes apparent at about 20 to 25 knots of true wind speed. It is very important that you maintain your control over the boat. In an emergency overpowering situation in heavy wind, the simplest and safest procedure is to sail more of a reach. Your fully battened sail will assist you. When you are going dead downwind and the mainsheet is in as tight as possible, the traveler is centered, and you are ready, release your halyard and pull your mainsail down as quickly as possible. Try to have your mast rotator parallel with the sail during this operation so there is no chance of the sail jamming in the sail groove.

CAPSIZING

Capsizing on a catamaran is no more cause for alarm than capsizing on any other centerboard or nonballasted boat. Swim the boat around so the sails face into the wind. Tie a righting line to the shroud on the dry hull. (If you don't have a righting line on board, undo the mainsheet from the block system and use it.) Be sure to release the mainsheet and jib sheet so the sails won't hold water, which would make righting more difficult. Also, if the sails are left sheeted, the boat may sail away without you when it comes up. Where you stand on the hull as you rotate the boat back out of the water will depend on the type of boat. On some boats with daggerboards you can stand on the board to get more leverage. On some you can't. Find out which kind you have before you get into this situation.

Stand on the submerged hull and lean out against your righting line as far as possible to provide leverage to right the boat. When the boat begins to right and come

over to you, duck in between the hulls for maximum safety. Do not drop the righting line until you are aboard, as there is always a possibility that the boat may sail away without you.

JIBING

The broad base, stability, efficient traveler system, and lack of a permanent backstay allow a catamaran to be jibed simply and easily. When jibing in unusually heavy conditions, assist the rig in the jibe in order to take some strain off the equipment. In heavy winds, trim the mainsheet, then assist the rig across the stern by hauling the traveler to center and then allowing it to pay out slowly on the opposite tack. In moderate winds, trim the mainsheet before jibing, then push your tiller to windward and complete your jibe, allowing the traveler to swing across on the new tack by itself.

APPARENT WIND

The apparent wind in catamaran sailing is usually forward of abeam. Since a catamaran's speed is normally a much higher percentage of the true wind speed than that of other boats, the apparent wind is much farther forward. It is not unusual to see single-hulled boats and catamarans on the same downwind course with the catamarans trimmed in much closer than the single-hulled boats. Because the catamarans are moving faster, their apparent wind is farther forward; since sails are trimmed to the apparent wind, their sails will be sheeted in tighter.

The traveler on a catamaran is more important in controlling the sail than it is on many other classes of boat. Most champion catamaran sailors trim their mainsail to the proper shape for the wind speed and direction and then use the traveler to obtain the optimum angle of attack as they sail on reaches. As the boat accelerates, they haul their travelers in toward the centerline; as the boat decelerates, they let the traveler out to maintain the same angle of attack. This is easy to achieve on a catamaran because of the very wide sheeting base and stability.

LAUNCHING, STORING, AND MAINTAINING YOUR BOAT

TRAILERS

Many sailors use trailers both to launch and to store their boats. This is the most versatile form of boat storage and lets you sail on a different body of water every weekend. You can store the boat in your driveway, which eliminates storage costs and the chance of vandalism.

There are two types of trailers. The boom variety emphasizes keel support; the frame type emphasizes hull support. Select a trailer that supports as much of the hull as possible. The trailer should meet local and state trailer regulations, permit dry launching, and provide maximum safety and comfort while being towed.

When pulling your boat and trailer with a vehicle, keep a few things in mind. Be sure your equipment rides well without shifting, chafing, and rattling. Balance is very important when trailering. Too much weight in the rear of the boat will cause your trailer to bob and sway. Check to see if your trailer has a recommended tongue weight and adjust the position of your boat to provide it.

Don't forget that you are really driving two vehicles, not one. Travel slowly and allow plenty of room to brake. An outside rearview mirror is very helpful, and lights on the rear of the trailer are a must.

Before launching a boat from a trailer, set the mast in place and attach the rigging and sails. Don't hoist the sails until you're in the water. Getting under way from a beach is simplified by using an outboard motor.

When launching your boat from a sandy beach, deflate your tires a little, as this will improve traction. Back into the water at right angles to the shoreline. Remember that to turn your trailer to the right, you turn the wheel to the left. To turn the trailer to the left, turn the steering wheel to the right.

RAMP LAUNCHING

In many parks, recreational facilities, and clubs, boats are launched from large concrete ramps that lead into the water. Always be aware of the power lines above the ramp and parking lot. You must be especially careful to keep your mast away from these wires.

Launching from a ramp takes great care, since the part that is in the water often develops a large amount of slippery growth. Watch your footing. Ramps are particularly dangerous around the edges because of deep water. Proceed down with caution.

When launching, back the trailer slowly into the water until the boat begins to float. Once the boat is floating, push it away from the trailer while a second person pulls the dolly out. Hold on to the boat at the bow, never allow it to get away from you and use bow and stern lines to move the boat to a dock nearby and secure it. Don't forget to use fenders.

If there is an offshore breeze, you can simply sail away. With an onshore breeze the waves break close to the ramp, so it is important to get away as quickly as possible. Never get between the boat and shore when there are breaking waves. To keep the boat from banging around, aim the bow directly into the waves.

When you are bringing the boat in, back the trailer into the water. Point the front of the trailer directly up the ramp so that it will be aligned with the bow pointing toward shore and the boat can easily be pulled out. Your centerboard should be up, the sails down, and the rudder out before you put the boat on the trailer. If you are lifting a boat out of the water, use three people, if possible, one on each side and one at the bow. If there are only two people, it is best to have one on each side.

If you are beaching the boat without a ramp, have the sails down, the centerboard up, and the rudder out before you get to the beach, and keep the boat outside the breaking waves until you are ready to lift it out. Watch for a smooth set of waves before taking it all the way in. Try to find a sandy part of the beach, one that is away from gravel. Again, never get between the hull of your boat and the shore, because the surf can roll the boat over on top of you. And whatever system you use, never leave your boat unattended.

MARINAS AND YACHT CLUBS

You may decide to keep your boat at a marina. Many marinas have launching ramps or a hoist, as well as dinghy service, docks, and a clubhouse with lockers and showers. Or you might choose to keep your boat at a yacht club. While most yacht clubs offer more limited services, they usually provide docks, a clubhouse, and probably swimming and sailing lessons. And of course yacht clubs provide a much more extensive social program and a chance to make friends with people of similar interests.

BOAT MAINTENANCE

To get the most out of your boat and sails, you must maintain them properly. Wash them down with fresh water every time after sailing. Salt can do a lot of damage to your boat's finish and working parts. Replace broken parts so that your boat is always in optimum working order. Be sure to store your boat properly. If you keep it on land, store it hull up to preserve the shape if you are leaving it for long periods. If you keep it in a berth, tie it properly to avoid damage from rough weather. Use covers to keep out water and leaves, etc.

Your sails also require care. Use sail covers, as synthetic sails are harmed by long exposure to sunlight. Use sail bags if you have them. Fold your sails smoothly to avoid wrinkling. (In light air an uneven surface will cause turbulence in the flow of air across the sail.)

When washing salt from your sails, use fresh water so they will dry properly. Never allow sails to flap in heavy wind; this weakens the fabric. Only hoist the sails to their design limits between the black bands on the mast.

Any boat with electrical devices such as lights and an electric-start motor will have a battery, wires and fuses. Check for loose or corroded connections and frayed wire insulation. Also make sure you have spare fuses and bulbs on board before casting off your dock lines.

A FINAL WORD

Simply finishing this book and its course of instruction does not make someone a proficient sailor. Only through practice will the skills taught in these lessons become a part of the individual. When you can react instinctively to a situation, instead of working through it mechanically, you've taken a major step toward becoming a competent sailor.

Review this book regularly. There will always be something that was not learned or fully understood the first time around. The review will stimulate you to think of all the things that can happen on a sailboat in terms of anticipation, preparation, and execution. Never think that you have learned it all. Nature-the wind and water-has a grand way of teaching humility to the overconfident.

Now that you have completed the Basic Sailing and Basic Coastal Cruising standards, you may wish to acquire actual certification. To do so, you should be tested by an American Sailing Association certified instructor and receive a signed ASA Sailing Log Book. Further information may be obtained directly from the American Sailing Association, P. O. Box 12079, Marina del Rey, California 90295, Phone (310) 822-7171, Fax (310) 822-4741, Email info@american-sailing.com, Website www.american-sailing.com

ANSWERS TO REVIEW QUESTIONS

PART ONE

Question 1.
A. Aloft
headstay 11
backstay 12
shroud 8
mast 9
boom 10
boom vang 14
topping lift 13
mainsheet 15
B. On Deck and Below
tiller 7
lifelines 3
rudder 6
stern 5
hull 1
bow 4
keel 2
C. Sails
jib 17
jib sheet 18
mainsail 16
head 19
clew 21
tack 20
luff 24
foot 25
leech 22
batten 23

Question 2.
b) into the wind

Question 3.
deck cleat B
winch E
block D
fairlead C
cam cleat A

Question 4.
displacement and planing

Question 5.
powerboat

Question 6.
false

Question 7.
true

Question 8.
5 persons

PART TWO

Question 1.
b) smooth air flow

Question 2.
b) close-hauled

Question 3.
c) eased out all the way

Question 4.
c) an accidental jibe

Question 5.
b) head to wind

Question 6.

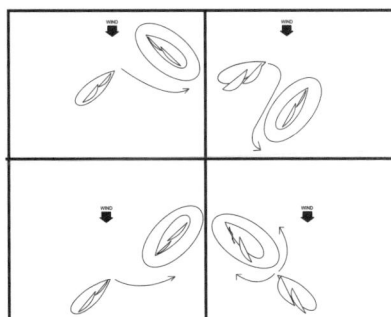

Question 7.
a) boat ahead and being overtaken
Question 8.

a) when overtaking,
c) when the power vessel is limited in its maneuverability by a narrow channel and
d) when the sailboat is also under power.

Question 9. A port tack boat shall give way to boat on starboard tack.

Question 10.
When two sailboats are approaching on the same tack, the windward boat shall stay clear of the leeward boat.

PART THREE

Question 1.
keep a person from falling overboard.

Question 2.
Heat Escape Lessening Position

Question 3.
Do remove wet clothing when in shelter
Do wrap in a sleeping bag or blank with external heat source.
Do call for medical assistance, even medium cases.

Question 4.
Do not administer fluids unless victim is totally conscious.
Do not massage victim.
Do not administer alcohol.

PART FOUR

Question 1.
fathoms, feet, and meters; meters

Question 2
a) port

Question 3.
c) splits into two routes.

Question 4.
1. swim area
2. rock
3. slow

Question 5.
anchor, chain, and rode

Question 6. a) acts as shock absorber
b) prevents rode from chafing on rocks

Question 7.
a) shelter
b) room to swing
c) sufficient water depth
d) good holding ground

Question 8.
a) nylon
b) Dacron
c) nylon
d) Dacron
e) polyethylene or polypropylene

Question 9.
fore and aft; maneuvering a vessel for docking and undocking

part five

Question 1.
self-bailing cockpit 6
through-hull fitting 5
pintle 3
gudgeon 2
rudderpost 4
tiller 1
turnbuckle 7
chainplate 8

Question 2.
a) left to right 4
b) right to left 1
c) toward us 3
d) away from us 2

Question 3.

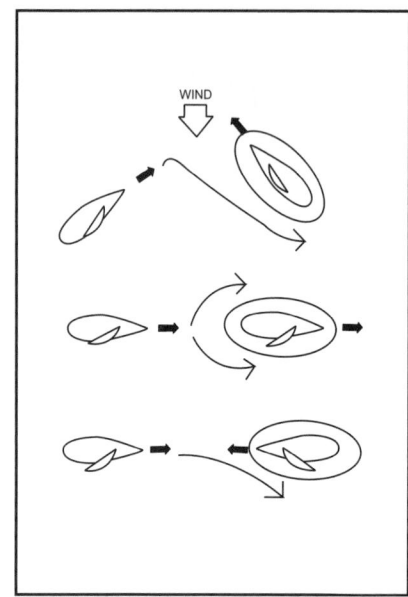

Question 4.
one short; one short; five or more short blasts

Question 5.
one prolonged blast

Question 6.
Type I

Question 7.
2 B-I or 1 B-II

Question 8.
Class B

Question 9.
d) all of the above (Note that other procedures are recommended, such as alerting authorities to your situation by radio and use of fire extinguishers.)

Question 10.
Class A

part six

Question 1.
a) bowline, a loop for attaching temporarily
b) clove hitch, for attaching to a spar temporarily
c) reef knot, for reefing the sails
d) round turn and two half hitches, for attaching to a spar or piling
e) figure eight, a stopper knot

Question 2.
b) 150% genoa

Question 3.
b) low pressure systems

Question 4.
b) cold fronts

Question 5.
a) cumulonimbus clouds: thunderstorms
b) low rolling clouds: line squalls

question 6.

a) Come about or jibe.
b) Determine the source and extent of the problem.
c) Position the boat to put the strain on the strongest part of the rig.
d) Determine another method of control.
e) Stop the engine and clear away the line.

FLOAT PLAN

Complete this plan before you go boating. Leave it with a reliable person either at a marina or elsewhere. Ask that person to notify the Coast Guard or other local authority if you do not return as scheduled.
DO NOT FILE THIS PLAN WITH THE COAST GUARD.
Cancel the plan when you return.

Name of your vessel _____

Your name _____ Telephone _____

Address _____

DESCRIPTION OF VESSEL

Type _____ Color _____

Color of Trim _____ Registration Number _____

Length _____ Sails _____ Make- _____

Engines: NumberType _____ Horsepower _____

Fuel Capacity _____ Canvas Top? _____ Color of Top _____

SURVIVAL EQUIPMENT (Check as appropriate)

PFDs _____ Flares-_____ Mirror _____ Signal Flag- _____

Smoke Signals _____ Signaling Flashlight _____

Food _____

Emergency Water _____

Anchor _____ Amount of Line _____ Paddle _____

Radio: Yes/No _____ Type _____ EPIRB _____ Frequencies _____

Raft or Dinghy _____

OTHER PEOPLE ON BOARD

Name	Age	Address and Telephone Number
_____	_____	_____
_____	_____	_____
_____	_____	_____

TRIP DETAILS

Depart: Date _____ Time _____ Return: Date _____ Time _____

Going to: _____ Via _____

Return via _____ Latest Time of Return _____

IF TRAILERING

Auto License _____ State _____ Type and Make _____

Trailer License _____ State _____ Color of Auto _____

Where Parked _____

NOTIFICATION

If Not Returned by _____ (time) Call the Coast Guard

at _____ or

Local Authority at _____

SAMPLE BOATING ACCIDENT REPORT

COMPLETE ALL BLOCKS (PRINT OR TYPE ALL INFORMATION. INDICATE THOSE NOT APPLICABLE BY "NA." THOSE UNKNOWN BY "UN")

1. OPERATOR'S NAME AND ADDRESS AGE _____

HOME PHONE (   )   WORK PHONE (   )

2. RENTED BOAT
- ☐ Yes
- ☐ No

3. OPERATOR'S EXPERIENCE

THIS TYPE OF BOAT	OTHER BOAT OPERATING EXPERIENCE
☐ UNDER 20 HOURS	☐ UNDER 20 HOURS
☐ 20 TO 100 HOURS	☐ 20 TO 100 HOURS
☐ 100 TO 500 HOURS	☐ 100 TO 500 HOURS
☐ OVER 500 HOURS	☐ OVER 500 HOURS

4. OWNER'S NAME AND ADDRESS

HOME PHONE (   )   WORK PHONE (   )

5. NUMBER OF PERSONS ON BOARD

6. NUMBER OF PERSONS TOWED (I.E. SKIING ETC.)

7. FORMAL INSTRUCTION IN BOATING SAFETY
- ☐ NONE
- ☐ USCG AUXILIARY
- ☐ US POWER SQUADRON
- ☐ AMERICAN RED CROSS
- ☐ STATE
- ☐ OTHER (SPECIFY)

VESSEL NO. 1 (YOUR VESSEL)

8. BOAT NUMBER	9. BOAT NAME	10. BOAT MANUFACTURER	11. BOAT MODEL	12. MFGR. HULL IDENT. NO.

13. TYPE OF BOAT
- ☐ OPEN MOTORBOAT
- ☐ CABIN MOTORBOAT
- ☐ AUXILIARY SAIL
- ☐ SAIL ONLY
- ☐ HOUSEBOAT
- ☐ RAFT
- ☐ CANOE
- ☐ KAYAK
- ☐ JET SKI/WETBIKE
- ☐ ROWBOAT
- ☐ OTHER (SPECIFY)

14. HULL MATERIAL
- ☐ WOOD
- ☐ ALUMINUM
- ☐ STEEL
- ☐ FIBERGLASS
- ☐ RUBBER/VINYL
- ☐ PLASTIC
- ☐ OTHER (SPECIFY)

15. PROPULSION
- ☐ OUTBOARD
- ☐ INBOARD
- ☐ INBOARD-OUTBOARD
- ☐ JET
- ☐ SAIL
- ☐ PADDLE/OARS
- ☐ OTHER (SPECIFY)

TYPE OF FUEL _____

16. BOAT DATA

NUMBER OF ENGINES _____   LENGTH _____
MAKE OF ENGINE _____   BEAM (WIDTH) _____
HORSEPOWER (TOTAL) _____   DEPTH (TOP OF INNER
YEAR BUILT _____   TRANSOM TO KEEL)
(ENGINE)   YEAR BUILT (BOAT) _____

17. PRIMARY BOAT USE
- ☐ RECREATIONAL
- ☐ COMMERCIAL
- ☐ FOR-HIRE
- ☐ WORK BOAT

18. PREVIOUS ACCIDENTS INVOLVING THIS BOAT

DATES

VESSEL NO. 2 (OTHER VESSEL INVOLVED)

19. BOAT NUMBER	20. BOAT NAME	21. BOAT MANUFACTURER	22. BOAT MODEL	23. MFGR. HULL IDENT. NO.

24. NAME OF OPERATOR AGE _____
HOME PHONE (   )
WORK PHONE (   )

25. ADDRESS

26. NAME OF OWNER
HOME PHONE (   )
WORK PHONE (   )

27. ADDRESS

28. WITNESSES

NAME	AGE	ADDRESS	TELEPHONE NUMBER
			( )
			( )
			( )

ACCIDENT DATE AND LOCATION

29. DATE OF ACCIDENT	30. TIME	31. NAME OF BODY OF WATER	33. LOCATION (AS PRECISELY AS POSSIBLE)
	_____ AM		
	_____ PM	32. LAST PORT OF CALL	

34. STATE	35. NEAREST CITY OR TOWN	36. COUNTY

ENVIRONMENTAL CONDITIONS

37. WEATHER
- ☐ CLEAR ☐ RAIN
- ☐ CLOUDY ☐ SNOW
- ☐ FOG ☐ HAZY

38. WATER CONDITIONS
- ☐ CALM
- ☐ CHOPPY
- ☐ ROUGH
- ☐ VERY ROUGH
- ☐ STRONG CURRENT

39. TEMPERATURE (ESTIMATE)
AIR _____ °F
WATER _____ °F

40. WIND
- ☐ NONE
- ☐ LIGHT (0 TO 6 MPH)
- ☐ MODERATE (7 TO 14 MPH)
- ☐ STRONG (15 TO 25 MPH)
- ☐ STORM (25 MPH AND OVER)

41. VISIBILITY
- ☐ GOOD
- ☐ FAIR
- ☐ POOR

42. WHEATHER ENCOUNTERED
- ☐ WAS AS FORECAST
- ☐ NOT AS FORECAST
- ☐ FORECAST NOT OBTAINED

THIS **CONFIDENTIAL REPORT** IS USED IN RESEARCH FOR THE PREVENTION OF ACCIDENTS,
AND A COPY IS FORWARDED TO THE UNITED STATES COAST GUARD.

(COMPLETE BOTH SIDES)

ACCIDENT DATA

43. OPERATION AT TIME OF ACCIDENT (CHECK ALL APPLICABLE)	44. TYPE OF ACCIDENT	45. IN YOUR OPINION, CAUSE OF ACCIDENT
☐ CRUISING ☐ DRIFTING ☐ MANEUVERING ☐ AT ANCHOR ☐ WATER SKIING ☐ TIED TO DOCK ☐ TOWING ☐ OTHER (USE ITEM 48) ☐ ACCELERATING	☐ GROUNDING ☐ COLLISION WITH FIXED OBJECT ☐ CAPSIZING ☐ COLLISION WITH FLOATING ☐ FLOODING OBJECT ☐ SINKING ☐ FALL OVERBOARD ☐ FIRE OR EXPLOSION (FUEL) ☐ FALL IN BOAT ☐ FIRE OR EXPLOSION (OTHER ☐ PERSON(S) HIT BY BOAT OR THAN FUEL) PROPELLER ☐ VESSEL(S) COLLISION ☐ OTHER (USE ITEM 48)	☐ WEATHER CONDITIONS ☐ RESTRICTED VISION ☐ EXCESSIVE SPEED ☐ FAULT OF HULL ☐ NO PROPER LOOKOUT ☐ FAULT OF MACHINERY ☐ OVERLOADING ☐ FAULT OF EQUIPMENT ☐ IMPROPER LOADING ☐ FATIGUE ☐ HAZARDOUS WATERS ☐ OTHER (SPECIFY) ☐ ALCOHOL _____ ☐ DRUGS

46. PERSONAL FLOTATION DEVICES (PFD)		47. FIRE EXTINGUISHERS
WAS THE BOAT ADEQUATELY EQUIPPED WITH COAST GUARD APPROVED PERSONAL FLOTATION DEVICES? ☐ YES ☐ NO WHERE THEY ACCESSIBLE? ☐ YES ☐ NO WHERE THEY USED? ☐ YES ☐ NO	WAS THE VESSEL CARRYING <u>NONAPPROVED</u> LIFESAVING DEVICES? ☐ YES ☐ NO WERE THEY ACCESSIBLE? ☐ YES ☐ NO WERE THEY USED? ☐ YES ☐ NO	WAS APPROVED TYPE FIRE FIGHTING EQUIPMENT ABOARD? ☐ YES ☐ NO WHERE THEY USED? (IF "YES", LIST TYPES(S) AND NUMBER) ☐ YES ☐ NO

48.   ACCIDENT DESCRIPTION

DESCRIBE WHAT HAPPENED AND WHAT COULD HAVE PREVENTED THIS ACCIDENT. (INCLUDE FAILURE OF EQUIPMENT.
EXPLAIN CAUSE OF DEATH OR INJURY, MEDICAL TREATMENT, ETC. USE SKETCH IF HELPFUL. IF NEEDED, CONTINUE DESCRIPTION ON ADDITIONA PAPER.)

GLOSSARY

abaft Toward the stern.

abeam At right angles to the centerline of a boat.

aboard On or in a boat; close to a boat.

aft, after Toward the stern.

aground With the hull or keel of a boat touching the bottom.

aloft Overhead.

amidships Between fore and aft; the middle of the boat.

anchor A device shaped so as to grip the

bottom It is secured to a line from the boat to hold it in the desired position.

astern Behind the stern of a boat.

athwartships Across the beam of a boat.

awash Immersed in water.

backstay A wire support from the mast to the stern of the boat.

bail To remove water from the boat.

ballast Weight placed in the bottom of the boat to give it stability.

bare poles With all sails down.

battens Thin wooden or plastic strips placed in pockets in the leech of a sail to help hold its form.

beam The width of a boat at its widest point.

beam wind A wind that blows across the boat from side to side.

bearing The compass (magnetic) direction from one object to another.

beat To sail to windward.

belay To make secure.

bend To secure (for example, a sail to a spar or a line to a sail).

bight Loop.

bilge The very lowest part of a boat's interior, where water is most likely to collect.

blanket To take wind from a sail

block A nautical pulley.

boat hook A device for catching hold of a

ring bolt or line when coming alongside a pier or picking up a mooring.

bolt rope Rope secured to the edge of a sail to give it strength and to facilitate adjusting foot and luff tension.

boom The spar to which the foot of the sail is attached with lacing, slides, or a groove.

boom vang A line to steady the boom when off the wind.

bow Forward part of the boat.

bowsprit A spar extending forward from the bow.

breast line Docking line leading roughly at right angles from the boat's sides.

bridle Rope span with ends secured for the sheet block to ride on.

broach To spin out of control and capsize or come close to a capsize; loss of steering.

buoy Any floating object anchored in one place to mark a position or provide a mooring.

by the lee On a run, having the wind coming slightly from the side on which the sails are trimmed.

can A buoy, used to mark a channel, colored green or black and given an odd number.

capsize To tip over.

careen To place a boat on her side so that work may be carried out on her underwater parts.

carry away To break or tear loose.

cast off To let go of a line when leaving the dock or mooring; to ease sheets.

catboat A sailboat with a single sail.

centerboard A shaped blade attached to the underside of the hull to give the boat lateral resistance when it is sailing to windward.

chafe To damage a line by rubbing.

chainplates Metal plates bolted to the

side of a boat to which shrouds are attached to support the rigging.

chock A device affixed to the deck and used as a guide for an anchor or mooring line.

claw off To clear a lee shore.

cleat A fitting used to secure a line under strain.

clew The outer comer of a sail.

close-hauled The most windward point of sail, on which the wind is at about 45 degrees.

close-winded Describes a craft capable of sailing very close to the wind.

coaming The raised protection around a cockpit.

cockpit The space at a lower level than the deck in which the tiller or wheel is located; a cockpit may be center or aft.

cringle A metal ring worked into the sail.

crutch Support for the boom when the sails are furled.

displacement The weight of water displaced by a boat.

dock The body of water in which the boat sits while tied up to a float or pier (often used to mean the float or pier itself).

downhaul A line attached to the tack of the sail, used to trim the draft forward.

draft 1) The depth or fullness of a sail. 2) The depth of the keel or centerboard in the water.

drift The leeway or movement sideways of a boat.

dry sailing Keeping a boat out of water when not in use.

ease To let out.

fairlead A fitting used to change the direction of a line, giving it a better angle from a sail or block to a winch or cleat.

fall The part of a tackle to which the power is applied in hoisting.

fathom A nautical measurement for the depth of water. One fathom is equal to six feet.

fetch A windward course by which a craft can make her destination without having to tack.

float A floating platform, usually accessible from shore, to which a boat is tied up when docked.

foot The bottom length of a sail.

fore-and-aft In the direction of the keel, from front to back.

forefoot The forward part of the keel, adjoining the lower part of the stem.

foremast The most forward mast of a sailboat having two or more masts.

foresail A jib.

fouled Entangled or clogged.

frames The skeleton of the ship, which holds the hull together and gives support.

free Sailing on any point of sail except close-hauled.

freeboard The distance from the top of the hull to the water.

full-and-by Sailing as close to the wind as possible with all the sails full.

furl To fold or roll a sail on a boom and then secure it with sail ties.

gaff A pole extending from a mast to support the head of a sail.

gasket A piece of rope or canvas used to secure a furled sail.

gear Any equipment pertaining to a sailboat.

genoa An overlapping foresail.

gimbal A device used for suspending the compass so it remains level.

give-way vessel A boat required to keep out of the way of another vessel.

gooseneck A device that secures the boom to the mast.

grommet A metal ring fastened in a sail.

ground tackle Anchor, rode, etc., used to secure a boat to her mooring.

gudgeon A fitting attached to the hull into which the rudder's pintles are inserted.

gunwale The rail of the boat at deck level.

guy A line or wire used to adjust and position the spinnaker pole.

halyard A line used to haul sails up and down the mast.

hard alee The command used in coming about to inform the crew that the helm is being pushed hard to leeward, turning the boat into the wind.

head The top of a sail.

head to wind With the bow headed into the wind and the sails luffing.

headsail Any sail used forward of the mast, a foresail.

headstay A forward stay supporting the mast.

headway Motion forward.

heave to To stop a boat by turning the bow to the wind and holding it there. A boat stopped this way is hove to.

helm The tiller or wheel mechanism by which the boat is steered.

hike To lean over the side of a boat to help counterbalance heeling.

hoist The vertical edge of a sail; to haul aloft.

hull The main body of the boat.

inboard Toward the centerline of the boat; mounted inside the hull.

in irons In the wind's eye and having lost all headway. A boat in irons will not go off **on either tack** Also called in stays.

jib A triangular sail set forward of the mainmast.

jibe To change tack on a downwind course. A boat begins to jibe at the moment when, with the wind aft, the foot of her mainsail crosses her centerline. The boat completes the jibe when the mainsail fills on the new tack.

jibstay A wire supporting the mast to which the luff of the jib is attached.

jumper A stay on the upper forward part of the mast.

keel A heavy fin filled with lead ballast under the hull. It prevents the boat from sideslipping by resisting the lateral force of the wind, and it gives the boat stability.

ketch A two-masted sailing vessel with a small after mast stepped forward of the rudderpost.

knot A nautical unit of speed: 6,076 feet or one nautical mile per hour.

lanyard A line fastened to an object, such as a pail, whistle, knife, or other small tool for purposes of securing it.

lay The twisting of a rope's strands.

lazarette A small space below deck, usually aft, where spare parts are kept or an outboard motor is mounted.

leech The after edge of a sail.

leeward Away from the wind (also lee).

lifeline A wire that encircles the deck to prevent crew members from falling overboard.

light sails Sails made of a lightweight material for use in light winds.

list A leaning sideways due to excess weight on one side.

locker A storage compartment on a boat.

lubber's line A short post inside a compass used as a reference point when steering or taking bearings.

luff 1) The forward vertical edge of a sail. 2) To alter course toward the wind until the boat is head to wind. 3) The flapping of a sail caused by the boat being head to wind.

mainmast The principal mast of a sailboat.

mainsail The largest regular sail on a modem sailboat.

mainsheet The line for controlling the main boom.

marconi A tall mast used with a jibheaded rig.

mizzen The shorter mast aft on a yawl or ketch.

mooring A heavy anchor or weight permanently in position.

mooring buoy A buoy fitted with a ring and used for mooring a boat.

nun A buoy with a conical top, found on the starboard hand on entering a channel and painted red. Nuns are numbered evenly.

offshore Away from the shore.

off the wind Sailing downwind or before the wind.

on the wind Sailing close-hauled.

outboard Away from the centerline of the boat; mounted on the stern.

outhaul The line that pulls the mainsail

away from the mast and tightens the foot of the sail along the boom.

painter A short piece of rope secured to the bow of a small boat and used for making her fast to a dock.

pay off To turn the bow away from the wind.

peak The upper after comer of a gaff sail.

pennant A three-sided flag.

pinch To sail so close to the wind as to allow the sails to luff.

pintle A bolt of metal secured to the rudder and fitting into the gudgeon. The pintle gives a swinging support to the rudder.

point To head close to the wind.

port The left side of a boat as one faces forward.

port tack A course with the wind coming from the port and the sails trimmed on the starboard side.

quarter That portion of a vessel's side near the stern.

rail The outer edge of the deck.

rake The angle of a boat's mast from the vertical.

reach Sailing with a beam wind.

ready about The command given to prepare for coming about.

reef To reduce the area of a sail.

rhumb line The straight-line compass course between two points; hence the shortest course, except over long distances, where the great circle course is shorter.

rig 1) In general, a boat's upper works. 2) To set up the spars and standing and running rigging of a sailboat.

rigging The wire or lines used to adjust sails.

roach The curve of the edge of the sail.

rode The line and chain that secure the anchor to the boat.

rudder A flat wooden shape fitted on the sternpost by pintles and gudgeons.

run Point of sail with the wind aft.

sail ties Lengths of webbing used to secure a furled sad to a boom.

scull To move the rudder rapidly back and forth to propel the boat forward.

seaway An area with rough or moderate waves.

secure To make safe.

set The direction of the leeway of a vessel or of tide or current.

shackle A U-shaped piece of iron or steel with eyes in the ends, closed by a shackle pin.

shake out To let out a reef and hoist the sail.

sheave The wheel of a block pulley.

sheet The line used to control the forward or athwartships movement of a sail.

shrouds Vertical wires that hold the mast upright.

skeg A continuation of the keel aft that protects the propeller and sometimes connects to the heel of the rudder.

spinnaker A balloonlike sail used on a downwind course.

splice To join rope by tucking the strands together.

spreader An athwartships support that holds the shrouds away from the mast.

spring line A line used when the boat is docked to keep her from moving forward and aft.

squall A brief storm that arrives suddenly.

stand-on vessel A vessel that maintains her course and speed.

standing rigging That part of a ship's rigging that is permanently secured and not movable (stays, shrouds, and spreaders).

starboard The right side of a boat as one faces forward.

starboard tack A course with the wind coming from the starboard and the sails trimmed on the port side.

stay A rope of hemp, wire, or iron used for supporting a mast fore-and-aft.

staysail A small triangular sail used forward of the mast on a reaching course.

stem The timber at the extreme forward part of a boat, secured to the forward end of the keel and supporting the bow planks.

step the frame into which the heel of a

mast fits or stops.

stern The after section of the boat.

stow To put away.

strake A row of planks in the hull.

swamp To fill with water.

tack 1) The forward lower corner of a sail, where the luff and foot meet. 2) Any course on which the wind comes from either side of the boat. 3) To change course by passing into the wind.

tackle An arrangement of ropes and blocks to give a mechanical advantage.

tender 1) A small boat employed to go back and forth to the shore from a larger boat. 2) Heeling easily when close-hauled.

thimble An iron ring grooved on the outside for a rope grommet.

thwart The athwartships seat in a boat.

tiller Steering instrument that controls the rudder.

topping lift 1) A line or wire to hold the boom off the deck when not in use (also called a boom lift). 2) A line from the mast to the spinnaker pole, controlling spinnaker pole height.

topside On deck.

transom The stern facing of the hull.

traveler A sliding fitting to which the mainsheet is attached, keeping the boom in the same place as it is moved in and out.

trim 1) To adjust the sails. 2) The position of the sails relative to the wind.

tuning The delicate adjustment of a boat's rigging, sails, and hull to the proper balance to assure the best sailing performance.

turnbuckle A threaded link that pulls two eyes together, used for setting up standing rigging.

veer A change of direction, as in the wind.

wake The waves from a boat.

waterline An imaginary line around the hull at the surface of the water when the boat is on an even keel.

weather The state of the atmosphere at a certain time and place.

well found Well equipped.

whip To bind the strands of a line's end with yarn or cord.

whisker pole A light spar extending from the mast and used to hold the jib out when sailing off the wind.

winch A mechanical device to aid in trimming a line. It consists basically of a coil, on which the line is wound, and a crank to do the winding.

windward Toward the wind, the opposite of leeward.

wing-and-wing Running before the wind with the sails set on both sides.

working sails The regular sails on a boat.

yacht General term for a boat used solely for the personal pleasure of the owner.

yawl A two-masted boat with a small after mast located abaft the steering gear.

INDEX

THE EVERYTHING®
PALEOLITHIC DIET SLOW COOKER COOKBOOK

Emily Dionne, MS, RD, LDN, CSSD, ACSM-HFS

Δadamsmedia

Avon, Massachusetts

John C. Hart Memorial Library
1130 E. Main Street
Shrub Oak, New York 10588

This book is dedicated to Brian.
Thank you for so many very special memories
that I will cherish forever, and for reminding
us all that life is far too short. I love you.

Copyright © 2013 by F+W Media, Inc. All rights reserved.
This book, or parts thereof, may not be reproduced
in any form without permission from the publisher; exceptions
are made for brief excerpts used in published reviews.

An Everything® Series Book.
Everything® and everything.com® are registered trademarks of F+W Media, Inc.

Published by Adams Media, a division of F+W Media, Inc.
57 Littlefield Street, Avon, MA 02322. U.S.A.
www.adamsmedia.com

ISBN 10: 1-4405-5536-2
ISBN 13: 978-1-4405-5536-7
eISBN 10: 1-4405-5537-0
eISBN 13: 978-1-4405--5537-4

The Everything® Paleolithic Diet Slow Cooker Cookbook contains material adapted and abridged from *The Everything® Gluten-Free Slow Cooker Cookbook* by Carrie S. Forbes, copyright © 2012 by F+W Media, Inc., ISBN 10: 1-4405-3366-0, ISBN 13: 978-1-4405-3366-2; *The Everything® Healthy Slow Cooker Cookbook* by Rachel Rappaport with B. E. Horton, MS, RD, copyright © 2010 by F+W Media, Inc., ISBN 10: 1-4405-0231-5, ISBN 13: 978-1-4405-0231-6; and *The Everything® Paleolithic Diet Cookbook*, by Jodie Cohen and Gilaad Cohen, copyright © 2011 by F+W Media, Inc., ISBN 10: 1-4405-1206-X, ISBN 13: 978-1-4405-1206-3.

Printed in the United States of America.

10 9 8 7 6 5 4 3 2 1

Always follow safety and common-sense cooking protocol while using kitchen utensils, operating ovens and stoves, and handling uncooked food. If children are assisting in the preparation of any recipe, they should always be supervised by an adult.

Many of the designations used by manufacturers and sellers to distinguish their products are claimed as trademarks. Where those designations appear in this book and F+W Media was aware of a trademark claim, the designations have been printed with initial capital letters.

This book is available at quantity discounts for bulk purchases.
For information, please call 1-800-289-0963.

Contents

Acknowledgments

I would like to thank all of my clients, family, friends, and coworkers who provided their inspiration and support, all of which is represented in this book by the hundreds of delicious recipes—none of which could have been created without their help. A special thank-you to my clients at MBX Training, for their specialized input into the performance nutrition recipes, tailored toward athletes like themselves. Another special thank-you to my parents, who graciously took care of Buddy on those many late nights spent slow cooking. I truly appreciate everyone's suggestions, insight, and patience.

Introduction

IT IS NO SECRET that the Paleolithic diet has been pegged as one of the most difficult diets to follow. Although many recipes call for just a few ingredients, the challenges revolve around the amount of planning ahead required to bring these recipes to fruition. Cue the slow cooker! Slow cooking introduces New Age cooking methods to Stone Age sustenance. It incorporates a diverse range of fresh produce, herbs, and spices in each and every scrumptious concoction, while encouraging creativity, patience, and an open mind. The cavemen of the Paleolithic era did not have the privilege of utilizing this modern-day appliance. However, they did have their own way of slow cooking, by the only source of heat that was available—fire.

Slow cooking helps simplify the entire recipe process, both the cooking as well as the preparation. Fortunately, for the fairly simplistic, three-food-group-limited Paleo diet, slow cookers add both versatility and flair. This book is comprised of an extensive array of delicious and nutritious Paleo cuisine, including breakfast, lunch, dinner, and dessert dishes, ethnic cuisine, kid-friendly entrées, appetizers, and much more. The sizes of slow cookers used in these recipes range from 2-quart to 6-quart, and cooking times vary from less than 1 hour, to greater than 10 hours.

The increasing popularity of the Paleo diet has led to the need for guidance in making it easier to follow, more convenient, and more conducive to our fast-paced, modern-day lifestyle. The Paleo way, sometimes referred to as eating "clean," can lead to a number of favorable health benefits for people of all ages and backgrounds, and as a result of some of these benefits, can also lead to improved sports performance in athletes. The diet is loaded with antioxidants, vitamins, minerals, and heart healthy fats, all of which provide anti-inflammatory benefits, which can decrease one's risk of developing chronic diseases, including diabetes, cancer, cardiovascular disease, and osteoporosis. Following the diet can improve disease markers in those already suffering, and speed an athlete's recovery from training and

competition, therefore improving strength gains, and ultimately, enhancing performance. The Paleo diet is also rich in fiber, which aids in regulating and improving digestion as well as maintaining more consistent energy levels, a key factor for both competitive athletes and avid exercisers. Some research also supports that this diet can improve an individual's weight management, overall body composition (i.e., decreased body fat percentage), and result in improvements in one's ability to control appetite.

There are some important modifications to the Paleo diet necessary to meet the specialized performance needs of athletes. Therefore, many of the recipes incorporate some "non-Paleo" foods such as starchy vegetables, sports drinks, and other liquid carbohydrates, in order to meet these needs. Two hours prior to competition, during competition, and up until ninety minutes following competition, specific non-Paleo foods should be consumed in order to prevent hindrance to performance, and to promote optimal recovery. Calcium and vitamin D supplements are sometimes recommended, depending on whether the athlete is willing to consume dairy or not and the amount of sunlight exposure he or she typically obtains. Consulting with a health care provider, team physician, or sports dietitian is important for athletes who follow the Paleolithic diet, especially for those just beginning the diet.

The hundreds of recipes included in the chapters to follow provide a diverse taste of the native cuisine of our primal ancestors, all slow cooked for your enjoyment. Remember, there are no rules when it comes to the types and amounts of fresh herbs, spices, fruits, and vegetables, so be creative, have fun, cook slow, and be well.

CHAPTER 1

Slow Cooking Nutritious and Delicious Cuisine for the Paleolithic Palate

The Paleolithic diet encompasses all principles of health and wellness. Adapting this lifestyle can help improve one's overall body composition, by both decreasing fat mass and increasing lean body mass. Some of the many potential health benefits of adopting a Paleolithic lifestyle include: improved health outcomes, decreased risk of disease, improved energy levels, and improved fitness levels and athletic performance. A major barrier to maintaining healthy behavior changes in today's society is time. Slow cooking is the perfect solution. With the use of a slow cooker, adopting a Paleolithic lifestyle can be simple and enjoyable.

The Paleolithic Era

Who would have thought that eating like a caveman would be a good idea? Little did we know how much knowledge our Paleolithic ancestors possessed. Even though they had to find, hunt, and kill most of their food, they were still making better choices than most in the world today. In addition, the exercise they endured while hunting their food was the icing on the cake. The Paleolithic humans had it right, while today's diets often include foods that are wreaking havoc on the human body.

Before the Neolithic time period, where development of agriculture and the domestication of animals became commonplace, Paleolithic humans were forced to survive off the land. They hunted wild game for protein and gathered fruits, vegetables, nuts, and seeds. There were no grains harvested, legumes cooked, or milk consumed past weaning. Our primal ancestors ate what they could find and they spent their lives hunting and gathering it. As a result, they were not exposed to many of the unhealthy additives present in some of our foods today.

Hunter-Gatherers

There are still some hunter-gatherers in existence today. They are peoples sustaining themselves and their families off of the land just as our ancestors of the Pleistocene epoch. Today, some examples of traditional hunter-gatherers that continue this lifestyle are the Bushmen of southern Africa, the Pygmies of central Africa, and the Spinifex people of western Australia. These tribes are practically free of the common ailments and killers of our generation today: heart disease, diabetes, arthritis, and cancer. Over time, issues with tooth decay, shorter life spans, infant mortality, and deficiencies such as iron were recorded more often. These are not issues that hunter-gatherers frequently faced.

Why is it that today's hunter-gatherer tend to be healthier than people in the rest of the world? From the outside, their lives appear to be much more difficult. They do not utilize modern medicine, modern shelter, or modern conveniences. They have no refrigeration to keep food for long periods of time. Yet, they survive and live healthier lives than most. Their genes are not constructed different than the rest of the population, and they are certainly not a "super species" of humans. The secret lies within their diet.

Today's Paleolithic Diet

Now you may be thinking that you need to move to the forest and take up hunting, fishing, and gathering to comply with today's Paleolithic diet. That could not be further from the truth. The Paleolithic lifestyle simply requires a shift in your thinking. First, you need to learn what foods are considered Paleo "yes" or Paleo "no." Next, an initial shopping list, an open mind, and a whole bunch of recipes will start you on the journey torward Paleolithic success. Transitioning to a Paleo style of eating does not have to be an arduous task. In fact, many of the recipes adored by families all over the world can be converted quite simply to Paleo recipes with a few careful ingredient choices and some fun substitutions. For example, pasta is a staple in many households, but it is not included in the Paleolithic diet. A fantastic alternative to pasta is spaghetti squash. This amazingly delicious member of the squash family softens when cooked in the oven for less than 45 minutes and with the light touch of a fork, can be pulled to form "strings" that resemble spaghetti.

ESSENTIAL

Paleolithic hunter-gatherers ate foods that were preagricultural. They did not farm the land or herd animals for sustenance. Grains such as wheat, oats, barley, quinoa, and rice were not a part of their diet. White potatoes and legumes, such as soybeans and peanuts, also were not included.

How to Be Successful on the Paleolithic Diet Plan

As with any lifestyle change, you are sure to face obstacles along the way. What will you be able to eat when you're out with your friends? What are you going to prepare for each meal every day? How will you survive without soda and popcorn at the movies? This plan is not easy to initiate, but there are some ways to help ease the transition. These few tips and tricks will make this plan seem more manageable, more comfortable, and simply more fun.

Storage and Cooking in Bulk

An important component of ensuring your success is planning ahead. It is critical that you shop and cook in large amounts and store meals in containers for the future. Otherwise, you will be cooking around the clock and feel overwhelmed. An effective strategy would be to develop a routine where you cook three or four meals at one time and store them in the refrigerator or freezer.

Slow Cookers

Typically, you can find slow cookers where you find most small appliances. These mini ovens enable you to pack the most flavor into your food and give even the most inexperienced cooks confidence in the kitchen. They are simple to operate and are practically foolproof, and best of all, you can throw everything in there and leave it to cook for hours at a time. Over the course of several hours your food will absorb the flavorings of spices and vegetables that you didn't know existed. This little invention creates a tasteful finished recipe that will leave you feeling like an accomplished chef.

Advantages to Slow Cooking the Stone Age Diet

Slow cooking is safe, easy, tasty, and even fun! Slow cooking is a slow process, and therefore, the time spent devoted to it is more appreciated, versus meals that require minimal time and preparation. It serves as the perfect way to counteract the hustle and bustle of today's society. It can help promote a *slower*, not-so-fast-paced lifestyle. The longer it takes to cook, the longer it should take to consume.

Slow cookers are extremely versatile. A slow cooker can accommodate a wide variety of dishes including soups and stews, main entrées, breakfast and brunch, meats, seafood, desserts, and even beverages. The Paleolithic diet is fairly restrictive, so incorporating the use of a slow cooker can help keep recipes new, fresh, and exciting.

Incorporating the use of slow cookers into the Paleo lifestyle helps increase acceptance and adherence. Ironically, it introduces some of the advantages of modern-day conveniences to an ancient, prehistoric way of life. Adding some of the benefits of today's fast-paced society through use of a slow cooker proves that quick and easy meal preparation can yield very healthy meals, and at the

same time, illustrates that a lifestyle based on ancient beliefs and practices, can actually be very convenient. In a sense, slow cooking helps reverse some of the negative impacts of the modern-day, fast-paced lifestyle. It also serves as a reminder that the longer it takes for a meal to cook, the longer it should take to eat it. Out with the fast. In with the slow.

FACT

Fifty percent of the ancient diet of the Paleolithic era was composed of fruits and vegetables, compared to a mere 10–15 percent of the modern diet. Ironically, all the fresh produce you desire is just miles away at the nearest grocery store. Our Stone-Age ancestors hand-picked their own.

A Menu the Whole Family Can Enjoy

The simplicity and safety of slow cooking allows for people of all ages to participate. Kid-friendly meals are very easily prepared. Therefore, encouraging kids to be involved in meal preparation teaches healthy cooking early on and decreases interest in other highly caloric, less nutritious foods. Teaching kids to cook at an early age improves the variety and nutrient density of their preferred food choices. It encourages autonomy and responsibility, while simultaneously instilling lifelong healthy behaviors.

ESSENTIAL

More frequent visits to the grocery store are a huge part of adhering to the lifestyle. This shouldn't be viewed as a chore however, but as a healthy experience that reinforces a new, healthier lifestyle with each visit! Engaging children in this experience is yet another positive step toward instilling *permanent* healthy habits.

There are a number of other potential health benefits kids can obtain from going Paleo. Traditional Paleo fare is free of many of the most common modern-day allergens, i.e., peanuts, milk, gluten, and soy. Avoiding allergens in popular and convenience foods can be extremely challenging for an

adult, never mind for a child. Paleolithic-inspired foods also help promote healthy brain development, as they are rich in important micro- and macro-nutrients such as the omega-3 fatty acids eicosapentaenoic acid (EPA) and docosahexaenoic acid (DHA), and antioxidants like vitamins E, C, and A, which help protect the body against free radical damage.

Incorporating "kid-friendly" meals and encouraging every child's participation in meal preparation is a positive step toward preventing childhood obesity. Slow cooking healthy, nutritious meals leaves kids feeling energized and focused versus sluggish and overly full from modern-day fast, convenient, processed foods. Kids who are more in tune with healthy eating are more health conscious, and are able to witness first hand the positive impact of healthy nutrition on their health and performance in sports and in the classroom.

Primal Food for Prevention and Health Promotion

Probably the most significant benefit of adhering to a Paleolithic lifestyle is the potential for decreasing one's risk of developing a number of chronic diseases such as cancer, diabetes, cardiovascular disease, osteoporosis, and so on. Decreasing your risk of developing diseases can of course, also be obtained from consuming a well-balanced, nutrient-dense modern-day diet, low in unhealthy fats, processed foods, refined carbohydrates, and preservatives. However, the popularity of Paleolithic nutrition continues to expand, and people of all ages, demographics, and fitness levels are climbing aboard and sailing back to ancient ways, perhaps in an attempt to reverse and/or avoid the negative impact that years of unhealthy eating habits and sedentary lifestyles have caused.

Heart Healthy

The high fiber, low saturated fat, and high antioxidant and micronutrient content of the Paleo diet has many heart healthy benefits. Such a diet composition can result in improved cholesterol profiles, decreased cardiac risk scores, and improved blood pressure status. It can promote a healthier heart and an overall healthier future.

Cancer Fighting

The Paleo diet provides a number of disease-fighting, cancer-preventing components. Its high dietary fiber content, coupled with an abundance of vitamins, minerals, and antioxidants, as well as the strict avoidance of processed trans fats and refined, processed sugars, together create a strong line of defense against numerous types of cancer.

Optimization of Overall Health and Wellness

Adherence to a Paleolithic lifestyle can also help in the prevention and management of chronic diseases like obesity (defined by a Body Mass Index, or BMI of > 30), diabetes, and osteoporosis. It encourages a naturopathic-based, organic, and more pure perception as well as a greater ownership of one's health and well-being. Self-awareness and establishing a more health conscious perception of oneself are important steps along the road to becoming and staying well.

FACT

Body mass index (BMI), which is calculated using an individual's weight (in kilograms) and divided by his or her height (in meters, squared), is used to classify whether someone is of normal weight, overweight, or in the obesity range. A BMI of 25–29.9 is considered overweight, and obesity is classified by a BMI greater than or equal to 30.

Prehistoric Metabolism

It is more than just what the cavemen put in their mouths that allowed them to maintain healthier weight profiles and a better overall body composition than their modern-day counterparts. Resting metabolism (your metabolic rate) naturally declines with age. This is due to the decrease in one's muscle mass over time, which in turn is due to the decline in physical activity over time. Paleolithic times did *not* promote or even allow for, any sort of sedentary lifestyle. To survive meant one had to move, hunt, gather, keep moving, and so on. Thus preserving their muscle mass for a longer period during adulthood.

ALERT

It is pretty difficult to gain weight on a diet comprised predominantly of fruits and vegetables! However, animal protein is a large component of the Paleo diet, and excess saturated fats and calories can easily be consumed, without careful consideration of food choices and meal preparation.

Longevity Without Medicine

Health and metabolism may have been more easily maintained in prehistoric times, despite the fact that advances in modern medicine were not available for them to take advantage of. If the two worlds collided—prehistoric lifestyle meets modern medicine—it could very well be the best of both worlds. Hence, the ever-growing popularity of Paleolithic nutrition.

Fuel for Fitness

Avid exercisers and competitive athletes are becoming increasingly interested in adopting a Paleolithic-themed lifestyle. As many engage in exercise to relieve stress and enhance overall health and wellness, their preference for a more pure, fresh, less processed, and more organic diet frequently ensues. Retracing the footsteps of our Paleolithic ancestors is an easy task for some, more challenging for others, yet tempting to many. It is important to set clear fitness and performance goals—and to ensure proper nutrition—in order to not only complement, but optimize these goals. When consistently and appropriately adhered to, the Paleolithic diet plan can play a key role in the pursuit of maximum performance.

Competitive athletes and others involved in periods of intense training and competition have more complex nutrient requirements. The work of Loren Cordain, PhD, a professor and well-known researcher in Paleolithic nutrition, laid the groundwork for the special considerations developed for athletes who follow the Paleolithic diet. Cordain's *The Paleo Diet for Athletes* recommends that athletes increase their consumption of essential carbohydrates to meet their specialized performance needs, and it provides nutrient

timing guidelines for doing so. The recommendations for implementing necessary variations to the Paleo diet are influenced by an increased need for carbohydrates before, during, and after training and competition. Non-Paleo starches and sugars are encouraged during these times, in order to adequately prefuel, maintain, and refuel. Adequate carbohydrates, fluids, and electrolytes are critical for preventing injury and enhancing recovery.

Awaken the Senses

The naturopathic-themed approach of the Paleo lifestyle to health and well-being promotes an overall wakening of the senses. The variety of fresh herbs and spices helps enhance enjoyment of eating. Adopting mindful eating practices creates more openness and acceptance to new foods, promoting a greater appreciation and understanding of where our foods actually come from. Slow cooking is a perfect way to illustrate the joy of mindful eating. It gives the experience of seeing and smelling, and thus savoring the food, even hours before sitting down to eat.

ESSENTIAL

Slow cooking allows for more variety and diversity, with the ability to use numerous fresh herbs, spices, and natural seasonings. Variety is crucial to preventing boredom, and thus maximizes adherence to a desired lifestyle; therefore, slow cooking Paleolithic dishes makes the lifestyle easier to stick with!

Processed Foods Out, Natural Fare In

Slow cooking, especially that of Paleolithic fare, prohibits the use of processed, packaged food products. Eating clean, in a sense, is enjoying cuisine free of additives, chemicals, and toxins, while embellishing wholesome, true ingredients. It serves as a twofold approach to health: Paleolithic nutrition helps eliminate the potentially negative impacts of the modern-day diet by simply avoiding the center of the supermarket, while enhancing overall nutritional intake by shopping solely along the perimeter.

Modernizing the Paleolithic Lifestyle

The conveniences of modern-day society place the world at our fingertips. Cavemen, with no access to any kind of technology or other conveniences of our modern-day lifestyle, survived and thrived on a Paleolithic lifestyle. Therefore, there is no reason it can't be done today. As technology and other modern advancements have evolved, there has been a corresponding decline in the significance placed on healthy eating and exercise. A lack of time is typically the most common excuse used for both. Isn't the purpose of technology to help make life easier, and better? Instead of allowing modern-day stressors to serve as a permanent excuse for achieving a healthy lifestyle, why not take advantage of these and use them as tools? Simplify. Slow cook!

Rise and Shine:
Slow-Cooking Breakfasts

Breakfast Burrito Filling

Wrap cooked ingredients in egg whites (pan-fried, and formed to a size similar to a tortilla), and serve with your favorite breakfast burrito toppings.

INGREDIENTS | SERVES 4

1¼ pounds lean boneless pork, cubed

12 ounces diced tomatoes with green chilies

1 small onion, diced

1 jalapeño, diced

½ teaspoon ground chipotle

¼ teaspoon cayenne pepper

¼ teaspoon ground jalapeño

2 cloves garlic, minced

Place all the ingredients into a 2-quart slow cooker. Stir. Cook on low for 8 hours. Stir before serving.

PER SERVING: Calories: 188 | Fat: 5g | Protein: 32g | Sodium: 70mg | Fiber: 0.5g | Carbohydrates: 2g | Sugar: 1g

"Hard Boiled" Eggs

This old-fashioned, hard boiled breakfast "staple," has never been so simply prepared.

INGREDIENTS | SERVES 12

1 dozen large eggs

1. Place 12 eggs in a 6-quart slow cooker. Cook on high for 2 hours.

2. Gently remove eggs and place in bowl of ice water (which loosens the shell for peeling). Peel, and enjoy!

PER SERVING: Calories: 72 | Fat: 5g | Protein: 6g | Sodium: 70mg | Fiber: 0g | Carbohydrates: 0.5g | Sugar: 0g

Slow Cooked Scrambler

Preparing a warm and hearty scrambled egg dish is a breeze in the slow cooker. A delicious start to the day.

INGREDIENTS | SERVES 2

1 tablespoon canola oil, plus more for greasing slow cooker

6 eggs

6 tablespoons coconut milk

Pepper, to taste

Seasonings of choice, to taste

1 cup chopped vegetables (of choice, e.g., mushrooms, onions, peppers)

1 teaspoon garlic, minced

1 teaspoon mustard

1. Turn a 4-quart slow cooker on low and place canola oil into the slow cooker. Grease the sides of the slow cooker with additional oil, as needed.

2. In a medium bowl, whisk together the eggs and coconut milk and season with pepper to taste. Add any other seasonings to the eggs and whisk the ingredients together.

3. Add 1 cup chopped vegetables of your choosing to the bowl, along with 1 teaspoon of minced garlic, and 1 teaspoon of mustard, and mix.

4. Transfer the egg mixture to the slow cooker, cover and cook on low for 1 hour.

5. Stir the eggs with a fork to help break them up to cook evenly. Cook the scrambled eggs, covered, for 1 more hour. Stir the eggs again with a fork.

PER SERVING: Calories: 362 | Fat: 31g | Protein: 20g | Sodium: 245mg | Fiber: 0.5g | Carbohydrates: 3g | Sugar: 1g

Breakfast Casserole

Cook this overnight and you're guaranteed to impress this season's holiday house guests!

INGREDIENTS | SERVES 4

1 pound lean ground beef (85% lean or higher)

1 small onion, diced

1 teaspoon ground black pepper

1 teaspoon garlic powder

1 teaspoon red pepper flakes

12 eggs

1 cup coconut milk

Canola oil for greasing the slow cooker (about 1 tablespoon)

1 small butternut squash, peeled, seeded, and sliced

1. In a skillet over medium heat, start to cook the ground beef. Add the onion and spices, cooking just until the onion is soft about 8–10 minutes (you don't need to finish cooking the beef—it will finish in the slow cooker).

2. In a large bowl, whip together eggs and coconut milk.

3. Grease the inside of a 4–6-quart slow cooker. Put in the squash, the beef/onion mixture, and then the egg/milk mixture. Stir and make sure that all of the food is covered by the egg/milk mixture. Cook on low for 8–10 hours. Slice and serve warm.

PER SERVING: Calories: 491 | Fat: 33g | Protein: 44g | Sodium: 293mg | Fiber: 1g | Carbohydrates: 5.5g | Sugar: 2g

Cinnamon Stewed Plums

Serve as a breakfast fruit, or as a dessert with a whipped topping.

INGREDIENTS | SERVES 4

½ cup honey

1 cup water

Dash salt

1 tablespoon fresh lemon juice

1 cinnamon stick

1 pound fresh ripe plums (about 8 small or 6 medium), pitted

1. Combine all ingredients in a 2- to 4-quart slow cooker and cook on low for about 6 hours, or until plums are tender.

2. Serve warm, chilled, or at room temperature.

PER SERVING: Calories: 181 | Fat: 0g | Protein: 1g | Sodium: 43mg | Fiber: 2g | Carbohydrates: 48g | Sugar: 46g

Ground Chicken and Carrot Quiche

This high protein recipe can be served for breakfast, lunch, or dinner.

INGREDIENTS | SERVES 2

6 large eggs
½ pound ground chicken, browned
1 cup shredded carrots
½ cup beef broth
5 tablespoons coconut milk
4 tablespoons fresh parsley
½ teaspoon coriander
Coconut oil, for greasing slow cooker

1. Crack the eggs into a medium bowl and beat well with wire whisk.

2. Add the chicken, carrots, and all remaining ingredients except coconut oil, and stir.

3. Grease bottom and sides of a 2- to 4-quart slow cooker with coconut oil. Add the egg mixture to slow cooker, cover, and cook on low for 1 hour.

4. Stir the eggs with a fork to help break them up for even cooking. Cover, and cook on low for 1 hour. Fluff with a fork and serve warm.

PER SERVING: Calories: 551 | Fat: 40g | Protein: 40g | Sodium: 538mg | Fiber: 2g | Carbohydrates: 8g | Sugar: 4g

Slow Cooked Eggs Florentine

This egg recipe can be prepared using a variety of vegetables.
Feel free to experiment with tomatoes, artichokes, zucchini, etc.

INGREDIENTS | SERVES 3

Cooking spray or coconut oil for greasing slow cooker

1 (10-ounce) package frozen, chopped spinach, thawed and drained

1 (8-ounce) can mushrooms, drained

¼ cup onion, chopped

6 large eggs, beaten

1 cup coconut milk

1 teaspoon black pepper

½ teaspoon dried oregano

½ teaspoon dried basil

½ teaspoon garlic powder

1. Spray a 4–6-quart slow cooker with nonstick cooking spray or grease with coconut oil.

2. Layer the spinach, mushrooms, and onions on bottom of slow cooker.

3. In a medium bowl, combine the eggs, coconut milk, pepper and all other seasonings, and pour mixture into slow cooker.

4. Cover and cook on high for 1½–2 hours or until center is hot. Spoon out onto individual plates, and serve warm.

PER SERVING: Calories: 341 | Fat: 27g | Protein: 18g | Sodium: 542mg | Fiber: 4g | Carbohydrates: 12g | Sugar: 3g

Southwestern Breakfast Bake

Perfect for brunch, or a special occasion late breakfast with family or friends, as this dish takes a minimum of 4 hours to cook.

INGREDIENTS | SERVES 8

8 large eggs

1 (7-ounce) can of green chilies, drained

2 cups coconut milk

1 cup sliced mushrooms

1 red bell pepper, seeded and diced

1 small onion, diced

1 cup diced tomatoes

¾ teaspoon lemon juice

½ teaspoon black pepper

2 (10-ounce) packages frozen spinach, thawed, undrained

1. Combine all ingredients (except spinach) in a bowl and whisk together.

2. Layer ⅓ of the spinach (about 3 ounces) on bottom of 4-quart slow cooker. Pour ½ of egg mixture on top of spinach. Put another layer of spinach (about 3 ounces) on top of egg mixture, and top with remaining egg mixture. Top with the remaining spinach. Cover and cook on low for 6–7 hours or on high for 4–5 hours.

3. Uncover a few minutes before serving, and cook on high to allow finished product to dry out.

PER SERVING: Calories: 227 | Fat: 18g | Protein: 11g | Sodium: 134mg | Fiber: 3g | Carbohydrates: 10g | Sugar: 4g

Paleo-Approved Zucchini Nut Bread

*Top this sweet bread with some apple butter, peach marmalade,
or other fruit spread found later in this chapter.*

INGREDIENTS | SERVES 8

3 eggs, beaten

½ cup sunflower oil

½ cup unsweetened applesauce (or
Awesome Applesauce, see Chapter 4)

1 teaspoon orange extract

¼ cup honey

2 teaspoons baking soda

1 teaspoon baking powder

1 teaspoon ground cinnamon

1 cup hazelnuts, ground to the
consistency of coarse meal

1 cup pecans, ground to the consistency
of coarse meal

1 cup almond powder

1 cup chopped walnut pieces

¾ pound zucchini, grated

Cooking oil spray

1. Preheat a round 5-quart slow cooker with the lid on at high for 15 minutes.

2. Blend together the first eight ingredients in a large bowl. Stir in the nuts and zucchini.

3. Spray the bottom and lower sides of the preheated slow cooker with the cooking spray oil.

4. Pour the batter evenly into the slow cooker. Cover and bake for 45–60 minutes, or until sides of the bread pull away from sides of slow cooker and the tip of a knife inserted into the center, held to the count of five, comes out clean.

PER SERVING: Calories: 238 | Fat: 17g | Protein: 8g |
Sodium: 406mg | Fiber: 3g | Carbohydrates: 17g | Sugar: 12g

Rubble Porridge

This Stone Age inspired hot cereal is loaded with fiber, vitamin E, and omega-3 fatty acids.

INGREDIENTS | SERVES 6

½ cup raisins and cranberries
¼ cup slivered almonds
¼ cup raw pumpkin seeds
¼ cup raw sunflower seeds
¼ cup unsweetened coconut
⅛ cup honey
2 tablespoons coconut butter, melted

1. Place all dry ingredients in a 4-quart slow cooker, add honey and butter, and toss well.

2. Cover (but vent with a chopstick) and cook on high for 2½–3½ hours, stirring periodically to prevent burning.

3. Cool porridge on parchment paper. Enjoy with almond or coconut milk.

PER SERVING: Calories: 160 | Fat: 9g | Protein: 4g | Sodium: 3mg | Fiber: 2g | Carbohydrates: 19g | Sugar: 14g

Apples Supreme

Enjoy the treasures of apple picking season with this melt-in-your-mouth dish, another recipe that can be served as a breakfast fruit or warm dessert.

INGREDIENTS | SERVES 8

4 Granny Smith apples, peeled, cored, and sliced

4 Golden Delicious apples, peeled, cored, and sliced

¾ cup honey

½ teaspoon ground cinnamon

½ teaspoon ground cloves

½ cup coconut butter

Place apples in a 4-quart slow cooker and toss with remaining ingredients. Cover and cook on low for 4–5 hours. Serve warm.

PER SERVING: Calories: 97 | Fat: 0g | Protein: 0g | Sodium: 2mg | Fiber: 1g | Carbohydrates: 26g | Sugar: 26g

Blackberry Jam

This easy low-sugar jam does not need to be canned; it will keep up to a month in the refrigerator.

INGREDIENTS | YIELDS 1 QUART

3 cups fresh blackberries

1¾ ounces no-sugar pectin

½ cup honey

¾ cup water

1. Place all the ingredients in a 2-quart slow cooker. Stir.

2. Cook on high, uncovered, for 5 hours. Using a fork or potato masher, smash the berries a bit until they are the texture you prefer. Pour jam into an airtight container.

3. Refrigerate overnight before using.

PER SERVING: Calories: 701 | Fat: 2g | Protein: 7g | Sodium: 16mg | Fiber: 23g | Carbohydrates: 181g | Sugar: 160g

Pear Clafouti

Clafouti is a soft pancake-like breakfast with fruit. If you choose to use a larger slow cooker than the specified 2½-quart sized, you will need to reduce the cooking time. When the sides are golden brown and a toothpick stuck in the middle comes out clean, the clafouti is done.

INGREDIENTS | SERVES 4

2 pears, stem and seeds removed, cut into chunks, and peeled if preferred

½ cup almond flour

½ cup arrowroot starch

2 teaspoons baking powder

½ teaspoon xanthan gum

⅓ cup honey

1 teaspoon ground cinnamon

2 tablespoons coconut butter, melted

2 eggs

¾ cup (full fat) coconut milk

1 tablespoon vanilla

1. Place pears in a greased 2½-quart slow cooker.

2. In a large bowl whisk together the almond flour, arrowroot starch, baking powder, xanthan gum, honey, and cinnamon.

3. Make a well in the center of the dry ingredients and add melted coconut butter, eggs, coconut milk, and vanilla. Stir to combine wet with dry ingredients.

4. Pour batter over pears. Cover slow cooker and vent lid with a chopstick or the handle of a wooden spoon.

5. Cook on high for 2½–3 hours or on low for 5–6 hours. Serve warm or cold drizzled with a slow cooked Paleo fruit sauce, like Cran-Apple or Summer Berry Sauce (see Chapter 4).

PER SERVING: Calories: 404 | Fat: 19g | Protein: 7g | Sodium: 291mg | Fiber: 5g | Carbohydrates: 56g | Sugar: 32g

Peach Marmalade

You can spread this on a Paleo fruit dish, or try on Paleo-Approved Zucchini Nut Bread (see recipe in this chapter).

INGREDIENTS | YIELDS 8 CUPS

2 pounds peaches, peeled, pitted, and chopped

½ cup (about 6 ounces) dried apricots, chopped

1 (20-ounce) can pineapple tidbits in unsweetened juice, undrained

2 medium oranges

1 small lemon

2 cups honey

2 (3-inch) cinnamon sticks

Innovative Peach Marmalade Uses

By keeping this marmalade the consistency of applesauce you have the added versatility of using it as a condiment to top cooked chicken breasts, easily mixing it with a Paleo barbecue or chili sauce to create a sweet and savory dipping sauce, or using it to replace applesauce in many different recipes.

1. Add peaches to a food processor or blender along with the apricots and pineapple (with juice).

2. Remove the zest from the oranges and lemon and add to the food processor or blender. Cut the oranges and the lemon into quarters and remove any seeds, then add to the food processor or blender. Pulse until entire fruit mixture is pulverized. Pour into a greased 4–6-quart slow cooker.

3. Add the honey to the slow cooker and stir to combine with the fruit mixture. Add the cinnamon sticks. Cover and, stirring occasionally, cook on low for 4 hours or until the mixture reaches the consistency of applesauce. When finished cooking, remove the cinnamon sticks.

4. Unless you process and seal the marmalade into sterilized jars, store in covered glass jars in the refrigerator for up to 3–4 weeks. The marmalade can also be frozen for up to 6 months.

PER SERVING: (1 cup) | Calories: 352 | Fat: 0g | Protein: 2g | Sodium: 5mg | Fiber: 3g | Carbohydrates: 94g | Sugar: 90g

Chai Tea

*Store any leftover tea in a covered container in the refrigerator.
It can be reheated, but leftover tea is best served over ice.*

INGREDIENTS | SERVES 12

5 cups water

6 slices fresh ginger

1 teaspoon whole cloves

2 (3-inch) pieces stick cinnamon

1½ teaspoons freshly ground nutmeg

½ teaspoon ground cardamom

1 cup honey

12 tea bags

6 cups coconut milk

Sweet Tip

If you prefer, you can omit adding the honey during the cooking process and allow each drinker to add the honey to his or her serving according to taste.

1. Add the water to a 4-quart slow cooker. Put the ginger and cloves in a muslin spice bag or a piece of cheesecloth that has been rinsed, wrung dry, and secured with a piece of kitchen twine; add to the cooker along with the cinnamon, nutmeg, and cardamom. Cover and cook on low for 4–6 hours or on high for 2–3 hours.

2. Stir in the honey until it's dissolved into the water. Add the tea bags and coconut milk; cover and cook on low for ½ hour. Remove and discard the spices in the muslin bag or cheesecloth, the cinnamon sticks, and the tea bags. Ladle into tea cups or mugs to serve.

PER SERVING: Calories: 312 | Fat: 24g | Protein: 2g | Sodium: 19mg | Fiber: 0g | Carbohydrates: 27g | Sugar: 23g

Autumn Inspired, Vanilla-Flavored Poached Fruits

Enjoy as breakfast or as dessert. Follow a Paleo dish with this concoction as a sweet end to a hearty meal.

INGREDIENTS | SERVES 5

2 Granny Smith apples, peeled, cored, and halved (save cores)

2 Bartlett Pears, peeled, cored, and halved (save cores)

1 orange, peeled and halved

⅔ cup honey

1 vanilla bean, split and seeded (save seeds)

1 cinnamon stick

1. Place apple and pear cores in a 4½-quart slow cooker.

2. Squeeze juice from orange halves into slow cooker and add the orange halves, honey, vanilla bean and seeds, and cinnamon.

3. Add apples and pears, and pour in enough water to cover the fruit. Stir, cover, and cook on high for 2–3 hours, until fruit is tender.

4. Remove apple and pear halves and set aside. Strain cooking liquids into a large saucepan and simmer gently over low heat until the liquid reduces by half and thickens. Discard apple and pear cores.

5. Dice apples and pears and add to saucepan to warm.

6. To serve, spoon fruit with sauce into bowls.

PER SERVING: Calories: 150 | Fat: 0g | Protein: 0g | Sodium: 2mg | Fiber: 1g | Carbohydrates: 40g | Sugar: 40g

Apple Butter

Depending on when you start this recipe, it can take up to 2 days to complete, but it is great for giving an "autumn-like" feel to just about any side dish, main entrée, dessert, or even a hot or iced beverage.

INGREDIENTS | YIELDS 5 CUPS

6 apples, peeled, cored, and quartered
½ tablespoon vanilla extract
⅔ cup honey
1 teaspoon ground cinnamon
¼ teaspoon ground cloves

1. Place apples and vanilla extract in a 4–6-quart slow cooker. Cover and cook on low for 8 hours.

2. Mash apples with a fork. Stir in honey, cinnamon, and cloves.

3. Cover and cook on low for 6 hours. Allow to cool at room temperature, or in refrigerator for 1–2 hours. Serve chilled or at room temperature.

PER SERVING: (1 cup) | Calories: 235 | Fat: 0g | Protein: 1g | Sodium: 2mg | Fiber: 3g | Carbohydrates: 62g | Sugar: 57g

Strawberry Jelly

Together with almond butter, they make the perfect pair—"AB & J" (almond butter and jelly).

INGREDIENTS | SERVES 24

1½ quarts red, ripe strawberries, washed and hulled

3¾ cups honey

¼ cup lemon juice

1. Place the strawberries into a 4-quart slow cooker. Stir in the honey and lemon juice. Cover and cook on high for 2½ hours, stirring twice.

2. Uncover and continue cooking 2 hours longer, or until preserves have thickened, stirring occasionally.

3. Ladle into hot, sterilized half-pint jelly jars, seal, and store in the refrigerator for up to 2 weeks.

PER SERVING: (3 ounces) | Calories: 173 | Fat: 0g | Protein: 0g | Sodium: 3mg | Fiber: 1g | Carbohydrates: 47g | Sugar: 45g

Pear Butter

Enjoy pear season, all year long! Drizzle over some fresh fruit salad for a sweet addition to a traditional breakfast favorite.

INGREDIENTS | SERVES 8

8 pears of any variety, peeled, cored, and sliced

2 cups water

¾ cup honey

Juice of 1 lemon

1 whole star anise

¼ teaspoon ginger

¼ teaspoon nutmeg

1. Place the all ingredients in a 6-quart slow cooker, cover, and cook on low for 10–12 hours.

2. Uncover and cook on low for an additional 10–12 hours until thick, and most of the liquid has been absorbed.

3. Allow to cool and remove the star anise before puréeing in blender. Store in airtight canning jars.

PER SERVING: (4 ounces) | Calories: 196 | Fat: 0g | Protein: 1g | Sodium: 5mg | Fiber: 5g | Carbohydrates: 53g | Sugar: 43g

Apricot Butter

Makes a tasteful substitute for orange marmalade.

INGREDIENTS | SERVES 8

5 ripe apricots: washed, peeled, pitted, and puréed in food processor
1½ cups honey
2 teaspoons ground cinnamon
1 teaspoon ground cloves
1½ tablespoons lemon juice

1. Pour puréed apricots into a 4–6-quart slow cooker and add honey, spices, and lemon juice. Mix well.

2. Cover and cook on high for 8–10 hours. Remove cover halfway through cooking. Stir periodically.

3. Store in refrigerator, in an airtight canning jar, or freeze.

PER SERVING: (4 ounces) | Calories: 413 | Fat: 0g | Protein: 1g | Sodium: 8mg | Fiber: 2g | Carbohydrates: 11g | Sugar: 109g

Blueberry Butter Bliss

A blueberry lover's dream. This antioxidant-rich spread proves blueberries do live up to their often referred to nickname, a superfood!

INGREDIENTS | SERVES 7

4 cups fresh blueberries, puréed
¾ cup honey
½ lemon zest
1 teaspoon cinnamon
¼ teaspoon grated nutmeg

1. Pour puréed blueberries into a 4–6-quart slow cooker and cover. Cook on low for 5 hours.

2. Remove lid and add the honey, lemon zest, and spices, mixing well. Turn heat up to high, and cook for another hour, uncovered.

3. Once butter is cooked down sufficiently, pour into canning jars and cover tightly.

4. Process canning jars in boiling water for 10 minutes. Store unopened jars in a cool, dark place.

PER SERVING: (4 ounces) | Calories: 161 | Fat: 0g | Protein: 1g | Sodium: 2mg | Fiber: 2g | Carbohydrates: 43g | Sugar: 38g

Blackberry and Apple Preserves

A not-so-traditional combination of two widely enjoyed, versatile fruits.

INGREDIENTS | SERVES 13

2 pounds cooking apples, peeled, cored, and chopped

3 cups honey

1¾ cups blackberries

2 tablespoons lemon juice

1 lemon rind, grated

1. Place all the ingredients in a 4–6-quart slow cooker, cover, and cook on high for 4–5 hours, stirring periodically.

2. Pour jam into warmed canning jars and allow to cool.

3. Cover and store in refrigerator for up to 2 months.

PER SERVING: (4 ounces) | Calories: 280 | Fat: 0g | Protein: 1g | Sodium: 4mg | Fiber: 2g | Carbohydrates: 75g | Sugar: 72g

Fig Jam

A versatile spread sure to liven up any Paleo breakfast sweet bread or fruit dish, and loaded with fiber and phytonutrients.

INGREDIENTS | SERVES 3 (½ CUP SERVINGS)

2 pounds fresh figs, peeled, cut into eighths

1 cup honey

½ cup water

1 lemon, diced, including the rind, seeds removed

3 tablespoons crystallized ginger, finely diced

1. Add all the ingredients to a 2–3-quart slow cooker. Cover, and cook on high for 4 hours.

2. Remove cover and cook an additional 1–2 hours, until mixture reaches a jam-like consistency.

3. While still hot, pour into clean, sterilized 4-ounce jars, and store covered in refrigerator for up to 3 weeks.

PER SERVING: Calories: 570 | Fat: 1g | Protein: 3g | Sodium: 9mg | Fiber: 9g | Carbohydrates: 152g | Sugar: 142g

Hot and Spicy Nuts

Serve these at a cocktail party as an alternative to plain salted nuts.
They are also delicious stirred into trail mix.

INGREDIENTS | YIELDS 2½ CUPS

2½ cups skin-on almonds or mixed nuts
1 teaspoon canola oil
½ teaspoon ground jalapeño
½ teaspoon powdered garlic
½ teaspoon ground cayenne
½ teaspoon ground chipotle
½ teaspoon ground paprika

1. Place the nuts into a 2–4-quart slow cooker. Drizzle with the oil. Stir. Add the spices, and then stir again to distribute the seasonings evenly.

2. Cover the slow cooker, and cook on low for 1 hour. Then uncover and cook on low for 15 minutes or until the nuts look dry.

PER SERVING: Calories: 1,417 | Fat: 122g | Protein: 51g | Sodium: 4mg | Fiber: 30g | Carbohydrates: 54g | Sugar: 9g

Slow Cooked Salsa

This may be the easiest salsa recipe ever, but it tastes so much fresher than jarred salsa.

INGREDIENTS | SERVES 10

4 cups grape tomatoes, halved
1 small onion, thinly sliced
2 jalapeño peppers, diced
⅛ teaspoon salt

1. Place all ingredients into a 2-quart slow cooker. Stir. Cook on low for 5 hours.

2. Stir and lightly smash the tomatoes before serving, if desired.

PER SERVING: Calories: 4 | Fat: 0g | Protein: 0g | Sodium: 0.5mg | Fiber: 1g | Carbohydrates: 1g | Sugar: 0.5g

Baba Ghanoush

This dish can be served as an appetizer, a side dish, a dip, or even a salad. Serve this with fresh vegetables.

INGREDIENTS | SERVES 12

1 (1-pound) eggplant
2 tablespoons tahini
2 tablespoons lemon juice
2 cloves garlic

Tahini Tips

Tahini is a paste made from ground sesame seeds. The most common tahini uses seeds that have been toasted before they are ground, but "raw" tahini is also available. The two can be used interchangeably in most recipes, but occasionally a recipe will specify one or the other. Look for tahini near the peanut butter, in the health food section, or with the specialty foods in most grocery stores.

1. Pierce the eggplant with a fork. Cook on high in a 4-quart slow cooker for 2 hours.

2. Allow the eggplant to cool. Peel off the skin. Slice it in half and remove the seeds. Discard the skin and seeds.

3. Place the pulp in a food processor and add the remaining ingredients. Pulse until smooth.

PER SERVING: Calories: 25 | Fat: 1g | Protein: 1g | Sodium: 4mg | Fiber: 2g | Carbohydrates: 3g | Sugar: 1g

Pumpkin Bisque

This simple soup is a perfect first course at a holiday meal or as a light lunch.

INGREDIENTS | SERVES 4

2 cups puréed pumpkin

4 cups water

1 cup unsweetened coconut or almond milk

¼ teaspoon ground nutmeg

2 cloves garlic, minced

1 large onion, minced

Make Your Own Pumpkin Purée

Preheat the oven to 350°F. Slice a pie pumpkin or an "eating" pumpkin into wedges and remove the seeds. Place the wedges on a baking sheet and bake until the flesh is soft, about 40 minutes. Scoop out the flesh and allow it to cool before puréeing it in a blender.

1. Place all ingredients into a 4-quart slow cooker. Stir. Cook on low for 8 hours.

2. Use an immersion blender, or blend the bisque in batches in a standard blender, to blend until smooth. Serve hot.

PER SERVING: Calories: 85 | Fat: 7g | Protein: 1g | Sodium: 12g | Fiber: 2g | Carbohydrates: 6g | Sugar: 2g

Beef Taco Filling, Paleo Style

Smoky hot chipotle peppers give this filling a rich spicy flavor. Try it wrapped in iceberg or romaine lettuce leaves and topped with shredded carrots, avocado, and tomato.

INGREDIENTS | SERVES 8

1½ pounds 94% lean ground beef

1 large onion, minced

15 ounces canned fire-roasted diced tomatoes

1 Anaheim pepper, minced

2 chipotle peppers in adobo, minced

½ teaspoon cumin

½ teaspoon cayenne pepper

½ teaspoon paprika

½ teaspoon garlic powder

½ teaspoon oregano

1. Sauté the beef and onion in a nonstick skillet for about 5–10 minutes, until just browned. Drain off any grease. Add to a 4-quart slow cooker. Break up any large pieces of beef with a spoon.

2. Add the remaining ingredients and stir. Cook on low for 7 hours. Stir prior to serving.

PER SERVING: Calories: 139 | Fat: 4g | Protein: 18g | Sodium: 56mg | Fiber: 0g | Carbohydrates: 2g | Sugar: 1g

Chicken Taco Filling, Paleo Style

Try different variations of this recipe using ground turkey or ground veal.

INGREDIENTS | SERVES 8

1½ pounds lean ground chicken

1 large onion, minced

15 ounces canned fire-roasted diced tomatoes

1 Anaheim pepper, minced

2 chipotle peppers in adobo, minced

½ teaspoon cumin

½ teaspoon cayenne pepper

½ teaspoon paprika

½ teaspoon garlic powder

½ teaspoon oregano

1. Sauté the chicken and onion in a nonstick skillet for about 4–8 minutes, until just browned. Drain off any grease. Add to a 4-quart slow cooker. Break up any large pieces of chicken with a spoon.

2. Add the remaining ingredients and stir. Cook on low for 7 hours. Stir prior to serving.

PER SERVING: Calories: 185 | Fat: 13g | Protein: 15g | Sodium: 65mg | Fiber: 0g | Carbohydrates: 2g | Sugar: 1g

Enchilada Filling, Paleo Style

This recipe is an excellent way to use up leftover chicken or turkey, and it makes enough filling for two 9" × 13" pans (8 enchiladas, using large lettuce leaves, per dish) of enchiladas. Make one pan and freeze the other for another time.

INGREDIENTS | SERVES 8

3 jalapeño peppers, halved
1 teaspoon canola oil
1 large onion, diced
3 cloves garlic, minced
1 teaspoon dried oregano
1 teaspoon ground cayenne
½ teaspoon cumin
28 ounces canned crushed tomatoes
¾ cup Chicken Stock (see Chapter 5)
1 tablespoon lime juice
4 cups shredded cooked chicken or turkey

Don't Overfill

Leave at least an inch of headroom in the slow cooker. The lid needs to fit tightly for the slow cooker to cook properly; otherwise the liquid ingredients may boil over, leaving you with a potentially dangerous situation and quite a mess.

1. Place the jalapeño peppers cut-side down on a broiler pan. Broil on low for 2 minutes or until they start to brown. Allow to cool, and then dice.

2. In a nonstick skillet, heat the oil over medium heat. Add the onions, garlic, and jalapeño peppers, and sauté until the onions are soft, about 5 minutes.

3. Add the onion mixture to a 4-quart slow cooker. Add the remaining spices, crushed tomatoes, stock, and lime juice. Cook on low for 5–6 hours, then add the shredded meat. Turn up to high and cook for an additional hour.

PER SERVING: Calories: 158 | Fat: 6g | Protein: 21g | Sodium: 93mg | Fiber: 1g | Carbohydrates: 4g | Sugar: 1g

Pork and Tomatillo Burrito Filling, Paleo Style

Serve this filling with tomatoes, lettuce, and avocado in large iceberg or romaine lettuce leaves.

INGREDIENTS | SERVES 2

½ pound boneless lean pork tenderloin roast

¾ cup diced tomatillos

¼ cup sliced onions

½ jalapeño, diced

1 tablespoon lime juice

1. Place all ingredients into a 2-quart slow cooker. Stir. Cook on low for 8–10 hours.

2. Use a fork to shred all of the contents. Toss to distribute the ingredients evenly.

PER SERVING: Calories: 147 | Fat: 3g | Protein: 24g | Sodium: 61mg | Fiber: 1g | Carbohydrates: 5g | Sugar: 3g

Stuffed Grape Leaves

Although there are many versions of grape leaves served across the Mediterranean, these grape leaves are inspired by Greece.

INGREDIENTS | SERVES 30

16 ounces jarred grape leaves (about 60 leaves)

Cooking spray, as needed

¾ pound 94% lean ground beef, chicken, or pork

1 shallot, minced

¼ cup minced dill

½ cup lemon juice, divided

2 tablespoons minced parsley

1 tablespoon dried mint

1 tablespoon ground fennel

¼ teaspoon freshly ground black pepper

2 cups water

1. Prepare the grape leaves according to package instructions. Set aside.

2. Spray a nonstick skillet with cooking spray. Sauté the meat and shallot until the meat is thoroughly cooked. Drain off any excess fat. Scrape into a bowl and add the dill, ¼ cup of the lemon juice, parsley, mint, fennel, and pepper. Stir to incorporate all ingredients.

3. Place a leaf, stem-side up, with the top of the leaf pointing away from you on a clean work surface. Place 1 teaspoon filling in the middle of the leaf. Fold the bottom toward the middle and then fold in the sides. Roll it toward the top to seal. Repeat until all leaves are used.

4. Place the rolled grape leaves in two or three layers in a 4-quart oval slow cooker. Pour in the water and remaining lemon juice. Cover and cook on low for 4–6 hours. Serve warm or cold.

PER SERVING: Calories: 21 | Fat: 1g | Protein: 3g | Sodium: 11mg | Fiber: 0g | Carbohydrates: 0g | Sugar: 0g

Slow Cooked Almonds with a Kick

These crunchy, heart-healthy snacks are hard to resist.

INGREDIENTS | SERVES 24

6 cups whole, unblanched almonds
4 tablespoons coconut oil
3 cloves garlic, minced
2–3 teaspoons coarsely ground pepper

1. Heat a 4-quart slow cooker on high for 15 minutes. Add the almonds.

2. Drizzle oil over almonds and stir. Sprinkle with garlic and pepper, and stir.

3. Cover, and cook on low for 2 hours. Stir every 30 minutes.

4. Turn heat up to high, and cook uncovered for 30 minutes, stirring every 15 minutes.

5. Turn heat to low and serve warm, or remove from heat and allow to cool.

PER SERVING: Calories: 138 | Fat: 12g | Protein: 5g | Sodium: 0.5mg | Fiber: 3g | Carbohydrates: 5g | Sugar: 1g

Eggplant Relish

Serve with grilled or raw veggies for dipping.

INGREDIENTS | SERVES 6

1 large eggplant, pierced all over with fork
2 tablespoons extra virgin olive oil
½ cup finely chopped tomato
¼ cup finely chopped onion
¼ cup almond yogurt
3 cloves garlic, minced
½ teaspoon dried oregano leaves
1–2 tablespoons lemon juice
Pepper, to taste

1. Place pierced eggplant in a 4-quart slow cooker, cover, and cook on low until tender, 4–5 hours. Cool to room temperature.

2. Cut eggplant in half and remove eggplant pulp (including the seeds) from the peel, with a spoon. Mash eggplant pulp and mix with olive oil, tomato, onion, almond yogurt, garlic, and dried oregano. Season with lemon juice and pepper and serve.

PER SERVING: Calories: 49 | Fat: 5g | Protein: 0g | Sodium: 2mg | Fiber: 0g | Carbohydrates: 2g | Sugar: 1g

Buffalo Chicken Wings

These spicy wings make the perfect tailgate treat.

INGREDIENTS | SERVES 12

4 tablespoons canola or coconut oil (or a combination of these)

4 tablespoons hot pepper sauce

1 tablespoon lime juice

Pepper, to taste

4 pounds chicken wings with wing tips removed, cut in half

Try 'em boneless!

For the boneless version of this classic appetizer, replace wings with 4 pounds of boneless, skinless tenders. Be prepared to eat with a fork! Serve as an appetizer as is, or on top a bed of salad greens.

1. Add oil, hot pepper sauce, and lime juice to a 4–6-quart slower cooker. Cook on high, about 15–20 minutes.

2. Add small amount of pepper to wings and broil in the oven until lightly browned, about 5–6 minutes on each side.

3. Add chicken wings to slow cooker, and stir to coat with the sauce. Cover and cook on high for 3–4 hours.

PER SERVING: Calories: 372 | Fat: 28g | Protein: 27g | Sodium: 233mg | Fiber: 0g | Carbohydrates: 0g | Sugar: 0g

Spiced Cashews

This fiery favorite can liven up any appetizer menu.

INGREDIENTS | SERVES 24

6 cups cashews

3 tablespoons olive or canola oil

3 tablespoons crushed dried rosemary leaves

1 tablespoon honey

¾ teaspoon cayenne pepper

½ teaspoon garlic powder

1. Heat a 2- to 4-quart slow cooker on high for 15 minutes; add cashews. Drizzle oil over cashews and toss; add remaining ingredients and toss.

2. Cover and cook on low for 2 hours, stirring every hour. Turn heat to high, uncover, and cook 30 minutes, stirring after 15 minutes.

3. Turn heat to low to keep warm for serving or remove from slow cooker.

PER SERVING: Calories: 20 | Fat: 2g | Protein: 0g | Sodium: 0mg | Fiber: 0g | Carbohydrates: 1g | Sugar: 1g

Appetizer Meatballs

Combine the cooked meatballs in a slow cooker with a sauce from Chapter 4, like Jalapeño-Tomatillo Sauce or Pink Tomato Sauce, to enhance the flavor of these versatile meatballs.

INGREDIENTS | YIELDS 24 MEATBALLS

1 pound lean ground beef
1 egg
2 tablespoons dried minced onion
1 teaspoon garlic powder
½ teaspoon pepper

1. Add all the ingredients to a large mixing bowl and combine with your clean hands. Shape the resulting mixture into approximately 24 meatballs.

2. Add meatballs to a 2- to 4-quart slow cooker, cover, and cook on high until meatballs are cooked through, about 4 hours.

3. Turn heat to low and keep warm before serving.

PER SERVING: (per meatball) | Calories: 29 | Fat: 1g | Protein: 4g | Sodium: 15mg | Fiber: 0g | Carbohydrates: 0g | Sugar: 0g

Slow Cooked Paleo Party Mix

Grab it while it's hot, because it won't last long once the guests arrive!

INGREDIENTS | SERVES 24

4 tablespoons canola oil
3 tablespoons lime juice
2 teaspoons garlic powder
2 teaspoons onion powder
1 cup raw almonds
1 cup raw pecans
1 cup raw walnut pieces
1 cup raw cashews
2 cups raw pumpkin seeds, shelled
1 cup raw sunflower seeds, shelled

1. Add canola oil to a 2-quart slow cooker. Then add the lime juice, garlic powder, and onion powder, and stir all together.

2. Next, add the nuts and seeds. Stir well until all are evenly coated. Cover and cook on low for 5–6 hours, stirring occasionally.

3. Uncover slow cooker, stir, and cook another 45–60 minutes, to dry the nuts and seeds.

4. Cool and store in airtight container.

PER SERVING: Calories: 207 | Fat: 19g | Protein: 7g | Sodium: 2mg | Fiber: 3g | Carbohydrates: 5g | Sugar: 1g

Spinach Bake

Serve with vegetable dippers or Paleo-friendly crisps!

INGREDIENTS | SERVES 8

1 (10-ounce) package frozen spinach, thawed, undrained

1 small onion, finely chopped

1 stalk celery, thickly sliced

1 clove garlic

2 tablespoons olive oil

½ teaspoon dried basil

½ teaspoon dried thyme

⅛ teaspoon ground nutmeg

Pepper, to taste

2 eggs

1. In a food processor, process the spinach, onion, celery, garlic, oil, basil, thyme, and nutmeg until finely chopped.

2. Season to taste with pepper. Add eggs and process until smooth.

3. Spoon the mixture into greased, 1-quart souffle dish, and place the dish inside a 6-quart slow cooker.

4. Cover and cook on low about 4 hours.

PER SERVING: Calories: 63 | Fat: 5g | Protein: 3g | Sodium: 48mg | Fiber: 1g | Carbohydrates: 3g | Sugar: 1g

Chicken Chowder

A warm, traditional taste of home. A great first course to a hearty poultry dish, on a cold winter's night.

INGREDIENTS | SERVES 5

1 pound skinless, boneless chicken thighs (cut up into chunks)

1 (14½-ounce) can diced tomatoes

1 (8-ounce) package of fresh, sliced mushrooms

1 large red onion, minced

4–6 cloves of garlic, minced

½ cup Chicken Stock (see Chapter 5)

½ cup dry red wine

1 teaspoon dried oregano

1 teaspoon dried basil

1 teaspoon ground pepper

1. Place all ingredients into a 4-quart slow cooker.

2. Cover and cook on low for 6 hours, stirring occasionally.

PER SERVING: Calories: 162 | Fat: 4g | Protein: 19g | Sodium: 239mg | Fiber: 1g | Carbohydrates: 8g | Sugar: 2g

Bison Stew

Bison contains fewer calories, less fat, and more iron per serving, than both beef and chicken!

INGREDIENTS | SERVES 4

2 small onions, sliced

6 whole, large carrots, peeled and sliced

1 bell pepper, diced

3 stalks celery, diced

2 jalapeño peppers, diced

2 pounds bison meat, cut into 1-inch cubes

1 (28-ounce) can fire-roasted tomatoes

½ cup Jalapeño-Tomatillo Sauce (see Chapter 4)

Handful of fresh cilantro, chopped

1 tablespoon oregano

Pepper, to taste

1. Place onions, carrots, bell pepper, celery, and jalapeño peppers in bottom of a 4–6-quart slow cooker. Add bison meat and all remaining ingredients.

2. Cover and cook on low for 6–8 hours. Serve hot.

PER SERVING: Calories: 95 | Fat: 1.5g | Protein: 2g | Sodium: 103mg | Fiber: 6g | Carbohydrates: 20g | Sugar: 9g

Coconut Shrimp

An irresistibly sweet way to enjoy a commonly served first course dish.

INGREDIENTS | SERVES 6

3½ cup Chicken Stock (see Chapter 5)

1 cup water

1 teaspoon ground coriander

1 teaspoon ground cumin

Cayenne pepper, to taste

1 lime, zested

⅓ cup lime juice

7 garlic cloves, minced

1 tablespoon fresh ginger, minced

1 large onion, chopped

1 red bell pepper, diced

1 large, whole carrot, peeled and shredded

½ cup flaked coconut

½ cup golden raisins

1½ pounds large or jumbo shrimp, peeled and thawed if frozen

Toasted coconut, for garnish

1. Mix the chicken stock, water, coriander, cumin, cayenne pepper, lime zest, lime juice, garlic, and ginger in a 4–6-quart slow cooker.

2. Stir in the onion, bell pepper, carrot, flaked coconut, and raisins.

3. Cover and cook on low setting for 3 hours.

4. Stir in the shrimp. Cover and cook another 30 minutes.

5. Serve garnished with toasted coconut.

PER SERVING: Calories: 232 | Fat: 4g | Protein: 28g | Sodium: 380mg | Fiber: 2g | Carbohydrates: 21g | Sugar: 12g

Carrot Pudding

Serve this pudding chilled in the summer heat and enjoy warm in the cold winter season.

INGREDIENTS | SERVES 4

4 large carrots, cooked and grated
1 small onion, grated
¼ teaspoon nutmeg
1 tablespoon honey
1 cup coconut milk
3 eggs, beaten
½ teaspoon lemon juice

1. Mix together carrots, onion, nutmeg, honey, milk, eggs, and lemon juice.

2. Pour into a 2- to 4-quart slow cooker and cook on high for 3–4 hours.

PER SERVING: Calories: 218 | Fat: 16g | Protein: 7g | Sodium: 110mg | Fiber: 2g | Carbohydrates: 15g | Sugar: 9g

Hot Cinnamon-Chili Walnuts

These seasoned walnuts are a surprising hit with chili powder, cinnamon, and honey.

INGREDIENTS | SERVES 6

1½ cups walnuts

¼ cup honey

2 teaspoons cinnamon

1½ teaspoons chili powder

2 teaspoons coconut oil

1. Combine all the ingredients and place in a greased 2½-quart slow cooker.

2. Cover slow cooker and vent lid with a chopstick or the handle of a wooden spoon. Cook on high for 2 hours or on low for 4 hours. If using a larger slow cooker, you will probably need to reduce the cooking time to only 1 hour on high, or 2 hours on low.

3. Pour walnut mixture out onto a baking sheet lined with parchment paper. Allow to cool and dry and then transfer to a container with an airtight lid. Store in the pantry for up to 2 weeks.

PER SERVING: Calories: 238 | Fat: 19g | Protein: 5g | Sodium: 8mg | Fiber: 3g | Carbohydrates: 16g | Sugar: 12g

Roasted Pistachios

Raw pistachios are available at Trader Joe's (www.traderjoes.com) or health food stores. Roasting your own lets you avoid salt on the nuts, which makes them a snack that perfectly matches your Paleo palate.

INGREDIENTS | SERVES 16

1 pound raw pistachios
2 tablespoons extra-virgin olive oil

Putting Roasted Pistachios to Work

You can make 8 servings of a delicious coleslaw alternative by mixing together 3 very thinly sliced heads of fennel; ½ cup roasted, chopped pistachios; 3 tablespoons extra-virgin olive oil; 2 tablespoons freshly squeezed lemon juice; and 1 teaspoon finely grated lemon zest. Taste for seasoning and add freshly ground black pepper, and additional lemon juice if desired. Serve immediately or cover and refrigerate up to 1 day.

1. Add the nuts and oil to a 2-quart slow cooker. Stir to combine. Cover and cook on low for 1 hour.

2. Stir the mixture again. Cover and cook for 2 more hours, stirring the mixture again after 1 hour. Store in an airtight container.

PER SERVING: Calories: 172 | Fat: 14g | Protein: 6g | Sodium: 0mg | Fiber: 3g | Carbohydrates: 8g | Sugar: 2g

CHAPTER 4

Sauces and Spreads

Jalapeño-Tomatillo Sauce

Serve this sauce over a fiery southwestern dish, for a little more spice.

INGREDIENTS | SERVES 4

1 teaspoon canola oil
2 cloves garlic, minced
1 medium onion, sliced
7 tomatillos, large, diced
2 jalapeño peppers, minced
½ cup water

1. Heat the oil in a nonstick pan over medium heat. Sauté the garlic, onion, tomatillos, and jalapeño peppers for 5–10 minutes, until softened.

2. Place the mixture into a 4-quart slow cooker. Add the water and stir. Cook on low for 8 hours.

PER SERVING: Calories: 14 | Fat: 1g | Protein: 0g | Sodium: 1mg | Fiber: 0g | Carbohydrates: 1g | Sugar: 0g

Fruity Balsamic Barbecue Sauce

Use this sauce in pulled pork, as a dipping sauce, over chicken or burgers, or even as a marinade.

INGREDIENTS | SERVES 20

¼ cup balsamic vinegar
2½ cups cubed mango
2 chipotle peppers in adobo, puréed
1 teaspoon honey

1. Place all ingredients into a 2-quart slow cooker. Stir. Cook on low for 6–8 hours.

2. Mash the sauce with a potato masher. Store in an airtight container for up to 2 weeks in the refrigerator.

PER SERVING: Calories: 19 | Fat: 0g | Protein: 0g | Sodium: 2mg | Fiber: 0g | Carbohydrates: 5g | Sugar: 4g

Lemon Dill Sauce

Serve this delicious, tangy sauce over salmon, asparagus, or chicken.

INGREDIENTS | SERVES 4

2 cups Chicken Stock (see Chapter 5)
½ cup lemon juice
½ cup chopped fresh dill
¼ teaspoon white pepper

Place all the ingredients into a 2–4-quart slow cooker. Cook on high, uncovered, for 3 hours or until the sauce reduces by one-third.

PER SERVING: Calories: 51 | Fat: 2g | Protein: 3g | Sodium: 179mg | Fiber: 0g | Carbohydrates: 6g | Sugar: 3g

A Peek at Peppercorns

Black peppercorns are the mature fruit of the black pepper plant, which grows in tropical areas. Green peppercorns are the immature fruit of the pepper plant. White peppercorns are mature black peppercorns with the black husks removed. Pink peppercorns are the dried berries of the Brazilian pepper.

Raspberry Coulis

A coulis is a thick sauce made from puréed fruits or vegetables. In this recipe, the slow cooking eliminates the need for puréeing because the fruit cooks down enough that straining is unnecessary. Delicious as both a breakfast fruit spread or sweet dessert topping.

INGREDIENTS | SERVES 8

12 ounces fresh or frozen raspberries
1 teaspoon lemon juice
2 tablespoons honey

Place all the ingredients into a 2-quart slow cooker. Mash gently with a potato masher. Cook on low for 4 hours uncovered. Stir before serving.

PER SERVING: Calories: 16 | Fat: 0g | Protein: 0g | Sodium: 0mg | Fiber: 0g | Carbohydrates: 4g | Sugar: 4g

Taste, Taste, Taste

When using fresh berries, it is important to taste them prior to sweetening. One batch of berries might be tart while the next might be very sweet. Reduce or eliminate honey if using very ripe, sweet berries.

Fennel and Caper Sauce

*Try this sauce over boneless pork chops or boneless, skinless chicken breasts
and grilled summer vegetables.*

INGREDIENTS | SERVES 4

2 fennel bulbs with fronds, thinly sliced

2 tablespoons nonpareil capers

½ cup Chicken Stock (see Chapter 5)

2 shallots, thinly sliced

2 cups diced fresh tomatoes

½ teaspoon freshly ground black pepper

⅓ cup fresh minced parsley

1. Place the fennel, capers, stock, shallots, tomatoes, and pepper in an oval 4-quart slow cooker.

2. Cook on low for 2 hours, and then add the parsley. Cook on high for an additional 15–30 minutes.

PER SERVING: Calories: 64 | Fat: 1g | Protein: 3g | Sodium: 108mg | Fiber: 5g | Carbohydrates: 13g | Sugar: 3g

Summer Berry Sauce

Drizzle this sauce over desserts and breakfast foods.

INGREDIENTS | SERVES 20

1 cup raspberries

1 cup blackberries

1 cup golden raspberries

½ cup water

½ teaspoon honey

Place all the ingredients into a 2-quart slow cooker. Lightly mash the berries with the back of a spoon. Cover and cook on low for 2 hours, then uncover and turn on high for ½ hour.

PER SERVING: Calories: 10 | Fat: 0g | Protein: 0g | Sodium: 0mg | Fiber: 1g | Carbohydrates: 2g | Sugar: 1g

Artichoke Sauce

Slow cooking artichoke hearts gives them a velvety texture.

INGREDIENTS | SERVES 4

1 teaspoon olive oil

8 ounces frozen artichoke hearts, defrosted

3 cloves garlic, minced

1 medium onion, minced

2 tablespoons capote capers

28 ounces canned crushed tomatoes

Cleaning Slow Cookers

Do not use very abrasive tools or cleansers on a slow cooker insert. They may scratch the surface, allowing bacteria and food to leach in. Use a soft sponge and baking soda for stubborn stains.

1. Heat the oil in a nonstick skillet over medium heat. Sauté the artichoke hearts, garlic, and onions for about 10–15 minutes, until the onions are translucent and most of the liquid has evaporated.

2. Put the mixture into a 4-quart slow cooker. Stir in the capers and crushed tomatoes.

3. Cook on high for 4 hours or on low for 8 hours.

PER SERVING: Calories: 24 | Fat: 1g | Protein: 0g | Sodium: 2mg | Fiber: 1g | Carbohydrates: 3g | Sugar: 1g

Pink Tomato Sauce

Try this creamier version of classic spaghetti sauce over chicken and a medley of oven-roasted vegetables.

INGREDIENTS | SERVES 8

1 tablespoon olive oil

1 large onion, diced

2 cloves garlic, minced

1 tablespoon minced fresh basil

1 tablespoon minced fresh Italian parsley

⅔ cup coconut or almond milk

1 stalk celery, diced

16 ounces canned whole tomatoes in purée

28 ounces canned crushed tomatoes

1. Heat the olive oil in a medium-sized nonstick skillet over medium heat. Sauté the onions and garlic for 5–10 minutes, until the onions are soft.

2. Add the onions and garlic to a 6-quart slow cooker. Add the herbs, milk, celery, and tomatoes. Stir to distribute the spices. Cook on low for 10–12 hours.

PER SERVING: Calories: 62 | Fat: 6g | Protein: 1g | Sodium: 8mg | Fiber: 0g | Carbohydrates: 3g | Sugar: 1g

Celery, the Star

Celery is often overlooked as an ingredient. It is perfect for slow cooking because it has a high moisture content but still remains crisp through the cooking process. Celery is also very low in calories and high in fiber.

Tomato and Chicken Sausage Sauce

Sausage is a delicious alternative to meatballs in this rich tomato sauce.

INGREDIENTS | SERVES 6

4 Italian chicken sausages, sliced

2 tablespoons tomato paste

28 ounces canned crushed tomatoes

3 cloves garlic, minced

1 large onion, minced

3 tablespoons minced basil

1 tablespoon minced Italian parsley

¼ teaspoon crushed rosemary

¼ teaspoon freshly ground black pepper

1. Quickly brown the sausage slices on both sides in a nonstick skillet, about 1 minute on each side. Drain any grease.

2. Add the sausages to a 4-quart slow cooker, along with the remaining ingredients. Stir.

3. Cook on low for 8 hours.

PER SERVING: Calories: 82 | Fat: 2g | Protein: 13g | Sodium: 88mg | Fiber: 1g | Carbohydrates: 3g | Sugar: 1g

Chipotle Tomato Sauce

Try this southwestern take on the classic Italian tomato sauce on "Paleo Pasta,"
or as salsa on a southwestern dish of choice.

INGREDIENTS | SERVES 6

3 cloves garlic, minced

1 large onion, minced

28 ounces canned crushed tomatoes

14 ounces canned diced tomatoes

3 chipotle peppers in adobo, minced

1 teaspoon dried oregano

1 tablespoon fresh cilantro, minced

½ teaspoon freshly ground black pepper

Place all the ingredients into a 4-quart slow cooker. Cook on low for 8–10 hours. Stir before serving.

PER SERVING: Calories: 19 | Fat: 0g | Protein: 1g | Sodium: 3mg | Fiber: 1g | Carbohydrates: 4g | Sugar: 2g

Know Your Slow Cooker

When using a new or new-to-you slow cooker for the first time, pick a day when someone can be there to keep tabs on it. In general, older slow cookers cook at a higher temperature than new models, but even new slow cookers can have some differences. It is a good idea to know the quirks of a particular slow cooker so food is not overcooked or undercooked. Tweak cooking times accordingly.

Bolognese Sauce

Also called Bolognese or ragù alla Bolognese, this sauce combines vegetables and meat to create the perfect sauce for pouring over just about any beef and veggie dish, to give it a little touch of Italian.

INGREDIENTS | SERVES 6

2 teaspoons olive oil
½ pound 94% lean ground beef
½ pound ground pork
1 large onion, minced
1 large carrot, minced
1 stalk celery, minced
3 ounces tomato paste
28 ounces canned diced tomatoes
½ cup coconut or almond milk
¼ teaspoon ground black pepper
⅛ teaspoon nutmeg

1. Heat the oil in a nonstick pan over medium heat. Brown the ground beef and pork, about 5–10 minutes. Drain off any excess fat.

2. Add the meats and the remaining ingredients to a 4-quart slow cooker. Cook on low for 8–10 hours. Stir before serving.

PER SERVING: Calories: 174 | Fat: 14g | Protein: 8g | Sodium: 148mg | Fiber: 1g | Carbohydrates: 6g | Sugar: 3g

Sun-Dried Tomato Sauce

Sun-dried tomatoes are an excellent source of lycopene, a micronutrient shown to be associated with cardiovascular health benefits and disease prevention.

INGREDIENTS | SERVES 4

1½ cups chopped sun-dried tomatoes
1 (28-ounce) can tomatoes, cut up
1 (14.5-ounce) can tomatoes, cut up
1 medium onion, chopped
2 cloves garlic, minced
1 cup chopped celery
⅔ cup chablis or other dry white wine
1½ teaspoons basil
1 teaspoon dried fennel seed
½ teaspoon oregano
½ teaspoon pepper
8 ounces of sliced mushrooms, optional

Place all the ingredients in a 4–6-quart slow cooker, cover, and cook on low for 6–8 hours.

PER SERVING: Calories: 156 | Fat: 1g | Protein: 6g | Sodium: 877mg | Fiber: 7g | Carbohydrates: 29g | Sugar: 17g

Spinach Marinara Sauce

Powerfully flavored and nutrient-rich. Goes well with chicken, beef, or turkey meatballs, or as a sauce over a vegetable medley side dish or main course.

INGREDIENTS | SERVES 8

1 (28-ounce) can peeled and crushed tomatoes, with liquid

1 (10-ounce) package frozen chopped spinach, thawed and drained

2⅔ (6-ounce) cans tomato paste

1 (4.5-ounce) can sliced mushrooms, drained

1 medium onion, chopped

5 cloves garlic, minced

2 bay leaves

⅓ cup grated carrot

¼ cup olive oil

2½ tablespoons crushed red pepper

2 tablespoons lemon juice

2 tablespoons dried oregano

2 tablespoons dried basil

1. In a 4–6-quart slow cooker, combine all the ingredients, cover, and cook on high for 4 hours.

2. Stir, reduce heat to low, and cook for 1–2 more hours.

PER SERVING: Calories: 154 | Fat: 8g | Protein: 5g | Sodium: 482mg | Fiber: 6g | Carbohydrates: 21g | Sugar: 11g

Ground Turkey Tomato Sauce

Packed full of fresh, natural flavor—an excellent completion to just about any Italian dish.

INGREDIENTS | SERVES 6

2 tablespoons olive oil

1 pound ground turkey

1 (14.5-ounce) can of stewed tomatoes

1 (6-ounce) can tomato paste

½ teaspoon dried thyme

1 teaspoon dried leaf basil

½ teaspoon oregano

½–1 teaspoon honey, optional

1 yellow onion, chopped

1 bell pepper, chopped

2 cloves crushed garlic

1 bay leaf

¼ cup water

4 ounces chopped or sliced mushrooms, fresh or canned, drained

1. Heat the olive oil in a skillet over medium heat. Add the ground turkey and cook for 5–7 minutes until brown.

2. While browning turkey, place stewed tomatoes, tomato paste, thyme, basil, oregano, and honey in a 4–6-quart slow cooker. Stir well and turn slow cooker to low heat.

3. Next, transfer browned turkey to slow cooker with slotted spoon. In pan with ground turkey drippings, sauté onion, pepper, garlic, and bay leaf for 3–5 minutes until softened.

4. To slow cooker, add the sautéed vegetables, water, and the chopped mushrooms. Cover and cook on low 4–6 hours. Thin with a little water if necessary.

PER SERVING: Calories: 211 | Fat: 13g | Protein: 15g | Sodium: 389mg | Fiber: 2g | Carbohydrates: 9g | Sugar: 5g

Cranberry Sauce

Serve this sweet-tart cranberry sauce with a holiday meal;
use it as a spread, or pour it over your favorite slow cooked dessert.

INGREDIENTS | SERVES 10

12 ounces fresh cranberries
½ cup freshly squeezed orange juice
½ cup water
½ teaspoon orange zest
½ teaspoon agave nectar

Place all ingredients into a 1½–2-quart slow cooker. Cook on high for 2½ hours. Stir before serving.

PER SERVING: Calories: 16 | Fat: 0g | Protein: 0g | Sodium: 1mg | Fiber: 2g | Carbohydrates: 4g | Sugar: 1g

Cran-Apple Sauce

Simple. Sweet. Loaded with antioxidants like vitamin C.

INGREDIENTS | SERVES 6

1 cup fresh cranberries
8 apples, peeled, cored and chopped
½ cup honey
1 cinnamon stick, halved
6 whole cloves

1. Combine cranberries, apples, and honey in a 4–6-quart slow cooker.

2. Place cinnamon and cloves in center of a 6" square of cheesecloth. Pull up around sides; tie to form pouch. Place in slow cooker.

3. Cover and cook on low for 4–5 hours or until cranberries and apples are very soft.

PER SERVING: (½ cup) | Calories: 197 | Fat: 0g | Protein: 1g | Sodium: 1mg | Fiber: 4g | Carbohydrates: 53g | Sugar: 46g

Mango Chutney

Chutney is a great complement to curry and meat dishes like pork, chicken, and fish.

INGREDIENTS | SERVES 4

4 cups mangoes, peeled, and chopped finely

3 cups apples, peeled, and chopped finely

1 cup raisins, golden

1 cup honey

1 cup lemon juice

¼ teaspoon cinnamon

¼ teaspoon allspice

1. Combine all ingredients in a 4-quart slow cooker. Simmer on low for 4–5 hours. Stir often.

2. Serve warm as a spread on top of pork, chicken, or fish, or as a dip.

PER SERVING: (8 ounces) | Calories: 531 | Fat: 1g | Protein: 3g | Sodium: 40mg | Fiber: 6g | Carbohydrates: 139g | Sugar: 122g

Rosemary-Mushroom Sauce

Used often as a marinade, as well as a sauce to enhance the flavor and texture of many slow cooked beef and chicken dishes.

INGREDIENTS | SERVES 4

8 ounces fresh mushrooms, sliced

1 large onion, thinly sliced

1 teaspoon olive oil

1 tablespoon crushed rosemary

3 cups Chicken Stock (see Chapter 5)

1. In a sauté pan set over medium heat, sauté the mushrooms and onions in olive oil for about 5 minutes, until onions are soft.

2. Place onions and mushrooms into a 4-quart slow cooker; add the rosemary and stock, and stir.

3. Cook on low for 6–8 hours or on high for 3 hours.

PER SERVING: Calories: 133 | Fat: 4g | Protein: 8g | Sodium: 65mg | Fiber: 5g | Carbohydrates: 15g | Sugar: 6g

Awesome Applesauce

*Serve warm or chilled, or as a complement to a main pork, chicken, or beef dish.
Or freeze for an icy, sweet summer treat!*

INGREDIENTS | SERVES 6

3 pounds Jonathan apples, peeled, and coarsely chopped
½ cup water
½ cup honey
Ground cinnamon, to taste

1. Combine all ingredients, except cinnamon, in a 6-quart slow cooker, and cover.

2. Cook on high until apples are very soft and form applesauce when stirred, about 2–2½ hours. Sprinkle with cinnamon just before serving.

PER SERVING: Calories: 86 | Fat: 0g | Protein: 0g | Sodium: 2mg | Fiber: 0g | Carbohydrates: 23g | Sugar: 23g

Slow Cooked Spicy Salsa

*Enjoy this salsa as a spicy, nutritious, low-calorie snack, or as a marinade
or complement to a slow cooked southern dish.*

INGREDIENTS | SERVES 16

10 fresh Roma or plum tomatoes, chopped
2 cloves garlic, minced
1 large onion, chopped
2 jalapeño peppers, stems removed and chopped (remove seeds for milder salsa)
1 large green bell pepper, chopped
¼ cup fresh cilantro leaves
½ teaspoon lemon juice

1. Place chopped tomatoes, minced garlic, and chopped onions in a 3–4-quart slow cooker.

2. Stir jalapeño peppers and bell peppers into the slow cooker. Cover and cook on high for 2½–3 hours.

3. When cool, combine mixture with cilantro leaves and lemon juice and blend in a food processor until desired consistency.

PER SERVING: (½ cup) | Calories: 14 | Fat: 0g | Protein: 0g | Sodium: 3mg | Fiber: 1g | Carbohydrates: 3g | Sugar: 2g

Homemade Ketchup

Condiments such as ketchup are generally gluten-free, but you always have to read the label and check with the manufacturer to make sure. Instead of worrying, you can make your own and know exactly what ingredients are in your specially made ketchup!

INGREDIENTS | SERVES 5

1 (15-ounce) can no-salt-added tomato sauce

2 teaspoons water

½ teaspoon onion powder

¾ cup honey

⅓ cup lime juice

¼ teaspoon ground cinnamon

⅛ teaspoon ground cloves

Pinch ground allspice

Pinch nutmeg

Pinch freshly ground pepper

⅔ teaspoon sweet paprika

1. Add all the ingredients to a 2½-quart slow cooker. Cover and, stirring occasionally, cook on low for 2–4 hours or until ketchup reaches desired consistency.

2. Turn off the slow cooker or remove the insert from the slow cooker. Allow mixture to cool, then put in a covered container (such as a recycled ketchup bottle). Store in the refrigerator for up to a month.

PER SERVING: (½ cup) | Calories: 156 | Fat: 0g | Protein: 0g | Sodium: 2mg | Fiber: 0g | Carbohydrates: 42g | Sugar: 42g

Ketchup with a Kick

If you like zesty ketchup, you can add crushed red peppers or salt-free chili powder along with, or instead of, the cinnamon and other seasonings. Another alternative is to use hot paprika rather than sweet paprika.

Plum Sauce

Plum sauce is usually served with egg rolls, which are generally not Paleo-approved. But this delicious sauce is also wonderful brushed on chicken or pork ribs; doing so near the end of the grilling time will add a succulent glaze to the grilled meat.

INGREDIENTS | SERVES 16

8 cups (about 3 pounds) plums, pitted and cut in half

1 small sweet onion, finely diced

1 cup water

1 teaspoon fresh ginger, peeled and minced

1 clove garlic, peeled and minced

¾ cup honey

½ cup lemon juice

1 teaspoon ground coriander

½ teaspoon cinnamon

¼ teaspoon cayenne pepper

¼ teaspoon ground cloves

1. Add the plums, onion, water, ginger, and garlic to a 4-quart slow cooker. Cover and, stirring occasionally, cook on low for 4 hours or until plums and onions are tender.

2. Use an immersion blender to pulverize the contents of the slow cooker before straining it or press the cooked plum mixture through a sieve.

3. Return the liquefied and strained plum mixture to the slow cooker and stir in honey, lemon juice, coriander, cinnamon, cayenne pepper, and cloves. Cover and, stirring occasionally, cook on low for 2 hours or until the sauce reaches the consistency of applesauce.

PER SERVING: Calories: 91 | Fat: 0g | Protein: 1g | Sodium: 3mg | Fiber: 1g | Carbohydrates: 24g | Sugar: 22g

Red Pepper Relish

This sauce adds a little kick, spicing up the flavor to just about any slow cooked entrée or side.

INGREDIENTS | SERVES 8

4 large red bell peppers, cut into thin strips

2 small Vidalia onions, thinly sliced

6 tablespoons lemon juice

¼ cup honey

½ teaspoon dried thyme

½ teaspoon red pepper flakes

½ teaspoon black pepper

1. Combine all the ingredients in a 1½-quart slow cooker and mix well.

2. Cover and cook on low for 4 hours.

PER SERVING: Calories: 61 | Fat: 0g | Protein: 1g | Sodium: 6mg | Fiber: 2g | Carbohydrates: 15g | Sugar: 12g

Paleo "Butterscotch-Caramel" Sauce

Here is a sweet and delicious way to enhance the flavor of just about any Paleo dessert.

INGREDIENTS | SERVES 24

½ cup coconut butter

2 cups (full fat) coconut milk

3 cups honey

2 tablespoons fresh lemon juice

1 tablespoon vanilla extract

1. Add the coconut butter, coconut milk, honey, and lemon juice to a 2-quart or smaller, slow cooker. Cover and cook on high for 1 hour or until the coconut butter is melted and the milk begins to bubble around the edges of the cooker. Uncover and stir.

2. Cover and cook on low for 2 hours, stirring occasionally.

3. Uncover and cook on low for 1 more hour or until the mixture coats the back of the spoon or the sauce reaches its desired thickness. Stir in the vanilla.

PER SERVING: Calories: 168 | Fat: 4g | Protein: 1g | Sodium: 5mg | Fiber: 0g | Carbohydrates: 36g | Sugar: 35g

Stocks, Soups, and Stews

Chicken Stock

Homemade chicken stock is much cheaper and tastier than storebought.

INGREDIENTS | YIELDS 3 QUARTS

1 (5–7 pound) chicken carcass

2 large carrots, peeled and cut into chunks

2 stalks celery, cut into chunks

2 medium onions, cut into chunks

2 parsnips, cut into chunks

1 head garlic

2 chicken wings

Water, as needed

Stock Options

Any leftover vegetables can be added to stock for extra flavor; fennel fronds, green onions, turnips, and red onion are all good choices. Depending on the recipe that the stock will be used in, adding items like dried chilies, ginger, or galangal root will customize the stock, making it an even better fit for the final product.

1. Place the carcass, carrots, celery, onions, parsnips, garlic, and wings into a 6-quart slow cooker.

2. Fill the slow cooker with water until it is 2 inches below the top. Cover and cook on low for 10 hours.

3. Strain into a large container. Discard the solids. Refrigerate the stock overnight.

4. The next day, scoop off any fat that has floated to the top. Discard the fat.

5. Freeze or refrigerate the stock and use within 1 week.

PER SERVING: (1 cup) | Calories: 31 | Fat: 1g | Protein: 2g | Sodium: 20mg | Fiber: 1g | Carbohydrates: 3g | Sugar: 1g

Beef Stock

A flavorful, easy to prepare stock, suitable for a variety of recipes.

INGREDIENTS | YIELDS 2 QUARTS

8 black peppercorns

5 sage leaves

4 thickly sliced large onions

4 medium carrots, thickly sliced

4 small stalks of celery, thickly sliced

2½ quarts water

2 ribs from cooked beef rib roast, fat trimmed

2 bay leaves

1 parsnip, peeled and sliced

1. Combine all the ingredients in a 6-quart slow cooker. Cover and cook on low for 6–8 hours.

2. Strain the stock through a double-layer of cheesecloth, discarding the solids.

3. Refrigerate 2–3 hours, until chilled. Remove fat from surface of stock.

4. Freeze or refrigerate the stock and use within 1 week.

PER SERVING: (1 cup) | Calories: 46 | Fat: 0g | Protein: 1g | Sodium: 49mg | Fiber: 2g | Carbohydrates: 11g | Sugar: 5g

Roasted Vegetable Stock

Use this stock in vegetarian recipes as a substitute for chicken stock or in other recipes as a flavorful alternative to water.

INGREDIENTS | YIELDS 5 QUARTS

3 medium carrots, peeled and coarsely chopped

3 parsnips, peeled and coarsely chopped

3 large onions, quartered

3 whole turnips

3 rutabagas, quartered

3 bell peppers, halved

2 shallots

1 whole head garlic

1 bunch fresh thyme

1 bunch parsley

5 quarts water

1. Preheat the oven to 425°F. Arrange the vegetables and herbs in a 9" × 13" baking pan lined with parchment paper. Roast for 30 minutes or until browned.

2. Add the vegetables to a 6-quart slow cooker. Add 5 quarts of water and cover. Cook on low for 8–10 hours. Strain the stock, discarding the solids. Freeze or refrigerate the stock and use within 1–2 weeks.

PER SERVING: (1 cup) | Calories: 46 | Fat: 0g | Protein: 1g | Sodium: 49mg | Fiber: 2g | Carbohydrates: 11g | Sugar: 5g

Turkey Stock

Popular during the holidays, this is the perfect way to put your leftover turkey to good use. This can also be used as a substitute in recipes calling for chicken stock.

INGREDIENTS | YIELDS 16 CUPS

10 black peppercorns
6 sprigs parsley
4 thickly sliced medium carrots
4 stalks celery, thickly sliced
4 quarts water
2 thickly sliced medium onions
2 leeks (white parts only)
1 turkey carcass, cut up
1 cup dry white wine, or water
1½ teaspoons dried thyme leaves
Pepper, to taste

1. Combine all the ingredients except pepper in a 6-quart slow cooker. Cover and cook on low for 6–8 hours.

2. Strain the stock through a double-layer of cheesecloth, discarding the solids. Season with pepper to taste.

3. Refrigerate 3–5 hours, until chilled. Remove fat from surface of stock.

4. Freeze or refrigerate the stock and use within 1 week.

PER SERVING: (1 cup) | Calories: 33 | Fat: 0g | Protein: 1g | Sodium: 29mg | Fiber: 1g | Carbohydrates: 5g | Sugar: 2g

Fish Stock

Use this fish stock in any fish or seafood dish instead of water or chicken stock.

INGREDIENTS | YIELDS 3 QUARTS

3 quarts water
2 large onions, quartered
Head and bones from 3 fish, any type
2 stalks celery, chopped
2 tablespoons peppercorns
1 bunch parsley

1. Place all the ingredients into a 4-quart slow cooker. Cook for 8–10 hours.

2. Remove all the solids. Refrigerate overnight.

3. The next day, skim off any foam that has floated to the top. Refrigerate and use within 1 week, or freeze.

PER SERVING: (1 cup) | Calories: 33 | Fat: 0g | Protein: 1g | Sodium: 29mg | Fiber: 1g | Carbohydrates: 5g | Sugar: 2g

Mushroom Stock

Shiitake mushrooms add a rich, bold flavor, and also provide a variety of beneficial phytonutrients. Be careful to not overcook this stock.

INGREDIENTS | YIELDS 2 QUARTS

1 quart water

12 ounces white mushrooms

6 stems of parsley (with leaves)

1 large onion, sliced

1 leek (white part only)

1 stalk of celery, sliced

2 ounces dried shiitake mushrooms

1 tablespoon minced garlic

1½ teaspoons black peppercorns

¾ teaspoon dried sage

¾ teaspoon dried thyme leaves

Pepper, to taste

1. Combine all the ingredients except pepper in a 6-quart slow cooker; cover and cook on low for 6–8 hours.

2. Strain, discarding solids; season to taste with pepper. Serve immediately, refrigerate and use within 1–2 weeks, or freeze.

PER SERVING: (1 cup) | Calories: 18 | Fat: 0g | Protein: 1g | Sodium: 11mg | Fiber: 1g | Carbohydrates: 4g | Sugar: 1g

Beef and Vegetable Stew

Fresh herbs brighten this traditional hearty stew. This recipe could be prepared with a variety of seasonal herbs, experiment for yourself!

INGREDIENTS | SERVES 4

2 teaspoons canola oil

1 large onion, diced

2 parsnips, diced

2 large carrots, peeled and diced

2 stalks celery, diced

3 cloves garlic, minced

1 tablespoon minced fresh tarragon

2 tablespoons minced fresh rosemary

1 pound lean beef top round roast, cut into 1" cubes

1½ cups water

1 bulb fennel, diced

1 tablespoon minced parsley

1. Heat the oil in a large skillet. Sauté the onion, parsnips, carrots, celery, garlic, tarragon, rosemary, and beef for 5–10 minutes, until the ingredients begin to soften and brown. Drain off any excess fat.

2. Place the mixture into a 4-quart slow cooker. Pour in the water. Stir. Cook on low for 8–9 hours.

3. Add the fennel. Cover and cook on high for an additional ½ hour. Stir in the parsley before serving.

PER SERVING: Calories: 227 | Fat: 7g | Protein: 27g | Sodium: 145mg | Fiber: 4g | Carbohydrates: 13g | Sugar: 4g

Bouillabaisse

With one bite, this slightly simplified version of the Provençal fish stew will convert anyone who is skeptical about cooking seafood in the slow cooker into a believer.

INGREDIENTS | SERVES 8

1 bulb fennel, sliced

2 leeks, sliced

2 large carrots, peeled and cut into coins

2 shallots, minced

5 cloves garlic, minced

2 tablespoons minced basil

1 tablespoon orange zest

1 tablespoon lemon zest

1 bay leaf

14 ounces canned diced tomatoes

2 quarts water or Fish Stock (see recipe in this chapter)

1 pound cubed hake or catfish

8 ounces medium peeled shrimp

1 pound mussels

1. Place the vegetables, garlic, basil, zests, bay leaf, tomatoes, and water or stock into a 6-quart slow cooker. Stir. Cook on low for 8 hours.

2. Add the seafood. Cook on high for 20 minutes. Stir prior to serving. Discard any mussels that do not open.

PER SERVING: Calories: 251 | Fat: 3.5g | Protein: 27g | Sodium: 384mg | Fiber: 8g | Carbohydrates: 31g | Sugar: 9g

Curried Cauliflower Soup

Orange cauliflower is an excellent variety to use in this recipe. It has 25 percent more vitamin A than white cauliflower and lends an attractive color to the soup.

INGREDIENTS | SERVES 4

1 pound cauliflower florets
2½ cups water
1 medium onion, minced
2 cloves garlic, minced
3 teaspoons curry powder
¼ teaspoon cumin

1. Place all the ingredients into a 4-quart slow cooker. Stir. Cook on low for 8 hours.

2. Use an immersion blender, or blend the soup in batches in a standard blender, until smooth.

PER SERVING: Calories: 46 | Fat: 1g | Protein: 3g | Sodium: 40mg | Fiber: 3g | Carbohydrates: 10g | Sugar: 3g

Curry Powder Power

Curry powder is a mixture of spices commonly used in South Asian cooking. While it does not correlate directly to any particular kind of curry, it is popular in Europe and North America to add an Indian flare to dishes. It can contain any number of spices, but nearly always includes turmeric, which gives it its distinctive yellow color.

No Bean Chili

For a variation, try this with lean beef sirloin instead of pork.

INGREDIENTS | SERVES 6

1 tablespoon canola oil

1 pound boneless pork tenderloin, cubed

1 large onion, diced

3 poblano chilies, diced

2 cloves garlic, minced

1 teaspoon cumin

1 teaspoon dried oregano

1 cup Chicken Stock (see recipe in this chapter)

15 ounces canned crushed tomatoes

2 teaspoons ground cayenne pepper

1. In a large nonstick skillet, heat the oil over medium heat. Add the pork, onion, chilies, and garlic. Sauté, 7–10 minutes until the pork is no longer visibly pink on any side. Drain off any fats or oils and discard them.

2. Pour the pork mixture into a 4-quart slow cooker. Add the remaining ingredients. Stir.

3. Cook on low for 8–9 hours.

PER SERVING: Calories: 157 | Fat: 5g | Protein: 19g | Sodium: 64mg | Fiber: 2g | Carbohydrates: 5g | Sugar: 2g

Using Herbs

As a general rule, 1 tablespoon minced fresh herbs equals 1 teaspoon dried herbs. Fresh herbs can be frozen for future use. Discard dried herbs after one year.

Mushroom and Onion Soup

This soup serves as an excellent opening course for a rich beef or pork dish.

INGREDIENTS | SERVES 6

6½ cups Chicken Stock (see recipe in this chapter)

3 cups thinly sliced onions

2 cups fresh mushrooms, sliced

1½ cups thinly sliced leeks

½ cup chopped shallots or green onions

1 teaspoon honey (optional)

Pepper, to taste

1. Combine all the ingredients except the pepper in a 6-quart slow cooker. Cover and cook on low 6–8 hours.

2. Season with pepper to taste.

PER SERVING: Calories: 191 | Fat: 4g | Protein: 11g | Sodium: 404mg | Fiber: 3g | Carbohydrates: 27g | Sugar: 12g

Acorn Squash Autumn Bisque

A seasonally delicious taste of fall. The yellow-orange color of squash is derived from its rich content of vitamin A. One cup of acorn squash provides more than 100 percent of the daily recommended amount of vitamin A.

INGREDIENTS | SERVES 6

2 cups Chicken Stock (see recipe this chapter)

2 medium sized acorn squash, peeled and cut into cubes

½ cup chopped onion

½ teaspoon ground cinnamon

¼ teaspoon ground coriander

¼ teaspoon ground cumin

½ cup unsweetened coconut milk

1 tablespoon lemon juice

Pepper, to taste

1. Combine the stock, squash, onion, cinnamon, coriander, and cumin in a 4-quart slow cooker. Cover and cook on high for 3–4 hours.

2. Blend the soup, coconut milk, and lemon juice in food processor until smooth.

3. Season with pepper to taste.

PER SERVING: Calories: 54 | Fat: 4g | Protein: 2g | Sodium: 11mg | Fiber: 1g | Carbohydrates: 3g | Sugar: 1g

Pumpkin Turkey Chili

Pumpkin keeps for 6 months whole, or for years canned; pumpkin is most often enjoyed in the fall, but can actually be enjoyed all year round.

INGREDIENTS | SERVES 6

2 red bell peppers, chopped
1 medium-sized onion, chopped
3–4 cloves of garlic, chopped
1 pound ground turkey, browned
1 (14.5-ounce) can pure pumpkin purée
1 (14.5-ounce) can diced tomatoes
½ cup water
1½ tablespoons chili powder
½ teaspoon black pepper
¼ teaspoon cumin

1. In a skillet over medium heat, sauté the peppers, onion, and garlic with the browned turkey for 5–7 minutes.

2. Transfer the turkey and veggies into a 4-quart slow cooker. Add the remaining ingredients.

3. Cover, and cook on low for 5–6 hours.

PER SERVING: Calories: 140 | Fat: 7g | Protein: 14g | Sodium: 188mg | Fiber: 2g | Carbohydrates: 6g | Sugar: 2g

Chicken and Mushroom Stew

A flagrant blend of sautéed chicken, vegetables, and herbs, best enjoyed on a late autumn night alongside a rich poultry dish.

INGREDIENTS | SERVES 6

16–24 ounces boneless chicken, cut into 1-inch cubes, browned (in olive oil)
8 ounces fresh mushrooms, sliced
1 medium onion, diced
3 cups diced zucchini
1 cup diced green pepper
4 garlic cloves, minced
1 tablespoon olive oil
3 medium tomatoes, diced
1 (6-ounce) can tomato paste
¾ cup water
1 teaspoon each: dried thyme, oregano, marjoram, and basil

1. Add browned chicken to a 4–6-quart slow cooker.

2. In a sauté pan over medium heat, sauté the mushrooms, onion, zucchini, green pepper, and garlic in olive oil for 5–10 minutes, until crisp-tender, and add to slow cooker.

3. Add the tomatoes, tomato paste, water, and seasonings.

4. Cover and cook on low for 4 hours or until the vegetables are tender. Serve hot.

PER SERVING: Calories: 222 | Fat: 6g | Protein: 28g | Sodium: 320mg | Fiber: 4g | Carbohydrates: 15g | Sugar: 9g

Southwestern Soup

A zesty and hearty creation with the perfect balance of herbs and seasonings.

INGREDIENTS | SERVES 4

1 pound pork tenderloin, cut into 1-inch pieces

1 cup chopped onion

1 green bell pepper, seeded and chopped

1 jalapeño pepper, seeded and minced

2 cloves garlic, minced

1 teaspoon chili powder

1 teaspoon ground cumin

¼ teaspoon freshly ground black pepper

5 cups Chicken Stock (see recipe in this chapter)

1 (14-ounce) can diced tomatoes

1 cup diced fresh avocado, for garnish

2 tablespoons chopped fresh cilantro leaves, for garnish

Lime wedges, for garnish

1. In the bottom of a 6-quart slow cooker, combine the pork, onion, bell pepper, jalapeño pepper, garlic, chili powder, cumin, and black pepper. Stir to combine.

2. Add stock and tomatoes. Cover and cook on low for 6–8 hours or on high for 3–4 hours.

3. When ready to serve, ladle soup into bowls and top with avocado and cilantro. Garnish soup with lime wedges.

PER SERVING: Calories: 266 | Fat: 9g | Protein: 29g | Sodium: 237mg | Fiber: 6g | Carbohydrates: 18g | Sugar: 6g

Tomato Vegetable Soup

The array of garden vegetables in this soup produces a light and fresh flavor with a "fall-ish" feel.

INGREDIENTS | SERVES 6

1 (28-ounce) can Italian plum tomatoes, undrained

2¼ cups beef broth

1 medium onion, chopped

1 large stalk celery, sliced

1 medium carrot, sliced

1 red bell pepper, chopped

1 teaspoon lemon juice

¾ teaspoon garlic powder

Pinch of crushed red pepper

Pepper, to taste

1. Combine all the ingredients except pepper in a 4–6 quart slow cooker. Cover and cook on high for 4–5 hours.

2. Process the soup in blender until smooth; season to taste with pepper. Serve warm.

PER SERVING: Calories: 50 | Fat: 1g | Protein: 3g | Sodium: 314mg | Fiber: 3g | Carbohydrates: 10g | Sugar: 6g

Zucchini Soup

This smooth and soothing blend of fresh herbs and spices is perfect for a cold, late autumn day.

INGREDIENTS | SERVES 8

4 cups sliced zucchini

4 cups chicken broth

4 cloves garlic, minced

2 tablespoons lime juice

2 teaspoons curry powder

1 teaspoon dried marjoram leaves

¼ teaspoon celery seeds

½ cup coconut milk

Cayenne pepper, to taste

Pinch of paprika

1. Combine all the ingredients, except the coconut milk, cayenne pepper and paprika in a 4–6-quart slow cooker, and cook on high for 3–4 hours.

2. Process the soup, with the coconut milk, in a blender until combined.

3. Season to taste with cayenne pepper. Serve warm, and sprinkle with paprika.

PER SERVING: Calories: 92 | Fat: 5g | Protein: 4g | Sodium: 531mg | Fiber: 1g | Carbohydrates: 9g | Sugar: 2g

Pumpkin and Ginger Soup

Relieve some stress with a hot cup of this comforting, seasonal favorite.

INGREDIENTS | SERVES 6

2 pounds pumpkin, peeled, seeded, and cut into cubes
3 cups chicken stock
1 cup chopped onion
½ cup dry white wine
1 tablespoon chopped ginger root
1 teaspoon minced garlic
½ teaspoon ground cloves
Pepper, to taste

1. In a 4-quart slow cooker, combine all ingredients except the pepper. Cover, and cook on high for 4–5 hours.

2. Place the soup in a food processor and blend until smooth.

3. Season to taste with pepper.

PER SERVING: Calories: 84 | Fat: 1g | Protein: 3g | Sodium: 14mg | Fiber: 2g | Carbohydrates: 15g | Sugar: 4g

Rosemary-Thyme Stew

Lots of rosemary and thyme give this surprisingly light stew a distinctive flavor.

INGREDIENTS | SERVES 4

1 teaspoon canola oil
1 large onion, diced
1 large carrot, peeled and diced
2 stalks celery, diced
2 cloves garlic, minced
3½ tablespoons minced fresh thyme
3 tablespoons minced fresh rosemary
1 pound boneless, skinless chicken breast, cut into 1" cubes
½ teaspoon freshly ground black pepper
1½ cups water or Chicken Stock (see recipe in this chapter)
1 cup diced green, red, and yellow peppers

1. Heat the oil in a large skillet. Sauté the onion, carrots, celery, garlic, thyme, rosemary, and chicken for 5–7 minutes, until the chicken is white on all sides. Drain off any excess fat.

2. Put sautéed ingredients into a 4-quart slow cooker. Sprinkle with black pepper. Pour in the water or stock. Stir. Cook on low for 8–9 hours.

3. Add the diced peppers. Cover and cook on high for an additional ½ hour. Stir before serving.

PER SERVING: Calories: 187 | Fat: 4g | Protein: 26g | Sodium: 173mg | Fiber: 3g | Carbohydrates: 10g | Sugar: 3g

Chicken Stew with Meat Sauce

This easy-to-make chicken stew is sure to please the entire family. Both kids and adults love this delicious recipe. Serve alone or pour over spaghetti squash as a Bolognese-type sauce.

INGREDIENTS | SERVES 4

1 pound (90% lean) grass-fed ground beef

4 boneless, skinless chicken breasts

1 (6-ounce) can organic tomato paste

1 (28-ounce) can diced organic tomatoes, no salt added

4 garlic cloves, chopped

4 large carrots, sliced

2 red bell peppers, diced

2 green bell peppers, diced

1 tablespoon dried thyme

2 tablespoons olive oil

1 tablespoon chili powder

1. In a medium sauté pan, cook ground beef until browned, about 5 minutes. Drain and place in a 4–6-quart slow cooker.

2. Wipe out the sauté pan and place it over medium-high heat. Brown the chicken breasts (5 minutes per side). Add to slow cooker.

3. Combine all the remaining ingredients in the slow cooker. Cook on high for 5 hours.

4. Serve over your favorite steamed vegetable.

PER SERVING: Calories: 469 | Fat: 14g | Protein: 56g | Sodium: 960mg | Fiber: 9g | Carbohydrates: 32g | Sugar: 17g

Slow Cookers Are Lifesavers

Slow cookers are the greatest appliance for the Paleo enthusiast. These little counter-top cookers allow you to cook easily and in bulk, which is important for a successful Paleolithic dieter.

Simple Ground Turkey and Vegetable Soup

This soup is easy to throw together with pantry ingredients.

INGREDIENTS | SERVES 6

1 tablespoon olive oil

1 pound ground turkey

1 medium onion, diced

2 cloves garlic, minced

1 (16-ounce) package frozen mixed vegetables

4 cups chicken broth

½ teaspoon pepper

1. In a large skillet over medium heat, add olive oil and heat until sizzling. Cook ground turkey until browned, about 5–6 minutes, stirring to break up the meat. Add meat to a greased 4-quart slow cooker.

2. In the same skillet, sauté onion and garlic until softened, about 3–5 minutes. Add to the slow cooker.

3. Add remaining ingredients. Cover and cook on high for 4 hours or on low for 8 hours.

PER SERVING: Calories: 254 | Fat: 11g | Protein: 19g | Sodium: 804mg | Fiber: 3g | Carbohydrates: 20g | Sugar: 1g

Stuffed Pepper Soup

All the flavor of stuffed peppers turned into a warm and satisfying soup.

INGREDIENTS | SERVES 6

1½ pounds ground beef, browned and drained

3 cups diced green bell peppers

2 cups butternut squash, peeled and diced

1 (28-ounce) can diced peeled tomatoes

1 (28-ounce) can tomato sauce

¾ cup honey

Seasonings of choice, (basil, thyme, oregano, onion flakes, etc.) to taste

1. Mix all the ingredients in a 4-quart slow cooker. Cover and cook on low for 3–4 hours or until the green peppers are cooked.

2. Turn heat to high and cook for 20–30 more minutes.

PER SERVING: Calories: 415 | Fat: 12g | Protein: 26g | Sodium: 951mg | Fiber: 6g | Carbohydrates: 56g | Sugar: 46g

Cincinnati Chili

This unusual regional favorite has a spicy sweet flavor that is wonderfully addictive! Serve over cooked "Paleo-Pasta" with any combination of the following toppings: diced raw onion, chopped green, red, yellow, or orange pepper, and shredded carrots.

INGREDIENTS | SERVES 8

1 pound ground beef
15 ounces crushed tomatoes in juice
2 cloves garlic, minced
1 large onion, diced
1 teaspoon cumin
1 teaspoon cacao powder
2 teaspoons chili powder
½ teaspoon ground cloves
1 tablespoon lemon juice
1 teaspoon allspice
½ teaspoon ground cayenne
½ teaspoon cinnamon

1. In a nonstick skillet, quickly sauté the beef until it is no longer pink, about 5–6 minutes. Drain all fat and discard it.

2. Place beef and all the other ingredients in a 4-quart slow cooker. Stir. Cook on low for 8–10 hours.

PER SERVING: Calories: 110 | Fat: 6g | Protein: 12g | Sodium: 45mg | Fiber: 1g | Carbohydrates: 3g | Sugar: 1g

Sauté the Meat When Making Chili

Even though it is not aesthetically necessary to brown the meat when making chili, sautéing meat before adding it to the slow cooker allows you to drain off any extra fat. Not only is it healthier to cook with less fat, your chili will be unappetizingly greasy if there is too much fat present in the meat during cooking.

Lone Star State Chili

Texans prefer their chili without beans, but you can add a can or two of rinsed and drained kidney beans if you prefer it that way. Serve this dish with baked corn tortilla chips and a tossed salad.

INGREDIENTS | SERVES 8

1 stalk celery, finely chopped

1 large carrot, peeled and finely chopped

1 (3-pound) chuck roast, cut into small cubes

2 large yellow onions, peeled and diced

6 cloves garlic, peeled and minced

6 jalapeño peppers, seeded and diced

½ teaspoon freshly ground pepper

4 tablespoons chili powder

1 teaspoon Mexican oregano

1 teaspoon ground cumin

1 teaspoon honey

1 (28-ounce) can diced tomatoes

1 cup beef broth

1. Add all of the ingredients to a 4–6-quart slow cooker, in the order given, and stir to combine. The liquid in your slow cooker should completely cover the meat and vegetables. If additional liquid is needed add more crushed tomatoes, broth, or some water.

2. Cover and cook on low for 8 hours. Taste for seasoning, and add more chili powder if desired.

PER SERVING: Calories: 60 | Fat: 1g | Protein: 2g | Sodium: 289mg | Fiber: 4g | Carbohydrates: 13g | Sugar: 6g

Hot Pepper Precautions

Wear gloves or sandwich bags over your hands when you clean and dice hot peppers. It's important to avoid having the peppers come into contact with any of your skin, or especially your eyes. As an added precaution, wash your hands (and under your fingernails) thoroughly with hot soapy water after you remove the gloves or sandwich bags.

Chicken Chili Verde

Enjoy this spicy chili over a southwestern-themed vegetable medley.
Avocado slices serve well as a festive garnish.

INGREDIENTS | SERVES 8

½ tablespoon olive oil

2 pounds skinless, boneless chicken breast, cubed

2 (28-ounce) cans whole peeled tomatoes, undrained

1 (4-ounce) can diced green chili peppers, undrained

1 teaspoon thyme

1 teaspoon oregano

1 teaspoon basil

1 tablespoon chili powder

2 teaspoons cumin

1 tablespoon honey

1 large onion, minced

3 cloves garlic, minced

½ cup water

1. Heat oil in a skillet over medium heat. Add the chicken. Cook, stirring frequently, until chicken is browned on all sides, about 1–2 minutes per side. Place browned chicken in a greased 4–6-quart slow cooker.

2. Add the remaining ingredients over the chicken in the slow cooker.

3. Cover and cook on high for 3 hours or on low for 6 hours.

PER SERVING: Calories: 195 | Fat: 4g | Protein: 26g | Sodium: 423mg | Fiber: 3g | Carbohydrates: 14g | Sugar: 8g

Paleo "Cream" of Mushroom Soup

This Paleo-approved "cream" of mushroom soup is a simple and light main dish. It's also a perfect Paleo-friendly base to use, when a recipe calls for canned cream soup.

INGREDIENTS | SERVES 4

2 tablespoons canola oil

2 tablespoons coconut butter

1 cup finely diced fresh mushrooms

4 tablespoons arrowroot powder

2 cups (full fat) coconut milk

½ teaspoon pepper

Cream Soup Variations

You can make any number of homemade cream soups with this recipe. If you would rather have cream of celery soup, use 1 cup of finely diced celery instead of the mushrooms. For a cream of chicken soup use 1 cup finely diced chicken and 2 teaspoons of poultry seasoning.

1. Heat the oil and coconut butter in a deep saucepan until sizzling. Add the diced mushrooms and cook until soft, approximately 4–5 minutes.

2. In a medium bowl whisk the arrowroot powder into the coconut milk. Slowly add to the mushrooms. Cook on medium heat for 5–10 minutes, whisking consistently, until slightly thickened.

3. Carefully pour cream soup into a greased 2½-quart slow cooker. Add pepper and any additional seasonings you would like. Cook on high for 2 hours or on low for 4 hours.

PER SERVING: Calories: 312 | Fat: 31g | Protein: 2g | Sodium: 15mg | Fiber: 0g | Carbohydrates: 10g | Sugar: 0g

Brown Stock

When you add ¼ cup of this concentrated broth to a slow cooked beef dish, you'll get the same, succulent flavor as if you first seared the meat in a hot skillet before adding it to the slow cooker. The broth also gives a delicious flavor boost to slow cooked tomato sauce or tomato gravy.

INGREDIENTS | YIELDS ABOUT 4 CUPS

2 large carrots, scrubbed
2 stalks of celery
1½ pounds bone-in chuck roast
1½ pounds cracked beef bones
1 large onion, peeled and quartered
Freshly ground black pepper, to taste
4½ cups water

1. Preheat the oven to 450°F. Cut the carrots and celery into large pieces. Put them, along with the meat, bones, and onions, into a roasting pan. Season with pepper. Put the pan in the middle part of the oven and, turning the meat and vegetables occasionally, roast for 45 minutes or until evenly browned.

2. Transfer the roasted meat, bones, and vegetables to a 4- or 6-quart slow cooker. Add the water to the roasting pan; scrape any browned bits clinging to the pan and then pour the water into the slow cooker. Cover and cook on low for 8 hours. (It may be necessary to skim accumulated fat and scum from the top of the pan juices; check the broth after 4, and again after 6, hours to see if that's needed.)

3. Use a slotted spoon to remove the roast and beef bones. Reserve the roast and the meat removed from the bones for another use; discard the bones.

4. Once the broth has cooled enough to handle, strain it; discard the cooked vegetables. Refrigerate the (cooled) broth overnight. Remove and discard the hardened fat. The resulting concentrated broth can be kept for 1 or 2 days in the refrigerator, or frozen for up to 3 months.

PER SERVING: (1 cup) | Calories: 33 | Fat: 0g | Protein: 1g | Sodium: 50mg | Fiber: 2g | Carbohydrates: 8g | Sugar: 4g

Pork Broth

Pork broth is seldom called for in recipes, but it can add layers of flavor when mixed with chicken broth in vegetable soups.

INGREDIENTS | YIELDS ABOUT 4 CUPS

1 (3-pound) bone-in pork butt roast
1 large onion, peeled and quartered
12 baby carrots
2 stalks celery, cut in half
4½ cups water

Pork Roast Dinner

To make concentrated broth and a pork roast dinner at the same time, increase the amount of carrots, decrease the water to 2½ cups, and add 4 peeled, medium sweet potatoes (cut in half) on top. Cook on low for 6 hours.

1. Add all the ingredients to a 4-quart slow cooker. Cover and cook on low for 6 hours or until the pork is tender and pulls away from the bone.

2. Strain; discard the celery and onion. Reserve the pork roast and carrots for another use. Once cooled, cover and refrigerate the broth overnight. Remove and discard the hardened fat. The broth can be kept for 1 or 2 days in the refrigerator, or frozen up to 3 months.

PER SERVING: (1 cup) | Calories: 29 | Fat: 0g | Protein: 1g | Sodium: 49mg | Fiber: 2g | Carbohydrates: 7g | Sugar: 3g

Seafood Stock

This recipe calls for using the shells only because the amount of time it takes to slow cook the stock would result in seafood that would be too tough to eat.

INGREDIENTS | YIELDS ABOUT 4 CUPS

2 pounds large or jumbo shrimp, crab, or lobster shells
1 large onion, peeled and thinly sliced
1 tablespoon fresh lemon juice
4 cups water

Fish or Seafood Stock in a Hurry

For each cup of seafood or fish stock called for in a recipe, you can substitute ¼ cup of bottled clam juice and ¾ cup of water. Just keep in mind that the clam juice is very salty, so adjust any recipe in which you use it accordingly.

1. Add the seafood shells, onion, lemon juice, and water, to a 4-quart slow cooker. Cover and cook on low for 4–8 hours.

2. Strain through a fine sieve or fine wire-mesh strainer. Discard the shells and onions. Refrigerate in a covered container and use within 2 days or freeze for up to 3 months.

PER SERVING: (1 cup) | Calories: 253 | Fat: 4g | Protein: 46g | Sodium: 341mg | Fiber: 1g | Carbohydrates: 6g | Sugar: 2g

Paleo "Cream" of Broccoli Soup

This Paleo-approved "cream" soup serves as a light meal on its own, or can be poured over a chicken or vegetable dish to enhance flavor and richness.

INGREDIENTS | SERVES 4

1 (12-ounce) bag frozen broccoli florets, thawed
1 small onion, peeled and diced
4 cups chicken broth
Freshly ground black pepper, to taste
1 cup (full fat) coconut milk

1. Add the broccoli, onion, broth, and pepper to a 2- or 4-quart slow cooker; cover and cook on low for 4 hours.

2. Use an immersion blender to purée the soup. Stir in the coconut milk. Cover, stir occasionally, and cook on low for 30 minutes, or until the soup is heated through.

PER SERVING: Calories: 241 | Fat: 16g | Protein: 8g | Sodium: 1,070mg | Fiber: 3g | Carbohydrates: 19g | Sugar: 2g

Caveman's Cabbage Soup

Slow cooking cabbage soup preserves the nutrients in the cabbage and other vegetables, versus other, higher temperature methods of preparation that tend to destroy many of the nutrients.

INGREDIENTS | SERVES 14

1 small head of cabbage
2 green onions
1 red bell pepper
1 bunch celery
1 cup baby carrots
4 cups chicken broth
4 cups water
3 cloves of garlic, minced
¼ teaspoon crushed red pepper flakes
¼ teaspoon dried basil
¼ teaspoon dried oregano
¼ teaspoon dried thyme
¼ teaspoon onion powder

1. Chop all vegetables and place them in a 6-quart slow cooker.

2. Pour in the broth and water.

3. Stir in garlic, pepper flakes, basil, oregano, thyme, and onion powder. Cover and cook on low for 8–10 hours.

PER SERVING: Calories: 49 | Fat: 1g | Protein: 2g | Sodium: 314mg | Fiber: 2g | Carbohydrates: 8g | Sugar: 3g

Pork and Apple Stew

If you prefer a tart apple taste, you can substitute Granny Smith apples for the Golden Delicious. (You can also add more apples if you wish. Apples and pork were made for each other!)

INGREDIENTS | SERVES 8

1 (3-pound) boneless pork shoulder roast

Freshly ground black pepper, to taste

1 large sweet onion, peeled and diced

2 Golden Delicious apples, peeled, cored, and diced

1 (2-pound) bag baby carrots

2 stalks celery, finely diced

2 cups apple juice

Optional: ¼ cup dry vermouth

Optional: 2 tablespoons brandy

Optional: 2 tablespoons honey

½ teaspoon dried thyme

¼ teaspoon ground allspice

¼ teaspoon dried sage

2 large sweet potatoes, peeled and quartered

1. Trim the roast of any fat; discard the fat and cut the roast into bite-sized pieces. Add the pork to a 4-quart slow cooker along with the remaining ingredients in the order given. (You want to rest the sweet potato quarters on top of the mixture in the slow cooker.)

2. Cover and cook on low for 6 hours or until the pork is cooked through and tender.

PER SERVING: Calories: 326 | Fat: 12g | Protein: 34g | Sodium: 226mg | Fiber: 4g | Carbohydrates: 18g | Sugar: 12g

Herbs and Spice Test

If you're unsure about the herbs and spices suggested in a recipe, wait to add them until the end of the cooking time. Once the meat is cooked through, spoon out ¼ cup or so of the pan juices into a microwave-safe bowl. Add a pinch of each herb and spice (in proportion to how they're suggested in the recipe), microwave on high for 15–30 seconds, and then taste the broth to see if you like it. Season the dish accordingly.

Lamb Stew

This high-protein concoction is a guaranteed Paleo crowd pleaser.

INGREDIENTS | SERVES 4

1½ pound boneless lamb shoulder, fat trimmed

1 cup Beef Stock (see recipe in this chapter)

6 medium carrots, cut into ¾" pieces

12 ounces turnips, cut into ¾" pieces

¾ cup chopped onions

½ tablespoon crushed garlic

¼ teaspoon thyme leaves

¼ teaspoon rosemary, crumbled

½ teaspoon black pepper

1. Cut lamb into 1½" chunks.

2. Combine all the ingredients into a 4-quart slow cooker and cook on low for 8–10 hours.

3. Before serving, skim off and discard fat.

PER SERVING: Calories: 532 | Fat: 32g | Protein: 32g | Sodium: 227mg | Fiber: 7g | Carbohydrates: 29g | Sugar: 14g

Texas Firehouse Chili

This no-bean chili is similar to dishes entered into firehouse chili cookoffs all over Texas.

INGREDIENTS | SERVES 4

1 pound cubed lean beef

2 tablespoons onion powder

1 tablespoon garlic powder

2 tablespoons Mexican-style chili powder

1 tablespoon paprika

½ teaspoon oregano

½ teaspoon freshly ground black pepper

½ teaspoon white pepper

½ teaspoon cayenne pepper

½ teaspoon chipotle pepper

8 ounces tomato sauce

1. Quickly brown the beef for 5–7 minutes in a nonstick skillet. Drain off any excess grease.

2. Add the meat and all of the remaining ingredients to a 4-quart slow cooker. Cook on low for up to 10 hours.

PER SERVING: Calories: 212 | Fat: 8g | Protein: 26g | Sodium: 359mg | Fiber: 2.5g | Carbohydrates: 9g | Sugar: 3g

Simple Tomato Soup

*This simple, healthy, three-step soup is made with canned tomatoes,
which are available year round at affordable prices. You can also make this soup
with about 4 pounds of chopped fresh tomatoes if you prefer.*

INGREDIENTS | SERVES 8

1 small sweet onion, finely diced

3 tablespoons coconut butter

3 (14.5-ounce) cans diced tomatoes

1 tablespoon honey

15 ounces Chicken Stock (see recipe in this chapter)

½ teaspoon lemon juice

1. In a small glass or microwave-safe bowl cook onions and coconut butter in the microwave on high for 1 minute to soften them.

2. Add onion mixture, tomatoes, honey, and chicken stock to a greased 4-quart slow cooker. Cook on high for 4 hours or on low for 8 hours.

3. After cooking period is over, turn off slow cooker. Add lemon juice to the soup. Allow soup to cool for about 20 minutes and then blend using an immersion blender or by pouring the soup (a little at a time) into a kitchen blender.

PER SERVING: Calories: 45 | Fat: 0g | Protein: 2g |
Sodium: 223mg | Fiber: 2g | Carbohydrates: 10g | Sugar: 6g

Beef, Pork, and Lamb

Tomato-Braised Pork

*Here the pork is gently cooked in tomatoes to yield meltingly tender meat.
If you'd prefer oregano or thyme in place of the marjoram, consider using a bit
less than what the recipe calls for, as these herbs tend to have a stronger flavor.*

INGREDIENTS | SERVES 4

28 ounces canned crushed tomatoes

3 tablespoons tomato paste

1 cup loosely packed fresh basil

½ teaspoon freshly ground black pepper

½ teaspoon marjoram

1¼ pounds boneless pork roast

1. Place the tomatoes, tomato paste, basil, pepper, and marjoram into a 4-quart slow cooker. Stir to create a uniform sauce. Add the pork.

2. Cook on low for 7–8 hours or until the pork easily falls apart when poked with a fork.

PER SERVING: Calories: 192 | Fat: 5g | Protein: 32g | Sodium: 166mg | Fiber: 1g | Carbohydrates: 3g | Sugar: 2g

Honey-Mustard Pork Loin

A mixture of mustard and honey keeps the pork from drying out during the long cooking time.

INGREDIENTS | SERVES 2

3 tablespoon Dijon mustard

1 tablespoon mild honey

½ pound pork tenderloin

1. In a small bowl, mix the mustard and honey. Spread the mixture on the pork tenderloin in an even layer.

2. Place into a 2-quart slow cooker. Cook on low for 6 hours.

PER SERVING: Calories: 170 | Fat: 3g | Protein: 25g | Sodium: 326mg | Fiber: 1g | Carbohydrates: 10g | Sugar: 9g

Pork Tenderloin with Sweet and Savory Apples

The tart apples sweeten over the long cooking time and nearly melt into the pork.

INGREDIENTS | SERVES 2

¼ teaspoon freshly ground black pepper
¾–1 pound boneless pork tenderloin
½ cup sliced onions
5 fresh sage leaves
2 cups peeled, diced Granny Smith apples

Pork Tenderloin Tip

Lean, boneless pork tenderloin is often sold in very large packages containing 2 or more tenderloins, with a combined weight that is frequently over 15 pounds. As a result, it can be very expensive. Buy pork tenderloin on sale, and cut the meat into meal-sized portions. Label and freeze the portions until they are needed.

1. Sprinkle pepper on the tenderloin. Place the onion slices on the bottom of a 1½–2-quart slow cooker. Add the tenderloin. Place the sage on top of the meat. Top with the diced apples.

2. Cover and cook on low for 8–10 hours.

PER SERVING: Calories: 261 | Fat: 5g | Protein: 47g | Sodium: 120mg | Fiber: 1g | Carbohydrates: 4g | Sugar: 2g

Beef and Coconut Curry

This Indian-inspired recipe combines the perfect blend of beef and vegetables, and the finished product is both sweet and savory.

INGREDIENTS | SERVES 4

2 tablespoons canola oil

2 pounds beef chuck roast, cut into 2-inch pieces

2 large onions, each cut into 8 wedges

4 cloves garlic, finely chopped

2 tablespoons finely chopped fresh ginger

12 ounces coconut milk

2 tablespoons honey

1 tablespoon curry powder

1 teaspoon cayenne pepper

1 pint cherry tomatoes

1. In a large skillet, warm oil over medium-high heat. Brown beef on all sides. Transfer to a 4-quart slow cooker along with onions, garlic, and ginger.

2. In a large bowl, whisk together the coconut milk, honey, curry powder, and cayenne pepper, and pour over meat. Cover and cook on low until meat is fork tender, about 4–5 hours.

3. Stir in cherry tomatoes and let them warm and soften in stew for 15–20 minutes.

PER SERVING: Calories: 315 | Fat: 25g | Protein: 4g | Sodium: 20mg | Fiber: 3g | Carbohydrates: 23g | Sugar: 14g

Curried Buffalo

This recipe using buffalo meat is made to impress even the most fussy Paleo eaters.

INGREDIENTS | SERVES 4

3 tablespoons arrowroot powder

3 tablespoons curry powder

1½ pounds of buffalo shoulder roast, cubed

3 large carrots, peeled and sliced

3 zucchini sliced

2 medium butternut squash, peeled and cubed

2 teaspoons crushed garlic

1 cup Beef Stock (see Chapter 5)

1. Combine the arrowroot and curry powder in a zip-top plastic bag.

2. Add buffalo to bag and shake gently until meat is coated.

3. Put vegetables and garlic into a 4-quart slow cooker, and then add the seasoned meat.

4. Pour stock over the meat and vegetables in the slow cooker. Cover and cook for 8–9 hours on low or 4–5 hours on high.

PER SERVING: Calories: 132 | Fat: 1g | Protein: 4g | Sodium: 101mg | Fiber: 7g | Carbohydrates: 29g | Sugar: 11g

Beef and Cabbage

The longer cooking time helps the flavors develop. But because the meat is already cooked, this meal is done when the cabbage is tender, or in about 4 hours on low. Serve over mashed turnip, cauliflower, or butternut squash.

INGREDIENTS | SERVES 4

1 pound cooked stew beef
1 small head of cabbage, chopped
1 medium onion, peeled and diced
2 large carrots, peeled and thinly sliced
2 stalks celery, sliced in ½" pieces
1 clove garlic, peeled and minced
2 cups beef broth
1 (14½-ounce) can diced tomatoes
¼ teaspoon honey
⅛ teaspoon freshly ground black pepper

1. Cut the cooked beef into bite-sized pieces and add it to a 4-quart slow cooker along with the cabbage, onion, carrots, and celery. Stir to combine.

2. Add the garlic, broth, tomatoes, honey, and pepper to a bowl; mix well and pour over the beef. Cook on high for 1 hour or until the cabbage has begun to wilt.

3. Reduce heat to low and cook for 3–4 hours or until cabbage is very tender. Adjust seasonings if necessary.

PER SERVING: Calories: 354 | Fat: 8g | Protein: 29g | Sodium: 241mg | Fiber: 12g | Carbohydrates: 43g | Sugar: 21g

Easy Leg of Lamb

Although lamb can be an expensive cut of meat, you can often find it on sale during the holidays. Stock up on several cuts and freeze them when you find good prices.

INGREDIENTS | SERVES 6

1 (4-pound) bone-in leg of lamb

5 cloves garlic, skin removed, and cut into spears

2 tablespoons olive oil

1 tablespoon dried rosemary

½ teaspoon ground pepper

4 cups Chicken Stock (see Chapter 5)

¼ cup red wine

1. Make small incisions evenly over the lamb. Place garlic spears into the slices in the lamb.

2. Rub olive oil, rosemary, and pepper over the lamb. Place lamb into a greased 4–6-quart slow cooker.

3. Pour stock and wine around the leg of lamb. Cook on high for 4 hours or on low for 8 hours.

4. Serve the roast lamb in bowls. Ladle the sauce from the slow cooker over each serving.

PER SERVING: Calories: 74 | Fat: 5g | Protein: 7g | Sodium: 15mg | Fiber: 1g | Carbohydrates: 3g | Sugar: 1g

Herbed Lamb Chops

This simple herb rub would make a fun holiday gift to give to friends or family members who enjoy cooking! Include this recipe with a small jar of the rub.

INGREDIENTS | SERVES 4

1 medium onion, sliced
1 teaspoon dried oregano
½ teaspoon dried thyme
½ teaspoon garlic powder
⅛ teaspoon ground pepper
2 pounds (about 8) lamb loin chops
1 tablespoon olive oil

1. Place the onion on the bottom of a greased 4-quart slow cooker.

2. In a small bowl mix together oregano, thyme, garlic powder, and pepper. Rub herb mixture over the lamb chops.

3. Place herb-rubbed lamb chops over the sliced onions in the slow cooker. Drizzle olive oil over the lamb chops.

4. Cook on high for 3 hours or on low for 6 hours, until tender.

PER SERVING: Calories: 43 | Fat: 3g | Protein: 0g | Sodium: 2mg | Fiber: 1g | Carbohydrates: 3g | Sugar: 1g

Easy Slow Cooker Pork Tenderloin

Slow cooker meals are a great way to cook for your family. Large quantities can be thrown into the cooker hours in advance. Most leftovers can be easily frozen for future meals.

INGREDIENTS | SERVES 4

1 pound lean pork loin, whole

1 (28-ounce) can diced tomatoes, no salt added

3 medium zucchini, diced

4 cups cauliflower florets

Chopped fresh basil, to taste

Garlic, to taste

1. Combine all the ingredients in a 2- or 4-quart slow cooker.

2. Cook on low for 6–7 hours.

PER SERVING: Calories: 58 | Fat: 1g | Protein: 3g | Sodium: 310mg | Fiber: 4g | Carbohydrates: 13g | Sugar: 6g

Low-Fat Meat Choice

Pork is a nice low-fat protein source. It is versatile for cooking and quite flavorful. This often-overlooked meat is a fantastic friend of the Paleolithic lifestyle.

Paleo Pulled Pork

This recipe was inspired by an elite athlete, Allie, a field hockey goalie, playing at the collegiate level. Allie often enjoys this pulled pork recipe as her postgame celebratory meal.

INGREDIENTS | SERVES 8

2½ pounds pork loin

1 large onion, chopped

1 (16-ounce) can unsalted organic tomato paste

3 tablespoons olive oil

2 cups lemon juice

½ cup unsalted beef broth

4 cloves garlic

¼ teaspoon cayenne pepper

½ teaspoon paprika

2 teaspoons chipotle chili powder

1 teaspoon thyme

1 teaspoon cumin

1. Combine all the ingredients in a 4–6-quart slow cooker.

2. Cook on low for 5 hours or until meat is softened completely.

3. Once cooled, shred with a fork and serve over a large dinner salad or a hot root vegetable medley.

PER SERVING: Calories: 116 | Fat: 6g | Protein: 3g | Sodium: 506mg | Fiber: 3g | Carbohydrates: 18g | Sugar: 9g

Apples-and-Onions Pork Chops

Try Sonya apples in this sweet and savory dish; they are crisp and sweet.

INGREDIENTS | SERVES 4

4 crisp, sweet apples, peeled and cut into wedges

2 large onions, sliced

4 thick cut boneless pork chops (about 1 pound)

½ teaspoon ground cayenne pepper

½ teaspoon ground cinnamon

¼ teaspoon allspice

¼ teaspoon ground fennel

1. Place half of the apple wedges in the bottom of an oval 4-quart slow cooker along with half of the sliced onions.

2. Top with a single layer of pork chops. Sprinkle with spices, and top with the remaining apples and onions.

3. Cook on low for 8 hours.

PER SERVING: Calories: 267 | Fat: 6g | Protein: 42g | Sodium: 94mg | Fiber: 2g | Carbohydrates: 7g | Sugar: 3g

Slow Cooking with Boneless Pork

Not only is there less waste associated with boneless pork chops or roasts, there is often less fat attached to the meat. Even without much fat, boneless pork is well suited to slow cooking. All of the moisture stays in the dish, ensuring tender pork.

Pot Roast with a Touch of Sweet

Serve this roast alongside a hearty potion of "Mashed" Cauliflower (see Chapter 10).

INGREDIENTS | SERVES 4

1 teaspoon freshly ground black pepper
1 teaspoon smoked paprika
1 teaspoon garlic powder
1 teaspoon onion powder
½ cup lime juice
½ cup tomato sauce
2 pounds beef chuck roast
1 large sweet onion, sliced thick
1 teaspoon coconut or olive oil
½ cup water
2 tablespoons red wine (optional)

1. In a small bowl, combine the pepper, paprika, garlic powder, and onion powder.

2. In a separate bowl, combine the lime juice and tomato sauce. Set aside.

3. Season all sides of the roast with the prepared spice mixture.

4. Place onion slices on the bottom of a 4-quart slow cooker.

5. Warm the oil in a large skillet over medium-high heat. Brown the roast on all sides in the skillet.

6. Place browned roast on top of the onions in the slow cooker. Turn heat to low, and add water and wine to the skillet.

7. Pour pan liquid over the roast, then the lime juice and sauce mixture on top. Cover and cook on low for 8 hours.

PER SERVING: Calories: 36 | Fat: 0g | Protein: 1g | Sodium: 164mg | Fiber: 2g | Carbohydrates: 7g | Sugar: 3g

Beef and Ginger Curry

*This hearty and spicy curry dish, typically served over rice,
is just as tasty over a bed of Paleo-approved carrots and cauliflower.*

INGREDIENTS | SERVES 4

1 pound stewing steak

1 tablespoon olive oil

Pepper, to taste

2 cloves garlic, minced

1 teaspoon chopped fresh ginger

1 fresh green chili, diced

1 tablespoon curry powder

1 (14-ounce) can stewed tomatoes, chopped

1 large onion, peeled and quartered

8–9 ounces Beef Stock (see Chapter 5)

1. In a frying pan, brown the steak in the olive oil for 5–10 minutes. Once browned, remove from pan, leaving juices. Season beef with pepper.

2. In the remaining juice from the steak, cook the garlic, ginger, and chili in the frying pan for 2 minutes, stirring frequently.

3. Season with curry powder. Mix in the chopped tomatoes.

4. Place the onion on bottom of a 2- or 4-quart slow cooker, and layer with browned beef.

5. Add mixture from pan to the slow cooker, and add the beef stock. Cover and cook on low for 6–8 hours.

PER SERVING: Calories: 82 | Fat: 4g | Protein: 2g | Sodium: 192mg | Fiber: 4g | Carbohydrates: 16g | Sugar: 5g

Roast Beef for Two

*Couples deserve a good roast dinner just as much as larger families.
So enjoy this one without having to eat leftovers for a week.*

INGREDIENTS | SERVES 2

½ teaspoon freshly ground black pepper

½ teaspoon fennel seeds

½ teaspoon crushed rosemary

½ teaspoon dried oregano

¾-pound bottom round roast, excess fat removed

¼ cup Caramelized Onions (see Chapter 10)

¼ cup Beef Stock (see Chapter 5)

1 clove garlic, sliced

1. In a small bowl, stir the pepper, fennel seeds, rosemary, and oregano. Rub it onto all sides of the meat. Refrigerate for 15 minutes.

2. Place the roast in a 2-quart slow cooker. Add the onions, stock, and garlic. Cook on low for 6 hours or on high for 3 hours. Remove roast and slice. Serve the slices topped with the onions. Discard any cooking juices.

PER SERVING: Calories: 266 | Fat: 11g | Protein: 38g | Sodium: 172mg | Fiber: 1g | Carbohydrates: 4g | Sugar: 1g

Ground Beef Ragout

Ragout is a term that generally refers to a slow cooked stew with a variety of vegetables that can be made with or without meat. Ground beef is used in this version for a very economical main dish. Serve over spaghetti squash or mashed cauliflower.

INGREDIENTS | SERVES 4

1 pound ground beef
2 medium onions, finely chopped
1 large green pepper, diced with seeds removed
1 tablespoon olive oil
1 (14.5-ounce) can Italian-style stewed tomatoes
3 medium carrots, cut into ½" slices
½ cup Beef Stock (see Chapter 5)
½ teaspoon ground pepper
1 medium zucchini, halved lengthwise and cut into ½" slices

Not a Fan of Zucchini?

Instead of using zucchini, use yellow squash, precooked sweet potatoes, parsnips, or even mushrooms. Use whatever vegetables you have on hand!

1. Brown ground beef in a skillet, discard grease, and spoon ground beef into a greased 4-quart slow cooker.

2. In the same pan, sauté the onions and green pepper in olive oil for 8–12 minutes until softened. Add onions and green pepper to slow cooker.

3. Add the tomatoes, carrots, stock, and pepper to the slow cooker. Stir to combine all the ingredients.

4. Cook on high for 4 hours or on low for 8 hours.

5. An hour prior to serving stir in the zucchini and allow to cook 10–20 minutes, until fork tender.

PER SERVING: Calories: 308 | Fat: 15g | Protein: 25g | Sodium: 264mg | Fiber: 5g | Carbohydrates: 20g | Sugar: 10g

Lamb with Garlic, Lemon, and Rosemary

You can use the spice rub in this recipe as a marinade by applying it to the leg of lamb several hours (or up to one full day) before cooking. The red wine in this dish can be replaced with chicken or beef stock (see Chapter 5).

INGREDIENTS | SERVES 4

4 cloves of garlic, crushed
1 tablespoon fresh rosemary, chopped
1 tablespoon olive oil
1 teaspoon ground pepper
1 (3-pound) leg of lamb
1 large lemon, cut into ¼" slices
½ cup red wine

1. In a small bowl mix together garlic, rosemary, olive oil, and pepper. Rub this mixture onto the leg of lamb.

2. Place a few lemon slices in the bottom of a greased 4-quart slow cooker. Place spice-rubbed lamb on top of lemon slices.

3. Add remaining lemon slices on top of lamb. Pour wine around the lamb.

4. Cook on low heat for 8–10 hours or on high for 4–6 hours.

PER SERVING: Calories: 763 | Fat: 52g | Protein: 62g | Sodium: 194mg | Fiber: 0g | Carbohydrates: 2g | Sugar: 0g

Pork Tenderloin with Nectarines

Pork combined with the flavor of ripe nectarines makes a lovely sweet and slightly tangy sauce. Serve sliced pork and sauce over steamed zucchini strips.

INGREDIENTS | SERVES 4

1¼ pounds pork tenderloin

1 tablespoon olive oil

4 ripe but firm nectarines, each cut into 4 wedges

2 tablespoons lemon juice

1. Rub pork tenderloin with olive oil. Place in a greased 4-quart slow cooker.

2. Pour nectarines on top of and around the pork tenderloin. Drizzle lemon juice over the pork and fruit. Cook on high for 3–4 hours or on low for 6–8 hours, until pork is very tender.

3. Remove pork from slow cooker and slice before serving. If needed, add pepper, to taste.

PER SERVING: Calories: 246 | Fat: 7g | Protein: 31g | Sodium: 76mg | Fiber: 2g | Carbohydrates: 15g | Sugar: 11g

Sirloin Dinner

Add a tossed salad and some mashed sweet potato or butternut squash, and this recipe makes a complete meal.

INGREDIENTS | SERVES 8

1 (4-pound) beef sirloin tip roast
2 tablespoons extra-virgin olive oil
½ teaspoon freshly ground pepper
1 teaspoon garlic powder
1 teaspoon onion powder
1 teaspoon ground cumin
1 teaspoon dried thyme leaves, crushed
½ teaspoon sweet paprika
2 turnips, peeled and cut into 2-inch pieces
2 parsnips, peeled and cut into 2-inch pieces
1 (1-pound) bag baby carrots
8 cloves garlic, peeled and cut in half lengthwise
2 large onions, peeled and sliced
½ cup dry red wine
1 cup beef broth
Freshly ground black pepper, to taste

Rare Sirloin Roast

If you prefer a rare roast, use a probe thermometer set to your preferred doneness setting. (130°F for rare.) You'll need to be close by so that you hear the thermometer alarm when it goes off. Remove the roast to a platter; cover and keep warm. Cover and continue to cook the vegetables if necessary.

1. To ensure the roast cooks evenly, tie it into an even form using butcher's twine. Rub the oil onto the meat.

2. In a small bowl, mix the pepper, garlic powder, onion powder, cumin, thyme, and paprika together. Pat the seasoning mixture on all sides of the roast. Place the roast in the slow cooker.

3. Arrange the turnips, parsnips, and carrots around the roast. Evenly disperse the garlic around the vegetables. Arrange the onion slices over the vegetables. Pour the wine and broth into the slow cooker. Season with pepper, to taste. Cover and cook on low for 8 hours.

4. Use a slotted spoon to remove the roast and vegetables to a serving platter; cover and keep warm. Let the roast rest for at least 10 minutes before carving. To serve, thinly slice the roast across the grain. Serve drizzled with some of the pan juices.

PER SERVING: Calories: 109 | Fat: 4g | Protein: 2g | Sodium: 75mg | Fiber: 3g | Carbohydrates: 14g | Sugar: 6g

Mango Pork Morsels

In this recipe, the mango provides natural sweetness and a tropical flair.
Plate and pierce each morsel with a toothpick.

INGREDIENTS | SERVES 10

1½ pounds lean pork loin, cubed

2 mangoes, cubed

3 cloves garlic, minced

1 jalapeño, minced

1 tablespoon salsa

¼ teaspoon freshly ground black pepper

2 teaspoons ground chipotle

1 teaspoon New Mexican chili powder

½ teaspoon oregano

2 tablespoons freshly squeezed juice from an orange

2 tablespoons lime juice

1. Quickly brown the pork in a nonstick skillet. Add the pork and mango to a 4-quart slow cooker.

2. In a small bowl, whisk together the garlic, jalapeño, salsa, pepper, chipotle, chili powder, oregano, and the orange and lime juices. Pour over the mango and pork. Stir.

3. Cook on low for 6 hours; remove the cover and cook on high for 30 minutes. Stir before serving.

PER SERVING: Calories: 29 | Fat: 0g | Protein: 0g | Sodium: 11mg | Fiber: 1g | Carbohydrates: 8g | Sugar: 6g

How to Cut Up a Mango

Slice the mango vertically on either side of the large flat pit. Using the tip of a knife, cut vertical lines into the flesh without piercing the skin. Make horizontal lines in the flesh to form cubes. Use a spoon to scoop out the cubes. Repeat for the other side.

Cabbage Rollatini

Serve alongside or atop a bed of mixed greens, and enjoy as a "taco salad."

INGREDIENTS | SERVES 12

1 tablespoon coconut oil

½ medium onion, ground in food processor

4 cloves garlic, ground in food processor

1 teaspoon dried basil

1 teaspoon cumin

1 teaspoon dried oregano

½ head cauliflower, ground in food processor

2 pounds ground meat (lean beef, chicken, or turkey)

½ cup almond flour

1 egg

½ teaspoon garlic powder

1 head green cabbage, leaves separated and heated (in microwave)

26 ounces of tomato sauce (jarred, or a sauce from Chapter 4)

1. Heat oil in a large skillet over medium heat. Add the ground onion, garlic, basil, cumin, and oregano and sauté for 2–3 minutes. Remove from heat.

2. In a large bowl, place the cauliflower, meat, almond flour, egg, and garlic powder. Combine thoroughly with your hands or a large spoon. Add in sautéed onion mixture and mix well.

3. Line a 4-quart slow cooker with 2 large cabbage leaves.

4. Scoop ½–¾ cup of the meat filling onto the stem end of the remaining cabbage leaves, and roll each cabbage leave as tightly as possible.

5. Place rolls in slow cooker, seam-side down. Pour tomato sauce evenly over top of cabbage rolls.

6. Cook on high for 4 hours. Serve warm, and spoon sauce and drippings over the rolls.

PER SERVING: Calories: 192 | Fat: 8g | Protein: 20g | Sodium: 386mg | Fiber: 4g | Carbohydrates: 11g | Sugar: 6g

Lunch Casserole

A filling, high-protein entrée, loaded with fiber, B-vitamins, and iron.

INGREDIENTS | SERVES 6

1½ pounds lean ground beef
1 large onion, chopped
2 tablespoons canola oil
2 cloves garlic, minced
6 ounces sliced mushrooms
½ teaspoon nutmeg
1 (10-ounce) package frozen spinach, thawed and squeezed dry
3 tablespoons arrowroot powder
6 eggs, beaten
¾ cup coconut milk, scalded

1. In a large skillet over medium heat, lightly brown the beef and onions for 5–10 minutes in the canola oil.

2. Drain the excess fat and place meat mixture in a well-greased 2- or 4-quart slow cooker.

3. Stir the garlic, mushrooms, nutmeg, spinach, and arrowroot powder into the meat mixture in the slow cooker.

4. In a small bowl, beat the eggs and coconut milk together. Pour over meat mixture in the slow cooker. Stir well.

5. Cover and cook on low for 7–9 hours or until firm.

PER SERVING: Calories: 365 | Fat: 22g | Protein: 34g | Sodium: 185mg | Fiber: 2g | Carbohydrates: 10g | Sugar: 2g

Barbecue Meatballs

This tangy, yet spicy meatball recipe goes well with some southern-inspired vegetables, or alone as a crowd-pleasing appetizer.

INGREDIENTS | SERVES 4

1½ cups chili sauce
1 cup Fig Jam (see Chapter 2), or grape jelly
2 teaspoons Dijon mustard
1 pound lean ground beef
1 egg
3 tablespoons arrowroot powder
½ teaspoon lemon juice

1. Preheat oven to 400°F.

2. Combine the chili sauce, jam, and mustard in a 2-quart slow cooker and stir well.

3. Cover and cook on high while preparing meatballs.

4. In a large mixing bowl, combine the remaining ingredients thoroughly. Shape into 20 medium-sized meatballs. Place meatballs on a broiler rack or in a baking pan and bake in oven for 15–20 minutes. Drain well.

5. Add meatballs to the sauce in slow cooker. Stir well to coat.

6. Cover and cook on low for 6–10 hours.

PER SERVING: Calories: 586 | Fat: 8g | Protein: 37g | Sodium: 1,496mg | Fiber: 8g | Carbohydrates: 102g | Sugar: 82g

Stuffed Cabbage

This is a wonderful dish to serve to guests. Although there is some preparation to do, you will have plenty of time to clean up before your guests arrive.

INGREDIENTS | SERVES 4

Water, as needed
1 large head cabbage
1 teaspoon canola or flaxseed oil
½ cup sliced onions
28 ounces canned whole tomatoes in purée
½ cup minced onions
1 egg
½ tablespoon garlic powder
½ tablespoon paprika
1 pound 94% lean ground beef

1. Bring a large pot of water to boil.

2. Meanwhile, using a knife, make 4 or 5 cuts around the core of the cabbage and remove the core. Discard the core and 2 layers of the outer leaves. Peel off 6–8 large whole leaves. Place the leaves in a steamer basket and allow them to steam over the boiling water for 7 minutes.

3. Allow the leaves to cool enough to handle. Dice the remaining cabbage to equal ½ cup.

4. In a nonstick skillet, add canola or flaxseed oil. Add the sliced onions and diced cabbage, and sauté for about 5 minutes until the onions are soft. Add tomatoes. Break up tomatoes into small chunks using the back of a spoon. Simmer about 10–15 minutes. Ladle one-third of the sauce over the bottom of a 4-quart oval slow cooker.

5. Place the minced onions, egg, spices, and beef into a medium-sized bowl. Stir to distribute all ingredients evenly.

6. Place a cabbage leaf with the open-side up and the stem part facing you on a clean work area. Add about ¼ cup filling to the leaf toward the stem. Fold the sides together, and then pull the top down and over the filling to form a packet. It should look like a burrito. Repeat until all the filling is gone.

7. Arrange the cabbage rolls, seam-side down, in a single layer in the slow cooker. Ladle about half of the remaining sauce over the rolls and repeat with a second layer. Ladle the remaining sauce over the rolls. Cover and cook on low for up to 10 hours.

PER SERVING: Calories: 282 | Fat: 8g | Protein: 34g | Sodium: 150mg | Fiber: 7g | Carbohydrates: 18g | Sugar: 9g

Meatloaf-Stuffed Green Peppers

This recipe is slightly different from traditional stuffed pepper recipes because it doesn't contain rice or potatoes to supplement the meat mixture. This is a great main dish option for those following low-carbohydrate food plans.

INGREDIENTS | SERVES 4

¼ cup almond flour

¼ cup coconut milk

1 pound ground beef

½ teaspoon lemon juice

½ teaspoon pepper

1½ teaspoons dried onion

1 egg

4 green peppers

⅓ cup water

1. In a large bowl mix together the almond flour and coconut milk, and set aside for 5 minutes.

2. Next, add the ground beef, lemon juice, pepper, dried onion, and egg to the mixture. Mix together well.

3. Carefully remove the tops, seeds, and membranes of the peppers. Fill each pepper with ¼ of the meatloaf mixture.

4. Place the stuffed peppers in a greased 4-quart slow cooker. Add ⅓ cup of water around the bottom of the stuffed peppers.

5. Cook on high for 3–4 hours or on low for 6–8 hours until green peppers are softened.

PER SERVING: Calories: 308 | Fat: 19g | Protein: 27g | Sodium: 97mg | Fiber: 3g | Carbohydrates: 8g | Sugar: 3g

CHAPTER 7

Poultry

Tuscan Chicken

This simple dish is perfect served over grilled or oven-roasted asparagus.

INGREDIENTS | SERVES 4

1 pound boneless, skinless chicken breast tenderloins

1 cup Chicken Stock (see Chapter 5)

4 cloves garlic, minced

1 shallot, minced

2 tablespoons lime juice

1 tablespoon lemon juice

1 tablespoon minced fresh rosemary

1. Place all the ingredients into a 4-quart slow cooker. Stir.

2. Cook on low for 4 hours or until the chicken is fully cooked.

PER SERVING: Calories: 141 | Fat: 3g | Protein: 25g | Sodium: 136mg | Fiber: 0g | Carbohydrates: 2g | Sugar: 0g

Coconut Mango Spiced Chicken

This simple, sweet, and spicy dish requires just four ingredients, and is easily prepared in just a few minutes.

INGREDIENTS | SERVES 4

1 can of coconut milk

1 large softball sized, (firm) mango, peeled and cut into cubes. (save mango pit)

1 pound of chicken (breasts or thighs), cut into cubes

1 tablespoon dried paprika flakes

1. Pour coconut milk into a 4-quart slow cooker.

2. Place the cubes of mango into the slow cooker, along with the pit of the mango. Add the chicken and paprika flakes. Stir well.

3. Cook on high for 3 hours or on low for 5–6 hours.

PER SERVING: Calories: 133 | Fat: 3g | Protein: 24g | Sodium: 131mg | Fiber: 1g | Carbohydrates: 1g | Sugar: 0g

Chicken Cacciatore

This recipe can be prepared using a variety of different vegetable combinations as substitutes for the mushrooms and green peppers, for example: sliced carrots, sliced zucchini and summer squash, eggplant, yellow or red pepper, etc.

INGREDIENTS | SERVES 6

6 skinless, boneless chicken breasts

21 ounces tomato sauce

9 ounces fresh mushrooms

2 green peppers, seeded and cubed

1 large onion, sliced

1–2 cloves garlic, minced

1. Place all ingredients in a 4-quart slow cooker. Cover and cook on low for 7–9 hours.

2. Serve warm over vegetable medley of choice.

PER SERVING: Calories: 319 | Fat: 7g | Protein: 53g | Sodium: 791mg | Fiber: 3g | Carbohydrates: 11g | Sugar: 7g

Pheasantly Pleasant

Wild game like pheasants move more frequently than the average chicken and therefore contain less saturated fat and calories per ounce.

INGREDIENTS | SERVES 6

2 pheasants, cut into small, 1–2" chunks

¼ cup almond flour, seasoned with pepper

4 tablespoons olive oil

4 tablespoons coconut butter

1 clove garlic

1 large onion, diced

1 cup sweet white wine

1 tablespoon honey

1 (10.75-ounce) can of chopped mushrooms

10 ounces chicken broth

1. Mix pheasant pieces in seasoned almond flour.

2. In a skillet over medium heat, sauté the pheasant for 5–7 minutes in oil and butter. Transfer pheasant to a 4-quart slow cooker.

3. Mash garlic clove in skillet juices, add onion, wine, honey, mushrooms, and broth. Heat to bubbling and simmer 5 minutes, and pour over pheasant in the slow cooker.

4. Cover and cook on low for 6–8 hours.

PER SERVING: Calories: 493 | Fat: 21g | Protein: 58g | Sodium: 381mg | Fiber: 1g | Carbohydrates: 10g | Sugar: 5g

No Crust Chicken Potpie

A traditional "comfort" food converted to satisfy even the hardest-to-please Paleo palate.

INGREDIENTS | SERVES 4

Butter-flavored cooking spray

10 ounces coconut milk

1 teaspoon dried parsley flakes

1 teaspoon dried onion flakes

1 (16-ounce) package frozen cauliflower, broccoli, and carrot blend

16 ounces skinned and boned, uncooked chicken breast, cut into ½-inch cubes

1. Spray a 4-quart slow cooker with butter-flavored cooking spray.

2. In the prepared slow cooker, combine coconut milk, parsley flakes, and onion flakes.

3. Stir in the frozen vegetables and chicken pieces. Cover and cook on low for 8 hours. Mix well before serving.

PER SERVING: Calories: 293 | Fat: 18 | Protein: 27g | Sodium: 166mg | Fiber: 3g | Carbohydrates: 7g | Sugar: 3g

Ground Turkey Joes

This easy, sweet and sour turkey dish comes together quickly and serves well over puréed cauliflower, mashed sweet potatoes, or turnips. If you prefer, you can also use ground chicken or ground beef as a substitute for the ground turkey.

INGREDIENTS | SERVES 4

2 teaspoons olive oil

1 pound lean ground turkey

½ cup onion, finely chopped

½ cup green pepper, finely chopped

1 teaspoon garlic powder

1 tablespoon prepared yellow mustard

¾ cup Homemade Ketchup (see Chapter 4)

3 tablespoons honey

¼ teaspoon lemon juice

½ teaspoon ground pepper

1. In a large skillet, heat olive oil over medium-high heat. Brown ground turkey, onion, and green pepper for approximately 5–6 minutes. Drain off any grease.

2. Add turkey mixture to a greased 2½-quart or 4-quart slow cooker. Add garlic powder, mustard, ketchup, honey, lemon juice, and ground pepper.

3. Mix ingredients together and cook on low for 4 hours or on high for 2 hours.

PER SERVING: Calories: 270 | Fat: 12g | Protein: 20g | Sodium: 108mg | Fiber: 1g | Carbohydrates: 22g | Sugar: 20g

Roast Chicken with Lemon and Artichokes

This is an elegant twist on a simple roast chicken. Marinated artichoke hearts add a hint of zest while fresh lemons give the dish a bright flavor reminiscent of summer.

INGREDIENTS | SERVES 4

1 small onion, quartered

1 large carrot, sliced

1 large lemon

3 cloves garlic

1 (4-pound) whole chicken

½ teaspoon freshly ground pepper

2 tablespoons olive oil

1 (6-ounce) jar marinated artichoke hearts

Make a Quick Lemon Sauce

Make a sauce using the liquids from the cooked chicken by straining them into a saucepan. Whisk in 2 tablespoons of almond flour and cook on low heat until thickened. The resulting sauce will have a fragrant aroma of lemon, artichokes, and garlic. Serve over green beans or asparagus, alongside a salad.

1. Grease a large 6-quart slow cooker with nonstick cooking spray.

2. Place the onion and carrot in the slow cooker. Cut the lemon in half. Place half of the lemon, along with the garlic cloves, into the cavity of the chicken.

3. Cut the remainder of the lemon into 4–5 large slices.

4. Place the chicken on top of the onions and carrots. Place lemon slices on top of the chicken. Sprinkle pepper over the chicken. Drizzle olive oil over the chicken. Cook on low for 6–8 hours or on high for 3–4 hours.

5. An hour before serving, place artichoke hearts (discarding the oil) over the top of the chicken.

PER SERVING: Calories: 611 | Fat: 21g | Protein: 96g | Sodium: 359mg | Fiber: 1g | Carbohydrates: 4g | Sugar: 2g

Chicken Paprikash

If you prefer not to cook with wine, replace it with an equal amount of chicken broth.

INGREDIENTS | SERVES 8

1 tablespoon coconut butter

1 tablespoon extra-virgin olive oil

1 large yellow onion, peeled and diced

2 cloves garlic, peeled and minced

3 pounds boneless, skinless chicken thighs

¼ teaspoon freshly ground pepper

2 tablespoons Hungarian paprika

½ cup Chicken Stock (see Chapter 5)

¼ cup dry white wine

2 cups (full fat) coconut milk

A Thought on Thinning

If the resulting sauce for the chicken paprikash is too thin, add more coconut milk.

1. Add the coconut butter, oil, and onion to a microwave-safe bowl; cover and microwave on high for 1 minute. Stir, re-cover, and microwave on high for another minute or until the onions are transparent.

2. Stir in the garlic; cover and microwave on high for 30 seconds. Add contents of the bowl to a greased 4–6-quart slow cooker.

3. Cut the chicken thighs into bite-sized pieces. Add the chicken to the slow cooker.

4. Stir in the pepper, paprika, stock, and wine; cover and cook on low for 6 hours or on high for 3 hours.

5. Stir in the coconut milk; cover and continue to cook long enough to bring the coconut milk to same temperature, about 30 minutes.

6. Sprinkle each serving with additional paprika if desired. Serve immediately.

PER SERVING: Calories: 343 | Fat: 20g | Protein: 35g | Sodium: 154mg | Fiber: 0g | Carbohydrates: 4g | Sugar: 1g

Curried Chicken in Coconut Milk

*Chicken base is available from Minor's (www.soupbase.com) or
Redi-Base (www.redibase.com), or you can use chicken bouillon concentrate.*

INGREDIENTS | SERVES 4

1 small onion, peeled and diced

2 cloves of garlic, peeled and minced

1½ tablespoons curry powder

1 cup coconut milk

¾ teaspoon chicken broth base

8 chicken thighs, skin removed

1. Add the onion, garlic, curry powder, coconut milk, and broth base to a 4-quart slow cooker. Stir to mix.

2. Add the chicken thighs. Cover and cook on low for 6 hours.

3. Use a slotted spoon to remove the thighs to a serving bowl. Whisk to combine the sauce and pour over the chicken.

PER SERVING: Calories: 292 | Fat: 18g | Protein: 29g | Sodium: 128mg | Fiber: 1g | Carbohydrates: 5g | Sugar: 1g

Poached Chicken

*Use this moist, tender poached chicken in any recipe that calls for cooked chicken.
It is especially good in salads and sandwiches.*

INGREDIENTS | SERVES 8

4–5 pounds whole chicken or chicken parts

1 large, whole carrot, peeled

1 stalk celery

1 medium onion, peeled and quartered

1 cup water

1. Place the chicken into an oval 6-quart slow cooker. Arrange the vegetables around the chicken. Add the water. Cook on low for 7–8 hours.

2. Remove the skin before eating.

PER SERVING: Calories: 310 | Fat: 8g | Protein: 54g | Sodium: 206mg | Fiber: 1g | Carbohydrates: 2g | Sugar: 1g

Tarragon Chicken

The tarragon infuses the chicken with flavor without added fat.

INGREDIENTS | SERVES 4

2 split chicken breasts
2 cups loosely packed fresh tarragon
1 medium onion, peeled and sliced
¼ teaspoon freshly ground black pepper

1. Place the chicken in a 4-quart slow cooker. Top with remaining ingredients. Cook on low for 7–8 hours.

2. Remove the chicken from the slow cooker. Peel off the skin and discard. Discard the tarragon and onion.

PER SERVING: Calories: 146 | Fat: 3g | Protein: 25g | Sodium: 138mg | Fiber: 1g | Carbohydrates: 3g | Sugar: 1g

Mango Duck Breast

Slow cooked mangoes soften and create their own sauce in this easy duck dish.

INGREDIENTS | SERVES 4

2 boneless, skinless duck breasts
1 large mango, cubed
¼ cup duck stock or Chicken Stock (see Chapter 5)
1 tablespoon ginger juice
1 tablespoon minced hot pepper
1 tablespoon minced shallot

Place all ingredients into a 4-quart slow cooker. Cook on low for 4 hours.

PER SERVING: Calories: 412 | Fat: 18g | Protein: 55g | Sodium: 225mg | Fiber: 0g | Carbohydrates: 3g | Sugar: 0g

Thyme-Roasted Turkey Breast

Slow cooked turkey is so moist there's no basting required!

INGREDIENTS | SERVES 10

2 large onions, thinly sliced
1 (6–7-pound) turkey breast or turkey half
½ cup minced thyme
½ tablespoon freshly ground black pepper
½ tablespoon dried parsley
½ tablespoon celery flakes
½ tablespoon mustard seed

1. Arrange the onion slices in a thin layer on the bottom of a 6–7-quart slow cooker.

2. Make a small slit in the skin of the turkey and spread the thyme between the skin and meat. Smooth the skin back onto the turkey.

3. In a small bowl, stir the pepper, parsley, celery flakes, and mustard seed. Rub the spice mixture into the skin of the turkey.

4. Place the turkey in the slow cooker on top of the onion layer. Cook for 8 hours. Remove the skin and onions and discard them before serving the turkey.

PER SERVING: Calories: 341 | Fat: 2g | Protein: 72g | Sodium: 146mg | Fiber: 1g | Carbohydrates: 4g | Sugar: 1g

Foolproof Chicken

The simplest chicken recipe there is, leaving no excuse to arrive home to a fully cooked chicken dinner, for just about any occasion.

INGREDIENTS | SERVES 6

3 pounds boneless, skinless chicken
24 ounces tomato sauce

Place chicken in a 4-quart slow cooker and add sauce. Cover and cook on low for 8 hours or on high for 4–5 hours. Once cooked, shred the chicken with a fork and enjoy.

PER SERVING: Calories: 282 | Fat: 6g | Protein: 49g | Sodium: 845mg | Fiber: 2g | Carbohydrates: 6g | Sugar: 5g

Hot Chicken Buffalo Bites

Love buffalo wings? Then you will love these chicken bites even more; they are made with juicy chicken breasts so you won't have to worry about bones. They are super easy and much less messy!

INGREDIENTS | SERVES 6

3 large chicken breasts, cut into 2-inch strips

2 tablespoons almond flour

¼ cup melted coconut butter

3 cloves garlic, peeled and minced

⅓ cup Frank's Red Hot sauce

Fresh Garlic Versus Garlic Powder

In a pinch you can use 1½ teaspoons garlic powder in this recipe. The garlic flavor won't be quite as pungent and rich as it is when you use fresh garlic, but it will still be easy and enjoyable.

1. Place chicken pieces into a greased 2½-quart slow cooker.

2. In a saucepan whisk together the almond flour and melted coconut butter for 2–3 minutes to toast the flour.

3. Slowly whisk in the garlic and Frank's Red Hot sauce. Pour sauce over chicken in the slow cooker.

4. Cover and cook on high for 3 hours or on low for 6 hours. Serve with celery and carrot sticks. If using a larger slow cooker, make sure to reduce cooking time by about half.

PER SERVING: Calories: 145 | Fat: 4g | Protein: 24g | Sodium: 461mg | Fiber: 0g | Carbohydrates: 1g | Sugar: 0g

Rotisserie-Style Chicken

Here is a delicious alternative to buying rotisserie chicken in your grocery store. This flavorful roast chicken is incredibly easy to make in your slow cooker. For a fast weeknight meal, cook the chicken overnight in the slow cooker and serve for dinner the next day.

INGREDIENTS | SERVES 6

1 (4-pound) whole chicken
2 teaspoons paprika
½ teaspoon onion powder
½ teaspoon dried thyme
½ teaspoon dried basil
½ teaspoon white pepper
½ teaspoon ground cayenne pepper
½ teaspoon black pepper
½ teaspoon garlic powder
2 tablespoons olive oil

Gravy

If you would like to make a gravy to go with the chicken, follow these directions: After removing the cooked chicken, turn slow cooker on high. Whisk ⅓ cup of almond flour into the cooking juices. Add pepper to taste and cook for 10–15 minutes, whisking occasionally, until sauce has thickened. Spoon gravy over chicken.

1. Rinse the chicken in cold water and pat dry with a paper towel.

2. In a small bowl mix together the paprika, onion powder, thyme, basil, white pepper, cayenne pepper, black pepper, and garlic powder.

3. Rub spice mixture over entire chicken. Rub part of the spice mixture underneath the skin, making sure to leave the skin intact.

4. Place the spice-rubbed chicken in a greased 6-quart slow cooker. Drizzle olive oil evenly over the chicken. Cook on high for 3–3½ hours or on low for 4–5 hours.

5. Remove chicken carefully from the slow cooker and place on a large plate or serving platter.

PER SERVING: Calories: 401 | Fat: 14g | Protein: 64g | Sodium: 231mg | Fiber: 1g | Carbohydrates: 1g | Sugar: 0g

Turkey in Onion Sauce

This is an African-inspired dish. Serve it over a mashed root vegetable or savory vegetable side dish of choice.

INGREDIENTS | SERVES 8

5 large onions, peeled and thinly sliced
4 cloves of garlic, peeled and minced
¼ cup fresh lemon juice
¼ teaspoon cayenne pepper
4 turkey thighs, skin removed
Freshly ground black pepper, to taste

1. Add the onions, garlic, lemon juice, and cayenne pepper to a 4-quart slow cooker; stir to combine. Nestle the turkey legs into the onion mixture. Cover and cook on low for 8 hours.

2. Remove the turkey legs and allow to cool enough to remove the meat from the bone. Leave the cover off of the slow cooker and allow the onion mixture to continue to cook for about 20–30 minutes, until the liquid has totally evaporated. (You can raise the setting to high to speed things up if you wish. Just be sure to stir the mixture occasionally to prevent the onions from burning.)

3. Stir the turkey into the onion mixture. Taste for seasoning and add pepper if desired. For more heat, add additional cayenne pepper, too.

PER SERVING: Calories: 42 | Fat: 0g | Protein: 1g | Sodium: 6mg | Fiber: 2g | Carbohydrates: 10g | Sugar: 4g

Homemade Turkey Breast

A versatile recipe for turkey that can then be used to top a lunch or dinner salad, or mix with some avocado and chopped grapes, for a tasty "turkey salad."

INGREDIENTS | SERVES 12

4 pound turkey breast, bone in, skin removed

Pepper, to taste

1 large onion, finely chopped

4 tablespoons coconut butter

4 tablespoons olive oil

2 cups Turkey Stock (see Chapter 5)

1. Season turkey liberally with pepper (and other herbs and spices of choice) and place in a 4-quart slow cooker.

2. Add onion to the slow cooker and place some onion inside the rib cavity.

3. Add the coconut butter, oil, and broth. Cover and cook on low for 7–9 hours or on high for 4–6 hours. Internal temperature of the turkey should read at least 165°F before it is removed from the slow cooker.

PER SERVING: Calories: 212 | Fat: 5g | Protein: 37g | Sodium: 113mg | Fiber: 0g | Carbohydrates: 1g | Sugar: 1g

Slow Cooker Southwestern Chicken Salad

Be creative and vary the vegetables in the recipe, or be bold and incorporate some hot chili peppers or jalapeños!

INGREDIENTS | SERVES 4

16-ounces Slow Cooked Salsa (see Chapter 3)
1 teaspoon pepper
1 teaspoon cumin
1 teaspoon chili powder
1 large onion, peeled, halved and sliced
1 cup frozen bell peppers
4 boneless, skinless chicken breasts
1 (14.5-ounce) can of diced tomatoes
Mixed salad greens
Avocado slices, for garnish

1. In a medium bowl, combine the salsa with the pepper, cumin, and chili powder.

2. Place the onions and peppers on the bottom of a 4-quart slow cooker.

3. Place the chicken breasts on top of the onions and peppers. Cover the chicken with the salsa and tomatoes. Cook on low for 8 hours.

4. Shred the chicken with a fork inside the slow cooker, and stir everything together to combine.

5. Serve over mixed salad greens garnished with avocado slices.

PER SERVING: Calories: 331 | Fat: 7g | Protein: 53g | Sodium: 540mg | Fiber: 2g | Carbohydrates: 10g | Sugar: 5g

Fall-Off-the-Bone Chicken

This rich French dish can stand on its own when served with just a tossed salad.

INGREDIENTS | SERVES 4

½ cup, plus 2 tablespoons almond flour

8 bone-in chicken thighs, skin removed

2 tablespoons coconut butter

2 tablespoons olive oil

1 medium yellow onion, peeled and diced

1 cup dry white wine

1 cup chicken broth

½–1 teaspoon dried tarragon

1 cup (full fat) coconut milk

Tarragon Chicken Cooking Times

After 3 hours on high, the chicken will be cooked through and ready to eat. Yet, if you prefer to leave the chicken cooking for a longer period, after 7–8 hours on low, the meat will be tender enough to fall away from the bone. You can then remove the bones before you stir in the coconut milk.

1. Add ½ cup flour and the chicken thighs to a gallon-sized plastic bag; close and shake to coat the chicken.

2. Add the coconut butter and oil to a large sauté pan and heat over medium-high heat. Add the chicken thighs; brown the chicken by cooking the pieces on one side for 5 minutes, and then turning them over and frying them for another 5 minutes. Drain the chicken on paper towels and then place in a 4–6 quart slow cooker. Cover the slow cooker. Set temperature to low.

3. Add the onion to the sauté pan; sauté until the onion is transparent, about 3–5 minutes. Stir in the remaining almond flour, cooking until the onion just begins to brown.

4. Slowly pour the wine into the pan, stirring to scrape the browned bits off of the bottom of the pan and into the sauce. Add the broth. Cook and stir for 15 minutes or until the sauce is thickened enough to coat the back of a spoon.

5. Stir the tarragon into the sauce, and then pour the sauce over the chicken in the slow cooker. Cover and cook on high for 3 hours or on low for 6 hours.

6. Pour the coconut milk into the slow cooker; cover and cook for an additional 15 minutes or until the milk is heated through. Test for seasoning and add additional spices and tarragon if needed. Serve immediately.

PER SERVING: Calories: 355 | Fat: 29g | Protein: 6g | Sodium: 273mg | Fiber: 2g | Carbohydrates: 12g | Sugar: 2g

Chicken and Artichokes

This is a dish that is great served with just a tossed salad to make it a complete meal.

INGREDIENTS | SERVES 4

8 boneless, skinless chicken thighs

½ cup Chicken Stock (see Chapter 5)

1 tablespoon fresh lemon juice

2 teaspoons dried thyme

1 clove of garlic, peeled and minced

¼ teaspoon freshly ground black pepper

1 (13-ounce) can artichoke hearts, drained

Add all the ingredients to the slow cooker; stir to mix. Cover and cook on low for 6 hours. If necessary, uncover and allow to cook for 30 minutes or more to thicken the sauce.

PER SERVING: Calories: 172 | Fat: 6g | Protein: 27g | Sodium: 123mg | Fiber: 0g | Carbohydrates: 1g | Sugar: 0g

Artichoke Hearts

You can use thawed frozen artichoke hearts in place of canned ones. Or, if all you have on hand are marinated artichoke hearts, drain them and add them to the recipe; simply omit the thyme and garlic if you do.

Honey-Glazed Turkey

If the turkey legs are large, you can remove the meat from the bone before serving and increase the number of servings to six or eight.

INGREDIENTS | SERVES 4

¼ cup Apricot Butter (see Chapter 2)

2 tablespoons honey

1 tablespoon fresh lemon juice

1 tablespoon Fruity Balsamic Barbecue Sauce (see Chapter 4)

1 teaspoon paprika

1 teaspoon lime juice

¼ teaspoon freshly ground black pepper

½ teaspoon dried rosemary

½ teaspoon dried thyme

4 turkey legs, skin removed

1 teaspoon arrowroot powder

1 teaspoon cold water

Turkey Salad

Complete Step 1–Step 3 of the Honey-Glazed Turkey recipe. Remove the turkey legs and allow to cool enough to remove the meat from the bones while you make the arrowroot slurry. Once the glaze is thickened, stir in the turkey meat. Serve on a bed of mixed greens.

1. Treat the insert of the slow cooker with nonstick spray. Turn the heat setting to high. Add the apricot butter, honey, lemon juice, and barbecue sauce. Once the mixture has heated enough to melt the apricot butter and honey into the mixture, stir in the paprika, lime juice, pepper, rosemary, and thyme.

2. Add the turkey legs, spooning the sauce over them. Cover, reduce the heat setting to low, and cook for 8 hours. Uncover, increase heat setting to high, and cook for ½ hour to reduce the pan juices.

3. Remove the turkey legs to a serving platter; cover and keep warm.

4. Add the arrowroot powder and water in a small bowl; stir to mix, and then thin with a little of the pan juices. Stir the resulting arrowroot powder slurry into the slow cooker. Cook and stir for 5 minutes or until thickened enough to coat the back of a spoon. Pour the glaze over the turkey legs and serve.

PER SERVING: Calories: 144 | Fat: 0g | Protein: 0g | Sodium: 4mg | Fiber: 1g | Carbohydrates: 13g | Sugar: 12g

Turkey Meatloaf

Instead of making the meatloaf entirely from ground turkey, you can use a combination of ground beef, ground pork, and ground turkey.

INGREDIENTS | SERVES 6

2 pounds ground turkey

1 large yellow onion, peeled and diced

2 stalks of celery, finely diced

1 green bell pepper, seeded and diced

2 cloves of garlic, peeled and minced

2 large eggs

1 cup arrowroot powder

2 teaspoons lemon juice

Freshly ground black pepper, to taste

½ cup Homemade Ketchup (see Chapter 4)

1 tablespoon honey

Optional: chili powder, to taste

Slow Cooker Liner

Instead of placing two pieces of heavy-duty aluminum foil across each other and over the sides of the slow cooker, you can instead line it with a Reynolds Slow Cooker Liner (*www.reynoldspkg.com*) and then place the nonstick foil piece inside the liner.

1. Add the ground turkey, onion, celery, bell pepper, garlic, eggs, arrowroot powder, lemon juice, and pepper to a large bowl; mix well with your hands. Form into a loaf to fit the size (round or oval) of your slow cooker.

2. Line the slow cooker with two pieces of heavy-duty aluminum foil long enough to reach up both sides of the slow cooker and over the edge, crossing one piece over the other. Place a piece of nonstick foil the size of the bottom of the slow cooker insert inside the crossed pieces of foil to form a platform for the meatloaf. (This is to make it easier to lift the meatloaf out of the slow cooker.)

3. Put the meatloaf on top of the nonstick foil. Spread the ketchup over the top of the meatloaf. Drizzle the honey and sprinkle the chili powder, if using, over the top of the ketchup. Cover and cook on low for 7 hours or until the internal temperature of the meatloaf registers 165°F.

4. Lift the meatloaf out of the slow cooker and place it on a cooling rack. Allow it to rest for 20 minutes before transferring it to a serving platter and slicing it.

PER SERVING: Calories: 377 | Fat: 14g | Protein: 29g | Sodium: 177mg | Fiber: 2g | Carbohydrates: 33g | Sugar: 12g

Cajun Chicken and Shrimp Creole

This light and savory surf and turf dish is jam-packed with flavor from a variety of fresh herbs and spices, and makes the perfect lunch-time portion.

INGREDIENTS | SERVES 6

1 pound boneless, skinless chicken thighs

1 red bell pepper, chopped

1 large onion, chopped

1 stalk celery, diced

1 (15-ounce) can stewed tomatoes, undrained and chopped

1 clove garlic, minced

1 tablespoon honey

2 teaspoons black pepper

1¼ teaspoons dried oregano

1¼ teaspoons dried thyme

1 teaspoon paprika

1 teaspoon garlic powder

1 teaspoon cayenne pepper

1 pound of large or jumbo shrimp, peeled, deveined, and cleaned.

1 tablespoon lemon juice

1 teaspoon lime juice

1. Place chicken in a 4½-quart slow cooker, along with all other ingredients except the shrimp and citrus juices.

2. Cover and cook on low for 7–9 hours or on high for 3–4 hours.

3. Add shrimp, lemon and lime juices, cover, and cook on low for 45 minutes–1 hour.

PER SERVING: Calories: 216 | Fat: 5g | Protein: 31g | Sodium: 284mg | Fiber: 3g | Carbohydrates: 12g | Sugar: 7g

CHAPTER 8

Fish and Seafood

Shrimp Fra Diavolo

Serve this spicy sauce over hot "Paleo pasta," i.e., spaghetti squash. Spaghetti squash is an excellent substitute for pasta. When cooked in the oven for 40–50 minutes, the squash becomes soft enough to lightly separate with a fork, forming an angel hair–like "pasta!"

INGREDIENTS | SERVES 4

1 teaspoon olive oil

1 medium onion, diced

3 cloves garlic, minced

1 teaspoon red pepper flakes

15 ounces canned diced fire-roasted tomatoes

1 tablespoon minced Italian parsley

½ teaspoon freshly ground black pepper

¾ pound medium shrimp, shelled

1. Heat the oil in a nonstick skillet. Sauté the onion, garlic, and red pepper flakes for 8–10 minutes, until the onion is soft and translucent.

2. Add the onion mixture, tomatoes, parsley, and black pepper to a 4-quart slow cooker. Stir. Cook on low for 2–3 hours.

3. Add the shrimp. Stir, cover, and cook on high for 15 minutes or until the shrimp is fully cooked.

PER SERVING: Calories: 116 | Fat: 3g | Protein: 18g | Sodium: 127mg | Fiber: 1g | Carbohydrates: 5g | Sugar: 1g

Slow Cooking with Shrimp

When slow cooking with shrimp, resist the temptation to put the shrimp in at the beginning of the recipe. While it takes longer to overcook foods in the slow cooker, delicate shrimp can go from tender to rubbery very quickly. For most recipes, 20 minutes on high is sufficient cooking time for shrimp.

Ginger-Lime Salmon

The slow cooker does all the work in this recipe, creating a healthy yet impressive dish that requires virtually no hands-on time.

INGREDIENTS | SERVES 12

1 (3-pound) salmon fillet, bones removed

¼ cup minced fresh ginger

¼ cup lime juice

1 lime, thinly sliced

1 large onion, peeled and thinly sliced

Cracked!

Before each use, check your slow cooker for cracks. Even small cracks in the glaze can allow bacteria to grow in the ceramic insert. If there are cracks, replace the insert or the whole slow cooker.

1. Place the salmon skin-side down in an oval 6–7-quart slow cooker. Pour the ginger and lime juice over the fish. Arrange the lime and then the onion in single layers over the fish.

2. Cook on low for 3–4 hours or until the fish is fully cooked and flaky. Remove the skin before serving.

PER SERVING: Calories: 166 | Fat: 7g | Protein: 22g | Sodium: 50mg | Fiber: 0g | Carbohydrates: 2g | Sugar: 1g

Salmon with Lemon, Capers, and Rosemary

Salmon is amazingly moist and tender when cooked in the slow cooker.

INGREDIENTS | SERVES 2

8 ounces salmon

⅓ cup water

2 tablespoons lemon juice

3 thin slices fresh lemon

1 tablespoon nonpareil capers

½ teaspoon minced fresh rosemary

1. Place the salmon on the bottom of a 2-quart slow cooker. Pour the water and lemon juice over the fish.

2. Arrange the lemon slices in a single layer on top of the fish. Sprinkle with capers and rosemary.

3. Cook on low for 2 hours. Discard lemon slices prior to serving.

PER SERVING: Calories: 165 | Fat: 7g | Protein: 22g | Sodium: 54mg | Fiber: 0g | Carbohydrates: 2g | Sugar: 1g

Romaine Wrapped Halibut Steaks

Enjoy this very healthy, lean seafood dish that is so tender it'll flake with just a light touch of a fork.

INGREDIENTS | SERVES 4

1 cup Chicken or Turkey Stock (see Chapter 5)

10–14 large romaine leaves

4 (4-ounce) halibut fillets

1 teaspoon bouquet garni or dried tarragon leaves

Pepper, to taste

½ cup fresh spinach, thinly sliced

Bouquet garni

A classic herb mixture frequently used for flavoring in meat and vegetable dishes. The herbs are typically tied together with cheesecloth, and removed before consumption. The herbs traditionally used include: dried parsley, thyme, bay leaf, and sage.

1. Pour stock into a 4-quart slow cooker. Cover, and cook on high for 20 minutes.

2. Immerse leaves of romaine (removing center stem) in boiling water for about 30 seconds, until wilted. Drain leaves.

3. Sprinkle halibut with herbs, pepper, and spinach. Wrap each fillet in 2–4 romaine leaves, placing lettuce seam-side down, and place in slow cooker.

4. Cover and cook on high for 1 hour, or until the fish is tender and can be flaked with a fork.

PER SERVING: Calories: 132 | Fat: 3g | Protein: 24g | Sodium: 69mg | Fiber: 0g | Carbohydrates: 1g | Sugar: 0g

Foiled Fish Fillets

A simple, low-cal, high-protein dish, that is ready in just 2 hours.

INGREDIENTS | SERVES 2

2 firm white fish fillets (e.g., tilapia)
1 small fennel bulb, thinly sliced
1 tomato, thinly sliced
1 red onion, sliced into rings
1 teaspoon of dried dill
1 lime, juiced
Pepper, to taste

1. Place fish fillets on aluminum foil and top with fennel, tomato, and onion.

2. Sprinkle on dill and lime juice. Fold the foil over and connect the edges, making a packet.

3. Place the packets into a 6-quart slow cooker. Cover and cook on high for 2 hours. Season to taste with pepper.

PER SERVING: Calories: 159 | Fat: 1g | Protein: 26g | Sodium: 83mg | Fiber: 3g | Carbohydrates: 11g | Sugar: 5g

Caveman's Catfish

First time trying catfish? This recipe is easily spruced up with the addition of a few or a combination of flavorful veggies (ie: tomatoes, onions, peppers, spinach, etc.).

INGREDIENTS | SERVES 4

4 catfish fillets
½ teaspoon dried dill
½ teaspoon dried basil
½ teaspoon dried thyme
2 lemons (1 juiced, 1 sliced into rings)

1. Place fish fillets on aluminum foil, sprinkle with spices, and squeeze the juice of 1 lemon over fish.

2. Place the lemon slices on the fish, and fold the foil over and connect the edges, making a packet.

3. Place the packets into a 6-quart slow cooker. Cover and cook on high for 2 hours.

PER SERVING: Calories: 160 | Fat: 5g | Protein: 26g | Sodium: 69mg | Fiber: 1g | Carbohydrates: 3g | Sugar: 1g

Orange Tilapia

A sweet taste of the sea. Serve with a medley of colorful summer vegetables.

INGREDIENTS | SERVES 4

4 tilapia fillets

2 tablespoons lime juice

1 tablespoon honey

1 (10-ounce) can of mandarin oranges, drained

Pepper, to taste

1. Place fish fillets on aluminum foil, drizzle with lime juice and honey, and pour on the drained oranges.

2. Fold the foil over the fish and connect the edges, making a packet. Place the packets into a 6-quart slow cooker.

3. Cover and cook on high for 2 hours. Add pepper to taste.

PER SERVING: Calories: 194 | Fat: 5g | Protein: 27g | Sodium: 72mg | Fiber: 1g | Carbohydrates: 11g | Sugar: 10g

Mahi-Mahi and Green Vegetable Medley

A super-healthy (and simply prepared) meal, packed with fiber, protein, iron, omega-3s, B-vitamins, and phytonutrients.

INGREDIENTS | SERVES 2

8 asparagus stalks
2 cups broccoli florets
2 cups fresh spinach
1 tablespoon olive oil
¼ teaspoon black pepper
½ teaspoon crushed red pepper flakes
¼ cup lemon juice
1 pound mahi-mahi

1. Place the vegetables in a 6-quart slow cooker.

2. In a separate bowl, combine the olive oil, pepper, red pepper flakes, and 1 tablespoon of lemon juice. Brush mixture on both sides of the mahi-mahi, and place fish on top of vegetables in the slow cooker.

3. Add remaining lemon juice. Cover and cook on low for 2–3 hours. The fish should flake easily with a fork.

PER SERVING: Calories: 296 | Fat: 9g | Protein: 45g | Sodium: 258mg | Fiber: 3g | Carbohydrates: 10g | Sugar: 2g

Shrimp Creole

This Big Easy-inspired recipe may also be made by substituting meat or another seafood for the shrimp.

INGREDIENTS | SERVES 2

1 (8-ounce) can tomato sauce

1 (28-ounce) can whole tomatoes, broken up

1½ cups diced celery

1¼ cups chopped onion

1 cup chopped bell pepper

1 clove garlic, minced

¼ teaspoon pepper

6 drops Tabasco sauce, or to taste

1 pound medium shrimp, deveined and shelled

1. Combine all the ingredients in a 4-quart slow cooker, except shrimp. Cook on high for 3–4 hours or on low for 6–8 hours.

2. Add shrimp during last hour of cooking, or during final 20 minutes, if cooking on high. Serve over hot veggies.

PER SERVING: Calories: 337 | Fat: 4g | Protein: 49g | Sodium: 998mg | Fiber: 6g | Carbohydrates: 24g | Sugar: 12g

Herbed Tilapia Stew

Any type of white fish fillets (such as haddock or cod) will also work in this recipe. Fish cooks very, very quickly even on the low setting in a slow cooker, so this is one recipe you will need to set a timer for.

INGREDIENTS | SERVES 6

2 pounds frozen boneless tilapia fillets

4 tablespoons canola oil

1 (14.5-ounce) can diced tomatoes, with juice

4 cloves garlic, minced

½ cup sliced green onions

2 teaspoons Thai fish sauce

2 tablespoons fresh thyme, chopped, or 1 teaspoon dried thyme

1. Grease a 4-quart slow cooker with nonstick cooking spray. Place all the ingredients in the slow cooker.

2. Cover and cook on high for 1½–2 hours or on low for 2½–3 hours. Watch the cooking time. If your fish fillets are very thin you may need to reduce the cooking time.

3. When fish is cooked through, fillets will easily separate and flake with a fork. Break the fish up into the tomatoes and cooking liquids.

PER SERVING: Calories: 87 | Fat: 9g | Protein: 0g | Sodium: 2mg | Fiber: 0g | Carbohydrates: 1g | Sugar: .0g

Scallop and Shrimp Jambalaya

This version of a "red" jambalaya originated in the French Quarter of New Orleans when saffron wasn't readily available. This Creole-type jambalaya contains tomatoes, whereas a rural Cajun jambalaya (also known as "brown jambalaya") does not.

INGREDIENTS | SERVES 8

2 tablespoons olive oil

1 large onion, chopped

2 medium celery stalks, chopped

1 medium green bell pepper, chopped

3 garlic cloves, minced

1 (28-ounce) can diced tomatoes, undrained

1 tablespoon parsley flakes

½ teaspoon dried thyme leaves

½ teaspoon salt

¼ teaspoon pepper

¼ teaspoon red pepper sauce

2 teaspoons gluten-free Creole seasoning

¾ pound uncooked, frozen scallops, thawed

¾ pound uncooked, peeled, deveined medium shrimp, thawed if frozen

¼ cup fresh parsley, chopped

1. In a large skillet, heat the oil over medium heat. Sauté the onions, celery, and bell pepper until softened, about 3–5 minutes. Add garlic and cook for 1 minute more.

2. Grease a 4-quart slow cooker and add sautéed vegetables and all the remaining ingredients except the shrimp and parsley.

3. Cover and cook on low for 6 hours or on high for 3 hours.

4. Add shrimp and continue to cook on low for 45 minutes to 1 hour, or until shrimp are bright pink. Serve jambalaya over a root vegetable medley and garnish with chopped fresh parsley.

PER SERVING: Calories: 103 | Fat: 4g | Protein: 10g | Sodium: 204mg | Fiber: 2g | Carbohydrates: 7g | Sugar: 4g

Mix It Up

Use your favorite type of seafood instead of shrimp or scallops. Try a combination of scallops, cod, or diced tilapia, halibut, mahi-mahi, etc.

Fish "Bake"

The stewed tomatoes help prevent the fish from overcooking and make a sauce perfect for serving the fish over steamed cabbage, or alongside a vegetable dish of your choice.

INGREDIENTS | SERVES 4

2 tablespoons olive oil

4 flounder or cod fillets

1 clove of garlic, peeled and minced

1 small onion, peeled and thinly sliced

1 green bell pepper, seeded and diced

1 (14½-ounce) can stewed tomatoes

½ teaspoon dried basil

½ teaspoon dried oregano

1 teaspoon dried parsley

Freshly ground black pepper, to taste

1. Add the oil to a 2- or 4-quart slow cooker. Use the oil to coat the bottom and the sides of the insert.

2. Rinse the fish fillets and pat dry with paper towels. Add to the slow cooker in a single layer over the oil.

3. Evenly distribute the garlic, onion, and green bell pepper over the fish. Pour the stewed tomatoes over the fish. Evenly sprinkle the basil, oregano, parsley, and pepper over the tomatoes.

4. Cover and cook on low for 6 hours or until the fish is opaque and flakes apart.

PER SERVING: Calories: 223 | Fat: 8g | Protein: 31g | Sodium: 134mg | Fiber: 1g | Carbohydrates: 3g | Sugar: 1g

Cioppino

Inspired by Erin, the natural-born chef, whose specialty is low-glycemic index–based cuisine.

INGREDIENTS | SERVES 6

2 tablespoons olive oil

1 large sweet onion, peeled and diced

2 stalks celery, finely diced

2 cloves garlic, peeled and minced

3 cups bottled clam juice or fish stock

2 cups water

1 (28-ounce) can diced or peeled Italian tomatoes

1 cup Zinfandel or other dry red wine

2 teaspoons dried parsley

1 teaspoon dried basil

1 teaspoon dried thyme

Dried red pepper flakes, to taste

1 teaspoon honey

1 bay leaf

1 pound cod, cut into 1-inch pieces

½ pound medium or large raw shrimp, peeled and deveined

½ pound scallops

1. Add the oil, onion, celery, and garlic to a 4-quart slow cooker. Stir to mix the vegetables together with the oil. Cover and cook on high for 30 minutes or until the onions are transparent.

2. Add the clam juice or fish stock, water, tomatoes, wine, parsley, basil, thyme, red pepper flakes, honey, and bay leaf. Stir to combine. Cover, reduce the slow cooker setting to low, and cook for 5 hours.

3. If you used whole peeled tomatoes, use a spoon to break them apart. Gently stir in the cod, shrimp, and scallops. Increase the slow cooker setting to high. Cover and cook for 30 minutes or until the seafood is cooked through. Ladle into soup bowls and serve immediately.

PER SERVING: Calories: 232 | Fat: 6g | Protein: 29g | Sodium: 168mg | Fiber: 1g | Carbohydrates: 6g | Sugar: 3g

Almond-Stuffed Flounder

Making this dish in the slow cooker lets you layer the fish and stuffing rather than stuffing and rolling the fillets. You can substitute sole for the flounder. Serve with a tossed salad and a seasoned vegetable medley of choice.

INGREDIENTS | SERVES 4

Nonstick spray

4 (4-ounce) fresh or frozen flounder fillets

½ cup slivered almonds

1 tablespoon freeze-dried chives, optional

Sweet paprika, to taste

¼ cup dry white wine, optional

1 tablespoon coconut oil

½ cup carrot, grated

1 tablespoon almond flour

¼ teaspoon dried tarragon

White pepper, to taste

1 cup (full-fat) coconut milk

1. Treat the insert of a 2- or 4-quart slow cooker with nonstick spray.

2. Rinse the fish and pat dry with paper towels. Lay 2 fillets flat in the slow cooker. Sprinkle the almonds and chives (if using) over the fillets. Place the remaining fillets on top. Sprinkle paprika over the fish fillets. Pour the wine around the fish.

3. Add the oil and carrots to a microwave-safe bowl. Cover and microwave on high for 1 minute; stir and microwave on high for 1 more minute. Stir in the flour, tarragon, and pepper. Whisk in half the milk. Cover and microwave on high for 1 minute. Stir in the remaining milk. Pour the sauce over the fish.

4. Cover and cook on low for 2 hours or until the fish is cooked through and the sauce is thickened.

5. Turn off the slow cooker and let rest for 15 minutes. To serve, use a knife to cut through all layers into four wedges. Spoon each wedge onto a plate (so that there is fish and filling in each serving). Sprinkle with additional paprika before serving if desired.

PER SERVING: Calories: 309 | Fat: 20g | Protein: 25g | Sodium: 108mg | Fiber: 2g | Carbohydrates: 6g | Sugar: 1g

Poached Swordfish with Lemon-Parsley Sauce

Swordfish steaks are usually cut thicker than most fish fillets, plus they're a firmer fish so it takes longer to poach them. You can speed up the poaching process a little if you remove the steaks from the refrigerator and put them in room temperature water during the 30 minutes that the onions and water are cooking.

INGREDIENTS | SERVES 4

1 tablespoon coconut butter

4 thin slices sweet onion

2 cups water

4 (6-ounce) swordfish steaks

1 lemon

2 tablespoons extra-virgin olive oil

2 teaspoons fresh lemon juice

¼ teaspoon Dijon mustard

Freshly ground white or black pepper, to taste, optional

1 tablespoon fresh flat leaf parsley, minced

Swordfish Salad

Triple the amount of lemon-parsley sauce and toss ⅔ of it together with 8 cups of salad greens. Arrange 2 cups of greens on each serving plate. Place a hot or chilled swordfish steak over each plate of the dressed greens. Spoon the additional sauce over the fish.

1. Use the coconut butter to grease the bottom and halfway up the sides of a 4-quart slow cooker.

2. Arrange the onion slices over the bottom of the slow cooker, pressing them into the butter so that they stay in place. Pour in the water. Cover and cook on high for 30 minutes.

3. Place a swordfish steak over each onion slice.

4. Thinly slice the lemon; discard the seeds and place the slices over the fish. Cover and cook on high for 45 minutes or until the fish is opaque. Transfer the (well-drained) fish to individual serving plates or to a serving platter.

5. In a small bowl add the oil, lemon juice, mustard, and white or black pepper, if using, and whisk to combine.

6. Immediately before serving the swordfish, fold in the parsley. Evenly divide the sauce between the swordfish steaks.

PER SERVING: Calories: 274 | Fat: 14g | Protein: 34g | Sodium: 160mg | Fiber: 1g | Carbohydrates: 3g | Sugar: 1g

Manhattan Scallop Chowder

*Serve this chowder with a tossed salad. Unlike the popular
New England version, this clam chowder is red!*

INGREDIENTS | SERVES 6

2 tablespoons coconut butter, melted

2 stalks celery, finely diced

1 medium green bell pepper, seeded and diced

1 large carrot, peeled and finely diced

1 medium onion, peeled and diced

2 medium butternut squash or turnip, scrubbed and diced

1 (15-ounce) can diced tomatoes

1 (15-ounce) can tomato purée

2 cups (bottled) clam juice

1 cup dry white wine

¾ cup water

1 teaspoon dried thyme

1 teaspoon dried parsley

1 bay leaf

¼ teaspoon freshly ground black pepper

1½ pounds bay scallops

Fresh parsley, minced, optional

Fresh basil, optional

1. Add the butter, celery, bell pepper, and carrot to a 4- or 6-quart slow cooker; stir to coat the vegetables in the butter. Cover and cook on high for 15 minutes. Stir in the onion. Cover and cook on high for 30 minutes, or until the vegetables are soft.

2. Stir in the squash, tomatoes, tomato purée, clam juice, wine, water, thyme, dried parsley, bay leaf, and pepper. Cover, reduce the temperature to low, and cook for 7 hours or until the squash are cooked through.

3. Cut the scallops so that they are each no larger than 1-inch pieces. Add to the slow cooker.

4. Increase the temperature to high, cover, and cook for 15 minutes or until the scallops are firm.

5. Remove and discard the bay leaf. Taste for seasoning and adjust seasonings if necessary. Ladle into soup bowls. If desired, sprinkle minced fresh parsley over each serving and garnish with fresh basil.

PER SERVING: Calories: 188 | Fat: 1g | Protein: 21g | Sodium: 583mg | Fiber: 3g | Carbohydrates: 17g | Sugar: 7g

Hatteras Clam Chowder

*This cozy, Paleo-creamy chowder is thickened by turnip, in place of potatoes.
Serve it with a fresh green salad or hearty main dish of your choice.*

INGREDIENTS | SERVES 4

1 small onion, diced and sautéed in olive oil (1 tablespoon)

2 medium turnips, peeled and diced

1 (8-ounce) bottle clam stock

2–3 cups water

½ teaspoon freshly ground pepper

2 (6.5-ounce) cans minced clams (do not drain)

1. Add cooked onions to a greased 2½-quart slow cooker.

2. Add turnips, clam stock, and enough water to cover (2–3 cups). Add pepper.

3. Cover and cook on high for 3 hours until turnips are very tender.

4. One hour prior to serving add in the clams along with broth from the cans and cook until heated through.

PER SERVING: Calories: 159 | Fat: 2g | Protein: 24g | Sodium: 149mg | Fiber: 1g | Carbohydrates: 10g | Sugar: 3g

CHAPTER 9

For the Vegetarian Paleo

Summer Style Vegetarian Chili

This light, meat-free chili is full of an array of summer vegetables. A very low-calorie, high fiber recipe loaded with vitamins and minerals.

INGREDIENTS | SERVES 8

1 bulb fennel, diced

4 radishes, diced

2 stalks celery, diced, including leaves

2 large carrots, cut into coin-sized pieces

1 medium onion, diced

1 shallot, diced

4 cloves garlic, sliced

1 habanero pepper, diced

12 ounces tomato paste

½ teaspoon dried oregano

½ teaspoon black pepper

½ teaspoon crushed rosemary

½ teaspoon cayenne

½ teaspoon ground chipotle

1 teaspoon chili powder

1 teaspoon tarragon

¼ teaspoon cumin

¼ teaspoon celery seed

2 zucchini, cubed

2 summer squash, cubed

10 Campari tomatoes, quartered

1. In a 4-quart slow cooker add the fennel, radishes, celery, carrots, onion, shallot, garlic, habanero, tomato paste, and all the spices. Stir.

2. Cook on low for 6–7 hours; then stir in the zucchini, summer squash, and tomatoes. Cook on high for an additional 30 minutes. Stir before serving.

PER SERVING: Calories: 109 | Fat: 1g | Protein: 5g | Sodium: 386mg | Fiber: 7g | Carbohydrates: 24g | Sugar: 13g

Spiced "Baked" Eggplant

Serve this as a main dish over a garden salad, or as a side dish, as is.

INGREDIENTS | SERVES 4

1 pound cubed eggplant
⅓ cup sliced onion
½ teaspoon red pepper flakes
½ teaspoon crushed rosemary
¼ cup lemon juice

Place all the ingredients in a 1½–2-quart slow cooker. Cook on low for 3 hours or until the eggplant is tender.

PER SERVING: Calories: 37 | Fat: 0g | Protein: 1g | Sodium: 6mg | Fiber: 4g | Carbohydrates: 9g | Sugar: 4g

Cold Snap

Take care not to put a cold ceramic slow cooker insert directly into the slow cooker. The sudden shift in temperature can cause it to crack. If you want to prepare your ingredients the night before use, refrigerate them in reusable containers, not in the insert.

Ratatouille

Ratatouille made in the slow cooker comes out surprisingly crisp-tender.

INGREDIENTS | SERVES 4

1 large onion, roughly chopped

1 eggplant, peeled and sliced horizontally

2 zucchini, sliced

1 cubanelle pepper, sliced

3 tomatoes, cut into wedges

2 tablespoons minced fresh basil

2 tablespoons minced fresh Italian parsley

½ teaspoon freshly ground black pepper

3 ounces tomato paste

¼ cup water

1. Place the onion, eggplant, zucchini, pepper, and tomatoes into a 4-quart slow cooker. Sprinkle with basil, parsley, and pepper.

2. In a small bowl, whisk the tomato paste and water together. Pour the mixture over the vegetables in the slow cooker. Stir.

3. Cook on low for 4 hours or until the eggplant and zucchini are fork tender.

PER SERVING: Calories: 102 | Fat: 1g | Protein: 5g | Sodium: 185mg | Fiber: 9g | Carbohydrates: 23g | Sugar: 13g

Slow Cooked Broccoli

A great way to cook a large amount of broccoli, while preserving all its nutrients.

INGREDIENTS | SERVES 5

1 pound fresh broccoli
½ cup water or chicken broth
2 tablespoons canola oil
½ teaspoon lemon juice
¼ teaspoon black pepper

1. Cut the main stalk off of fresh broccoli with a sharp kitchen knife, and then rinse the broccoli under cool running water. Place the broccoli into a 2-quart slow cooker.

2. Pour ½ cup of water into the slow cooker with the broccoli. Place canola oil into the cooker.

3. Add lemon juice and black pepper. Cover and cook on low for 3 hours or until the broccoli is tender.

4. Serve immediately or allow to stay warm in the cooker for another hour.

PER SERVING: Calories: 89 | Fat: 6g | Protein: 3g | Sodium: 135mg | Fiber: 2g | Carbohydrates: 7g | Sugar: 2g

"Roasted" Roots

A perfect substitute for meats that typically call for a starchy side.

INGREDIENTS | SERVES 6

1 pound baby carrots

12 ounces turnip, peeled and cubed

1 medium onion, chopped

2 cloves garlic, minced

2 tablespoons water

3 tablespoons olive oil

¼ teaspoon lemon juice

⅛ teaspoon pepper

1. Combine the vegetables, water, olive oil, lemon juice and pepper in a 3–4-quart slow cooker and stir to combine.

2. Cover and cook on low for 7–9 hours or until vegetables are tender when pierced with a fork.

PER SERVING: Calories: 110 | Fat: 7g | Protein: 1g | Sodium: 97mg | Fiber: 4g | Carbohydrates: 12g | Sugar: 6g

Caveman Caponata

An extremely flavorful, high fiber, nutrient-dense vegetable entrée.
The high fiber content makes this meat-free dish very filling.

INGREDIENTS | SERVES 4

1 pound plum tomatoes, chopped

1 eggplant cut into ½" pieces

2 medium zucchini cut into ½" pieces

3 stalks celery, sliced

1 large onion, finely chopped

½ cup chopped parsley

1 teaspoon lemon juice

2 tablespoons lime juice

1 tablespoon honey

¼ cup raisins

¼ cup tomato paste

¼ teaspoon freshly ground black pepper

1. Combine tomatoes, eggplant, zucchini, celery, onion, parsley, lemon and lime juice, honey, raisins, tomato paste, and pepper in 4-quart slow cooker.

2. Cover and cook on low for 5½ hours. Do not remove cover during cooking.

PER SERVING: Calories: 129 | Fat: 1g | Protein: 4g | Sodium: 169mg | Fiber: 8g | Carbohydrates: 31g | Sugar: 20g

Zucchini Casserole

This highly nutritious and delicious vegetable compilation is the perfect lunch-time portion.

INGREDIENTS | SERVES 2 (MEAL-SIZED PORTIONS)

4 medium zucchini, sliced and unpeeled

1 red onion, sliced

1 green pepper, cut in thin strips

1 (16-ounce) can diced tomatoes, undrained

1 teaspoon lemon juice

½ teaspoon pepper

½ teaspoon basil

1 tablespoon canola oil

1. Combine all the ingredients, except the canola oil, in a 2-quart slow cooker. Cook on low for 3 hours.

2. Drizzle casserole with canola oil. Cook on low for 1½ hours more.

PER SERVING: Calories: 201 | Fat: 9g | Protein: 8g | Sodium: 356mg | Fiber: 8g | Carbohydrates: 30g | Sugar: 19g

Gone Nuts over Broccoli

A traditional, "go-to" vegetable with a little kick! This recipe promises to prevent you from becoming bored with broccoli.

INGREDIENTS | SERVES 8

2 pounds broccoli florets, washed and trimmed

12 cloves garlic, peeled

½ teaspoon black pepper

1 cup large raw hazelnuts

2 tablespoons olive oil

2 lemons, juiced

1. Place broccoli in a 4-quart slow cooker and add garlic, pepper, hazelnuts, olive oil, and lemon juice and toss.

2. Cover and cook on high for 2 hours or on low for 4 hours.

PER SERVING: Calories: 169 | Fat: 13g | Protein: 6g | Sodium: 38mg | Fiber: 5g | Carbohydrates: 13g | Sugar: 3g

Slow Cooked Paleo-Stuffed Portobello

Portobello mushrooms are a rich source of antioxidants, all of which are generally preserved through cooking, unlike other vegetables whose phytonutrient compounds are often destroyed during the cooking process.

INGREDIENTS | SERVES 2

4 large portobello mushrooms, stems removed and chopped, centers removed

1½ cups cherry tomatoes, chopped

¼ cup arrowroot powder

3 tablespoons olive oil

¼ cup lime juice

1 tablespoon dried basil

½ teaspoon lemon juice

½ teaspoon black pepper

1. Place mushroom centers and stems, tomatoes, arrowroot powder, olive oil, lime juice, basil, lemon juice, and pepper in a large mixing bowl. Mix well.

2. Place mushroom caps on bottom of a greased 6-quart oval slow cooker. Spoon mixture on top of mushrooms. Cover and cook on low for 4–7 hours.

PER SERVING: Calories: 261 | Fat: 21g | Protein: 1g | Sodium: 7mg | Fiber: 2g | Carbohydrates: 20g | Sugar: 3g

Sweet and Savory Acorn Squash

This rich-tasting, sweet side serves well as a substitute for the starch often called for in recipes. This is so flavorful and filling, it can also suffice as a main lunch-time dish.

INGREDIENTS | SERVES 4

¾ cup honey
1 teaspoon ground cinnamon
1 teaspoon ground nutmeg
2 small acorn squash, halved and seeded
¾ cup raisins
4 tablespoons coconut butter
½ cup water

1. In a small bowl, combine the honey, cinnamon, and nutmeg.

2. Spoon honey mixture into the squash halves. Sprinkle with raisins.

3. Top each half with 1 tablespoon of the coconut butter.

4. Wrap each squash half individually in aluminum foil, and seal tightly.

5. Pour the water into a 4–6-quart slow cooker. Place the squash, cut side up, in the slow cooker. Cover and cook on high for 4 hours or until the squash is tender.

6. Open the foil packets carefully to allow steam to escape.

PER SERVING: Calories: 280 | Fat: 0g | Protein: 1g | Sodium: 7mg | Fiber: 2g | Carbohydrates: 75g | Sugar: 68g

Acorn Squash Casserole

Try this recipe using other seasonal fall vegetables like butternut squash or eggplant. Round out this classic comfort cuisine and serve with pumpkin or sweet potato soup.

INGREDIENTS | SERVES 6

2 medium acorn squash, sliced and peeled

1 red onion, sliced

1 green pepper, cut in strips

16 ounces diced fresh tomatoes, unpeeled

1 teaspoon lemon juice

½ teaspoon pepper

½ teaspoon basil

1 tablespoon coconut oil

1. Combine all the ingredients, except coconut oil, in a 2-quart slow cooker.

2. Cover and cook on low for 3 hours.

3. Drizzle the casserole with coconut oil and cook another 1½ hours on low.

PER SERVING: Calories: 25 | Fat: 0g | Protein: 1g | Sodium: 5mg | Fiber: 2g | Carbohydrates: 6g | Sugar: 3g

Sautéed Fennel with Orange

Fennel is crunchy and a bit sweet, and is most often associated with Italian cuisine.

INGREDIENTS | SERVES 4

3 small fennel bulbs, halved

1 (13-ounce) can chopped tomatoes

1 small orange, juiced and rind grated

2 tablespoons honey

Pepper, to taste

1. Place the halved fennel in a 4–6-quart slow cooker.

2. In a large mixing bowl, combine the remaining ingredients. Pour mixture over the fennel in the slow cooker.

3. Cover and cook on high for 4–5 hours.

PER SERVING: Calories: 59 | Fat: 0g | Protein: 1g | Sodium: 131mg | Fiber: 2g | Carbohydrates: 15g | Sugar: 13g

Vegetable Fajita Filling

Use large lettuce or cabbage leaves as the fajita "wrap,"
or serve over a starchy or seasonal root vegetable.

INGREDIENTS | SERVES 3

3 large onions, thinly sliced and separated

2 large sweet peppers, 1 red and 1 green, julienned

2 tablespoons olive oil

½ teaspoon paprika

Pepper, to taste

1. Place all the ingredients into a 4–6-quart slow cooker and toss well.

2. Cover and cook on high for 3½–4 hours.

PER SERVING: (1 cup) | Calories: 163 | Fat: 9g | Protein: 3g | Sodium: 10mg | Fiber: 5g | Carbohydrates: 19g | Sugar: 9g

Spaghetti Squash and Garden Veggies

Spaghetti squash is frequently used as a pasta substitute in Paleo recipes, due to its similarities in appearance, texture, and taste.

INGREDIENTS | SERVES 2

1 spaghetti squash
1–2 cups water
2 tablespoons olive oil
1 large onion, diced
2 cloves garlic, minced
5 roma tomatoes, chopped
3 tablesppons chopped fresh basil
Fresh ground pepper, to taste

1. Pierce the spaghetti squash several times with a fork. Place it in a 4–6-quart slow cooker and cover with 1–2 cups of water.

2. Cover and cook on low for 6–8 hours or high for 3–4 hours. Remove from slow cooker and let it cool. Drain the water from the slow cooker.

3. While the squash is cooling, heat oil in a large nonstick skillet over medium-high heat. Sauté the onion for 5–10 minutes until tender, and the add the garlic and stir. Turn off heat.

4. Slice the cooked squash in half, seed it, and use a fork to shred the strands from the squash and return the strands to the slow cooker.

5. Add the onion, garlic, and oil mixture to the slow cooker.

6. Add the tomatoes and toss so that they become warm.

7. Add the basil and toss. Serve warm and sprinkle with pepper to taste.

PER SERVING: Calories: 175 | Fat: 14g | Protein: 2g | Sodium: 18mg | Fiber: 3g | Carbohydrates: 12g | Sugar: 6g

Garlicky Vegetable Soup

Garlic is a versatile vegetable with multiple health benefits such as its blood pressure and cholesterol-lowering capabilities, as well as its high antioxidant profile which aids in reducing inflammation and lowering the risk of developing diseases like cancer.

INGREDIENTS | SERVES 4

5 heads garlic, peeled, each clove peeled

6 cups Roasted Vegetable Stock (see Chapter 5)

1 (6-ounce) can tomato paste

1 large yellow onion, diced

¼ teaspoon lemon juice

2 tablespoons olive oil

Fresh basil, for garnish

1. Place all the ingredients, except the oil and basil, into a 4–6-quart slow cooker. Stir.

2. Cover and cook on low for 8 hours or on high for 5 hours.

3. Add olive oil. Use an immersion blender or blend the soup in batches in a standard blender until smooth.

4. Garnish with basil and serve.

PER SERVING: Calories: 120 | Fat: 7g | Protein: 2g | Sodium: 343mg | Fiber: 3g | Carbohydrates: 17g | Sugar: 8g

Baked Sweet Potatoes

The simplest way to prepare this carbohydrate-rich side dish, perfect for the Paleo-athlete.

INGREDIENTS | SERVES 2

2 large sweet potatoes

1. Wash off the sweet potatoes but don't dry them. You'll want the moisture in the slow cooker.

2. Stab each sweet potato with a fork 5–6 times. Place the sweet potatoes in the slow cooker.

3. Cover the slow cooker and cook on low for 5–6 hours.

PER SERVING: Calories: 112 | Fat: 0g | Protein: 2g | Sodium: 72mg | Fiber: 4g | Carbohydrates: 26g | Sugar: 5g

Paleo "Pasta" Palooza

Serve this "pasta" tossed with fresh herbs, pepper, and your favorite Paleo-friendly sauce (see Chapter 4).

INGREDIENTS | SERVES 1

2 cups water
1 spaghetti squash

1. With a skewer or large fork, puncture several holes in the spaghetti squash.

2. Pour water in a 2-quart slow cooker and add the whole squash. Cover and cook on low for 8–9 hours.

3. Split the squash and remove the seeds. Use a fork to shred the strands from the squash, which will resemble angel hair pasta. Transfer the "spaghetti" strands to a bowl and top with sauce of your choice.

PER SERVING: Calories: 52 | Fat: 1g | Protein: 4g | Sodium: 6mg | Fiber: 4g | Carbohydrates: 11g | Sugar: 7g

Walnut-Stuffed Slow Cooked Apples

Walnuts are an excellent source of omega-3s, vitamin E, and a variety of other phytonutrients and antioxidants.

INGREDIENTS | SERVES 4

¼ cup coarsely chopped walnuts

3 tablespoons dried currants

¾ teaspoon ground cinnamon, divided

4 medium Granny Smith apples, cored

1 cup honey

¾ cup apple cider

1. In a small bowl, combine first 2 ingredients. Add ¼ teaspoon cinnamon, stirring to combine.

2. Peel top third of each apple; place apples in a 2-quart or smaller, slow cooker. Spoon walnut mixture into the cavity of each apple.

3. In a mixing bowl, combine the remaining ½ teaspoon cinnamon, honey, and apple cider, stirring to combine. Pour over apples in the slow cooker.

4. Cover and cook on low for 2¾ hours. Remove the apples with a slotted spoon.

5. Spoon ¼ cup cooking liquid over each serving.

PER SERVING: Calories: 264 | Fat: 0g | Protein: 0g | Sodium: 20mg | Fiber: 0g | Carbohydrates: 68g | Sugar: 66g

Apple and Sweet Potato Casserole

This sweet and simple dish is loaded with vitamins C and A, and would be perfect for Thanksgiving or even as a dessert!

INGREDIENTS | SERVES 6

4 large sweet potatoes, peeled and sliced

1 (15-ounce) can apple pie filling (or the Crustless Apple Pie in Chapter 14)

2 tablespoons coconut butter, melted

Canned Shortcuts

Using apple pie filling in this recipe is an easy way to add apples, spices, and sweetness without a lot of hassle. Apple pie filling is good not only with sweet potatoes, but also with a breakfast dish, or a Paleo-approved, slow cooked cake or bread recipe.

1. Grease a 4-quart slow cooker with nonstick cooking spray. Place the sweet potatoes in the bottom of the slow cooker.

2. Add the apple pie filling and coconut butter to the slow cooker. Cover and cook on high for 3–4 hours until the sweet potatoes are fork tender.

PER SERVING: Calories: 75 | Fat: 0g | Protein: 1g | Sodium: 48mg | Fiber: 3g | Carbohydrates: 17g | Sugar: 4g

Herb-Stuffed Tomatoes

Serve these Italian-influenced stuffed tomatoes with a simple salad for an easy, light meal.

INGREDIENTS | SERVES 2

2 large tomatoes

1 stalk celery, minced

1 tablespoon minced fresh garlic

2 tablespoons minced fresh oregano

2 tablespoons minced fresh Italian parsley

1 teaspoon dried chervil

1 teaspoon fennel seeds

¾ cup water

1. Cut out the core of each tomato and discard. Scoop out the seeds, leaving the walls of the tomato intact.

2. In a small bowl, stir together the celery, garlic, and spices. Divide into 2 even portions, and stuff 1 portion into the center of each tomato.

3. Place the filled tomatoes in a single layer in a 4-quart slow cooker. Pour the water into the bottom of the slow cooker. Cook on low for 4 hours.

PER SERVING: Calories: 48 | Fat: 0g | Protein: 2g | Sodium: 29mg | Fiber: 3g | Carbohydrates: 10g | Sugar: 5g

Leek, Turnip, and Carrot Potage

Potage is a classic French home-style soup that is perfect for a blustery winter day.

INGREDIENTS | SERVES 6

4 cups sliced leeks

4 medium-sized (size of a potato) turnips, peeled and cubed

2 large carrots, peeled and diced

5 cups water

½ teaspoon white pepper

1. Place all the ingredients into a 4-quart slow cooker. Cook on low for 7 hours.

2. Purée using an immersion blender, or purée in batches in a blender. Serve piping hot.

PER SERVING: Calories: 69 | Fat: 0g | Protein: 2g | Sodium: 89mg | Fiber: 3g | Carbohydrates: 16g | Sugar: 6g

CHAPTER 10

Sides

"Steamed" Artichokes

Choose artichokes that are all the same size so they will finish cooking at the same time.

INGREDIENTS | SERVES 4

4 large artichokes
1 cup water
1 lemon, cut into eighths, seeds removed
2 tablespoons lemon juice
1 teaspoon dried oregano

1. Place the artichokes stem-side down in an oval 4-quart slow cooker. Pour the water into the bottom of the slow cooker. Add the lemons, lemon juice, and oregano.

2. Cook on low for 6 hours or until the leaves are tender.

PER SERVING: Calories: 83 | Fat: 0g | Protein: 6g | Sodium: 156mg | Fiber: 9g | Carbohydrates: 19g | Sugar: 2g

Poached Figs

Use these poached figs in any recipe that calls for cooked figs, or eat them as is.

INGREDIENTS | SERVES 4

8 ounces fresh figs
1 cup water
1 vanilla bean, split
1 tablespoon raw honey

1. Put all ingredients into a 2-quart slow cooker. Cook on low for 5 hours or until the figs are cooked through and starting to split.

2. Remove the figs from the poaching liquid and serve.

PER SERVING: Calories: 58 | Fat: 0g | Protein: 0g | Sodium: 3mg | Fiber: 2g | Carbohydrates: 15g | Sugar: 13g

Shopping for Figs

Look for figs that are plump and soft but not squishy. The skin should not be split or oozing. Store figs in the refrigerator or in a cool dark cabinet until ready to use.

Roasted Garlic

Roasted garlic is mellow enough to eat as is, but it is also great in any recipe that would benefit from a mild garlic flavor.

INGREDIENTS | YIELDS 4 HEADS OF GARLIC

½ tablespoon olive oil

4 heads garlic

1. Pour the oil onto the bottom of a 2-quart slow cooker. Place the garlic in a single layer on top of the oil.

2. Cook on low for 4–6 hours or until the garlic is very soft and golden. To serve, simply squeeze the garlic out of the skin.

PER SERVING: (1 tablespoon) | Calories: 15 | Fat: 2g | Protein: 0g | Sodium: 0mg | Fiber: 0g | Carbohydrates: 0g | Sugar: 0g

Caramelized Onions

So sweet it feels like dessert! Serve over beef or pork as a sweet way to complement a basic traditional dish.

INGREDIENTS | SERVES 2

1 extra large onion, peeled and sliced thin

1 tablespoon olive oil

1 clove garlic, minced

1. Spray the insert of a 3–4 quart slow cooker with nonstick spray, add ingredients in order listed, stir, and cover.

2. Cook on high for 10–12 hours.

PER SERVING: Calories: 62 | Fat: 7g | Protein: 0g | Sodium: 0mg | Fiber: 0g | Carbohydrates: 1g | Sugar: 0g

Blackberry Compote

Try this on slow cooked pineapple or apples.

INGREDIENTS | SERVES 6

2 cups blackberries
¼ cup raw honey
¼ cup water

Place all ingredients into a 2-quart slow cooker. Cook on low for 3 hours, remove the lid, and cook on high for 4 hours.

PER SERVING: Calories: 64 | Fat: 0g | Protein: 1g | Sodium: 1mg | Fiber: 3g | Carbohydrates: 16g | Sugar: 14g

Strawberry-Rhubarb Compote

Try this over fruit salad or another sweet treat.

INGREDIENTS | YIELDS 1½ CUPS

1 pound strawberries, diced
½ pound rhubarb, diced
2 tablespoons lemon juice
1 tablespoon lemon zest

1. Place all ingredients into a 3½–4-quart slow cooker. Cook on low for 2 hours.

2. Lightly mash with a potato masher.

3. Cook on high, uncovered, for 1 additional hour.

PER SERVING: Calories: 201 | Fat: 2g | Protein: 5g | Sodium: 20mg | Fiber: 13g | Carbohydrates: 48g | Sugar: 25g

Rhubarb Facts

The leaves of the rhubarb plant are toxic, but the stalks are perfectly edible. Despite being a tart vegetable, rhubarb is most often served in sweet dishes where its tartness contrasts with a sweeter ingredient like strawberries.

Dill Carrots

The carrots in this side dish keep a firm texture even when fully cooked.

INGREDIENTS | SERVES 6

1 pound carrots, cut into coin-sized pieces
1 tablespoon minced fresh dill
⅓ teaspoon olive or canola oil
3 tablespoons water

1. Place all the ingredients in a 2-quart slow cooker. Stir. Cook on low 1½–2 hours or until the carrots are fork tender.

2. Stir before serving.

PER SERVING: Calories: 31 | Fat: 0g | Protein: 1g | Sodium: 53mg | Fiber: 2g | Carbohydrates: 7g | Sugar: 4g

Dill Details

Dill is a delicate plant that has many culinary uses. The seeds are used as a spice, and fresh and dried dill, called dill weed, are used as herbs. Dill is an essential ingredient in dill pickles and gravlax, a type of cured salmon.

Slow Cooked Brussels Sprouts

A traditional "not-so-favorite" turned decadent and delicious!

INGREDIENTS | SERVES 4

1 pound Brussels sprouts, trimmed
¾ cup Chicken Stock (see Chapter 5)
2 tablespoons canola oil
3 tablespoons coconut butter
3 tablespoons finely chopped shallots

1. Place Brussels sprouts into a 4–6 quart slow cooker and pour the chicken stock over them.

2. Add the canola oil, coconut butter, and shallots.

3. Cover and cook on low for 3 hours or until sprouts are tender.

PER SERVING: Calories: 120 | Fat: 7g | Protein: 4g | Sodium: 33mg | Fiber: 4g | Carbohydrates: 12g | Sugar: 3g

Rosemary-Thyme Green Beans

In this recipe, the slow cooker acts like a steamer, resulting in tender, crisp green beans.

INGREDIENTS | SERVES 4

1 pound green beans
1 tablespoon minced rosemary
1 teaspoon minced thyme
2 tablespoons lemon juice
2 tablespoons water

1. Place all the ingredients into a 2-quart slow cooker. Stir to distribute the spices evenly.

2. Cook on low for 1½ hours or until the green beans are tender. Stir before serving.

PER SERVING: Calories: 40 | Fat: 0g | Protein: 2g | Sodium: 9mg | Fiber: 4g | Carbohydrates: 9g | Sugar: 4g

Stewed Tomatoes

For an Italian variation on these tomatoes, add basil and Italian parsley.

INGREDIENTS | SERVES 6

1 (28-ounce) can whole tomatoes in purée, cut up
1 tablespoon minced onion
1 stalk celery, diced
½ teaspoon oregano
½ teaspoon thyme

Place all the ingredients into a 2-quart slow cooker. Stir. Cook on low for up to 8 hours.

PER SERVING: Calories: 24 | Fat: 0g | Protein: 1g | Sodium: 192mg | Fiber: 2g | Carbohydrates: 6g | Sugar: 3g

Stewed Cinnamon Apples

These apples are wonderful with pork. The longer they are cooked, the softer they become.

INGREDIENTS | SERVES 4

1 teaspoon honey
1 tablespoon ground cinnamon
2 tablespoons lemon juice
2 tablespoons water
4 crisp apples, cut into wedges

1. Place the honey, cinnamon, lemon juice, and water into a 4-quart slow cooker. Stir until the honey dissolves. Add the apples.

2. Cook on low for up to 8 hours. Stir before serving.

PER SERVING: Calories: 88 | Fat: 0g | Protein: 1g | Sodium: 2mg | Fiber: 3g | Carbohydrates: 24g | Sugar: 18g

Fig and Ginger Spread

Use as a breakfast fruit spread atop a Paleo breakfast bread recipe, or to liven up a basic Paleo dessert.

INGREDIENTS | SERVES 25

2 pounds fresh figs
2 tablespoons minced fresh ginger
2 tablespoons lime juice
½ cup water
¾ cup honey

1. Place all the ingredients in a 2-quart slow cooker. Stir. Cook on low for 2–3 hours. Remove the lid and cook an additional 2–3 hours, until the mixture is thickened.

2. Pour into airtight containers and refrigerate for up to 6 weeks.

PER SERVING: Calories: 58 | Fat: 0g | Protein: 0g | Sodium: 1mg | Fiber: 1g | Carbohydrates: 15g | Sugar: 14g

Apple and Pear Spread

Make the most of in-season apples and pears in this easy alternative to apple or pear butter.

INGREDIENTS | YIELDS 3 QUARTS

4 Winesap apples, peeled, cored and sliced

4 Bartlett pears, peeled, cored and sliced

1 cup water or pear cider

½ cup honey

¼ teaspoon ginger

¼ teaspoon cinnamon

¼ teaspoon nutmeg

¼ teaspoon allspice

1. Place all the ingredients into a 4-quart slow cooker. Cook on low for 10–12 hours.

2. Uncover and cook on low for an additional 10–12 hours or until thick and most of the liquid has evaporated.

3. Allow to cool completely then pour into the food processor and purée. Pour into clean glass jars. Refrigerate for up to 6 weeks.

PER SERVING: (½ cup) | Calories: 35 | Fat: 0g | Protein: 0g | Sodium: 1mg | Fiber: 0g | Carbohydrates: 9g | Sugar: 9g

Honey-Drizzled Brussels Sprouts and Pearl Onions

*A sweeter, more fun way to enjoy vegetables. You'll be surprised how quickly
your family asks for "more Brussels sprouts!"*

INGREDIENTS | SERVES 4

8 ounces small Brussels sprouts
8 ounces frozen pearl onions, thawed
1¼ cups water
1 tablespoon canola or flaxseed oil
¼ cup honey
White pepper, to taste

1. In a 4-quart slow cooker, add Brussels sprouts, onions, and water. Cover and cook on high for about 2 hours or until Brussels sprouts are soft. Drain.

2. Add the oil and honey to the cooked sprouts. Cover and cook on high for about 10 minutes, or until glazed.

3. Season to taste with white pepper.

PER SERVING: Calories: 89 | Fat: 0g | Protein: 2g | Sodium: 17mg | Fiber: 2g | Carbohydrates: 23g | Sugar: 19g

Greek-Style Asparagus

A slight Mediterranean touch induces a delicious aroma.

INGREDIENTS | SERVES 8

1 pound asparagus, trimmed

1 (28-ounce) can petite-diced tomatoes, undrained

½ cup onion, chopped

4 cloves garlic, minced

¾ teaspoon dried oregano

¾ teaspoon basil

Pepper, to taste

1. Combine all the ingredients, except the pepper, in 2-quart or smaller slow cooker and cover.

2. Cook on high for about 4½ hours or until the asparagus is tender. Season to taste with pepper.

PER SERVING: Calories: 17 | Fat: 0g | Protein: 1g | Sodium: 2mg | Fiber: 1g | Carbohydrates: 4g | Sugar: 2g

Sweet Beets

New research has shown an association between nitrates, such as those naturally occurring in beets, and in increased performance in endurance sports. Serve this dish warm alongside roast pork or beef, or cold with sliced meats.

INGREDIENTS | SERVES 6

1½ pounds beets

2 cups hot water

¼ cup red onion, finely chopped

¼ cup honey

2 cloves garlic, minced

¼ cup raisins

4 tablespoons toasted walnuts

2–3 tablespoons lemon juice

1 tablespoon coconut oil

Pepper, to taste

1. Combine the beets and water in a 4–6-quart slow cooker. Cover and cook on high for about 2–2½ hours or until the beets are tender.

2. Drain and peel the beets, and cut into ¾" cubes. Combine cubed beets and remaining ingredients, except the pepper, in the slow cooker.

3. Cover and cook on high for 20–30 minutes. Season with pepper to taste.

PER SERVING: Calories: 147 | Fat: 3g | Protein: 3g | Sodium: 93mg | Fiber: 4g | Carbohydrates: 29g | Sugar: 23g

Tangy Green Beans

This versatile side dish can dress up just about any meal.
Try adding additional ingredients like slivered almonds or cranberries.

INGREDIENTS | SERVES 4

4 cups frozen green beans, thawed
¼ cup chopped onion
¼ cup chopped green bell pepper
¼ cup lime juice
2 tablespoons honey
⅛ teaspoon black pepper

1. Combine all the ingredients in a 2-quart or smaller slow cooker. Stir to distribute evenly.

2. Cover, set to low, and cook for 5 hours. Serve warm.

PER SERVING: Calories: 72 | Fat: 0g | Protein: 2g | Sodium: 8mg | Fiber: 3g | Carbohydrates: 18g | Sugar: 13g

Slow Cooker Cabbage

This high-fiber, low-calorie vegetable is rich in antioxidants and an excellent source of vitamins C and K.

INGREDIENTS | SERVES 3

1 large head of red cabbage, washed and coarsely sliced
6 tart apples, cored and quartered
2 medium onions, coarsely chopped
2 cups hot water
⅔ cup lime juice
6 tablespoons coconut butter
3 tablespoons honey
2 teaspoons lemon juice

1. Place all the ingredients in a 2-quart slow cooker.

2. Cover and cook on low for 8–10 hours or on high for 3 hours. Stir well before serving.

PER SERVING: Calories: 325 | Fat: 1g | Protein: 6g | Sodium: 64mg | Fiber: 13g | Carbohydrates: 83g | Sugar: 63g

Pumpkin Butter

*Serve with apple slices, pear slices, drizzled over butternut squash
or on top of a Paleo-friendly dessert of your choice.*

INGREDIENTS | SERVES 8

6 cups pumpkin purée
2¼ cups honey
1 teaspoon cinnamon
¾ teaspoon ground ginger
½ teaspoon ground cloves
¼ teaspoon ground nutmeg
Juice of 3 lemons

1. Add all the ingredients to a 4–6-quart slow cooker. Cook the mixture on low for about 4–4½ hours, until it becomes thick and smooth.

2. Pour the finished pumpkin butter into sterilized pint or half pint jars, and seal.

PER SERVING: Calories: 298 | Fat: 0g | Protein: 1g | Sodium: 5mg | Fiber: 1g | Carbohydrates: 81g | Sugar: 79g

Glazed Carrots

*The slow cooker is an excellent way of preparing carrots,
just be sure to allow enough time for them to cook.*

INGREDIENTS | SERVES 3

3 cups thinly sliced carrots
2 cups water
¼ teaspoon lemon juice
3 tablespoons coconut butter
2 tablespoons chopped pecans
3 tablespoons honey

1. Combine carrots, water, and lemon juice in 2-quart or smaller slow cooker. Cover and cook on high for 2–3 hours or until the carrots are fork tender.

2. Drain well; stir in the remaining ingredients.

3. Cover and cook on high for 20–30 minutes.

PER SERVING: Calories: 141 | Fat: 4g | Protein: 2g | Sodium: 82mg | Fiber: 4g | Carbohydrates: 29g | Sugar: 23g

Carrot Nutmeg Pudding

Carrots are often served as a savory side dish. In this recipe the carrots have just a little bit of honey added to bring out their natural sweetness.

INGREDIENTS | SERVES 4

4 large carrots, grated
2 tablespoons coconut butter
½ teaspoon freshly grated nutmeg
2 tablespoons honey
1 teaspoon vanilla
1 cup coconut milk
3 eggs, beaten

1. Add carrots and coconut butter to a large glass, microwavable bowl. Cook on high for 3–4 minutes, until carrots are slightly softened.

2. Stir in remaining ingredients and pour into a greased 2½-quart slow cooker. Cook on high for 3 hours or on low for 6 hours. Serve hot or cold.

PER SERVING: Calories: 231 | Fat: 16g | Protein: 6g | Sodium: 110mg | Fiber: 2g | Carbohydrates: 18g | Sugar: 13g

Butternut Squash with Walnuts and Vanilla

Butternut squash has a very mild and slightly sweet flavor. Often people who don't like sweet potatoes enjoy this alternative side dish. Many grocery stores now sell butternut squash that has been peeled and precut into cubes, which can make meal preparation a breeze.

INGREDIENTS | SERVES 4

1 butternut squash (about 2 pounds), peeled, seeds removed, and cut into 1" cubes
½ cup water
½ cup honey
1 cup chopped walnuts
1 teaspoon cinnamon
4 tablespoons coconut butter
2 teaspoons grated ginger
1 teaspoon vanilla

1. Grease a 4-quart slow cooker with nonstick cooking spray. Add the cubed butternut squash and water to slow cooker.

2. In a small bowl mix together the honey, walnuts, cinnamon, coconut butter, ginger, and vanilla. Drizzle this honey mixture evenly over the butternut squash.

3. Cook on high for 4 hours, on low for 6–8 hours, or until the butternut squash is fork tender.

PER SERVING: Calories: 328 | Fat: 19g | Protein: 5g | Sodium: 4mg | Fiber: 2g | Carbohydrates: 40g | Sugar: 36g

Sweet and Sour Red Cabbage

Cabbage is often overlooked when it comes to weekly meals, which is unfortunate considering how nutritious it is. The tart apples, honey, and lime juice give the cabbage a tangy pickled flavor. Try this recipe as a side to roast pork.

INGREDIENTS | SERVES 6

1 large head red cabbage, sliced

2 medium onions, chopped

6 small tart apples, cored and quartered, and peeled (if preferred)

1 cup hot water

1 cup apple juice

⅓ cup honey

⅔ cup lime juice

½ teaspoon caraway seeds

3 tablespoons coconut butter, melted

3 tablespoons canola oil

1. Place the cabbage, onions, and apples into a greased 4-quart slow cooker.

2. In a medium bowl whisk together the water, apple juice, honey, lime juice, and caraway seeds. Pour over the cabbage.

3. Drizzle coconut butter and canola oil over everything and cover slow cooker. Cook on high for 3–4 hours or on low for 6–8 hours. Stir well before serving.

PER SERVING: Calories: 253 | Fat: 7g | Protein: 3g | Sodium: 32mg | Fiber: 6g | Carbohydrates: 49g | Sugar: 39g

Lemon-Garlic Green Beans

Lemon zest and sliced garlic add a fresh and bright flavor to these slow cooked green beans. Fresh green beans are sturdy enough to withstand very long cooking temperatures without getting mushy.

INGREDIENTS | SERVES 4

1½ pounds fresh green beans, trimmed

3 tablespoons olive oil

3 large shallots, cut into thin wedges

6 cloves garlic, sliced

1 tablespoon grated lemon zest

½ teaspoon pepper

½ cup water

1. Place the green beans in a greased 4-quart slow cooker. Add the remaining ingredients over the top of the beans.

2. Cook on high for 4–6 hours or on low for 8–10 hours. If you like your beans more crisp, check them on high after about 3½ hours or on low after about 6 hours.

PER SERVING: Calories: 150 | Fat: 11g | Protein: 3g | Sodium: 12mg | Fiber: 5g | Carbohydrates: 14g | Sugar: 6g

Honey-Ginger Carrots

Carrots and honey are a naturally delicious pair. Honey brings out the pure sweetness in baby carrots and fresh ginger gives this dish extra bite!

INGREDIENTS | SERVES 4

1 (16-ounce) package baby carrots, peeled

2 tablespoons freshly squeezed orange juice

1 tablespoon honey

½ teaspoon freshly grated ginger

1 tablespoon orange zest

1 tablespoon fresh parsley

Storing Orange, Lemon, and Lime Zest

To keep fresh citrus zest on hand at all times, freeze it! Place zest in snack-sized zip-top bags and take out as much as you need when it's called for in a recipe. The zest should stay fresh for up to 6 months in the freezer.

1. Place the baby carrots in a greased 2½-quart slow cooker.

2. In a small bowl mix together orange juice, honey, ginger, and orange zest. Pour over carrots. Cook on high for 3–4 hours, on low for 6–7 hours, or until carrots are fork tender.

3. Serve carrots by spooning a little bit of the honey-orange sauce over them and then sprinkling a little bit of fresh parsley over each plate.

PER SERVING: Calories: 58 | Fat: 0g | Protein: 1g | Sodium: 88mg | Fiber: 3g | Carbohydrates: 14g | Sugar: 10g

Stuffed Onions

Serve these onions with a salad and a steamed vegetable.

INGREDIENTS | SERVES 4

4 medium onions, peeled

1 pound ground beef or lamb

¼ teaspoon ground allspice

¼ teaspoon dried dill

3 tablespoons fresh lemon juice, divided

2 teaspoons dried parsley

Freshly ground black pepper, to taste

1 large egg

1–2 tablespoons almond flour

2 tablespoons extra-virgin olive oil

1 cup chicken broth

1. Cutting across the onions (not from bottom to top), cut the onions in half. Scoop out the onion cores.

2. Chop the onion cores and add to the ground beef or lamb, allspice, dill, 2 tablespoons of the lemon juice, parsley, pepper, and egg; mix well.

3. Fill the onion halves with the meat mixture. (The meat will overflow the onions and form a mound on top.) Sprinkle the almond flour over the top of the meat.

4. Add the oil to a deep 3½-quart nonstick skillet or electric skillet and bring it to temperature over medium heat. Add the onions to the pan, meat side down, and sauté for 10 minutes or until browned.

5. Arrange the onions in a 4-quart slow cooker so that the meat side is up. Mix the remaining tablespoon of lemon juice into the broth; pour the broth around the onions. Cover and cook on high for 4 hours, on low for 8 hours, or until the onion is soft and the meat is cooked through.

PER SERVING: Calories: 367 | Fat: 22g | Protein: 27g | Sodium: 361mg | Fiber: 2g | Carbohydrates: 15g | Sugar: 5g

Moroccan Root Vegetables

Moroccan Root Vegetables make an excellent side to a slow cooked chicken or pork dish.

INGREDIENTS | SERVES 8

1 pound parsnips, peeled and diced
1 pound turnips, peeled and diced
2 medium onions, chopped
1 pound carrots, peeled and diced
6 dried apricots, chopped
4 pitted prunes, chopped
1 teaspoon ground turmeric
1 teaspoon ground cumin
½ teaspoon ground ginger
½ teaspoon ground cinnamon
¼ teaspoon ground cayenne pepper
1 tablespoon dried parsley
1 tablespoon dried cilantro
14 ounces vegetable broth

1. Add the parsnips, turnips, onions, carrots, apricots, prunes, turmeric, cumin, ginger, cinnamon, cayenne pepper, parsley, and cilantro to the slow cooker.

2. Pour in the vegetable broth. Cover and cook on low for 9 hours or until the vegetables are cooked through.

PER SERVING: Calories: 118 | Fat: 1g | Protein: 2g | Sodium: 85mg | Fiber: 7g | Carbohydrates: 28g | Sugar: 13g

"Mashed" Cauliflower

Use as a starch substitute in any recipe calling for potatoes, rice, pasta, or polenta, to make it a Paleo-friendly meal.

INGREDIENTS | SERVES 4

1 head cauliflower, steamed and drained
1 tablespoon coconut butter
Freshly ground black pepper, to taste

Process cauliflower in a food processor with coconut butter and pepper until smooth. Serve warm.

PER SERVING: Calories: 36 | Fat: 0g | Protein: 3g | Sodium: 43mg | Fiber: 3g | Carbohydrates: 7g | Sugar: 3g

CHAPTER 11

For the Little Cavemen: Kid-Friendly

Mini Caveman Squash (Baby Food)

This recipe makes about 6 servings (or fewer), depending on age and appetite!

INGREDIENTS | SERVES 3

2 yellow squash, peeled and cubed

¼ cup water

1. Place the squash in a 4–6-quart slow cooker, add water, cover, and cook on high for 3 hours.

2. Use a blender or food processor to purée into baby food.

PER SERVING: Calories: 21 | Fat: 0g | Protein: 2g | Sodium: 3mg | Fiber: 1g | Carbohydrates: 4g | Sugar: 3g

Mini Caveman Green Beans (Baby Food)

This recipe can be doubled, or even tripled, depending on how many "little cavemen" are at home, and how far ahead you wish to plan for.

INGREDIENTS | SERVES 6

1 (12-ounce) bag of frozen green beans

¼ cup water

1. Place the green beans in a 4–6-quart slow cooker, add water, cover, and cook on high for 3 hours.

2. Use a blender or food processor to purée into baby food.

PER SERVING: Calories: 17 | Fat: 0g | Protein: 1g | Sodium: 4mg | Fiber: 2g | Carbohydrates: 4g | Sugar: 2g

Mini Caveman Sweet Potatoes (Baby Food)

Turnips or winter squash could also be used here, in place of the sweet potatoes.

INGREDIENTS | SERVES 6

2 medium-sized sweet potatoes

¾ cup water

1. Place the sweet potatoes in a 4–6-quart slow cooker, add water, cover, and cook on high for 3 hours.

2. Use a blender or food processor to purée into baby food.

PER SERVING: Calories: 37 | Fat: 0g | Protein: 1g | Sodium: 25mg | Fiber: 1g | Carbohydrates: 9g | Sugar: 2g

Mini Caveman Carrots (Baby Food)

This could also be used to incorporate puréed carrots into another recipe to thicken a soup, for example.

INGREDIENTS | SERVES 6

12 ounces of carrot sticks, sliced thin and chopped

¼ cup water

1. Place the carrots in a 4–6-quart slow cooker, add water, cover, and cook on high for 3 hours.

2. Use a blender or food processor to purée into baby food.

PER SERVING: Calories: 23 | Fat: 0g | Protein: 1g | Sodium: 39mg | Fiber: 2g | Carbohydrates: 5g | Sugar: 3g

Stewed Fruit

An easy way to help the little ones at home meet their 5-a-day (fruit and vegetable) needs. This recipe is jam-packed with vitamin C and fiber.

INGREDIENTS | SERVES 6

16 ounces prunes, pitted

8 ounces dried apricots

8 ounces dried pears

3 cups water

½ cup honey

2 tablespoons fresh lemon juice

1 teaspoon finely grated lemon zest

½ vanilla bean or ½ teaspoon vanilla

1. Combine all the ingredients together in a 2-quart slow cooker and cook on low until the fruit is tender, 6–8 hours.

2. Serve warm or at room temperature.

PER SERVING: Calories: 379 | Fat: 1g | Protein: 3g | Sodium: 11mg | Fiber: 9g | Carbohydrates: 101g | Sugar: 75g

Chicken Tenders

A Paleo-approved version of a traditional kid-friendly favorite. Partners perfectly with a side of Turnip Tots.

INGREDIENTS | SERVES 4

2 tablespoons olive oil

1 clove of garlic, minced

6 sprigs of fresh thyme, stripped and chopped

1 tablespoon lemon zest

¼ cup lemon juice

1 pound chicken breast tenders

Pepper, to taste

1. In a large mixing bowl, combine the olive oil, garlic, chopped thyme, lemon zest, and lemon juice.

2. Season the chicken tenders with pepper.

3. Spray a 2 quart slow cooker with nonstick cooking spray. Place chicken in the slow cooker, and pour olive oil mixture over chicken, stirring until coated.

4. Cover and cook on low for 4–6 hours.

PER SERVING: Calories: 65 | Fat: 7g | Protein: 0g | Sodium: 4mg | Fiber: 0g | Carbohydrates: 2g | Sugar: 0g

"Roasted" Root Veggies

You won't have to beg the kids to eat their veggies with this yummy recipe.
You won't even have to ask them twice!

INGREDIENTS | SERVES 10

1½ pounds sweet potatoes
1 pound parsnips
1 pound carrots
2 large red onions, coarsely chopped
¾ cup sliced cranberries
1 tablespoon honey
3 tablespoons olive oil
2 tablespoons lemon juice
½ teaspoon freshly ground pepper
⅓ cup chopped fresh flat-leaf parsley

1. Peel the sweet potatoes, parsnips, and carrots and cut into 1½" pieces.

2. Combine the parsnips, carrots, onions, and cranberries in a lightly greased 6-quart slow cooker; layer sweet potatoes over the top.

3. In a small bowl, mix together the honey, olive oil, lemon juice, and pepper; pour over vegetable mixture. (Do not stir.)

4. Cover and cook on high for 4–5 hours or until vegetables are tender. Toss with parsley just before serving.

PER SERVING: Calories: 193 | Fat: 4g | Protein: 2g | Sodium: 75mg | Fiber: 7g | Carbohydrates: 38g | Sugar: 16g

Turnip Tots

A Paleo-approved substitute for "Tater Tots," and the perfect accompaniment to Paleo Chicken Tenders. Serve with Homemade Ketchup (see Chapter 4).

INGREDIENTS | SERVES 4

4 medium turnips, peeled and cubed
2 tablespoons canola oil
2 tablespoons honey
1 tablespoon brown mustard
¼ teaspoon pepper

1. Place the turnips in a 2- or 4-quart slow cooker, drizzle with canola oil and toss.

2. In a small bowl, mix together the remaining ingredients, and drizzle over turnips, and toss.

3. Cover and cook on low for 5 hours. Serve alongside chicken tenders.

PER SERVING: Calories: 127 | Fat: 7g | Protein: 1g | Sodium: 82mg | Fiber: 2g | Carbohydrates: 17g | Sugar: 13g

Good Ol' Fashioned AB & J! (Almond Butter and Jelly)

Combine the finished product with some Strawberry Jelly (see Chapter 2), and there you have an AB & J!

INGREDIENTS | YIELDS 16 OUNCES

2 cups almonds
Olive oil, as needed (about 2–3 teaspoons)

1. Place almonds in food processor and turn on.

2. Add olive oil as needed, depending on creaminess desired.

3. Serve almond butter "sandwiches" by using frozen banana slices, or apple slices, and smoothing almond butter and jelly (see Strawberry Jelly in Chapter 2) between 2 fruit slices (or any other Paleo-friendly, creative version).

PER SERVING: (1 ounce of almond butter) | Calories: 68 | Fat: 6g | Protein: 3g | Sodium: 0mg | Fiber: 1g | Carbohydrates: 3g | Sugar: 0g

Paleo Stuffed Peppers

Peppers are chock-full of great vitamins and minerals that kids need. These peppers are so fun to eat, kids won't know how healthy they are.

INGREDIENTS | SERVES 4

4 red bell peppers
2 tablespoons olive oil
3 cloves garlic, chopped
1 large onion, chopped
1 pound ground chicken
2 green bell peppers, chopped
1 cup diced celery
1 cup sliced mushrooms
2 tablespoons chili powder
1 tablespoon cumin
1 (28-ounce) can organic, no-salt-added diced tomatoes
1 (6-ounce) can organic, no-salt-added tomato paste

1. Cut off the tops of red peppers and remove seeds and ribs. Set aside.

2. In skillet, heat the olive oil, and sauté garlic and onion for 2 minutes.

3. Add ground chicken and cook until browned, about 5 minutes.

4. Add green peppers, celery, mushrooms, chili powder, and cumin, and continue cooking for 5 minutes.

5. Stuff mixture into red peppers and place in a 4-quart slow cooker.

6. Pour diced tomatoes and tomato paste over peppers and cook on high for 5 hours.

PER SERVING: Calories: 385 | Fat: 25g | Protein: 23g | Sodium: 159mg | Fiber: 6g | Carbohydrates: 17g | Sugar: 9g

Soft "Shell" Beef Tacos

The romaine leaves could also be placed on the broiler until crispy, for use as a "hard" taco shell.

INGREDIENTS | SERVES 12

2 (16-ounce) jars mild or medium tomato-based salsa

2 tablespoons lime juice

5 teaspoons chili powder

1½ pounds beef chuck pot roast, fat trimmed

12 large leaves of romaine lettuce (for use as taco "shells")

3 cups shredded lettuce

1 avocado, diced

1. Spoon 1 cup salsa into a small bowl; set aside.

2. In a 4-quart slow cooker, combine remaining salsa with lime juice and chili powder.

3. Add beef, cover and turn heat to low. Cook for 10–12 hours. Shred the meat, using 2 forks, and spoon into a serving bowl.

4. Lay out the romaine leaves for use as taco "shells," and place a small portion of slow cooked beef on each.

5. Place shredded lettuce, diced avocado, and reserved salsa in small separate bowls for serving. Add toppings to tacos, wrap lettuce leaves tight, and enjoy.

PER SERVING: Calories: 56 | Fat: 3g | Protein: 2g | Sodium: 464mg | Fiber: 3g | Carbohydrates: 8g | Sugar: 3g

Slow Cooked Sloppy Joeys

Serve over mashed cauliflower, turnips, or winter squash.

INGREDIENTS | SERVES 4

1 pound lean ground beef or turkey meat

1 (6-ounce can) tomato paste

2 tablespoons honey

1 tablespoon onion flakes

1 tablespoon paprika

1 teaspoon ground cumin

1 teaspoon lemon juice

½ teaspoon garlic powder

¼ teaspoon dry mustard

¼ teaspoon celery seed

¼ teaspoon black pepper

1 cup warm water

1 teaspoon almond meal

1. Place meat, tomato paste, honey and seasonings into a 4-quart slow cooker. Add water and almond meal, and stir.

2. Cover and cook on low for 6–7 hours or on high for 3–5 hours. Serve warm.

PER SERVING: Calories: 234 | Fat: 6g | Protein: 26g | Sodium: 414mg | Fiber: 3g | Carbohydrates: 18g | Sugar: 14g

Slow Cooked Burgers

Serve these no-bun Paleo burgers with Sweet Potato "fries"
(recipe in this chapter) and Homemade Ketchup (see Chapter 4).

INGREDIENTS | SERVES 2

2 preformed (4-ounce) lean hamburger patties, frozen
⅛ teaspoon lemon juice
¼ teaspoon onion powder
¼ teaspoon dried basil
¼ teaspoon dried thyme
¼ teaspoon dried oregano

1. Insert a wire rack into a 6-quart slow cooker and place frozen patties on rack.

2. Drizzle lemon juice and seasonings on top.

3. Cover and cook on high for 60–90 minutes. Drain on paper towels before serving. Serve with slow cooked sweet potato "fries" (see recipe in this chapter).

PER SERVING: Calories: 318 | Fat: 26g | Protein: 19g | Sodium: 77mg | Fiber: 0g | Carbohydrates: 0g | Sugar: 0g

Sweet Potato "Fries"

Serve alongside a Paleo burger and drizzle with Homemade Ketchup
(see Chapter 4), honey, or some honey mustard.

INGREDIENTS | SERVES 2

2 medium-sized sweet potatoes, sliced into thin wedges

¼ cup water

2 tablespoons canola oil

1. Place sweet potato wedges into a 4-quart slow cooker and add water.

2. Drizzle canola oil over sweet potatoes.

3. Cover and cook on high for 2–3 hours. Remove cover and continue cooking for 20–30 minutes, until desired browning occurs.

4. Serve alongside slow cooked burgers (see recipe in this chapter).

PER SERVING: Calories: 232 | Fat: 14g | Protein: 2g | Sodium: 72mg | Fiber: 4g | Carbohydrates: 26g | Sugar: 5g

Lemonade

Serve cold on a hot summer day, or warm on a cold winter's night!

INGREDIENTS | SERVES 6 (1 CUP SERVINGS)

5 cups water
¾ cup lemon juice
¾ cup honey
2" piece ginger root, sliced

1. Combine all the ingredients in a 2-quart or smaller slow cooker.

2. Cover and cook on high for 2–3 hours (if mixture begins to boil, turn heat to low).

3. Turn to low to keep warm for serving, or chill and serve over ice.

PER SERVING: Calories: 135 | Fat: 0g | Protein: 0g | Sodium: 14mg | Fiber: 0g | Carbohydrates: 37g | Sugar: 36g

Orange Juice

A thirst-quenching breakfast beverage, and an old-fashioned favorite.

INGREDIENTS | SERVES 6 (1 CUP SERVINGS)

5 cups water
5 oranges, juiced
¾ cup honey
2" piece ginger root, sliced

1. Combine all the ingredients in a 2-quart slow cooker.

2. Cover and cook on high for 2–3 hours (if mixture begins to boil, turn heat to low).

3. Allow to cool and serve chilled.

PER SERVING: Calories: 180 | Fat: 0g | Protein: 1g | Sodium: 8mg | Fiber: 3g | Carbohydrates: 48g | Sugar: 45g

Candied Butternut Squash

Butternut squash has a delicious natural sweetness and is an excellent replacement for sweet potatoes. Also, you can now buy ready cut and peeled butternut squash in many grocery stores (in the produce section), making this recipe incredibly easy to assemble.

INGREDIENTS | SERVES 4

4–5 cups butternut squash, peeled, seeded, and cubed

⅓ cup honey

1 tablespoon orange zest

½ teaspoon ground cinnamon

½ teaspoon ground cloves

Add all the ingredients to a greased 4-quart slow cooker. Cook on high for 3–4 hours or on low for 6–8 hours, until squash is fork tender.

PER SERVING: Calories: 168 | Fat: 0g | Protein: 2g | Sodium: 9mg | Fiber: 4g | Carbohydrates: 44g | Sugar: 27g

Butternut Squash Versus Sweet Potatoes

Wondering which might be better for you? Actually both are extremely healthy choices. Per serving, sweet potatoes have more fiber than the squash, but one cup of butternut squash contains fewer calories and fewer total carbohydrates. Both are high in vitamins A and C. In many recipes, they can be used interchangeably.

Saucy Brown "Sugar" Chicken

*Kids will love the sweet and sour flavors of honey and Dijon mustard in this
super simple slow cooker chicken. Serve chicken over butternut squash, or alongside
a slow cooked, baked, or steamed and mashed sweet potato.*

INGREDIENTS | SERVES 4

4 skinless, boneless chicken breasts

1 (12-ounce) jar peach salsa

¼ cup honey

1 tablespoon Dijon mustard

Slow Cooker Sundays

If you have multiple slow cookers you can make several main dishes at one time on Sunday afternoons. The ready-made meals can then be stored in the refrigerator for up to 5 days or frozen. You will save money and time by having homemade slow cooked meals already prepared.

1. Place chicken breasts in a greased 4-quart slow cooker.

2. In small bowl mix together the salsa, honey, and mustard. Pour over chicken in the slow cooker.

3. Cook on high for 3–4 hours or on low for 6–8 hours.

PER SERVING: Calories: 336 | Fat: 6g | Protein: 50g | Sodium: 319mg | Fiber: 0g | Carbohydrates: 18g | Sugar: 17g

"French Fry" Casserole

A kid favorite that the whole family will love. Frozen sweet potato fries, ground beef, and a simple slow cooked, Paleo-approved cream sauce make a tasty weeknight meal. Serve with a salad or steamed green beans.

INGREDIENTS | SERVES 4

1 pound ground beef

1 tablespoon coconut butter

½ onion, finely diced

1 cup mushrooms, sliced

½ green pepper, diced

2 tablespoons arrowroot powder

1⅓ cups (full-fat) coconut milk

½ teaspoon pepper

3 cups frozen sweet potato fries (shoestring cut)

Paleo Shortcuts

You can make several batches of Paleo-approved cream sauce at the beginning of the week to make meals even easier to put together. Simply make a batch, pour in a glass jar with an airtight lid, and store in the refrigerator for up to 1 week.

1. Brown ground beef in a skillet on medium heat, for approximately 3–5 minutes. Pour cooked ground beef into a greased 2½-quart or larger slow cooker.

2. In a medium-sized saucepan, melt the coconut butter. Add the onion, mushrooms, and green pepper. Cook for 3–5 minutes until softened.

3. Mix the arrowroot powder with the coconut milk and slowly add to cooked vegetables. Whisk together for 5–10 minutes over medium heat until thickened.

4. Pour the cream sauce over ground beef in the slow cooker. Sprinkle with pepper.

5. Top casserole with sweet potato fries. Vent the lid of the slow cooker with a chopstick to prevent extra condensation on the fries. Cook on high for 3–4 hours or on low for 5–6 hours.

PER SERVING: Calories: 224 | Fat: 11g | Protein: 23g | Sodium: 76mg | Fiber: 1g | Carbohydrates: 6g | Sugar: 1g

Gingerbread Pudding Cake

This somewhat messy concoction is a guaranteed kid-friendly favorite.

INGREDIENTS | SERVES 6

½ cup almond flour
½ cup arrowroot powder
1 cup honey, divided
1 teaspoon baking powder
¼ teaspoon baking soda
1¼ teaspoons ground ginger
½ teaspoon ground cinnamon
¾ cup coconut milk
1 egg
½ cup raisins
2¼ cups water
½ cup coconut butter

1. Grease a 4-quart slow cooker with nonstick cooking spray.

2. In a medium bowl, whisk together the almond flour, arrowroot powder, ½ cup honey, baking powder, baking soda, ginger, and cinnamon.

3. Stir coconut milk and egg into the dry ingredients. Stir in raisins (batter will be thick). Spread gingerbread batter evenly in the bottom of the prepared slow cooker.

4. In a medium saucepan, combine the water, remaining ½ cup honey, and coconut butter. Bring to a boil; reduce heat. Boil gently, uncovered, for 2 minutes. Carefully pour water/honey mixture over the gingerbread batter.

5. Cover and vent lid with chopstick or the end of a wooden spoon. Cook on high for 2–2½ hours until cake is cooked through and a toothpick inserted about ½" into the cake comes out clean. (It may not look like it's all the way cooked through.)

6. Remove slow cooker insert from the cooker. Allow to cool for 45–60 minutes to allow "pudding" to set beneath the cake.

7. To serve, spoon warm cake into dessert dishes and spoon "pudding sauce" over the warm cake.

PER SERVING: Calories: 369 | Fat: 12g | Protein: 4g | Sodium: 156mg | Fiber: 2g | Carbohydrates: 69g | Sugar: 54g

CHAPTER 12

Ethnic Cuisine

Caribbean Chicken Curry

Traditional Jamaican curries are cooked for long periods of time over the stove top, making them a logical fit for the slow cooker. The spices meld together and the chicken is meltingly tender.

INGREDIENTS | SERVES 8

1 tablespoon Madras curry powder

1 teaspoon allspice

½ teaspoon ground cloves

½ teaspoon ground nutmeg

1 teaspoon ground ginger

2 pounds boneless, skinless chicken thighs, cubed

1 teaspoon canola oil

1 large onion, chopped

2 cloves garlic, chopped

2 jalapeño peppers, chopped

⅓ cup light coconut milk

1. In a medium bowl, whisk together the curry powder, allspice, cloves, nutmeg, and ginger. Add the chicken and toss to coat each piece evenly.

2. Place the chicken in a nonstick skillet and quickly sauté for about 5–7 minutes, until the chicken starts to brown. Add to a 4-quart slow cooker along with the remaining spice mixture.

3. Heat the oil in a nonstick skillet and sauté the onions, garlic, and peppers for about 5–7 minutes, until fragrant. Add to the slow cooker.

4. Add the coconut milk to the slow cooker. Stir. Cook on low for 7–8 hours.

PER SERVING: Calories: 167 | Fat: 7g | Protein: 22g | Sodium: 99mg | Fiber: 1g | Carbohydrates: 2g | Sugar: 1g

Italian Chicken

This tastefully simple Italian favorite calls for just 6 ingredients

INGREDIENTS | SERVES 6

6–8 boneless, skinless chicken breast tenderloins

2 bay leaves

½ teaspoon black pepper

½ teaspoon dried oregano

½ teaspoon dried basil

32-ounce jar or homemade tomato sauce

1. Add chicken to the bottom of a 4-quart slow cooker and sprinkle seasonings over chicken.

2. Pour sauce over seasoned chicken. Cover the chicken completely with sauce.

3. Cover and cook on low for 6 hours or on high for 3½–4 hours. Serve with an Italian vegetable medley.

PER SERVING: Calories: 395 | Fat: 8g | Protein: 69g | Sodium: 1,148mg | Fiber: 8g | Carbohydrates: 8g | Sugar: 6g

Greek Stew

This dish is loaded with fresh herbs and aromatic vegetables, it is just bursting with flavor.

INGREDIENTS | SERVES 10

3 tablespoons coconut oil

3 pounds grass-fed beef cut into 1½" cubes

1 medium onion, chopped

10 large garlic cloves, lightly crushed

1 cup tomato purée (canned or fresh)

½ cup dry red wine

2 tablespoons lemon juice

2 bay leaves

1 cinnamon stick

4 whole cloves

Freshly ground black pepper, to taste

1 pound small pear onions (optional)

2 tablespoons currants (optional)

1 cup walnut halves

1. In a Dutch oven, heat 3 tablespoons oil over medium-high heat, then brown the beef on all sides, about 5 minutes. Add the meat in batches, so the pot does not get overcrowded. Remove the meat and place in bowl so the juices are caught in the bowl.

2. Add the chopped onion and garlic cloves to the Dutch oven, stirring, until the onions are translucent, about 4 minutes.

3. Add the tomato purée, wine, and lemon juice to de-glaze the Dutch oven.

4. Pour the meat and its juices back into the Dutch oven.

5. Add the bay leaves, cinnamon, cloves, and season with pepper.

6. Place all the ingredients in a 4 or 6-quart slow cooker, and cook on high for 4 hours.

PER SERVING: Calories: 308 | Fat: 17g | Protein: 31g | Sodium: 174mg | Fiber: 1g | Carbohydrates: 5g | Sugar: 2g

Asian Pepper Steak

Serve with Asian vegetables like bok choy and Chinese cabbage.

INGREDIENTS | SERVES 4

2 pounds steak (sirloin is preferable, but any other good cut will do)

2 tablespoons coconut oil

Pepper, to taste

1–2 cloves of garlic, minced

¼ cup wheat-free tamari

1 (16-ounce) can diced tomatoes

1 large green pepper, sliced in thin strips

1 small onion, sliced

1. On a chopping board, cut the steak on an angle to make strips about a ½" thick.

2. In a large frying pan, add the oil and heat over medium heat. Sauté the steak for 10–15 minutes, until it lightly browns.

3. Drain excess fat, liberally coat the meat with ground pepper and put the meat in a 4- or 6-quart slow cooker.

4. Add garlic and tamari, and mix so that the steak is thoroughly coated. Cook on low for 6 hours.

5. One hour before serving, add tomatoes, green peppers, and onions, and turn the slow cooker to high. Cook for 1 hour and then serve piping hot.

PER SERVING: Calories: 383 | Fat: 16g | Protein: 49g | Sodium: 129mg | Fiber: 2g | Carbohydrates: 8g | Sugar: 5g

Creole Chicken

Top this recipe with some salsa to give it even more of a kick, and/or garnish with avocado slices.

INGREDIENTS | SERVES 4

4 skinless chicken breasts
Pepper, to taste
Cajun seasoning, to taste
1 (14.5-ounce) can stewed, chopped tomatoes
1 stalk of celery, diced
1 green pepper, diced
3 cloves of garlic, minced
1 large onion, minced
4 ounces fresh mushrooms
1 fresh green chili, seeded and chopped

1. Place chicken in a 4-quart slow cooker. Season with pepper and Cajun seasoning.

2. Stir in the tomatoes, celery, green pepper, garlic, onion, mushrooms, and green chili.

3. Cook on low for 10–12 hours or on high for 5–6 hours.

PER SERVING: Calories: 302 | Fat: 6g | Protein: 52g | Sodium: 286mg | Fiber: 2g | Carbohydrates: 7g | Sugar: 3g

German Coleslaw

Serve with some slow cooked chicken salad or seafood recipe. Red or yellow peppers could be substituted here for the green peppers to give it a bit more color, like confetti!

INGREDIENTS | SERVES 4

1 teaspoon celery seed
1½ cups lime juice
1½ teaspoons mustard seed
1 teaspoon turmeric
1 teaspoon lemon juice
8 cups shredded cabbage
2 green peppers, chopped fine
1 large onion, chopped fine

1. In a saucepan over high heat, bring the celery seed, lime juice, mustard seed, turmeric, and lemon juice to a boil.

2. Place all vegetables into a 2-quart or smaller slow cooker.

3. Pour boiling liquid over vegetables. Cover and let stand, without heat, for 2 hours. Will keep crisp for 3–4 weeks in refrigerator.

PER SERVING: Calories: 70 | Fat: 1g | Protein: 3g | Sodium: 30mg | Fiber: 5g | Carbohydrates: 15g | Sugar: 8g

Ethiopian Chicken Stew

The eggs increase the protein, vitamin E, and omega-3 content of this recipe.

INGREDIENTS | SERVES 8

1 (14.5-ounce) can diced tomatoes, undrained

1½ pounds boneless, skinless chicken thighs

¼ cup lemon juice

2 tablespoons coconut butter

3 large onions, diced

1 tablespoon paprika

1 teaspoon ground ginger

1 teaspoon cayenne pepper

1 teaspoon ground turmeric

½ teaspoon black pepper

2 cups water

8 hard-boiled eggs

1. Place tomatoes into a 6-quart slow cooker. Add the chicken thighs and lemon juice. Add the coconut butter, onion, and all the spices.

2. Add the water. Cover and cook on low for 6–8 hours or on high for 4–5 hours.

3. Ladle into bowls with a peeled hard-boiled egg in each individual bowl.

PER SERVING: Calories: 210 | Fat: 9g | Protein: 24g | Sodium: 151mg | Fiber: 2g | Carbohydrates: 9g | Sugar: 4g

"Jamaica-Me" Some Salmon

This Caribbean-themed favorite is a guaranteed hit. The variety of herbs and spices leave it exploding with flavor.

INGREDIENTS | SERVES 2

1 teaspoon onion powder

½ teaspoon ground cinnamon

¼ teaspoon black pepper

¼ teaspoon chipotle chili powder

⅛ teaspoon ground nutmeg

⅛ teaspoon ground ginger

⅛ teaspoon ground cloves

⅛ teaspoon dried thyme

2 teaspoons honey

1 teaspoon lemon juice

1 pound salmon

1. Combine all the spices, herbs, honey, and lemon juice in a bowl.

2. Place the salmon on aluminum foil and rub (or brush) both sides of salmon with ingredients from the bowl. Fold over the foil and connect the sides, making a pocket. Fold sides to prevent fluids from leaking out from foil, and place pocket in a 6-quart slow cooker.

3. Cover and cook on low for 2 hours. When done, salmon should flake easily with a fork.

PER SERVING: Calories: 348 | Fat: 14g | Protein: 45g | Sodium: 100mg | Fiber: 1g | Carbohydrates: 8g | Sugar: 6g

Indian Lamb Curry

Lamb is a rich source of iron and zinc, as well as an excellent source of protein.

INGREDIENTS | SERVES 6

⅓ cup canola oil

3 medium yellow onions, chopped

4 cloves garlic, peeled and minced

1 (2") piece of ginger, peeled and grated

2 teaspoons ground cumin

1½ teaspoons cayenne pepper

1½ teaspoons ground turmeric

2 cups Beef Stock (see Chapter 5)

3 pounds boneless leg of lamb, cut into 1" cubes

6 cups baby spinach

1⅓ cups coconut milk

1. In a large frying pan over medium-high heat, warm the oil. Add onions and garlic, and sauté until golden, about 5 minutes.

2. Stir in the ginger, cumin, cayenne, and turmeric, and sauté until fragrant, about 30 seconds.

3. Pour in stock, raise heat to high, and deglaze the pan, stirring to scrape up the browned bits on the bottom. When broth comes to a boil, remove pan from heat.

4. Put lamb in a 4 or 6-quart slow cooker, and add contents of frying pan. Cover and cook on high for 4 hours or on low for 8 hours.

5. Add baby spinach to slow cooker and cook, stirring occasionally, until spinach is wilted, about 5 minutes.

6. Just before serving, stir in coconut milk. Spoon into shallow bowls and serve hot.

PER SERVING: Calories: 712 | Fat: 56g | Protein: 44g | Sodium: 162mg | Fiber: 2g | Carbohydrates: 9g | Sugar: 3g

Thai Curried Chicken

This chicken dish can be served wrapped in large lettuce leaves,
or over a Thai-themed vegetable medley.

INGREDIENTS | SERVES 8

2½ pounds boneless, skinless chicken breasts, cut into 1" cubes

½ cup Thai green curry paste

2¼ cups coconut milk

24 ounces broccoli florets

12 ounces cremini mushrooms, sliced

3 tablespoons fish sauce

½ cup honey

Juice of 1 lime

½ cup basil leaves, chopped

2 teaspoons almond meal

2 tablespoons water

1. In a 6-quart slow cooker, place the chicken, curry paste, and coconut milk. Stir to combine. Cover and cook on low for 4 hours.

2. Turn the cooker on high, and add the broccoli and mushrooms.

3. In a separate bowl, whisk together the fish sauce, honey, and lime juice, and add this mixture to the slow cooker. Cover and cook for 30 minutes, then uncover and cook for 30 minutes more.

4. Stir in the basil.

5. In a separate bowl, whisk the almond meal with 2 tablespoons of water, and add this mixture to the slow cooker. Stir, and cook for an additional 15–30 minutes, until the liquid has thickened slightly.

6. Serve hot, or rolled up in a lettuce leaf.

PER SERVING: Calories: 384 | Fat: 18g | Protein: 34g | Sodium: 200mg | Fiber: 3g | Carbohydrates: 26g | Sugar: 19g

Vietnamese Cucumber Soup

This is a simple, 6-ingredient soup, easily prepared and ready in under 3 hours.

INGREDIENTS | SERVES 6

2 quarts water

1 pound of ground pork, or beef, or chicken, or turkey

6 tablespoons fish sauce, divided

⅛ teaspoon black pepper

4 large cucumbers peeled, halved, de-seeded, and sliced

2 green onions, chopped

1. Get the water simmering in a large pot (to be placed inside a large slow cooker).

2. In a large bowl, combine the meat with 2 tablespoons of the fish sauce. Add the pepper, and mix thoroughly.

3. Make meatballs out of the meat mixture and then transfer into boiling water, along with the cucumber slices. Cook for 15 minutes, and be sure to remove any foam and discard. Transfer the whole boiling pot into slow cooker.

4. Add the green onions and 4 remaining tablespoons of fish sauce. Cover and cook on high for 1½–2 hours.

PER SERVING: Calories: 198 | Fat: 16g | Protein: 13g | Sodium: 52mg | Fiber: 0g | Carbohydrates: 0g | Sugar: 0g

Amish Apple Butter

Traditionally flavored with warm spices and sweetened with honey, this condiment is called a "butter" due to its thick consistency and soft texture. Since apple butter needs a long, unhurried cooking period to caramelize the fruit and deepen the flavors, the slow cooker is the most suitable modern cooking appliance in which to make it.

INGREDIENTS | YIELDS 8 CUPS

10 cups (about 5 pounds) Gala apples, peeled, cored, and quartered

1 cup honey

3 tablespoons lemon juice

1½ teaspoons ground cinnamon

½ teaspoon ground cloves

½ teaspoon allspice

Old-Fashioned Apple Butter Making

Apple butter used to be made in large copper pots while simmering over a hot fire all day long. It was often done by a church group, or a large family who could share the responsibility of stirring the pot throughout the long day to prevent it from burning. Once finished, the apple butter would be canned and sold to raise money for a good cause or shared among all who helped make it.

1. Place the apples in a greased 4-quart slow cooker.

2. Pour honey and lemon juice over the apples and add cinnamon, cloves, and allspice. Stir to coat apples.

3. Cover and cook on low for 14–16 hours until the apple butter is a deep, dark brown and is richly flavored.

4. Ladle into pint jars and store in the refrigerator for up to 6 weeks. You can also process and can the apple butter if you prefer.

PER SERVING: Calories: 132 | Fat: 0g | Protein: 0g | Sodium: 3mg | Fiber: 0g | Carbohydrates: 36g | Sugar: 35g

African Soup

Feel free to play around with the seasonings in this unique soup.
A small pinch of curry powder would be an excellent addition.

INGREDIENTS | SERVES 6

2 tablespoons olive oil

2 medium onions, chopped

2 large red bell peppers, seeded and chopped

4 cloves garlic, minced

1 (28-ounce) can crushed tomatoes, with liquid

8 cups Roasted Vegetable Stock (see Chapter 5)

¼ teaspoon ground black pepper

¼ teaspoon chili powder

⅔ cup natural almond or cashew butter

½ cup fresh chopped cilantro

Nut Allergies and Intolerances

Nut allergies are very serious and can be life threatening. If you have a child or family member who has nut allergies, use sunflower butter in this recipe instead.

1. Heat olive oil in a large skillet. Cook onions and bell peppers until softened, usually 3–4 minutes.

2. Add garlic and cook for 1 minute more, stirring constantly. Add cooked vegetables to a greased 6-quart slow cooker.

3. Add tomatoes and their liquid, broth, ground pepper, and chili powder to the slow cooker. Cover and cook on high for 4 hours or on low for 8 hours.

4. One hour prior to serving stir in the almond butter. Heat for an additional 45–60 minutes, until soup has been completely warmed through. Garnish with cilantro.

PER SERVING: Calories: 154 | Fat: 5g | Protein: 3g | Sodium: 245mg | Fiber: 7g | Carbohydrates: 26g | Sugar: 15g

Greek Lemon-Chicken Soup

Lemon juice and egg yolks make this soup a lovely yellow color.
It's a unique soup that's perfect for a spring luncheon.

INGREDIENTS | SERVES 4

4 cups Chicken Stock (see Chapter 5)

¼ cup fresh lemon juice

¼ cup shredded carrots

¼ cup chopped onion

¼ cup chopped celery

⅛ teaspoon ground white pepper

2 tablespoons canola oil

2 tablespoons almond flour

4 egg yolks

½ cup diced, cooked boneless chicken breast

8 slices lemon

1. In a greased 4-quart slow cooker, combine the chicken stock, lemon juice, carrots, onion, celery, and pepper. Cover and cook on high for 3–4 hours or on low for 6–8 hours.

2. One hour before serving, blend the oil and the flour together in a medium bowl with a fork. Remove 1 cup of hot broth from the slow cooker and whisk with the oil and almond flour. Add mixture back to the slow cooker.

3. In a small bowl, beat the egg yolks until light in color. Gradually add some of the hot soup to the egg yolks, stirring constantly. Return the broth/egg mixture to the slow cooker.

4. Add the cooked chicken. Cook on low for an additional hour. Ladle hot soup into bowls and garnish with lemon slices.

PER SERVING: Calories: 181 | Fat: 14g | Protein: 6g | Sodium: 43mg | Fiber: 2g | Carbohydrates: 9g | Sugar: 3g

Mediterranean Chicken Casserole

Raisins may seem like an odd ingredient to add to a main dish, but they provide a slightly sweet flavor that beautifully complements the tomatoes and spices.

INGREDIENTS | SERVES 4

1 medium butternut squash, peeled and cut into 2" cubes

1 medium bell pepper, seeded and diced

1 (14.5-ounce) can diced tomatoes, undrained

4 boneless, skinless chicken breast halves, cut into bite-sized pieces

½ cup mild salsa

¼ cup raisins

¼ teaspoon ground cinnamon

¼ teaspoon ground cumin

¼ cup chopped fresh parsley

1. Add the squash and bell pepper to the bottom of a greased 4-quart slow cooker.

2. Mix the tomatoes, chicken, salsa, raisins, cinnamon, and cumin together and pour on top of squash and peppers.

3. Cover and cook on low for 6 hours, on high for 3 hours, or until squash is fork tender.

4. Remove the chicken and vegetables from slow cooker with slotted spoon. Ladle remaining sauce from slow cooker over the vegetables and chicken. Garnish with parsley.

PER SERVING: Calories: 189 | Fat: 3g | Protein: 26g | Sodium: 331mg | Fiber: 3g | Carbohydrates: 15g | Sugar: 10g

Asian Inspired Honey-Glazed Chicken Drumsticks

It can be a challenge to eat at Chinese restaurants when you are abiding by the Paleolithic lifestyle. But this Asian-inspired chicken is a great substitute for take-out! Serve with a salad and egg drop soup.

INGREDIENTS | SERVES 4

2 pounds chicken drumsticks
1 tablespoon melted coconut butter
¼ cup lemon juice
¾ cup honey
1 teaspoon sesame oil
3 cloves garlic, crushed
½ teaspoon ground ginger

1. Place the chicken drumsticks in a greased 4-quart slow cooker.

2. In a glass measuring cup whisk together the melted butter, lemon juice, honey, sesame oil, garlic, and ginger.

3. Pour the honey sauce over the drumsticks. Cook on high for 3–4 hours or on low for 6–8 hours.

PER SERVING: Calories: 571 | Fat: 21g | Protein: 44g | Sodium: 192mg | Fiber: 0g | Carbohydrates: 54g | Sugar: 53g

Sesame Oil

Sesame oil is a highly flavorful oil made from pressing either toasted or plain sesame seeds. It provides a unique nutty and earthy flavor to savory dishes. A little goes a long way, and it's not very expensive. It can be found at most grocery stores in the Asian food aisle.

Moroccan Chicken

This dish was inspired by traditional North African tagines (stews) and adapted for the slow cooker. Serve over mashed sweet potatoes.

INGREDIENTS | SERVES 6

½ teaspoon coriander

½ teaspoon cinnamon

1 teaspoon cumin

3 pounds (about 8) boneless, skinless chicken thighs, diced

1 large onion, thinly sliced

4 cloves garlic, minced

2 tablespoons fresh ginger, minced or ½ teaspoon dried ginger

½ cup water

4 ounces dried apricots, halved

1. In a large bowl, combine the coriander, cinnamon, and cumin. Toss chicken in the spice mixture.

2. Place onion, garlic, ginger, and water into a 4-quart slow cooker. Place chicken on top of vegetables. Place dried apricots on top of chicken.

3. Cover and cook on low for 5–6 hours.

PER SERVING: Calories: 326 | Fat: 9g | Protein: 45g | Sodium: 197mg | Fiber: 2g | Carbohydrates: 15g | Sugar: 11g

Swiss Steak

Minute steaks are usually tenderized pieces of round steak. You can instead buy 2½ pounds of round steak, trim it of fat, cut it into 6 portions, and pound each portion thin between 2 pieces of plastic wrap. Serve Swiss Steak over mashed root vegetables.

INGREDIENTS | SERVES 6

½ cup almond flour
¼ teaspoon freshly ground black pepper
6 (6-ounce) beef minute steaks
2 tablespoons canola oil
2 teaspoons coconut butter
½ stalk celery, finely diced
1 large yellow onion, peeled and diced
1 cup beef broth
1 cup water
1 (1-pound) bag baby carrots

1. Add the almond flour, pepper, and steaks to a gallon-sized plastic bag; seal and shake to coat the meat.

2. Add the oil and coconut butter to a large skillet and bring it to temperature over medium-high heat. Add the meat and brown it for 5 minutes on each side. Transfer the meat to a 4-quart slow cooker.

3. Add the celery to the skillet and sauté while you add the onion to the plastic bag; seal and shake to coat the onion in flour. Add the flour-coated onion to the skillet and, stirring constantly, sauté for 10 minutes or until the onions are lightly browned.

4. Add the broth to the skillet and stir to scrape up any browned bits clinging to the pan. Add the water and continue to cook until the liquid is thickened enough to lightly coat the back of a spoon. Pour into the slow cooker.

5. Add the carrots. Cover and cook on low for 8 hours.

6. Transfer the meat and carrots to a serving platter. Taste the gravy for seasoning, and add more pepper if desired. Serve alongside or over the meat and carrots.

PER SERVING: Calories: 392 | Fat: 22g | Protein: 39g | Sodium: 284mg | Fiber: 4g | Carbohydrates: 11g | Sugar: 5g

Mexican Pork Roast

Serve this pork over Mexican-themed vegetables, or as
Paleo-friendly "burritos," wrapped in lettuce wraps.

INGREDIENTS | SERVES 4

1 tablespoon olive oil

1 large sweet onion, peeled and sliced

1 medium carrot, peeled and finely diced

1 jalapeño pepper, seeded and minced

1 clove of garlic, peeled and minced

¼ teaspoon dried Mexican oregano

¼ teaspoon ground coriander

¼ teaspoon freshly ground black pepper

1 (3-pound) pork shoulder or butt roast

1 cup chicken broth

1. Add the olive oil, onion, carrot, and jalapeño to a 4–6-quart slow cooker. Stir to coat the vegetables in the oil. Cover and cook on high for 30 minutes, or until the onions are softened. Stir in the garlic.

2. In a small bowl, combine the oregano, coriander, and black pepper. Rub the spice mixture onto the pork roast.

3. Add the rubbed pork roast to the slow cooker. Add the chicken broth. Cover and cook on low for 6 hours or until the pork is tender and pulls apart easily.

4. Use a slotted spoon to remove the pork and vegetables to a serving platter. Cover and let rest for 10 minutes.

5. Increase the temperature of the slow cooker to high. Cook for about 10–20 minutes, and reduce the pan juices by half.

6. Use 2 forks to shred the pork and mix it in with the cooked onion and jalapeño. Ladle the reduced pan juices over the pork.

PER SERVING: Calories: 576 | Fat: 28g | Protein: 68g | Sodium: 530mg | Fiber: 1g | Carbohydrates: 8g | Sugar: 2g

Tuscan Chicken and Turkey Stew

You don't need a lot of ingredients to create a stew full of hearty and warm Tuscan flavors.

INGREDIENTS | SERVES 4

1 pound boneless, skinless chicken thighs

8 ounces ground turkey

1 (26-ounce) jar pasta sauce

1 can green beans, drained

1 teaspoon dried oregano

Change It Up

Don't like green beans or don't have them available in your pantry? Try this recipe with different vegetable combinations like mushrooms or artichokes.

1. Cut chicken thighs into bite-sized pieces. Place chicken into a greased 4-quart slow cooker.

2. Add the remaining ingredients. Stir to combine, and cook on high for 4 hours or on low for 8 hours.

PER SERVING: Calories: 391 | Fat: 14g | Protein: 36g | Sodium: 1,067mg | Fiber: 6g | Carbohydrates: 28g | Sugar: 17g

CHAPTER 13

Foods for Optimal Performance and Enhanced Recovery

Italian Tomato Sauce with Turkey Meatballs

Using roasted garlic eliminates the need for sautéing, making this recipe a snap to put together. Serve with "Paleo Pasta" as a pregame meal.

INGREDIENTS | SERVES 4

12 ounces frozen turkey meatballs

1½ tablespoons minced basil

1 medium onion, minced

1 head roasted garlic (about 2 tablespoons), peels removed

28 ounces fire-roasted tomatoes

1 teaspoon crushed red pepper flakes

Defrost the meatballs according to package instructions. Place in a 4-quart slow cooker with the remaining ingredients. Stir. Cook on low for 3–6 hours. Stir before serving.

PER SERVING: Calories: 138 | Fat: 7g | Protein: 15g | Sodium: 80mg | Fiber: 1g | Carbohydrates: 3g | Sugar: 1g

Sweet Potato Soup

As a postcompetition or training snack, it provides both fluid and carbohydrates to help refuel and rehydrate.

INGREDIENTS | SERVES 4

3 sweet potatoes, peeled and cubed

2 cups Chicken or Roasted Vegetable Stock (see Chapter 5)

1 (15-ounce) can of sliced mangoes, undrained

¼ teaspoon ground allspice

½ cup coconut milk

1. Place all ingredients, except coconut milk, in a 4-quart slow cooker. Cover and cook on low for 8 hours or on high for 4 hours.

2. When sweet potatoes are soft, blend in blender and stir in coconut milk.

PER SERVING: Calories: 155 | Fat: 7g | Protein: 3g | Sodium: 67mg | Fiber: 4g | Carbohydrates: 22g | Sugar: 5g

Paleo Meatballs and Sauce

These meatballs are so close to the original, you won't know the difference. This recipe can also be served with "Paleo Pasta," before or after competition to either fuel or refuel.

INGREDIENTS | YIELDS 12 MEATBALLS

1 (16-ounce) can diced, no-salt-added tomatoes

1 (4-ounce) can organic, no-salt-added tomato paste

2 pounds grass-fed ground beef

1 cup chopped celery

1 cup chopped onion

1 cup chopped carrots

4 finely chopped garlic cloves

3 eggs

½ cup flaxseed meal

1 tablespoon oregano

1 teaspoon black pepper

¼ teaspoon chili powder

1. Pour canned tomatoes and tomato paste into a 4-quart slow cooker.

2. Place all remaining ingredients in a large bowl and mix well with clean hands.

3. Roll resulting meat mixture into 2–3 ounce (large, rounded tablespoon) balls and add to slow cooker.

4. Cook on low for 5 hours minimum.

PER SERVING: (1 meatball) | Calories: 134 | Fat: 5g | Protein: 18g | Sodium: 82mg | Fiber: 1g | Carbohydrates: 3g | Sugar: 1g

Sweet Potatoes with an Orange Twist

This delicious dish gives you a sweet helping of performance fuel.

INGREDIENTS | SERVES 4

2 pounds sweet potatoes, peeled and cubed

½ cup honey

½ cup coconut butter

1 teaspoon vanilla extract

1 teaspoon ground cinnamon

½ teaspoon ground nutmeg

1 medium orange, juiced

½ cup toasted chopped pecans

1. Place sweet potatoes in bottom of a 4- or 6-quart slow cooker.

2. Mix honey, coconut butter, vanilla, spices, and orange juice together. Stir into sweet potatoes. Cook on high for 2 hours or on low for 4 hours.

3. Stir in toasted pecans prior to serving.

PER SERVING: Calories: 422 | Fat: 10g | Protein: 5g | Sodium: 125mg | Fiber: 8g | Carbohydrates: 83g | Sugar: 45g

Sweet Potato Casserole

Inspired by Lauren, an aspiring field hockey player and fitness guru, this recipe is loaded with carbohydrates, and is a rich source of lots of beneficial vitamins and minerals. A great way to recharge after a long, hard workout.

INGREDIENTS | SERVES 6

2 pounds sweet potatoes, peeled and mashed

¼ cup canola oil

1⅓ cups honey, divided

1 tablespoon freshly squeezed orange juice

2 eggs, beaten

½ cup coconut milk

½ cup chopped pecans

2 tablespoons arrowroot powder

2 tablespoons coconut butter

1. Lightly grease a 4- or 6-quart slow cooker. Mix mashed sweet potatoes, canola oil, and ½ cup honey together in a large bowl.

2. Beat in orange juice, eggs, and coconut milk. Transfer to slow cooker.

3. In a medium bowl, combine the pecans, the remainder of the honey, the arrowroot powder, and the coconut butter. Spread evenly over the top of the sweet potatoes.

4. Cover and cook on high for 3–4 hours.

PER SERVING: Calories: 571 | Fat: 21g | Protein: 6g | Sodium: 111mg | Fiber: 6g | Carbohydrates: 96g | Sugar: 69g

Postgame Potent Pecans, Paleo Style

This recipe provides a blend of protein, fat, carbohydrates, calories, and even electrolytes to satisfy any athlete looking to recharge.

INGREDIENTS | SERVES 9

3 cups pecan halves

1 egg white

1 teaspoon cinnamon

¼ teaspoon cayenne, or more to taste

1 cup honey

1. Place pecans in a 2-quart or smaller slow cooker, add egg white, and stir until evenly coated.

2. In a small bowl, stir the cinnamon, cayenne, and honey together and pour mixture over pecans, stirring until evenly coated.

3. Cover and cook on low for 3 hours, stirring every hour.

4. Uncover slow cooker, stir, and cook uncovered another 30–45 minutes, until pecans are dry. Cool and store in airtight container.

PER SERVING: Calories: 368 | Fat: 26g | Protein: 4g | Sodium: 8mg | Fiber: 4g | Carbohydrates: 36g | Sugar: 32g

Chicken and Sweet Potato Stew

An easy way to meet pregame carbohydrate and fluids requirements, and very low in fat to ensure optimal digestion.

INGREDIENTS | SERVES 4

1 pound boneless, skinless chicken breasts, cubed

12 ounces sweet potatoes, peeled and cubed

12 ounces Chicken Stock (see Chapter 5)

1 large green bell pepper, sliced

2–3 teaspoons chili powder

½ teaspoon garlic powder

¼ cup cold water

2 tablespoons almond meal

Pepper, to taste

1. Combine all ingredients except water, almond meal, and pepper in a 4-quart slow cooker. Cover and cook on high 4–5 hours.

2. In a small bowl, combine the almond meal and water. Add to the slow cooker, stirring 2–3 minutes. Season to taste with pepper.

PER SERVING: Calories: 247 | Fat: 5g | Protein: 27g | Sodium: 205mg | Fiber: 5g | Carbohydrates: 22g | Sugar: 5g

Homemade Tomato Juice

Rehydrate and replenish. A perfect, postexercise thirst quencher, loaded with electrolytes.

INGREDIENTS | SERVES 4

10 large tomatoes, seeded and sliced

1 teaspoon lemon juice

¼ teaspoon black pepper

1 tablespoon honey

1. Place tomatoes in a 2-quart slow cooker. Cover; cook on low for 4–6 hours.

2. Press tomato mixture through a sieve. Add remaining ingredients and chill.

PER SERVING: Calories: 99 | Fat: 1g | Protein: 4g | Sodium: 23mg | Fiber: 6g | Carbohydrates: 22g | Sugar: 16g

Sweet Potato Gratin with Leeks and Onions

The combination of sweet and savory makes this a fascinating, unique, and delicious dish.

INGREDIENTS | SERVES 6

2 leeks, white part only, rinsed and chopped

2 large sweet onions, such as Vidalias, peeled and finely chopped

2 stalks celery with tops, finely chopped

4 tablespoons olive oil

4 sweet potatoes, peeled and sliced thinly

1 teaspoon dried thyme

½ teaspoon ground black pepper

3 cups coconut milk

1½ cups arrowroot powder

2 tablespoons coconut butter, cut in small pieces

1. In a skillet over medium heat add the leeks, onions, celery, and olive oil. Sauté for 3–5 minutes, until softened.

2. Grease a 4-quart slow cooker with nonstick cooking spray.

3. Layer the sweet potato slices in the slow cooker with the sautéed vegetables. Sprinkle thyme and pepper on each layer as you go along. Finish with a layer of potatoes.

4. Add the coconut milk until it meets the top layer of potatoes. Then add the arrowroot powder. Dot with the coconut butter.

5. Cover and cook on high for 4 hours, on low for 8 hours, or until the potatoes are fork tender. In the last hour of cooking, vent the lid of the slow cooker with a chopstick or wooden spoon handle to allow excess condensation to escape.

PER SERVING: Calories: 530 | Fat: 33g | Protein: 5g | Sodium: 71mg | Fiber: 5g | Carbohydrates: 58g | Sugar: 7g

Beef and Sweet Potato Stew

This rich, deeply flavored beef stew with sweet potatoes is inspired by Lara— an aspiring young field hockey player who adheres to a strict gluten-free diet.

INGREDIENTS | SERVES 8

¾ cup almond flour

1½ teaspoons lemon juice, divided

1½ teaspoons ground black pepper, divided

1¼ pounds stew beef, cut into 1" chunks

¼ cup olive oil, divided

1 medium yellow onion, diced

2 cups peeled and diced carrots

¾ pound cremini mushrooms, cleaned and cut in half

6 cloves garlic, minced

3 tablespoons tomato paste

1 pound sweet potatoes, peeled and diced

4½ cups Beef Stock (see Chapter 5)

1 bay leaf

1½ teaspoons dried thyme

1 tablespoon honey

1. In a large zip-top plastic bag, place flour, 1 teaspoon lemon juice, and 1 teaspoon pepper. Add beef and close the bag. Shake lightly, open bag, and make sure that all of the beef is coated in flour and seasoning. Set aside.

2. In a large skillet, heat 2 tablespoons of olive oil over medium heat. Cook beef in small batches until browned on all sides, about 1 minute per side. Add beef to a greased 4–6-quart slow cooker.

3. In the same skillet, heat the remaining 2 tablespoons of olive oil. Add onion and carrots, and cook until onions are translucent, about 5 minutes.

4. Add mushrooms and garlic, and cook for another 2–3 minutes.

5. Add tomato paste and heat through. Deglaze the pan, scraping the stuck-on bits from the bottom of the pan. Add cooked vegetable mixture on top of the beef in the slow cooker.

6. Add the sweet potatoes, stock, bay leaf, and thyme to the slow cooker. Cover and cook on low for 8 hours or on high for 4 hours.

7. Before serving, add honey and remaining lemon juice and pepper.

PER SERVING: Calories: 260 | Fat: 12g | Protein: 18g | Sodium: 578mg | Fiber: 3g | Carbohydrates: 20g | Sugar: 7g

Cabbage and Beef Casserole

A lower-carbohydrate beefy casserole using cabbage and tomato sauce.

INGREDIENTS | SERVES 6

2 pounds ground beef
1 small onion, chopped
1 head cabbage, shredded
1 (16-ounce) can tomatoes
½ teaspoon garlic powder
¼ teaspoon ground thyme
¼ teaspoon red pepper flakes
½ teaspoon oregano
8 ounces tomato sauce

1. In a large skillet, brown the ground beef for about 5–6 minutes. Remove ground beef to a bowl and set aside. In the same skillet, sauté onion until softened, about 3–5 minutes.

2. In a greased 4–6-quart slow cooker, layer cabbage, onion, tomatoes, garlic powder, thyme, pepper flakes, oregano, and beef. Repeat layers, ending with beef. Pour tomato sauce over casserole.

3. Cook on low for 8 hours or on high for 4 hours.

PER SERVING: Calories: 269 | Fat: 8g | Protein: 35g | Sodium: 429mg | Fiber: 5g | Carbohydrates: 15g | Sugar: 9g

Lamb and Root Vegetable Tagine

This exotic dish provides a rich source of long-lasting carbohydrates with the combination of dried fruit and root vegetables.

INGREDIENTS | SERVES 6

1 tablespoon olive oil
2 pounds leg of lamb, trimmed of fat and cut into bite-sized chunks
½ large onion, chopped
1 clove garlic, minced
½ teaspoon pepper
1 cup Chicken Stock (see Chapter 5)
½ pound (about 2 medium) sweet potatoes, peeled and cut into 1" chunks
⅓ cup dried apricots, cut in half
1 teaspoon coriander
1 teaspoon cumin
¼ teaspoon cinnamon

1. In a large skillet, brown the cubed lamb in olive oil, approximately 1–2 minutes per side. Add lamb to a greased 4-quart slow cooker.

2. Cook the onion and garlic in the same skillet for 3–4 minutes until soft and then add to the slow cooker.

3. Add remaining ingredients to slow cooker. Cook on high for 4 hours or on low for 8 hours.

PER SERVING: Calories: 393 | Fat: 24g | Protein: 29g | Sodium: 111mg | Fiber: 2g | Carbohydrates: 15g | Sugar: 6g

Orange Chicken

Serve this dish over stir-fry vegetables, or a puréed starchy or root vegetable.

INGREDIENTS | SERVES 8

3 pounds boneless, skinless chicken breasts

1 small onion, peeled and diced

½ cup freshly squeezed orange juice

3 tablespoons orange marmalade (or Peach Marmalade, see Chapter 2)

1 tablespoon honey

1 tablespoon lemon juice

1 teaspoon Dijon mustard

1 tablespoon arrowroot powder mixed with 2 tablespoons hot water

2 tablespoons grated orange zest

1. Grease the slow cooker with nonstick cooking spray.

2. Cut the chicken breasts into bite-sized pieces. Add the chicken and the onion to the slow cooker.

3. In a small bowl, mix together the orange juice, marmalade, honey, lemon juice, and mustard. Pour over the chicken in the slow cooker.

4. Cover and cook on low for 5–6 hours or until chicken is cooked through.

5. About 10 minutes before serving, whisk in the arrowroot powder slurry. Leave the slow cooker uncovered, turn the temperature to high, and continue to cook for 10 minutes to thicken the sauce. Serve with orange zest sprinkled on top.

PER SERVING: Calories: 235 | Fat: 4g | Protein: 36g | Sodium: 208mg | Fiber: 0g | Carbohydrates: 11g | Sugar: 9g

Chicken and "Paleo-Approved" Dumplings

Fluffy Paleo dumplings float on top of a savory chicken stew.
The perfect combination of protein and energy producing carbohydrates.

INGREDIENTS | SERVES 4

4 chicken breasts, cut into chunks

4 cups Chicken Stock (see Chapter 5)

1 teaspoon ground pepper

2 celery stalks, thinly sliced

2 large carrots, thinly sliced

½ large onion, finely chopped

1 cup almond flour

1 cup arrowroot starch

1 teaspoon xanthan gum

1 tablespoon honey

3 teaspoons baking powder

⅓ cup coconut butter

2 eggs, lightly beaten

1 cup coconut milk

1. Place the chicken in a greased 4–6-quart slow cooker. Add chicken stock, pepper, celery, carrots, and onion. Cook on high for 3–4 hours or on low for 6–8 hours.

2. In a mixing bowl whisk together the flour, arrowroot starch, xanthan gum, honey, and baking powder.

3. Cut the coconut butter into the dry ingredients with two knives or a pastry cutter until the mixture resembles small peas. Make a well in the center of the dry ingredients and add the eggs and coconut milk. Gently mix the wet ingredients into the dry ingredients until you have a fluffy dough.

4. Thirty minutes before serving, carefully drop the dough in golf ball–sized spoonfuls into the hot chicken broth. Place the lid on the slow cooker and do not open it for 30 minutes so the dumplings will rise and cook through.

5. Serve dumplings with broth and chicken in large bowls.

PER SERVING: Calories: 658 | Fat: 33g | Protein: 47g | Sodium: 653mg | Fiber: 6g | Carbohydrates: 48g | Sugar: 8g

Turkey Meatballs with Tangy Apricot Sauce

These easy turkey meatballs obtain their flavor from the tasty, sweet and sour combination.
An excellent and valuable pregame or postgame fuel (or refuel) source.

INGREDIENTS | SERVES 4

1 pound ground turkey

¾ cup almond flour

1 egg

¼ cup finely diced onions

¼ cup finely diced celery

½ teaspoon ground pepper

1 tablespoon olive oil

1 cup apricot preserves (or Peach Marmalade, see Chapter 2)

¼ cup Dijon mustard

Are Meatballs Paleo-Approved?

Meatloaf and meatballs are usually made with wheat bread crumbs. To make meatloaf or meatballs Paleo-friendly, simply replace the bread crumbs called for in a recipe with almond flour and/or arrowroot powder.

1. In a large bowl mix together the ground turkey, almond flour, egg, onions, celery, and ground pepper. Roll into small meatballs (about 16–20). The meatball mixture will be slightly wet.

2. Heat olive oil in a large skillet. Add meatballs to hot skillet and brown on all sides, about 1 minute per side.

3. Grease a 2½-quart slow cooker. Add browned meatballs to the slow cooker.

4. In a small bowl mix together the preserves (or marmalade) and mustard. Pour the sauce over the meatballs. Cook on high for 3 hours or on low for 6 hours.

5. If using meatballs as an appetizer instead of a main course, you can turn the slow cooker to the warm setting and heat them for up to 2 hours.

PER SERVING: Calories: 350 | Fat: 25g | Protein: 26g | Sodium: 307mg | Fiber: 3g | Carbohydrates: 7g | Sugar: 2g

Apricot Pork Sirloin Roast

A pork sirloin roast is low in fat, yet it cooks up tender and moist. If you prefer gravy instead of sauce, simply mix the reduced pan juices with some full-fat coconut milk.

INGREDIENTS | SERVES 8

15 pitted prunes (dried plums)

12 dried apricots, pitted

½ cup boiling water

1 cup Chicken Stock (see Chapter 5)

1 cup apple juice

1 (3½–pound) pork sirloin roast, trimmed of fat and silver skin

4 large sweet potatoes, peeled and quartered

Freshly ground pepper, to taste

1 tablespoon arrowroot powder

2 tablespoons cold water

1. Add the prunes and apricots to a 6-quart slow cooker. Pour the boiling water over the dried fruit; cover and let set for 15 minutes.

2. Add the chicken stock, apple juice, pork sirloin roast, sweet potatoes, and pepper. Cover and cook on low for 5–6 hours or until the internal temperature of the roast is 160°F.

3. Remove the meat and sweet potatoes from the cooker; cover and keep warm.

4. Turn the cooker to high. Use an immersion blender to purée the fruit.

5. In a small bowl, mix the arrowroot powder into the cold water. Once the liquid in the slow cooker begins to bubble around the edges, slowly whisk in the arrowroot liquid. Reduce the heat to low, and simmer the sauce for several minutes, stirring occasionally, until thickened.

6. Place the pork roast on a serving platter and carve into eight slices. Arrange the sweet potatoes around the pork. Ladle the sauce over the meat. Serve immediately.

PER SERVING: Calories: 398 | Fat: 7g | Protein: 46g | Sodium: 265mg | Fiber: 4g | Carbohydrates: 36g | Sugar: 17g

Roast Pork with Cinnamon Cranberries and Sweet Potatoes

You can substitute Peach Marmalade (see Chapter 2) for the orange marmalade and orange juice called for in this recipe. Doing so will add a subtle taste of peaches and pineapple to the dish, too.

INGREDIENTS | SERVES 6

1 (3-pound) pork butt roast

Freshly ground pepper, to taste

1 (16-ounce) can sweetened whole cranberries

1 medium onion, peeled and diced

¼ cup orange marmalade

½ cup freshly squeezed orange juice

¼ teaspoon ground cinnamon

¼ teaspoon ground cloves

3 large sweet potatoes, peeled and quartered

1 tablespoon arrowroot powder, optional

2 tablespoons cold water, optional

1. Place the pork, fat side up, in a 4-quart slow cooker and add pepper to taste.

2. In a medium bowl, combine the cranberries, onion, marmalade, orange juice, cinnamon, and cloves, and stir to mix. Pour over the pork roast in the slow cooker.

3. Arrange the sweet potatoes around the meat. Cover and cook on low for 6 hours or until the pork is tender and pulls apart easily.

4. To serve with a thickened sauce, transfer the meat and sweet potatoes to a serving platter. Cover and keep warm. Skim any fat off of the pan juices. (You'll want about 2 cups of juice remaining in the cooker.) Cover and cook on the high setting for 30 minutes, or until the pan liquids begin to bubble around the edges. In a small bowl, combine the arrowroot powder with the water. Whisk into the liquid in the slow cooker. Reduce temperature setting to low, and continue to cook and stir for an additional 2 minutes, or until it is thickened and bubbly.

PER SERVING: Calories: 390 | Fat: 8g | Protein: 52g | Sodium: 154mg | Fiber: 2g | Carbohydrates: 26g | Sugar: 12g

Sweet and Sour Shrimp with Pineapple

Serve over a generous portion of seasonal vegetable blend. Shrimp is a great source of high quality protein, and combined with all the vegetables and simple sugars, this dish makes an excellent protein/carb combo; the perfect recipe for optimal recovery.

INGREDIENTS | SERVES 4

3 (8-ounce) cans pineapple chunks, drained and 1 cup juice reserved

2 (6-ounce) packages frozen green beans, thawed

¼ cup arrowroot powder

⅓ cup, plus 2 teaspoons honey

2 cups Chicken Stock (see Chapter 5)

1 teaspoon ground ginger

1 pound medium or large shrimp, peeled, deveined, and cleaned

¼ cup lemon juice

1. Place pineapple and green beans in a 2- or 4-quart slow cooker.

2. In a medium saucepan combine the arrowroot powder, honey, and chicken stock. Add 1 cup reserved pineapple juice and ginger.

3. Bring saucepan contents to a boil for 1 minute, and then pour into the slow cooker.

4. Cover and cook on low for 4½–5½ hours.

5. Add shrimp and lemon juice. Cover and cook on low for 30 minutes.

PER SERVING: Calories: 375 | Fat: 2g | Protein: 25g | Sodium: 177mg | Fiber: 5g | Carbohydrates: 68g | Sugar: 53g

Hawaiian Fruit Compote

A must-have pregame/training, last minute energizer.

INGREDIENTS | SERVES 6

3 cups pineapple, coarsely chopped

3 grapefruit, peeled and sectioned

3 cups fresh peaches, chopped

3 limes, peeled and sectioned

1 mango, peeled and chopped

2 bananas, peeled and sliced

1 tablespoon lemon juice

1 (21-ounce) can cherry pie filling

Slivered almonds, optional

1. Place all the ingredients except the almonds, in a 2-quart slow cooker. Mix well.

2. Cover and cook on low for 4–5 hours or on high for 2–3 hours.

3. Serve topped with almonds, if desired.

PER SERVING: Calories: 180 | Fat: 1g | Protein: 3g | Sodium: 3mg | Fiber: 6g | Carbohydrates: 47g | Sugar: 34g

Pear Slush

Fulfills the two most important postworkout needs: replenishes carbohydrate stores and rehydrates!

INGREDIENTS | SERVES 6

1 pound fresh pears, cored (Bosc are preferred)

1¼ cups water

¼ cup honey

½ teaspoon ground cinnamon

1 tablespoon lemon juice

Ice Fruit

Enjoy this deliciously cool, thirst-quenching treat as a postgame snack—to cool down; or as a pregame energizer, for a last minute burst of high-quality carbohydrates and fluids.

1. Place the pears, water, honey, and cinnamon in a 2-quart slow cooker. Cover and cook on high for 2½–3½ hours. Stir in the lemon juice.

2. Process pear and syrup mixture in a blender until smooth. Strain mixture through a sieve, and discard any pulp.

3. Pour liquid into a 11" × 9" baking dish, cover tightly with plastic wrap, and transfer to freezer.

4. Stir every hour with a fork, crushing any lumps as it freezes. Freeze 3–4 hours or until firm.

PER SERVING: Calories: 87 | Fat: 0g | Protein: 0g | Sodium: 3mg | Fiber: 2g | Carbohydrates: 23g | Sugar: 19g

Apple Freeze

Inspired by Buddy, and his never-ending love for frozen applesauce.

INGREDIENTS | SERVES 6

1 pound fresh apples, cored (Golden Delicious are preferred)

1¼ cups water

¼ cup honey

½ teaspoon ground cinnamon

1 tablespoon lemon juice

1. Place the apples, water, honey, and cinnamon in 2-quart slow cooker. Cover and cook on high for 2½–3½ hours. Stir in the lemon juice.

2. Process apple and syrup mixture in a blender until smooth. Strain mixture through a sieve, and discard any pulp.

3. Pour liquid into a 11" × 9" baking dish, cover tightly with plastic wrap, and transfer to freezer.

4. Stir every hour with a fork, crushing any lumps as it freezes. Freeze 3–4 hours or until firm.

PER SERVING: Calories: 80 | Fat: 0g | Protein: 0g | Sodium: 3mg | Fiber: 1g | Carbohydrates: 21g | Sugar: 19g

CHAPTER 14

Stone Age Sweet Treats: Slow Cooked Desserts

"Baked" Apples

Serve these lightly spiced apples as a simple dessert or as a breakfast treat.

INGREDIENTS | SERVES 6

6 baking apples
½ cup water
1 cinnamon stick
1 knob peeled fresh ginger
1 vanilla bean

Baking with Apples

When baking or cooking, choose apples with firm flesh such as Granny Smith, Jonathan, McIntosh, Cortland, Pink Lady, Pippin, or Winesap. They will be able to hold up to long cooking times without turning to mush. Leaving the skin on adds fiber.

1. Place the apples in a single layer on the bottom of a 4–6-quart slow cooker. Add the water, cinnamon stick, ginger, and vanilla bean. Cook on low for 6–8 hours or until the apples are tender and easily pierced with a fork.

2. Use a slotted spoon to remove the apples from the insert. Discard the cinnamon stick, ginger, vanilla bean, and water. Serve hot.

PER SERVING: Calories: 77 | Fat: 0g | Protein: 0g | Sodium: 1mg | Fiber: 2g | Carbohydrates: 21g | Sugar: 16g

Slow Cooked Pineapple

Slow cooking makes pineapple meltingly tender.

INGREDIENTS | SERVES 8

1 whole pineapple, peeled
1 vanilla bean, split
3 tablespoons water or rum

Cooking with Vanilla Beans

Vanilla beans have a natural "seam" that can easily be split to release the flavorful seeds inside. After using a vanilla bean, wash it and allow it to dry. Then place it in a container with a few cups of sugar for a few weeks to make vanilla sugar.

Place all ingredients into a 4-quart oval slow cooker. Cook on low for 4 hours or until fork tender. Remove the vanilla bean before serving.

PER SERVING: Calories: 57 | Fat: 0g | Protein: 1g | Sodium: 1mg | Fiber: 2g | Carbohydrates: 15g | Sugar: 11g

Paleo Brownie Bowls

Who ever said brownies were "Paleo No" foods? Perish the thought!

INGREDIENTS | SERVES 2

½ cup almond butter
¼ cup honey
⅛ cup cocoa powder
1 teaspoon vanilla extract
1 egg
¼ teaspoon baking soda
Dash pumpkin pie spice
Dash ground ginger (optional)
2 ceramic coffee mugs

1. Combine all the ingredients in a large mixing bowl and mix well. Grease coffee mugs with some coconut oil, so your brownie doesn't get stuck all over the sides of the mug.

2. Pour even amounts of the batter into mugs, and set them inside a 4-quart slow cooker. Don't fill the mugs any more than about halfway full; the batter will rise and bubble over if mugs are too full.

3. Cover, and cook on high for about 1½–2 hours, depending on desired cake-like consistency. Knife should be mostly clean, after inserted and removed, from center of brownie.

4. Remove lid and allow to cool before serving.

PER SERVING: Calories: 183 | Fat: 3g | Protein: 4g | Sodium: 195mg | Fiber: 2g | Carbohydrates: 38g | Sugar: 35g

Warm Spiced Fruit

This recipe can be used with a variety of different fruits. Serve as dessert or as a sweet addition to a slow cooked breakfast, brunch, or dinner dish of choice.

INGREDIENTS | SERVES 8

1 (28-ounce) can peach slices, drained

1 (16-ounce) can pineapple tidbits with natural juices, undrained

1 (28-ounce) can pear slices, drained

1 (15-ounce) can mixed chunky fruit

½ cup maraschino cherries, drained

½ cup honey

4 tablespoons coconut butter

1 tablespoon almond meal

1½ teaspoons ground cinnamon

1 teaspoon ground nutmeg

1. Combine all the ingredients in a 4-quart slow cooker; stir gently.

2. Cover and cook on low for 4–6 hours or on high for 2–3 hours.

PER SERVING: Calories: 257 | Fat: 1g | Protein: 1g | Sodium: 15mg | Fiber: 6g | Carbohydrates: 66g | Sugar: 60g

Cranberry-Apple Compote

An easy, succulent taste of fall.

INGREDIENTS | SERVES 6

4 cups of apples, peeled, cored, and sliced

½ cup sliced cranberries

⅓ cup honey

2 tablespoons coconut oil

1 teaspoon ground cinnamon

¼ teaspoon ground nutmeg

¾ cup chopped walnuts and almonds

1. Combine all the ingredients, except the nuts, in a 3–4-quart slow cooker.

2. Cover and cook on high for 1½–2 hours or until apples are tender.

3. Sprinkle each serving with nuts.

PER SERVING: Calories: 221 | Fat: 10g | Protein: 3g | Sodium: 1mg | Fiber: 3g | Carbohydrates: 36g | Sugar: 30g

Sweet and Spicy Walnuts

A perfect sweet and savory snack, guaranteed to please just about any palate.

INGREDIENTS | SERVES 12

2 tablespoons coconut oil

¼ cup honey

1 teaspoon ground ginger

1 teaspoon curry powder

½ teaspoon cayenne

¼ teaspoon onion powder

¼ teaspoon garlic powder

3 cups shelled walnuts

1. Pour coconut oil into a 2–4-quart slow cooker, turn on high and allow to melt.

2. While oil is melting, in a separate bowl, mix honey and seasonings together.

3. Once oil as melted, add walnuts to slow cooker and stir. Add honey and seasoning blend to slow cooker, and stir until evenly coated.

4. Cover and cook on high for 1 hour. Stir the nuts, recover, and cook for another hour.

5. Remove cover and cook an additional 20–30 minutes, until the nuts are dry. Cool and store in airtight containers.

PER SERVING: Calories: 214 | Fat: 19g | Protein: 5g | Sodium: 1mg | Fiber: 2g | Carbohydrates: 10g | Sugar: 7g

Bananas Foster

Not just good . . . Heavenly. Words just cannot describe the level of deliciousness this recipe creates.

INGREDIENTS | SERVES 3

3 overripe bananas
4 tablespoons coconut butter
⅓ cup honey
1 teaspoon vanilla extract

1. Place bananas into a plastic zip-top plastic bag, and mash.

2. Squeeze banana pulp into a 2-quart slow cooker. Add coconut butter, honey, and vanilla.

3. Cover and cook on low for 3–4 hours or on high for 1–2 hours.

PER SERVING: Calories: 224 | Fat: 0g | Protein: 1g | Sodium: 3mg | Fiber: 3g | Carbohydrates: 58g | Sugar: 46g

Vanilla Infused Fruit Cocktail

Try this recipe with a different fruit combination each time.

INGREDIENTS | SERVES 8

16 ounces prunes, pitted
8 ounces dried apricots
8 ounces dried pears
3 cups water
½ cup honey
2 tablespoons fresh lemon juice
1 teaspoon finely grated lemon zest
½ vanilla bean or ½ teaspoon vanilla

1. Combine all the ingredients together in a 4–6-quart slow cooker.

2. Cook on low for about 6–8 hours or until the fruit is tender.

3. Serve warm or at room temperature.

PER SERVING: Calories: 284 | Fat: 0g | Protein: 2g | Sodium: 9mg | Fiber: 7g | Carbohydrates: 75g | Sugar: 57g

Island-Inspired Fruit Crisp

An irresistible blend of tropical fruit and coconut flavors.

INGREDIENTS | SERVES 6

2 (21-ounce) cans apricot pie filling

1 (7-ounce) package tropical blend mixed dried fruit bits

1 cup crushed almonds and walnuts

⅓ cup toasted coconut

How to Toast Coconut

Spread coconut flakes in a shallow baking pan and bake in a preheated oven at 350°F for 5–10 minutes, or until golden brown. Watch closely to avoid burning, and shake the pan once or twice while cooking.

1. Lightly coat the inside of a 3½–4-quart slow cooker with nonstick cooking spray.

2. Combine the pie filling and dried fruit bits in slow cooker.

3. Cover and cook on low for 2½ hours. Remove liner from cooker, if possible, or turn off cooker.

4. In a small bowl combine the nuts and coconut. Sprinkle over fruit mixture in cooker.

5. Let stand, uncovered, for 30 minutes to cool slightly before serving.

6. To serve, spoon warm mixture into dessert dishes.

PER SERVING: Calories: 186 | Fat: 9g | Protein: 4g | Sodium: 7mg | Fiber: 5g | Carbohydrates: 25g | Sugar: 1g

Caveman "Choc" Pot

A Paleo-approved, delectable chocolate mousse-like dessert.

INGREDIENTS | SERVES 8

5 egg yolks
2 cups coconut milk
½ cup honey
1 tablespoon vanilla extract
¼ cup unsweetened cocoa powder

1. Place an oven-safe dish inside of a 6-quart slow cooker and add water around the dish, making a water bath. Fill water until it reaches the halfway point of the dish.

2. Whip egg yolks, coconut milk, honey, vanilla, and cocoa powder together and pour mixture into dish. Cook on high for 2–4 hours.

3. Unplug the slow cooker, let dish cool and remove from slow cooker. Keep in refrigerator for 2–3 hours before serving.

PER SERVING: Calories: 214 | Fat: 15g | Protein: 3g | Sodium: 13mg | Fiber: 0g | Carbohydrates: 20g | Sugar: 18g

Perfect Pear O' Sweetness

The attractive finished product makes for a great holiday dish.

INGREDIENTS | SERVES 8

8 firm ripe pears, peeled
½ cup sliced cranberries
¾ cup honey
¼ teaspoon ground ginger
¼ teaspoon ground cinnamon
⅛ teaspoon ground cloves
1 lemon, juiced
2 tablespoons lime juice

1. Stand the pears upright in a 6-quart slow cooker. Sprinkle on the cranberries.

2. In a separate bowl, combine the honey, ginger, cinnamon, and cloves, and spoon on top of the pears. Pour the lemon and lime juice evenly over the contents.

3. Cover and cook on low for 4 hours or on high for 2 hours.

PER SERVING: Calories: 219 | Fat: 0g | Protein: 1g | Sodium: 3mg | Fiber: 6g | Carbohydrates: 59g | Sugar: 47g

Paleo Poached Peaches with Raspberry and Vanilla

This can be made with either Marsala wine or sherry.

INGREDIENTS | SERVES 6

⅔ cup Marsala wine

⅔ cup water

⅓ cup honey

6 firm, ripe peaches, pitted and halved

1 vanilla bean, slit lengthwise

2 teaspoons arrowroot powder

1 cup raspberries

1. Pour the wine, water, and honey into a saucepan and bring to a boil.

2. Place the peach halves and vanilla bean into 4–6-quart slow cooker, and pour on hot syrup from saucepan.

3. Cover slow cooker and cook on low for 1–1½ hours or until hot and tender.

4. Remove peaches and vanilla bean. Scrape seeds from vanilla bean and return seeds back to cooking syrup in slow cooker.

5. Mix the arrowroot powder with about ½ teaspoon water to create a paste, and stir into syrup.

6. Cook on high for 15 minutes, stirring periodically. Pour thickened syrup over peaches, add the raspberries, and serve warm or chilled.

PER SERVING: Calories: 170 | Fat: 1g | Protein: 2g | Sodium: 4mg | Fiber: 4g | Carbohydrates: 36g | Sugar: 31

Chunky Apple-Cherry Sauce

Enjoy warm as a breakfast fruit, or chilled as a sweet summer treat.

INGREDIENTS | YIELDS 6 (½-CUP) SERVINGS

5 Golden Delicious apples, peeled, cored, and sliced

2 tablespoons water

¼ cup honey

½ cup cherry preserves

1. Place apple slices in a greased 4–6-quart slow cooker. Add water, honey, and toss to coat the apples. Cover and cook on low for 6–7 hours.

2. Stir in the cherry preserves.

3. Serve warm or allow to cool and serve chilled.

PER SERVING: (½ cup) | Calories: 118 | Fat: 0g | Protein: 0g | Sodium: 9mg | Fiber: 0g | Carbohydrates: 30g | Sugar: 25g

Pumpkin Pie Pudding

A flavorful, festive, and favorite holiday treat.

INGREDIENTS | SERVES 8

1 (15-ounce) can solid pack pumpkin, softened

1 (12-ounce) can coconut milk

¾ cup honey

½ cup almond meal

2 eggs, beaten

2 tablespoons coconut butter, melted

2 tablespoons honey

2 teapsoons pumpkin pie spice

1 teaspoon coconut extract

1. In a large bowl stir together pumpkin and ¼ cup of the coconut milk, stirring until well blended with the pumpkin.

2. Add remaining coconut milk and the remaining ingredients, and beat until blended.

3. Transfer to a 3–4-quart slow cooker, coated with nonstick cooking spray.

4. Cover and cook on low for 6–8 hours, until pudding is set when lightly touched with finger.

PER SERVING: Calories: 271 | Fat: 14g | Protein: 5g | Sodium: 27mg | Fiber: 2g | Carbohydrates: 38g | Sugar: 33g

Crustless Apple Pie

Adjust the cooking time depending on the type of apple you use.
A softer Golden Delicious should be cooked through and soft in the recommended
cooking times, but a crisper Granny Smith apple may take longer.

INGREDIENTS | SERVES 8

Nonstick spray

8 medium apples, washed, cored and sliced

3 tablespoons freshly squeezed orange juice

3 tablespoons water

½ cup pecans, chopped

⅓ cup honey

¼ cup coconut butter, melted

½ teaspoon cinnamon

1. Treat the slow cooker with nonstick spray. Arrange apple slices over the bottom of the slow cooker.

2. Add the orange juice and water to a small bowl or measuring cup; stir to mix. Evenly drizzle over the apples.

3. In a small bowl, add the pecans, honey, coconut butter, and cinnamon, and mix well. Evenly crumble the pecan mixture over the apples.

4. Cover and cook on high for 2 hours or on low for 4 hours. Serve warm, or chilled, if desired.

PER SERVING: Calories: 171 | Fat: 5g | Protein: 1g | Sodium: 1mg | Fiber: 3g | Carbohydrates: 34g | Sugar: 29g

Paleo "Butterscotch–Caramel" Glazed Nuts

These nuts taste even better when sprinkled over some Crustless Apple Pie.

INGREDIENTS | SERVES 32

4 cups raw almonds, pecan halves, or walnut halves

½ cup Paleo "Butterscotch-Caramel" Sauce (see Chapter 4)

1½ teaspoons cinnamon, optional

1. Add all the ingredients to a 1-quart slow cooker. Stir to coat the nuts. Cover and cook on low for 3 hours, stirring at least once an hour.

2. Uncover and, stirring the mixture every 20 minutes, cook on low for 1 more hour, or until the nuts are almost dry.

3. Evenly spread the nuts on a lined baking sheet until completely cooled. Store in a covered container.

PER SERVING: Calories: 79 | Fat: 6g | Protein: 3g | Sodium: 0mg | Fiber: 2g | Carbohydrates: 5g | Sugar: 3g

Cinnamon-Spiced Apple Butter

If you're using a less tart apple, add the honey ¼ cup at a time, until you reach desired sweetness. Serve over a slow cooked dessert or breakfast dish.

INGREDIENTS | YIELDS 6 (½-CUP) SERVINGS

8 large or 12 medium Granny Smith apples
½ cup apple juice
¾ cup honey
2 teaspoons ground cinnamon
½ teaspoon allspice
½ teaspoon ground cloves

1. Wash, peel, core, and quarter the apples. Add to a 2-quart slow cooker along with the juice. Cover and cook on high for 4 hours.

2. Use an immersion blender to purée the apples. Stir in the honey, cinnamon, allspice, and cloves. Taste for seasoning and adjust if necessary.

3. Reduce the temperature of the slow cooker to low. Cook uncovered for 2 hours or until the apple butter is thick and dark. Store in the refrigerator for several weeks or freeze until needed.

PER SERVING: (½ cup) | Calories: 141 | Fat: 0g | Protein: 0g | Sodium: 3mg | Fiber: 1g | Carbohydrates: 38g | Sugar: 37g

Winter Warmer

Escape the bitter cold and warm up with this hot, comforting drink.

INGREDIENTS | SERVES 6

1 small cinnamon stick, broken into 1 inch pieces
¼ teaspoon ground cloves
¼ teaspoon nutmeg
¼ cup lemon juice
⅔ cup honey
1 bottle dry red wine
Thin lemon slices, for garnish

1. Combine all the ingredients, except the lemon slices, in a 2-quart slow cooker.

2. Heat on high for 1 hour, or until hot, then reduce to low to hold temperature for serving.

3. Ladle into cocktail glasses and top each serving with a lemon slice.

PER SERVING: Calories: 217 | Fat: 0g | Protein: 0g | Sodium: 9mg | Fiber: 0g | Carbohydrates: 35g | Sugar: 32g

Orange Pudding Cake

Creamsicle and Orange Julius fans will love this dessert. It also works well with lemon juice and lemon zest instead of the orange. The beaten egg whites act as the leavening; the pudding forms on the bottom as the cake cooks.

INGREDIENTS | SERVES 6

4 large eggs, separated
⅓ cup fresh orange juice
1 tablespoon orange zest, grated
3 tablespoons coconut butter, softened
1½ cups coconut milk
1 cup almond flour
1 cup honey

1. Add the egg yolks, orange juice, orange zest, and coconut butter to a food processor; process for 30 seconds to cream the ingredients together. Continue to process while you slowly pour in the coconut milk.

2. In a medium bowl, combine the almond flour and honey. Stir to mix.

3. Pour the egg yolk mixture into the bowl and stir to combine it.

4. Add the egg whites to a separate chilled bowl; whip until stiff peaks form. Fold into the cake batter.

5. Pour into a greased (with nonstick spray) 2-quart or smaller slow cooker. Cover and cook on low for 2–2½ hours or until the cake is set on top.

PER SERVING: Calories: 445 | Fat: 25g | Protein: 10g | Sodium: 57mg | Fiber: 2g | Carbohydrates: 54g | Sugar: 49g

Lemon Pudding Pie

Try this recipe with a Paleo-approved "crumb" topping.

INGREDIENTS | SERVES 6

¾ cup honey
¼ cup arrowroot powder
3 eggs, whisked
1 cup coconut milk
¼ cup lemon juice
1 teaspoon vanilla extract

1. Coat a 4-quart slow cooker with cooking spray.

2. In a small bowl, stir the honey and arrowroot powder together.

3. In a separate bowl, stir the eggs, coconut milk, lemon juice, and vanilla.

4. Combine the 2 mixtures and stir to form batter. Pour into slow cooker, cover, and cook on high for 2–4 hours, until the center has set and browned.

5. Let sit for 20 minutes before serving.

PER SERVING: Calories: 262 | Fat: 11g | Protein: 4g | Sodium: 44mg | Fiber: 0g | Carbohydrates: 42g | Sugar: 35g

Apple-Date "Crisp"

Golden Delicious apples are suggested here, but go ahead and try a different type of baking apple of your choice.

INGREDIENTS | SERVES 6

6 cups peeled and thinly sliced Golden Delicious apples

2 teaspoons lemon juice

⅓ cup chopped dates

1⅓ cups finely chopped almonds

½ cup almond flour

½ cup honey

½ teaspoon ground cinnamon

½ teaspoon ground ginger

Dash of ground nutmeg

Dash of ground cloves

4 tablespoons coconut butter

1. Combine apples, lemon juice, and dates in a bowl, and mix well. Transfer mixture to a 4½-quart slow cooker.

2. In a separate bowl, combine the almonds, flour, honey, cinnamon, ginger, nutmeg, and cloves. Cut in coconut butter with 2 knives or a pastry blender. Sprinkle nut mixture over apples and smooth down.

3. Cook on low for 4 hours. Serve warm.

PER SERVING: Calories: 290 | Fat: 15g | Protein: 7g | Sodium: 2mg | Fiber: 5g | Carbohydrates: 38g | Sugar: 31g

Paleo Crisp Variations

Experiment with a variety of Paleo-approved crisp ingredients like walnuts and pecans. Try using coconut or canola oil, or a combination of the two, instead of coconut butter.

Toasted Hazelnuts and Dates

Hazelnuts should be toasted on a baking sheet in a preheated, 350°F oven for 8–10 minutes before using.

INGREDIENTS | SERVES 8

2 cups pitted dates, soaked in water overnight

⅔ cup boiling water

½ cup honey

Strips of peel from 1 lemon (yellow part only)

¼ cup hazelnuts, shelled and toasted

1. Drain the dates and place in a 4½-quart slow cooker.

2. Add boiling water, honey, and lemon peel. Cover and cook on high for 3 hours.

3. Discard lemon peel. Place dates in serving dishes and sprinkle with hazelnuts.

PER SERVING: Calories: 212 | Fat: 2g | Protein: 2g | Sodium: 2mg | Fiber: 4g | Carbohydrates: 51g | Sugar: 46g

Peach Cobbler

Cobbler is a versatile sweet dish that can be enjoyed as a warm and tasty eye opener or as a post dinner dessert.

INGREDIENTS | SERVES 8

2 (16-ounce) packages frozen peaches, thawed and drained

¾ cup plus 1 tablespoon honey, divided

2 teaspoons ground cinnamon, divided

½ teaspoon ground nutmeg

¾ cup almond flour

6 tablespoons coconut butter

1. Combine the peaches, ¾ cup honey, 1½ teaspoons cinnamon, and the nutmeg in a bowl. Transfer to a 4½-quart slow cooker.

2. In a separate bowl, combine the flour with remaining honey, and remaining cinnamon.

3. Cut in coconut butter with 2 knives or a pasty blender, and then spread mixture over peaches.

4. Cover and cook on high for 2 hours.

5. Serve warm.

PER SERVING: Calories: 211 | Fat: 6g | Protein: 3g | Sodium: 1mg | Fiber: 3g | Carbohydrates: 42g | Sugar: 38g

Paleo "Yes" and "No" Foods

In order to ensure your success on the Paleolithic diet, you need to stock your pantry with fresh, organic produce and grass-fed and barn-roaming meats. Feel free to experiment with items you would not normally choose. That will spice things up and keep you interested in the diet. Also listed here are the foods you should avoid, including processed grains, potatoes, legumes, and dairy.

Paleo "Yes" Foods

Protein

- Alligator
- Bass
- Bear
- Beef, lean and trimmed
- Bison
- Bluefish
- Caribou
- Chicken breast
- Chuck steak
- Clams
- Cod
- Crab
- Crayfish
- Egg whites
- Eggs
- Flank steak
- Game hen breasts
- Goat
- Grouper
- Haddock
- Halibut
- Hamburger, extra lean
- Herring
- Liver (beef, lamb, goat, or chicken)
- Lobster
- London broil
- Mackerel
- Marrow (beef, lamb, or goat)
- Mussels
- Orange roughy
- Ostrich
- Oysters
- Pheasant
- Pork chops
- Pork loin
- Pork, lean
- Quail
- Rabbit
- Rattlesnake
- Red snapper
- Salmon, wild-caught
- Scallops
- Scrod
- Shrimp
- Tilapia
- Tongue (beef, lamb, or goat)
- Trout
- Tuna, canned, unsalted
- Tuna, fresh
- Turkey breast
- Veal, lean
- Venison

Leafy Vegetables

- Arugula
- Beet greens
- Bitterleaf
- Bok choy
- Broccoli rabe
- Brussels sprouts
- Cabbage
- Celery
- Chard
- Chicory
- Chinese cabbage
- Collard greens
- Dandelion
- Endive

- Fiddlehead
- Kale
- Lettuce
- Radicchio
- Spinach
- Swiss chard
- Turnip
- Watercress
- Yarrow

Fruiting Vegetables

- Avocado
- Bell pepper
- Cucumber
- Eggplant
- Squash
- Sweet pepper
- Tomatillo
- Tomato
- Zucchini

Flowers and Flower Buds

- Artichoke
- Broccoli
- Cauliflower

Bulb and Stem Vegetables

- Asparagus
- Celery
- Florence fennel
- Garlic
- Kohlrabi
- Leek
- Onion

Sea Vegetables and Herbs of All Types

Fruits

- Apple
- Apricot
- Banana
- Blackberries
- Blueberries
- Cantaloupe
- Cherries
- Coconut
- Cranberries (not dried)
- Figs
- Grapefruit
- Grapes
- Guava
- Honeydew melon
- Kiwi
- Lemon
- Lime
- Mandarin orange
- Mango
- Nectarine
- Orange
- Papaya
- Passion fruit
- Peaches
- Pears
- Persimmon
- Pineapple
- Plums
- Pomegranate
- Raspberries
- Rhubarb

- Star fruit
- Strawberries
- Tangerine
- Watermelon
- All other fruits are acceptable

Fats, Nuts, Seeds, Oils, and Fatty Proteins

- Almond butter
- Almonds
- Avocado
- Brazil nuts
- Canola oil
- Cashew
- Cashew butter
- Chestnuts
- Coconut oil
- Flaxseed oil
- Hazelnuts/filberts
- Macadamia butter
- Macadamia nuts
- Olive oil
- Pecans
- Pine nuts
- Pistachios
- Pumpkin seeds
- Safflower oil
- Sesame seeds
- Sunflower butter, unsweetened
- Sunflower seeds
- Udo's oil
- Walnut oil
- Walnuts

Paleo "No" Foods

Legume Vegetables

- American groundnut
- Azuki beans
- Black-eyed peas
- Chickpeas (garbanzo bean)
- Common beans
- Fava beans
- Green beans
- Guar
- Indian peas
- Kidney beans
- Lentils
- Lima beans
- Mung beans
- Navy beans
- Okra
- Peanut
- Peanut butter
- Peas
- Pigeon peas
- Pinto beans
- Red beans
- Rice beans
- Snow peas
- Soybean and soy products
- String beans
- Sugar snap peas
- White beans

Dairy Foods

- All processed foods made with any dairy products
- Butter

- Cheese
- Cream
- Dairy spreads
- Frozen yogurt
- Ice cream
- Ice milk
- Low-fat milk
- Nonfat dairy creamer
- Powdered milk
- Skim milk
- Whole milk
- Yogurt

Cereal Grains

- Barley
- Corn
- Millet
- Oats
- Rice
- Rye
- Sorghum
- Wheat
- Wild rice

Cereal Grain-Like Seeds

- Amaranth
- Buckwheat
- Quinoa

Starchy Vegetables

- Starchy tubers
- Cassava root
- Manioc
- Potatoes and all potato products

- Sweet potatoes or yams (unless after workout to replenish gylcogen)
- Tapioca pudding

Salt-Containing Foods, Fatty Meats, and Sugar

- Almost all commercial salad dressings and condiments
- Bacon
- Beef ribs
- Candy
- Canned salted meat or fish
- Chicken and turkey legs, thighs, and wings
- Chicken and turkey skin
- Deli meats
- Fatty ground beef
- Fatty pork cuts
- Frankfurters
- Ham
- Ketchup
- Lamb roast
- Olives
- Pickled foods
- Pork rinds
- Processed meats
- Salami
- Salt
- Salted nuts
- Salted spices
- Sausages
- Smoked, dried, and salted fish and meat
- Soft drinks and fruit juice
- Sugar

Paleo Athlete Modifications

Pre-Exercise Fuel: At least two hours before exercise or competition

Goals
- Consume low fiber and low glycemic index carbohydrates
- Include protein
- Hydrate

Examples: fruit (lower in fiber), i.e. applesauce, homemade smoothies (with fruit, small amount of fruit juice, and a few tablespoons of protein powder), sports bars (low in fiber and fat)

During Exercise Fuel: Per hour of exercise

Goals
- Consume higher glycemic index carbohydrates, approximately 60 grams per hour
- Prevent dehydration

Examples: Sports drinks are best during training and competition, especially in hot and humid climates.

Post-Exercise Fuel: Within thirty minutes, and until ninety minutes after

Goals
- Replace carbohydrate stores (a.k.a. muscle glycogen)
- Promote muscle repair and recover (protein)
- Rehydrate (fluid and electrolytes)

Examples: liquid carbohydrates (i.e. sports drinks with protein); protein drink/homemade smoothies; non-Paleo foods are encouraged here (sports drinks; jelly; fruit juices; starchy vegetables) along with lean proteins (chicken, turkey, tuna, etc.)

Adapted from *The Paleo Diet for Athletes*. © 2005. Loren Cordain, PhD and Joe Friel, MS.

Paleo Substitutions

INGREDIENT	PALEO SUBSTITUTIONS
cow's milk	coconut, almond, macadamia, or hazelnut milk
bacon	uncured bacon and meats
deli meat	fresh cut chicken or turkey breast, thinly sliced
salad dressing	oil and lemon or lime juice
vinegar	lemon or lime juice
starch	spaghetti squash, butternut squash, acorn squash
sugar	raw honey
soda	fruit-infused water, iced tea
salt	lemon juice, spices, fresh herbs
butter	nut oils, coconut butter
peanut butter	all other nut and seed butters
cookies	fresh fruit
chocolate	cacao
commercially prepared meat	grass-fed, barn-roaming meat
farm raised fish	wild-caught fish
baked desserts	baked fruit
wheat flour	almond flour
breadcrumbs	arrowroot powder
cream	full-fat coconut milk or coconut butter

Standard U.S./Metric Measurement Conversions

VOLUME CONVERSIONS

U.S. Volume Measure	Metric Equivalent
⅛ teaspoon	0.5 milliliters
¼ teaspoon	1 milliliters
½ teaspoon	2 milliliters
1 teaspoon	5 milliliters
½ tablespoon	7 milliliters
1 tablespoon (3 teaspoons)	15 milliliters
2 tablespoons (1 fluid ounce)	30 milliliters
¼ cup (4 tablespoons)	60 milliliters
⅓ cup	90 milliliters
½ cup (4 fluid ounces)	125 milliliters
⅔ cup	160 milliliters
¾ cup (6 fluid ounces)	180 milliliters
1 cup (16 tablespoons)	250 milliliters
1 pint (2 cups)	500 milliliters
1 quart (4 cups)	1 liter (about)

WEIGHT CONVERSIONS

U.S. Weight Measure	Metric Equivalent
½ ounce	15 grams
1 ounce	30 grams
2 ounces	60 grams
3 ounces	85 grams
¼ pound (4 ounces)	115 grams
½ pound (8 ounces)	225 grams
¾ pound (12 ounces)	340 grams
1 pound (16 ounces)	454 grams

OVEN TEMPERATURE CONVERSIONS

Degrees Fahrenheit	Degrees Celsius
200 degrees F	95 degrees C
250 degrees F	120 degrees C
275 degrees F	135 degrees C
300 degrees F	150 degrees C
325 degrees F	160 degrees C
350 degrees F	180 degrees C
375 degrees F	190 degrees C
400 degrees F	205 degrees C
425 degrees F	220 degrees C
450 degrees F	230 degrees C

BAKING PAN SIZES

American	Metric
8 × 1½ inch round baking pan	20 × 4 cm cake tin
9 × 1½ inch round baking pan	23 × 3.5 cm cake tin
1 × 7 × 1½ inch baking pan	28 × 18 × 4 cm baking tin
13 × 9 × 2 inch baking pan	30 × 20 × 5 cm baking tin
2 quart rectangular baking dish	30 × 20 × 3 cm baking tin
15 × 10 × 2 inch baking pan	30 × 25 × 2 cm baking tin (Swiss roll tin)
9 inch pie plate	22 × 4 or 23 × 4 cm pie plate
7 or 8 inch springform pan	18 or 20 cm springform or loose bottom cake tin
9 × 5 × 3 inch loaf pan	23 × 13 × 7 cm or 2 lb narrow loaf or pate tin
1½ quart casserole	1.5 litre casserole
2 quart casserole	2 litre casserole

Index

We Have

EVERYTHING

on Anything!

John C. Hart Mem Lib (Shrub Oak)

3 1030 15337994 6

With more than 19 million copies sold, the Everything® series has become one of America's favorite resources for solving problems, learning new skills, and organizing lives. Our brand is not only recognizable—it's also welcomed.

The series is a hand-in-hand partner for people who are ready to tackle new subjects—like you!

For more information on the Everything® series, please visit *www.adamsmedia.com*

The Everything® list spans a wide range of subjects, with more than 500 titles covering 25 different categories:

Business	History	Reference
Careers	Home Improvement	Religion
Children's Storybooks	Everything Kids	Self-Help
Computers	Languages	Sports & Fitness
Cooking	Music	Travel
Crafts and Hobbies	New Age	Wedding
Education/Schools	Parenting	Writing
Games and Puzzles	Personal Finance	
Health	Pets	

RECEIVED JAN 2 5 2013

Team Members Receive Special Preference

To our members the ASA means more than certification and Vessel Assist educational excellence. It's smart business! When you join the ASA, you become a member of America's strongest and fastest growing team. Check out these membership benefits!

Each issue is packed with news and information for active sailors who need to know. Articles on navigation, cruising, learning to sail and stories about real people and their adventures make American Sailing one of the premiere journals of its kind. Only ASA members can get American Sailing; don't look for it in stores.

 **Marine Insurance Discounts**

Boat owners can save a bundle with ASA membership. Save at least 5% over regular, quoted rates. With today's insurance costs that can really add up!

Rental, Charter and Instruction Discounts
Present the ASA membership card at selected charter companies and sailing schools throughout the United States and you sail at a preferred rate. Worldwide charter companies including The Moorings and Stardust Marine honor the ASA card for charter and travel discounts

ASA Travel Service!
Unbelievable 10% rebate on all airline tickets. Hundreds of hotels throughout the United States offer ASA members discounts up to 50%. These aren't second rate hotels and you will certainly recognize Hilton, Radisson and Ramada to name a few.

ASA Gold Mastercard
Put your name under the ASA logo on a gold Mastercard that offers a competitive interest rate, no annual fee the first year and up to $15,000 credit limit. A portion of each purchase also goes to the ASA charitable educational fund.

Vessel Assist

The Boat Owner's Auto Club you cannot afford not to belong to!

FREE ONE YEAR MEMBERSHIP in Vessel Assist is available to all ASA members. An Associate Membership in VA entitles you to:

- Group rate insurance program
- Free towing, free jump starts and free delivery of necessary parts, fuel, etc.
- 24 hour toll free dispatch and claims center
- Coverage worldwide on any boat you own or legally charter
- Immediate and reliable member response
- Fully insured U.S. Coast Guard licensed professional
- Ungrounding when soft aground, on-scene service
- First Alert Cruise Log Float Plan Service
- Special discounted rates for services at a home berth non-emergency service and savings on fuel, parts, etc. from marine vendors

Free One year subscription to SAIL Magazine, America's most popular sailing magazine.

Discounts on Books! Videos! Sailing Gear!

PLUS LOTS MORE!
Join the Team!

- ❏ $39 one-year individual
- ❏ $55 two-year individual
- ❏ $20 additional family member, per year
- ❏ $75 one-year family (list additional members)
- ❏ $99 two-year family (list additional members)
- ❏ $300 individual lifetime membership
- ❏ $500 family lifetime membership (list additional members)

Name _____

Street Address _____

City _____ State ____ Zip _____

❏ Check or M.O. ❏ Mastercar ❏ Visa ❏ Amex

Card # _____ Expires _____

Signature _____

You and the ASA
A continuing relationship

An ASA school doesn't just teach people how to sail. It teaches them how to sail better; to become more competent and confident in their abilities. A broad curriculum of courses allows you to continue seeking new challenges ... reaching for new heights. We'll teach you how to cruise coastal waters; how to skipper your own charter boat; how to navigate with electronics and by the stars; how to set off across oceans. You can learn it all or any single aspect of sailing which interests you. Experienced sailors are welcome too and can receive internationally recognized credentials through successfully completing the appropriate examination. With an ASA school, you are assured of professional training and the best value for your sail education dollar.

The ASA Progression

The ASA curriculum is composed of seven levels, from basic sailing to ocean passagemaking. Certification at any of these levels opens the door to an expanded world of sailing opportunity. Your ASA Log Book outlines in detail the Standards and Certification requirements for all levels of training. Below is a brief description of the various levels.

1. ASA BASIC SAILING-Daysail a boat up to approx. 26 feet in moderate wind and sea without supervision. No previous navigation or sailing skills required.

2. BASIC COASTAL CRUISING-Skipper or crew aboard a 20 to 30-foot auxiliary sailboat in moderate winds and sea. ASA Basic Sailing certification required. Basic Sailing and Basic Coastal Cruising courses can be taken simultaneously.

3. BAREBOAT CHARTERING-Skipper or crew a 30 to 50-foot auxiliary sailboat by day in coastal waters. Boat systems and maintenance included. Basic Coastal Cruising Certification required.

4. COASTAL NAVIGATION-Navigational theory required to safely navigate a sailboat in coastal or inland waters. Meets Advanced Coastal Cruising Standard. No previous certification required.

5. ADVANCED COASTAL CRUISING–Skipper or crew a 30 to 50-foot auxiliary sailboat, day or night, in coastal waters, in any weather. Certification in Basic Coastal Cruising and Coastal Navigation required.

6. CELESTIAL NAVIGATION-Celestial navigation theory required to safely navigate a vessel on an offshore passage. Meets Offshore Standard. No previous certification required.

7. OFFSHORE-Skipper or crew a 30 to 50-foot auxiliary sailboat, day or night, offshore, in any weather. Certification in Advanced Coastal Cruising and Celestial Navigation required.

EXPERIENCED SAILORS TAKE NOTE ... You need not enroll in a course of instruction to receive Certification-credentials will be awarded upon successful completion of the appropriate examination taken at an ASA sailing school. Challenge the Standards and receive the credentials you deserve to back up your experience!

220 • SAILING FUNDAMENTALS

ACKNOWLEDGMENTS

My many thanks for help of every kind to

Hunter Yachts
Karina Paape
Marti Betz
Kathy Thompson
Janice Jobson
Lenny Shabes
Peter Isler
Fred Hills
Charles E. Kanter
Mark Robinson
Hank Bernbaum
Daniel Maxim
John Van Osdol
Julia Garver

Clyde Hungerford
Dudley Overton
John Peterson
Erik Macklin
Cynthia Shabes
Carole Bright
Evelyn DeChantillon
Kathy Christensen
Greg Hillman
Flor Restrepo
Harry Munns
Joan Gilmore
Charlie Nobles
Robert McCreary

Welcome to the EVERYTHING Series!

These handy, accessible books give you all you need to tackle a difficult project, gain a new hobby, comprehend a fascinating topic, prepare for an exam, or even brush up on something you learned back in school but have since forgotten.

You can choose to read an Everything® book from cover to cover or just pick out the information you want from our four useful boxes: e-questions, e-facts, e-alerts, and e-ssentials.

We give you everything you need to know on the subject, but throw in a lot of fun stuff along the way, too.

We now have more than 400 Everything® books in print, spanning such wide-ranging categories as weddings, pregnancy, cooking, music instruction, foreign language, crafts, pets, New Age, and so much more. When you're done reading them all, you can finally say you know Everything®!

QUESTION

Answers to common questions

FACT

Important snippets of information

ALERT

Urgent warnings

ESSENTIAL

Quick handy tips

PUBLISHER Karen Cooper

MANAGING EDITOR, EVERYTHING® SERIES Lisa Laing

COPY CHIEF Casey Ebert

ASSOCIATE PRODUCTION EDITOR Mary Beth Dolan

ACQUISITIONS EDITOR Lisa Laing

SENIOR DEVELOPMENT EDITOR Brett Palana-Shanahan

EVERYTHING® SERIES COVER DESIGNER Erin Alexander

Visit the entire Everything® series at *www.everything.com*

W9-BUG-470

THE

EVERYTHING

PALEOLITHIC DIET
SLOW COOKER COOKBOOK

Dear Reader,

This book will help you overcome the barriers of adhering to the very popular and healthy, but sometimes not-so-easy-to-follow, Paleolithic diet. Many people find it difficult to fully immerse themselves in this fairly strict lifestyle. However, by incorporating the use of a slow cooker into your daily routine (for far more than just dinner entrées), you will find the Paleo way of eating simpler, more palatable, and more enjoyable than you ever thought possible!

The Paleolithic diet, often referred to as the Caveman diet, consists solely of foods consumed during the Paleolithic era, which concluded roughly 10,000 years ago. Obviously there was no technology back then, and therefore no packaged, processed, or genetically enhanced foods. No wonder there was no evidence of any unhealthy, overweight, disease-stricken cavemen! Leading a Paleolithic lifestyle—consuming only natural, preservative-free, fresh foods (or even modified versions of them)—can help you obtain positive health benefits, hence its popularity. Some of these benefits include: an improved health and wellness profile, a decreased risk of chronic disease due to the diet's high antioxidant content, and more energy to live, work, and play!

Cheers,

Emily Dionne

Pump Jacks. These movable platform supports are raised and lowered to suit the task. When you pump the lever with your foot they ride up and down a pair of doubled 2x4s. You can add accessory brackets to make a handy elevated workbench. Pump jacks also operate as freight elevators for raising large or heavy objects.

Pump Jacks. This affordable type of scaffolding rides on doubled 2x4s set vertically.

Roofing Materials

Composition Shingles

Composition shingles are relatively simple to apply, last 15 to 20 years, and come in a wide variety of colors, profiles and textures. These shingles, which are by far the most common roofing material in North America, are made with felt, wood fiber, or most typically these days, fiberglass mat impregnated with asphalt and coated with mineral granules. Most shingles have adhesive beneath the tabs to keep them from curling or blowing back. They are flexible and therefore adaptable, and can wrap almost all roof shapes and contours. They also suit every climate in North America.

Shingles can be applied to any roof that has a slope of 4 in 12 (4 inches of vertical rise for every 12 inches of horizontal run) or more. With double felt underlayment, they can be applied to a roof with a slope as low as 2 in 12 if shingle tabs are sealed down.

Often composition shingles are applied over an old roof of the same type. Three layers can be built up before all must be torn off (more than three layers are permissible only if the framing can bear the weight, and nails must be long enough to penetrate at least ¾ inch into the decking). If a tear-off is required, repair sheathing and remove all loose or protruding nails. Staples are used on new roofs and on roofs that have been stripped of old roofing.

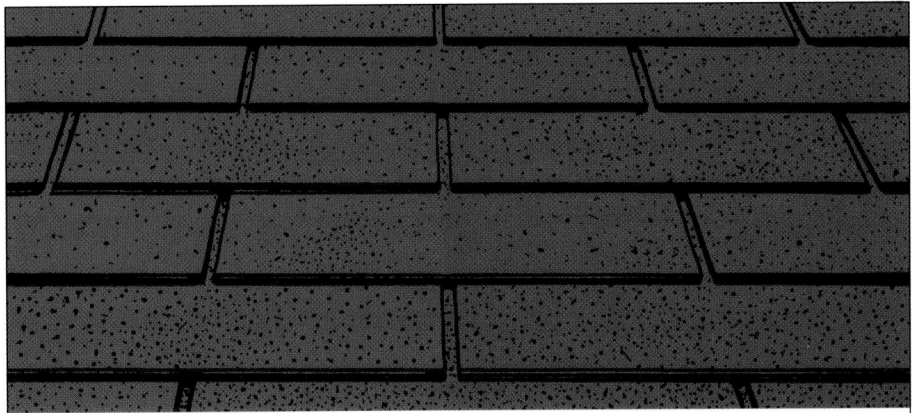

Composition Shingles. By far the most common roofing material in North America, composition shingles are relatively simple to apply, last 15 to 20 years, and are available in a wide variety of colors, profiles, and textures.

Types of Shingles

There are many styles of composition shingles. You can purchase them with three tabs that suggest three slate or wooden shingles, with two tabs, or strip shingles with no tabs. Also available are multi-layered textured shingles designed to look like wood shakes.

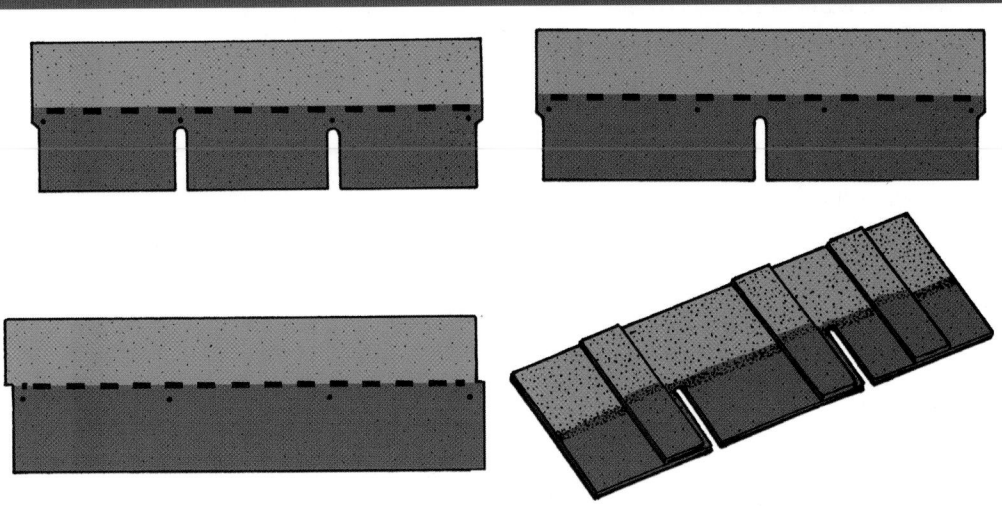

Roll Roofing

Ideal for porches with shallow slopes, garages, and utility buildings, roll roofing is quick and easy to apply. It is the least expensive option for roofs that have a very slight pitch. Roll roofing is not as attractive as composite shingles, but roofs with very shallow pitches are not visible from the ground anyway. One type of roll roofing, sometimes called selvage, is designed to be applied with a half-lap to provide double coverage. Selvage can be used with slopes as low as 1 in 12 (1 inch rise per 12 inches of run). Roll roofing is 36 inches wide and is available in a variety of colors. It can be applied with nails revealed (on slopes of 2 in 12 or more) or with nails covered by the roofing (on more shallow slopes).

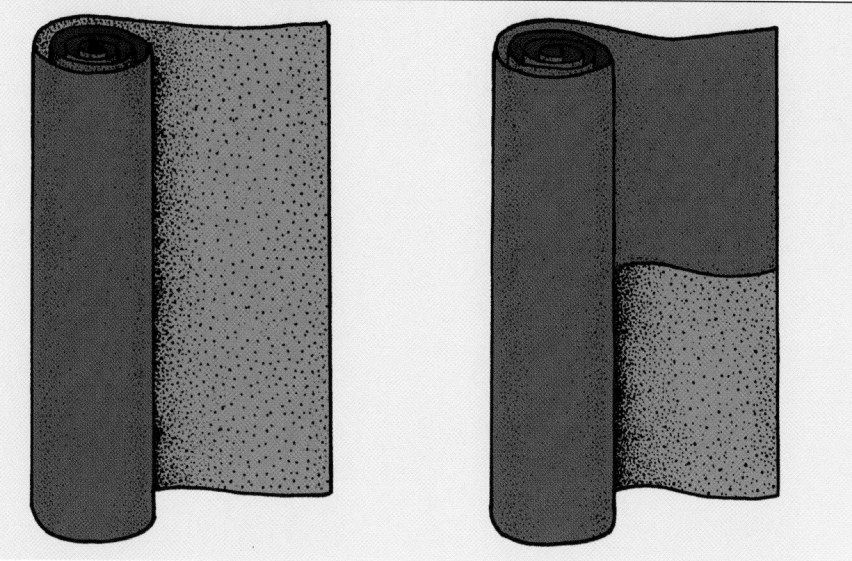

Roll Roofing. Roll roofing is 36 in. wide and comes in two types. One type has mineral granules covering the entire face and is applied with courses overlapping only 2 in. The other type, sometimes called selvage, has granules on only half its face. Roofing cement or hot asphalt is applied to the non-granule side, which is then covered with the next course of roofing. This double coverage roofing is for very slight pitches.

Wood Shingles & Shakes

Among the most beautiful roofing materials are red cedar shingles and shakes. They have twice the insulation value of asphalt shingles, are lighter in weight than most other roofing materials, and are very resistant to hail damage. They also are well-suited to withstand the freeze-thaw conditions of variable climates. Wood shingles are machine cut and smoothed on both sides, while shakes are thicker and rough on at least one side. Pressure-injected fire retardant, as indicated by the industry designation "Certi-Guard," conforms to all state and local building codes for use in fire hazard regions. Given periodic coatings of wood preservative, shingles and shakes serve for 50 years or more. The drawbacks of using them include their high cost and slow application time.

Shakes differ from wood shingles in that they are split on one face and machine smoothed on the other. They vary in thickness and have a rustic, varied appearance. Because the rough surface of the split face sometimes allows water back under the shakes, a layer of underlayment (asphalt-saturated felt or fiberglass) is used between each course.

Both shingles and shakes require 1x4 sheathing spaced to suit the desired exposure. Along the roof rake and roof eaves 1x6 sheathing supports underlayment and seals the roof.

Wood Shingles and Shakes. Although quite simple, the installation of wood shingles and shakes is a time-consuming job.

Wood Fiber Shingle Panels. A relatively new product, these panels install quickly and weather to a shingle-like gray.

Slate. One of the oldest roofing materials, slate is beautiful, long lasting and very expensive.

Wood Fiber Shingle Panels.

Another wood shingle option that is suitable for roofs with a 4 in 12 slope is hardboard shingle panels. With scored nailing and alignment lines to ease application, these shingles are installed in half the time it takes to apply cedar shakes. The panels do not crack with age and weather to a light gray. Shingle panels are 12x48 inches.

Slate

Fireproof and extremely durable as well as beautiful, slate is among the oldest roofing material. Today it is also among the most expensive. In addition it requires special framing (designed to bear a heavier weight) and special furring. Difficult to cut and apply, slate roofing is definitely a job left to the professionals.

Synthetic Slate. Made of cement-impregnated non-asbestos fiber, synthetic slate looks like the real thing but weighs a lot less. Synthetic slate does not contain combustible materials and therefore carries the highest fire rating (Class A) from Underwriters Laboratories. Some brands carry a warranty of 40 years. Synthetic slate is an expensive material. It typically is used on homes where historically appropriate

Synthetic Slate. Cement-impregnated fiber creates a long-lasting imitation of the real thing.

materials are required. The material is difficult to cut and must be nailed carefully to avoid cracking the shingles. This is another job for experienced professionals.

Built-Up Roofing

Built-up roofing is suitable only for flat roofs and roofs with very slight pitches. For this reason it is used on many contemporary, flat-roofed homes and on slightly pitched porch roofs. Because it requires hot asphalt,

a contractor must handle this job and the roof must have a minimum slope of ¼ inch per foot (no roof can have a slope of less than this anyway).

The oldest type of built-up roofing consists of several alternating layers of hot asphalt and felt. The final layer of asphalt is topped with pea gravel.

An increasingly common form of built-up roofing employs a large sheet of modified bitumen membrane to improve protection for flat or slightly sloped roofs. There are two types: plasticized, also called atacitic polypropylene (APP), and rubberized, also called styrene-butadiene-styrene (SBS). These relatively new materials are less prone to damage caused by ultraviolet rays. They have a higher melting point and therefore are slower to soften in direct sunlight. They also are more stable than roll roofing or felt. Since the application of plasticized roofing involves heating the bottom of the material with a propane torch, a contractor is required for the job. Granules or foil are added as a final layer for ultraviolet protection.

One advantage to using rubberized roofing is its ability to stretch in extreme temperatures. It may be heat welded, or applied with hot asphalt or a cold adhesive. Both rubberized and plasticized roofing benefit from a layer of fiberglass membrane for additional strength.

Metal Roofing

Widely used on commercial buildings, metal roofing is increasingly marketed for residential use. Depending on slope and framing, metal roofing can be installed over old roofing. It costs as much as three times more than conventional roofing but can last from 20 to 50 years with almost no maintenance. Unlike the old galvanized tin roofs, metal roofing today is made of steel with an alloy coating of aluminum and zinc. A wide spectrum of colors are available.

Many different profiles are available but the simple standing seam style (with overlapping ridges that run parallel to the eaves) is the most appropriate for older homes that might have had a tin roof at one time. This material usually requires professional application, and while the popularity of metal roofing is quickly increasing, a network of qualified residential contractors is only slowly developing.

Clay and Concrete Tile

Clay tile roofs, often used in the West, Southwest, and parts of the South, can last as long as the house itself. New fiber-reinforced concrete tiles, both flat and traditional barrel-shaped are less costly, easier to install, more uniform in appearance, and have most of the attributes of traditional tile. Beyond replacing cracked or missing tiles, the do-it-yourselfer probably will want to hire a professional for this difficult job.

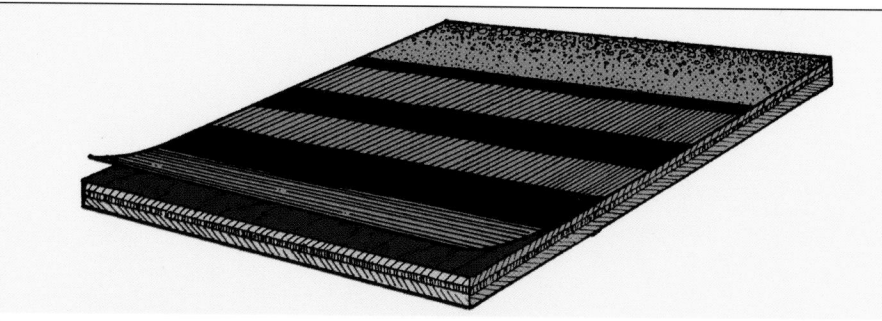

Built-Up Roofing. This material derives its name from the layers that combine to create a water-resistant surface. Pea gravel protects the roof from ultraviolet rays.

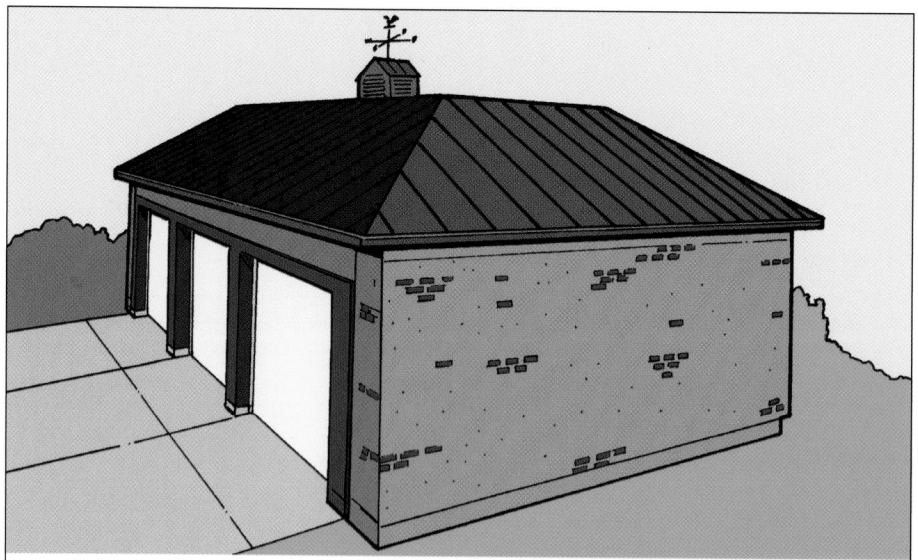

Metal Roofing. Metal roofing is making a comeback. With minimal maintenance it lasts up to 50 years.

Concrete Tile. Concrete tile roofs require special framing and expert installation. Repairs are within the skill of the do-it-yourselfer, but whole roof installation is still left to the professionals.

repairs

Tracing Roof Leaks

The best way to detect a leak is to locate dampness or a trail of discoloration in the attic. Do not, however, expect the leak to be directly above a damp ceiling or wall. Most likely the leaking water has traveled beneath the roofing material and down a rafter or truss member before appearing on the interior ceiling or wall.

The best way to find a leak is to examine the underside of the roof from the attic. If your attic does not have a floor be careful to step only on the floor joists (never step on the insulation between the joists). Better yet, set boards or a piece of ½-inch plywood perpendicular to the joists. Make sure the ends of the lumber extend far enough past each joist to prevent tipping.

With a powerful light source inspect the undersides of the sheathing in the general area where the stain has appeared. Sheathing is usually made up of plywood but yours may be made of shiplap planks. In the case of very old houses, you may find no roof sheathing, only lath nailed across the rafters with wooden or slate shingles nailed on top of the lath. Good sheathing or lath is uniformly aged and completely dry even after a rain. Check for dampness and discoloration and pay special attention to the places where the roof is penetrated by the chimney, air vent, or plumbing vent pipes. If sheathing is dark, damp, or crumbling, check for wood rot by probing with a screwdriver. Rotten wood must be replaced.

Water always runs in a downward direction so once you find dampness search for the source of the water's path above the moisture. Water may pool on flat surfaces, but it always finds its way downward, even if it runs along what appears to be a horizontal surface.

When the leak is discovered mark the area to be repaired. If you are going to make the repair immediately, pierce through the sheathing from underneath with a nail, extended drill bit, or awl. If not, measure from the attic wall framing and ridge or eaves. Allow for the thickness of the wall and the outward extension of the eaves when taking measurements.

Making Emergency Roof Repairs

Damage from fallen tree limbs, violent storms, and exceptional snow buildup is an unwelcome surprise. Here are some interior and exterior solutions to leaks.

Limiting the Damage. Limit the water damage as quickly as possible by placing a bucket as close to the leak as possible. Remove and discard soaked attic insulation. A string attached to the leak guides the water to the bucket.

Providing Protection. Cover large areas of damage with a fiber-reinforced plastic dropcloth. Place boards under the dropcloth to create a high spot that will carry water away from the damaged area.

Fixing a Shingle. To fix a broken or missing shingle in an emergency situation, slip a piece of scrap sheet metal or aluminum flashing under the damaged shingle. Tap it with a block of wood to force it under the course above.

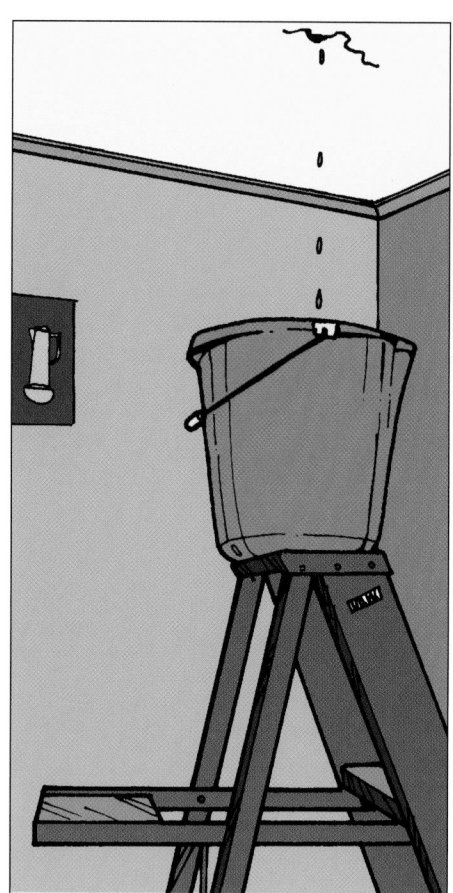

Limiting the Damage. Catch the water as soon as possible; mop up and remove any soaked materials.

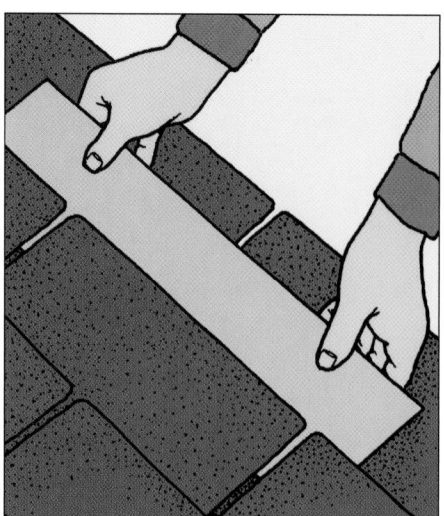

Fixing a Shingle. A simple piece of metal shoved under a shingle tab holds until a more permanent patch is made.

Providing Protection. Cover the leak if possible to prevent additional damage.

Locating Trouble Spots

If your roof has a leak check the trouble spots to determine where the leak originates. Trouble spots are those places well known for causing leaks. They include valleys, flashing along walls and around objects that penetrate the roof (such as chimneys, air vents, and plumbing stacks), rotting doors, gutters, eaves encrusted with ice, and popped nails. Keep in mind that almost all flat roofs eventually experience problems.

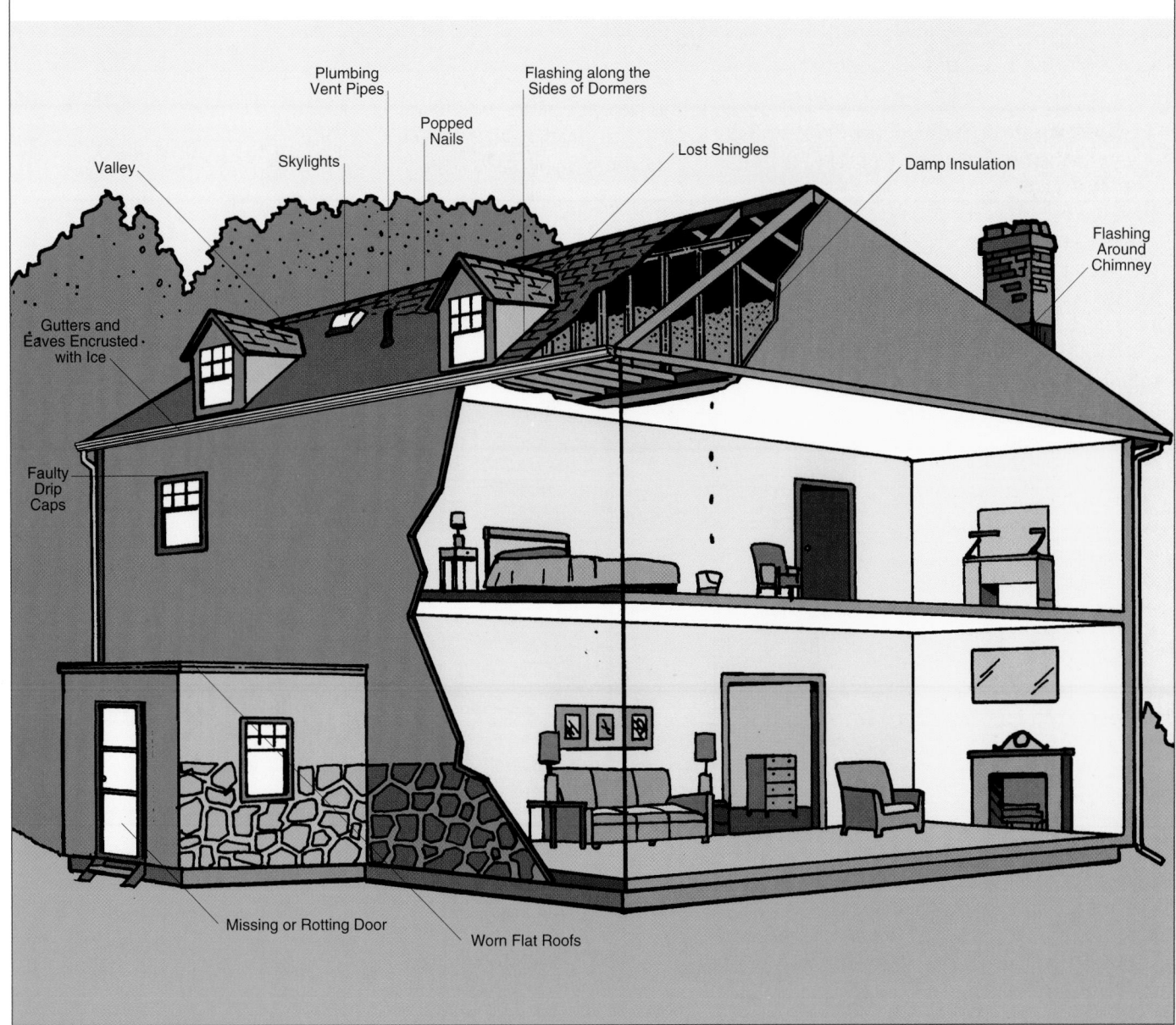

Valley · Gutters and Eaves Encrusted with Ice · Faulty Drip Caps · Plumbing Vent Pipes · Skylights · Popped Nails · Flashing along the Sides of Dormers · Lost Shingles · Damp Insulation · Flashing Around Chimney · Missing or Rotting Door · Worn Flat Roofs

Making Temporary Roof Repairs

Equipped with hammer, pry bar, galvanized roofing nails, roofing cement, and spare shingles, a do-it-yourselfer can quickly make repairs to protect the home temporarily. When dealing with shingles remember to tuck the topmost edge of new shingles or patches beneath the course above. This overlap sheds water in a downward direction.

To temporarily repair wind-torn shingles, glue down both sides of the tear with roofing cement. Nail both sides and apply cement over the heads of the nails. Applying a small amount of cement to the shank of the nail before hammering it home creates an especially good seal. In a similar fashion, curled shingles are glued down with roofing cement. This is best done on a hot day when the shingles are warm and supple. Nail them if necessary, coating the nail shanks and heads with roofing cement.

Repairing Blisters on Built-Up Roofs

With time, blisters may appear on built-up roofs. This occurs because moisture that is trapped under one of the layers of the roof expands due to extreme heat and causes bubbles to form. The bubbles must be lanced, flattened, and resealed to eliminate the possibility of a future leak.

1 **Splitting the Blister.** Begin by lancing the blister with a utility knife. Take care not to damage the layers underneath. Allow moisture beneath the blister to dry.

2 **Applying Roofing Cement.** Before flattening, apply a generous layer of roofing cement into the blistered area. Be sure to work the cement well under the interior edges. Nail the patch in place.

3 **Applying a Patch.** Use a piece of 90-pound roofing paper to cut out a patch that is at least 3 inches larger than the blistered area in all directions. Nail it and cover the entire area with roofing cement.

4 **Re-applying Gravel.** If weather permits let the patch dry for several days. Then pour roofing tar (not cement) onto the patch and evenly sprinkle pea gravel over the patch so that it matches the rest of the roof.

Patching Flat Roofs

Worn roofing, popped nails, and separated seams are the most common problems. Standing water on low spots often forces leakage. One advantage of having a leak on a flat roof is that it is easier to work on than an angled roof. A disadvantage is that water can find any gaps left in the patch and the patch itself can act as a dam, eventually creating another leak-prone pool. Follow these steps carefully, filling all gaps while keeping the profile of the patch as smooth as possible.

1 **Cutting Away Damaged Roofing.** A tear or crack is repaired by cutting a rectangular

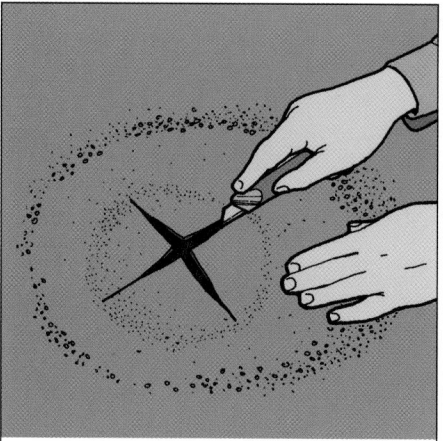

1 Cut the blister open with a utility knife without damaging the layers underneath.

2 Push roofing cement under the edges of the blister.

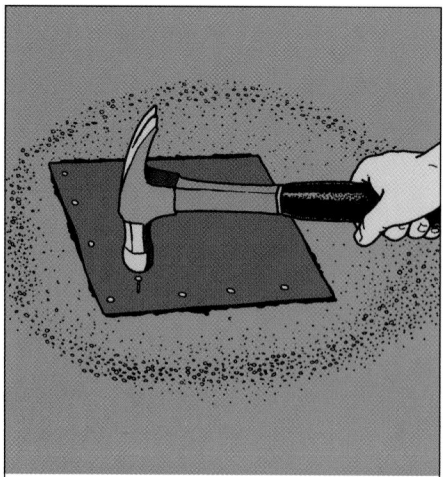

3 Cut a patch larger than the damaged area, and nail every 2 in. around the perimeter.

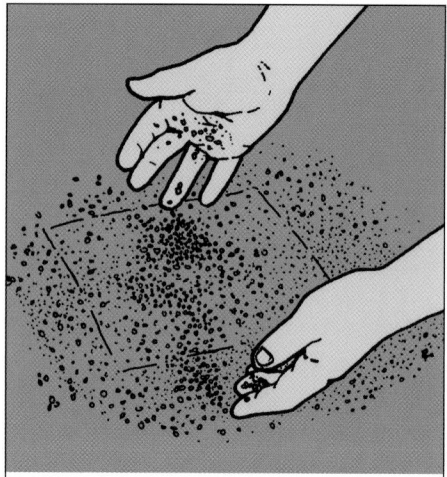

4 After letting the patch dry, coat the area with roofing tar and cover it with pea gravel.

patch. You can use a piece of composite shingle or roll roofing for the patch. Cut the patch larger than the area of the crack and use it as a guide for cutting into the roofing

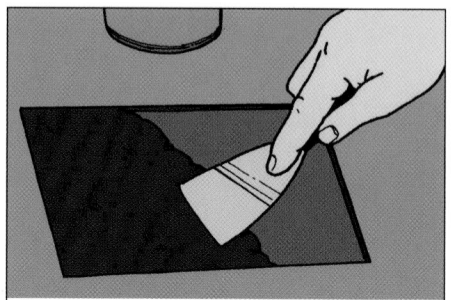

1 Enlarge the cavity for the new patch by cutting away the damaged area.

material. Cut into the old roofing and remove the damaged area.

2 **Cementing the Patch.** Use a putty knife to smooth roofing cement into the area you have cut

2 Work an ample layer of roofing cement under the edges of the cavity.

out. Be sure to work cement well under the cut edges. If there is more than one layer of roofing, add layers of cement and equal size patches until the surface of the patch is even with the surface of the roof.

3 Nailing and Applying Cement. Nail around the edges of the patch and apply another layer of cement. This time overlap the joint of the patch by at least 2 inches.

4 Adding a Final Cover. Add a final cover of roofing material, once again overlapping the patch area by at least 2 inches. Press down firmly but do not nail. If nails have popped out, nail them down and coat the heads with roofing cement.

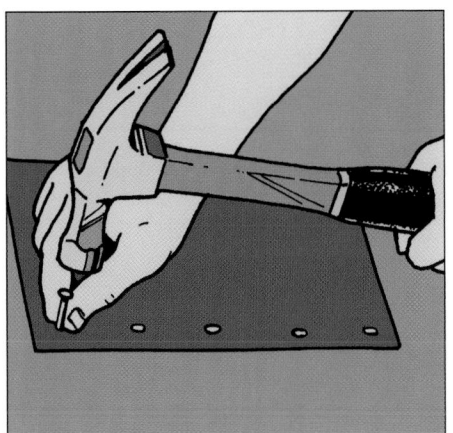

3 Nail and apply cement 2 in. beyond the edges of the patch.

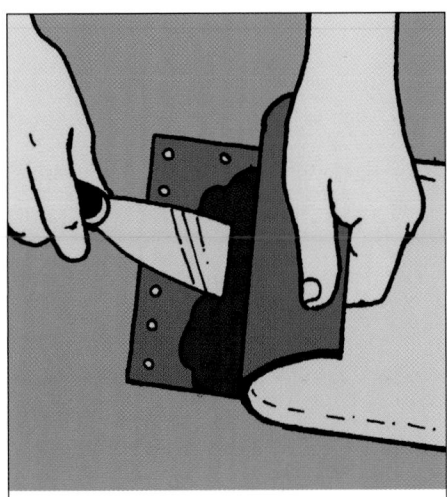

4 Cement in place a final covering that is 2 in. longer and wider than the cutout.

Making Permanent Shingle Repairs

If the roof is sound except for some isolated shingle damage, there is a way to repair composition shingles. To make your working area as safe and convenient as possible while making these repairs, note the information on ladders and roof brackets. (See pages 7–9.)

1 Removing Nails. Each shingle is held in place by two sets of four nails: one set directly pierces the shingle and the other pierces the shingle after passing through the course above. Remove the damaged shingle by first pulling out the nails that pass through the shingle above into the damaged shingle. Then pull out the nails that pass directly through the damaged shingle. To get at the nails, hold the tabs back and use a flat prybar to pry out the nails. You may need to release the adhesive seals by levering underneath with the pry bar, but be careful not to crack the shingle when working in cooler weather.

2 Replacing the Shingle. Slip a new shingle in place, aligning it with the tabs on either side. If the weather is warm enough to make the tabs supple, simply bend them up and nail the shingle in place with galvanized roofing nails.

If you are making the repair in cool weather, you may want to use the flat end of a crowbar or pry bar to hammer the nail. Hammer on the bar as near as possible to the nailhead without hitting the shingles.

3 Sealing the Shingle. Place a small amount of roofing cement under the tabs and press down. This holds shingles down until they settle into place with warm weather.

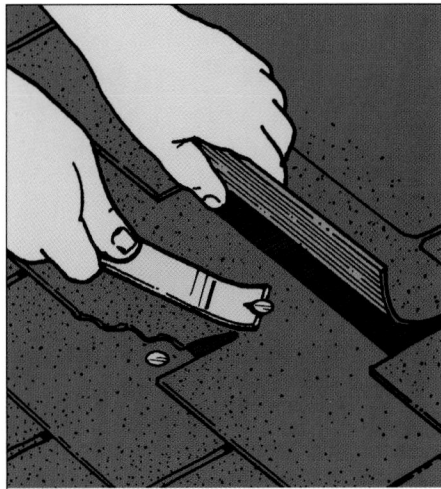

1 Use a pry bar to pry out nails in the the damaged shingle and in the course above.

2 Slip a new shingle into place aligned with the tabs on either side.

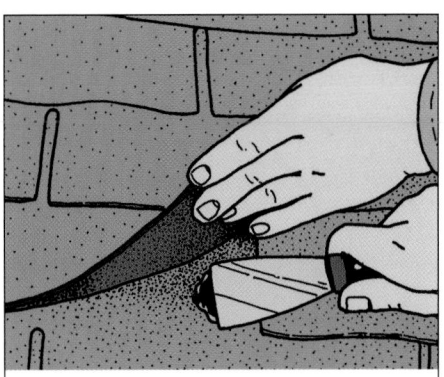

3 Use roofing cement to hold down the tabs that were bent back.

Repairing Wood Shingles & Shakes

1 Splitting and Removing the Shingle. Replacing wood shingles and shakes can be complicated because shingles and shakes are not flexible and crack relatively easily. If a shingle is badly rotted or cracked, remove it by splitting it with a chisel or the sharp end of a pry bar. Pull out the pieces carefully without damaging the 24-inch strip of heavy-duty roofing felt (called underlayment) that lays beneath each course of shingles.

2 Cutting Nails. Use a hacksaw blade (wrap electrical tape around one end to spare your fingers) to cut the nails that remain under the shingle that overlaps the area. Cut them as flush to the shingle.

3 Cutting a Replacement Shingle or Shake. Use the hatchet end of a roofing hammer to split a shingle or shake to size. Use a utility knife or block plane to fine tune the width for a ⅛- to ¼-inch gap on both sides of the replacement shingle.

4 Installing the New Shingle. Slip the shingle into place. Then tap it with a block of wood until it is within 1 inch of the course line. Toenail it in place, driving two 4d galvanized nails just at the course edge. Use a nail set to drive the nails home without damaging the shingle above.

5 Forcing the Shingle into Place. Use a block to hammer the shingle under the course. As you do so, the nailheads move under the overlapping course sealing them tightly.

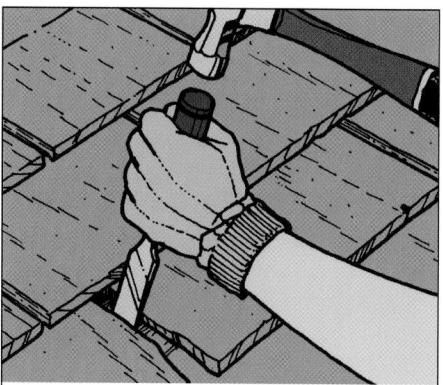

1 Remove the damaged shingle by splitting it in several places with a wood chisel.

2 With a hacksaw blade cut off the nails under the course above. Cut nails flush to the shingle.

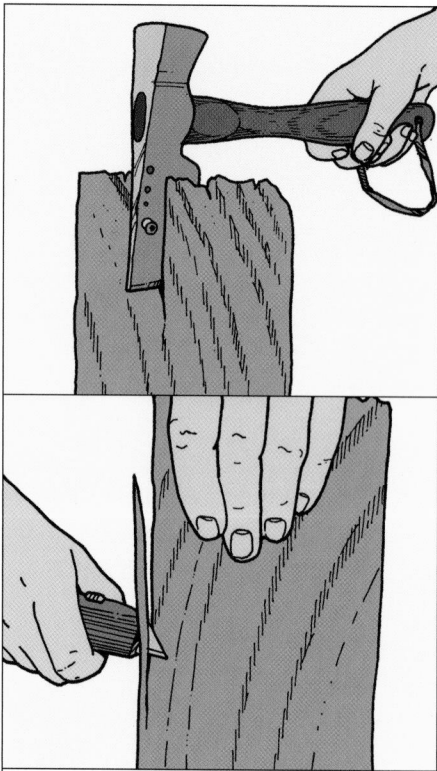

3 Split the shingle to size (top). Shave the shingle to the exact width (bottom).

4 Tap the new piece 1 in. short of the course line. Toenail with two 8d galvanized nails.

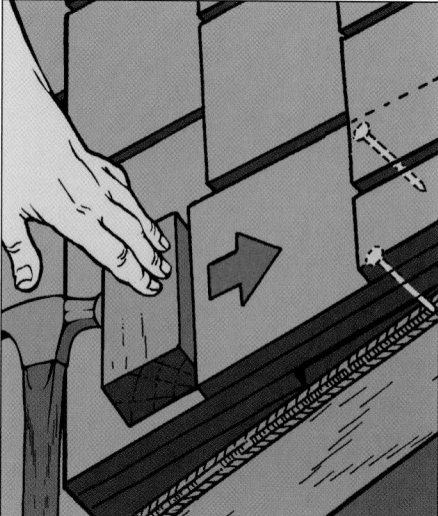

5 Force the new shingle into place by hammering the piece of scrap.

Repairing a Ridge Shingle

A crack in the ridge (usually caused by a fallen tree limb) is repaired by cutting a shingle tab to size and cementing it in place. Bend the patch gently to match the curve of the ridge and slip one edge of it under the lip of the ridge shingle nearest the damage.

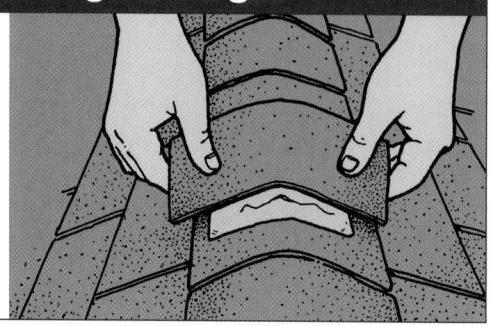

Repairing & Replacing Flashing

Flashing is the crucial water barrier between the roof and vertical surfaces such as chimneys, vents, and walls. It is made of sheet metal or roll roofing. Flashing fails when it rusts, becomes punctured or loosens. Complete flashing replacement is best done after removing a roof or before a new layer of roofing is installed. Roofing cement works wonders for breakdown maintenance until thorough repairs can be made.

Flashing leaks often are the result of bent or loose metal flashing, or worn or punctured roll roofing. Simply bend pieces of metal flashing to their original shape, then renail and caulk with asphalt. Flashing that is fitted into mortar joints on chimneys sometimes loosens. In this case, chip out the loose mortar and replace with mortar or latex mortar caulk.

Repairing Fascia & Eaves Damage

If the eaves are in disrepair, weather and small animals may invade the roof. An ideal time for eaves replacement is before adding a new roof or a new layer of roofing. Eaves damage typically is caused by faulty gutters and deteriorated roofing. Eaves repairs require a good working platform (ideally scaffolding) and an assistant.

1 **Removing the Gutter.** To rebuild a section of eaves, remove the overlapping run of gutter. First detach the gutter from the downspout by removing the sheet metal screws. Both ends of the gutter must be supported until lowered to the ground.

2 **Removing Damaged Wood.** Pry off the damaged fascia from the rafter ends. If a complete fascia board is not removed, make a cut over the middle of a rafter end.

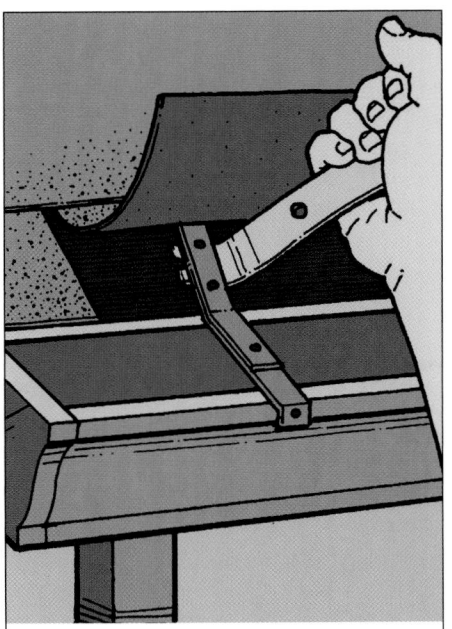

1 Pull back a shingle tab to reveal the nails holding the strap of the gutter hanger.

Choose a location for the cut and pull the nails out with a "cat's paw" nail remover. Then mark the cutting line and make the cut with a hand saw. Sometimes the end of the rafter may be too chewed up to provide good nailing when replacing the board. If this is the case add a sister (a small nailing block nailed to the side of the rafter) flush to the end.

3 **Replacing Eaves Fascia.** Cut new boards to length and prime on both sides. With the help of an assistant nail the board in place. (If you are working alone, this old carpenter's trick helps: Hammer a nail into the top edge of the new fascia, then bend it over and use it as a hook to hold one end in place while you nail the other end.)

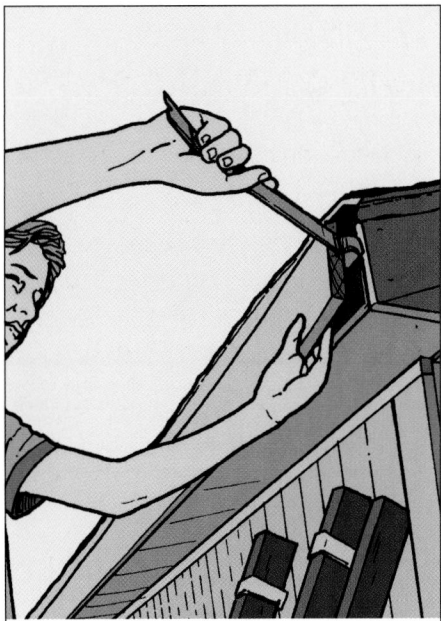

2 Pry off damaged fascia. To remove a section cut over a rafter, start from the saw cut.

3 Use a bent nail in the top of the fascia to hook one end in place while you nail the other end. Attach the new fascia with two 8d galvanized nails into each rafter. Toenail slightly at joints.

Repairing Cracks & Splits

Minor cracks (up to ½ inch) are patched with roofing cement. For a larger cracks, apply a couple of dabs of roofing cement to the underside of a piece of sheet aluminum and slip it under the shingle. Bowed shingles or shakes are remedied by splitting the bowed shingles lengthwise with a chisel. Remove about ¼ inch of the shingle at the split so it lays down flat. Drill pilot holes and nail either side of the split. Finish the job by applying a coat of roofing cement over the split.

4 Straightening New Wood. Rafter ends are seldom even. Hammer two 8d galvanized nails (one above the other) where the fascia touches a rafter end. Stretch a cord or chalkline from end to end of the fascia. Note where the face of the board cups or bows out. Tap from behind in cupped sections and insert builder's shim between the rafter and the fascia. Prime replacement molding. Then cut and nail in place, overlapping fascia joints for a seamless finish.

5 Replacing Damaged Soffit. If the fascia is damaged, the soffit is probably damaged as well and will need to be replaced. Sizes and materials vary but the procedure is roughly the same. Remove the damaged area, including trim found beneath the soffit. Be sure that you add the replacement where there is a rafter end for nailing. Cut the replacement piece to size and use the damaged piece as a guide to mark the locations of the rafters on the replacement piece. Tack two 8d nails at each mark. (It is easier than trying to start the nails upside down.) Tack a nail into the wall of your house to support one end of the soffit as you push it into place.

6 Getting a Tight Fit. Tack the soffit in place but do not drive the nails home. Pry the soffit outward with a prybar until you have a tight joint between the fascia and the soffit. Complete nailing and replace trim if necessary.

4 Set a taut line as a guide for straightening replacement fascia. Hammer outward from under the eaves to correct an inward bow.

5 Soffit damage often occurs where there is fascia damage. After removing the damage, cut a new piece to size. Mark nailing points and start nails before pushing the new soffit into place.

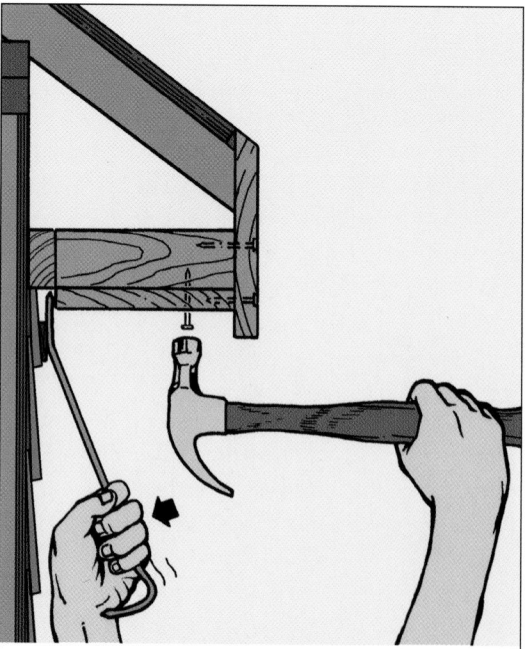

6 Pry the soffit outward for a tight, straight fit with the fascia. Replace any soffit trim previously removed.

flashing

Tear-Off or Reroof?

A reroofing job consists of applying new roofing material over the existing surface. This is less expensive and easier than a "tear-off" job, which requires that the old roofing be stripped off and hauled away.

Old tile and slate roofs cannot be covered over. Because they are heavy and impossible to nail through, they must be torn off. Roll roofing placed over any other surface (even shingles) is unsightly. If the house can take another layer of roofing, make sure there is a sound foundation for nailing and an even surface for the new shingles.

1 Counting the Layers. The first step in determining whether or not you can reroof is to check the rake of the roof to determine how many roofing layers exist. The rake is the sloped edge of the roof. Remember that drip edge sometimes is applied before reroofing and may hide evidence of previous layers. Once the number of layers is determined, check local roofing codes for the maximum number of roofing layers allowed. The answer varies depending on the type of roofing materials and the pitch of the roof. For wood shingles, codes typically allow the original roof plus one reroof. For asphalt shingles, codes typically allow the original plus two reroofs. Ask your local building inspector for specifics.

2 Checking for Solid Sheathing. All rotten boards under the old roofing must be replaced. Go into the attic and examine all suspicious spots including voids and separating plywood. Check for rot by poking with a screwdriver. If the rot is limited to a few places, you need only remove the old roofing and replace the boards in those spots. If necessary, build up the roofing above the replacement sheathing with extra layers of shingles to make a flush surface for the new roof.

3 Checking Surface Conditions. Do not expect the new roofing to smooth over dips and waves found in

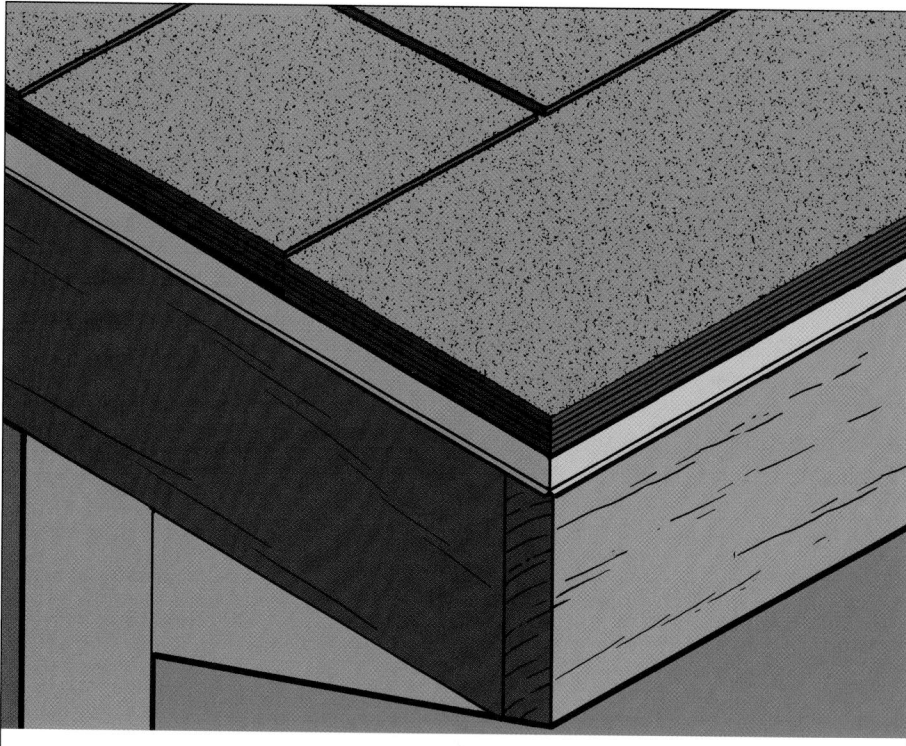

1 The rake edge reveals the number of layers of roofing that exist.

2 Check between rafters for any signs of deterioration of the sheathing.

the old roofing. If the surface of the old roofing is not uniformly flat, it must be removed. Shake roofs, shingle roofs that have curled excessively, and old-style interlocking shingles must be torn off.

Caution: *If you reroof when a tear-off is called for, the results may include costly structural damage to your home and possible fines for violating local codes.*

3 Make sure old roofing lays flat before adding a new layer of roofing.

Tear-Off Techniques

Removing an old roof is a matter of hard physical work, and although no special skills are required, a bit of planning and preparation makes the job less difficult.

Tearing-off creates a massive amount of debris, so plan ahead by calling several dumpster rental companies to get the best price. If you tell them the square footage of the roof and the number of roofing layers that are to be torn off, they can estimate the size and number of containers needed. Choose the location for the dumpster carefully, minimizing damage to landscaping and limiting carrying distance as much as possible.

Warn your neighbors ahead of time and get their permission if you need to place the dumpster on their property. Place dropcloths wherever debris is likely to fall; nails and broken shingles wreak havoc with the lawn mower. If you are lucky, the shingles may come off in large groups. (This indicates that they were not nailed down properly.) Usually shingles come off two or three at a time.

1 Starting at the Top. Begin at the ridge, and work your way down. (This is especially important for wood shingles so debris does not fall through the open sheathing.) Tear off wood shingles or shakes by sliding a crowbar or prybar underneath and pulling sharply upward. This loosens several rows at a time.

2 Saving Old Flashing. Remove flashing carefully so it can be used as a template for new flashing. If old shingles and nails are removed with care, the flashing can be reused. In the case of chimney flashing where the upper part may be embedded in mortar, you may be able to carefully bend the flashing out of the way rather than go through the trouble to remove it.

3 Inspecting the Deck. Once you have removed the old roofing, inspect all of the sheathing and replace broken or rotten pieces with a material of the same thickness. On older homes the sheathing may be ⅞ inch to 1 inch thick. Plywood sheathing is not available in thicknesses greater than ¾ inch. Use extra layers of felt or roofing materials to make up the difference.

1 Use a crowbar to tear off shingles, working from the ridge downward.

2 If old flashing is in good condition pull it back to allow for the new roof, then reuse it.

Tear-Off Techniques. If the dumpster sits in a public access area, rope off the area and provide signs in accordance with local ordinances.

3 Replace damaged areas of the decking before reroofing.

3 Flashing

Applying Underlayment

1 Rolling out the Felt. Roofs that have been stripped down to the sheathing require a layer of underlayment before flashing and reroofing. Check the instructions on the roofing material that you are using to determine whether you need 15- or 30-pound felt. Be sure the deck is dry before starting the job. There is no need for extensive nailing unless you plan to leave the felt exposed for a few days, or if you are working in windy conditions. The nailing for the shingles will hold the felt permanently in place. Roofing nails are acceptable but ¼- to ⁵⁄₁₆-inch staples are quicker to apply and usually do the trick just as well. A staple hammer (also known as a hammer tacker) speeds up the job. Be sure nails or staples are hammered completely flush.

2 Overlapping Courses. Overlap the felt 2 inches. (White lines printed on the felt provide a 2-inch guide.) It must be flat and smooth. When working in the hot sun lay only as much as you can cover with roofing in an hour or so as heat causes exposed felt to buckle.

3 Trimming for Stacks and Vents. Underlayment is installed before flashing. Trim it back so that it does not buckle from being too close to the vents or stacks.

Preparing to Reroof

Even if the job does not require tearing off the old roofing, there is plenty of serious preparation to take care of before reroofing. The deck must be cleared for the new roof.

■ Ridge shingles are removed with a flat bar or levered off with a flat shovel. Be careful to sweep away all debris—especially loose nails (top left).

■ To ensure a smooth-looking roof nail down curled shingles and fill in spaces where shingles have cracked off (top right).

■ Remove protruding nails or hammer them flush. Sweep well; a loose nail wedged under a shingle is a leak just waiting to happen (bottom left).

■ Remove all exposed old flashing, such as the vent stack flashing shown. Exposed metal flashing in the valleys, called open valley flashing, can be left if you are sure it will last 25 more years (bottom right).

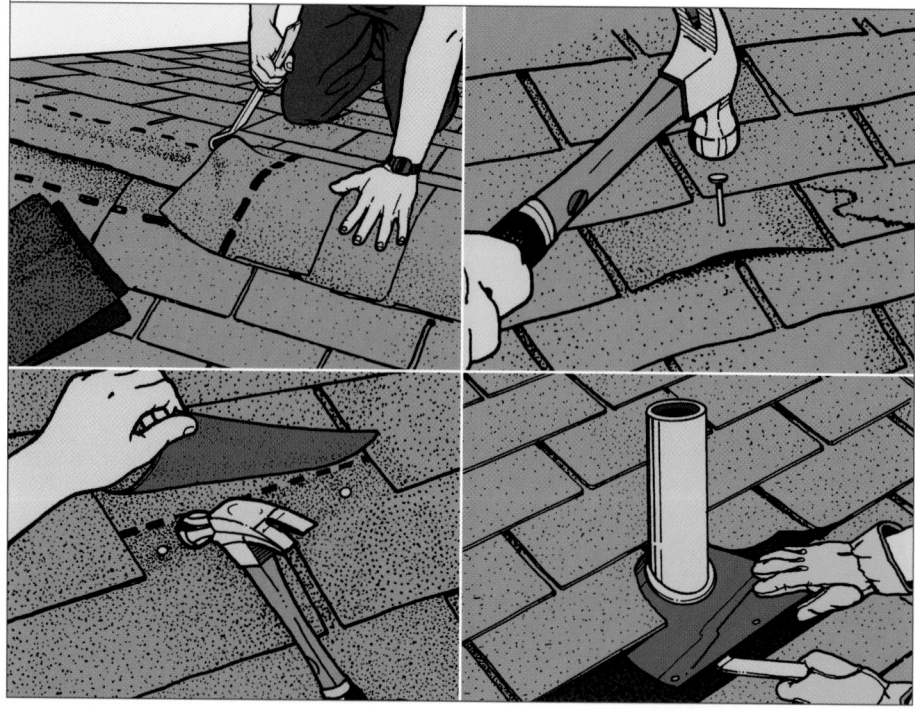

1 Unroll the felt and tack the upper corner of the end. Cut to fit after fastening.

2 The felt overlaps 2 in. lengthwise. Allow at least 4 in. in places that overlap on the side.

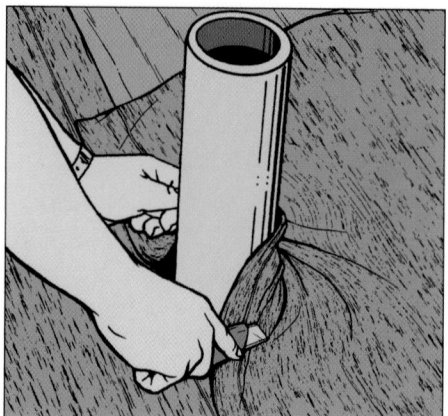

3 Cut carefully around vent stacks so that the felt lays flat and does not create gaps.

Applying Flashing

Flashing is applied in places where regular roofing materials cannot prevent leaks. It is found around vent pipes, chimneys and skylights, and also is used in valleys that connect two sections of roof, in places where the roof meets a side of the house, and on the ends of eaves and rakes. Flashing is made of galvanized sheet metal, aluminum or copper. Roofing cement is used in conjunction with flashing but cement alone can't do the job. If the original flashing did its job well, use it as a guide for applying new pieces. Keep sections of the old flashing for templates and install the new flashing in the same place and manner as the old. If the old flashing leaked and you cannot locate the source of the problem, it is best to call in a professional.

The nails used must be made of the same material as the flashing. A mixture of aluminum, tin, steel or copper may cause corrosion or discoloration.

If you find that the roof suffered from blistering, wore out prematurely, had an exceptional number of buckled shingles, and you find evidence of moisture damage in rafters or attic insulation, it may be an indication that the roof needs additional vents. In the case of roof vents, the rule of thumb is one square foot of ventilating area per 150 square feet of attic space. If you determine that the roof needs additional vents now is the time to install them.

Valley Flashing

Valley flashing is installed on top of the underlayment, but beneath the roofing. The two basic types of valley treatments are called open and closed. If the flashing material is visible after the roof is finished it is considered open. If the roofing material covers the flashing it is considered closed. Open flashing works for all types of roofs. On the other hand, closed flashing is used only for composition shingles. Open valleys are essential for wooden shingles, slate and tile because the nature of materials do not allow them to overlap to make a closed valley. Open valleys also are commonly used with asphalt shingles that have metal or roll roofing flashing. Open valley flashing is the more complicated to apply, but provides greater protection, especially from torrential downpours and the slow melt of heavy snow.

Installing Open Valley Flashing

If you are reroofing a roof that has open flashing be certain that the old flashing will last as long as the new roof. If not, you may have to remove the old flashing by cutting out a section of the old roofing wide enough to allow its removal. Install new flashing and fill in the remaining space with roofing material.

W-Metal. For open valleys it is preferable to use preformed W-metal (so called because in profile it looks somewhat like the letter W). This type of flashing has a ridge bent in the middle to prevent water from rushing down one roof slope and under the shingles on the other slope.

In an open valley the exposed portion of the flashing is wider at the bottom than at the top to allow better drainage. On either side of the valley, snap chalk lines that begin 6 inches apart at the top and widen at the rate of about ⅛ inch per foot as they descend.

Waterproofing Shingle Underlayment

A roof depends on gravity to make water run down and off, but when held back by ice, or during intense driving rain, water can work its way up and under even properly installed shingles. Because normal felt underlayment is not completely waterproof, especially around nail holes, water can work its way in. For those who experience harsh winters, it's reassuring to know you can install additional insurance against water damage.

Waterproof shingle underlayment is a special material made of asphalt and elastic polymers designed to adhere tightly to roof sheathing and around the shanks of nails driven through it. This self-sealing attribute ensures that water cannot get past it, even where you drive a nail.

Install the underlayment along those areas where ice dams and driving rain can create a problem, or where water tends to accumulate: along the eaves, around skylights, in valleys, in saddles, or on low-pitched roofs. Normal felt underlayment should still be installed in non-critical areas, and metal flashing should still be used, as per ordinary roof installation.

Waterproofing shingle underlayment must be installed over bare sheathing. Installation is a two-man job. Unroll the underlayment while your assistant peels off the plastic film backing. Carefully set the material in place. During installation, the material is slightly tacky, but can be lifted and repositioned if necessary. However, once it's installed and exposed to sunlight, the underlayment locks tight.

It's important to know what waterproof shingle underlayment can and cannot do. The underlayment will protect those vulnerable areas of your roof from leaks; it does not prevent the formation of the ice dams that form those leaks. Proper insulation and ventilation of your attic are essential to avoid ice damming in the first place. In addition, since the underlayment is a complete vapor barrier, it can prevent the escape of moisture from your attic. To prevent condensation-related problems, make sure that your attic is adequately ventilated.

Types of Drip Edge

The ends of eaves and rakes often need to be protected by more than just the overhang of the roofing material. Install preformed eaves and rake flashing (called drip edge) along the eaves before underlayment is applied and along rakes after the underlayment is down. Cut corners carefully with a tin snips, both for the sake of appearance and for better coverage. Nail the drip edge to the roof sheathing every 8 to 10 inches. Do not nail the drip edge to the fascia.

Wrap-around end-cap flashing covers the edges of old roofing layers. Be sure flashing overlaps at corners. For example, rake flashing must overlap eaves flashing so water is shed downward without working its way beneath the flashing **(A)**.

For roofing trimmed flush with the fascia, this type of end-cap covers the edges of layers and keeps water and ice from backing under the old shingles **(B)**.

A canted drip edge of this variety carries the water away from the fascia **(C)**.

This type of drip edge is designed to contain pea gravel on a built-up roof **(D)**.

Sometimes called drip cap, this flashing adds a lip to the roof edge that overlaps the gutter **(E)**.

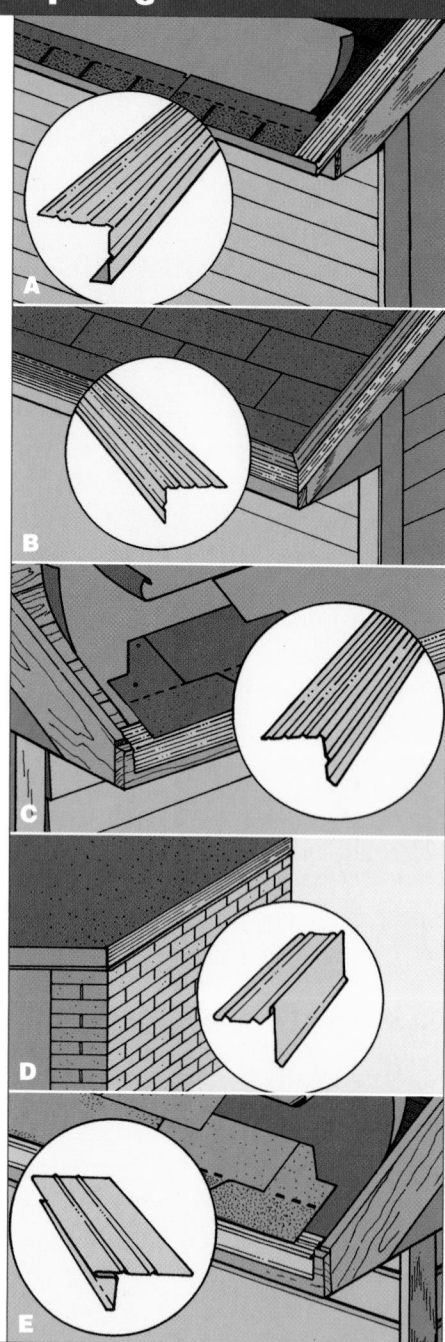

For best results paint galvanized flashing with primer on both sides before installing. Let the flashing run wild (temporarily overhang) past the eaves and the top of the valley. Carefully trim both ends flush after it is nailed in place. Place the nails about 6 inches apart in rows ½ inch from the edges. If you need to use more than one piece of metal, nail the first piece at the bottom of the valley and lap the second piece over it by 6 inches. Dab nailheads with roofing cement.

Roll Roofing Valleys. A less costly and less durable option for open valleys is roll roofing. Typically used with asphalt shingles, two layers of roll roofing are applied: One layer is 18 inches wide (the full width of the roll cut lengthwise in half) and one is 36 inches wide (full width). The 18-inch piece is laid granule side down while the 36-inch piece is laid granule side up. Strike a chalk line down the center of each piece to center it in the valley. Nail one side only at first. Before nailing the other side, press the roofing firmly into the valley to eliminate voids that might become punctured later. Mark the valley with chalk lines 6 inches apart at the top of the valley. The bottom is 6 inches wide plus ⅛ inch per foot of descent. The shingles overlap the chalk line and later are trimmed. The uppermost corner of the shingle is nipped diagonally to direct water flow into the valley. A final dab of roofing cement applied after shingles are trimmed keeps water from working under the roofing. (See page 44.)

Flashing Options

Flashing is available in a variety of forms starting with aluminum coil on the least expensive end of the spectrum and copper sheeting on the most expensive end. Aluminum is readily available in widths ranging from 10 to 36 inches. Colors vary as well with the most typical being white, black and brown.

W-bend galvanized steel flashing is available in 8- to 10-foot lengths, 20 to 24 inches wide. If you would like to bend the flashing for a custom fit, rent a break (a device typically used to neatly bend aluminum siding soffits and trim). They are simple to use and available at most rental shops.

Full-Width Roll Roofing Placed Granules Up

18" Strip of Roll Roofing Placed Granules Down Under Full-Width Roll Roofing

Chalk Line Guides for Shingles

Installing Roll Roofing Valleys. Two layers of roll roofing, one 18 in. wide, the other 36 in. wide, make a nonmetallic valley for use with composition shingles.

Installing Closed Valley Flashing

An extra layer of underlayment is placed in a closed valley. For added protection in harsh climates add a 24-inch-wide sheet of aluminum or galvanized metal. Shingles are laid over the flashing in an alternating fashion or they are half-laced (trimmed down the center of the valley where one plane of shingles overlaps the other).

Installing a Half-Laced Valley. The half-laced (sometimes called half-woven) valley is another type of closed valley. One layer of roofing overlaps the other and is trimmed instead of woven. The overlap is put on the face of the roof that bears the most water. The bottom layer of shingles overlaps the valley by at least 12 inches. After trimming, adhere the topmost layer with roofing cement. No nails are applied within 6 inches of the center of the valley.

Installing Continuous Flashing

Use this simple type of flashing only in places where the joint is horizontal. For example, the joint at which the front wall of a dormer meets the roof, or where a shed roof is attached to a wall. Lay your last course of roofing so that the tops of the shingles butt the wall.

Installing Closed Valley Flashing. Such a valley is woven (or laced) together with courses from either side of the valley alternately overlapping each other. Each overruns the valley by at least a tab and a half.

Installing a Half-Laced Valley. The half-laced valley is a type of closed valley. The overlap is put on the face of the roof that bears the most water.

1 Score the flashing material, and sandwich it at the bending point between two 1x4s.

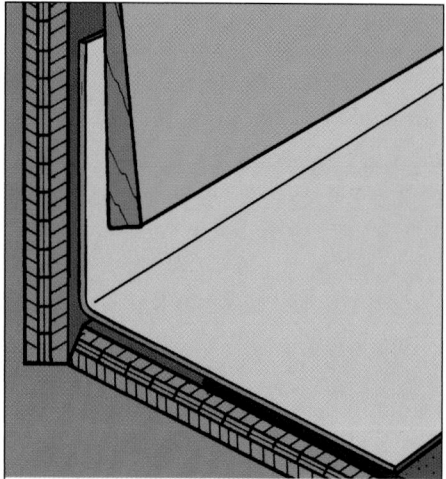

2 Siding overlaps flashing so that water sheds downward on top of, not under, the flashing.

3 Cut tabs off shingles, and press them into roofing cement applied to the flashing.

If necessary, adjust the exposures in the last two courses so the last course, which will be trimmed to butt the wall, is at least 8 inches wide.

Note: When reroofing it may be possible to continue to use old flashing. If the old flashing is in good repair and you think it will last the life of the new roofing, seal the new roofing to the flashing with roofing cement.

1 **Bending Flashing.** Continuous flashing typically is a strip of metal at least 9 inches wide, bent to match the angle of the joint to be covered. Position the bend so that there will be at least 5 inches of flashing on the wall and 4 inches on the roof. Use clamps and boards to bend the metal neatly. Alternately you can rent a break (typically used to form aluminum soffits and trim caps) to custom-bend aluminum flashing. (It does not work for galvanized steel.)

2 **Attaching the Flashing.** Put roofing cement on the last course of shingles. On walls that have wood siding, slip the the flashing behind the siding and then press it into the cement. You don't need to nail the flashing to the wall. Nail the flashing to the siding with roofing nails every 2 or 3 feet.

3 **Covering the Flashing.** Cut the tabs off as many shingles as you need for the course. Coat the flashing with roofing cement. Press the tabs into the roofing cement leaving gaps between each that approximate the cutouts between tabs on an intact shingle. Tabs cut from a standard shingle will cover the flashing plus about 1 inch more. Do not nail the tabs. Use a caulk gun to apply a bead of roofing cement along the flashing junction.

Flashing Brick or Stucco

If the wall is masonry or stucco, the job is more difficult because the flashing must be set into the wall.

1 **Bending Lip on Flashing.** Using two boards, clamp the sheet metal or aluminum flashing so that ½ inch protrudes freely over the edge.

Use a hammer to bend that same ½ inch of flashing so that it sticks up at a 90-degree angle.

2 **Cutting the Slot.** Use a piece of chalk to mark a line about 5 inches above the surface of the roof. Use the nearest mortar line if it is a masonry wall. Then use a circular saw (with a masonry blade) or a chisel to cut a ½-inch-deep slot along that line. Bend the flashing a second time so that it fits on the roof.

3 **Sealing with Mortar.** Stuff the slot with mortar or silicone caulk, and press the top lip of the flashing into the slot.

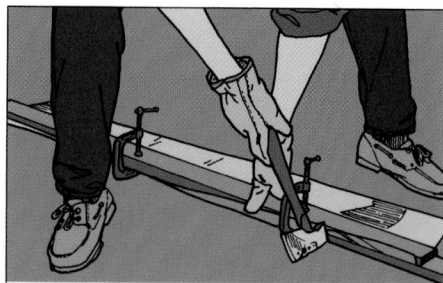

1 Score a line on the flashing, and bend the lip as shown.

2 Open the mortar line using a chisel or circular saw with a masonry blade.

3 Fill the chiseled mortar lines with mortar or caulk, and set the flashing in place.

Flashing Vents & Soil Stacks

Vents and soil stacks are covered with sleeves. A flap at the base of the sleeve makes a waterproof seal. These sleeves are available in a variety of styles and materials including lead, sheet metal, rubber and plastic. All types are easy to install.

Shingle up to the base of the vent or stack. Cut the shingle around the stack, apply roofing cement and slip on the sleeve (left).

Shingles overlap the upper half of the vent sleeve. Cut the overlapping courses around the stack, leaving a ½-inch gap. Cement the tabs to the sleeve (right).

Flashing a Chimney

This job is probably the most complicated part of roofing a house. Old flashing pieces can be used as templates, but keep in mind that by reroofing or tearing off the old roof, the dimensions of the flashing have changed. Chimney flashing typically consists of base flashing (which wraps the front of the chimney), step flashing (which is placed up the sides of the chimney), cricket flashing (a peaked piece that diverts water from the upslope side of the chimney) and pieces of counter flashing (also called cap flashing which hangs over all the other flashing pieces).

If the chimney is 24 inches or wider, construct a cricket along the upper side of the chimney. This helps keep water and snow from building up in this critical area.

Before flashing, complete all final roofing up to the base of the chimney and no further.

Step Flashing

Use step flashing on a shingled roof where the roof meets the sloping side of a wall or a chimney. (For roll or panel roofing use continuous flashing.) Step flashing requires that each piece of flashing overlaps the one below it. The flashing is interlaced with the shingles as well. You can purchase step flashing precut, or you can cut the flashing into shingle-like pieces 10 inches long and 2 inches wider than the exposure of the roofing. For example, if the shingle exposure is 5 inches, each shingle is cut 10 x 7 inches. Install the flashing so that it has the same exposure as the shingles, nailing the the top edge into the roof only so the nails are covered by shingles.

In the illustration at right, the roofing exposure (the amount of roofing material visible in each course) is 5 inches.

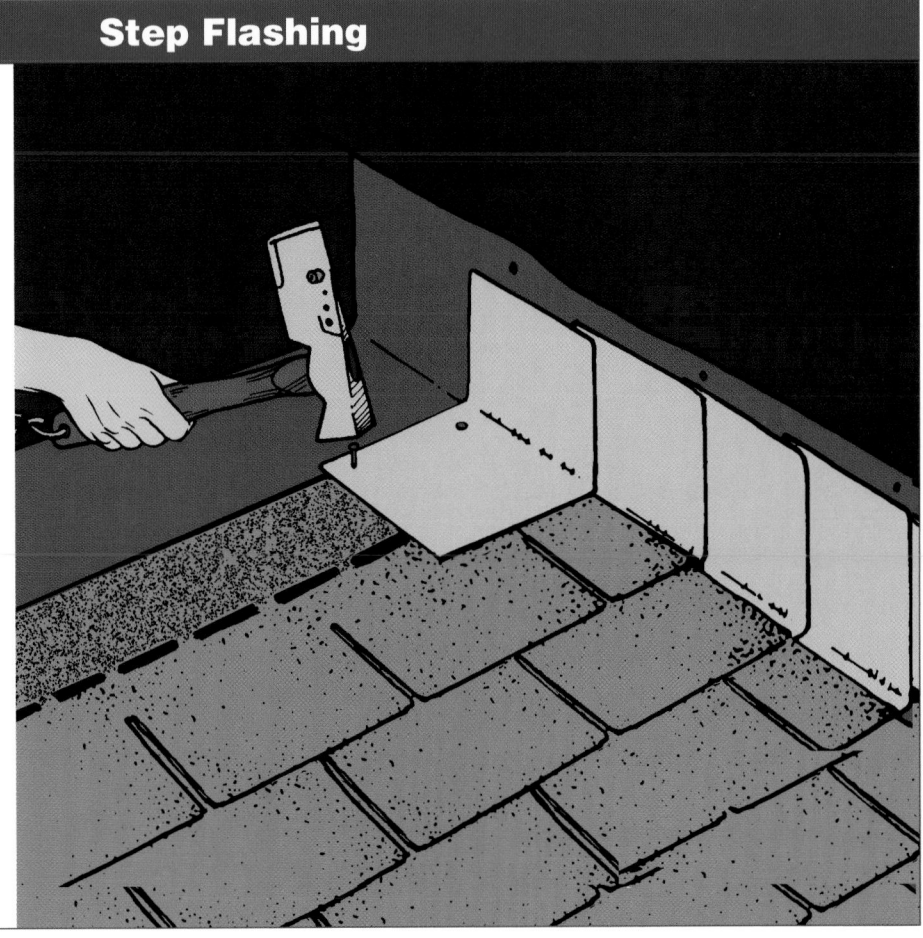

1 Adding Base Flashing. Base flashing is applied at the base of the chimney. Make your own by bending a piece of aluminum with a straightedge. For a simple jig to make this bend and to add a lip to the flashing, see page 28. After bending the aluminum, mark where it intersects the open mortar line and bend a lip along the upper edge. Wearing gloves, use tin snips to cut wings that wrap around the sides of the chimney. Seal the lip of the flashing in the mortar line with mortar or caulk. Overlap the roofing with the lower edge of the flashing.

2 Applying Step Flashing. Install step flashing as you shingle the roof, nailing it as shown on page 29. Cement each step to the roof but not the chimney, as the roof may settle independently.

3 Fitting Counter Flashing. Counter flashing is a layer that sheds water onto step flashing. With a large sheet of paper, make a template, or have one made by a sheet metal shop that stair-steps down according to mortar lines. The lips of the flashing are set ¼ inch into the mortar line. Trace the outline onto the sheet metal, and cut it with tin snips. Use the edge of a screwdriver to score the lines along which the lips bend. Use two scraps of wood to clamp and bend the lips. Set the finished flashing in place, mortaring or caulking the lips into the chimney. Do not connect the counter flashing to the other flashing pieces because the roof and the chimney are on different foundations and thus settle independently. Do not smear the bottom pieces with caulk or roofing

cement because this attaches them to both roof and chimney.

4 Adding a Cricket. A cricket keeps water, snow and debris from piling up behind a chimney. The height of the cricket is one-half the width of the chimney. Crickets are made of wood that is roofed over or sheet metal exposed as flashing. Given a sketch of what is needed, a sheet-metal shop will cut and break a cricket for you. If you are going to do it yourself, the simplest approach is to add a 2x6 frame behind the chimney. One 2x6 is cut on an angle so that it can be nailed horizontally with a second stub piece to support it at the chimney. Two scraps of ½-inch CDX plywood cut to incline at roughly 45 degrees form a miniature roof. To finish the job, apply felt, flashing, and roll roofing.

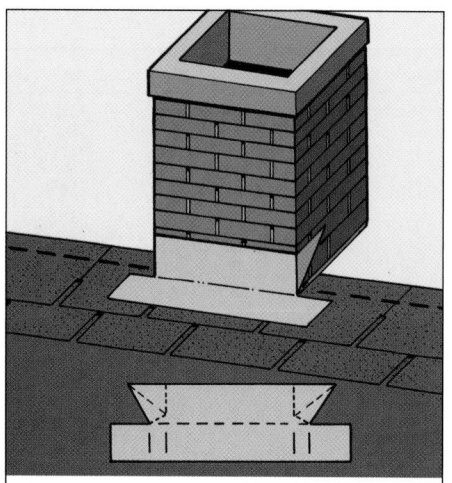

1 Cut the base flashing, and use roofing cement to carefully attach it to the roofing.

2 Install the step flashing as the roofing is applied to the chimney.

3 Set counter flashing into the mortar line in overlapping sections or in one continuous piece.

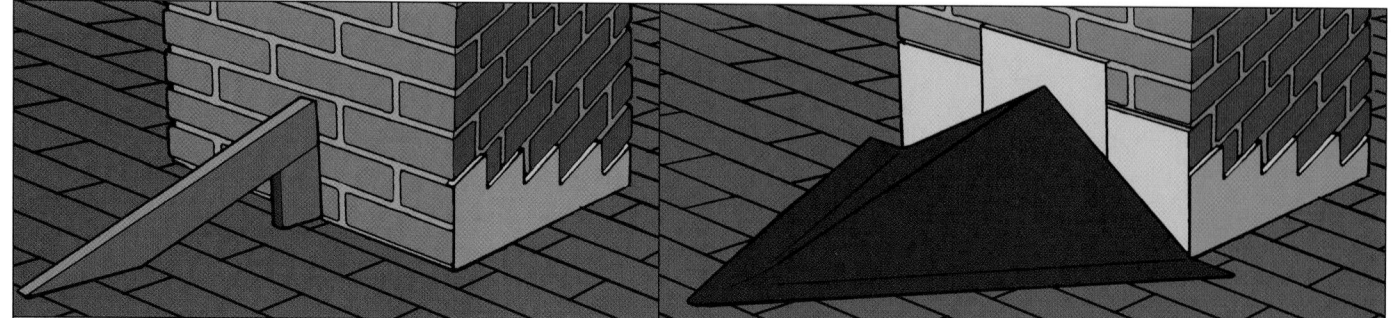

4 Framing for a cricket consists of no more than one horizontal ridge piece supported by one vertical piece (left). Nail two pieces of ½-in. plywood to the ridge piece and the deck. Install flashing, and then cover with roll roofing (right). Allow the roll roofing to overlap the roof by 4 or 5 in.

asphalt shingles

Selecting Composition Shingles

Shingles are purchased by the square, which is enough shingles to cover 100 square feet at the recommended exposure. Shingles typically are packaged 80 to the square, though larger shingles are packaged 64 to the square. Each square is made up of bundles of paper-wrapped blocks of shingles. Most squares are made up of three bundles, but heavier squares are made up of four.

The durability of shingles used to be rated by the weight of the square. The heavier the square, the thicker and longer-lived the shingle. Today shingles are given lifetime ratings of 15, 20, and 25 years. Prices rise accordingly. Colors include white, black, and shades of brown, green, gray, and blue. Pressed texture and granule coloration combine to produce shingles that resemble wood shingles and shakes.

When selecting a color, remember that roofs last 20 years, far longer than the latest fashion trends. Neutral blacks, whites, and grays remain the most popular colors.

Composition shingles can be applied to any roof that has a slope of 4 in12 (4 inches rise for every 12 inches of run) or more. With double felt underlayment, they can be applied to a roof with a slope as low as 2 in 12 if shingle tabs are sealed down.

Deciding to Reroof

Composition shingles are a versatile material and can be used to cover almost anything that accepts a nail.

Composition Shingles. Nail down warped shingles and fill voids. Usually only three layers of shingles are allowed; check your local codes.

Wood Shingles. Add thin, beveled strips (sometimes called horse feathers) to fill the voids between courses, and notch in 1x4s at the rakes and eaves to create a smooth platform for a new layer of roofing.

Roll Roofing. If the slope is at least 4 in 12, roll roofing makes a smooth bed for a new layer of composition shingles. Remove all loose nails before reroofing.

Tile and Slate Roofs. Tile and slate roofs, as well as metal and fiberglass panels, are impossible to nail through and therefore cannot be reroofed with composition shingles. Shakes are too uneven to take new roofing and must be removed as well.

Estimating Materials on Gabled Roofs

You need to be able to tell your local lumberyard or roofing supplier how many squares (100 square feet) of roofing you need. By determining the square footage of your roof and adding 10 percent for ridges and waste, you can estimate costs and order materials. It is safest and most convenient to take as many measurement as you can from the ground. With a simple gable roof, you can take all the measurements without a ladder. But you'll have to climb up to directly measure details such as dormers. Here's how to measure your roof with little or no climbing:

Different Types of Composition Shingles

Composition shingles come in a variety of styles and colors to complement the architectural and color scheme of your house. Here are three of the most common composition shingle styles you will find.

Standard Three-Tab Shingles. These are the most common style in North America today. They typically are sold 80 shingles per square, three bundles per square (left).

Shadow Line Three-Tab Shingles. The illusion of thickness is created by a line of darkened granules. These too come 80 shingles per square, three bundles per square (center).

Mock Wood Shakes. Added thickness and the clever use of color give mock wood shingles their wood-like appearance. Because they are thicker and heavier, they are sold only 64 shingles per square, four bundles per square (right).

1 To determine the area of the roof, sketch a simple bird's-eye view. Divide the plan into squares, rectangles, and triangles.

1 **Sketching the Roof.** From the ground make a rough sketch of your roof. Include all planes of the roof including valleys, dormers, and chimneys. Do not worry about getting it to scale. Next, reduce the diagram to a series of triangles, rectangles, and squares, drawing in dotted lines where appropriate. (Later these shapes are calculated for area.)

2 **Measuring Gable and Eaves Lengths.** First measure the length of your house on one of the eave sides. Include the gable overhang in your measurement. To determine how far the overhangs protrude, stand directly under them and measure to the house. This will give you a rough measurement of the length of the eave that's close enough for estimating materials. Mark the eave length on your drawing.

Now measure the width of the gable end, again including overhangs. Jot down this measurement, but don't put it on the drawing yet.

3 **Measuring Slope.** The purpose of the next two steps is to deter-

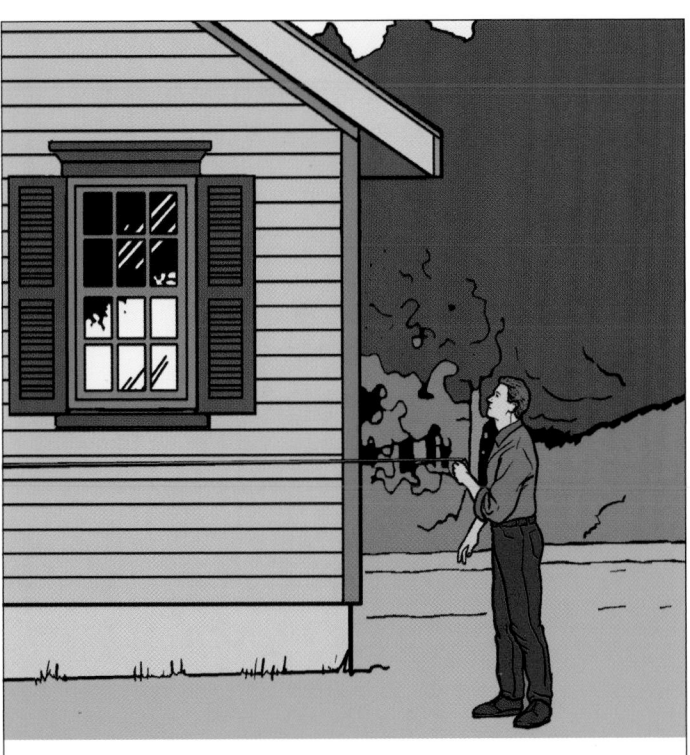

2 Measure the length of the eave end and gable end of your house. Include any overhangs in your measurement.

3 Use a level and a ruler to determine the slope of your roof.

mine the length of the rake, which is one sloped edge of your roof. When you know the length of the rake and the length of the eaves, you can multiply them to get the square footage of your roof.

First, calculate the slope of the roof. Slope is expressed as inches of roof rise (unit rise) per 12 inches of roof run (unit run). A 6-in-12 roof rises 6 inches per 12 inches of run. The slope of the roof is determined from the ground by using a spirit level and a ruler. Mark the level 12 inches from one end. Stand back from a gable, and hold the level so that one end appears to touch the eaves. Make sure the level is exactly horizontal. At the 12-inch mark on the level, hold the ruler upright and note the number of inches to the rake. This is the rise. Almost all house slopes are expressed in whole inches. For example, 4 in 12, 6 in 12, etc.

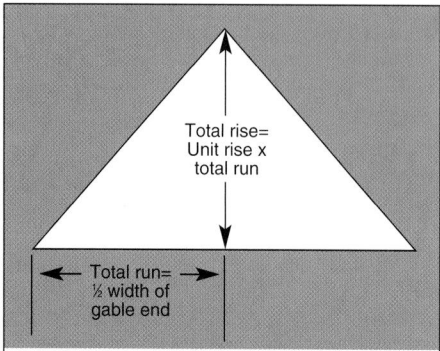

4 From the length of the gable and the slope of the roof, calculate the total rise of the gable.

4 Determining Total Rise. Let us say for example that the gable end of your house is 20 feet wide including the overhangs. That means the base of the triangle you are calculating, or the total run of the roof, is 10 feet long. Let us also assume you have determined that the slope is 6 in 12. This means that in a total run of 10 feet, the roof rises 5 feet.

5 Calculating Rake Length. This is an opportunity to put your high school geometry to use. Remember the Pythagorean theorem? This useful formula asserts that if you know the measurements of two sides of a right triangle, the third can be computed. This means that if you know the length of a gable (which you measured from the ground) and you know its height, you can determine the length of the rake.

The total rise squared times the total run squared gives us the length of the rake squared. In our example, the 10-foot total run squared equals 100. The 5-foot total rise squared equals 25. Added together they equal 125, which is the rake squared. The square root of 125 is 11.18, so the rake is 11 feet 2 1/8 inches long. Now multiply the rake length by the length of the eaves. Then you have the area of one side on the gable roof.

6 Calculating the Area. If you are dealing with a simple gable roof with no dormers, just double the area of one side of the roof and add 10 percent for waste and ridge cap

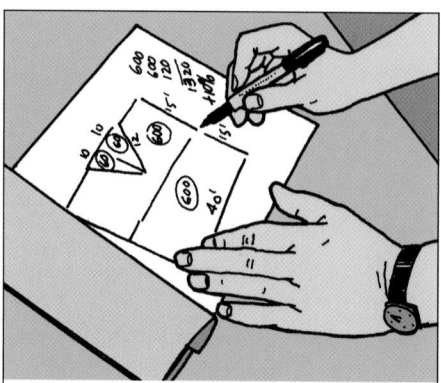

6 With the measurements in place, you can calculate the total area of your roof.

shingles. Divide the square footage by 100 for the total number of squares needed. If your rake is 11.18 feet long and your eave end is 40 feet long, one side of your roof will be 447.2 square feet. Both sides will be 894.4 square feet. You need nine squares to cover the roof. Adding 10 percent, you should order 10 squares.

If you have dormers, climb up on the roof and measure their length and width directly. When all measurements are determined, compute the area of each roof plane using the following formulas: One side of a rectangle or square multiplied by an adjacent side yields the area; the area of a right triangle equals one half the base multiplied by the height. Again, total all areas and add 10 percent for waste and extras. Do not subtract for chimneys, air vents, and small skylights. Then divide by 100 for the total number of squares needed.

You'll need one 36-inch x 144-foot roll of felt underlayment per three squares of shingles.

Storing Shingles

Composition shingles have adhesive blobs that, when warmed by the sun, seal each tab. For this reason, shingles must be stacked out of the sun. Bundles also must be protected from the rain. Shingles are best stored on a skid and covered with plastic.

The most physically demanding part of roofing is getting the shingles on the roof. Many suppliers offer this service which is well worth the additional expense (right).

If the job is going to be spread over several evenings and weekends, carry up only as many shingles that can be applied in a day. Partial bundles can be carried across one's padded head, or whole bundles can be supported on one padded shoulder (center right). Most shingle bundles weigh about 75 pounds.

If you would rather not carry the shingles up by hand, use a ladderveyor (below). Be sure to read the ladder safety tips found on pages 7–9.

A bundle set on either side of the ridge forms a level base for stacking additional bundles. Doing this provides an open work area (below right).

Installing the Starter Course

Composition shingles overlap each other, covering the roof with two layers of roofing. To provide the first layer at the eaves edge, a starter course is applied. The starter course is always necessary whether reroofing over old shingles, applying shingles on a new roof, or applying shingles after a tear-off. The procedure is slightly different for reroofs than it is for a new roof or tear-off.

Working with a Reroof

Adding Drip Edge. If shingles at the edge of the eaves are deteriorated cut them back flush with the fascia, or old drip edge below. Add a metal drip edge to prevent moisture from getting under the shingles. This protects the fascia boards from rot and provides a finished appearance and a straight, strong edge. Apply the drip edge with roofing nails.

Applying Reroof Starter. When reroofing, the starter strip is just wide enough to cover the exposure of the first course of old shingles. Make a starter strip by cutting the tabs off of several shingles. The resulting strip is 4 to 5 inches wide.

Trim 3 inches off one side of the first strip so that no joints between strips fall over joints between old roofing shingles. Nail it in place with four nails at 3 or 4 inches above the eaves edge. If you added a drip edge bring the edge of the starter course even with the edge of the drip edge. If you did not use a drip edge allow the starter strip to extend ¼ to ⅜ inch beyond the edge of the eaves.

Starting a New Roof or Tear-Off

Apply a starter course directly on top of the roofing felt or ice guard. Cut the tabs off of full shingles. Trim 3 inches off one side of the first shingle so that joints are staggered rather than lined up with the first course of shingles below. Staggering joints prevents leaks. Apply the starter course so that it is flush with the drip edge. (The asphalt strips will be 1 inch above the drip edge.) If there is no drip edge, allow the starter strip to overhang the edge of the eaves by ¼ to ⅜ inch. Be sure any nails will be covered by shingles above.

Adding Drip Edge. If the edges of existing shingles are deteriorated cut them back and add a drip edge.

Applying Reroof Starter. Cut the tabs off shingles for starter strips. Trim 3 in. to stagger the joints.

Starting a New Roof or Tear-Off. Starter strips go on top of roofing felt or ice guard.

Ice Guard. This material is available in rolls that are simple to install. Heavy snow areas get two courses.

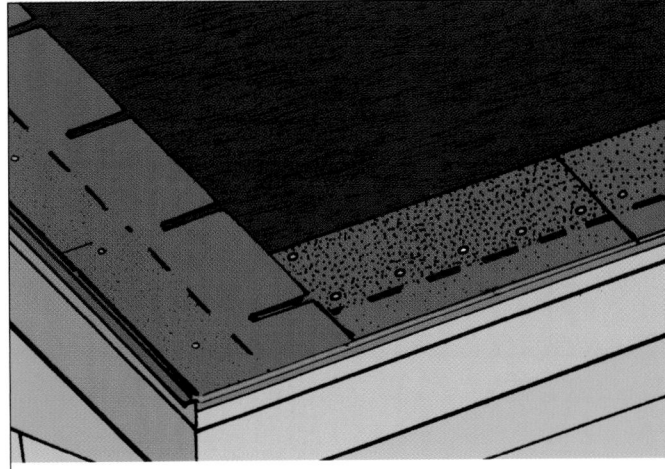

Applying Rake Edge. If the rake edge is badly worn, nail whole shingles, upper edge out, along the rake.

Ice Guard. Local building codes may require that you install a roll roofing ice guard to prevent leaks from ice dams. The material can be purchased in rolls that are simply rolled out and nailed down. There are no joints, so you do not have to worry about staggering. Some products are self-adhesive, so you don't have to nail it; others are "self-sealing."

Applying Rake Edge. If the rake edge (the roof edge above the gable) is badly deteriorated, supplement the new shingles with a border of whole shingles applied along the rake edge. Keep the upper edge of the shingle toward the rake edge with tabs inward. Allow ¼- to ⅜-inch overhang. Nail every 10 to 12 inches, 3 to 4 inches in from the edge.

Applying the First Courses

The edge of the roof does not follow a straight line in most cases and cannot be used as a guide for straight courses of shingles. All of the first course shingles must overhang the drip edge by the same ¼ to ⅜ inch, so it is okay to align the first course to the drip edge and then snap a chalk line to align the second course. Make a mark near both rakes to indicate how far up the roof you want the bottom of the course to be. Hold the chalk receptacle downward to fully coat the line with chalk. Then stretch the line taut across the two marks; pull up on it; and release to make the line.

You'll be working on an extension ladder to install the starter course along the eaves. While you are installing the starter course, add four more courses along the eaves to provide room for roof cleats. By doing these courses along with the starter course, you'll minimize the number of times you have to move the ladder. While up there, renail and adjust gutter hangers as necessary.

Tips for Cutting Shingles

■ Hook blades specially made for cutting roofing fit in a standard utility knife.

■ Some roofers prefer straight blades because you can use them to "gang-cut" through several shingles at the same time. Gang-cutting is handy when you are cutting lots of tabs for a ridge or hip. Granules quickly dull the blades of utility knives, so be sure to have plenty of extras on hand. Shingles tear when cut with a dull blade.

■ In cool weather it is faster to cut shingles from the side that is not granulated.

■ When a neat, straight cut is required (as when cutting off a tab at the end of a course) a metal square can be used as a straightedge guide in which to run the blade.

Applying the First Courses. The edge of the roof may not be straight so you must snap a chalk line to establish a straight second course.

Tips for Fastening

Whether you choose to hammer nails or apply staples driven by a pneumatic gun, the following tips help to achieve a secure fastening job:

Use zinc-coated nails to prevent corrosion.

■ Avoid exposing fasteners. Each row of shingles must cover the fasteners of the previous course.

■ Do not drive the fastener so deep that its head breaks the surface of the shingle.

■ A nail that penetrates too easily may work its way out. Remove it and seal the hole.

■ Always drive fasteners in straight so that the heads lay flat. Nail heads that stick up at an angle can wear through the shin-gle above.

■ If the fastener does not penetrate properly remove it, patch the deck, and drive another fastener nearby.

■ Do not nail into or above an adhesive strip.

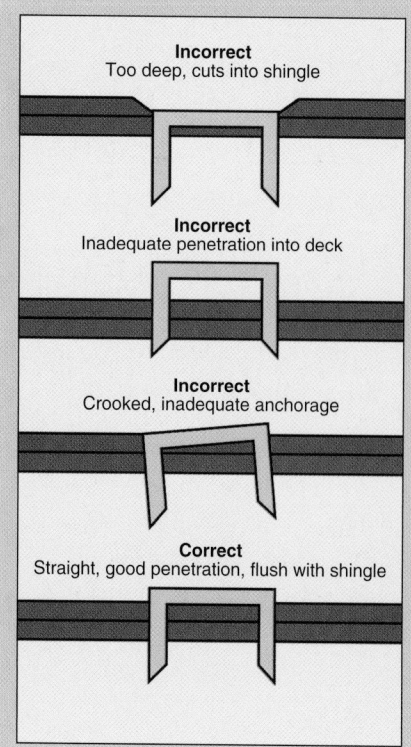

Incorrect
Too deep, cuts into shingle

Incorrect
Inadequate penetration into deck

Incorrect
Crooked, inadequate anchorage

Correct
Straight, good penetration, flush with shingle

Nailing Shingles Properly

Shingles are typically attached with four nails; one at each end and one above each tab slot. In windy areas some roofers use six nails, adding one to either side of each tab slot. Note that nails are positioned just beneath the adhesive, but above the tops of the slots. Nails also must be long enough to penetrate the sheathing by ¾ inch. This rule applies whether fastening the shingles to a new roof or to a reroof.

Basic Shingling

Nothing is more frustrating than hammering four to six nails into a shingle only to find that it is crooked. The procedure below will help you get the shingle aligned right the first time.

1 **Lining Up the Shingle.** Begin by aligning the upper corner of the shingle with the upper corner of the shingle already in place. Tack a nail to hold it in place.

1 Align the upper corner of the new shingle with the upper corner of the adjacent shingle.

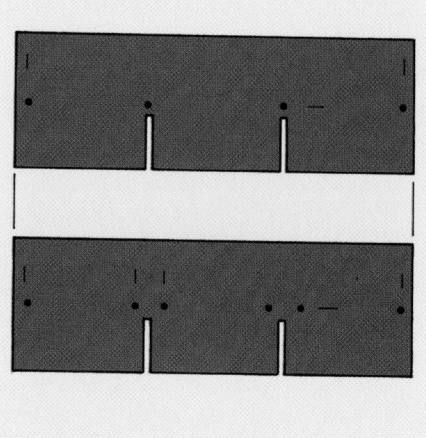

Nailing Shingles Properly. Either 4 or 6 nails are used to hold shingles. Nail in the pattern shown above.

2 **Tacking Opposite End.** Position the opposite end of the shingle. (Some people do this by simply eyeballing where the tab hits the shingle on the previous course. Others use the gauge built into a roofing hammer.) Tack in place.

3 **Checking and Nailing.** Give the shingle a quick double-check for alignment. Then, beginning from the left (if you are right-handed)

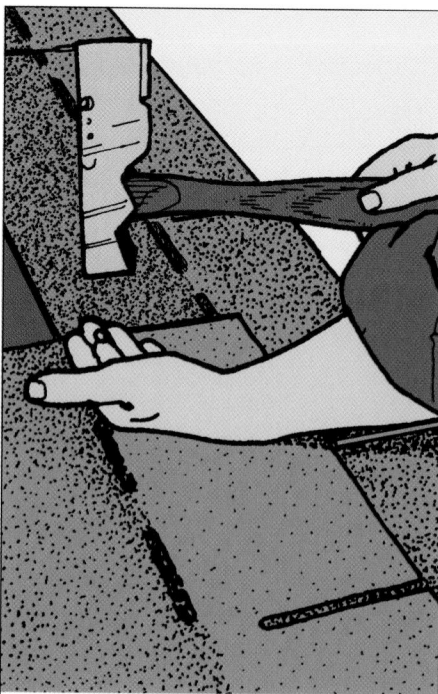

2 Position the opposite edge of the shingle and tack it in place.

nail the first tacked nail home and work across the course, carefully flattening out bulges. If necessary, remove one of the tacked nails to eliminate buckling.

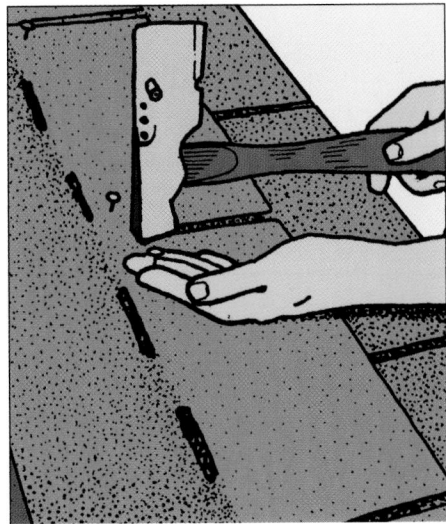

3 Drive in the tacked nails across the shingle.

Choosing a Shingle Pattern

Before nailing skills are put to work, you must choose a shingle pattern. Each pattern requires standard three-tab shingles, which are positioned differently to achieve different effects. Each offsets the tab cutouts of overlapping courses by a different distance.

Six-Inch Method. The most common method of aligning shingles is called the 6-inch method. Each course starts at a 6-inch offset to the course below. This is handy because it neatly cuts tabs in half and therefore minimizes waste. The result is a neat arrangement where each tab lines up with the tab two courses above or below.

Four- and Five-Inch Methods. Though the 6-inch method is the easiest to cut and apply, some builders are concerned with the way every other vertical cutout lines up and as a result creates a flow path that may erode shingles. This issue is still being debated, but there are other patterns that avoid the prob-

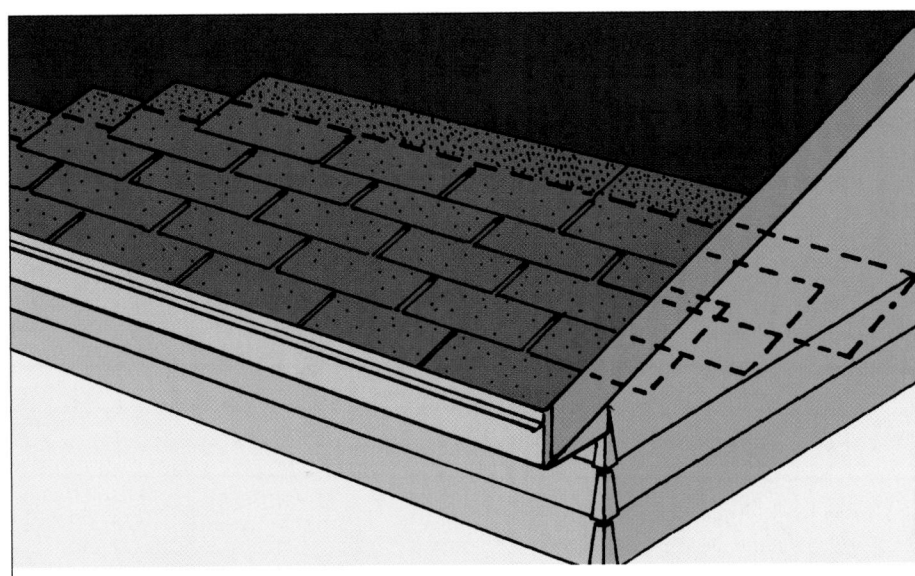

Six-Inch Method. The 6-in. method is the easiest and most common shingling pattern. Alternating tab cutouts are aligned.

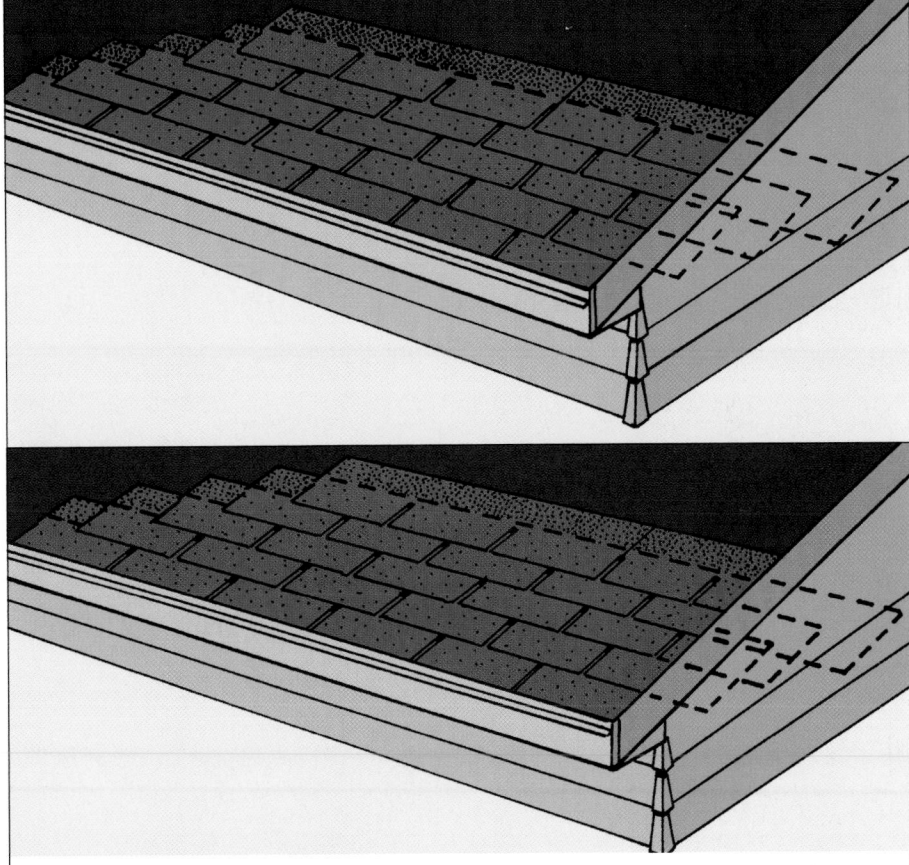

Four- and Five-Inch Method. A pleasing diagonal effect results when shingles are trimmed in 5 in. increments (top). The 4-in. method is even more abruptly diagonal. Tab cutouts align vertically only every fourth course (bottom).

lem altogether. The 5-inch method provides a bit more offset and more of a diagonal pattern to the shingles.

The 4-inch method is diagonal in appearance with two full shingles between tab slots.

Choosing to Hammer

Professional roofers who nail by hand are a vanishing breed. As a do-it-yourselfer you have two options. If you are able to set aside a block of time to complete the roof in one go you can rent a pneumatic stapler (ask the rental dealer to demonstrate safe use of the equipment). However, renting equipment results in added expenses and the additional time it takes to learn how to use that equipment. Breaking out a simple hammer is often the better choice. The following is a professional nailing technique that speeds a hammering job along.

Holding a Handful. Hold a dozen or so nails loosely in your hand. Using only one hand work a nail around so it hangs head up between your fingers. (left)

Hammering the Nail Home. Position the nail on the shingle using the nail hand only. Nail it. (center)

Working Nails into Position. While one hand is nailing, the other hand is busy readying the next nail. (right)

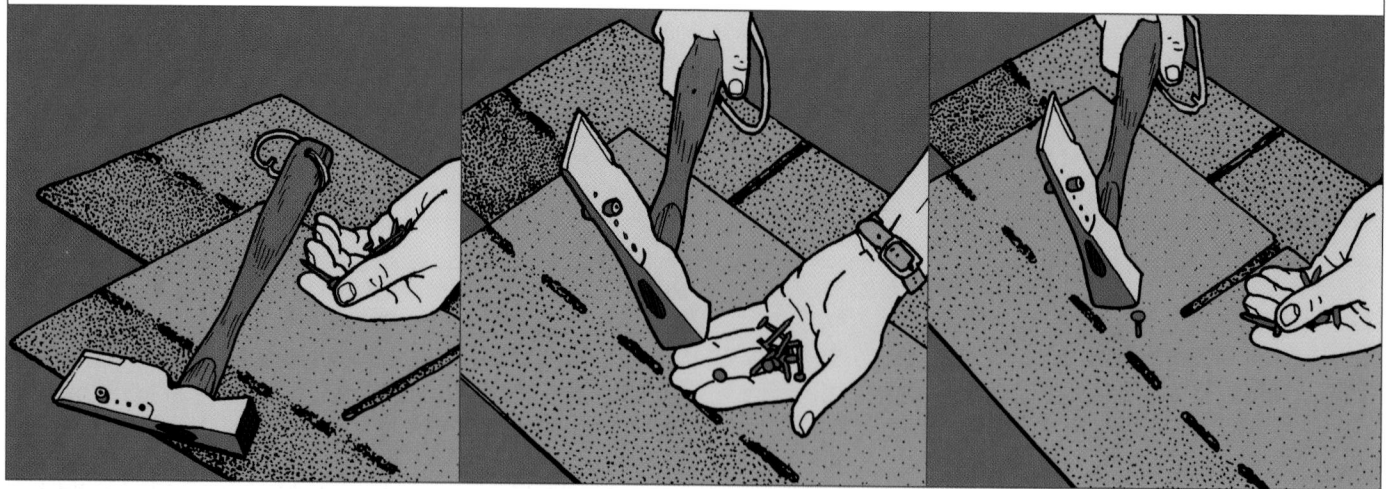

Using a Roofing Hammer

A roofing hammer speeds up any roofing job and although it is a relatively expensive tool, it is worth the investment if you are doing a large roofing job. A roofing hammer's heavy weight is an advantage for quickly whacking nails home, but be careful of its serrated head which is especially hard on fingers if you miss the nail.

With a built-in course gauge set according to the exposure desired, this hammer is far more precise and much faster than simply eyeballing the top of the shingles. The guide pin can be set in any one of the several holes for the desired course depth (left).

Hook the pin on the course below and let the bottom edge of the shingle rest against the heel of the hammer (center).

The hatchet side of the hammer is designed for splitting wood shingles to size (right). It is less useful for composition shingles, but is still good for chopping out old roofing cement or flashing.

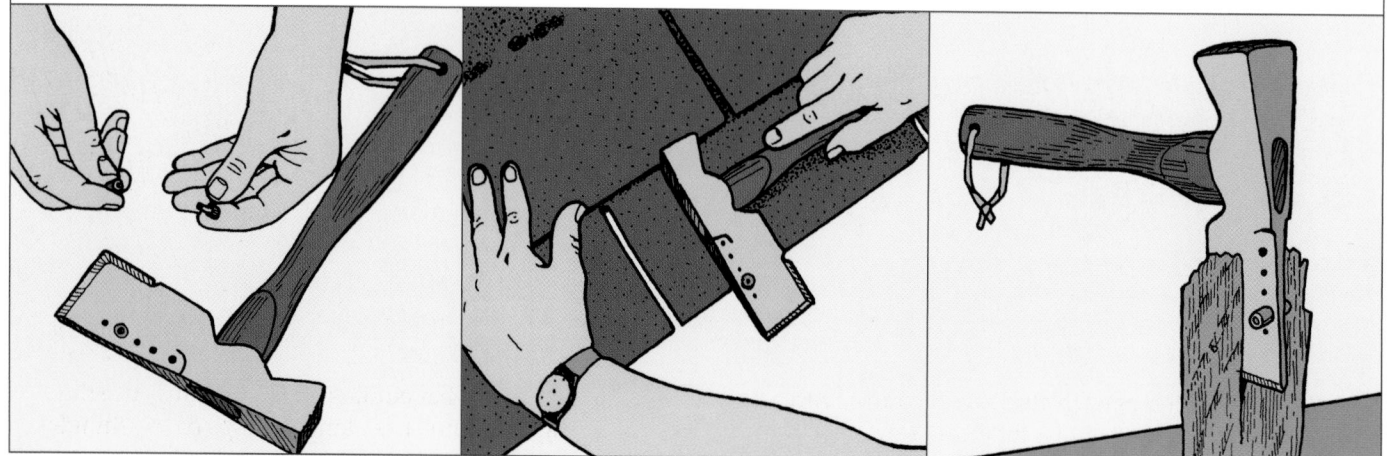

Random Shingling. With random shingling, each course is offset a multiple of 3 inches. The order of the multiples—whether they be 3, 6, 9, or 12 inches of offset—varies. The effect is a helter-skelter look with some of the character of random-width wood shingles or slates.

Shingling a Stair-Step Pattern

At this point the roof is prepared for shingling, the shingles are ordered, and the shingling pattern has been chosen. The following is a step-by-step approach to the 6-inch pattern. Except when it comes to the amount of shingle that must be trimmed, the same instructions apply to the other shingling patterns.

Rather than working across the roof one row at a time (and moving ladders, cleats, etc. each time) experienced roofers stair-step as many courses as they can safely reach—and as far across as roof brackets permit. By building up a stair-step pattern of shingles along the left-

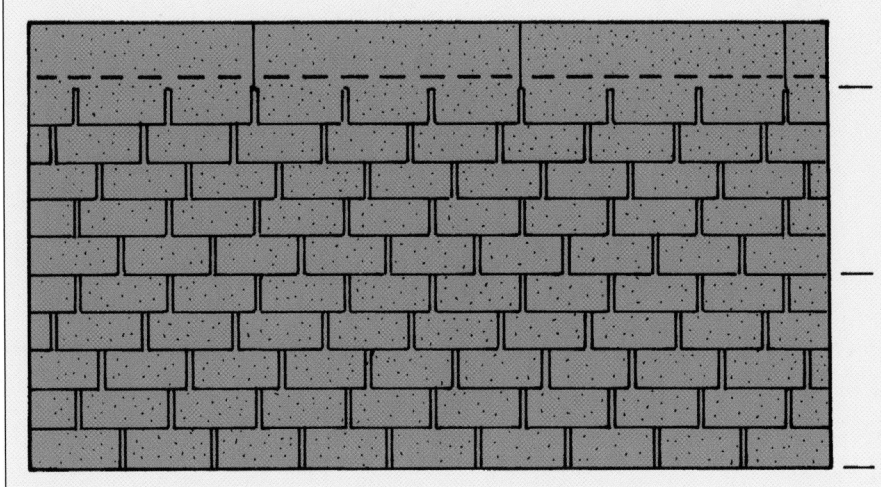

Random Shingling. This random pattern uses 3-in. cutouts in a varied order to achieve a look similar to wood shingles or slate.

hand eaves of the roof (left-handed shinglers work from the right side of the roof), you can add on a series of whole shingles without moving the roof cleats.

1 Precutting Shingles. Set up a work area on the ground. A 4x4-ft. scrap of plywood on a sawhorse is ideal. Using an angle square and a utility knife equipped with a roofing hook blade, cut a series of partial

shingles so you can stair-step up five courses. (Save scrap pieces for possible use as filler at the opposite end of the roof.)

2 Starting the Course. The first shingles are placed over the eaves course (the first course of shingles laid on top of the starter course). Double-check to be sure seams between shingles do not line up with seams in the starter course.

1 A stair-step pattern starts each course with a shingle half a tab less than the course above.

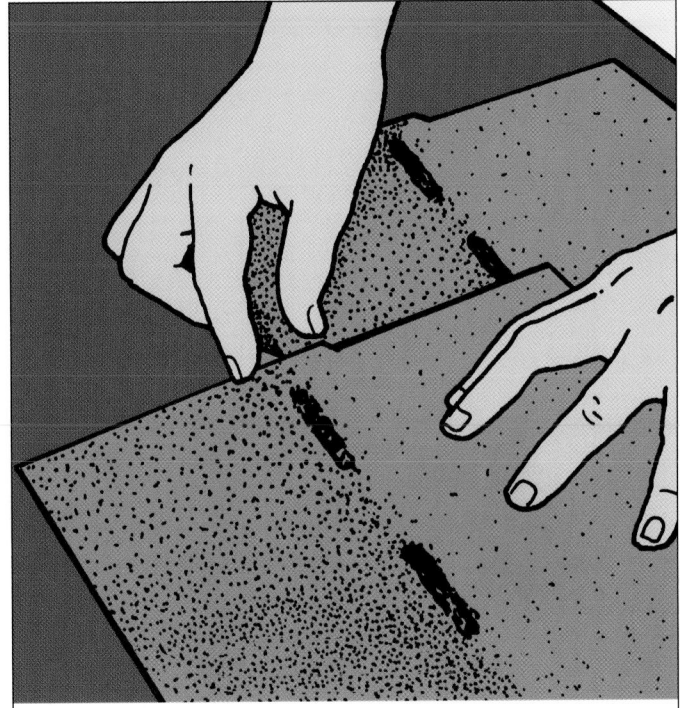

2 To ensure that cutouts align vertically, use the alignment notches along the tops of the shingles.

3 Stair-step the pieces in place along the rake edge.

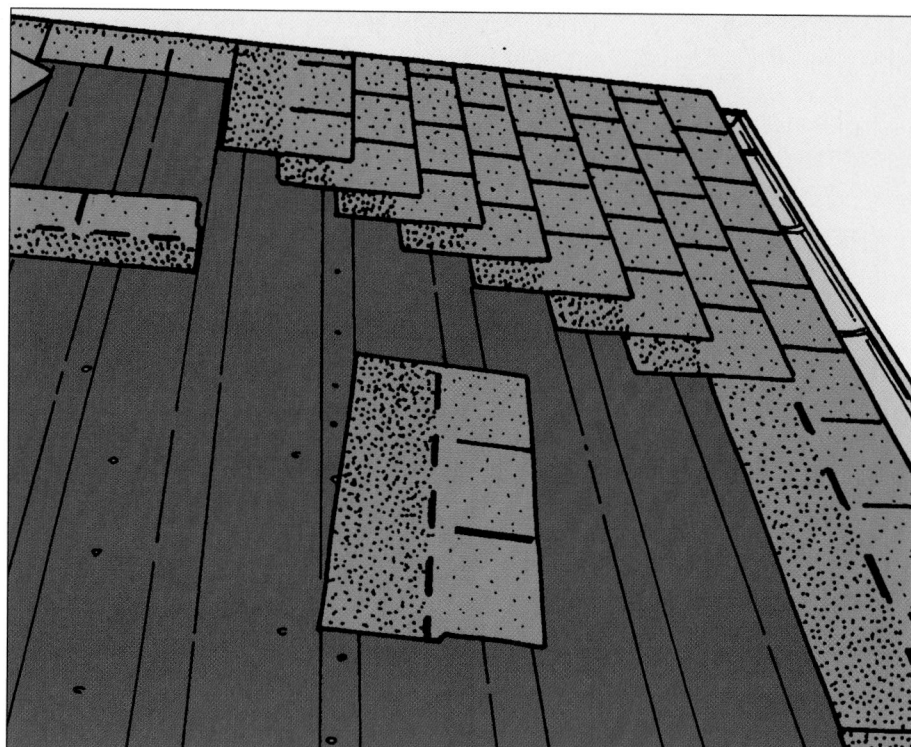

4 Measure every 12 courses or so to check that courses are running parallel to the eaves.

3 Building the Stair-Step.
Remove one half of a tab from a shingle and use this shingle to begin the second course. If you are using a roofing hammer use the gauge to keep course depth consistent. Continue adding partial shingles along the rake to achieve the stair-step pattern. Once the pattern is complete you can add course after course of whole shingles.

4 Checking and Aligning.
Almost all composition shingles have alignment notches in the middle of each tab along the upper edge of the shingle. These are especially useful when beginning courses. Pinch one side of the alignment notch upright so the new shingle butts against it. Roofs seldom are perfectly square. If correction is needed strike a chalk line as a guide for the next course.

Nesting

When applying new shingles directly over the old, the roof first must be brushed to remove any debris or loose granules. New shingles are then "nested" over the old shingles. This maintains the old exposure and provides a quick way to align the new shingles because you push the tops of the new shingles against the bottom tabs of the old. The result is a smooth, uniform covering.

Nesting is simple. Begin by trimming the tabs off a whole shingle to make a starter strip. It fits just between the eaves edge and the bottom of the second course of shingles. Note that the tab adhesive provides a good seal at the eaves. In positioning the starter strip be sure to adequately overlap tab cutouts on the first course of the old roof. Once the starter strip is in place proceed with the courses, positioning them so that cutouts offset the old cutouts by 3 inches.

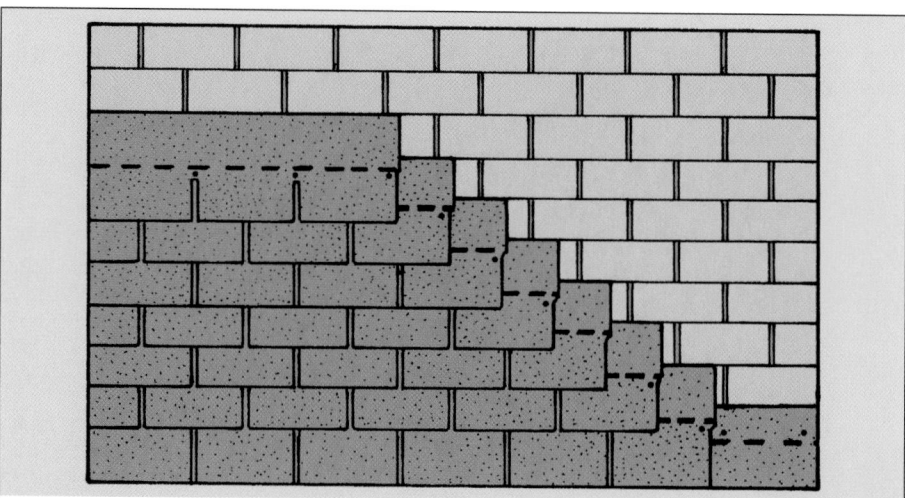

Nesting. The nesting method of applying new shingles over old provides even coverage and quick course alignment.

Ribbon Courses

A ribbon course adds interest to the standard 6-inch pattern.

After six courses have been applied cut a 4-inch-wide strip lengthwise off the upper section of a shingle. Nail it as the seventh course ¼ inch below the top of the cutouts of the sixth course. Then reverse the 8-inch-wide leftover scrap and nail it on top of the 4-inch strip (left). Cover both with the next full course. Doing this creates a three-ply edge also known as the ribbon (right).

Working on Steep Roofs

It is extremely difficult to work on a high-pitched roof. A scaffold is a necessity in these situations. Unless you own a scaffold and are experienced in using it, it's best to hire a contractor to handle steep roofs.

Roofs that exceed a slope of 21 in 12 (a mansard roof is likely to have this sort of slope) render factory-applied, self-sealing adhesive ineffective. This is because the extreme pitch makes it impossible for heat and gravity to complete the seal. In this case use extra sealant. Put a quarter-size dab of quick-setting roofing cement under each tab as you shingle. Also, apply six fasteners to each shingle: One at each end and two above and to each side of each tab cutout.

Working on Low Slopes

Water tends to be blown under shingles applied to low slopes, so special precautions must be taken. Where the rise is 2 to 4 inches in 12, use square-tab shingles with double underlayment and roofing cement. (A roof with a slope of less than 2 in 12 cannot be covered with tab shingles. Use roll or built-up roofing instead.) Apply a double thickness of underlayment, lapping each course over the preceding one by 19 inches. Start with a 19-inch strip at the eaves. If you live in a cold climate, protect against ice dams by cementing together the two felt layers up to a point 2 feet inside the interior wall line of the house.

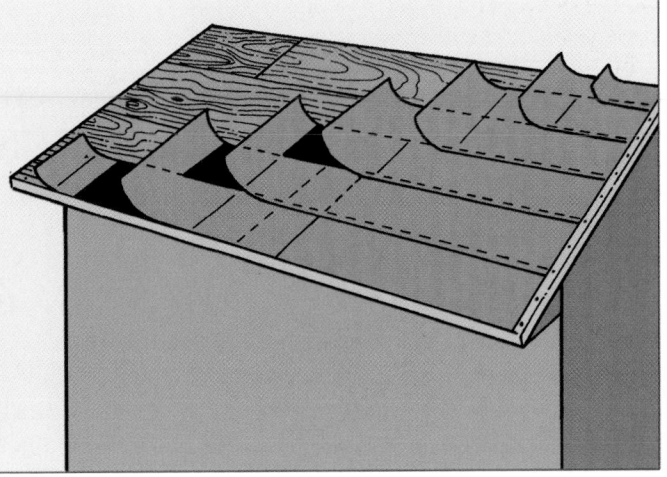

Roofing the Valleys

Valleys are among the most difficult and most important areas to roof. A valley forms the junction between two planes on a roof and must carry off a great deal of water. The two types of valleys are called open and closed. Open valleys create a channel down which water flows. Closed valleys are shingled over completely. The valley is the most vulnerable section of a roof. During a torrent, water is sometimes driven under shingles on either side of the valley, causing leaks. Always avoid stepping in a valley when working on the roof.

Building Open Valleys

1 Applying Roll Roofing. Fill in the valley with an 18-inch piece of roll roofing. Roll out the length needed from a 36 inch-wide roll. Then flip it over, strike a line at 18 inches, and cut with a utility knife. Roll it up again before carrying it up to the roof.

Coat the valley with roofing cement and lay the piece of roll roofing granule-face down. Drive a nail every 12 inches down one side. Nail the other side after nesting the piece completely into the valley, leaving no voids beneath. Then center a full-width (36-inch) piece over it, granules down. Nail along one edge only. Let the roofing run wide, which means you just let extra lengths of roofing flop over the ridge and eaves to be trimmed later. Split the roofing at the ridge and eaves so it lays flat.

Trim the lower edge flush with the eaves and cut a slight radius at the inside corner on the intersection of the eaves.

2 Shingling and Trimming. Use a chalk line to mark the center of the valley. Continue installing shingles until they reach the valley. Make sure the last shingle in each course ends within 3 inches of the centerline. Then strike guidelines for trimming the shingles. Start the lines 6 inches apart at top and let them diverge ⅛ inch per foot toward the eaves.

3 Nipping Corners. Slip a scrap of roofing under the shingles and trim the new shingles using a utility knife with a hook blade. Be careful not to pierce the roll roofing. When one side is completely trimmed work your way back up the other side, trimming the uppermost corner of each shingle. This prevents the corner from catching water and pulling it under the shingle.

4 Nailing and Cementing Shingles. Nail the shingles at least 4 inches from the trim edge. Use roofing cement to seal down the shingles.

1 Open valleys have a central channel of doubled roll roofing laid granule face down.

Chalk Line

2 After shingling the roof, snap a chalk line to trim the valley.

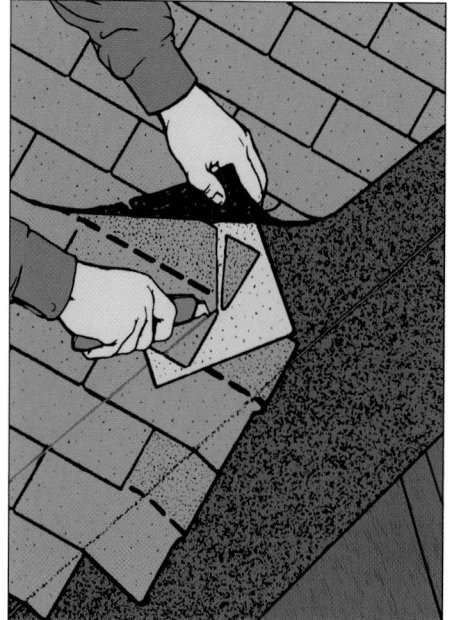

3 Use a utility knife to trim the uppermost corner off each shingle along the valley.

4 Cement shingles to each other and to the roll roofing in the valley.

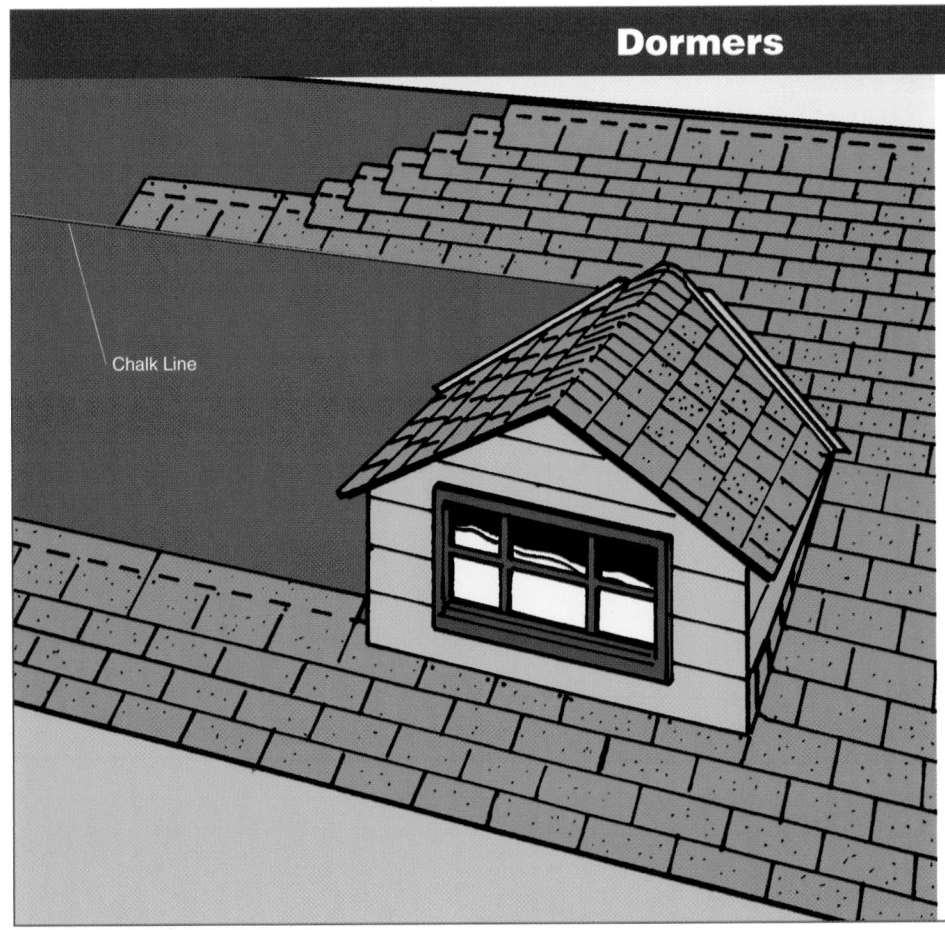

Chalk Line

As the valley leads you up one side of the dormer, you probably are wondering how to evenly match the courses of shingles on the other side. Once you have worked your way to a dormer and have completed one valley, continue the topmost course past the ridge of the dormer. Chalk a line that extends the course. If possible, check the trueness of the extended line by measuring down from the roof ridge. Nail along the top of the course only so that shingles may be slipped under it later.

Once the course is extended about 10 feet, strike parallel chalk lines 36 inches apart to serve as a guide for aligning cutouts as the other side of the dormer is shingled. As you complete shingling on the other side of the dormer, check course alignment as well. Fortunately, shingles are a forgiving material and slight adjustments, if made over several courses or shingles, are not noticeable.

Building Closed Valleys

Closed valleys have no channel and are created by continuing the roofing material across the valley. A woven valley (sometimes referred to as a laced valley) is the quickest type of closed valley to install. A slightly more time-consuming variation is the half-weave valley (sometimes called closed-cut or half-laced valley) in which the overlapping layer of roofing is neatly trimmed.

Both types begin with one layer of 36-inch-wide roll roofing. Hold the roll roofing in place with temporary nails tapped lightly into the surface 1 inch from the outer edge of the valley. (The nails from the shingles fasten it permanently later.) Be careful to work roofing into the valley cavity. This job is easier done on a warm day, as warm shingles become pliable enough to lay down completely and without voids. Trim excess at eaves. At the ridge, allow the piece to flop over the opposite roof face.

Building Closed Valleys. A woven valley is made up of interlacing shingles from adjacent roof faces. The job is done quickly, but does not offer the best protection or appearance.

Full Weave. In this case, overlaps stack up on one side to compensate for the difference in pitch. Do not nail within 6 in. of the centerline of a valley.

Half Weave. One group of shingles is laid across the valley. Shingles on the opposite side are trimmed to bisect the valley with a crisp line.

Full Weave. Complete shingling adjacent planes of the roof that meet at the valley. With a helper, complete the shingling of each plane, weaving the shingles by laying alternate shingles down at each course and pushing them into the valley. Clip the uppermost corner of every overlapping shingle. Apply two nails at the side of the shingle that crosses the valley.

Do not nail within 6 inches of the centerline of a valley. If the pitch of the roof differs on either side of the valley you may have to weave as many as three shingles on one side to one on the other.

Half-Weave. The half-weave valley is a variation on the woven valley. Begin by laying down roll roofing as described. Completely shingle one side of the roof overlapping the valley at least 12 inches beyond the centerline. Next, shingle the opposite side letting the shingles overlap the finished side. Clip the uppermost corner of every overlapping shingle. Do not nail within 6 inches of the centerline of the valley. Strike a chalkline down the center of the valley and trim the shingles. Trim corners nearest the valley and seal shingles with roofing cement.

Air Vents & Plumbing Stacks

Shingling around Air Vents.

Reroofing (or tearing off and adding a new roof) presents the opportunity to add new air vents to the attic. Old, dented vents also can be replaced while you are on the roof. The roofing principles for handling air vents and plumbing stacks are the same: Flashing covers shingles below the object, shingles overlap the flashing above the object. Adhere the vent with a coating of roofing cement.

Shingling around Air Vents. Install air vents so that shingles cover at least the top half of the vent flashing. Work roofing cement under the flashing. Nail the bottom edges with galvanized roofing nails, and cover the heads with roofing cement.

Shingling around Stacks. The most thorough way to roof around a stack is to remove the flashing. Older homes have lead flashing while newer homes have aluminum or vinyl flashing. (Replacement stack flashing can be readily purchased if the old flashing is damaged.) Continue the courses of roofing beneath the vent, notching them with a utility knife to fit around the pipe. Nail and cement the flashing into place so that it covers the courses below. Continue the courses so that those halfway above the pipe overlap the flashing. Notch them as necessary and seal with roofing cement.

The flashing around a plumbing stack overlaps the same shingles that the stack pierces. Trim an overlapping tab so that it surrounds the stack. Use roofing cement to seal the job.

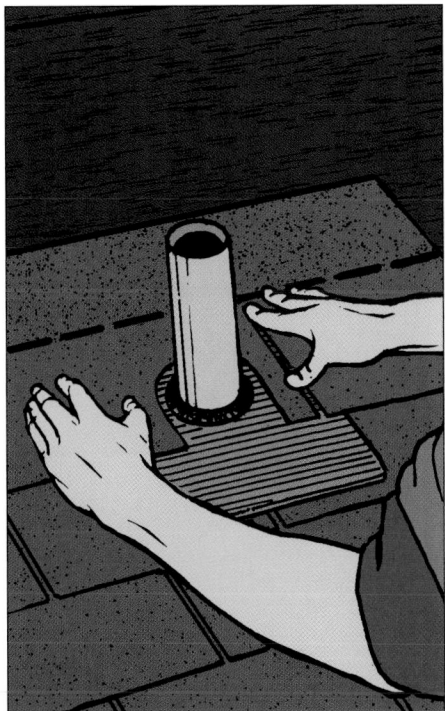

Shingling around Stacks. Fit the vent collar onto the stack and over the new roofing. Fasten it with roofing cement. Shingles should overlap only the upper half of the vent collar. Trim the overlapping shingles around the stack, maintaining a ½-in. gap. Seal the shingle tabs down with roofing cement.

Shingling Ridges

The ridge of your roof runs from the peak of one gable to the peak of the other. It's the point at which both slopes come together. Here's how to shingle the ridge.

1 Gang-Cutting Tabs. Ridges are made by cutting single tabs off of shingles. The easiest way to do this is to stack a bunch of shingles neatly together. Use a square as a guide as you cut through the first shingle to separate the tabs. Taper the cuts slightly as shown in the drawing. Then you can use the top shingle as a guide to slice through the shingles below.

2 Trimming Final Course. Wrap ridge shingle piece over the ridge to check whether you need another course of shingles on either slope. Trim the last course of shingles to fit just up to the ridge.

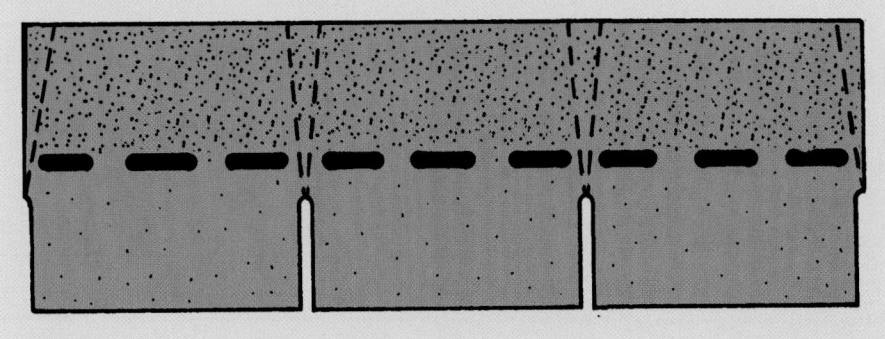

1 Cut single tabs from whole shingles and taper the unexposed area as shown.

2 Apply and trim the final course of shingles. Trim the last course of shingles on each slope to end at the ridge.

A caulk gun loaded with a tube of roofing cement is a handy tool when it comes to finishing up the job. It can be used to seal tabs where roof cleats were suspended, to seal nails on gutter hangers, to coat bolts that hold antennas to the roof, and to seal tabs that may have curled at the edges (below).

Strike a chalk line where the shingles overlap the rake by ¼ to ⅜ inch. Then use a utility knife to trim the rake edges (right).

3 **Wrapping the Ridge.** Strike a chalk line on the most visible side of the house, usually the front. Wrap a single tab over the ridge, making sure the alignment notch centers the very apex. Use this as a guide for snapping the line. If there is a prevailing wind direction in your area, work toward it. Apply one nail at either side of each tab and just in front of the sealant line.

4 **Topping it off.** Nail the final shingle, and cover the nailheads with roofing cement. Seal each tab with roofing cement for a truly windproof ridge.

5 **Mitering Ridge Shingles.** Begin the ridge of a hip roof with a single tab mitered to suit the shape of the eaves. Position the tab, mark along the eaves line at either side, and cut using a square as a guide. Work along the ridge in the same way you would for a gable ridge (see page 47). At the top of the hip ridge, miter adjacent tabs and overlap them with a tab that has been specially cut and folded into a cap.

3 Strike a chalk line, and apply the shingles with a 5-in. exposure.

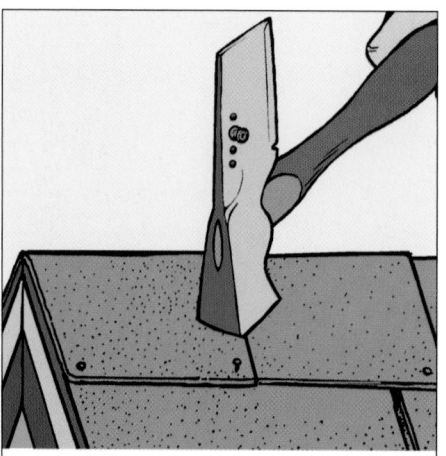

4 To prevent water seepage and wind damage, seal each tab with roofing cement.

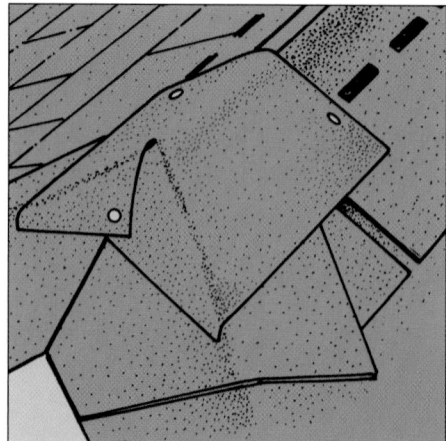

5 Use mitered ridge shingles to begin a hip roof ridge, and cap it with a cut and folded shingle.

wood shingles

Roofing with Wood

Wood shingles and shakes usually are made of Western red cedar, a long-lasting, straight-grained wood. The grain is what gives the wood surprising strength whether it is cut thick or very thin. Even after years of weathering, wood does a much better job of shedding water than might be expected. In addition, wood shingles and shakes resist heat transmission twice as well as composition shingles.

Wood shingles often require more maintenance than other roofing options, especially if you live in a harsh climate. In such areas it is advisable to treat wood shingles and shakes with a preservative every five years or so. Regular cleaning also is recommended to clear away debris that traps moisture and breeds fungus, mildew, rot, and insect borers. Wood shingles and shakes are not fire resistant and some local codes may even require that the wood be pressure treated. Some localities have banned wood roofing altogether; be sure to check your local codes before deciding to use wood shingles or shakes. In addition, check with your insurance company to see if your premiums will be affected.

Choosing Between Shingles & Shakes

Shingles are thinner than shakes and are sawn smooth on both sides. Shakes often are split by hand rather than cut and have a very irregular surface. They are thicker and therefore more durable than shingles which typically last no more than 20 to 25 years. There are two common types of shakes used in residential roofing. One type, called tapersplit, is split on both sides. Tapersplits are made by hand. The other type, called handsplit and resawn, is split from the block and then sawn to produce two shingles, each with one split and one sawn face.

Straight-split shakes do not taper in thickness (as do all other wood shin-

gles and shakes) and are not intended for residential use.

Both shakes and shingles are available in number 1, 2, and 3 grades. Grade number 1 is cut from heartwood, a clear (knot-free), completely edge-grained wood that is the more resistant to rot than the other grades. It is also the most expensive of the grades. Buy the best grade you can afford. Grade number 2 has a limited amount of sapwood. (Sapwood is less rot-resistant than heartwood.) In addition, number two grade has some knots and is flat grained. It is acceptable for residential roofing. Use grade number 3 shingles or shakes for outbuildings only. Shingles also come in a grade 4 which has large knots and is only acceptable for a starter course. Shakes don't come in grade 4.

The shingle length needed is determined by the desired exposure (the length of shingle exposed to weather). Exposure is determined by pitch. Shingle widths vary from 3 to 9 inches.

Reroofing with Shingles & Shakes

With the proper preparation you can shingle over a roof of wood shingles.

However, you cannot shingle over shakes due to their irregular shape. Both shingles and shakes can be installed over composition shingles.

In order to install shingles and shakes, the roof must have a large enough slope. The reason for this is simple. Unlike self-sealing composition shingles or roll roofing, voids remain between courses of wood shingles and shakes. With enough pitch for quick runoff this poses no problem, but when installed on a low-slope, roof shingles are not protected from windblown rain and snow.

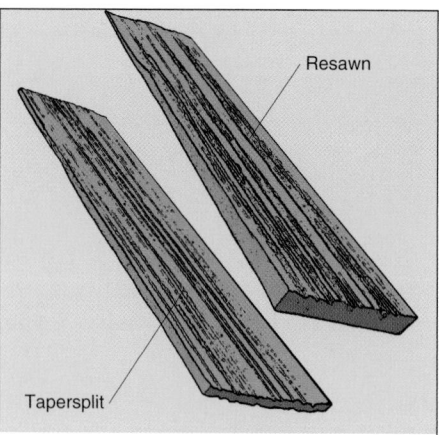

Wooden Shakes. Handsplit and resawn shakes have a split top face and a sawn bottom face. A tapersplit is handmade by splitting on both sides.

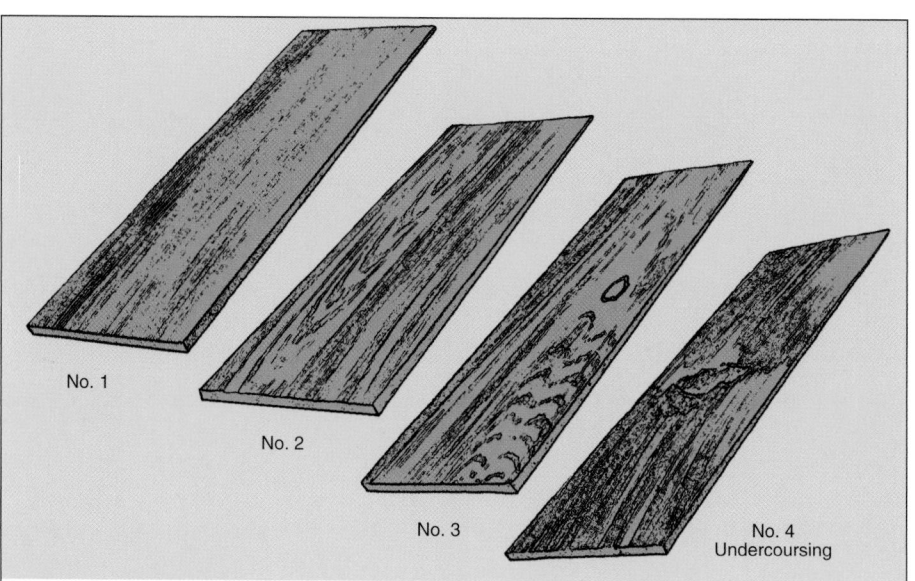

Wooden Shingles. Shingles come in four grades with clear heartwood being the best and undercoursing being the worse.

Shingles are not recommended for roofs with less than a 3-in-12 slope. (See pages 33–34.) Shakes are not recommended for roofs with a slope of less than a 4 in 12. Exposure also must be limited for slight slopes. For example, with a 3-in-12 slope, 16-inch shingles must have a maximum of 3³/₄-inch exposure (5 inches on a 4-in-12 slope). Eighteen-inch shingles may be exposed a maximum of 4¹/₄ inches (5¹/₂ inches on a 4-in-12 slope). Shingles that are 24 inches long can have the greatest exposure (5³/₄ inches on a 3-in-12 slope and 7¹/₂ inches on a 4-in-12 slope).

Nailing Patterns

Apply shingles and shakes with only two nails per shingle. As the courses overlap, four nails pierce each shingle or shake. Place nails about ¾ inch from each edge and 1 to 2 inches above the lowest edge of the overlapping course. Stagger joints at least 1¹/₂ inches.

Nailing Guides. To keep courses straight, tack a 1x4 guide in place for each course or use the adjustable gauge on a roofing hammer.

Building Special Helpers

Wood shingles and shakes are slippery compared to the gritty grab of composition shingles, so its a good idea to use a toeboard to help keep yourself and your materials on the roof. A toeboard is simply a long 2x4. Use three shakes or shingles as shown to shim the toeboard off the roof, giving you a deeper toe hold. Use 16d or 20d nails through the toeboard, shims, roofing and sheathing and into the rafter below. For a handy place to nest a bundle of shingles, nail two scrap shingles upright on the toeboards. Use a toeboard every 3 or 4 feet up the roof.

A simple seat with a spiked base that grips the newly applied shingles also comes in handy. Build it with plywood and 1x4s. Drill ¹/₁₆-inch pilot holes and screw the pieces together with 6x1⅝ galvanized deck screws. Drive roofing nails through the 1x4s before attaching them to the seat. The nails stick into the roof to keep you from sliding.

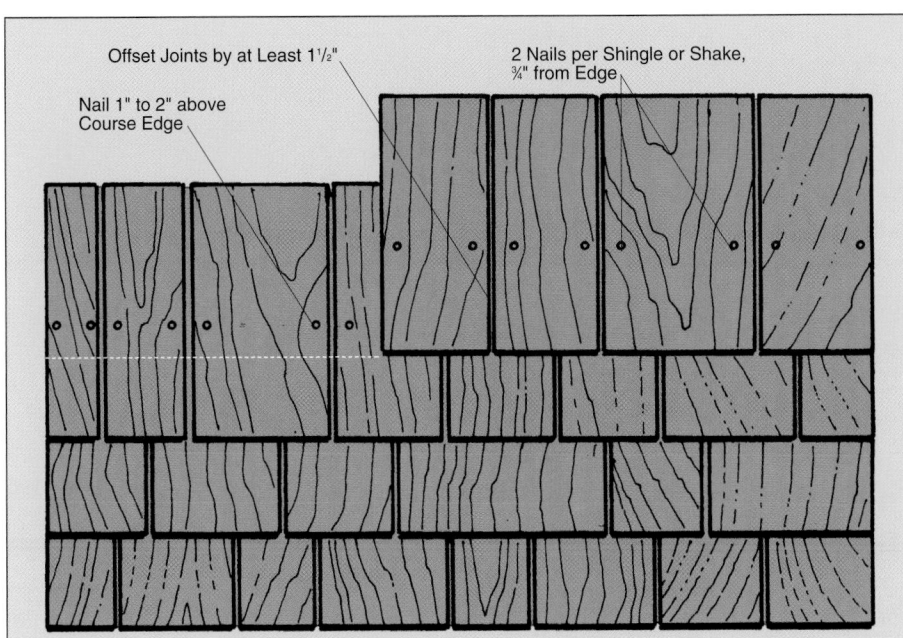

Offset Joints by at Least 1¹/₂"

Nail 1" to 2" above Course Edge

2 Nails per Shingle or Shake, ¾" from Edge

Nailing Patterns. Each shingle or shake is applied with two nails. Due to overlapping courses, four nails ultimately hold each shingle.

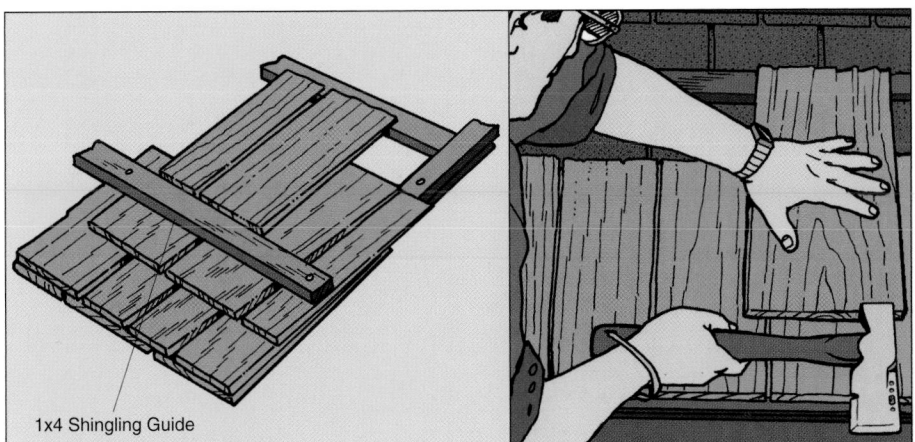

1x4 Shingling Guide

Nailing Guides. For quick application and a crisp finish use a guide board for positioning shingles or shakes (left). A roofing hammer with an adjustable course guide speeds up the job of aligning shingles (right).

Applying Sheathing & Underlayment

Wood roofing benefits greatly from ventilation so it almost always has spaced sheathing. The space allows shingles to dry after rain thereby preventing rot. Solid sheathing, however, still is used at ridges, eaves, rakes, and places exposed to great amounts of wind and snow.

Always use 30-pound felt underlayment when installing shakes. The irregular shape of the shakes allows plenty of air circulation. For wood shingles use underlayment only in areas where ice may collect and at the eaves and rakes.

Before laying shakes (not shingles) nail a drip edge along the eaves.

Begin by laying a full sheet of felt. All subsequent sheets are 18 inches wide. If you cannot purchase 18-inch felt, cut the sheets to size.

When adding a layer of new shingles over old, ventilation channels are made by installing a new underlayment. This process includes removing old shingles, furring out the ridge, renewing the valley flashing and adding a 1x6 nailer at the eaves and rakes.

By adding a similar system of underlayment wood shingles can be installed on top of composition shingles. Trim back the composition shingles where they extend beyond the edge of the roof before installing underlayment.

Covering Wood Shingles

1 **Removing the Ridge.** Use a flat shovel or crowbar to remove the old ridge.

2 **Renewing the Valley.** Fur out the valley to bring it to the level of the original shingles. Resurface with new flashing.

3 **Reinforcing the Ridge.** Beveled siding turned upside down reinforces the ridge and counteracts the bevel of the last course of shingles.

4 **Sheathing Rake and Eaves.** Use the sharp edge of a roofing hammer to cut away shingles along the rake and eaves. Open a cavity into which a 1x6 piece of sheathing can be nailed.

1 The first step in adding a new layer to an old wood roof is to pry off the old ridge with a crowbar or a flat shovel.

2 Use 1x3s to fill in the valleys so they will be flush with the old roof. Resurface by installing W-metal flashing.

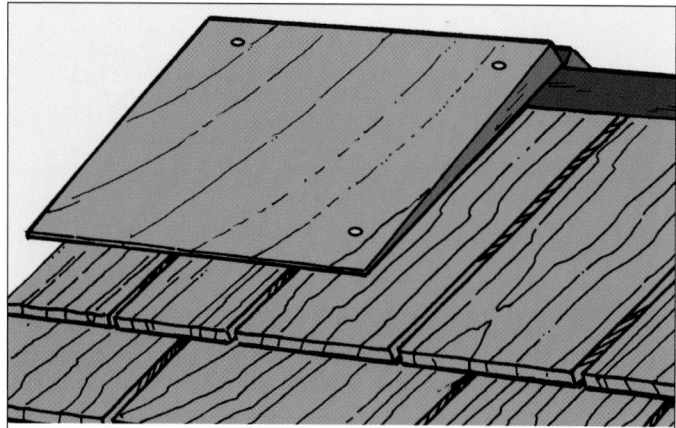

3 Use beveled cedar siding turned upside down to reinforce the ridge and counteract the bevel of the last course of old shingles.

4 Cut away rake and eaves shingles with the sharp edge of a roofing hammer to make room for 1x6 sheathing.

Covering Asphalt Shingles

1 Trimming Back. Use a sharpened roofing hammer to cut away the overhang created by the old composition shingles.

2 Applying Solid Sheathing. Using 8d galvanized nails, add 1x6 sheathing to provide a solid nailing surface at the ridge, rakes, and eaves. Use pairs of 1x3s in the valleys.

3 Applying Ventilation Strips. Space 1x3s a distance equal to the desired exposure of the shingles. Metal flashing is applied to the valley before installing shingle courses. (See page 52.)

1 Trim the old shingles flush to the rake with a utility knife or sharp roofing hammer.

2 Sheathe ridge, rakes, eaves and valley with 1x6 boards fastened with 8d galvanized nails.

3 Ventilation strips, sometimes called "skip" sheathing, allow air to pass between the shingles and the asphalt roof. The strips are made of 1x3s.

Installing Shingles

1 Aligning First Shingles. Lay a starter course that overhangs the eaves by 1 inch. To establish a straight line tack a shingle at either end of the eaves, positioning it so it overhangs the rake by ¼ to ⅜ inch and the eaves by 1 inch.

2 Lining Up the Starter Course. Tack a nail into the butt of each starter shingle at the end of the eaves and run a line between the two. Use the line as a guide for laying the starter course.

3 Adding Courses. Leave ⅛- to ¼-inch spaces between shingles. Always stagger spaces at least 1½ inches as courses overlap. Snap a chalk line to ensure a straight second course. Set your roofing hammer (if you have one) to the correct exposure and use it as a guide for placing the shingles. Snap a chalk line to check alignment every three or four courses. Use 3d nails for 16- and 18-inch shingles, and 4d for 24-inch shingles. Always use galvanized nails.

4 Cutting Valley Shingles. Use a spare shingle to transfer the angle of the valley to the shingles that will be installed. Align the butt of the shingle at the eaves line, mark the angle and cut. Once you have captured this angle, shingles can be gang cut down on the ground.

5 Using a Guide for Valleys. A piece of one-by carefully placed (not nailed) in the valley provides a simple guide for aligning shingles along the valley. Allow the final course at the top of the roof to extend above the ridge line. Stretch a chalkline even with the ridge line and snap it on the shingles. Score the overhang with a utility knife. Press downward slightly to snap off the excess. Finish hips and ridges with factory-made ridge shingles. (See page 56.)

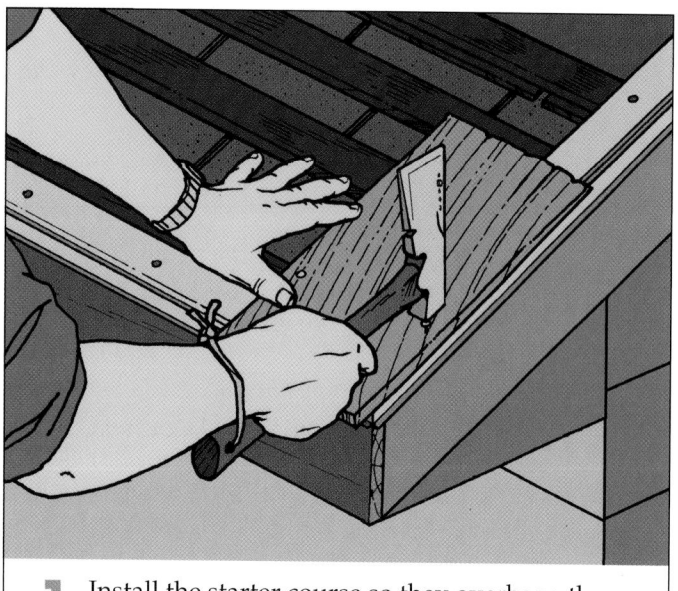
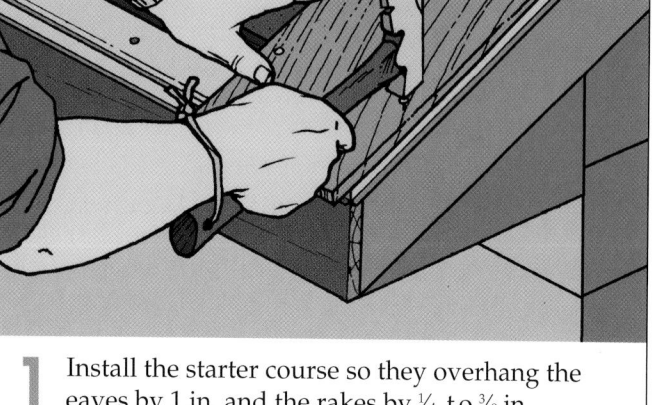

1 Install the starter course so they overhang the eaves by 1 in. and the rakes by ¼ to ⅜ in.

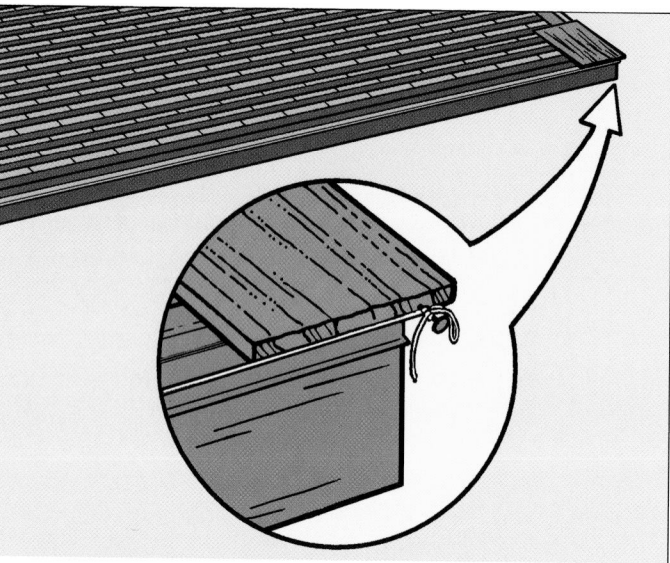

2 Run a line from a nail in the butt of the starter shingles. This line is a guide for the first course.

3 Each shingle receives two nails about ¾ in. from the edge. Use galvanized nails.

4 A spare shingle transfers the angle of the valley to the shingle to be installed.

5 A piece of 1x4 laid in the valley simplifies shingle alignment. Do not nail the 1x4.

Installing Shakes

1 Applying Roll Underlayment. Unlike shingles, shakes require 18-inch underlayment sandwiched between each course. The underlayment helps shed water and blocks windblown rain. Before laying the first course, install 36-inch-wide, 15- or 30-pound felt underlayment at the eaves. (The felt weight depends on local code.) If you live in a climate with a lot of rain and snow it is best to consider shakes only if the roof has a slope of at least 6 in 12. The irregular pattern that results with shakes provides a major advantage in that you can reroof over composition shingles or solid sheathing. The irregular pattern allows for airflow which is crucial to wood shingles and shakes.

2 Gauging Each Course. Shakes are available in 18- and 24-inch lengths. Typical exposures are 7½ inches for 18-inch shakes and 10 inches for 24 inch shakes. You can use your hammer as an exposure guide by measuring up the handle and wrapping a piece of tape around the desired length of exposure.

Begin applying shakes with a doubled starter course that overhangs the eaves by 2 inches and the rakes by 1½ inches. To establish a straight eaves line, tack in place two shakes; one at either end of the eaves. Position each shake so it protrudes 2 inches beyond the drip edge. Hammer a nail into the edge and run a line taut between the two shakes. Each shake just touches the line as the starter course is applied. Set a similar line for the rake. Each shake receives two nails about ¾-inch from the edge. Use 7d galvanized nails for shakes.

Leave a ½-inch gap between shakes. When a course is completed install an 18-inch-wide strip of 30-pound felt underlayment. Position the bottom edge of the felt above the shake butt at a distance equal to twice the weather exposure. Offset the gaps between shingles in neighboring courses by at least 1½ inches.

3 Marking Valley Shakes. Lay a spare shake parallel with the valley and over a shake that has been lined up even with the eaves edge. Mark a line and cut the shake. Use this shake as a template for gang-cutting shakes on a table saw.

4 Using a Guide for Valleys. A piece of one-by carefully placed (not nailed) in the valley provides a simple guide for aligning shakes that border the valley. Trim underlayment between shake courses to 2 inches short of the guide board.

5 Extending Final Courses. Allow the final courses at the top of the roof to extend above the ridge. Snap a chalk line at the ridge height and trim shakes with a circular saw. Finish hips and ridges with factory-made ridge shakes.

1 Begin by installing 36-in.-wide underlayment along the eaves.

2 Install 18-in.-wide underlayment between courses of shakes.

3 Use a spare shake to transfer the angle of the valley.

4 Trim underlayment 2 in. short of the 1x4 guide board.

5 Strike a line and use a circular saw to cut shakes at the ridge.

Finishing Shingles & Shakes

1 Installing the Ridge. Precut, factory-made ridge shingles are well worth the money. Begin by striking a line along the side of the ridge that is most visible from the ground. Use ridge shingles at either end of the ridge to set the chalkline. Alternate the mitered joint of the ridge shingles as you work up the ridge.

2 Alternating Overlap. If working on a peak, begin applying the ridge shingles at the end farthest from prevailing weather so that shingles overlap away from the weather. Alternate the overlap of the mitered joint of the precut ridge shingles. On the ridge of a hip roof, double the starter course at the eaves.

3 Nailing Ridge Shingles. Drive two nails into the midpoint of each ridge shingle and just beyond the point of overlap of the next course.

Note: When installing shakes wrap the last course of underlayment over the ridge.

4 Installing Stack Flashing. When applying shingles or shakes around plumbing stacks, bring the courses of shingles past the vent, and notch them with a keyhole saw or sabre saw. Cut two layers of felt slightly smaller than the base of the stack flashing. The felt fills in variations in the grain. Seal the flashing to the shingles beneath with two layers of 30-pound felt.

5 Notching Shingles around the Stack. Notch the next course in place. Shingles and shakes permit flexibility around the vent; it is okay for some water to flow beneath the shingles.

6 Surrounding the Stack. With wood shingles (unlike composition shingles) it is possible to completely wrap the stack without causing a back flow. To increase coverage you may choose to drop a shingle down from the final course so that it overlaps the stack flashing.

1 Use ridge shakes to set guides. Then strike a chalk line along the most visible roof plane.

2 Alternate ridge miters to avoid the chance of moisture seepage along the ridge.

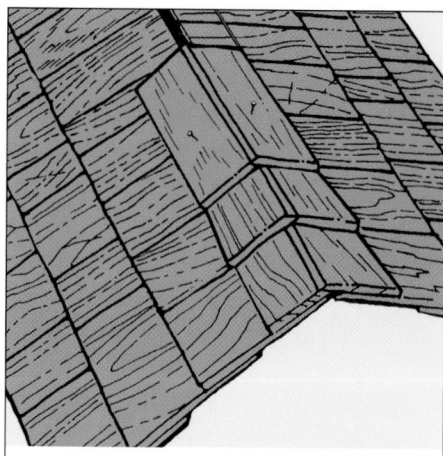

3 Apply two nails: one on each side of the ridge and behind the overlap of the next ridge shingle.

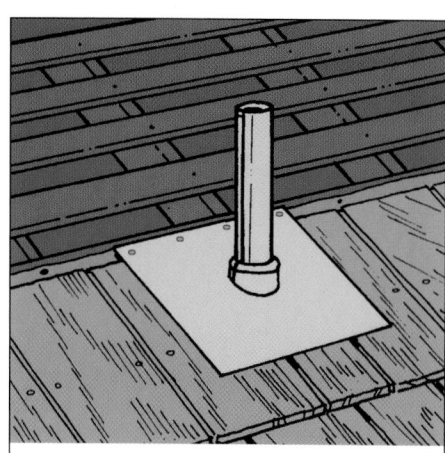

4 Vent flashing overlaps at least one course. Nail the upper edge to the sheathing only.

5 Overlap the stack flashing, notching shingles 1 in. from the stack.

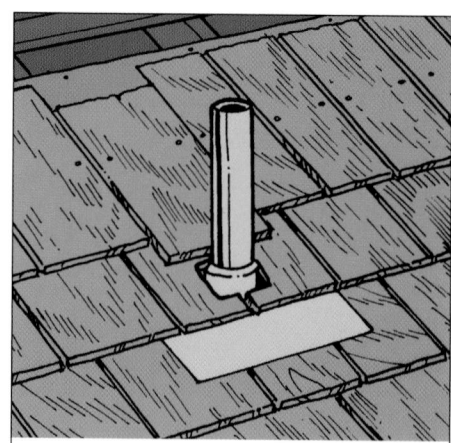

6 Notching is allowed as water flow escapes beneath the shingles and on top of the flashing.

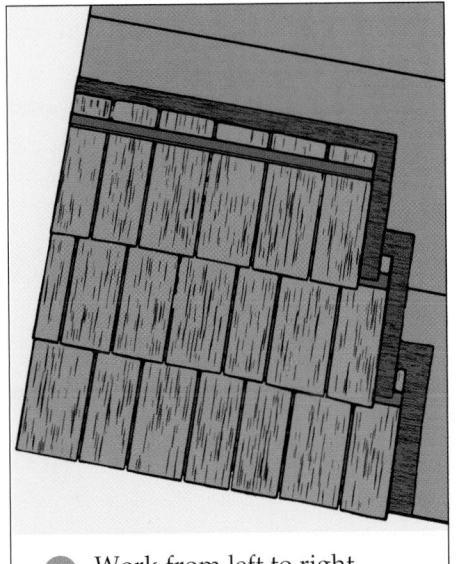

1 Two layers of panels form the starter course.

2 Work from left to right. Offset each course by 6 in.

Panelized Shingles

Wood shingles and shakes are available in prebonded panels, and although they are more expensive than regular shingles and shakes, they also are much quicker to install. Manufacturers claim that panels are installed twice as fast as composition shingles and four times faster than individual shakes or shingles. The panels are glued together in two- and three-ply sections that are 8 feet long. The panels are available in exposures ranging from $5\frac{1}{2}$ inches (for shingles) to 9 inches (for shakes). They are applied on roofs with pitches that are 4 in 12 or greater. Each panel has a score line that is used to align courses. One fastener per shingle or shake holds each panel in place (7 fasteners per panel).

1 Applying the Starter Course. If the roofing is to be applied directly over sheathing, first cover the sheathing with an underlayment of 15-pound felt. (Skip the felt if you are covering composition shingles.) Apply two layers of panels for the starter course, overhanging the eaves by $1\frac{1}{2}$ inches and the rake by 2 inches. Nail the first layer of the starter course with two nails halfway up both ends. Then remove the felt backing from panels to be used on the second layer and nail them in place with seven nails, offsetting them by at least $1\frac{1}{2}$ inches. Use No. 13 gauge, $\frac{7}{32}$-inch-head, rust-resistant nails or 2-inch-long, $\frac{7}{16}$-inch crown corrosion-resistant staples. Because the felt backing of the panels extends 4 inches on the right side of each panel, they must be laid from left to right.

2 Applying Additional Courses. Offset the second and subsequent courses by 6 inches. Trim 6 inches off the first panel of the second course, 12 inches off the third course, 18 inches off the third course, and so on. The seventh course panel will be about 7 inches long. Save the trimmings—they can be used on the opposite rake. Each panel is scribed at the exposure line for a quick and easy guideline.

3 Trimming Valleys. Cover valleys with 36-inch felt and lay down W-metal valley flashing. (See page 25.) Trim courses as they are applied so that they are at least $1\frac{1}{2}$ inch from the centerline of the valley.

4 Roofing around Obstructions. Adjust courses as you approach a vent stack or other obstruction so you can notch the shingles without cutting into the nailing bar. Courses can be adjusted up to 2 inches per course without becoming noticeable. Make sure each course has no more than a 9-inch exposure. Adjust the courses as you approach the ridge. The goal is to end up with full-depth panels. Before installing the last course, wrap a 10-inch-wide piece of felt over the ridge. Use standard precut ridge shingles to finish the job. (See page 56.)

3 Trim panel ends to $1\frac{1}{2}$ in. between the center of the valley and the trimmed edge.

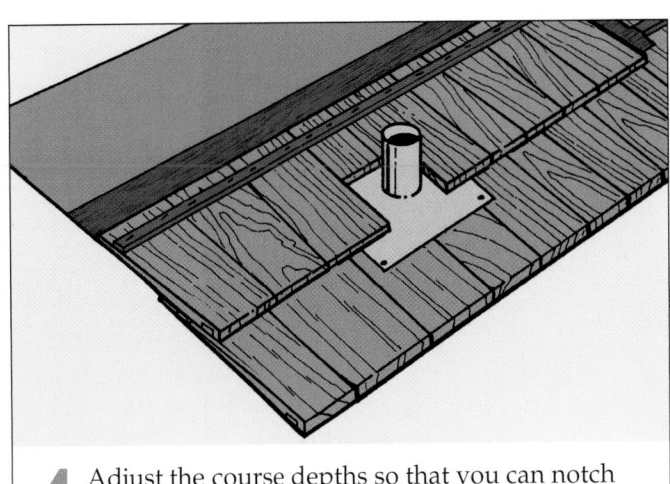

4 Adjust the course depths so that you can notch for vents without cutting the nailing bar.

Wood-Fiber Panels

Wood-fiber panels are another handy alternative to wood shingles. They are embossed with deep shadow lines and random-cut grooves that mimic the look of shakes. These 12 x 48-inch panels are applied lengthwise across the roof. They overlap with a shiplap joint between courses and a lap joint between shingles in the same course. The panels can be applied over solid sheathing or over old roofing (if the surface is sound and a layer of felt is added first). Cut the panels with a circular saw equipped with a plywood-cutting blade.

Wood-fiber panels are quick and easy to install and after a few months they weather to a silver-like gray that is very similar to cedar shingles. They can be used on roofs that have a 4-in-12 or greater slope.

1 Applying the Starter Course. Before installing wood-fiber shingles, apply a drip edge, 18 inch-wide, 30-pound felt at the eaves and 36 inch-wide, 30-pound felt underlayment. Cut 2½-inch-wide panel starter strips, applying them so that they overlap the eaves by 1 inch and the rakes by 2 inches. As you apply the the first course of full panels, offset the joints by 15 inches. Apply 8 fasteners per panel: Begin with one centered over the shiplap joint and end with one 3 inches in from the edge. Use 11-gauge roofing nails that penetrate ¾ inch into the deck, or 16-gauge staples that penetrate 1 inch into the deck.

2 Applying Subsequent Courses. Add the subsequent courses, offsetting end joints by at least 15 inches. The panels have two kinds of grooves in them: One type mimics the ridges found in a hand-split shake, the other type is deeper and mimics spaces between shingles. For appearance sake avoid lining up the deeper grooves even though functionally it makes no difference. Wood fiber panels have two score lines for your convenience: One for aligning the course, the other as a guide for nailing. Still, check the alignment every six or eight courses by measuring up from the eaves. Strike a chalk line if adjustment is needed.

3 Preparing the Valleys. Line the valleys with 36-inch felt and 24-inch-wide W-metal. Trim panels to within a minimum of 4 inches from the centerline of the valley and clip 2 inches off the topmost corner of each panel along the valley.

4 Finishing Ridges and Hips. Ridges and hips are finished with manufactured caps that are scored with guidelines for spacing. After wrapping the ridge or hip with a 10-inch piece of felt, apply three fasteners in a triangular pattern to each shingle. Be careful to stay 1 inch inside of the overlap line.

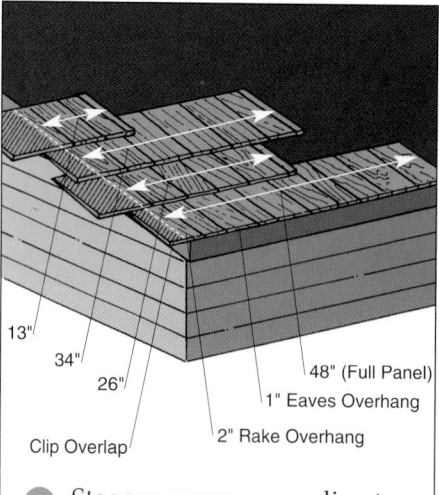

1 Cut and fasten a 2½-in. starter strip over drip edge, 18-in.-wide felt and 36-in.-wide felt.

2 Stagger courses according to the pattern shown to achieve the best appearance and protection.

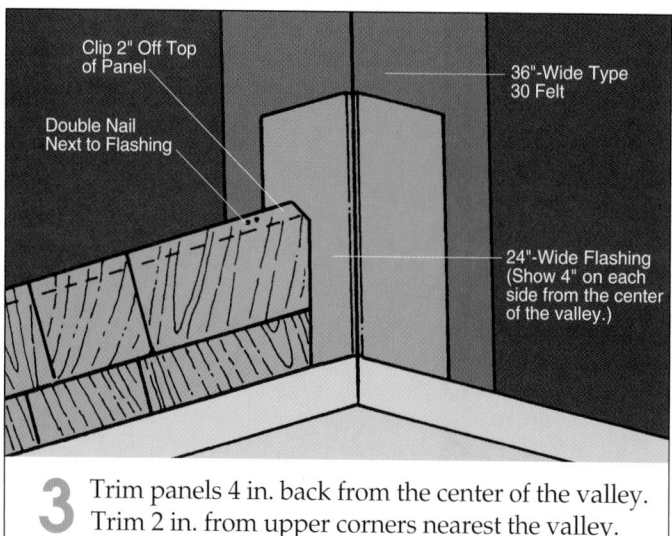

3 Trim panels 4 in. back from the center of the valley. Trim 2 in. from upper corners nearest the valley.

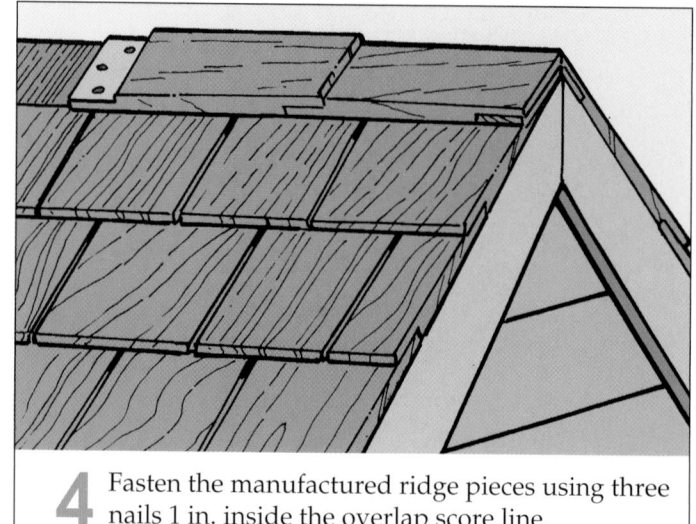

4 Fasten the manufactured ridge pieces using three nails 1 in. inside the overlap score line.

built-up roofing

Coping with Flat Roofs

Experience has proven that an absolutely flat roof leads to trouble. To avoid standing water which eventually causes leaks, a roof must have a minimum pitch of ¼ inch per foot. If you are reroofing consider sheathing the roof to give it the minimal incline.

Roll roofing and built-up roofing are the most common techniques used to cover flat roofs. (Composition shingles are not used on roofs with a slope of less than 2 in 12; wood shingles are not used on a slope of less than 3 in 12; and shakes are not used on a slope of less than 4 in 12.) Of the two methods, roll roofing is quicker and easier to handle. Built-up roofing requires special equipment that cannot readily be rented. It is included in this chapter only to faciltate hiring a professional to do the job.

Installing Roll Roofing

Roll roofing provides a quick, inexpensive roofing solution. Essentially made of the same material as composition shingles, roll roofing provides only one layer of covering as opposed to three layers. Compared with shingling, roll roofing is installed very quickly. A lot of territory is covered in a short time although it helps to have an assistant.

The life of roll roofing is typically 5 to 12 years. Given its plain appearance and short life, single-layer roll roofing is best used on sheds or in places where the roof is not visible. It may be used on slopes that are flatter than those normally covered by shingles, especially if a concealed nail application is used. Double-coverage selvage roll roofing is used for roofs that are nearly flat.

Roll roofing is more fragile than other roofing options. In temperatures below 45 degrees the material may crack. You can work in colder conditions if you warm the rolls first. The roofing cement and lap cement must be kept at a temperature above 45 degrees, so store it indoors if you are working in cold weather.

Make sure the roofing has not curled at the edges or puckered in the middle. If it has, cut it into pieces 12 to 18 feet long and stack the pieces on a flat surface. Depending on the air temperature they will take an hour to one day to flatten.

Underlayment is not required, but since it is easy to install and so inexpensive, it is worth the extra effort. Install drip edge at the rakes and eaves before roofing. (See page 26.)

Even small pebbles and sticks eventually poke through roll roofing, so sweep the surface with extra care.

Roll Roofing Option

An option to installing roll roofing horizontally to the rakes is to install it vertically. This eases the job when working on highly pitched roofs. Overlap pieces by 2 inches. Cement the seam and nail every 3 inches. Horizontal seams (where a new piece of roll roofing continues the vertical run) also must overlap 2 inches. Cement the seam and nail every 3 inches.

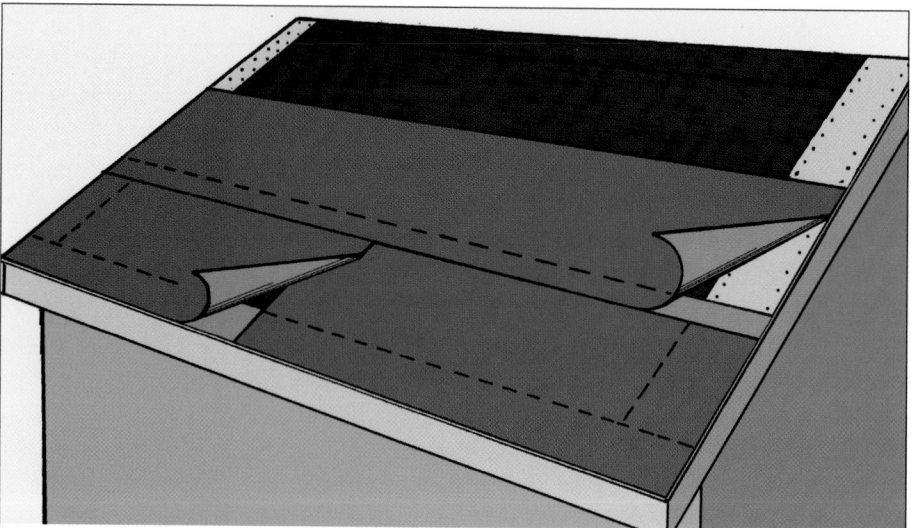

Installing Roll Roofing. Applied with nails and roofing cement, roll roofing is a quick and inexpensive option.

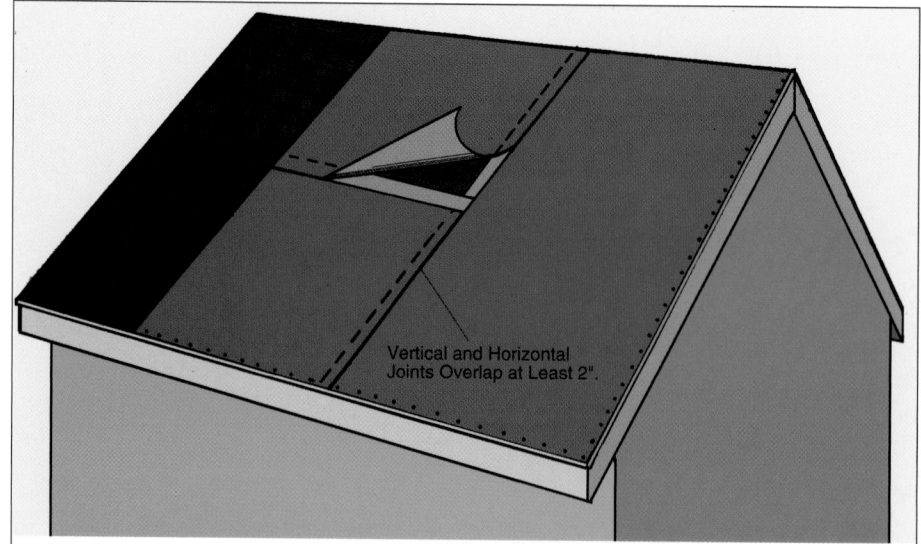

Vertical and Horizontal Joints Overlap at Least 2".

Roll Roofing Option. An alternative for a highly pitched roof is to apply roll roofing parallel to the rake.

Exposed-Nail Method

The exposed-nail method is the quickest and easiest way to install roll roofing.

1 Installing the First Course. First protect each valley with an 18-inch-wide sheet, taking extra care to lay it completely flat. If the material is raised above the sheathing it will tear later if someone walks on it.

The eaves may be uneven so do not use it as a guide for aligning the first sheet. Instead snap a chalk line 35½ inches up from the eaves and run your first sheet so that it overhangs the eaves by ½ inch. Add 2 inches of roofing cement at eaves and nail all seams and edges every 3 inches. Use galvanized roofing nails to penetrate the sheathing by at least ¾ inch. Once you have "aimed" the sheet and put some nails down, you can't fix it if you find that it is headed off course. Avoid puckers and folds. Cut the course long enough so that some roofing overhangs the rake. When the roof is complete use a utility knife to trim the course flush with the edge of the drip edge. If you are reroofing and there is no drip edge, strike a line so the new roofing can be trimmed flush with the previous layer.

2 Nailing and Cementing. Snap a chalk line 2 inches down from the top of the first sheet, and carefully spread lap cement above this line.

3 Cutting and Nailing. Use the roll of roofing itself as a guide to a straight, rough cut. Use the chalk line as a guide to nail down the next sheet. The lap cement seals all nails.

4 Covering Ridges and Hips. Cover ridges and hips after you have roofed both sides. Cut a piece of roll roofing 12 inches wide; snap chalk lines down from the ridge on either side; apply lap cement above those lines; and nail down the ridge sheet.

1 Position roll roofing along the eaves overlapping the edge by ½ in. Align to a chalk line snapped 35½ in. from the bottom edge.

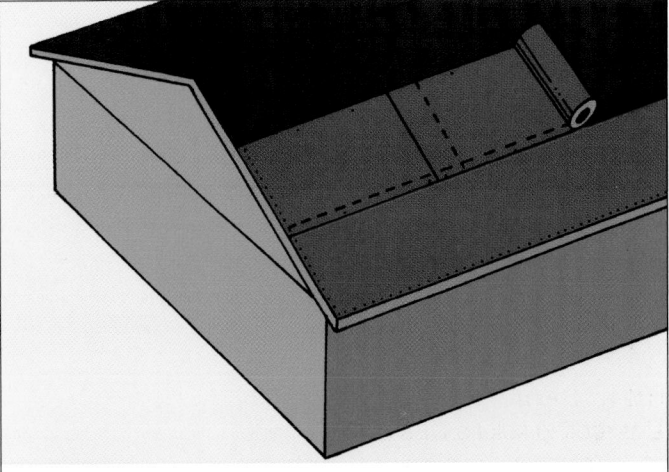

2 Strike a line 2 in. down from the top of the last course. Cement the seam, pressing down to ensure adhesion. Nail at 3 in. intervals.

3 Roll to edge and then fold the roll back on itself. Use the roll as a cutting guide. Cut more roofing than needed and trim as a final step.

4 Cut a 12-in. piece of roll roofing. Snap chalk lines down from the ridge, and apply lap cement above those lines. Nail down the ridge roofing.

Concealed-Nail Method

The concealed-nail method is ideal for low-slope roofs (1 in 12 or less) where slow-moving water might work its way under nailheads.

1 Adding Strips to Roof Edges. When installing a new roof begin by attaching 9-inch-wide starter strips of roll roofing along rakes and eaves. Use nails spaced 4 inches apart and ¾ inch from the edge. These strips provide a surface to which the cement adheres.

2 Installing the First Course. Snap a chalk line 35½ inches from the eaves as a guide for rolling out the first course of roofing. This allows the 36-inch wide roll to over-hang the eaves by ½ inch. Attach the first course to the chalk line, nailing the top edges only. Nail every 4 inches, ¾ inch from the top of the course. Trowel a rough 2-inch-wide layer of roofing cement under the first course at the eaves and the rake. Press down the seams to make sure they stick.

3 Installing Remaining Courses. Mark course overlaps as you go, by snapping a chalk line 6 inches down from the top of each course. Align the bottom of the next course and nail along the top edge only. Then go back and apply roofing cement at the rakes and at the over lap with the course below.

4 Covering Valleys. Begin by covering each valley with an 18-inch-wide sheet of roll roofing. Be careful to lay it completely flat. As courses of roll roofing are added onto roofs adjacent to the valley, let each run 12 inches past the valley. Cement (do not nail) seams within 6 inches of the center of the valley. Then add roofing to the opposite face of the roof, again letting it overlap the valley. Trim down the center of the valley and cement into place.

5 Covering Ridges and Hips. Ridges and hips are covered after both sides are roofed. Cut a piece of roll roofing 12 inches wide, snap chalk lines 6 inches down. From the ridge on either side, apply lap cement above those lines, and seal down the ridge.

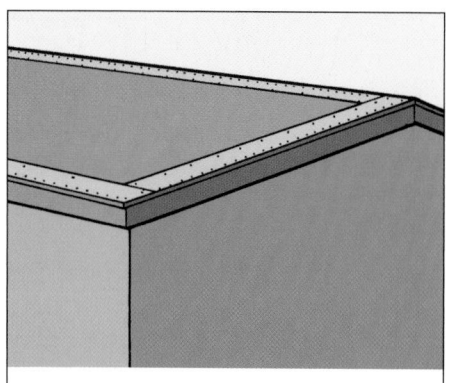

1 Cut 9-in. strips to be nailed ¾ in. in from the edge at 4-in. intervals to the rakes and eaves of the roof.

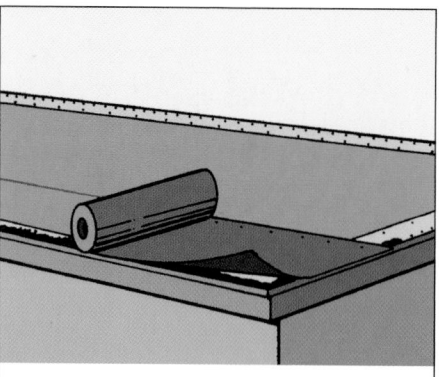

2 Strike a line 35½ in. from eaves edge as a guide for rolling out the roofing. Nail at top edge only.

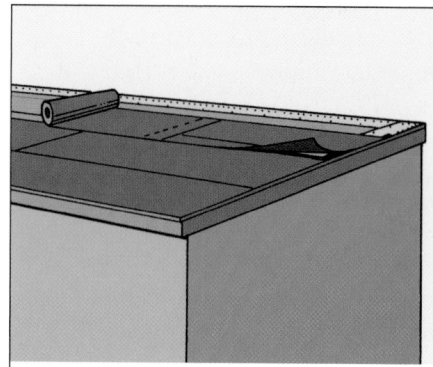

3 Install remaining courses overlapping them 6 in. Nail at top edges, and cement course overlaps and rakes.

4 After roofing the valley, add the courses of roofing so that courses overlaps each other. Trim down the center of the valley.

5 Cover the ridge with a 12-in. strip sealed in place with roofing cement.

Double Coverage Roll Roofing

Buy double coverage roll roofing (sometimes called selvage roofing) for those roofs that are nearly flat (up to 1 in 12). This material is applied with a 19-inch overlap called the selvage and 17-inch mineral-coated exposure. Selvage can be applied over shingle or roll roofing although it is best to remove old roofing, repair the sheathing and install drip edges. Each roll covers 51 square feet. Because of the thorough overlap it provides a double layer of roofing. Be sure to purchase the type that is applied with cold cement rather than hot asphalt.

1 Applying the Starter Strip. Double coverage roofing is applied directly to sheathing. Cut away the 17-inch mineral-coated section to be used as the starter strip. Use a broom-handled brush to apply a 17-inch-wide layer of roofing cement along the eaves. Then press the starter strip into the cement, and roll it with a roofer's roller. (These can be rented.) Nail in two rows of nails at 12-inch intervals across the the surface.

2 Adding the Course. Position the first course over the starter strip. Nail it in place, with two horizontal rows of nails. Position the rows 4½ inches and 13 inches from the top of the course. Space nails in rows about 12 inches apart. Roll back the sheet and coat the selvage surface thickly with roofing cement.

3 Sealing Vertical Overlaps. Vertical seams are cemented rather than nailed and overlap by 6 inches. Nail the first sheet along the edge, spacing nails 4 inches apart and 1 inch in from the edge. Apply cement to the overlapping sheet, covering the first sheet 5½ inches in from its nailed edge. Nail the overlapping sheet in place (again nailing only on the selvage area). Press down the vertical seam for adhesion. Do not nail the exposed area.

1 Apply roofing cement along the eaves. Use the selvage section as a starter strip.

2 Nail selvage of first full course. Apply cement under mineral-coated exposure.

3 Overlap vertical seams by 6 in. Apply cement, and seal. Nail the selvage area only.

4 Seal hips and ridges with a selvage section starter, and cement on next section.

4 Sealing Hips and Ridges. Finish hip and ridges by repeating the same procedure in miniature. Cut sections 12 inches wide from a roll of double coverage roofing. (Include both the selvage and exposed areas.) Snap a line, and apply a starter strip using only the selvage section of one piece. Nail the selvage section, spacing the nails at 4-inch intervals. Hammer one additional nail 1 inch in from the edge. Trowel on cement and add the next section as you would a shingle.

5 Trimming Rakes. As with roll roofing it is easiest to let the roofing overhang the rake and trim it when the roof is covered. Strike a line

5 Snap a chalk line, and use a utility knife to trim excess material at the rakes.

so that ¼ inch of roofing overhangs the drip edge. Use a hook blade utility knife to trim the rake.

For extra protection use double layers of standard roll roofing. Cut a 19-inch strip as a starter course. Cement the starter strip to the deck and nail it every 12 inches. Overlap the starter course forming a 17-inch exposure. Apply roofing cement between layers and nail only the overlapped area. Overlap each course 6 inches vertically, cementing it and nailing every 2 inches where the next course will overlap.

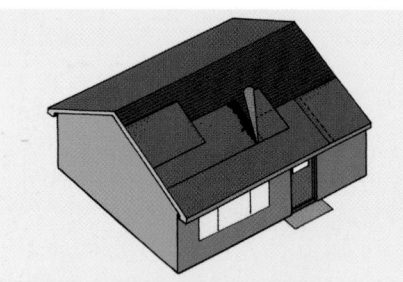

Built-Up Roofing

During the last 30 years many flat-roofed sections of homes, and in some cases whole homes, have been covered with a built-up roof (BUR). Do-it-yourselfers easily can patch built-up roofing. (See page 16.) Installing an entire built-up roof requires specialized equipment. If you have a built-up roof and foresee major repairs or replacement, you will want to know the components of built-up roofs and how to judge a professional crew.

Leaving it to the Professionals

Most built-up roofs are covered with three to five layers of heavy roofing

Modified Bitumen Roofing

Believed to be the most effective roofing for flat and low-incline roofs, the installation of modified bitumen roofing is a job for professional roofers. Large sheets of roofing material are applied over layers of nailed felt. The material is lapped by 4 inches and usually sealed with a torch. (Hot tar or roofing cement is sometimes used.) Unlike other roofing techniques that call for gravel, modified bitumen roofing is covered with aluminum paint.

Leaving it to the Professionals. Because of the need for applicators such as these, built-up roofing jobs are left to the professionals.

felt coated with hot asphalt. A mineral surface of gravel or crushed rock often tops the job.

Depending on the number of layers applied and the way in which they are applied, a contractor guarantees the work for 10 to 20 years. If you hire a professional make sure that a guarantee is in the contract.

Tools used by contractors range from simple mops and buckets to high-cost spraying equipment. The best job requires hot roofing, in which the asphalt coating is heated in large kettles before being applied. Built-up roofing is thick but not indestructible. When a roof begins to split or develops deep alligatoring (checked cracks that resemble alligator skin) it is time to have it inspected.

If serious alligatoring appears within a year or so of installation, the hot asphalt probably was laid too thickly and the job needs to be redone. Sometimes within several years of installation the roofing comes apart from the roof below or pulls away from other surfaces such as adjoining walls. (This is called delaminating.) These problems are caused when the surface of the roof is not completely cleared of debris or water before installation. If alligatoring or delaminating occurs, the roof must be redone.

Flashing Built-Up Roofs. The greatest potential for trouble is found in the places where the roof deck meets a vertical wall. A cant strip is placed in such a corner to soften the angle between roof and wall and to keep water from standing in the joint. Tile or metal flashing ideally overlaps the roofed surface.

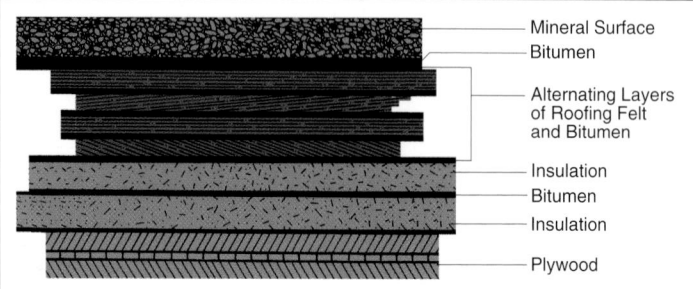

Built-up Roofing. As its name implies, built-up roofing consists of several layers, beginning with plywood sheathing.

Mineral Surface
Bitumen
Alternating Layers of Roofing Felt and Bitumen
Insulation
Bitumen
Insulation
Plywood

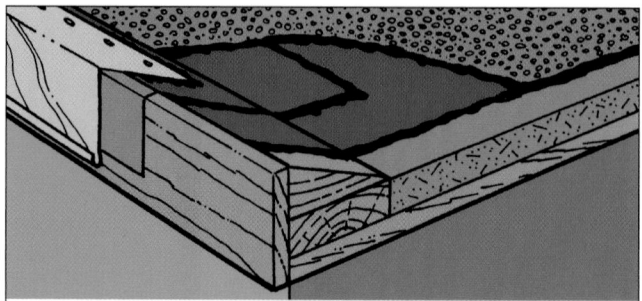

Flashing Built-up Roofs. Beveled strips of wood and a layer of flashing protects vulnerable joints.

other roofing

Slate Roofing

Slate is the most expensive roofing option; even its very long life (from 50 to 100 years) hardly makes it financially practical. But nothing else provides the rugged-yet-classy look of slate. Slate can be placed over a layer of composition shingles only if the slope of the roof is 4 in 12 or more and only if a structural engineer has confirmed the roof framing can bear slate's 7-pound-per-square-foot weight. If you are an experienced do-it-yourselfer who is willing to embark on a major project, you might consider buying slating tools and learning the craft. However, slating is a skill that demands considerable investment—an investment better put toward the cost of hiring a professional.

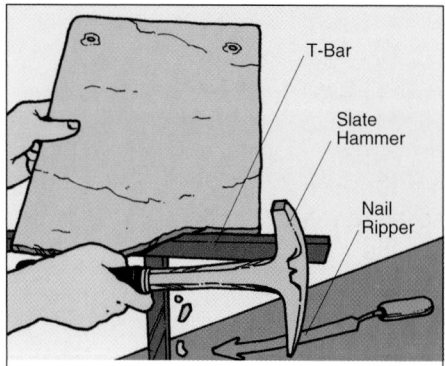

Slate Roofing. Applying a slate roof requires three specialized tools: A nail ripper, a hammer equipped with a sharp edge and a point, and a T-bar for trimming.

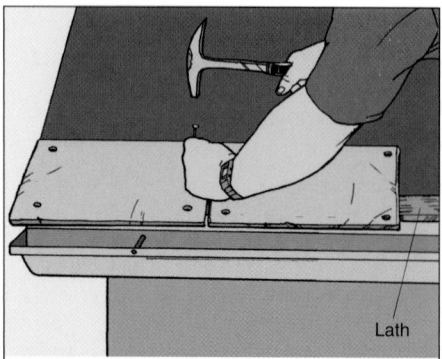

Shimming the Starter Course. A piece of lath is nailed to the roof under the starter course. This gives the first course an upward tilt at the eaves.

Slate is simply unprocessed stone that has been mined from the ground and cut to size. It is available in a wide variety of grades and thicknesses, so ask a salesman how long your selection is expected to last. Slate comes in many colors, from gray to shades of green, purple, and red. Some colors fade after years of exposure. Slate also can be smooth or rough surfaced. Different colors and textures may be used on a single roof, but be wary of this: You may not like the patterns that emerge.

Slate is heavy. Just how heavy depends on the grade. Be sure your roof can handle the load. Many local codes require specific reinforcements if you want to put slate over an existing roof. Copper flashing is recommended because it is long-lasting and looks good with slate.

The professionals use three simple but specialized tools: a nail ripper, which is used to cut off a nail level to the surface; a hammer equipped with a sharp edge for cutting slate and a point for poking nailholes in the slate; and a T-bar which aids in trimming.

Fiber-Cement Roofing. If you love the look of slate but you do not have the money to put into it, you can use a compromise material. New varieties of slate-like fiber-cement roofing are light, attractive, and warranted for 40 years. These new products not only look a lot like slate, but they also share much of its durability and are worth investigating. As with slate, they are typically contractor installed.

Installing Slate

The following list outlines the basic procedures used for installing a slate roof.

Shimming the Starter Course. Slate tilts slightly upward at the eaves, extending ½ inch beyond the rake and 1 inch beyond the eaves. Use a piece of lath to shim the starter course, which is made up of slates set lengthwise.

Installing Felt Underlayment. Slate often is laid on one layer of 30-pound

roofing felt. Some contractors prefer to use individual felt strips under each course to provide additional cushioning.

Installing the Slates. Two nails, installed in pre-punched holes, hold each slate. The slates are set so their beveled edges show. There is a ⅛-inch gap between slates.

Offsetting the Gaps. The gaps between slates are offset by at least 2 inches.

Installing Felt Underlayment. Slates are cushioned by felt underlayment between courses.

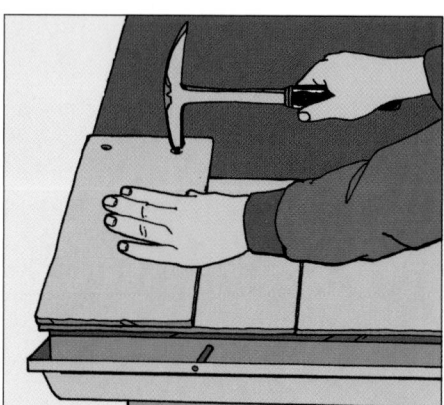

Installing the Slates. Each slate is held in place by two nails in pre-punched holes.

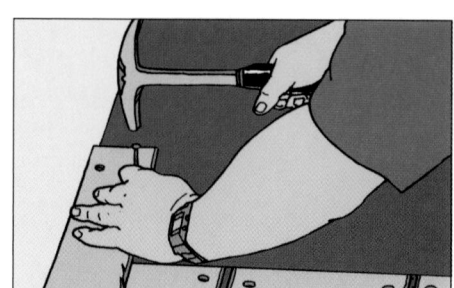

Offsetting the Gaps. An offset of at least 2 in. is used between gaps between slates.

Capping the Ridge. All of the slates at the ridge are the same width. The peak overlap is alternated from one side of the roof to the other.

Capping the Ridge. The ridge is capped with slates that are the same width. The overlap at the peak is alternated from one side of the roof to the other. Slates are fastened to the ridge with two nails.

Working with Slate

■ Use solid copper- or zinc-coated nails. These are nailed through factory-punched holes in each slate.

■ Give slate roofs extra pitch (called canting) at the eaves. Before slating, a ¼-inch-thick strip of wood is nailed along the eaves. This causes the bottom course of slate to turn upwards slightly. It also gives the roof a classic appearance and provides additional drip protection for the fascia.

■ To prevent cracking the slate courses, use proper scaffolding. (Or make sure your contractor uses proper scaffolding.)

■ Slate nails do not penetrate metal flashing. Unlike the nails used with shingle roofs, these nails have no way of sealing themselves.

■ Use plenty of roofing cement under hip and ridge slates. All exposed nailheads also must be covered with cement.

■ Slates must lap over the underlying course by at least 3 inches.

■ Slates with hairline cracks should be discarded; cracks only worsen over time.

Maintaining & Repairing Slate

There is little maintenance involved when it comes to a slate roof. The only thing you have to worry about is debris that traps moisture along eaves and degrades the slate. Broken slates can be replaced, but you will need a slate ripper to remove the damaged portion.

1 Clipping Nails. Slip the nail under the slate to be replaced. Hook the ripper onto the shaft of a nail that holds the slate in place. Hammer the ripper to cut the nail. Repeat with the second nail to release the slate.

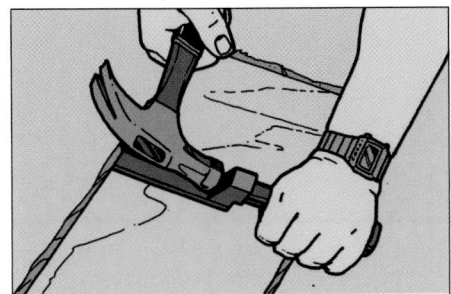

1 Hammer the nail ripper to cut the nails holding a damaged shingle.

2 Cutting a Replacement. Cut slate to size with a carborundum circular saw blade. You also can use a nail set to punch a series of holes along the cut line, and then holding the cut line even with the edge of a bench or other hard edge, crack off the excess. Wear goggles.

3 Marking Nailholes. Slip a new slate into the space and mark for nailholes in the crack between shingles in the overlapping course. If two cracks overlap the replacement shingle make a mark at both. Then remove the slate and use a ⅛-inch masonry bit to drill holes.

4 Nailing the Gap. Put back the slate and use a nail set to gently drive an 8d galvanized finishing nail flush with the slate surface.

5 Covering the Nailhead. Use two screwdrivers to gently pry the overlapping slates. Cut a piece of copper roughly 5x6 inches and bend it until it is slightly cupped. Slip the cupped copper sheet over the nailhead to seal it. Friction holds the the sheet in place.

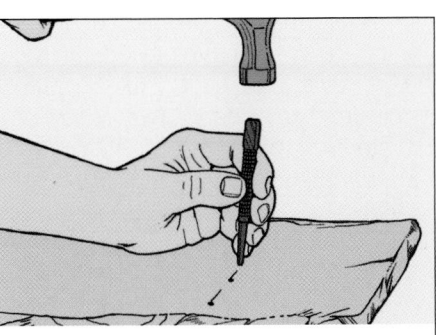

2 To cut slate, punch a series of holes on the back of the slate and then sever along the line.

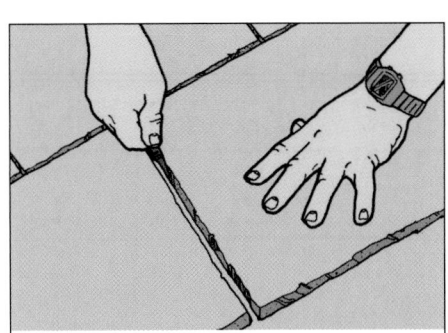

3 Position the replacement slate, and mark holes for nailing between the overlapping shingles.

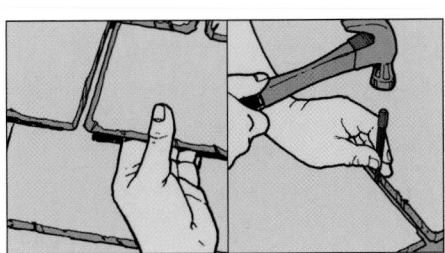

4 Replace the slate, and use a nail set to drive galvanized nails flush with the slate surface.

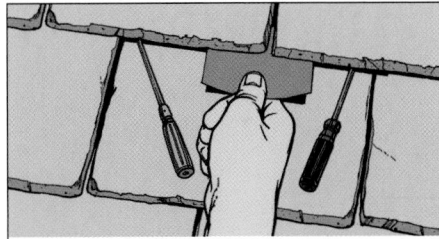

5 Gently pry up overlapping shingles, and slip in a cupped piece of copper over the nailhole.

Tile Roofing

Like slate, classic clay tiles last from 50 to 100 years and possess a timeless quality few other materials have to offer. Tiles also are expensive and very heavy, weighing as much as 1,000 pounds to the square. Concrete tiles are a smart substitute. They look good, last almost as long as clay tiles, and are light enough to be installed on some standard roofs intended for composition shingles.

If you are considering a tile or concrete tile roof, consult your roofing supply source and local building department to make sure your roof can handle the tiles you choose. Do not tile over a roof that has a slope flatter than 3 in 12.

Although more difficult to apply than shingles, tiles can be installed by a skilled do-it-yourselfer. In addition to the tools used for installing composition shingles, you also will need a circular saw with a masonry-cutting blade.

Caution: Wear protective goggles when cutting tiles.

If you can fit it into your budget, use copper nails rather than galvanized nails. An advantage to using copper nails is that they are soft enough to cut through should you have to replace a tile. Copper nails also allow enough give so that if you nail them too far into the tiles, the tiles will not crack as the decking moves with temperature variations. Hammer all nails, no matter what kind, to within a nickel's thickness of the tile surface.

Preparing the Deck

Although there are various ways to install tile, a few basics prevail. Your tiles will come with instructions pertaining to whether or not they require underlayment. Some tiles are nailed directly to sheathing, while others require battens to be laid first. Battens are 1x2 strips of redwood or pressure-treated pine that are spaced at intervals that match the tile exposure. (14 inches is typical.) Further preparations also may be called for, such as one 2x2 along all ridges and hips, 1x2 starter strips along eaves and rakes, or 1x3 nailed to rake rafters to allow the tiles to extend further sideways. Check manufacturer's instructions.

Use flashing that will last as long as your tiles. Copper is best. Apply metal drip edge along the eaves before the underlayment (if any) is installed. Along the rakes, the drip edge is installed after the underlayment. Take special care in the valleys; first put down 90-pound mineral-surfaced roll roofing, then W-metal that is at least 24 inches wide. (See page 25.) Cover hips and ridges with a double layer of felt.

Tile Alternatives. Tiles are designed to interlock so the amount of exposure is always readily apparent. Nail them down to the sheathing or "hang" them on the battens. If your roof has a slope of 7 in 12 or steeper or if you live in an area subject to high winds, fasten every third or fourth course with metal clips.

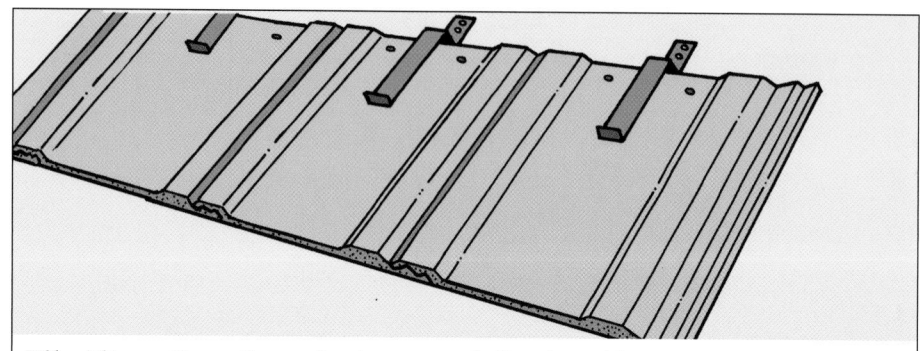

Tile Alternatives. Some tiles have metal clips for additional hanging support.

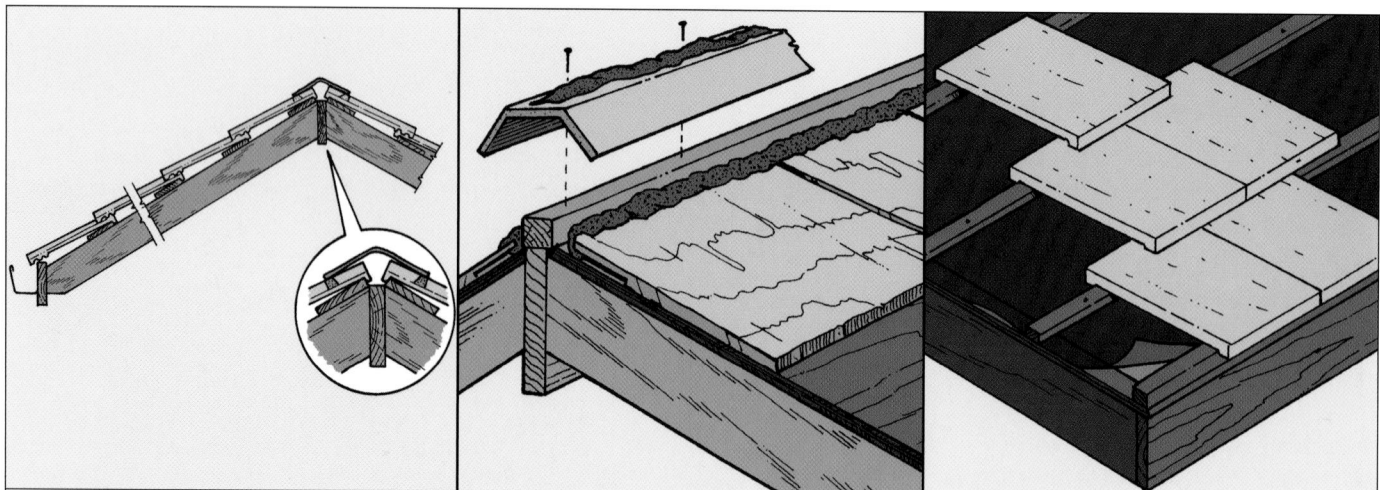

Preparing the Deck. Tiles are attached to battens and interlock between courses (left). Some tiles can be directly attached to roof sheathing. The ridge is sealed with mortar and a cap (center). Concrete tiles lock onto 1x2 battens attached to the decking (right).

Installing Clay Barrel Tile

1. Setting the Tile Width. The positioning of the tiles is crucial. (You cannot end at a rake with half a tile.) Snap a chalk line as a guide along the eaves. Tiles hang over the eaves by 2 inches. Nail the gable rake tiles in place, overlapping the drip edge. By dividing the total length of the eaves by the width of a tile, determine the distance each tile will be set apart and mark the drip edge accordingly. Tiles provide about 1 inch of sideways leeway where they overlap the previous tile. Set the eaves closure tiles flush with the eaves edge and nail in place.

2. Setting the Tile. Apply roofing mastic where one tile overlaps the other. Set the first tile in place, and nail with a 6d nail.

3. Nailing the First Course. Install six tiles using the marks along the rake and the horizontal chalk line as positioning guides. Double-check your width calculation to make sure the course ends with a full-width tile.

4. Adding the Second Course. Work up the roof in stair-step fashion. Overlap the tiles by at least 3 inches.

5. Finishing the Course. Lay the left-hand rake tiles. Toenail a 1x3 nailer that runs from eaves to ridge. Position it so that it lines up with holes in the tile that are provided for nailing. Nail the last tile of each course to this nailer.

6. Laying the Ridge. Lay a bed of tinted mortar, and set ridge starter tiles. Apply the hip and ridge tiles over the ridge, overlapping each by at least 3 inches.

7 Other Roofing

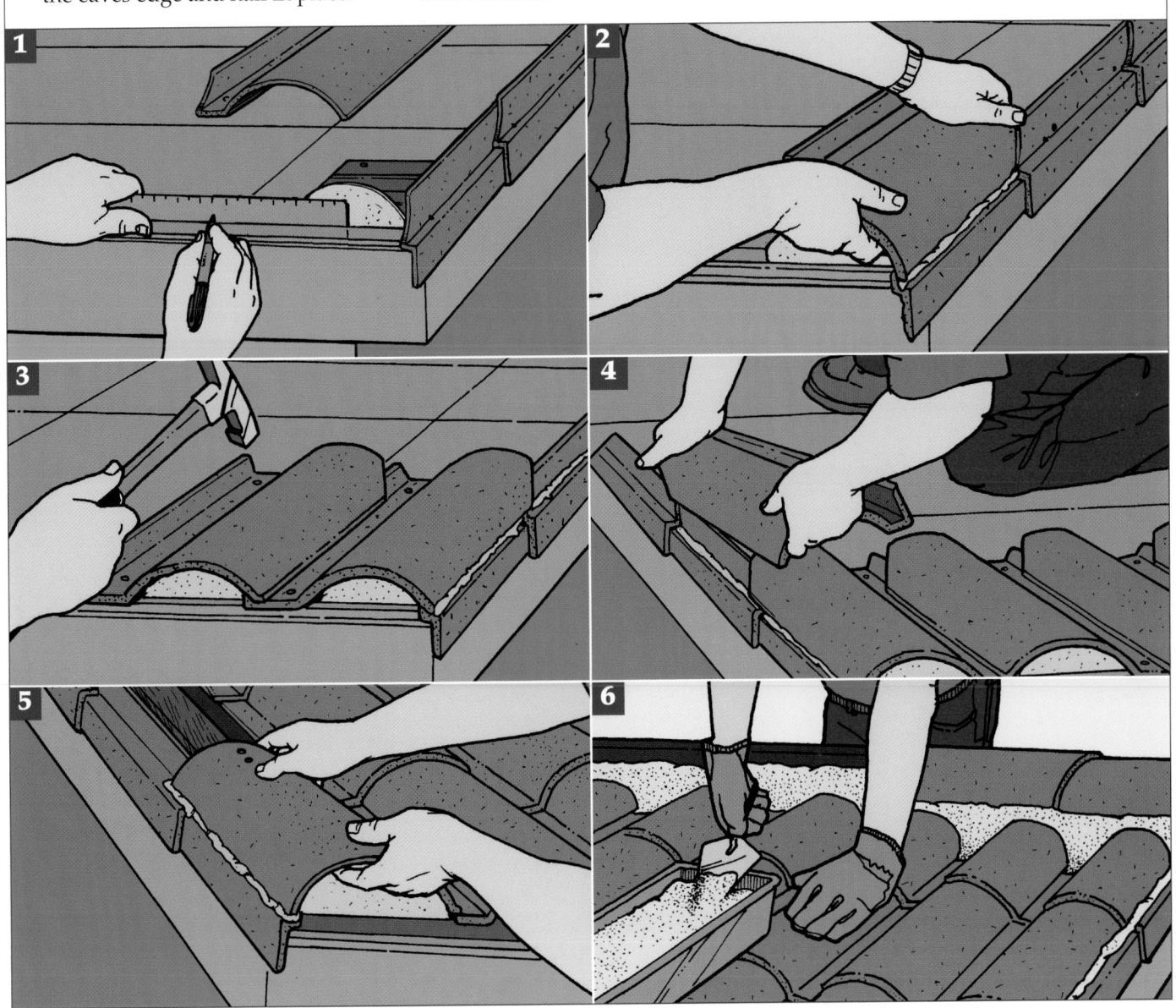

Working with a Professional

Before committing to a contractor, check his/her references and make sure he/she is certified to install the material you have chosen. Visit nearby sites and use the following tips to help evaluate the contractor:

Use of Sealant. Tape sealant is used within joints, but almost never on the surface where it can be seen (and where it can wear off with time). Too much reliance on sealant might be a sign that the contractor is not installing the material correctly. Expect some visible sealant in places where ridge panels join and around the vent stack sleeves.

Signs of Quality Work. Check that panels are straight, and that details at the rakes and eaves are neat. Denting, particularly in the valley, is a sign of poor craftsmanship. Check that stack penetrations are neat and that minimal sealant is used on them.

Check for Other Metals. Lead stack sleeves, steel antenna wires, and copper gutters all contain a metal that corrodes the roofing. An experienced contractor knows to replace these problem items.

Few Exposed Fasteners. The standing seam system has exposed fasteners only on the rake and eaves trim, and then only sparingly. If exposed fasteners are used they must be coated, long-life fasteners.

Get the Manual. Manufacturers want their systems to be applied correctly and most will not hesitate to send you a manual. Use it as a guide to asking the right questions.

Metal Roofing

The metal roof is experiencing new popularity. This may be due to the success of metal roofs on commercial buildings, or perhaps the historical appropriateness of metal roofing on older homes. Metal boasts a longevity surpassed only by slate and tile—at a considerably lower cost.

Standing-seam panel roofing is the most common type of metal roofing for residential use. These panels, which run vertically, usually are made of aluminum or galvanized steel, but in some cases they are made of zinc and aluminum-coated steel. Since the panels are painted, they offer more color options than other types of roofing. Metal roofing is ideal for restoring older homes that originally had metal roofs.

This light material (one pound per square foot) is suitable for covering old roofs and may even be used over three layers of composition shingles (if local codes permit). For roofs that have irregularities, narrow, textured and dull-finish panels are best.

The metal roofing shown here can cover a roof with a slope of at least 3 in 12. Other metal roof systems handle roofs with slopes as slight as ¼-inch in 12 (usually a job for built-up roofing). However, the experience and special equipment of a contractor is needed for its installation.

The installation process involves laying 12- to 16½-inch panels and correctly joining them at the seams, wall flashing, valleys and ridges. The panels are precut to the exact length ordered up to 40 feet long. (For this reason horizontal seams are very

Metal Roofing. Metal roofing requires some special tools and experience to install.

unlikely on most homes.) Metal roofing can be applied to plywood decking with an underlayment of 30-pound felt. Laying and joining the panels is not difficult, but handling eaves edges, rakes, wall flashing valleys, and ridges requires experience.

Installing Metal Roofing

As mentioned, installing metal roofing requires some special tools and experience. Here's an overview of what is involved.

Installing Felt and Eaves Trim.
Thirty-pound felt provides a moisture barrier over plywood decking. Metal roofing is applied vertically, completing a 12- to 16½-inch panel from eaves to ridge before applying the next. Check the squareness of the roof and adjust for irregularity. Eaves trim is screwed in place, and sealant is applied to the edge before panels are clipped in place.

Applying the First Rake Edge.
After the first vertical panel has been set, the first rake edge (applied on either side of the roof, depending on the installer's preference) is applied over the panel. Underlayment overlaps the rake edge.

Joining the Panels.
Clips and sealant join the panels. Clips are applied every 12 inches where high winds prevail, every 18 inches elsewhere. No adhesive is necessary to seal the sheets to the decking. Do not step on the seams. In fact, walk on the sheets as little as possible. Scratched finishes may void the warranty.

Installing Valley Flashing.
Valley flashing is set on a piece of 30-pound felt underlayment that lines the valley. Channels running parallel in the valley are sealed and screwed to it and hold the edge of the panels.

Sealing Ridge Flashing.
At the ridges, flashing is sealed to "Z" strips that are fastened between the standing seams.

Installing Felt and Eaves Trim. Trim is installed and sealed before panels are installed.

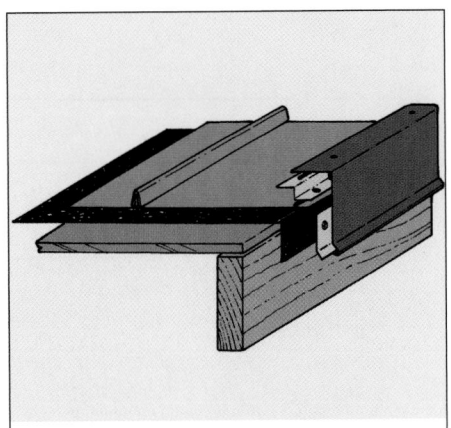

Applying the First Rake Edge. The first rake edge is appled after the first vertical panel has been set.

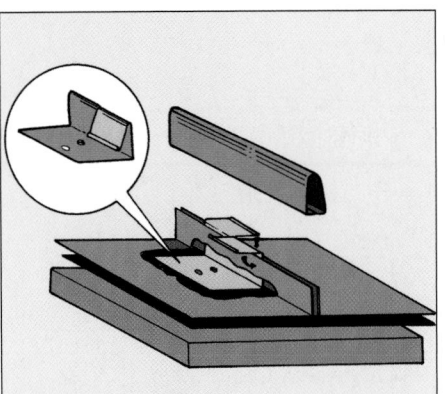

Joining the Panels. Clips and sealant join the panels. No adhesive is needed to seal the sheets.

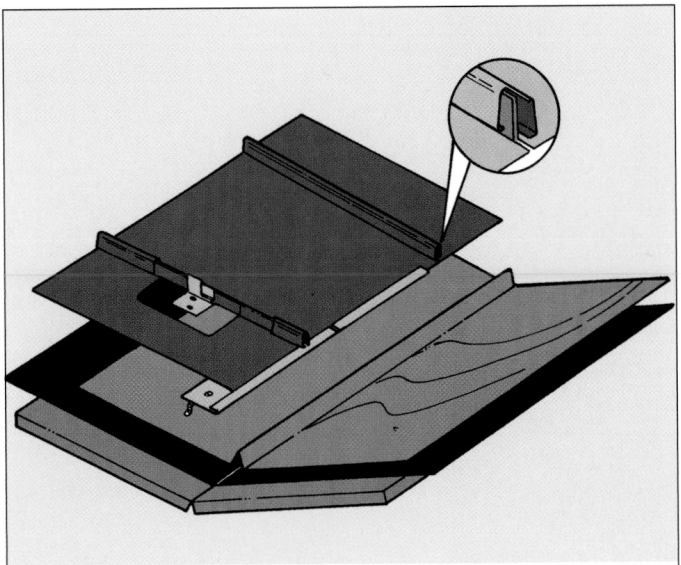

Installing Valley Flashing. Channels running parallel in a valley are sealed and screwed in.

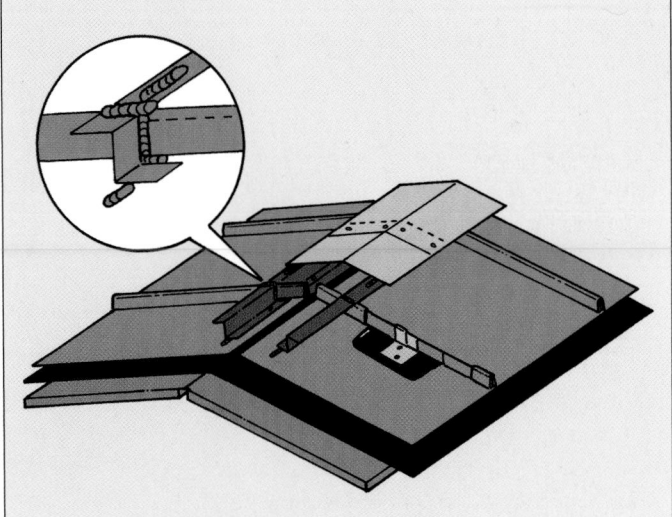

Sealing Ridge Flashing. At the ridges, flashing is sealed to "Z" strips that are fastened between the seams.

Panel Roofing

Corrugated panel roofs made of fiberglass provide a watertight, yet translucent covering for decks, carports, and greenhouses. In addition, corrugated aluminum and galvanized metal panels are easy to install and are long-lasting solutions for utility buildings. Panels of both types typically are sold along with manufacturer-specific nails, filler strips and caulk. Install according to manufacturer's instructions.

Panel roofing is a quick and easy roofing solution, but keep in mind that fiberglass easily chips and metal tends to dent and bend—both are problems that cannot be fixed. The panels expand and contract with temperature changes and if not installed correctly this causes the roof to come detached. In addition to the roofing material, the job requires filler strips (pieces of wood shaped to fit the contours of the panels) and special nails (aluminum for aluminum roofs, steel for steel roofs) fitted with plastic washers.

1 Framing the Panel. Install 1x4 framing set on two-by rafters in accordance with local municipal codes. In areas of heavy snow, slope must be at least 8 in 12. No underlayment or drip edge is required. Panels also can be added over old roofing by applying 1x4 nailers every 2 to 4 feet. Use nails that penetrate the sheathing by at least ¾ inch.

2 Installing the Panels. In places where a complete seal against the weather is necessary, place filler strips under the roofing at the eaves. The strips are shaped to conform to the profile of the panels. Install the filler strips as you work your way across the the roof, beginning with the first full-width panel. Panels typically are 26 inches wide. Nail four nails across the panel where it rests on a framing piece. When working with steel and fiberglass, predrill a hole for each nail. Nail carefully so the roofing is snug to the framing but not indented. Overlap panels 1 inch lengthwise. Lay a bead of adhesive caulk across the length of each seam where panels overlap. For translucent fiberglass panels use clear silicone caulk. Panels are available in lengths up to 20 feet. If you need more than one panel from eaves to ridge, overlap by 12 inches on slopes greater than 4 in 12; 18 inches on lower slopes.

3 Installing Ridge Cap. Install ridge cap at ridges and hips. Some styles require filler strips, while others are shaped to fit the roofing. Nail at ridges according to the manufacturer's recommended pattern. Do not nail edges that will be overlapped. Overlap panels with the ridge cap by at least an inch. Overlap sections of ridge panel by 6 inches.

1 In accordance with local codes, construct framing out of 1x4s.

2 Allow panels to overhang rake by ¼ to ⅜ in., and eaves by 2 in. Overlap panels side-by-side 1 in.

3 Install ridge cap at ridges and hips. Some styles require filler strips while others are shaped to fit the roofing. Overlap panels with the ridge cap by 1 in.

ventilation

Ventilating the Roof

Whether the attic space is insulated from above or below, adequate ventilation coming from the underside of the roof deck must be provided. Ventilation allows heat to escape, preventing ice buildups on the eaves in winter and an overheated roof in summer. Ice buildups deteriorate the structure and cause water leaks inside the house, while dark-colored organic roofing, such as composition shingles, does not last as long if subjected to temperature extremes.

Ventilating a roof requires making a path for air to get into and out of the space between the roof deck and the insulation. The best way to ensure air movement through the roof is to locate the intake port at a low point on the roof and the exhaust port at a high point.

Incoming Air. The most effective way for air to enter the roof is through vents that are placed in the soffits (which are found at the lowest points on the roof). Continuous soffit strip vents provide the most reliable port for intake air, while rectangular vents are next on the list. Round ventilator plugs are easy to install, but usually are too small to provide adequate airflow. Insulation baffles ensure a clear pathway for air to travel between the rafters.

Outgoing Air. Stale air escapes through the top of the roof through gable vents on the end walls, turbine vents on the roof, or ridge vents, also found on the roof. Continuous ridge vents are the preferred type for pitched roofs, while gravity vents are best installed where ridge vents are not feasible, such as in a hip roof. For houses that have open attics and insulated attic floors, vents located in the gable ends may suffice if the openings are large enough. Gable vents also can be used in a finished attic above an insulated flat ceiling.

Ventilating Unheated Attics

Unheated attics are the easiest type to ventilate. Air enters through vents in the eaves, rises naturally toward the roof deck, and exits through a continuous vent on the ridge, gable vents on the end walls, or roof vents placed high on the roof. If an airway is maintained under the roof (where the ceiling insulation abuts the eaves), the moving air keeps the roof ventilated, but does not affect the insulated ceiling below.

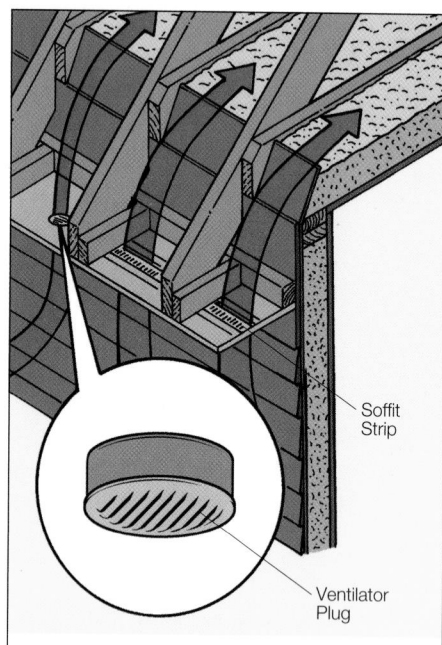

Incoming Air. The best way to let air into the roof is through soffit vents. Ventilator plugs, continuous soffit strip vents, and rectangular vents are most often used.

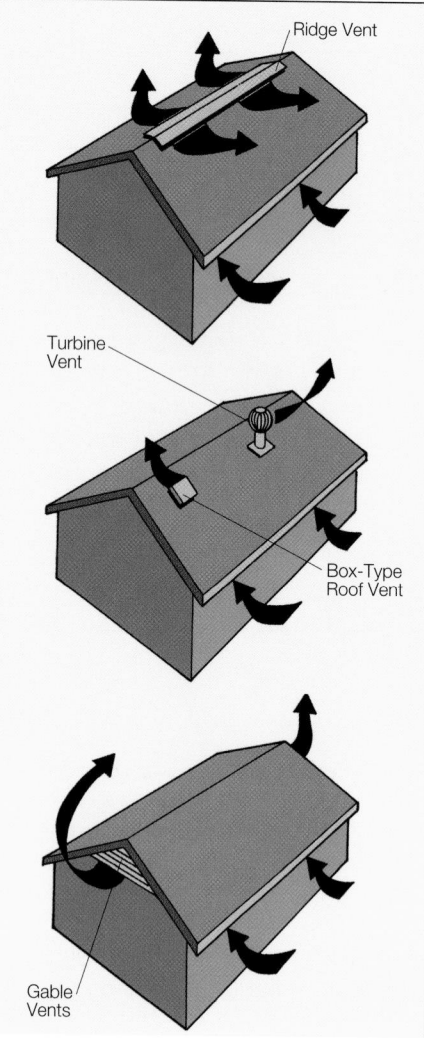

Outgoing Air. Air exhaust options include ridge vents, turbines, box-type vents, and gable vents.

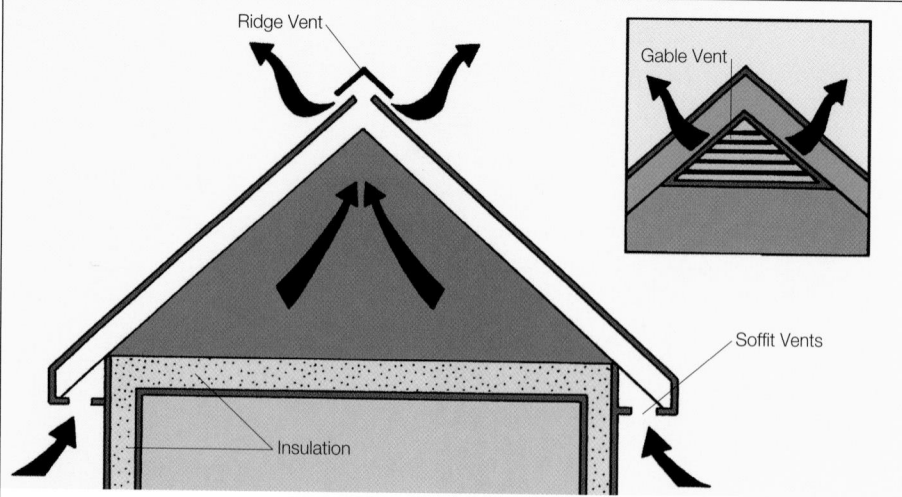

Ventilating Unheated Attics. An unheated attic is ventilated easily by installing soffit vents for air to come in and a ridge vent, gable vent, or roof vent for air to escape.

Calculating Adequate Roof Ventilation

The amount of area needed to provide for roof ventilation depends on whether or not the ceiling has a vapor barrier. If there is a vapor barrier allow one square foot of free ventilating area for every 150 square feet of house area. If there is no vapor barrier double this amount. The total free ventilating area must be divided equally between the intake and exhaust ports. Because the thickness of vanes or wires in a venting device reduces the airspace, use oversized vents to compensate. For example, if the vent has a screen with ⅛-inch-square holes, divide the area of the screen by 1.25 to get the free ventilating area. If the vents used consist of louvers backed by screens, divide by 2.25. The following example shows how to size soffit and ridge vents for a 25x40-foot house that has a vapor barrier in the ceiling:

1. Figure the area of the roof: 25 multiplied by 40 equals 1000 square feet.

2. The free ventilating area equals 1000 divided by 150, or 6.66 square feet. To convert feet to inches, multiply 6.66 by 144 to get 959 square inches. You need half of this amount (480 square inches) for the soffit vents and the other half for the ridge vents.

3. Each 8x12-inch louvered soffit vent used has an area of 96 square inches. Divide this number by 2.25 to get 43 square inches (rounded off) of free area. The number of vents needed is 480 square inches divided by 43, which is 11. Use five or six on each side of the roof.

4. The product literature that comes with the ridge vent provides information concerning the necessary free ventilating area per lineal foot. One rolled ridge vent product yields 17 inches, so the house in this example needs a strip equal to the free area required at the ridge: 480 square inches divided by 17 equals 28 feet.

Ventilating Heated Attics

Providing ventilation in a heated attic is a bit trickier than working with an unheated one, but the same principles apply. The important thing is to maintain at least 2 inches of clearance between the underside of the roof deck and all insulation. This allows the air to travel from the eaves to the top of the roof. If the eaves provide a space of 10 inches or more, simply choose insulation that has a thickness that allows for this additional 2-inch airspace. Most likely though, a combination of blanket insulation between the rafters and rigid insulation attached to the underside of the rafters will be necessary to achieve the desired R-value, while retaining an adequate amount of airspace.

Ventilating Cathedral Ceilings

Like the roof deck above heated attics, cathedral ceilings must contain an airspace above insulated cavities. Unlike attics, however, not

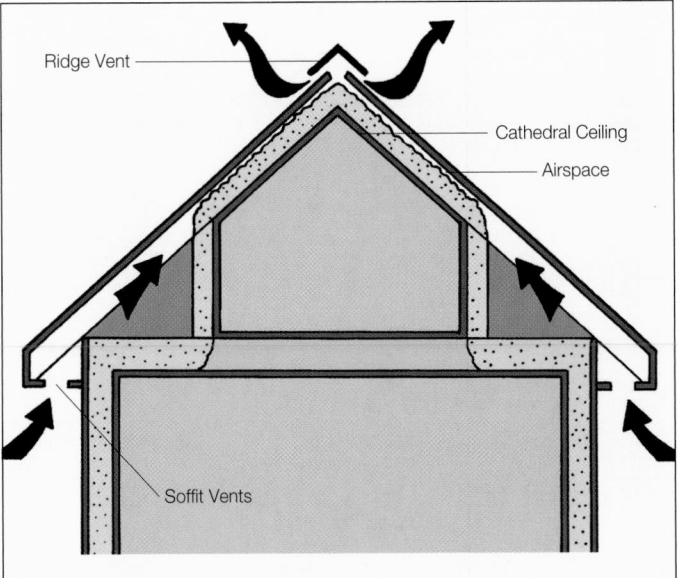

Ventilating Heated Attics. Leave a 2-in. airspace between the insulation and roof deck to allow air to circulate from the intake to exhaust vent.

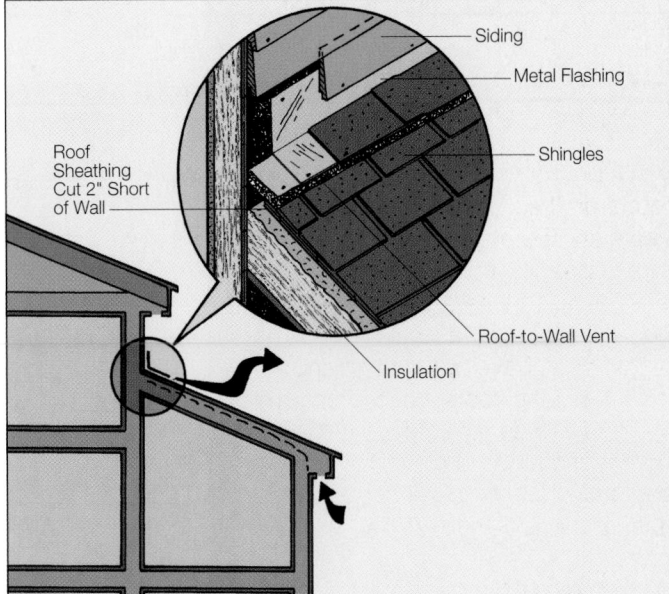

Ventilating Cathedral Ceilings. Special roof-to-wall vents provide ventilation in places where the roof abuts a wall.

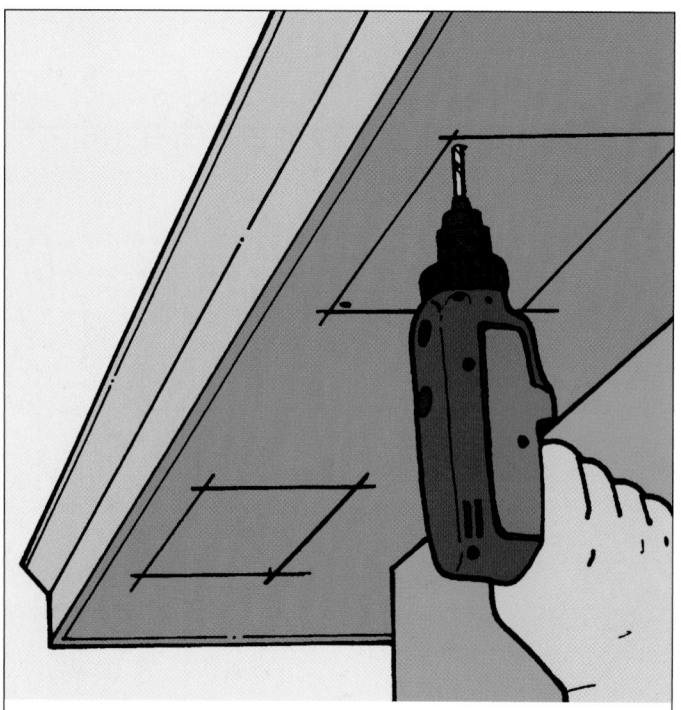

1 Use the vent as a template to mark the cutouts. Use a ¾-in. drill bit to drill a starter hole at one corner of the marked box.

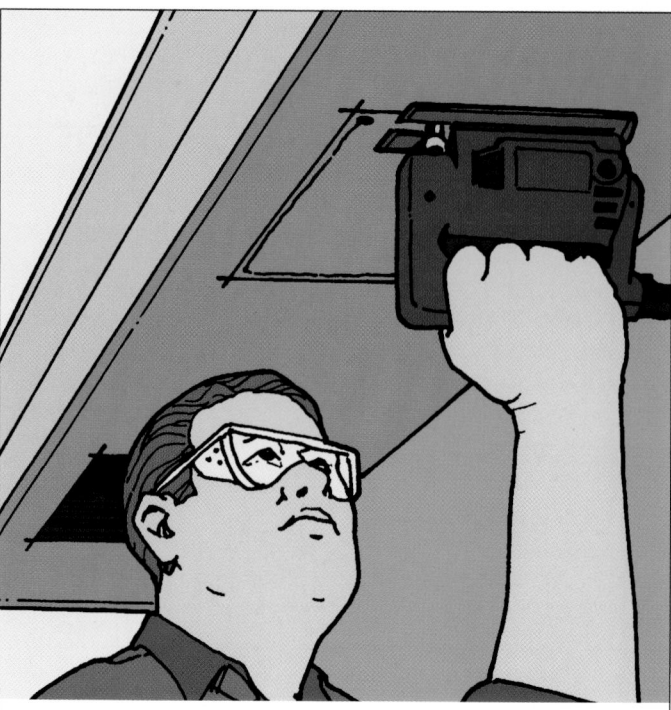

2 Insert the blade of a saber saw into the starter hole, and cut the opening.

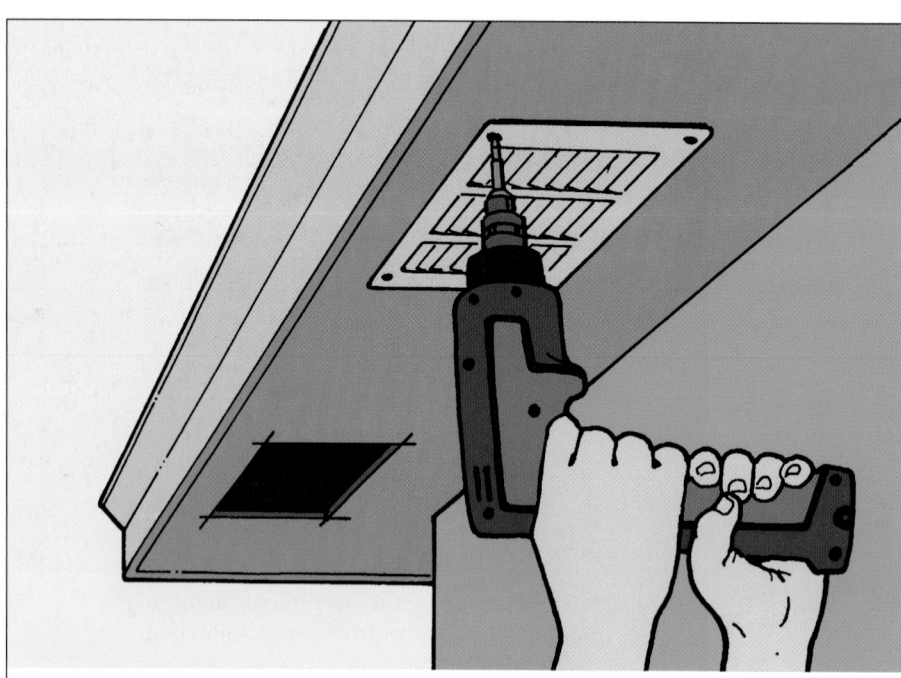

3 Use an electric drill equipped with a Phillips bit to screw the vent to the soffit.

every cathedral ceiling has an easy escape port such as a roof ridge. If not, other ways must be designed to allow air to escape. Special roof vents are available for cathedral ceilings and almost any other special

conditions, such as a low roof that abuts a vertical wall.

Choosing a Soffit Vent

Continuous soffit strip ventilators work well and are easy to install into

a new soffit. However, installing them into an existing soffit often requires tearing the soffit apart. Two better options in this case include rectangular roof vents and ventilator plugs.

Installing Rectangular Soffit Vents

Those who decide to use rectangular soffit vents can use the guidelines found on page 75, "Calculating Adequate Roof Ventilation," to determine the size and quantity needed at each soffit.

1 **Drilling a Starter Hole.** Mark the location of the vent on the soffit and, using a ¾-inch drill bit, drill a starter hole at one corner of the marked rectangle.

2 **Cutting the Opening.** Insert the blade of a saber saw into the starter hole, and cut the opening.

3 **Attaching the Vent.** Secure the vent to the soffit using the screws that are supplied with the vent. An electric drill equipped with a Phillips bit makes the job a lot easier.

1 Mark the center of each hole, and use an electric drill equipped with a hole saw bit to cut a 2½-in. diameter hole.

2 Push an aluminum or plastic plug into the hole until the flange is against the soffit.

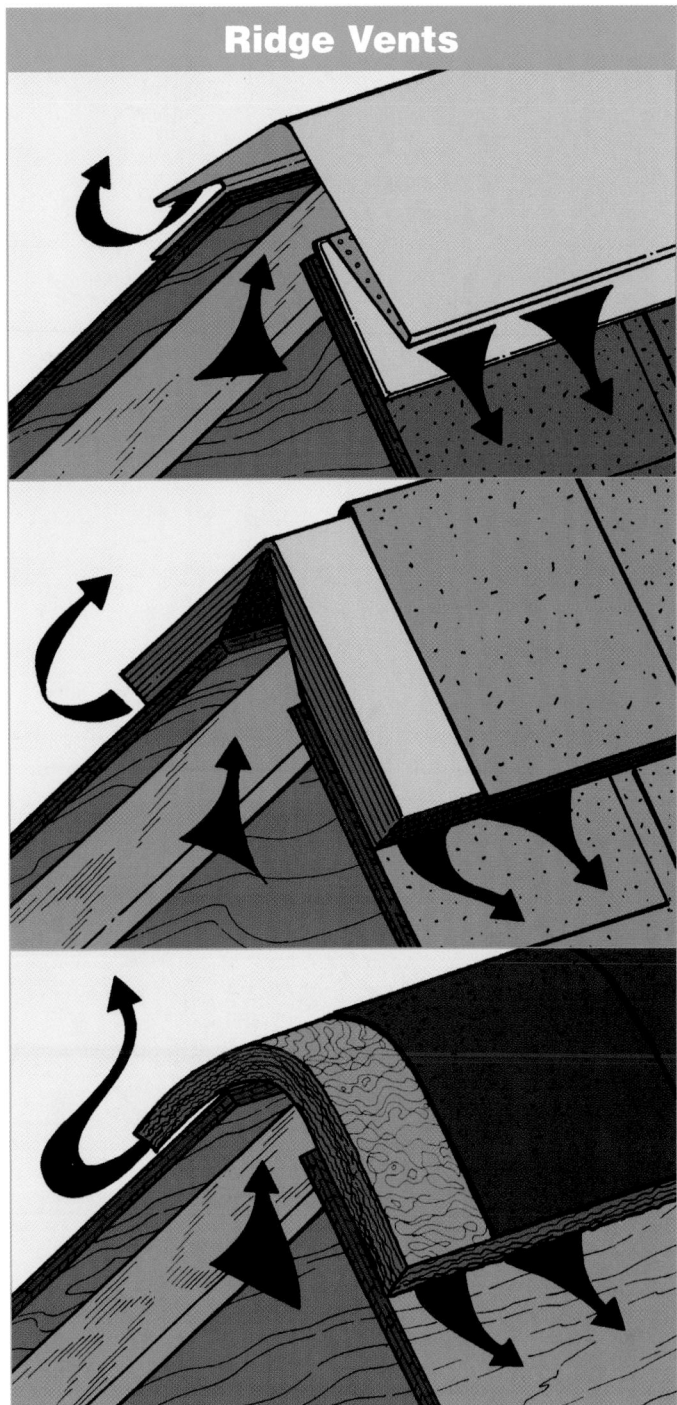

Ridge vents come as rigid lengths of metal (top), composite materials (middle), or in rolls of an air-permeable material (bottom). The lower two are designed to accept roof shingles.

Installing Plug Vents

Ventilator plugs usually do not yield the free area required by the guidelines on page 75, but it is better to use them than to have no ventilation at all. Use at least two plugs per rafter bay.

1 **Cutting Holes.** Each rafter bay requires two holes. Mark the center of each hole and use an electric drill equipped with a hole saw bit to cut a 2½-inch-diameter hole. If you do not have an electric drill, mark off the outline of the hole, drill a starter hole on the edge, and use a keyhole or saber saw to cut the hole.

2 **Inserting the Plug.** Push an aluminum or plastic plug into the hole until the flange is flush with the soffit.

8 Ventilation

1 Cut a 2-in.-wide slot along each side of the ridge, leaving 6 in. of each end uncut.

2 Uncoil a rolled vent (left) or secure a rigid vent (right) along the slot and over the uncut ends of the roof.

Installing a Ridge Vent

Ridge vents are made of various materials and may be packaged in rigid sections or rolls. A well-designed vent allows air to escape, but keeps out rain and snow. Because the ridge vent sits on top of the roof, it is highly visible. Keep this in mind when choosing a vent. Many homeowners opt for one that can have shingles installed on top.

1 Cutting an Opening. Use a circular saw with a carbide-tipped blade to cut a 2-inch slot along each side of the ridge. Start the cut 6 inches from one end of the ridge, and end it 6 inches from the other end. Set the blade depth to cut through the roofing and sheathing only, leaving the rafters uncut.

Caution: Wear goggles and make sure you have solid footing when cutting with a saw. Install roofing cleats if necessary to support yourself on the roof. Lay out the extension cord so that there is no chance of tripping on it.

2 Attaching the Vent. Uncoil the vent (if it's packaged in rolls) or secure a rigid vent to the ridge. Extend the vent to cover the uncut 6-inch portions of roof at each end.

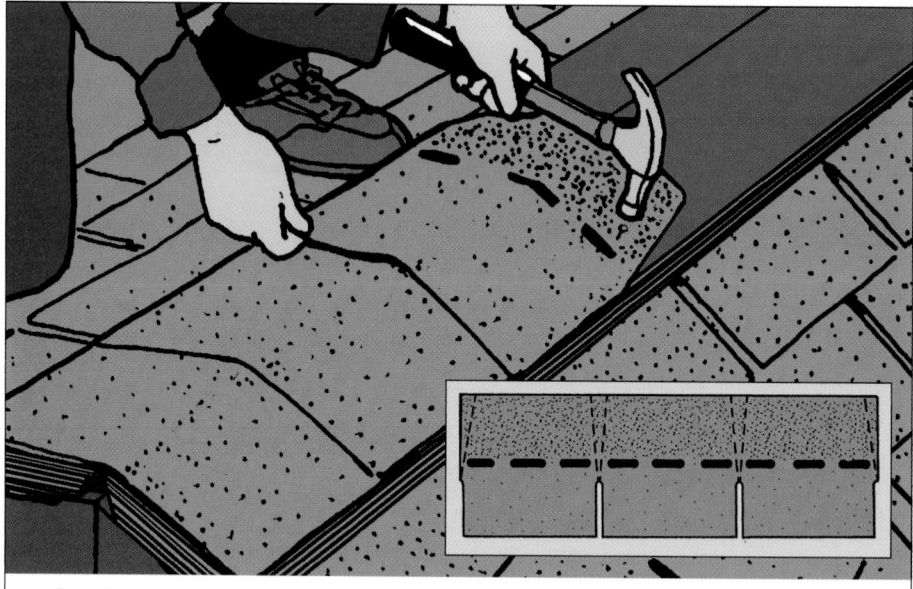

3 Three ridge shingles are cut from one composition shingle (inset). Place ridge shingles over the top of the vent. Without compressing the vent material, drive the nails through the shingles and vent and into the sheathing.

If you're using a metal vent that is not intended to be topped with shingles, nail the flanges to the roof using aluminum roofing nails.

3 Topping the Vent. For ridge vents that are designed to be covered with shingles, cut three ridge shingles from one three-tab composition shingle. Place the first shingle over one end of the ridge vent, aligning it with the edge of the shingles along the roof rake. Nail the shingle through the part to be covered by the next shingle. Using roofing nails that are long enough to penetrate into the sheathing, install one nail at each side of the ridge. Put the next shingle in place over the nails, and continue.

Alignment notch A cutout projection or slit on the ends or sides of shingles that acts as a guide in application to secure a proper exposure.

Asphalt A bituminous compound, dark brown or black in color, used in the manufacture of asphalt roofing shingles.

Blind nailing Nails driven so that the heads are concealed.

Built-up roofing An outer covering of a comparatively flat roof, consisting of several layers of saturated and/or saturated-and-coated felt, each layer mopped with hot tar or asphalt as laid. The top layer is finished with a mineral or rock covering or with a special coating.

Butt That portion of a shingle exposed to the weather, also called the tab of the shingle.

Closed valley A valley in which the roofing material is laced or woven through the valley intersection.

Collars or vent sleeves Sheet-metal-flanged collars placed around vent pipes to seal the roofing around the vent pipe openings.

Counter flashing Strips of metal, roofing, or fabric inserted so as to shed water onto the base flashing.

Course Horizontal unit of shingles running the length of the roof.

Cricket A small peaked saddle built behind the chimney or over an entry. Its purpose is to divert water to either side.

Cutout Slot or notch in a shingle that makes tabs look like individual shingles.

Deck The structural skin of a roof over which roofing is applied. Most homes built within the last 40 years use plywood for this purpose. (See Sheathing.)

Double coverage A method of applying roof shingles that provides two complete layers of protection.

Drip course First course of shingles at the eaves.

Eaves Edge of roof that projects over the outside wall.

Exposure Portion of shingle exposed to the weather, measured from butt of one shingle to butt of next course.

Fascia Horizontal trim at eaves that covers the rafter ends.

Flashing Material used to prevent seepage of water around any intersection or projection in a roof, including vent pipes, chimneys, adjoining walls, dormers, and valleys.

Gable The triangular area of exterior wall of a building.

Hip The line of intersection of two sloping roof planes with walls that are not parallel to each other.

Hip roof A roof which rises from all four sides of a building.

Lacing or Weaving Interweaving of a course of shingles at an intersection of a roof; e.g., at 90-degree angles in a valley.

Laid to the weather (See Exposure)

Lap To overlap the surface of one shingle or other type of roofing material with another; also the length of such an overlap.

Lean-to roof Has one slope only and is built against a higher wall.

Open valley Type of valley on a roof in which roofing material is trimmed and flashing is exposed.

Pitch Height from the joist to the ridge, divided by the span, or width of the building; expressed as a ratio of rise to span.

Ridge The horizontal line at which two roof planes meet when both roof planes slope down from that line.

Roll roofing Roofing laid from a roll of material.

Roofer's cement A quick-setting asphalt adhesive for use with roofing materials.

Run The horizontal distance from the eaves to a point directly under the ridge of a roof.

Rake A slope or inclination of a roof; the same as the slope.

Run wild To leave a piece of roofing or other material untrimmed until fastened.

Seal down An asphalt adhesive factory applied so that the shingles, once installed, have a concealed strip of sealing compound that securely bonds each shingle to provide wind resistance.

Sheathing The wooden foundation of a roof, also known as the deck. Typically made of ½-inch construction-grade plywood; older homes may have shiplap or planks.

Slope The degree of inclination of a roof plane in inches of rise per horizontal foot.

Soffit The finished underside of an eaves.

Soil stacks (See Vents)

Span The horizontal measurement from eaves to eaves.

Square An area of exposed roofing 10 feet square or comprising 100 square feet.

Square butt shingles Strip shingles that usually have two or three tabs formed by cutouts or slots.

Standing seam The vertical ridge formed where two panels of metal roofing are joined.

Starter course The first course of shingles installed on a roof, starting at the lower edge of the eaves. It is covered by the first course.

Starter strip Mineral-surfaced roll roofing applied at eaves line before application of shingles. Fills spaces of cutouts and joints.

Stepped flashing Flashing along a roof slope against a wall or chimney. Usually consists of L-shaped units that fit into the joint between the roof and the wall.

Storm collar A flashing unit for prefabricated chimney pipe.

Valley The line of intersection of two roof slopes.

Vent An outlet for air (e.g., vent pipe in a plumbing system, ventilating duct).

Vent sleeves or Collars Sheet-metal-flanged collars placed around vent pipes to seal off the roofing around the vent pipe opening.

Weaving or Lacing Interweaving of a course of shingles where there is an intersection in a roof for drainage (e.g., valley).

index

2 1982 01507 1214

MAY 26 2004